MULTICULTURAL BUSINESS ETHICS AND GLOBAL MANAGERIAL MORAL REASONING

Kamal Dean Parhizgar

Robert Parhizgar

University Press of America,® Inc.
Lanham · Boulder · New York · Toronto · Oxford

Copyright © 2006 by
University Press of America,® Inc.
4501 Forbes Boulevard
Suite 200
Lanham, Maryland 20706
UPA Acquisitions Department (301) 459-3366

PO Box 317
Oxford
OX2 9RU, UK

Library of Congress Control Number: 2006920828
ISBN-13: 978-0-7618-3428-1 (paperback : alk. paper)
ISBN-10: 0-7618-3428-1 (paperback : alk. paper)

To Parhizgar Family Members: Ozra Mitra Esfandiari,
Suzan Parhizgar, and Fuzhan Parhizgar
with whom we have a very happy life.

We have written the book of
Multicultural Business Ethics and Global Managerial Moral Reasoning;
So we care about humanity and humaneness in the book above.

You can forget our names or remember them as you wish;
So we will be remembered by the book of
Multicultural Business Ethics and Global Managerial Maral Reasoning.

Parhizgars

CONTENTS

Chapter 10: Morality and Ethics in Global
Business Social Darwinism......437

Chapter 11: Justice, Law, and Social Contracts
Between Businesses and Society......473

FOREWORD

Multicultural Business Ethics is a fascinating and multi-faceted topic in global business. To begin with, there is no general agreement on "Multicultural Business Ethics" and maybe for judgmental reasons, there cannot be a general understanding. A multitude of parameters, mostly human behavioral variables, impact and determine the core definition of the topic. Until such human behavioral variables are globalized it is impossible, at least unlikely, to develop a universal definition of Multicultural Business Ethics. Otherwise what is ethical, moral, and legal in one culture might be unethical, immoral, and even illegal in another. The failure of repeated attempts at creating a legal framework for the legality of global business practices, going back to the Foreign Corrupt Businesses Act of the 1970s, is an indication of the magnitude of the problem. At least legality is subject to a modicum central (governmental) control, whereas ethicality has no central controlling body.

Kamal Dean Parhizgar and Robert R. Parhizgar have undertaken the colossal task to establish the framework for analyzing Multicultural Business Ethics and Global Managerial Moral reasoning. This comprehensive study of the subject is a pioneering work for which the authors deserve everyone's gratitude and admiration. They have chosen to analyze global business ethics from a managerial perspective. The first five chapters set the broad and somewhat philosophical framework for their detailed analysis of the specific topics to follow. The enormity of their task becomes evident in the remaining chapters when they identify different elements determining cultural behavior in general, and related to business decision-making in particular.

The father-son authors rely heavily on the personal experiences of the father as well as extensive academic research undertaken by both. Professor Parhizgar's in-depth knowledge of global business, gained through some forty years of researching, teaching, and practicing international business gives him a unique perspective of the issue. This is amply supplemented by Robert's equally significant experience as a scientist. Together, they are able to present a well-rounded view of multicultural business ethics. This is one of several aspects of this book that makes it a major contribution to the discipline.

It should be noted that the application of business ethics to the global environment is a relatively new phenomenon in business research. Recent years have witnessed a noticeable increase in the level of interest in – and consequently a growing number of attempts at – developing a theoretical framework of analysis for global business ethics. The Parhizgars' contribution is, nevertheless, the first attempt at doing so on a comprehensive scale. Furthermore, their selection of "global managerial moral reasoning" as their sub-topic and their examination of each element of ethics within this broad framework adds greatly to the value of their work.

The authors identify twelve related objectives for their work early in the book and proceed to fully accomplish all of them. Their perspective is both balanced and refreshing. They acknowledge that their research on global business ethics has lead them to "a multitude of opinions, from the notion that the very concept of business ethics is an oxymoron to the idea that the thoughtful and objective consideration of business ethics is a necessity for the continuity of the human race" and everything in between. This balanced perspective is evident throughout the book. The authors' view is also refreshing when they identify Multicultural Business Ethics as a "positive phenomenon, associated with accelerated novelty and the creation of global honesty." In short, the authors have been very successful in writing a book based on research findings without losing their own valid view of the topic.

Multicultural Business Ethics and Global Managerial Moral Reasoning is a major contribution to the discipline. It offers scholars and students of global business a framework on which to build their future research agenda. For that Professor Kamal Dean Parhizgar and Robert R. Parhizgar have earned everyone's respect and gratitude.

Khosrow Fatemi, President
Eastern Oregon University
La Grande, Oregon
July 2005

AKNOWLEDGEMENTS

We are sincerely indebted to the many philosophers, scholars, and writers who have provided us their thoughtful contributions to facilitate our writings. Also, we would like to acknowledge, with thank, the many people who contributed to this book directly and indirectly. Without the help of our family, friends, and colleagues, this book could never have been completed. These people have encouraged and helped us; for this we owe them a great deal of gratitude. There are just too many people to thank, so we cannot thank everyone individually. But we do want to identify some individuals who have been especially helpful in the long and arduous process of writing this book. Several colleagues have expressed their support and contributed substantially to the final product. Particularly, we want to thank the following:

Professor Khosrow Fatemi, President of the Eastern Oregon University; Professor Ray M. Keck III, President of Texas A&M International University; Professor Erdener Kaynak, Pennsylvania State University, Harrisburg; Professor John P. Kole, Dean of the College of Business Administration, at California East Bay University – Hayward; and our colleagues at Texas A&M International University: Provost Dan Jones, Associate Provost Faridoun Farrokh; Professor Tagi Sagafi-nejad; Professor John Michael Patrick; Professor Michael Landeck; Mrs. Jessica Whitt Ratliff; Hafizul Islam; and Mrs. Linda Lee Gribble.

Special Thanks to Professor Manouchehr Mohseni Parsa, University of Teheran, Iran; Professor Charles W. Rudiger, Dowling College; Professor Kamal Fatehi, Georgia State University, Kennesaw; and Professor Cyrous Kooros, Nicole State University.

We want particularly to thank Mr. David Chao, Acquisition Editor; Ms. Audrey Babikirk, Senior Production Editor; and Ms. Beverly Baum, Production Editor and the staff at the University Press of America, Inc. They have been especially helpful in encouraging and guiding us through the project from the beginning of publication to end. We appreciate the time and effort that they put into this project.

Finally, we owe our family members Ozra Mitra Esfandiari, Suzan S. Parhisger, and Fuzhan F. Parhizgar a special debt of gratitude for putting up with us during the many hours that a project like this consumes. Our family's support was vital to completion of this project. We hope that this textbook is worthy of interest in its contribution toward understanding and comprehending multicultural business ethics in the world in which we live.

Kamal Dean Parhizgar, PhD
Robert R. Parhizgar MS (MD-MBA Candidate)

INTRODUCTION

If you turn on major global broadcasts like CNN and Al-Jezeera, if you have satellite and/or Internet connections, and read newspapers, magazines, and professional journal articles or analyze your daily social life, you will find events, crisis, or problems that relate to business activities. Through your personal moral and global ethical convictions you question quickly:

Who is at fault?
Who is greedy or generous?
Who is fair or unfair?
Who is just or unjust?
Who is liable and should pay damages?
Who acted responsibly?
Who did not?

Then you wonder: Are these issues and problems inherent in the nature of human beings, or are they holistic by-products of sociocultural and politico-economical beliefs and desires of interest groups among nations? Multicultural business ethics is an invisible aspect of business. It intersects between an individual's desire and group interests and raises special curiosity in the minds of many producers and consumers around the world. The magnitude of competitive international enterprises makes it imperative that producers and consumers develop multicultural "codes of ethics," "codes of behavior," and "codes of conduct" in order to deal with today's cultural diversity. The diverse cultural and religious need must be viewed as a reality in international business operations.

Multicultural business ethics is a positive phenomenon, associated with accelerated novelty and creation of global honesty. It stands alone in its concern with contentious problems such as political ideologies, ethnicity, race, gender, color, and religious faiths. In multinational environments, the most problematic issue is the friction generated by organizational and operational functions along with the consideration and integration of different cultural values and perceptions within the mission of an organization.

With this in mind, we can find a multitude of opinions, from the notion that very concept of business ethics is an oxymoron to the idea that the thoughtful and objective consideration of business ethics is a necessity for the continuity of the human race. Within such a magnitude of socio-ethnic perceptions, artistic artifacts, and finally religious faiths with a variety of beliefs, ideas, doctrines, and material and non-material hierarchies, all have made our lives very complex. Clearly, these phenomena prompt the reflective person or entity not to make fun of multicultural business ethics, but rather to think more deeply about the nature and purposes of businesses and society.

In the twentieth century, we witnessed how ignorance, fanaticism, prejudices, in humaneness, and atrocity mingled with religious cultural egoism and political racism ignored the spiritual dimension of humanity. At the beginning of the third millennium, the global notion of ethicality and morality temporarily started to collapse by the unexpected crisis of September 11, 2001. On that global day, like other crucial days in the history of mankind, all governments and people from different economical, social, legal, and religious faiths acted noticeably to make this world more safe and secure.

Understanding multicultural business ethics and global moral reasoning is crucial to every manager who belongs to and leads within a multinational organization. In recognition of the development and rapidly growing importance of international relations and the need to educate future managers and professional experts, the American Assembly of Collegiate Schools of Business (AACSB) now requires business schools to multiculturalize their curriculum with business ethics.

Multicultural Business Ethics and Global Moral Reasoning is a sort of imaginative coverage of multi-moral, ethical, and legal cultural differences and similarities for future use by students in both fields of domestic and international businesses. Topics in this text are presented in a smooth and logical fashion. The authors' intention was to establish, as powerfully as possible, a frame of reference that expressed this judgment and method of study that was appropriate to multicultural business transactions. Several business ethics texts are available to the community of scholars. This book was written not only to be useful for practicing international management, but also to be used for understanding and appreciating similar and different ethical and moral values among nations. This text also will be useful for students majoring in other areas, such as political science, international relations, public administration, health and medical care administration, and educational administration.

DISTINCTIVE PERSPECTIVES

Many conceptual dimensions ensure that this text is linked to current issues facing multicultural organizations. Multicultural business ethics is not aimless, but it is in fact a goal-oriented effort. Its goal is related directly not only to ethics and morality but also to the application of business law, economics, finance, and the like. It is also concerned with what home and host cultures and societies value. In the global free-market economy multicultural business ethics examines what producers and consumers believe in and why they expect honesty and integrity. In particular, the authors have become convinced that all multinational managers have to travel this route for a more synergistic understanding of their own personal aspirations and societal goodness.

THE PURPOSE OF THIS BOOK

In an era of highly sophisticated technology we have found no significant evidence related to the holistic important issues of multicultural understanding, spiritual aspirations, and material comforts among people from different cultural backgrounds. We are living in an era moving from the sectarian religious faiths to mutual understanding of human dignity and societal integrity; from the Cold War's competitive forced-technology to an exchange and alliance of technology between the East and West; from simple cultural dependency to multicultural sufficiency; from national to multinational free market economy; from representative democratic societies to participatory democracies; and from oligopolistic industries to multiple, optional conglomerate enterprises.

Multinational corporations and the World Wide Web (WWW) play a special role, not only in building cross-cultural bridges among home and host nations, but also they provide innovative multicultural business ethics through their informational and practical knowledge-based resources. Multicultural business ethics can gather peoples' thoughts and efforts along with their natural resources to use towards more effective, efficient, and productive managerial outcomes.

Multicultural Business Ethics and Global Managerial Reasoning presents a fresh view on the separation of ethics and morality. The separation of these two phenomena creates distinguishing what people value individually and collectively. In this text, authors are concerned with at least twelve related objectives:

- To cover major philosophical views concerning ethics and morality.
- To revisit and examine theoretical foundations of morality and ethicality.
- To analyze foundational beliefs concerning different theories of ethics and morality.
- To define territorial characteristics of goodness and badness in individual and group intentions by expressing and valuing humanity and humaneness.
- To cover major global historical and contemporary issues in business ethics.
- To present the desire of stakeholders and managerial frameworks and practices for identifying and evaluating their business means and ends in the global business world.
- To present actual business events and managerial ethical dilemmas in a straightforward analysis by case study.
- To provide a critical ground for thinking concerning the future ethical and moral issues related to scientific advancements and technological developments in biosciences, biotechnological research, and biobusinesses.
- To offer academic and journalistic findings and stories to explain how

- To highlight ethical and moral dilemmas in the field of multicutural business ethics.
- To ask different questions at the end of each chapter in order to update readers' views concerning business ethics.
- To motivate readers by viewing contents of each chapter and illustrate current applications of chapter contents in judging ethical, moral, and legal issues.

In addition to providing concrete frameworks for analyzing and discussing a wide range of ethical issues we need to understand that global interdependence is no longer a matter of belief, ideology, and choice, but also it is an inescapable reality. The authors of this text addressed themselves, in a way that is both sound and thought provoking, to the importance of multicultural ethics in multinational organizational management. Their views, of course, are based on a fundamental focus (the managerial perspective of multicultural synergy).

Multicultural ethics is a provocative effort of modern human life to create innovative thoughts and methods through application of international value systems. Multicultural business ethics is making possible an understanding among all cultures. It is not the only intent of the authors of this book to present a prescription for multicultural business ethics, but also to help develop a sense of understanding of the magnitude of multicultural value systems in order to maximize overall human spiritual efforts. However, in the field of global business, managers should promote the pride of all common cultural values in home and host countries. Multinational corporations should provide appropriate room for the growth and development of cultural values (in sum a paradigm of global multiethical value system).

BOUNDARIES OF MULTICULTURAL BUSINESS ETHICS

Multicultural business ethics is the study of philosophical views, conceptual perceptions, and spiritual bindings constituting multinational corporate management systems. The field of multicultural business ethics is a multidisciplinary rather than interdisciplinary phenomenon. Multicultural business ethics covers an enormous spiritual territory. It is a research-oriented field and this book will be a valuable source of reference for both practitioners and academicians.

Multicultural ethical understanding is expanding because of diverse natures of communication and contacts among nations. This is a growing discipline that will add new conceptual and scientific thoughts for improving moral, ethical, and legal relationships between home and host countries. In addition, rapid demographic movements, expansion in tourism and trade industries, development in scientific resources, changing job specifications, and legal requirements all are forcing multinational corporations to advance their organizations into more global understandings. By analyzing ethical philosophies, virtues, values, motives, and beliefs of an increasingly multicultural workforce, multinational managers have to pay serious attention to global competitiveness in productivity and equally to the integrity of their organizational performance. Therefore, multicultural business ethics is a field that deals with the composition of a multinational workforce in a competitive free market economy with different culturally oriented consumers. In sum, this text will create new valuable challenges for multinational managers.

THE FEATURES OF THIS BOOK

This book is deeply rooted in variety of ethical and moral behavioral patterns for producers and consumers. It is not the first to seek multiethical understanding within the contextual boundaries of competitive partnership among nations, and hopefully it will not be the last. It is written with a multidimensional perspective to help readers gain multilateral advantages by addressing the needs of multicultural ethical management. By understanding the foundations and applications of multicultural business ethics, we mean to blend ethical values with capitalizing on multinational resources towards the creation of an honest and just competitive qualitative outcome.

One of the most valuable contributions of this book is to identify and clarify the terms, meanings, and processes of the theoretical foundations of deontological, utilitarian, hedonistic, eudaemononistic, and teleological beliefs and practices in different nations. This book serves all types of business as well as public administration in terms of understanding multinational organizations and management complexities.

This book will help students understand the specific identity of many ethical, moral, and legal foundations of people around the globe. It will inspire them to appreciate the structural operations and managerial decision-making processes in order to understand new missions, strategies, and policies. It also helps multinational managers build their ethical philosophies, in order to better match their corporate fitness with their environmental conditions. There are several features that this text has developed. These features are as follows:

Global Scope

Multiple sections on globalization, internationalization, moralization, ethicalization, and legalization of business transactions are included in this edition. Traditional cultural diversity and contemporary multicultural ethics in the field of business are presented throughout the text.

Cross-Disciplinary Approaches

Topics related to philosophy, science, religion, art, law, morality, ethics, business, society, and multicutural management are deeply analyzed and enlarged.

Clear and Perceptive Presentations

Philosophical grounds, theoretical concepts, and pragmatic principles of morality and ethicality with examples are written to enhance learning endeavors. Although the intended primary readers of this text are business students, it may also serve as a useful additional reference in other disciplines such as public administration, educational administration, health and medical care administration, and bioethics.

A Variety of Cases

At the end of each chapter, readers will find appropriate and related cases concerning the application of each chapter's concepts and contents. Also, at the end of each case, there are several questions for instructors and students to provide a lively springboard for class discussions and the application of moral and ethical theories. Also, the case studies vary in kind and length, but they are intended to permit instructors and students to pursue further some of the issues discussed in each chapter and to analyze them in more specific contexts.

Emerging perspectives

We looked at business ethics through multiculturalization and multinationalization of business entities in the twenty-first century. Special attention has been paid to socio-cultural, politico-economical, and religious dimensions of the world in which we live.

STRUCTURE OF THE BOOK

Chapter 1 provides a general view of business ethics. It familiarizes the reader with judgmental implications concerning managerial decision-making processes and operations. It also provides specific views concerning moral absolutism, ethical relativism, and legal doctrines concerning multicultural environments of businesses.

Chapter 2 introduces different definitions and distinctions among moral, ethical, and legal perceptions concerning business transactions. It provides an analytical foundation for viewing speculative moral understandings, pragmatic ethical knowledge, and limits of legal self-interest and self-discipline in the field of global business management.

Chapter 3 contains a discussion of the "micro-level" approach to moral theories: idealistic, hedonistic, eudaemonistic, and authentic. By analyzing optimistic, moderate, and pessimistic theoretical foundations of each moral theory, both classical and more temporary ways of thinking and acting are presented. In addition, individual styles of moral beliefs are discussed in this chapter.

Chapter 4 contains a discussion of the "macro-level" social approaches to ethical theories: relativism, deontologicalism, teleologicalism, and utilitarianism. Globally, by analyzing principles, arguments, and applications of each theory according to their religious faiths, cultural value systems, and political ideological doctrines you will be familiar with multicultural ethical and moral perspectives of most nations around the world.

Chapter 5 extends the level of analysis to philosophical means and ends in moral, ethical, and legal business responsibilities within multicultural corporations and discusses problems and issues between home and host countries. The chapter answers these questions: (1) how should intellectual property rights, privacy and ownership rights, and eudaemonistic and hedonistic means and ends be examined? (2) how can ethical principles and practices enhance relationships between both domestic and global corporations?

Chapter 6 contains definitions of the paradigm of multicultural ethics and business knowledge management. It answers the questions: (1) how should scientists, technologists, marketers, and managers be familiar with acquisition and application of knowledge? (2) what are moral and ethical knowledge? what are multiethical integrated knowledge-based foundations of scientific, technological, artistic, and philosophical know-why, know-what, know-where, know-how, and know-whose knowledge?

Chapter 7 defines moral virtues, ethical values, and the corporate stakeholders' convictions. It introduces the stakeholder and issues of management methods for studying social responsibility in relationships at individual, group, and organizational levels. These analyses provide for and encourage the incorporation of moral principles and ethical values from the entire book.

Chapter 8 defines managerial trust, rights, and duties. Although the content of this chapter is based on socialized approaches of multicultural business ethics, the concepts of trust, rights, and duties can be used to examine and explain corporate integrity through prodigical synergistic outcomes. Specifically, different theories on behalf of sellers and buyers such as positivism, negativism, libertarianism, and fatalism are analyzed in this section.

Chapter 9 describes inherent ethical issues concerning econo-political ideologies: capitalism, socialism, communism, humanism, and imperialism. Within such a magnitude, different types of businesses from honest to dishonest such as the honest, the camouflaged, the *multi-fin-pols*, the *multi-corp-mags*, the hoodlum, the hoodwinker, and the business ring are defined and analyzed. In addition, ethical and moral issues related to invisible and visible power players such as global alliances (e.g., Illuminaties, Freemasons, the Council on Foreign Relations, the Builderbergers, the Club of Rome, the United Nations, and the Trilateral Commission), are presented and analyzed.

Chapter 10 argues major ethical and moral issues concerning Global Social Businesses Darwinism. The major philosophical foundations of the evolutionary business Darwinism ideology and outcomes are analyzed.

Chapter 11 presents the main theories of justice, law, and social contracts between businesses and society. The justice philosophies of equalitarian and equitability are presented. Different systems such as compensatory, retributive, procedural, commutative, and distributive justice theories and practices are explained. In addition, different international court systems such as the court of law and remedies at law, the court of equity and remedies in equity, and the Islamic *sharia* courts are presented.

Chapter 12 begins by addressing general ethical and moral foundations in the workplace. It discusses the values-driven relationships between employers and employees and how the outcomes of these relationships affect organizational ethical outcomes. It also examines how employer-employee contracts bind parties to legitimate contractual promises. In addition, within the contextual boundaries of bilateral contracts between employers and employees, it looks at how both parties respect the state of civil liberties in the workplace. In addition, this chapter addresses gender ethics in the workplace.

Chapter 13 extends the level of analysis to domestic and multinational corporations and discusses ethical issues concerning legitimate and illegitimate capital flights around the world.   This section defines, analyzes, and explains ethical and moral circulation of dirty-money, soft-money, free-money, money cleansing, and money-power in the international community. It examines how different types of front businesses clean these types of money.

Chapter 14 addresses ethical and moral integrity, loyalty, and accountability of professionalism, paraprofessionalism, occupationalism, and vocationalism. This chapter provides a framework for examining codes of ethics, codes of behavior, and codes of conduct within contextual boundaries of these groups of people. It provides concrete frameworks for making ethical and moral distinctions concerning altruistic and egoistic desires of employees in an organization. In addition, this section analyzes what duties, responsibilities, and accountability business entities have to the public.

Chapter 15 presents professional integrity and organizational loyalty in relation to whistle blowing. Aligning ethical and moral convictions is a dominant theme in the chapter, along with examining the management of mechanistic functional systems. In particular, this chapter examines the means and ends of whistle blowing. The chapter analyzes how employees can be loyal to their professions, organizations, and nations. The following questions are asked:

- What are employees' professional obligations to the welfare and integrity of society?
- Who owns employees' knowledge and experiences?
- When and how should or should not an employee blow the whistle and inform the public of an organization's wrong doings?

INTENDED AUDIENCES

The primary users of this text would be college students. Its secondary users would be multicultural researchers and it can be used as a reference book. The third users would be academicians, as a new multidisciplinary source for conceptualizing the further path of their research. Understanding principles of multiculturalism, cultural diversity, ethics, morality, and legality in the field of business requires a very broad-based knowledge. This text provides such a base. This book will help readers understand the specific identity of many cultures. It is unique in several ways. First, it provides a view of cultural philosophies broadened to the more common interpretation of cultural economy. In the field of international business, it provides a frame of reference, that religious, governmental, and regional forces are crucial synergistic role players in an international free market economy. Second, it has gathered information from the wave of ever changing management literature that promotes changes in the international marketplace. Third, this text addresses a blending of ideas of multicultural business ethics from diverse cultural values in order to provide a compelling call for more understanding, cooperation, and above all multicultural synergy. Finally, the authors have cited both theoretical and practical information, and studied applications of both ethical and moral values, for better understanding and crystallizing the necessity of paying attention to the needs of producers and consumers.

CHAPTER 1

AN OVERVIEW:
THE NATURE OF GLOBAL BUSINESS ETHICS

When a business is lost, something is lost;

When liberty is lost, democracy is lost;

When the judiciary system is lost, justice is lost;

When reputation is lost, a personality is lost;

When morality is lost, dignity is lost;

When ethics is lost, integrity is lost;

When honesty is lost, faith is lost;

When decency is lost, humanity is lost;

When honor is lost, all is lost.

CHAPTER OBJECTIVES

When you have read this chapter you should be able to do the following:

- Develop conceptual skills in order to analyze global business ethics.
- Develop a framework of analysis to enable you to discuss how to ethically manage international organizations.
- Define ethics, morality, and legality.
- Understand the importance of ethical, moral, and legal behavior in the workplace.
- Understand the complexity of international business transactions.
- Analyze the religious and secular motives of humanity.
- Grasp the magnitude of today's global business responsibilities.
- Review the historical and contemporary ethical, moral, and legal business dilemmas.
- Analyze the contemporary dimensions of international economic value systems.
- Confirm your relative strength of ethical beliefs.

THOUGHT STARTER

It seems clear that the business operations of today are no longer limited by their national market boundaries, and that they are faced with intensive global competition. Global business is changing at a rapid pace through borderless E-commerce alteration and elimination of national and political boundaries. Nevertheless, legally, businesses are faced with antitrust laws. If customers find that pricing systems are too high, for instance, they may think this must be due to the producer's *selfish nature* of profit making and risk being labeled monopolists. Monopolistic businesses, therefore, must be broken up. Also, if customers feel that prices are too low, they may perceive that businesses are probably examples of *cutthroat competition.* Therefore countervailing tariffs or duties and higher taxes should be imposed to maintain the integrity of the domestic market. If a business strategy is avoiding both these paths by setting a common price within the competitive market, neither too high or too low, but just right; customers may consider such businesses oligopolies. Whatever businesses do, they may be perceived as guilty. Some critics blame businesses by claiming they manipulate the customers' minds by showering them with ads and promotions in order to gain their selfish profits.

Ecologists and environmentalists claim that natural resources are vanishing and they blame businesses and the greedy appetite of businesspeople. As result, if anybody has any trouble of any kind, blame the businesspeople. Even if a customer spills her cup of coffee miles away from the seller's establishment (e.g., McDonald's case), the court finds that business with unlimited chain liability.

Businesspeople accumulate capital through profit-making processes and investments. They decide which line of products should be expanded and accelerated by examining the marketplace demand (Peikoff, 1999: 15). They crystallize their production objectives through the integration of natural resources, human discoveries, labor efforts, and marketing information strategies. These activities depend on risky decisions and actions on which abundance and prosperity need to be focused.

Philosophically, for investors profit making is viewed as the result of conscious deliberation in the course of gaining and losing. Since profitability is ideally a kind of legitimate payment earned by moral virtue through an honest deal between buyers and sellers, it is a payment for scientific thoughts, technological breakthroughs, and customer satisfaction. Profit making is the prime mover of the efficient, effective, and productive economy by creating global mass markets and products and services for every income level. In sum, profit is the final product of the wealth of intellect and knowledge. It is, primarily, the product of intellectual values and moral virtues. Therefore, businesses must be oriented not only towards profitability, but also towards ethical worldliness. Businesspeople must have intellectual civility in their minds and good moral character in their decisions and actions.

PLAN OF THIS CHAPTER

People often complain that business leaders, including some direct investors, are less honest than before. Whether this perception is true or not, it needs to be analyzed on the basis of moral and ethical convictions. Consumers are always worried about whether they are treated fairly, justly, and rightly by businesspeople. Given this potential antipathy, it is sometimes not difficult to observe that some global business corporations act in an amoral way and ignore their moral and ethical commitments to their customers. Today, the situation for global business leaders is more critical than ever before, because there is a high probability of getting caught for immoral, unethical, and illegal business transactions.

An objective of this chapter is to provide the theoretical and practical knowledge needed in today's global business ethics environments. In this opening chapter, we will introduce many issues that lay down a foundation for later discussions. We will start with a brief analysis of the changing ethical perspectives of global business. The primary focus of this chapter is to study the urgency of moral, ethical, and legal influences on individual and group behavior in international business environments. This chapter illuminates the introductory perspectives of global business ethics.

THE BUSINESS OF BUSINESS ETHICS

International management practices reflect the societal ethical values, moral virtues, and legal beliefs within which business organizations exist. Moreover, technological innovations, societal movements, political events, and economic forces have changed over time and are changing human faith, beliefs, and behavior now and in the future. In today's increasingly competitive international free market economy, managers cannot succeed on their domestic cultural understanding skills alone. They must also have ethical, moral, and legal interactive knowledge and communication skills. Cherrington and Cherrington (1989: 30) spotted twelve categories of business ethics:

> Taking things that don't belong to you.
> Saying things you know are not true.
> Giving or allowing false impressions.
> Buying influence or engaging in conflict of interest.
> Hiding or divulging information.
> Taking unfair advantage.
> Committing acts of personal decadence.
> Perpetrating interpersonal abuse.
> Permitting organizational abuse.
> Violating rules.
> Condoning unethical actions
> Balancing ethical dilemmas

From the global business view, Payne, Raiborn, and Askvik (1997: 1727) indicate:

> Additionally, the growing interdependence of socially, politically, economically, and legally diverse countries has caused multinational corporate entities to reexamine a variety of their existing policies. Among these revisions are strategic management philosophies, strategic alliance partnerships, competitive products and/or services positions, total quality management, and ethical-legal conducts.

These revisions mandate to international managers the creation of new missions on the basis of both domestic and global perspectives, with ever-increasing awareness of corporate conglomerate multiculturalization, and multiethical visions.

It seems clear that the dynamic environment of today's global business is the subject of much criticism in light of varying unethical decisions and immoral conducts. The result is negative and can have wide-ranging repercussions, including bad publicity, bad reputation, consumer suspicion, boycotts, government intervention, and lawsuits. Although many businesses recognize the need to establish a sound philosophy of business, they nevertheless tend to view the real world without ethical and moral perspectives. Several questions address the mission of a contemporary global corporation:

- What are the core cultural values and political beliefs of a corporation?
- What are global businesses for, and whose values, beliefs, and interests may be at risk?
- Are they binding countries, institutions, corporations, and people in an interdependent global economy? If the answer is yes, then who will be helped or harmed by these global corporations?
- Are these global corporations established solely to make profit? If the answer is yes, then how will the corporation's decisions and operations preserve the core values and beliefs of all stakeholders?
- Are they established to assess cost-profit analysis?
- How should people from different countries have access to natural resources, products, and services?
- Who should manage and control natural resources?
- Who should make ethical and moral decisions and take actions?
- How do we know what decision or action is right?
- Can an international business transaction be right?
- What must we do to make it right?
- What should we do to have it end right?

Thus, to investigate the right decisions and actions, we need to probe the real nature of cost and benefit analysis within the contextual boundaries of ethical, moral, and legal reasoning of ethicists, liberalists, and pragmatists. Our initial concern is to state precisely what kind of decision, action, and behavior or thought of global business is ethical, moral, and legal. Do we believe that global business ethics are transactional compromises between buyers and sellers? Does business ethics comprise moral principles and standards that guide behavior in the world of business (Fraedrich and Ferrell, 1991: 5). By reading this book, you will be able to judge what should be business ethics.

MORALITY, ETHICS, AND LAW

Is Business Ethics a Fad?

Why do some people label business ethics a fad? Perhaps they believe the ethical issue will go away over time. We truly wish ethical problems would simply disappear like the hula-hoop, a bona fide fad that came and went with the 1960s (Trevino and Nelson, 1995: 7). Is there any single common standard of business ethics in an increasingly interdependent traditional trade economy or in the contemporary global E-commerce?

In responding to the above question, global management needs to be concerned with the right answers. The right way to do business in the international free market economy is not necessarily a matter of aligning our actions with either the home or the host socio-cultural and econo-political value systems. Yet international managers struggle to carve out some form of consensus on business ethics and moral behavior, especially in the areas where the international law does not seem to cover the significant bases. International managers need to make their decisions on the basis of their moral and ethical commitments.

Morality is a dynamic behavioral deliberation of an individual's intellect and wisdom to pursue good causes. The word order is distinct from the real (natural) order of existing things and the logical (artificial) order, formed by people. Both natural and artificial orders are caused by good reason.

Ethics is a speculative and/or practical collective cultural value system. Ethics is concerned with groups' psychosocial actions and deals with good deeds in a society. Philosophers have formulated ethics to be speculative and demonstrative of good thoughts and behavior (deontologicalism) and some have tended to identify ethics completely with the practical good end-results (utilitarianism).

Legality is not a static phenomenon. It is dynamic. The law sets rules for behavior, rules that change on the basis of time and circumstances. When rules are broken, the consequence is punishment. The law sets behavioral standards and initiates an expected system for compliance.

Regarding the question of what legally should be done in profit-making processes; we might want to say that certain *shoulds* are universally compelling. However, ethics provides options, often disconnected from official sanctions, because not all activity that is legal could be right. In a general term, law concerns what we must do, ethics concerns what we should do (Halbert and Ingulli, 2000: 1) and morality concerns what we actually need to do. The problem in international business transactions is sometimes related to specific issues in which there are similarities between home and host countries' laws and ethics, and in other cases there are differences. Ethics in business becomes somewhat like business politics. Is there any moral obligation and ethical commitment either in international politics or global business ethics?

Much has not been written and said about the ethical and moral problems and issues for international corporate commitments and responsibilities. Every nation seems to be concerned with these issues. This may be in part because multinational corporations are proportionately powerful and influential in mapping international econo-political diplomacy. They provide employment opportunities, produce needed products and services, and earn profits for their shareholders. Also, they create problems such as polluting the air and water and in some cases ignore human rights. They are admired, envied, hated, feared, and frequently despaired of by both admirers and critics (Farmer and Hogue, 1973: vii). Therefore, business ethics is not a *fad*. It is a *fact*.

Is Business Ethics Just a Myth or a Real Logic?

Ethical myth and millennial vision are characterized by what may be called traditional consciousness. Emphasis is on the past and on the scarce and timeless understanding of life. Some philosophers have emphasized on the similarities between the myth and ideology, others have stressed the differences. This disagreement stems in part from the tendency to describe the numerous connections between the myth and ideology. Perhaps this point can be illustrated by an analogy. If chemists were so impressed by the frequency of the hydrogen-oxygen complex that they failed to define the two elements independently, they would be unable to deal with them when they occurred separately in pure form, or, more commonly, when they appeared in compound with other elements. To define them separately, however, would in no sense be denial the phenomenon water. It is, to be sure, quite unusual for myth or ideology to appear in pure forms. But it is very common for them to be found in compound with other systems. Ethical myth and political ideologies are frequently interrelated in a complex compounded situation. For such a reason we need to identify what we mean by ethical myth.

In the pre-modern world culture, people had two separate ways of perceiving, speaking, and acquiring knowledge. Greek scholars have called these views *mythos* and *logos*. *Mythos* or myths are specific types of descriptive stories in the realm of supernatural beings and are designed to explain some of the big issues concerning the condition of human existence, such as where we came from, why we are here, and how we account for the things in our world. They are, in other words, stories of our search for significance, meaning, and truth (Ferraro, 1995: 321). Myths deal with timeless truths and meanings like an ancient form of psychology (Gates, 2000).

There are many religious, heroic, and literary myths in human history. In the field of business for example, the Rockefeller's dime campaign myth is one of the events that has attracted much attention. When John D. Rockefeller was at the zenith of his power, as the founder of the Standard Oil Company, he handed out dimes to rows of eager children who lined the street. This event was created by a group of public relation experts, who believed the dime campaign would counteract his widespread reputation as a monopolist who had ruthlessly eliminated his competitors in the oil industry. Rockefeller believed he was fulfilling moral, ethical, and humanitarian responsibilities by passing out dimes to hungry children. His strategy was to unethically and immorally to gauge the price of oil and earn money, and then give away a dime to hungry children. However, the Rockefeller's dime campaign myth was not a complete success, because the Standard Oil Company was broken up under the Sherman Act of 1890 (Kreithner 1998: 131).

Business in American society, is primarily concerned with expansion and profitability. Profitability is a social contract. On the one hand, it is a contract between workers and capital holders, and on the other hand it is a legitimate agreement between society and organizations or between sellers and buyers, whose mandate and limits are set by legal systems. If people believe in a universal cause for existence, then international moral rights exist without the need for legal fortification. International business law faces a number of problems stemming directly from the simple fact that sourcing pluralistic gain is suspicious. It carries a partisan message of distrust among customers, distributors, and suppliers. Such a lack of confidence in its inherent ability gives little reason to provide international support by all involved parties. Thomas Friedman (2000: 20) has indicated his views for accelerating the trend toward globalization as follows:

> Today, more than ever, the traditional boundaries between politics, culture, technology, finance, national security, and ecology are disappearing. You often cannot explain one without referring to the others, and you cannot explain the whole without reference to them all.... I wish I could say I understood all this when I began my career, but I didn't. I came to this approach entirely by accident, as successive changes in my career kept forcing me to add one more lens on top of another, just to survive.

Nevertheless, contemporary American multidomestic businesses are more than legal entities engaged in manufacturing and sale of products and/or performance of services for making profit. Multidomestic corporations are synergistic legal entities of those stakeholders, who have offered their resources and efforts to conduct their business affairs within and beyond home and host countries to provide services to customers for profitable returns. They are holistic embodiments of the varied resources of the different stakeholders who shape their existence. Many investors from all over the world invest their capital in the American multidomestic corporations in order to make a profit. Also, they have assurance that their capital and investments are safe. Nevertheless, international investors are not concerned about any ethical and moral code of behavior in American society. Their sole objective is to make more money through their investments. More particularly, American multidomestic corporations are explicitly concerned only with the legality of business transactions.

According to the amoral myth of businesses, people are not explicitly concerned with moral and ethical transactions. They are not unethical or immoral; rather, they are being legal. The prominent business advisor Peter Drucker (1980: 191) has written that ethics is a matter for one's private soul. Following his reasoning, he states that a management job is to make human strength productive. Some of the multinational business oriented people believe that ethical values and moral behaviors are not relevant to the business world. They believe business is business and since the nature of business is concerned with exploitation of profitable resources, there is no room for ethical and moral standards. However, a 1987 Conference Board survey of 300 companies worldwide provides a gauge of ethical awareness in the global market economy. This survey revealed seven items as having widespread agreement (80 percent or more saying yes) as ethical issues for global businesses:

- Unauthorized payments,
- Affirmative action,
- Employee privacy,
- Environmental issues (Brooks, 1989: 117; Berenheim, 1987).

OBJECTIVE AND SUBJECTIVE MORALITY, ETHICALITY, AND LEGALITY

Morality and ethics are directly related to an individual's conscientious decisions and actions. These are viewed as products of personal and societal judgments concerning good and bad, right and wrong, just and unjust, and fair and unfair of those decisions and actions. There are two inherent views attached to the attributions of such justifications, namely, objective and subjective morality and ethics. Some people simply accept the ethical principles of their society without personally examining them, and some others question whether what society holds to be right is really right. Within such a complex cognitive testing system, there are objective and subjective judgments. Nevertheless, conscience is the power of intellect or rational ability to conceive the truth through truthful meaning of reasoning. Intellectual freedom enquiry is the bedrock of scientific discoveries, national progress, moral reasoning, ethical tolerance, and personal autonomy. The traditional academic career requirement of publish or perish, morally, ethically, and legality should not allow researchers to convert publish or perish into a vehicle whereby publish and perish all human civilization.

Conscience is an act of an individual's moral conviction. It is an act of a societal ethical opinion that can cause the notions of objective and subjective morality and ethics. The distinction between what an individual believes to be right and what is actually right refers to subjectively right and objectively right decisions and actions. This means that what an individual is judging now, from a moral point of view could be perceived as a cognitive phenomenon. A decision or an action is objectively right if that decision or action is in conformity with the ethical law of society. Therefore, a decision or an action is subjectively right if an individual believes that a decision or an action is moral. There is one condition for a decision or an action to be objectively and subjectively right. If an individual believes telling the truth is right, and the statement he/she declares is correct, then the action of giving the statement is both subjectively and objectively right. Otherwise, that statement may be subjectively right and objectively wrong. For example, if bribery or payola is a popular cultural tradition in a country and if I am mistaken about the morality of bribery, then I may believe it to be moral for me to take bribes, even though it is actually (objectively) immoral. Or conversely, a decision or an action can be subjectively wrong and objectively right (De George, 1995: 38).

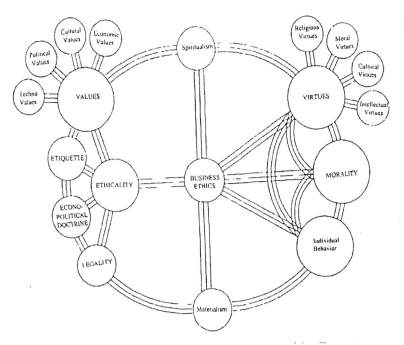

Figure 1.1: Effects of Morality, Ethicality, and Legality on the Logic of

Human life is viewed as an integral sum of morality, ethicality, and legality. All of these characteristics are highly related to the interrelationships of people in society. Humans perceive their activities on the basis of two major phenomena: (1) spirituality, and (2) materiality. Business ethics has been viewed as a societal integration of all aspects of human socialization (see Figure 1.1).

Regardless of different views on multicultural business ethics, in the postmodern industrial era, *logos* or logic deals with pragmatic realities. Logic or reason as a scientific type of realism deals with a dominated form of the modern cognitive study of human intention, objectives, and processes through six major stages:

- Acquisition of knowledge.
- Comprehension of problems.

- Analyzing factorial interrelated processes.
- Synthesizing theoretical and pragmatic solutions.
- Formulating, selecting, and applying the viable and reliable solutions.
- Evaluating the consequential results of thinking and acting.

The objectives in one stage are likely to make use of and build on the behaviors found in the preceding stages. While we are primarily concerned with the cognitive domain of conscience, we have done something to reveal the connectivity between cognitive and pragmatic knowledge. This is the exact meaning of ethical behavior. Ethical logic is concerned with cognitive causes, pragmatic processes, and synthesized effects. Thus, the ethical behaviors in the diffusive cognitive-pragmatic domain are largely characterized by a rather high degree of consciousness on the part of reality.

The so-called acquisition of knowledge and application of knowledge as a dual use phenomenon has provided humanity with good and bad consequences. Scientific knowledge is arguably politically neutral but its technological application is not. Scientific discoveries in physics, chemistry, engineering, and cybernetic systems have brought vast benefit to mankind while simultaneously generating even some harmful side effects in humans and in the environment. Poste (2001: IV) indicates: "Assuming that the current political (September 11 incident) will act to heighten defenses against bioterrorism is sustained, this will spawn big new commercial opportunities and is likely to spark the emergence of a life sciences defense industry." Therefore, the logic behind establishment and development of a new industry is based on necessity.

TRANSETHICAL BUSINESS CHALLENGES

It is now a commonly accepted truism that global businesses are more than international entities engaged in manufacturing and selling products and/or rendering services for profit. It is also perceived that global enterprises are holistic embodiments of multicultural values and beliefs of different stakeholders who shape their existence. More particularly, global businesses are synergistic expressions of those who have offered their resources and efforts to conduct their business affairs within and beyond both home and host countries. They provide services to consumers for fees. Furthermore, global businesses are expendable and successful -- at best because of different cultural perceptions and can always slip out of hand (Parhizgar, 1999: 43).

Walton (1977: 25-27) generalizes the challenges to commercial activities at international, national, and corporate levels in the following manner:

- **Global:**

  o   The finite biosphere of water, soil, and air is producing a revolution in though comparable (said anthropologist Margaret

Mead) to the Copernican revolution. Selling more may yield to selling less -- but better. Mankind is more interdependent than ever before and a parochial nationalistic view by corporate or government executives will not help. Economist Harold Isaacs has said that: We are experiencing on a massively universal scale a conclusive ingathering of men in their numberless grouping of kinds tribal, racial, ethnic, religious, national. ... Yet the more global our science and technology, the more tribal our politics; the more we see of the plants the less we see of each other. Perhaps this is the great moral paradox of the century. A fundamental problem is the lopsided distribution of the world's resources, both material and human. Definitely needed are mechanisms whereby the world's resources can be better identified, better managed and more equitably distributed. A consequence of the uneven distribution of resources is the need to cope with the growing power and growing demands of third-world countries defined mainly as non-Caucasian people largely in Africa, Caribbean, India, and the South Sea Islands. These third-world people, determined to overthrow cultural and political domination by the West, will influence the formation of a new transcultural ethics. The new imperative will be either do in Rome what the Romans do or do in Rome what Americans do in America. To find a new ethic of compromise Western man must begin to understand their literary and philosophical traditions. .. Critical to all efforts to increase prosperity and share it with others throughout the globe is the multinational corporation whose power must be channeled into mutually satisfactory efforts.

- **Domestic:**

  o The older sense of Manifest Destiny for America has been rejected in favors of a more modest view of both our capabilities and our rights vis-à-vis those of other nations.
  o The legitimacy of American capitalism, based on the moral system of rewards rooted in the Protestant sanctification of work, is under increasing strain.
  o If the politicalization of social decision-making continues at present rates the point will soon be reached when ethics will be defined simply as obedience to the law and this would be disastrous.
  o Neither the free enterprise and pluralistic economic system nor the political democratic systems have yet developed instruments for coping with long-range problems.
  o Because the need for large-scale organizations (oligopolies) is explicitly recognized, the meaning of competition must be redefined.

- **Business:**

  o The distinction between old-fashioned capitalism and modern enterprise is basic and the corporate executive accepts his obligations to the larger society.

  o The identifying mark of the new enterprise system is professional responsibility defined as the sophisticated balancing of claims by various interest groups-stockholders, employees, customers, and the larger public.

  o A renewed emphasis on human values requires the corporation to develop a working climate wherein each individual can constructively translate personal aspirations important to him into performance and results important to others.

  o Moral improprieties by the few have given a black (blind) eye to the entire corporate community so that ethical renewal is essential. But the norms for making ethical assessments are not static but changing sometimes clear and often ambiguous.

  o Professions other than management (notably law and accounting) performance of the modern corporation.

  o The clamor for corporate reform will encourage large enterprises to reassess the composition of their boards to assure a greater range of competence and representation.

The transethical principles for doing business in the contemporary global market have changed drastically. Those corporations that understand the new international rules for doing business in a free world economy will prosper; those that cannot may perish (Mohrman and Mitroff, 1987: 37). A sense of prosperity permits global corporations to appropriately search for opportunities created by the new socio-transethical considerations The basic perception is that instant reform in the global transethical business is emerging.

GLOBAL BUSINESS ORGANIZATIONS

Ethical and moral philosophies of global business mandate corporations to become legitimate not simply because they are efficient, effective, and productive, but because they represent a holistic worldwide accountability. Today global enterprise leaders who act together can do more than anyone could do singly for the goodness of humanity.

Since in the international free market economy there is a multicultural milieu, nations have not created a unified system of moral standards, ethical value systems, and legal principles. In other words, there is no universal agreement among buyers and sellers how to responsibly and accountably close their deals. Accordingly, there is no universal applicability of judgments in moral, ethical, and legal business transactions among nations. There are similarities and differences among nations in global, continental, and local business transactions. The first obvious step is to seek understanding of those basic forces in the global marketplace and within the environments of global, multinational, transnational, international, foreign, and domestic corporate moral, ethical, and legal systems. Having once catalogued the major transformations that characterize these entities, critical decisions and actions can be reconsidered to respond constructively. Some factors are very important in understanding the nature of all kinds of international business entities. These factors are as follows:

- Ownership
- Investment
- Styles of management
- Controlling systems
- Marketing segmentation
- Autonomy of subsidiaries
- Profitability
- Consumer profiles

An alternative way to view what is meant by transethical business is to distinguish foreign businesses from domestic.

A domestic business operates in only one country, and a global business in more than one. The definitions adopted here are broad and include firms involved in exports and imports of goods and services, as well as those with financial operations around the world. For the clarity of the terms used in this text you will find definitions of different types of business entities in this chapter. It is important to recognize specific differences in the way that a business is conducted domestically and/or internationally. The subsequent discussion identifies the differences between firms described as foreign and domestic businesses. Differences in firms' operations are identified in a magnitude of two extreme conditions: global and domestic, (see Figure 1.2). Most companies combine attributes of both global and domestic markets in their operations. Nevertheless, it is helpful to distinguish between the two extremes.

There are several issues in the field of global business that need to be clarified. These issues could be perceived as inbound and outbound of the organization and the nations such as investment, operation, the rule of origin, plant location and relocation, legal territories, foreign sales relative to domestic sales, foreign profit relative to domestic, foreign employment relative to domestic, and foreign investment relative to domestic.

Furthermore, other issues are related to the stakeholders such as market shares, product positions, plant condition, subsidiary operations, consumer and customer efficacy, and shareholder and stockholder rights. In addition to these issues, number and type of ownership, the form of overall corporate ownership, the makeup of top corporate management authorities, the mix of foreign and domestic management, and technical personnel in various locations, moral and cultural boundaries, organizational affiliations, alliance and joint venturing partnerships, private, public, or government agencies, and profit, non-profit, and not-for-profit corporations are considered the main issues in analyzing an organizational structure.

It is important to realize that for specific ethical, moral, and legal analysis, more precise definitions and finer distinctions may be appropriate. Some authors distinguish among these different forms of business organizations. Parhizgar (2000: 1-23) defined all these entities as follows:

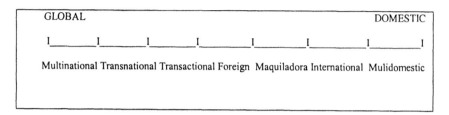

Figure 1. 2: Magnitude of the Two Extreme Conditions of Global and Domestic Corporations

Global Corporations (GCs)

A *Global Corporation* is a business entity that obtains the factors of production from all countries without restriction and/or discrimination against it by both home and host countries. It markets its products and/or services around the globe for the purpose of making profit (e.g., The World Bank Group and The International Finance Corporation-IFC). These organizations around the globe serve their investors, managers, employees, and consumers regardless of their socio-cultural and econo-political differences.

Multinational Corporations (MNCs)

A *Multinational Corporation* is a highly developed organization with a deep worldwide involvement in obtaining the factors of production from multiple countries around the world, manufactures its products, and markets them in specific international markets (e.g., Exxon in the energy sector; General Motors in the automobile industry; Mitsui & Co, Ltd. in the wholesale business; IBM in the computer industry; E. I. du Pont de Neours in the chemical industry; and General Electric in the electrical equipment industry).

Transnational Corporations (TNCs)

A *Transnational Corporation* refers to a business entity whose *management* and *ownership* are divided equally among two or more nations. These corporations acquire their factors of production around the world and market them in specific countries (e.g., Royal Dutch/Shell Group headquarters are located in the Netherlands and the United Kingdom). The European countries most commonly use the term transnational corporation.

Transactional Corporations (TACCs)

A *Transactional Corporation* is a domestic corporation which operates its activities on the basis of a particular form of reciprocal trading practices that facilitates the exporting and importing of goods and/or services without any flow of money. They trade goods and services with different goods and/or services. Usually transactional corporations countertrade activities consisting of three types of transactions: barter, counterpurchase, and compensatory arrangements.

Barter: Two parties as sellers and buyers directly exchange products and/or services without any flow of money.

Counterpurchases: Two parties as sellers and buyers concurrently agree to trade a given percentage of their trade contract value in the form of products and/or services. Ethically, both parties agree to exchange products with products and or with services.

Compensatory Arrangements: As an example, a selling company agrees to sell technological machineries to a buyer company solely for the purpose of completing a production system in exchange for receiving its full payment, in the form of products of those machineries, as the result of the sale. Ethically, the buying party is under obligation not to resell those technologies to other nations without the consent of the seller.

Foreign Corporations (FCs)

A *Foreign Corporation* is a business entity that has its assets invested by a group of foreigners to operate its production system and markets its products and/or services in host countries for the purpose of making profit. These corporations are controlled and managed by foreigners to the extent in which they adhere to all rules and regulations of the host countries (e.g., Japanese Sanwa Bank in the United States).

International Corporations (ICs)

An *International Corporation* is a domestic and/or a multidomestic entity that operates its production activities in full-scale at home and markets its products and/or services beyond its national geographic and/or political borders. In return, it imports the value added monetary income to its own country's GNP.

It engages in exporting goods, services, and management (e.g., Wal-Mart Company).

Multidomestic Corporations (MDCs)

A *Multidomestic Corporation* is a domestic business entity that is owned by a group of businesses for the purpose of synergistic profitability. Such a company conducts its business transactions in home and host countries through separate local, and foreign entities in home and host countries (e. g., The Walt Disney World and Time Warner).

Super-National Corporations (SNCs)

A *Super-National Corporation* is a small domestic business entity that creates large market shares and product positions in the regional markets. Specifically, SNCs are emerging from the E-commerce. SNCs are heavily dependent on mass communication, logistics and mass transportation services: sea, air, and land. The E-commerce companies are heavily dependent on the international telecommunication industry (e.g., Yahoo and Amazon.Com.).

Maquiladora Corporations (MCs)

A *Maquiladora Corporation* is known as the twin plant, production sharing, or inbound organization, which is allowed the duty-free importation of machinery, raw materials, and components, inbound production and outbound manufactured products, between neighboring countries. The word maquila is derived from the Spanish verb maquilar, which translates as to do work for another. The current usage of the word describes the Mexican corporations being paid a fee for processing and refining raw materials and/or assembling manufacturing parts for foreign corporations. Maquilas are applying Fordism techniques to assemble parts for foreign manufacturers (e.g., 2,500 Maquiladoras on the border of the United States and Mexico). Maquilas are assembly plants in Mexico under special custom treatment and foreign investment regulations, whereby they import duty-free parts and components into Mexico, on a temporary basis, and export finished, refined, and assembled goods and products from Mexico to the United States or Japan. These plants pay only a value added tax on exports. The number of Maquiladora has increased significantly from 12 plants in 1965 to 2,500 in 1977, employing over 740,000 workers with cheaper wages (Parhizgar and Landeck, 1997: 427).

BUSINESS ETHICS IN
GLOBAL ENVIRONMENTS

In global business environments, ethics can be a misleading because different nations perceive ethical value systems differently. Ethical and moral perceptions are conceived as the individual beliefs about what is right and wrong, good and bad, just and unjust, fair and unfair. The major implication in global business is that people with different beliefs establish different ethical standards and apply different values and principles in their judgments. Consequently, international ethical values are relative, not absolute standards of thoughts and behaviors for all people. Whether or not the behavior of a person is ethical depends on who is being examined and who is the judge about the ideas, events, and people. Internationally, there is no single way to ensure that a corporate manager makes ethical decisions. Written codes of conduct often look great, but they may have no effect if employees do not believe or feel that top management do not take the codes of ethics seriously (Parhizgar, 1999: 16).

In our contemporary international free market economy, multiethicalism can have a profound impact on people's lives. Global E-commerce is emerging from multi-functional, multi-disciplines, multi-media, and multi-conducts among sellers and buyers. Nations in such commercial E-environments come into frequent contact with what Gudykunst (1994: 4) calls strangers:

> Namely people who are not members of our groups and who are different on the basis of moral virtues, ethical principles, cultural values, political ideologies, legal doctrines, religious faith, ethnical backgrounds, different gender perceptions, or other group characteristics.

Consequently the world becomes a multiethical global village.

Multiethics are like snapshots taken from different angles and distances of societies at different times within the context of multicultural organizations. No multiethical single picture or perspective can depict multifaceted characters of human behavior, because diversified value systems differ in focus and scope of ethics, morality, and legality (Harvey and Allard, 1995:3). When a company becomes multidomestic and/or multinational, it creates miniatures of itself in other markets. These companies are staffed by other nationalities and ethnicities and gain a wide degree of autonomy. In practice, it will often be quite difficult to classify the predominant value systems in globalize corporations. However, it should be relatively easy to identify the sources of value systems in both home and host countries.

In globalization of a firm, there is a fundamental requirement for definition and classification of conceptual and practical value systems that reflect the central elements defining the rights and duties of producers and consumers. Since these values are central to the concepts of moral, ethical, and legal practices of businesses, the definitions and classifications of value systems should be internationally known through the United Nations. Although there is a

United Nations International Court of Justice (World Court-WC), the power to enforce the judgments of this court is bound only by the parties' honor to comply with the WC rulings: if a ruling is not economically or politically expedient for the rebuked party, noncompliance is likely (Payne, Raiborn, and Askvik, 1997: 1728).

THE OLD ENVIRONMENTS OF GLOBAL BUSINESS ETHICS

The international business trade has a long history. Slaves were perhaps the first global unethical and immoral commodities to be traded among colonial powers. At the height of slavery, in just one decade of the Eighteenth century over 300,000 slaves were shipped to the Americas from Liverpool, England, for a gross of 15,186,850 British Pounds. At 50 pounds a head, slaves were among the most valuable merchandise that could be shipped. In the post industrial revolution the slave trade, like its twin, the opium trade, defined a triangle. Slaver traders took goods from Europe to Africa, where they exchanged them for slaves; ferried the slaves to the Americas, where they were sold to cotton or sugar plantations; brought the proceeds back to Liverpool, Bristol or London, England in the form of rum, cotton, tobacco or other fashionable new world produce (Honigmann, 2000: V).

In 1851, Bostonian I. M. Singer invented the first sewing machine. In 1867, the Singer Sewing Machine Company became the first American international conglomerate business when it built a factory in Glasgow, Scotland. By the end of the 1880s, the company had become an international conglomerate with branches in Montreal, Russia and Australia. In 1874 Singer was selling more than half of its machines in foreign markets: 126,694 out of 241,679 total sold (Jackson, Miller, and Miller, 1997: 173). Colgrove (1999) reported:

> Singer Company filed for Chapter 11 bankruptcy protection. She questions: How many of us believed that Singer worked out their problems and ought another Singer machine over the last 10 years? I know I was one of them. I purchased a Singer Quantum CXL in 1995. The store where I purchased the machine closed its doors within two months of my purchase. I was forced to deal with the Singer Company for all my problems. .... and they were many. On the third time of the machine being shipped out to be replaced, I asked the customer service representative, if this was common with this machine. He answered: "You use it too much," left me speechless. For the $1,500.00 I spent, I expected to use the machine.

Another example is James Cash Penny. As a young man, Penny opened his first butcher store in Denver, Colorado with $300.00 that he borrowed from his mother's life savings. The departing butcher advised Penny that his success would depend heavily on trade from a nearby hotel. To keep the hotel as a customer, the former butcher explained, all you have to do is to buy the chef a bottle of whisky a week. Penny regularly made the gift and business was good, but gradually the opinion of his father, who reviled alcohol, preyed more and more on his mind. He made a decision not to make profit in such a manner, stopped giving the bribe, and at the age of 23 was flat broke when the shop failed. Penny later started the Golden Rule Department Store in Denver and with honesty he expanded the J. C. Penny's Department Store around the U. S. (Steiner and Steiner, 1994: 181).

THE NEW ENVIRONMENTS OF GLOBAL BUSINESS ETHICS

In the first decade of the Twentieth century, New Jersey had been the leader in offering easy terms for corporations. In 1913, prodded by Governor Woodrow Wilson who argued that such a pro-business atmosphere was immoral, the New Jersey legislature decided to increase restrictions on its corporations. The new law lasted only four years, but by then most of the state's corporations had moved to Delaware (Clarkham, 1994: 174).

Around 1920, social economy began to drift away from the traditional capitalists (the owners) into the hands of professional managers who owed their position and power to function and performance (Drucker, 1980: 191). In the mid Twentieth century, Watson (1963: 3) reports that of the top twenty-five industrial corporations in the United States in 1900, only two remained in that select company in 1963. One retained its original identity; the other was a merger of seven corporations on that original list. Two of those twenty-five corporations failed, three others merged and dropped behind. The remaining twelve continued in business, but each had fallen substantially in its standing. One way speculates at length about immoral and unethical behaviors of managers as a cause of the decline or fall of these corporations.

In the late 1990s, scientific discoveries and technological innovations created knowledge wealth and money-power. Then, money-power safeguarded knowledge wealth, intellectual property power, and new industrial billionaires such as the former Chief Executive Officer of Microsoft, Bill Gates. However, in the modern global business, the intellectual property power cannot and will not be able to establish and maintain scientific ethics unless it initiates responsibility and accountability among multidomestic and multinational corporations.

In order to create an ethical money-power structure and convert it into stakeholder power, it needs to first establish the efficient legal infrastructure through socio-ethical responsibility and accountability. However, legal infrastructure spells out only the foundation of the right decisions and actions. Businesspeople need to voluntarily impose ethics in their decisions and actions. Aristotle states that responsibility follows knowledge. Nevertheless, knowledge does not carry responsibility and accountability. Instead, knowledgeable people can be responsible or irresponsible. Finally, in the beginning of the Twenty First century, the borderless E-commerce has emerged and conquered the international business transactions. People criticize their peers for immoral and unethical decisions and actions other than their own (Carroll, 1975). Among all managers, those at the lower levels have reported feeling the most pressure to compromise their ethics (Baumhart, 1961: 6).

In today's global market, consumers and producers frequently find themselves faced with ethical dilemmas. A prominent boutique manager in Beverly Hills, California found that during 1970s and 1980s, the Beverley Hills customers bought very expensive dresses a few hours before Hollywood parties and wear them for a few hours, then returned them to the boutique the next day and requested a full refund. The manager had to honor the customer demands. In order to make a profit, the manager resoled those returned dresses to other customers as new dresses. Do you find any unethical and immoral behavior in such a business process by both sellers and buyers?

CLASSICAL AND CONTEMPORARY VIEWS OF THE BUSINESS WORLD

The primary focus of this book is to study moral, ethical, and legal influences on individual and group behavior in organizations. These are three major behavioral ordinations of reason for people who strive to achieve a common good. Ordination of reason signifies the establishment of cognitive and behavioral orders in a search for proper ends through good means. Ordination provides peace and harmony among people. Not all ordinations establish practical patterns of expected excellent behaviors. One kind of ordination gives you ideas, another kind gives you contents, and the other one binds you with perceptual commitments. All these ordinations are rooted in variations such as generalizing, understanding, and defining fundamental principles and distinctive outcomes of these three phenomena. Managers should understand ethical, moral, and legal ordinations. These three ordinations are covered in their full expositions in multiethical organizations.

The various ordinations for an individual's behavior (ethical, moral, and legal means and ends) are the three major topics in this section. In addition, the notions of sensational and emotional pleasure respond to the degree of enjoyment and pleasure. The rational decisions and actions provide long-term happiness. Sometimes the means justify the ends or *vice versa*. Researchers have found that the expression of emotions and grief is in fact a transcultural universal. There are a number of different terms, however, that are used transculturally to express grief, such as depression, sadness, despair, the blues, helplessness, hopelessness, powerlessness, feeling low, gloom, and listlessness. In addition, dejection, sorrow, anguish, unhappiness, melancholy, and woe are also words used to express grief and associated emotions.

Historically, conservative cultures have been driven to seek a surer foundation than motives to legitimize actions and behavior. In contrast, modern cultures are driven to seek practical motives based on objectively oriented data gathering to value peoples' competitive actions and behaviors. Consequently, one thing seems certain and it is that in advanced industrialized, developed, developing, and decaying societies, ethics, morality, and legality play important roles in people daily lives. Table 1.1 composes classical and contemporary views of the modern world.

Historically, both conservative and modern cultural views have articulated their positions on more specific political, educational, economic, cultural, social, and medical issues in all societies and they have shaped expected patterns of behaviors between homogeneous faiths and beliefs. For example, Roman Catholicism has a rich tradition of formally applying its core values to the moral aspects of industrial relations (Shaw, 1996: 12). Judaism does not demand social isolation or adoption of a unique style of life. Jews need to provide alternatives when a need is felt. Moslems believe in religious scripture (Koran) that has formulated social justice.

CLASICAL CULTURAL WORLD PWERSPECTIVE	CONTEMPORARY INDUSTRIAL WORLD PERSPECTIVE
Religious principles: Faith	Econo-political ideologies: Beliefs
Eternal spiritual life	Worldwide material life
End-result orientations	Mean-result orientations
Theoretical-life	Practical-life
Intuitive behavior	Rationalized behavior
Destiny by God's will	Human-made decisions and actions
Religious obedience	Legal compliance
Mystery-to-be-accepted	Mystery-to-be discovered
Community sense of value	Individual sense of value
Service beyond self: Charity	Service for self-interest: Egoism
Compassion	Survival-of-the-fittest (Darwinism)
Equality	Justice
Individual natural rights	Individual's legal privileges
Absolutism ethics	Relativism Ethics
Stabilized economy	Dynamic economy
Exploitation	Exploration
Fixed price	Market price
Cooperation	Competition
Imitation	Innovation

Table 1.1: Comparison of the Conservative and Modern Industrial Views of the Cultural World

In the first instance, through the modern industrialized views, the free market mechanism sought to make energized people richer. Note how sociocultural, econo-political and religious doctrines partially and to some extent holistically played important roles to influence an individual's daily behavior. People have learned from both religious faith and political ideologies how to appreciate moral thoughts and ethical principals.

Moral behavior deals with an individual's ultimate state of psychosocial doctrines and religious faith. These manners are related to the individual's behavioral ends. The ethical behavior deals with pluralistic means in actions. The ethical pluralistic beliefs can create a qualitative ordination to facilitate ultimate sociocultural ends. The legal behavior deals with the econo-political ordination of reason to be enforced for the common good.

As you look at changes in the history of the industrialized world, you will observe how science and technology played important roles in all societies and changed peoples' perceptions. Today, global citizens are living in an age of moral, ethical, and legal confusion. They are prone to periodic outbreaks of amoral dynamic forces. Individuals try to preserve their natural rights. Governments of many countries prevent individuals from exercising their potential rights. The content of these rights, obligations, and bans by governments and interest groups are constantly changing. Since these changes deeply affect the lives of many people, there are likely to be disagreement between governments, interest groups, and ordinary people. People desire to maintain their moral virtues, ethical values, and legal principles in order to protect their rights. However, because of changing socio-cultural and econo-political mechanisms of life, people are increasingly exposed to behavioral collisions not only between countries, but also within the countries.

FROM THE BUREAUCRATIC SYSTEM TO COSMOCRATIC BUSINESS ENVIRONMENTS

Globalization of the New World Order has caused businesses to depart from the state of segmented political ideologies and return to the free trade world of nature. Stepping into cyberspace business is no reason to abandon the worthy ethical and moral obligations of the traditional commercial processes. Free trade among nations without government and/or interest group interference will be only practical reality between producers and consumers. In reality, E-knowledge has created a virtual world. In such a virtual environment a new elite group of Global Digital Citizens (GDCs) whose power lies in their ideas, share their speculative discoveries and pragmatic innovativeness through global multi-connected contacts. The Internet as a wild and lawless frontier allows GDCs to do what they have always done more quickly and cheaply, and sometime in different ways. Websites are accessible from countries of which the owner of the websites may never have been familiar with consumer cultures and *vice versa*. This can cause difficulties for both global digital producers and consumers. For example, Randall and Treacy (2000: 6) state: "The UK Virgin Atlantic Airline recently ran into difficulties when advertised (Via its UK-based Website) a transatlantic fare in terms which were entirely conventional in the UK (such as:

"Fly from London to New York for $x return, plus taxes and booking fee."
Please contact your local travel agents for details)." In the U.S. marketplace,
however, it is not enough simply to refer to the fact that additional charges are
payable. A company (in the U.S.) must set out the exact cost of the taxes and
booking fees. While the Virgin Atlantic Airline incurred only a relatively trivial
fine, the adverse publicity was potentially damaging to the company's reputation
and integrity. Likewise, the consumer protection laws of Germany put
significant restrictions on discounts and other benefits that a retailer can offer to
consumers.

In the cyberspace business, people still live physically in ideological
segmented societies, but mentally they are proceeding in highly cosmocratic
multi-natural environments. A New York City cosmocrat is more likely to
communicate via E-mail to global peers around the world than talk to the people
next door. This is a return to the rules of nature, where moral and ethical good
senses and reasons are the best reliable choices. These cosmocrats constitute a
more better off pursuing constraints on their actions for restraints being accepted
by others. On the one hand, bureaucrats believe that most people are not
sufficiently enlightened to seek their own interest, so they advocate that people
need to follow the bureaucrat-guided laws. Yet an elite based on the best and the
highest power competitive edge, bureaucrats compete with cosmocrats with
money-power, and cosmocrats compete with bureaucrats with their brainpower.
On the other hand, in the global digital space, cosmocrats are competing with
bureaucrats to become a self-conscious power group to help all nations with
different cultures in order to establish a better life. So each power group is trying
to provide sufficient information for people to make good choices. Cosmocrats
possess the brains and a good deal of the knowledge-power.

Cosmocrats are defined by their ethical values, moral attitudes, and
intellectual lifestyles rather than just by their bank accounts. Cosmocrats rely on
their brainpower. These global digital cosmocrats (GDCs) can freely express
their ideas through the Internet. Being in an E-civil world, means that we accept
the responsibility of obeying moral obligations and ethical responsibilities.
Cosmocrats are not only found in the business world. They are also Global
Digital Sabbatical Professors who are navigating scholars through distance
learning around the world in order to educate people. The global sabbatical
professors abide by their professional ethical values and mutual contracts with
the community of scholars, and submit their disputes to impartial professional
arbitrators. Therefore, global digital citizens become a self-conscious class with
their genetic traits in blood, dominated by national cultural values in taste, and
civilized by their personal opinion in morals, and professionalized intellectually
in ethics. This seems to say that GDCs are the same worldwide and share ethical
values.

Two preferred ethical and moral commitments are endemic to cosmocrats.
The first is an emphasis on cosmocratic productionism and consumerism. This
means that knowledge, information, and science are highly integrated in a
unified fashion. E-commerce and the E-information motivate cosmocrats to be a

source of reliable updated commercial knowledge. They strive for converting E-business into a general global platform for ethical and moral considerations. The second is the desire and passion of the E-academicians to stay in the domain of current knowledge creativity. Such a far-reaching state of thought will be created through global free communication -- most notably through the Internet.

ETHICAL BEHAVIOR IN THE GLOBAL BUSINESS WORLD

Why Be Ethical in Global Business Transactions?

Today, there has been a growing concern about the globalization of business ethics. Contrary to the belief that ethical and moral value systems are just buzzwords, they are often the major predictors of success or failure in either an industry or a company strategy. Kirrane (1990: 53) indicates that the very term, business ethics, tends to raise cynicism. People shake their heads and woefully recite recent scandals. The business world of the past century is full of scandals. For example, near the turn of the Twentieth century, Henry Ford that he was planning to sell his shares of Ford Motor Company stock to General Motors started a rumor. The original eleven stockholders of the Ford Company, alarmed by the false rumors, sold their stocks back to Henry Ford at a bargain price (Dahlinger, 1978: 124). In the mid-1960s, a major Korean political party asked a Gulf Oil Company for a $10 million donation. The CEO personally negotiated it down to $4 million, still a huge sum. In another incident, Lockheed made an estimated $25 million in payments as payola in connection with sales of its Tristar L-1011 aircraft in Japan (Tong and Welling, 1981).

The baby-food manufacturer Beech-Nut Company sold flavored sugar water as pure apple juice in the early 1980s. The company was found guilty to 215 criminal counts and paid over $25 million in fines. The investigators found no apple juice in the product that claimed it was 100% pure apple juice. They found that the allegedly 100% pure apple juice was actually a 100 percent fraudulent chemical cocktail (Hartley, 1993: 112).

Business Week (January 10, 1977) reported that the scorecard on questionable bribery payments made overseas by the United States corporations indicated that 175 companies had admitted shelling out more than $300 million during the early 1970s.

The Charles Keading, President of the failed Lincoln Savings and Loan, was notorious in his behavior to influence federal regulators into changing regulations that would benefit him and his family members on the Lincoln payroll. Keating used S&L funds to buy or subsidize vacation homes, private jet airplanes, and works of arts. Keating also hired three of his son-in-laws to executive positions that paid as much as $1.2 million a year. He was the subject of a brilliant (notorious brilliant) BPS documentary, Other People's Money, (Barton, 1995: 83).

Conspiracy to commit immoral, unethical, and illegal actions is obviously a punishable offense. Indeed, the generally light penalties given to executives and managers (usually a very light financial fine and or a requirement for community service) may actually motivate some managers to take the risks associated with dishonesty (Barton, 1995: 83). For example, a federal jury convicted James J. McDermott Jr., former Chief Executive of Keefe Bruyette & Woods, on the charge of leaking inside information about banking mergers to his mistress, an actress who performed in adult movies under the name Marlilyn Star. The case marks the first time a Wall Street chief executive has been charged and convicted of insider trading, said the Security Exchange Commission (SEC) - (*Financial Times*, 2000: 1).

Universal codes of ethics are established or justified by preference to principles, and the same principles can establish different rules in different circumstances and hence for different societies. Since the business operations in the international market may be conceived as ethical relativism, businesses do not follow those ethical principles. They can be relative in the sense that they are not binding under certain types of conditions. For example, a former employee of the Bank of New York, Russian-born Lucy Edwards and her husband Peter Berlin, plead guilty to laundering $7 billion in suspected Russian funds through accounts at the Bank of New York. This illegal capital flight may be a cause of the disassembly of the Russian economy, and is an apparent abuse of the American and international banking system (Williams, 2000: 2). In a New York federal court, Edwards and Berlin admitted that they set up a branch of a foreign bank without regulatory permission, operated an illegal wire transfer business, fraudulently obtaining visas, bribed an American official, evaded U.S. taxes, accepted illicit payments, and laundered them offshore. The confessions represented a major break in the case, described as the largest money laundering investigation ever (Catan, 2000:18). Do you think the CEO of the Bank of New York was not involved in a $7 billion capital flight? It is not a surprise, in contemporary Russian culture, to find immoral and unethical behaviors such as bribery and money laundering. Allocation of $7 billion from one country to another raises questions concerning the existence of a profile of immoral principles and unethical practices in the international banking industry and involves many governmental and banking industry authorities.

Another similar case indicates that on February 17, 2000, Swiss justice sources confirmed a report in *Le Temps* newspaper, which said documents traced payments from Merkata Trading, a Swiss-based construction company, through offshore company accounts owned by Mr. Pavel Borodin, the former top Kremlin official, and his associates in connection with two government contracts worth about $500 million. Victor Stolpolvskikh, a former Moscow representative of Mabetex, another Swiss-based construction company, runs Markata Trading. Merkata paid $60 million in bribes to Pavel Borodin for winning Russian government construction contracts. According to the documents in the possession of Geneva investigators, Mr. Daniel Devaud, the investigating magistrate of the Swiss Justice Department, formed and issued the basis of the international warrant for Borodin's detention and extradition to Switzerland (Williams, 2000: 2). It is apparent from International Monetary Fund (IMF) reports that the international financial authorities and politicians have shown a growing concern and distrust of the behavior of Russian businesspeople in general and the large government corruption in particular. As the participants in the fifty-second American Assembly at Arden House, on April 1977, the IMF pointed out in their final report: "Corporations must realize that some of their actions-action taken in their view in the best interest of the corporation may produce consequences on both business and the society at large that trigger disapproval" (Nelson, 1977: vii). The above cases and others are only a few examples that are worrying or plaguing the international ethical and moral value systems.

The topic of business ethics includes not only the question of the moral or immoral motivations of businesspeople, but it also includes a range of issues that arise in the depth of socio-cultural values and econo-political beliefs. Today, global business environments essentially comprise multiple complex webs that are highly interrelated and integrated interest groups (hereafter called stakeholders). Each group of stakeholders is distinguished by its unique set of objectives. For example, a multinational corporation (MNC) is itself an amalgamation of several home and host stakeholder groups (e.g., shareholders, stockholders, bondholders, employees, management, customers, consumers, suppliers, home and host governmental authorities, etc.). Each of these interest groups can be further subdivided into voting versus non-voting shareholders, secured versus unsecured creditors, and unionized versus non-unionized employees with various economic, and cultural and political expectations (Dobson, 1990: 481).

Contrary to the belief that multinational corporate success or failure in globalization of their firms is often the result of decision-making processes, in most cases it has been observed that the practice of marketing global of products and/or services depends upon the realization of the corporate ethical, moral, and legal commitments to their stakeholders. For example, Cargill, the U.S. agribusiness group, will pay $100 million to the Pioneer Company to settle the allegation that it used genetic material stolen from Pioneer. Pioneer is a subsidiary of Dupont. The settlement reflects damages for past infractions. Pioneer had alleged that one of its former employees took corn-breeding material with him when he went to work for Cargill's seed business in 1989. The settlement will allow the Cargill Company to go ahead with the sale of its North American seed operations. It had planned to sell these to AgrEvo Company, the German Agri-Chemical Group, for about $650 million in 1998. Also under the settlement, Cargill Company agreed to immediately destroy improperly obtained material in its own corn-breeding program. Fritz Corrigan, executive vice-president of Cargill Company admitted that: "The episode had been painful and Pioneer's allegations had revealed that our seed business hadn't always met with up to our high ethical standards" (Tait, 2000: 17). This incident reveals that unethical and illegal decisions and actions can create harsh consequences for a company.

Along the above line of mismanagement, de Jonquieres (2000: 8) reveals that the recent report, by Templeton College, Oxford, says the findings show that many large multinational companies are not particularly good at managing their foreign activities, and that strong core competence does not guarantee international commercial success. The report is based on an analysis of 214 of the companies in 1999 Fortune Global 500 list. It finds their foreign activities accounted on average for 36 percent of their assets and 39 percent of revenues, but generated only 27 percent of their profits in 1998. The report found many of the poorest performers were European and Japanese companies, with Japan accounting for 11 of the 20 lowest ranked companies. Thirteen of the 20 companies with best foreign performance were headquartered in the U.S. The best-performing sectors were pharmaceuticals, soaps, and tobacco. Go to almost any pharmacist in Africa, parts of Asia or Latin America and the chances are, you will find medicines stamped with the same three words: Made in India. For years, India has been the world's supplier of generic and pirated medicines. An astonishing 23,000 drug companies, some of them little more than back street operations, others mini-multinationals, produce tablets, syrups, and infusions (Shanker and Pilling, 2000: 12)

GLOBAL CODES OF BUSINESS ETHICS

Globalization has multiplied the ethical problems facing organizations (Deresky, 1997: 493). Yet business ethics has not yet been global. While domestic American companies may use general guidelines for appropriate behavior based on federal law and the value structure rooted in the nation's Judeo-Christian heritage, such guidelines are not consistently applicable overseas (Laczniak and Naor, 1985). Traditional cultural, religious, and political beliefs are weakening in the wake of globalization of the free market economy, particularly in securities market.

David Hume (1955) stated that the epithets sociable, good-natured, humane, merciful, graceful, friendly, generous, beneficent, or their equivalents, are known in all languages, and universally express the highest merit human nature is capable of attaining. However, there is a discernible difference between past and present views and practices on ethical violations in the field of international business. Although many instances of unethical behavior and events have occurred throughout international business history, there has also been universal consensus on the need for international codes of business conduct (Dobson, 1990: 484). Among these consensus concerns are the responsibilities of the International Monetary Fund (IMF), the Securities and Exchange Commission (SEC.), the Environmental Protection Agency (EPA), the Earth Summit (ES), the Organization for Economic Cooperation and Development (OEDC), the International Chamber of Commerce (ICC), the International Labor Organization (ILO); and the Center for Traditional Corporations (CTC).

The International Monetary Fund (IMF) was originally founded by fifty nations in Bretton Woods for regulating and supervising the lending of foreign currency to its member countries and to stabilize the international exchange rates. Furthermore, IMF attempts to coordinate and monitor economic and financial policies of the various nations through research and consultation. It allows devaluation of a nation's currency up to 10 percent, but anything above this requires formal approval from IMF.

The U.S. Securities and Exchange Commission (SEC) is the result of the Great Depression that centered on direct involvement by the federal government in business during the Roosevelt administration. The Securities Act of 1933 and the Securities and Exchange Act of 1934 increased federal regulation of the stock market and restored investor confidence. The SEC, through legislation, enables the regulation of the nation's stock exchanges, in which shares of stocks are bought and sold and requires full disclosure of financial profiles of companies that wish to sell stocks and bonds to the public.

From another ethical environmental dimension, the Earth Summit (ES) took place for the first time in Rio de Janeiro, Brazil on June 3, 1992. Participants of the ES were representatives from 178 nations. Among environmental issues were pollution of the oceans, air, and lands, global warming, acid rain, and rain forest depletion that transcend national borders. These issues were supposed to be regulated among nations, through treaties between neighboring countries and among different nations (Manakkalathil, 1995: 29). However, the environmental pollution remained in tact, so that the ES only highlighted the difficulties of international agreement on environmental issues. It is a natural order in the universe that everything depends on everything else. Within every ecosystem, there are complex chained interdependencies among all mineral elements, plants, animal species, and weather. If one species of plant or animal and/or one mineral element is eradicated, there will be a chain reaction that affects all other ecosystem processes in some way. Through culturalogical auditing, we can find different cultures within a continuum of harmony with nature and against nature. In an ethical assessment, we can conclude the human race, specifically industrialized nations, consciously neglected their own survival environments. It is ironic to see how industrialization, development, and progress are destroying the ecosystem and replacing them with human-made eugenic species such as cloning. The future of the Earth and species of plants and animals, including human beings, is within the hands of biotech corporations and industry.

Environmental Protection Agency (EPA) is one of the eco-friendly organizations that promotes resource conservation and regulates the transportation and disposal of hazardous waste. Corporations need to conduct environmental audits as protective measures. The environmental resource conservation audits include voluntary surveys, assessments, and inspections of a firm's environmentally related activities. The EPA allows companies to correct the problems themselves before it brings criminal charges (Raclin, 1995: 4).

Getz (1990: 567) analyzed international codes of conducts:

The Organization for Economic Cooperation and Development (OEDC) is the primary policy-determining organization for industrialized nations. Existence of this international agency is the result of the third world countries that complained against unethical and immoral operations of some multinational corporations. Consequently, a code of conduct for MNCs was drafted as a response to these complaints.

However, it should be noted that the OCED's non-binding guidelines for MNCs addressed five major issues: competition, financing, taxation, employment/industrial relations, and science/technology. These traditional guidelines apply only to MNCs and governments alike. One drawback, however, is that developed, newly industrialized, developing, and agricultural countries cannot agree on interpretation of the guideline. It should be noted that the United States produces 22 percent of the world's carbon dioxide emissions (Jackson, Miller, and Miller, 1997: 500).

The International Chamber of Commerce (ICC) is an employer's federation operating on an international level and serves as a liaison with the United Nations. This organization is concerned with both fair treatment of MNCs and conditions promoting the international flow of capital and skills. ICC guidelines address international investment policies, ownership, management, finance, fiscal policies, legal framework, labor policies, technology policies, and commercial policies. The ICC also created the International Court of Arbitration as a forum for dispute settlements. The possibility of arbitration (rather than litigation) is a final international peaceful settlement among disputing international parties, corporations, governments, and nations.

The International Labor Organization (ILO) is a United Nations agency. It comprises union, employer, and government representation whose mission is to ensure that humane conditions of labor are maintained. One declaration of the ILO focuses on eight main issues concerning direct investments in developing countries: (1) Equality of opportunity and treatment, (2) Security of employment, (3) Wages, (4) Benefits, (5) Conditions of work, (6) Safety/health, (7) Freedom of association, and (8) Collective bargaining.

The Center for Traditional Corporations (CTC) is another entity that is affiliated with the United Nations. The CTC's mission is to maximize the contributions of transnational corporations to economic development and growth and to minimize the negative effects of the activities of these corporations. Ketz (1990: 567) identifies the proposed text of the draft code of transnational corporation:

The four codes place different emphasis on the MNC-host government relationship. The UN/CTC code includes more principles on this topic than the other codes. That is clearly understandable given that one goal of the code is to facilitate a change in the international economic system toward the establishment of a New International Economic Order. Most transnational corporations do not feel obligated to implement their business strategies according to the guidelines set forth in these codes.

ASSESSING THE VALUES OF HUMAN GLOBAL BUSINESS ENVIRONMENTS

To assess the worth of a person's life is ambiguous. One must specify to whom it is valuable. Are we assessing our lives on the basis of monetary values or on the basis of non-monetary values? Every aspect of a social life carries specific material and spiritual values -- ideal ones and the real ones by which people actually operate. These values guide the individual's worth of life through functioning in a society. Nevertheless, the personal value of a life is its value to the person whose life it is.

McIntyre (1983: 145) identifies five ways of determining the value of a human life: (1) Calculating the present value of estimated futures earning that are forgone due to premature death. (2) Calculating the present value of the losses others experience because of a person's death. (3) Examining the value placed on an individual life by presently established social policies. (4) Using the willingness to pay method where people are asked how much they would be willing to pay to reduce the probability of their death by a certain amount. (5) Looking at the compensation people accept as wage premium for dangerous jobs or hazardous occupation.

If your life's worth is based on the concept of material worth, you may specifically say that economic values are those that relate to desirable monetary purchase power of your living necessities. If it is based on the spiritual concept of worth, your moral and ethical values are those that relate you to desirable conduct, motives, and attitudes interacting with other people. Therefore, people assess their life's worth through two major dimensions: material and spiritual.

From the standpoint of a financial view, corporations need to make legitimate profits to survive. Businesses face unexpected costs such as lawsuits, unpredictable economic hardships, technological change, shorter product life cycles (PLCs), heavy taxation, and ecological incidents (e.g., earthquake, hurricane, volcano, flooding, tornados, drought, and fire). Businesses need to survive and pursue their profit making objectives. Legitimacy of a business is based on cost-benefit analysis in relation to the quality of its products and/or services. The question is: what type of costs and with what percentage of return for a business can be a legitimate one? There are several strategies for corporations to apply such assessments in order to survive. Some strategies emphasize serving customers with effective products, while others prefer to rip customers off and make profit. Others pursue their profitability to the extent of abusing and taking the lives of people with unsafe products.

It is true that without profit or surplus, no company can provide new equipment, new training programs, new research, or development facilities. If no company improves its operational facilities, society is left with aging plants and equipments, mediocre employees, and decaying operations. Without profit, there is no corporation to provide high quality, safe, and effective products and services.

Always, we need to trade off benefits with costs. The economic goals of a corporation are to present society with healthy and safe products. Businesses need to safeguard the environment in which to earn and spend money income. Businesses provide incentives to both Gross Domestic Profit (GDP) and Gross National Profit (GNP) and share their innovations in their own industries. These benefits improve the quality of life for citizens. Businesses must make profit to survive, but it should not be by ripping off their customers and polluting their environments.

In ethical and moral terms, we need to ask these questions: What should be the rate of profitability compared to proportionate quality of services to be rendered to customers? With what qualitative cost assessments, value systems, and quantitative cost-benefit techniques should we evaluate businesses? Painfully, people around the world are driven to determine just what human life is worth. Questions in regard to the value of life in the field of business explore this theme: Do we really believe that each human's life has infinite value or is a human life finite and is it the result at times in the assessment of costs and benefit analysis? It does not matter whether you dislike these questions or whether you refuse to think about them. In the end, we assess the real value of humanity. If you look at a back ticket of a commercial airline, you will find how much your life is worth in the case of an airplane crash. According to the International (Warsaw Convention) Notice:

> If the passenger's journey involves an ultimate destination or stop in a country other than the country of origin, the Warsaw Convention may be applicable and the Convention governs and in most cases limits the liability of carriers for death or personal injury to passengers is limited in most cases to proven damages not to exceed U. S. $75,000 per passenger.... For such passengers traveling by a carrier not party to such special contracts or on a journey not to, from, or having an agreed stopping place in the United States of America, liability of the carrier for death or personal injury to passengers is limited in most cases to approximately U.S. $10,000 or U S. $20,000 (American Airline Ticket, 2000).

In industrialized nations, human life and body parts are valued through monetary and budgetary assessments. Each person, on the basis of their inherent valuing characteristics, is valued differently at different times, situations, positions, circumstances, businesses, and industries. Values of people are different during life, post life, and pre-skeleton conditions.   Today, in the international organ transplant industry; body organs carry different values depending on whether the person is alive or really deceased. As another example, brown eggs cost more than white eggs, and from large through extra-large to jumbo there is an orderly progression of prices, with a premium for size and color. There are many supermarkets in the biotech cyber-eugenic industry in human eggs, too. A couple advertised in newspapers on the campuses of such universities such as Harvard, Princeton, and Stanford, offering $50,000.00 for the eggs of a woman who was 5'10" or taller and had scored at least 1,400 on her SATs (Rothman, 1999: A52). The cutting edge of developmental genetic research is advancing via the creation of the right gene in the right environment.

Japanese culture has been viewed as a materialistic culture. In October 1999, members of the Diet, the Japanese parliament, called for regulations ob the banking and loan industry's inhumane debt collection methods. The loan default rate in Japan is extremely low. The Japanese, culturally, are ashamed to admit bankruptcy. Nichiei, a Japanese consumer finance company, asked a loan guarantor to raise money by selling body parts in order to pay back the loan for Y5.7 millions. Eisuke Arai, a Twenty Five-year-old employee of the Nichiei company's debt collector offered a Sixty Two-year-old debtor Y3 million ($29,000) for his kidney and Y1 million for his eyeball to help him to finance a loan he had guaranteed to a now-bankrupt company. Arai said to the debtor: "You have two eyeballs and two kidneys, don't you? Many of our borrowers have only one kidney.... I want you to sell your heart as well, but if you do that you will die. So I will bear with you sell everything up to that." Traditional Japanese banks are shrinking their loan portfolios and leaving many individuals and small businesses with nowhere else to turn. Japanese consumer finance companies enjoy huge margins, benefiting from a cost of funding of about 2.3 percent and an ability to charge interest rates of up to 40 percent for loans without collateral (Abraham, 1999: 1).

In addition, in different industries and professions, people are valued differently. For example, in the movie industry a young star is valued more than an old one. In the professions of medicine, law, academia, and politics, older people are more valued more than younger ones. In the car insurance industry, young people are more valuable for insurance companies because of their highly risky scores and higher premiums. In the judiciary system of the United States, in most occasions children are more valuable than adults. In the global gender labor market assessments, males are more valuable than females. In contrast, in the 2, 500 maquiladora companies in the north of Mexico, young female workers are more valuable than young males. As another example, since the 1960s women have made many inroads into media careers, but they are still a distinct minority. As Table 1.2 shows, women are 33.7 percent of the work force in television, but only 16.8 percent of news directors (Gibbons, 1992: 88).

Table 1 2: Salary Average Across Media Industry

Businesses	%Women	Median salary for women	Median salary for men
Daily papers	39 0	$30,887	$36,959
Weekly papers	44 1	$17,917	$23,750
Television	33 7	$25,000	$25,961
Radio	32 4	$18,611	$21,176
Newsmagazines	45 9	$58,750	$68,333
Wire services	25 9	$41,071	$44,844

Source: Data from Sheila Gibbons, (Ed), (*Media Report to Women*.. Vol 20, (Fall, 1992), 88

Viewing the costs and benefit analysis in industrialized nations, if people and their legislative representatives do not like the idea that a certain number of accidental deaths are inevitable, they need to pass more laws to protect people. This will create higher safety costs enacting new safety laws, or pressuring businesses and government to build safer roads, carries more costs. When deciding what to do, one must ask what are the priorities of cost and benefit analysis? For example, is the automobile's safety more important than the profit of auto industry or vice versa? Should customers be forced to accept more safety costs to avoid loss of life? Should some types of vehicles be banned because they are too dangerous? Should auto and jetliner industries provide cheaper transportation in spite of the risks involved? What rights do manufacturers and customers have? Who should decide what the ethical, moral, and legal relationships should be established and enforced at the local, national, and global levels? There are many cases and incidents related to the above questions. One of those controversial cases is the Ford Pinto Fire.

Gioia (1995: 80) reported that Ford Company had begun selling the Ford Pinto in 1970. Ford decided to battle the foreign competition in the small car market. This decision came after a hard fight between Ford President Semon Bunky Knudsen and Lee Iacocca, who had risen quickly within the company because of his success with the Mustang. Iacocca suggested designing and manufacturing Ford Pinto. (see Exhibit 1.1). The final decision ultimately was in the hands of the CEO, Henry Ford II, who not only agreed with Iacocca, but also promoted him to position of president after Knudsen was forced to resign. The typical time span from conception to production of a new model was more than three to five years. However, Iacocca wanted to launch the Pinto in just over two years.

As a consequence, when it was discovered through crash testing that the Pinto's fuel tank often ruptured during rear-end impact, it was too late and costly to do much about it in terms of redesign. Between the years 1970-1978, hundreds of thousands of cars burned every year, taking 3,000 lives annually. Despite the crash test results, Ford decided to go with its gas tank design. Iacocca set an important goal known as the limits of 2000; the Pinto could not cost more than $2,000.00 and could not weigh more than 2,000 pounds. Having decided to go ahead with normal production plans, the Pinto's problems soon surfaced with many accidents. By early 1973, Ford's recall coordinator received field reports suggesting that Pintos were susceptible to exploding in rear-end collisions at very low speeds (under Twenty Five miles per hour). No recall was initiated because of the high costs. Finally, a lawsuit was filed and settled in February 1978, when a jury awarded a judgment of over $125 million against Ford Company (later reduced to $6 million by a judge who nonetheless accused Ford of callous indifference to human life). This judgment was based on convincing evidence that Ford chose not to spend the extra $11.00 per car to correct the faults in the Pinto gas tanks that its own crash testing had revealed.

Ford representatives argued that companies must make cost-benefit decisions all the time. They claimed that it was an essential part of business, and even though everyone knows that some people will die in auto accidents, buyers want costs held down; therefore, people implicitly accept risks when they buy cars. As a result, the Ford Company preferred to not recall Pintos and bear the $137 million loss.

Exhibit 1 1: Cost-Benefit Analysis of the Ford Company for Ford Pintos

Component	1971Costs per victim
Future productivity losses	
Direct	$132,000 00
Indirect	41,300 00
Medical Costs	
Hospital	700 00
Other	425.00
Property Damage	1,500 00
Insurance Administration	4,700 00
Legal Costs and Court fees	3,000 00
Employer Losses	1,000 00
Victim's Pain and Suffering	10,000 00
Funeral	900 00
Assets (Lost Consumption)	5,000 00
Miscellaneous Accident Cost	200 00
TOTAL PER FATALITY	$200,725 00

COSTS	
Sales:	11 million cars, 1 5 million light trucks
Unit cost:	11,000,000 ' ($11) + 1,500,000 ' ($11) = $137 million

BENEFITS	
Savings	180 burn deaths, 180 serious burn injuries, 2100 burned vehicles
Unit Cost:	$200,000 per death, $67,000 per injury, $700 per vehicle
Total Benefit:	180 ' ($200,000) + 180 ($67,000) + 2,100 ' ($700) = $49 5 million

RESULT	(Recall costs) $137 million - (actual accidental cost) $49 5 million = $87 5 Million (profit)

Source: Dennis Gioia, In L. K Trevinio, and A N. Katherine, *Managing Business Ethics: Straight Talk About How To Do It Right*, (New York: John Wiley & Sons, Inc , 1995), 80-85.

A 1071 study from the National Highway Traffic Safety Administration, disclosed how industries value human life in relation to cost and benefit analysis. They have broken down the estimated cost to society every time someone is killed in a car collision. Dowie (1977: 51) framed the case of Ford Pinto in a sensational analysis: One wonders how long the Ford Motor Company would continue to market lethal cars were Henry Ford II and Lee Iacocca serving twenty-year terms in Leavenworth for consumer homicide. It should be noted that Lee Iacocca, as a capable CEO of the former Ford Company, was selected in 1980 as the savior of the Chrysler Company.

HUMANITY AND HUMANENESS

When we analyze moral, ethical, and legal reasoning, we refer to a multitude of objective and subjective judgments concerning right and wrong, good and bad, fair and unfair, and just and unjust. Through objective moral reasoning, judgments are associated with universal rightness and wrongness of a decision and an action. The moral reasoning is based on whether if an action or a decision is right for me, it is also right for anybody else. For example, the universal view on honesty applies for everyone the same way at every place and any time.

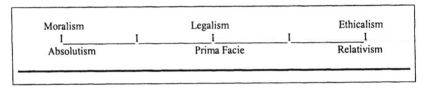

Figure 1.3: The Magnitude of Absolutism and Relativism

Through subjective antinomianism reasoning, sometimes people refuse to judge others and their own decisions and actions. They cannot give reasons for decisions and actions being right or wrong, and fair or unfair, just or unjust. They often take the position: There is no objective morality, or Amorality is purely subjective (De George, 1995: 39). They consider themselves to be personally moral when they act, as they believe they should. The antinomianism reasoning refuses subjective guilt and blame with objective guilt and blame. They abandon universal moral absolutism and believe in legal relativism.

Moral absolutism also carries with it moral obligations. There is a point of balancing between moral absolutism and ethical relativism: *prima facie* (see Figure 1.3). If something is true, then it is *prima facie*. We reason that for something to be right if it is *prima facie*. Just as one *prima facie* obligation may conflict with another and may be overridden, so one *prima facie* right may conflict with another *prima facie* right and may be overridden. For example, the right to live is more important than the right to property. However, in the time of conflict, it is reversed. In some cultures the right to live is viewed as the fundamental value, while in other cultures the right to property overrides the right to live. In the latter case legally the intruder's life is permitted to be taken by the property owner who is in danger of losing his/her life.

Moral absolutism mandates all human beings respect two fundamental values: (1) humanity and (2) humaneness. It should be noted that ethics is the progressive intention and action of both humanity and humaneness. The term *humanity* refers to the totality of two major attributes that distinguishes the right to live for all human beings as distinct from other creatures and denotes the essential human qualitative values or characters such as compassion, sympathy, and consideration for the suffering of other human beings. These two principles stem from the original attributes of the human species that give rise to morality as an absolute institution C the *sentience* (the power perception by the senses), the *rationality* (the power of mind by wisdom) of people, and the attributes that lie at the universal core of absolutism of morality. Humanity, therefore, is the notion that to be treated without deceit or violence is more than a right. A person has a right to have his/her full human particularity taken into account by those who enter into relations with that person. Above all, most of the key terms in humaneness and humanity denote qualities of tolerance of pain and suffering and recognition of the universal moral absolute worth of the basic autonomy of every human being.

The term *humaneness* refers to general characteristics of those people who tend to be refined, polite, and compassionate. It is characterized by tenderness and compassion for the suffering or distressed conditions of human beings. While humanity refers to both characteristics of human beings such as kindness and weakness or goodness and badness, humaneness takes into account only the noble spiritual aspects of human beings. A humane person is specifically one who has actuated by benevolence in his/her treatment of others. In the term of ethics, the humane doctrine characterizes a person's obligations to be concerned wholly with the welfare of the human race. For clarity of moral absolutism and ethical relativism, the following pages will be devoted to these subject matters.

Moral Absolutism

Choice and deliberation are two major component parts of a *will*. We need to understand the nature of moral obligations (goodwill) for an individual in order to make a right choice. An individual can make a choice on the basis of either sensational or intellectual reasoning. Sensational choices can end up with pleasure (appropriate sensational and emotional enjoyments) or pain (excessive sensational and emotional deprivations). In contrast, intellectual choices can end up with happiness (appropriate usage of intellect) and avoidance of misery (inappropriate usage of wisdom). Simple emotional acts of desires are not choices of an individual's will. Emotional desires are acts for achieving pleasure. An individual's will is an intellectual satisfactory intention of reasoning. Intellectual choices are not necessarily connected with pleasure or pain, but are connected with happiness and satisfaction. Also, intellectual choices are associated with self-volition, that is, as being very intent on getting what they seek. Therefore, managers need to act on the basis of their will. What type of will? Good will.

Deliberation is a pragmatic work out of ones reason. We consider and evaluate reasons for or against doing something. We still need to understand the nature of choice itself because the act of choice may cause misunderstanding. Morally, a right choice should be based on good will. It should follow the intellectual reasoning for specifying the right means and ends. A manager without intellectual deliberation and good choices cannot be an effective leader. A good manager needs to apply sufficient good will, useful knowledge, and reliable information in order to make good moral choices and take good actions.

The moral absolutism philosophy holds that there are eternal virtues and universal values in humanity that are always and everywhere applicable as long as human beings exist (e.g., the existence of God for religious people; honesty, integrity, dignity, courage, etc.). The roots of moral absolutism begin with certain Platonic and Aristotelian doctrines that attained great popularity in later centuries. We can see ourselves as fleshing out a neo-Aristotelian conception of the human form. Aristotle argued that humans are rational and social beings, and that these two qualities distinguish them from other animals. As such, they form the ground for certain fundamental dispositions or universal virtues such as truthfulness, perceptiveness, prudence, kindness, friendliness, justice, and so on (Nussbaum, 1993: 243). Plato believed a moral person is one who is wise, temperate, courageous, and just. In absolutist terms, desires and passions function harmoniously under the governance of intellectual reasoning. Therefore, moral behavior entails the process of absolute definition, classification, and generalization of human characteristics. Moral principles serve as step stones in the mores, customs, traditions, and laws of different societies and formulate theories about the role of morals in society; or they may study the relationship between technological and ethical-cultural change; or they may report the facts, points of view, and actions taken in specific cases of moral conducts. The manager, above all, needs to grasp the great ideal of the *absolute goodness*, and this requires the rigorous cultivation of pure intelligence. Moralists want to keep alive the absolute values they consider worthwhile and improve the moral quality of their community (Albert, Denise, and Peterfraund, 1984: 1). Moralists seek to win others over to their ethical convictions and to exhort them to act in accordance with absolute truth. In addition, absolute beliefs in good manners are primarily persuasive and prescriptive quality of character. Some absolutists hold that the principles of morality are absolute. These principles create moral virtues, cultural values, and legal standards for having good behavior. Absolutist moralists believe that all moral principles, norms, and standards are everywhere and always the same. In the absolute moral sense, there are different versions of valuing self. For example, Sigmund Freud believed that in a general sense we could distinguish among the *ego, superego*, and *id*. The *ego*'s assertions are so called *selves* because they originated with the ego, a metapsychological construct representing the executive agency in an individual's mind. The ego tries to mediate between an individual's internal and external worlds in an effort to maintain an absolute, and homoeostatic state of existence (Freud, 1926: Vol. 20). According to Freud (1926: Vol. 19) the *superego*, in a metapsychological sense, represents society within the psyche and gives rise to a conscience, morality, and ideals. The superego internalizes the demands of socializing forces, thereby fulfilling a self-observation function. The superego also demands reparation of wrongdoing, and occasionally inflicting self-punishment in the process. The *id's* assertions remain after ego and superego assertions have been dismantled. They give rise to a compulsion to repeat earlier experiences, beliefs, and situations, whatever the costs, and to the tendency of organism toward a state of entropy (Freud, 1926, Vol. 18).

Since morality is related to an individual's universal virtuous excellence, ethics serves to harmonize conflicting psychosocial interests between an individual and other people. Ethics is concerned with psychosocial actions and deals with good deeds in a society. In contrast, morality is an abstract signifying the moral order of an individual's behavior.

Ethical Relativism

According to the above definitions, there are some differences between moral absolutism and ethical relativism. While moral absolutism justifies means by ends, ethical relativism justifies ends by means. This means that an action can be ethical if that action is extenuating circumstances be taken into account. In dealing with principles that establish standards for actions, ethicists have much in common with casuists. What we mean by casuists? Casuists are those moralists who study and resolve cases of conscience or conduct. Moralists have an interest in normative behavior, that is, the regulation of personal conduct. Moralists' distinctive function, however, is a deliberative one in which the principles of mercy is due to their humane characteristics. The relativism is that sort of comparative means which range from little, just enough, and sufficient to justify a cause of action. According to Aristotle (1987: 138), ethical relativism is a state involving voluntary choices, and only unethical actions that are involuntary, can be excused. The two factors that may lead to involuntary behavior are excusable ignorance and convincible incapacity to perform an action. Both excusable ignorance and convincible incapacity diminish ethical wrongdoing. A business owner may be ignorant of facts or the consequences of an act. According to Steiner and Steiner (1994: 181) circumstances leading to incapacity arise when: (1) A course of action may impose unrealistically high cost, (2) there may be no power to influence an outcome, (3) no alternative exists, and (4) External force may compel action.

Ethical relativists hold that people are different; consequently, their ideas and ethical beliefs are different. When two people hold different moral virtues, both can be right because both carrying virtuous thoughts and actions. In order to prove something is good, people have a multitude of good choices. There are two perceptual paths to make good choices: (1) Apply *contextual variables* which include size, degree of credibility, validity, reliability, circumstances, contingencies, certainties, and interdependencies of an ethical issue to the maxim of excellence. Then the conclusion is based on these relative contextual factors, (2) to apply *structural variables* that include constituencies' differentiation, formalization, centralization, internalization, externalization, status systems, taxonomy, and classification.

People have many choices. What exactly is meant by the contextual and structural claims? A first form of ethical judgment involves stating that both of the two conflicting virtuous judgments are right because they are searching for revealing the truth through different paths of truth discovery. In the first form, contextually, a moral judgment is based on a mathematical view of moral language and the logic of moral discovery. A second form, structurally, holds that judgments of right and wrong are determined by applicability of moral principles and interdependent structural facts. For the clarity of these two terms you will find the following explanations.

Contextual Ethical Relativism: *Contextual ethical relativism* has been divided into three phases within three levels of attending to a judgment: (1) Preliminary hypothetical perceptions, (2) discovering factual elements and events, and (3) arriving in and concluding final judgments.

While in each phase, the division points between objective and subjective points of judgment are based on conscious awareness. They are arbitrary and contain sub-judgments to represent a continuum. The range of the continuum extends from an extremely minimum position to an extremely positive position. Conscious ethical awareness is almost a cognitive value judgment. It is based upon a pluralistic social value system. This means that the only accepted formula to treat people ethically is in a common perception and be used the expression of valuable objectives. Therefore, a valuable objective could be mathematically implied from one to an unlimited number of values. Furthermore, contextual ethical values are the worth of those things, phenomena, or behaviors of people. We cannot deny the relative judgmental qualitative values compared to the quantitative values. For example, for a shoplifter who steals a piece of merchandise from a retail store with today's market value of $5.00 and $0.50 on sale tomorrow, the ethical relativism judgment will not focus on quantitative values of the merchandise, instead it will focus on the qualitative inherent action of the shoplifter's intention and action which indicates a wrong doing. Behavioral judgments through contextual ethical views emphasize the characteristics of beliefs and attitudes of people. At this stage of ethical judgment, we are not concerned with the factorial relationships among values of the merchandise but rather with the internalization and externalization of a set of specified ideals and values of good behavior compared with wrong behavior.

Viewed from another standpoint, ethical judgments are derived from the prime beliefs in which the conscience of the individual is concerned with preservation of the qualitative mind-set values of good and bad behavior. An important element of ethical judgment, characterized by contextual relativism, is that it is motivated not only by the desire to comply or obey good behavior, but by the individual's commitment to the underlying value guiding the societal value system.

Those who maintain relativism contextual ethics claim that right and wrong decisions and actions are based on cultural value systems. These forms of ethical relativism deserve some attention because business transactions occur in different countries with different cultural beliefs, ideas, values, expectations, and traditions. So global business managers are faced with contradictory situations between home and host cultural value systems. These forms of ethical relativism indicate that in order to be ethical in both environments we need to get to the middle ground of legalism judgments in order for our judgments to be applied to both home and host countries through similar and mutual value systems.

PERSPECTIVE	ATTRIBUTION	CONCLUSIVE OPINION
RELIGION	Nudity is sinful.	Nudity corrupts faith and is evil.
MORALITY	Nudity is ugly.	Nudity degrades personal character.
ETHICS	Nudity is shameful.	Nudity abuses the human body's integrity.
LAW	Nudity is conditional.	Nudity is permissible under licensing.
PASSION	Nudity is enjoyable.	Nudity satisfies the lustful image.
ARTISTIC	Nudity is aesthetic.	Nudity exhibits natural beauty.
PSYCHOLOGICAL	Nudity is tempting.	Nudity motivates appetitive curiosity.
SCIENTIFIC	Nudity is a natural curious fact.	Nudity discovers right and wrong causes of abnormality.
PROFESSIONAL	Nudity is posing.	Nudity personifies exhibitive characters.
SOCIOLOGICAL	Nudity is not acceptable.	Nudity is a dangerous social disorder.
PSYCHOSOCIAL	Nudity is appealing.	Nudity is an intrinsic sexual deceitful technique.
BUSINESS	Nudity attracts attention.	Nudity impresses viewers for product attractiveness.

Table 1.3: Conclusive Contextual Ethical Relativism

Today, the universality of a behavioral culturalogical approach indicates that preferred levels and modes of ethical perceptions in all cultures are not the same. However, the ingredients of the perceptions are similar in all cultures. For example, let us start with how nudity appeals in international advertising. The fascinating motive is not to judge about how much sexually appealing something is in an international advertising. Contrary to the cultural impressions, sexual appeal in advertising may be viewed as a sinful and/or unethical and immoral act in one culture and a joyful, praising and/or legal acts in another culture. Different cultures around the world possess different views on nudity. Table 1.3 illustrates how people perceive nudity through different perspectives.

Structural Ethical Relativism: In a geological analogy, we can view by structural ethical relativism as the physical terrain of a landscape such as hills and rivers; the ethical and valuable decisions and actions of organizational incumbents are equivalent to the amount of rainfall and wind. The physical terrain has a significant effect on the amount of rainfall or wind. In turn, the amount of rainfall or wind can cause the terrain to change slowly. Of course, there can be sharp changes in the landscape due to natural disasters such as hurricanes, volcanic eruptions, flooding, tornadoes, earthquake, and drought.

AMERICAN CULTURE	AUSTRALIAN CULTURE	ASIAN CULTURE	MIDDLE EASTERN CULTURE
Nudity is legal under appropriate licensed conditions.	Nudity is a common perception in its aesthetic cultural behavior.	Nudity is a hidden agenda in personal perception for enjoying sexual life.	Nudity is illegal, immoral, unethical, ugly, and sinful behavior.
Nudity in advertising has the effect of reducing brand recall.	Nudity in advertising is more effective on men than women.	Nudity in advertising is a part of the popular culture.	Nudity in advertising is prohibited by all means and ends
Nudity in advertising is viewed as a psychological stimulation for companionship.	Nudity in advertising is viewed as a cultural appeal for attraction of more tourists.	Nudity in advertising is viewed as a sense of cultural hospitality.	Nudity in underground advertising is viewed as a motive for individual's sexual curiosity.

Table 1.4: Nudity Cultural Appealing in Advertising

At the level of structural ethical relativism, we are concerned with ascribing worth to phenomena, behavior, object, an individual, etc. The term *belief*, which is defined as the emotional acceptance of a proposition or doctrine upon what one implicitly considers adequate ground   (English and English, 1958: 64), describes quite well what may be thought of as the dominant characteristic here. Beliefs carry varying degrees of certitude. In structural ethical relativism, there are multitudes of valuing degrees from good to excellence.

At the lowest level, we are concerned with the minimum requirement to be good; that is, there is more of a devotion to strive for achieving the highest degree of excellence. One of the distinguishable characteristics of structural ethical relativism is a progressive trend in consistency of efforts become closer to the ideal of thoughts towards excellence. It is consistent enough so that others may perceive a person as holding a belief in the value of moving towards excellence. At the level of structural ethical relativism, we are moving up from the first step of goodness to the last step of excellence. Such a movement is both sufficiently consistent with others that they can identify the valuing criteria, and sufficiently committed that people respect the values of those perceptions that appear in their own judgments.

Therefore, at the stage of structural ethical relativism, there are sub-objectives that express the relative values of goodness of internalized characteristics of a person and the mere acceptance of externalized value systems and commitments or convictions in the usual connection of deep involvement toward excellence. Ethical values at this stage imply not just to the existence of harmony among the individual's internalized values and the social externalized group values, but the dynamic pluralistic movement of people to become sufficiently committed to the social values, to seek, pursue, and want excellence.

CHAPTER SUMMARY

Contrary to the belief that global corporate success or failure in globalization of their firms is often the result of the decision-making processes, in most cases it has been observed that the practice of globalization of products and/or services marketing strategies depends upon realization of the corporate ethical, moral, and legal commitments to their stakeholders. International management practices reflect the societal ethical values, moral virtues, and legal beliefs within which business organizations exist. Moreover, the technological innovations, societal movements, political events, and economic forces have changed over time and are continuing to change human faith, beliefs, and behavior in the future. The right way to do business in the global free market economy is not necessarily a matter of aligning our actions with either the home or the host socio-cultural and econo-political value systems. Yet international managers struggle to carve out some form of consensus judgments for business ethics and moral behavior, especially in areas where the international law does not seem to cover the significant bases. International managers need to make their decisions on the basis of their own moral, ethical, and legal commitments.

Morality is a dynamic behavioral deliberation of intellect and wisdom. Distinct from both the real (natural) order of existing things and the logical (artificial) order formed by people is the moral order. Both natural and artificial orders are caused by reason.

Ethics is a speculative and/or practical collective cultural value systems. Ethics is concerned with psychosocial actions and deals with good deeds in a society. Philosophers have formulated ethics in order to speculate and demonstrate good thoughts and behaviors (deontologicalism) and some have tended to identify ethics with the practical good end-results (utilitarianism).

Legality is not a static phenomenon. It is dynamic. The law sets rules for behavior. Rules change on the basis of time and circumstances. When rules are broken, the consequence is with punishment. The law sets behavioral standards and initiates an expected system for compliance. Regarding the question of what should be done legally in the profit-making processes, we might want to say that certain *shoulds* are universally compelling. The topic of business ethics includes not just the questions of the moral or immoral motivations of businesspeople, but also it includes a range of issues that arise from the depth of socio-cultural values and econo-political beliefs. Today's global business environments essentially comprise multiple complex webs that are highly interrelated and integrate different interest groups (hereafter called stakeholders). Each group of stakeholders is distinguished by their unique set of objectives. For example, a multinational corporation (MNC) is itself an amalgamation of several home and host stakeholder groups (e.g., shareholders, stockholders, bondholders, employees, management, customers, consumers, suppliers, home and host governmental authorities, etc.). Each of these interest groups can be further subdivided into voting versus non-voting shareholders, secured versus unsecured creditors, and unionized versus non-unionized employees with various economic, cultural, and political expectations.

QUESTIONS FOR DISCUSSION

- State and explain the definition for morality.
- State and explain the definition for ethics.
- State and explain the definition for legality.
- How do you define humanity and humaneness?
- Explain the distinction between morality and ethics.
- Explain the distinction between ethics and legality.
- Explain the difference between moral and amoral behavior.
- Do you think business ethics is a fad?
- Do you think business ethics is a myth?
- Describe practical knowledge.
- Explain the distinction between bureaucrats and cosmocrats.
- Do you find any global codes of business ethics in the international markets?
- Explain your life worth in different industries.

- What is the material objective of ethics?
- Cite an example of a situation you are familiar with where the "right" answers just was not obvious.
- What is the subject matter of ethics that is based on relativism?
- Are the principles of the universal moral certain? Explain why.
- Are you convinced that business ethics should be considered in the global business transactions?
- Explain the difference between contextual and structural ethical relativism.

CASE STUDY

THE GERON CORPORATION: ETHICAL AND UNETHICAL ISSUES IN STEM CELL BUSINESS

Geron Corporation is a biopharmaceutical entity that has been focused on discovering, developing, and commercializing therapeutic and diagnostic products for drug efficacy. This corporation has a monopolistic international licensing control over its field. Such strength has made it the leader in stem-cell research worldwide. Geron Corporation has three major missions: regenerative organ cloning, reproductive cloning and therapeutic cloning.

GERON'S CORPORATE STRUCTURE

Geron Corporation is a small corporation based out of Menlo Park, California. The CEO of Geron is Thomas Okarma (MD & PhD). The latest reported headcount of employees was 112. This count seems to be relatively small for a corporation that is on the cutting edge of its biotechological field. Regardless of employees' highly specialized capabilities, this company has been successful as the leader in its field of biotechnology because it is a highly oriented scientific focused entity. The financial resources of this organization are not so great. The number of outstanding shares was 21,860,000. The value of the stock for the last fifty-two weeks (July 1, 2000 – through May 31, 2001) was quite volatile. The lowest value on March 22, 2001 was $9.125 and the highest on September 25, 2000 was $30.25. The return on investment (ROI) was negative 20.41 as compared to the Biotechnology Industry's (BI) positive 4.90. The return on equity (ROE) was at negative 34.56 as compared to positive 7.48 for the industry average. By reviewing these figures, we found some problems for investors. This indicated that Geron was not achieving managerial objectives very effectively. The goal of Geron's regenerative medicine is to produce transplantable cells that provide therapeutic benefits without triggering immune rejection of the transplanted cells. This could be used to treat numerous chronic diseases such as diabetes, heart disease, stroke, Parkinson's disease and spinal cord injury.

PROBLEMS AND ISSUES

There are several problems and issues concerning humanity in the field of biotechnology. Some major issues and problems strike at the heart of ethical, moral, and religious beliefs and faiths as follows:

- Can the stem-cell research in cloning human beings change human natural characteristics for good or evil?
- Is it extremely dangerous to attempt changing the path of human reproductive system to the artificial one?
- How can trial and error in cloning research be beneficial to the human species?
- Is there sufficient extrapolated data from all animal species in order to use it as the scientific foundation for reproductive cloning in the human species?
- Is it true that the possible cloning of human species would be an extremely dangerous procedure and contaminate human races?
- Is it simply an unethical and immoral decision and action to subject humans to unpredictable and irreversible risks?
- Isn't it true that cloning humans will challenge fundamental religious and cultural concepts concerning ethical and spiritual wellbeing?
- Will cloning human beings eradicate kinship among human beings?
- What does it means to be natural parents, a brother, a sister, or a family, and should cloned humans marry each other?
- Can cloning create different species of human beings for different subjective expected tasks?
- As potatoes and tomatoes genes have been synthesized into *"Pomatoes"* will human genes and animal genes be synthesized into new species?
- By advancement and development of the stem cell biotechnology and reproduction of cloned humans what will happen to the natural and artificial gene=s owners property rights? Who are going to be parents of cloned children with what natural and legal parental rights?
- How will businesses order their workers for different organizational tasks to reproduce their future human resource needs?
- Will future cloned human workers belong to business corporations that paid the cloning costs B slavery?
- Can commercialization of women eggs, body parts including ovaries tissues and men sperm, tissues, and body parts create unethical, immoral, and inhumane consequences for future generations?

PAYING THE PRICE

In licensing gene patents, commercial biotech institutions are trying to make sufficient profits in order to fund their research projects. Such a commercial use of the patent system is very clear. The fact is, the patent system is geared toward patent holders locking up products and procedural processes unless and until they get the cash they demand. The University of Wisconsin through [WiCell

Reseach Institute Inc.] has indicated that it will be enforcing its patent on stem cell extraction. Geron, which helped fund the university's research, and has a contract with the university to do certain types of research itself, has a licensing agreement for third parties that one researcher has called punitive.

Internationally, there are two general opposing views concerning human cloning: choice and force:

- Those people who are against human cloning believe that it is immoral and unethical to clone human beings.
- Others believe that it is a fundamental right to reproduce human beings in any way you want. If you want to mix genes with others, then that is your choice. But if you want to reproduce only with your genes, then it is your right.

In both philosophical views there are specific costs that clients have to pay. For example, governmental funding in the field of embryonic stem-cell research is very restricted. Up to date there are sixty-four lines of cells, each created by destroying a single embryo. The worth of each cell-line is estimated to be billion of dollars. Nearly half of the cell lines come from a mere two institutions: Goteborg University in Sweden is listed as having nineteen cell lines, and a privately held San Diego company in California, CyThera, is said to have derived nine cell lines. The Wisconsin Alumni Research Foundation (WARF), is listed as having five cell lines. WARF distributed cell lines from those that were created at the University of Wisconsin with funding from Menlo Park, California based Geron. BresaGen, an Australian, company has four stem-cell lines and the rest belong to both private and public institutions in different countries.

Geron, with the Roslin Institute (co-creators of Dolly, the cloned sheep), is studying how to use genetically modified pigs as sources for human organ transplants. Geron is also working with Celera Genomics to develop stem cells for a variety of medical purposes, as well as with Merix Bioscience to develop telomerase-based cancer vaccine. These research programs will attract enormous wealth for the future of Geron Corporation.

ANALYSIS

In November 1998, two independent teams of U.S. biomedical scientists reported that they had succeeded in isolating and culturing stem cells obtained from human embryos and fetuses. An international scientific consensus recognized that human embryos are biologically human beings beginning at fertilization and acknowledged the physical continuity of human growth and development from the one-cell stage forward. Humanity has certain basic questions before it. By analyzing ethical and moral values of life in the terms of socio-cultural and politico-economical inquiries is it right to justify the ownership of the stem cell as ends by its means? What is the value of life? Is it going to be based on privatization of human life by stem-cell technology? Should researchers and biotech corporations and/or governments own the endowment of mankind? Is it right to destroy life or potential life for the ability to do research and the possibilities of potential life saving technologies? These and other similar questions raise moral and ethical implications that all nations need to address them in their future politico-economical policy.

On the two poles of an ethical and unethical magnitude, one pole illustrates that the moral imperative to save lives through medical research should receive unquestionable financial support, while on the pole is strongly believes that the benefits to others, whatever it may be, cannot justify the destruction of human life.

The two poles of arguments represent two very different options that are ethically and morally grounded in their own righteousness. Both anti-abortion and pro-medical research groups are on the side of life. Both are opposed to one another. On one side we have life issues that are technically related to life-enhancement rights to be protected and on the other side we have new life issues that are related to privileges to be endowed.

CASE CONCLUSION

When analyzing the mission of Geron Corporation, we need to examine ethical, moral, and legal issues associated with human embryonic stem-cell research. We need to examine three different problems related to human beings: therapeutic cloning, regenerative medicine, and reproductive stem cell cloning. All of three activities need sufficient funding by some source either by government or private sector. Stem-cell research should not be banned when human beings are faced with severe diseases such as cancer, heart attacks, and severely burned skins. The biotechnological innovativeness in these areas should be continued in order to cure patients. In regard to reproductive stem cell cloning, we need to assess the ethical and moral consequences of creating, adjusting, and reinventing the human species. This will be related to future generations. This needs to be handed to tomorrow's generation.

In conclusion, if anything is to be gained or lost from the cruel atrocities committed against humanity in life sciences, is it the lesson that ethical utilitarian devaluation of one group of human beings should be in question. We need to pay attention to the religious faiths which indicate that the natural processes from the beginning of humanity emerged million years ago have been exclusively associated with God's power. From now such a process will be undertaken by a group of businesspeople that are money-power oriented for achieving profit purposes. These biobusiness oriented groups will not be guided by any professional codes of ethics or occupational codes of conduct. They are looking for fulfillment of capitalistic ideology in a global free market economy to maximize their wealth. By stem-cell technology nobody will be left over in future. The cloned human species will yield the human race unspeakable power over its existence. Only hunger for wealth, power, and reputation will show us the results of today's decision in future.

CASE QUESTIONS FOR DISCUSSION

We are repeating the problems and issues concerning outcomes of Geron Corporation as follows:

- Can the stem-cell research in cloning human beings change human natural characteristics for good or evil?
- Is it extremely dangerous to attempt to change the path of human reproductive system to the artificial one?
- How can trial and error in cloning research be beneficial to the human species?
- Is there sufficient extrapolated data from all animal species in order to use it as the scientific foundation for reproductive cloning in the human species?
- Is it true that the possible cloning of the human species would be an extremely dangerous procedure and contaminate human races?
- Is it simply an unethical and immoral decision and action to subject humans to unpredictable and irreversible risks?
- Isn't it true that cloning humans will challenge fundamental religious and cultural concepts concerning ethical and spiritual wellbeing?
- Will cloning human beings eradicate kinship among human beings?
- What does it mean to be natural parents, a brother, a sister, or a family, and should cloned humans marry each other?
- Can cloning create different species of human beings for different subjective expected tasks?
- As potatoes and tomatoes genes have been synthesized into *Pomatoes,* will human genes and animal genes be synthesized into new species?
- By advancement and development of the stem cell biotechnology and reproduction of cloned humans what will happen to the natural and artificial gene owner's property rights? Who are going to be parents of cloned children with what natural and legal parental rights?
- How will businesses order their workers for different organizational tasks to reproduce their future human resource needs?
- Will future cloned human workers belong to business corporations paid the cloning costs (slavery)?
- Can commercialization of women's eggs, body parts including ovaries tissues and men's sperm, tissues, and body parts create unethical, immoral, and inhumane consequences for future generations?

CASE SOURCES

<http:/www.stemcellresearch.org/statement/statement.htm> (09/23/2001).

<http://www.bio.org/laws/tstm061901.htm > (9/23/2001).

<http:://dir.yahoo.com/Business_and_Economy/Business_to_Business/S../Geron _Corporation> (9/20/2001).

<http://biz.yahoo.com/p/g/gern/html> (9/20/2001).

<http: //yahoo.marketingguide.com/mgi/ratio/A1208.html> (9/20/2001).

<http://busidesc.asp?target+%2Fstocks%Fcompanyinformation%2Fbusinedesc &Ticker+GER> (9/20/2001).

<http://forbes.com/2001/08/27/0827stem.html> (9/20/2001).

<http://www.msnbc.com/news610155.asp?pne ¦ msn> (8/7/01).

<http://moneycentral.msn.com/investor/research/profile.asp?Symbol+GERN> (9/23/2001).

CHAPTER 2

COMPARATIVE ANALYSIS OF MORALITY, ETHICALITY, AND LEGALITY

When things are not going well,
we turn to science and technology to fix them.

When people are not progressing well,
we turn to education to enhance them.

When businesses are not functioning well,
we turn to government to regulate them.

When organizations are not operating well,
we turn to law to bring them into order.

When humanism is not considered well,
we turn to ethics and morality to enrich it.

CHAPTER OBJECTIVES

When you have read this chapter, you should be able to do the following:

- Define morality, ethics, and legality.
- Identify differences between ethical and moral definitions.
- Explain the ultimate objectives of moral behavior and codes of ethical conducts.
- Identify component parts of moral, ethical, and legal intentions and actions.
- Describe speculative and practical moral, ethical, and legal knowledge.
- Understand the meaning of commitments.
- Know the meaning of appetite and greed.
- Analyze conscience awareness and cognitive judgments.
- Know the difference between choice and force.
- Know bureaucratic and cosmocratic business characteristics.

THOUGHT STARTER

Morality consists of acts in accordance with maximum self-intellectual reasonableness in which people must come to review their own behavior in order to enhance their daily intentions and actions. Ethics concerns itself with peoples' societal conduct, activity, and behavior such that they are done knowingly and deliberately and to a large extent willingly and collectively. Ethics is concerned with the construction of a societal rational system through the application of moral principles that are called virtues. Legality is a practical reasoning that determines means in relation to some given ends. Law formalizes socio-cultural and econo-political contracts under which the community limits the *harm* that members can do to the social fabric. The recent incidents of Firestone's recall of 6.5 million tires on August 9, 2000 placed Ford Company as the second international car manufacturer in a controversial ethical and legal situation. As a tire manufacturer, Firestone (part of the Bridgestone group) has served Ford Company as a major subcontract-supplier in the U.S. auto industry. After the Ford Pinto scandal, the Ford Explorer incidents have positioned Ford Company in another controversial ethical and legal situation. Ford Company has been dealing with Firestone for almost 80 years. In the recent resulting accidents almost 90 people have been killed and 250 people injured driving Ford Explorers. These incidents put the importance of Ford Company's customer service reputation above all else. The resulting unethical and illegal cover-up safety of the two companies has accelerated a daily barrage of negative coverage. These accidents in the U.S., Venezuela, Saudi Arabia, and elsewhere have spawned a wave of personal injury lawsuits. The questions could be asked:

- Are these incidents viewed as a tire issues or a vehicle issues?
- Should we blame Firestone or Ford Company for the defects of their products separately or collectively?
- In the case that Firestone is legally liable what is the ethical responsibility of Ford Company?

PLAN OF THIS CHAPTER

The primary concern of this chapter is to first define morality, ethics, and law. Second is to identify moral, ethical, and legal ordinations in terms of two fundamental distinctions: (1) whether these phenomena are speculative understanding or (2) they are pragmatic knowledge. Speculative understanding refers to a phenomenon or an object in which nothing is effective directly, and hence the phenomenon or object is placid. Pragmatic knowledge, on the contrary, is concerned precisely with a phenomenon or an object insofar as it is dynamic and tangible. In addition, speculative understanding and pragmatic knowing are either for the sake of simply an individual's *conscience awareness* and *cognitive judgments* or for the sake of *formative* and *summative* knowledge application to ordinate people's behavior or their societal interactions. Striving for such judgmental perceptions mandates that people be involved within the context of intellectual deliberation, time, and often-legal costs. Such a managerial judgment varies culture to culture. Therefore, our initial concern in this chapter is to identify precisely what kinds of speculative information or pragmatic knowledge are moral, ethics, and legal. For example, in the U.S., the First Amendment right to free expression has created a different attitude in the business world. Section 509 of the Telecommunications Decency Act of 1997 provides that an informant as a service provider is not to be considered as a publisher of material provided by a third party. This act protects the service provider in relation to any actions taken by it in good faith to restrict access to specific materials that the provider might consider obscene, lewd, lascivious, filthy, excessively violent, harassing, or otherwise objectionable (Randall and Treacy, 2000: 6).

THE EFFECT OF AWARENESS
AND COGNITION ON BEHAVIOR

Conscience Awareness

Conscience awareness merely says that an individual ought to fulfill universal excellent objectives. This type of commitment is contingent upon affordability and solvency of knowers to deliberate their views without fear of retaliation by power holders. For example, the relationship between a lender and borrower on the basis of conscience awareness is based on speculative knowledge by either choice or by force. The connection between choice and force of the will is usually so close that the two seem to be one in the end. Since choice is an intrinsic deliberated voluntary will, it mandates an individual conform to conscious commitments. On the other hand, force is an extrinsic involuntary commitment to fulfill psychosocial commitments. Therefore, a situation at the stage of complex moral, ethical, and legal acts is based on the following conditions: Both lenders and debtors must, at a minimum, respect the universal moral rights. For the purpose of the purported rights, there are at least three conditions that must be considered: (1) the rights must protect something of great mutual importance to both lenders and debtors, (2) the rights must be subject to substantial and recurrent opportunities and threats, and (3) the obligations or burdens imposed by the mutual rights must satisfy a fairness-affordabilty test for both lenders and debtors (Parhizgar and Jesswein, 1998: 141).

Cognitive Judgments

Cognition is the insight knowledge that people express their judgments about conceiving an object or an event in a rational way. The cognitive, rational, or intellectual component of an attitude is what most people understand is to be the reason for an expression of self-behavior based upon conscious awareness, knowledge, and understanding. Attitude is the positive and free will aspect of human behavior. An attitude utilizes conscious awareness such as expectancies, demands, and incentives. Since cognition is based on conceptual rational judgments, an attitude is based upon holistic feelings, thinking, and behaving. Attitude is differentiated from the reality of past experiences. Cognitive information is based on truth and reality. Cognitive perception is a purposive behavior that is directed toward understanding the real nature of an object, a phenomenon, or an event. For example, in the field of international management, the cognitive judgment concerning bribery, dishonesty, and perjury depends on conditional situations. There is a problem with cognitive perceptions. Cognitive perceptions are based upon socio-economic conditions, cultural orientations, and psychological understanding of the cause-effects of some attributions. This variation in cognitive perception is based on perceptual judgment (not conceptual judgment), and cognitive perceptions become very subjective. Nevertheless, the cognitive perceptual component of an attitude may be logical or illogical, rational or irrational, and/or relevant or irrelevant to an object. This perceptual knowledge may be true, partially true, or totally false. For example, shoplifting is a bad attitude among some customers. In some cultures the attitude of shop lifting in a monopolistic industry may be conceived as a logical attitude because consumers believe that a business owner is ripping customers off on the basis of their daily necessities. In another culture the attitude of shoplifting is a bad attitude because people conceive it within an industry that there are many competitors with varieties of pricing systems and it increases an unfair pricing system. Therefore, the consumer-producer relationship is based on reciprocal satisfaction. People believe that it is not right for both parties to rip each other off and/or to steal something from each other. In such an analogy, the matter of justification of perceptual attitudes is based upon choice, not force. In a monopolistic market customers are exposed to force while in a competitive free market economy, customers are dealing with choice. However, within the boundary of conceptual cognition, the actions of ripping customers off and stealing merchandise from businesses are not viewed as moral, ethical, or legal.

BEHAVIORAL ORDINATIONS

Getting ourselves out of the state of nature is simply a matter of good sense and reason. Hobbes (1588-1679) said the state of nature is the beginning point for our development. There are three major behavioral *ordinations* of reasons to people who strive for achieving a common good: (1) constructive ideas, (2) valuable contents, and (3) cultivation of a sense of commitment. Ordination of reason signifies the establishment of cognitive and behavioral orders to search for proper ends through good means. Not all ordinations can establish practical patterns of expected valuable contents, and the other one binds you with decisive commitments. These are rooted in variation of generalization, understanding, defining fundamental principles, and distinctive outcomes of our natural life. The various ordinations for the individual's behavioral ethical, moral, and legal means and ends are the three major topics in this section. In addition, the notions of sensational and emotional pleasure, rational happiness, and the means and ends will be discussed in the following pages.

Constructive Ideas

We are what we either positively and/or negatively think. Whatever we are conceiving and perceiving is determined by our ability to think critically. If our thinking is overly unrealistic, our cognitive judgments will lead us to a fantasized world. If our thinking is overly optimistic, it will enhance our intellectual ability to recognize the real characteristics of things in which we should properly rejoice them. If an individual thinks about his/her life positively, they will feel positive about it and they will be able to pursue a fruitful life. The most important source of critical thinking within the contextual existent domain of our identity is conscientious awareness. It explicitly puts our intellectual ability into words, phrases, and ideas. Conscientious awareness provides us with a psychological reinforcement within our personality in order to express our identity and autonomy. Also, conscientious awareness facilitates critical thinking to make corrections in our judgments. The truth is that since very few people realize the powerful role of critical thinking, they can gain significant command over their independent thinking. Such a superlative spiritual characteristic allows an individual not to be victimized and/or harmed by greedy and selfish people.

Valuable Contents

Life is swiftly changing. With each passing day, we confront with new challenges. The pressure to cope with those challenges is very intense. New global realities are deeply affecting our lives. We first need to think and then act, not first act and then think. Critical thinking inspires people to move towards novelty through learning, analyzing, and experiencing new things. Ordinary people are accustomed to reutilized, habitual, automated, and fixed procedures. They are afraid to be changed, because they do not desire to progress and develop their intellectual abilities. They are satisfied with what they have learned and accustomed to do them over and over. These types of people are viewed as imitators, because they do not convince themselves to think critically.

Critical thinking is very complex. It requires a periodical radical revision in adaptability to the divergent points of view. The world in which we now live requires us to continually and rapidly reevaluate, reanalyze, and relearn innovative techniques. In short, there is a new world facing us everyday. In order to be able to digest new changes, we need to critically and periodically enhance our judgments with the power of the mind to command itself, to procession itself, and to determine how to increase the quality of our work and our lives.

Cultivation of a Sense of Commitment

The ability to define and to set priorities concerning the ethical and moral mandates in the field of business requires the cultivation of a sense of commitment. Business managers need to establish commitments in their behavior during the decision-making processes and actions and quickly analyze their outcomes rationally rather than just sensationally or emotionally. Commitment to ethical, moral, and legal principles in the scientific communities is old as human civilization (e.g. Socratic Oath in Medicine). However, including ethics in business curriculum programs and practices is new. Nash (1996: 11) indicates: "In the early 1980, I found two articles that shed light on what I should call the analytic/normative dichotomy in my teaching." Peter Drucker (1981: 30) and Mark T. Lilla (1981) raised the controversial issue whether the study of ethics should ever be included in the business curriculum. Drucker argued for an axiomatic ethics of interdependence, based on a Confucian moral model. He advocated measuring each ethical transgression against a universal ethics of sincerity: Actions which are appropriate to the spirit of interdependence and, hence, promote harmony in specific relationships are right behavior Drucker (1980: 191). Also, Drucker (1980: 191) indicates: "Around 1920, social power in economy began to drift away from the traditional capitalists, the owners of the nineteenth century into the hands of professional managers, who owed their position and power to function and performance."

This indicated that human civilization is evolving from a traditional moral model to the cosmocratic ethical one. In the modern cosmocratic societies, power would follow professional functions rather than property or the consent of the governed. In supporting this proposition, Lilla (1980: 5) urged that pragmatic ethics should be taught to professional students in order to do the right things through duties and virtues of democratic moral behavior. For Lilla, the correct behavioral virtues are rather obvious: courage, tenacity, and prudence. Lilla would have ethics instructors be, first of all, good human beings who preach, witness, and exemplify what is moral.

In order to be committed to the ideal of professional knowledge, we need to understand the nature of professions. Scientifically, all professions are not following a generic methodology to learn and perform their jobs. They require the theoretical pragmatic acquisition of different levels of data, information, and knowledge. They require different types of searching, learning, and applying data, information, and knowledge when they make the best sense to acquire them. What all professions have in common is ethical and moral responsibilities and commitments to preserve their professional integrity. Professionals need sincere commitments to preserve the sanctity of their professions. They need commitments to fair-mindedness in order to minimize human suffering. They should be committed to a more just world and serve rational rather than irrational ends. In the field of business, we have observed how Arthur Andersen Company (an auditing company) repeatedly betrayed its professional integrity and commitments by providing phony and incorrect data and information to the public in the stock market and provided unethical, immoral, and illegal loopholes for some interest groups including managers in order to gain free-money. Arthur Andersen's practical unprofessional activities were subject to a lack of intellectual virtues, to a tendency to violate the public trust, to betray the Certified Public Accountancy (CPA) and converted it into an unethical and illegal vested interest to destroy the financial life of many investors in the stock market. These incidents should make us worry about where we look for probable weaknesses and how to recognize likely strengths in all professions. Also, we need to understand the differences between the ideal of professional commitments and the manner in which professionals practice their professions in the real world.

SEPARATION OF MORAL AND ETHICAL BEHAVIOR

Let us first begin our discussion with how we perceive morality and ethicality. Then we link morality and ethicality to legality. By looking at Figure 2-1, we may understand the differences among terms and processes of these phenomena. Within the analytical domain of this chapter, we have raised some questions concerning the understanding of the main domain of moral, ethical, and legal understanding as follows:

- Do we perceive primarily the common understanding of moral, ethical, and legal ordinations as *speculative* understanding or do we view them primarily as the *pragmatic* knowledge of how to behave according to the commonality of our cultural beliefs?

- In other words, are moral, ethical, and legal contemplations serving the intellectual means for our behavioral ends, or are we examining the people's behavioral manifestation of their thoughts and emotions as the prime objectives for achieving our ends?

Figure 2-1: Interrelatedness of Morality, Ethics, and Law

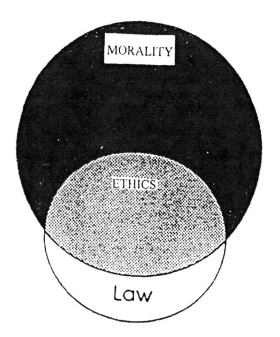

These questions are not simple to answer. If we presume that moral virtues, ethical values, and legal principles are practical in the sense that they are considered, then how people's intentions and actions should be coordinated? In general terms, we are examining the nature of moral, ethical, and legal intentions and actions (see Tables 2.1 and 2.2).

It should be noted that some writers believe ethics and morality are the same. Morality is based on an individual's spiritual commitments toward the end-result of excellence. Ethics is based on conceptual collectively known cultural values (e.g., ideas, beliefs, reactions, anti or pro-actions) by the intellectual reasoning of a homogeneous group of people. Ethics, also, deals with human social acts in order to direct people to a meaningful end.

Table 2.1: Analysis of Positive Perceptual Attributions of Religious Faiths, Moral Judgments, Ethical Behavior, and Legal Actions

Perceptual Attributions	Positive Attitudes	Expected Consequences (Earthly)	Expected Consequences (Heavenly)
Religious Faith: Family Orientation	Virtuous intentions	Conscious awareness	Spiritual revelation
Moral Judgments: Individualistic Orientation	Conscientious normative judgments	Syllogistic reasoning for philanthropic helps	Universal order of goodness and tranquility
Ethical Behavior: Pluralistic Orientation	Conscious cognitive behavior	Social praiseworthines s and honorable reception	Blessing wishes and solemn ritual happiness
Legal Decisions and Actions: Collectivistic Orientation	Meritorious compliance, jurisprudence, sociological jurisprudence, and legal realism jurisprudence	Material goodness; peace of mind; advocacy for just, fair, and right decisions and actions	XXX

The laws and regulations are based upon ideological, econo-political, and social doctrines in order to establish happiness primarily through maintaining peace and order. The in-depth analysis in analyzing of these subject areas may be formed by the following questions:

- What are fundamental definitions, classifications, and generalizations of moral, ethical, and legal conceptions?
- What conditions make the discussion of business ethics and moral conducts possible today?
- What does the current discussion of both domestic and international businesses mean in terms of the way that people from different cultures think about the morality of global business obligations and commitments?
- In order to understand the holistic means and ends of our organizational behavior, we need to define morality, ethics, legality and their applications in human relations. Understanding human thoughts and activities is impossible without defining their theoretical and practical boundaries. This is true about ethics and morality. Whatever the

advantages are, a shared meaning does two things. First, it allows us to insure that all meanings and attributes mean the same thing when discussants and practitioners use a term or refer to an idea. Second, we closely ally this to the first that discussants and practitioners can pursue carefully defined terms.

Table 2.2: Analysis of Negative Perceptual Attributions of Antagonistic Beliefs, Immoral Judgments, Unethical Behavior, and Illegal Actions

Perceptual Attributions	Negative Attitudes	Expected Consequences (Earthly)	Expected Consequences (Heavenly)
Antagonistic Beliefs: Family Orientation	Sinful and filthy intentions	Conscious remorse and condemned intentions	Godly Dissatisfaction and forbidden intentions
Immoral Judgments: Individualistic Orientation	Shameful, improbable, and faulty judgments	Damned reactionary vindication	Psychological exonerated punishment
Unethical Behavior: Pluralistic Orientation	Blameworthy and condemned reactions	Social hatred and abhorrent abominations	Presumption of eternal painful, distressful, and miserable life
Illegal Decisions and Actions: Collectivistic Orientation	Chaotic, anarchic, terrorist, fraudulent, criminal, defaulted, deceptive, and corruptive conducts	Punishment, imprisonment, fine, torturous, exoneration, and execution	XXX

Therefore, many philosophers and social scientists spend their efforts analyzing and defining ethics, morality, and legality. These phenomena address what is truthfulness and falsehood, goodness and badness, rightness and wrongness, justness and unjustness, honesty and dishonesty, responsibility and irresponsibility, fairness and unfairness, worthiness and worthlessness, and the like.

The distinction between conscientious objectives marks the prevailing virtue of the intellect and wisdom of human beings of the mind and conscious behavior of the body. Both make morals and ethics different. In making a distinction between morality and ethics, we discover that the challenge of morality consists of intellectual generalization in universal reasoning, and that the challenge of ethics exist more in the stimulation of its question than in the finality of its answer. Moral absolutism, which assumes that all moral issues can be measured by one universal standard regardless of cultural, religious, and political differences, has been offered an alternative view to ethical relativism.

Etymologically, religious faiths, political ideologies, and cultural values are the three foundations of moral and ethical views among people. They have different meanings and perceptions concerning what are common good for individuals and groups. Most writers have stated that the term *moral* is essentially equivalent to the term *ethical*. Albert, Denise, and Peterfreund (1984) stated: "Etymologically, these terms are identical, the former (moral) being derived from the Latin word *mores*, the latter (ethics) from the Greek word *ethos*, both words are referring to customary behavior." Both terms may be used with two different antonyms. Ordinarily, the opposite of moral is taken to be immoral, so that we mean by a moral person one who is good and does what is right, and by an immoral person one who is bad and does what is wrong. However, moral may also be used in a wider sense to refer simultaneously to right and wrong thoughts and actions. Then, moral's antonym is *amoral*. In this usage, people are moral in the sense that certain of their actions are subject to judgments of right and wrong. The same analysis may be used with the term ethically: Its antonym may be either unethical; that is, it may refer to what is wrong, or it may have as an antonym nonethical, in which case it would apply to objectives that are not subject to moral or ethical evaluation.

In some cases, such as the American business culture, people believe in amoral behavior. An amoral behavior relies on a partial truth while it conceals a good deal of the whole truth. Some American business people perceive their moral obligations as showing a partial truth primarily to be able to sell their products and make profit. To them, an individual and/or a business entity to earn a profit, it needs to produce goods and/or provide services for customers. According to this philosophy, people and/or businesses are not explicitly concerned with ethics. They are concerned with law. They do not consider themselves as unethical or immoral; rather they are amoral as far as they feel that ethical considerations are inappropriate in business (De George, 1995: 5).

There is still another sense of understanding that the words ethics and morals are used differently in other cultures. For example, in the Persian culture the words of *Akhlagh* for ethics and *Khooy* for morality have been perceived separately through the philosophy of *Eshragh* (Illuminationism). Illuminationism means that the intellectual enlightenment should search for revelation through truthful scriptures. This behavior is based upon the divine inspiration of truth and the observation of rational and logical reasoning for the blessing in earthly life and revelation in eternal life after death (Parhizgar, 2002: 297). Therefore, discovering the intellectual truth and acting on the whole truth can provide soundness behavior.

The Buddhist cultural value system involves paying attention to *mundane* (such as earthly refinement) and individual problems (such as health), to salvation, and to morality. There are many facets related to such an ethical and moral goodness. Seen from this perspective, the dominant view in the Asian culture is *monistic*. *Monism* is a doctrine in which moral and ethical behaviors are considered as ultimately one unit of reality. Therefore, in such a cultural perception, there is no separation between morality and ethics (Yinger, 1970: 45).

Shaw (1996: 4) stated: "In everyday parlance, we interchange 'ethical' and 'moral' to describe people we consider good and actions we consider right. And we interchange 'unethical' and 'immoral' to describe what we consider bad people and wrong action." French and Granrose (1995: 9) stated:

> We use these terms (ethics and morality) interchangeably between the words ethics and morals is that the first is derived from Greek word, the second from a Latin one. Both words originally referred to the customs or habits of a society or an individual.

As we have seen, there is no agreement among philosophers and scholars in regards to a unified and generalized definition concerning the phenomena of morals and ethics. Some people object to the term ethics and prefer to characterize ethical problems as religious problems. For example, in the American culture, the subject of business ethics refers to legal market liability, business and external environment, and corporate responsibility. The Germans prefer to call it *Wirtschaftsethik*, which exactly translated means the ethics of relationship between economics and society.

On the other hand, some philosophers and scholars make a distinction between morality and ethics. They define morality refers to human conducts and values and ethics referring to the study of those areas. Walton (1977: 6) defines ethics as a critical analysis of human acts to decide their rightness or wrongness in terms of two major criteria: truth and justice. De George (1995: 19) defined:

> Morality is a term used to cover those practices and activities considered importantly right and wrong; the rules that govern those activities; and the values that are embedded, fostered, or pursued in those activities and practices. Ethics is a systematic attempt to make sense of our individual and social moral experience, in such a way as to determine the rules that ought to govern human conduct, the values worth pursuing, and the character traits deserving development in life.

Oesterle (1957: 5) defined ethics as "the science that deals with those acts that proceed from the deliberative will of man, especially as they are ordered to the end of man." Since ethics is formally practical knowledge, morality is the sound knowledge of what constitutes good or bad actions.

Through a spiritual aesthetic view, morality is the very delightful, intelligible, and beautiful conscious awareness. It is an individual's knowledge. Many people feel that morality is personal and that no one should force such views on others. According to this position, people are entitled to their own personal moral understandings and judgments. In contrast, many people hold another position with respect to different countries and cultures, and believe that all members of a society must abide by their cultural values. This view is another popular form of ethical relativism.

Table 2.3: Analytical Comparative Description of Moral, Ethical, and Legal Perceptions

MORALITY	ETHICALITY	LEGALITY
Psychosocial concern for excellence	Sociocultural concern for goodness	Econo-political concern for peace and harmony
Morality is the matter of an individual's choice	Ethics as the matter of cultural valuable norms	Legality is the socio-political mandated enforcement
Spiritual concern for happiness	Passionate concern for social satisfaction	Prudential concern for a secured life
Conscious concern for self-enhancement	Conscious concern for self-refinement	Citizen concern for social development and growth
Religious concern for revelation	Humanitarian concern for community welfare	Obligatory concern for community ordination
Fear of God and shameful self-blame	Fear of social group condemnation	Fear of court's punishment and fines
Conceptual faith for mental synergy	Societal beliefs for behavioral energy	Legal expectation for profitable prodigy
Universal concern for intellectual power	Natural concern for appetitive power	Legal concern for legitimized power
Searching for the ends of self-excellence	Searching for the means of self-confidence	Searching for the minimal means and ends of goodness
Building individual dignity and loyalty toward trustfulness	Building collective integrity and loyalty toward worthiness	Building personal records of decriminalization
Developing and maintaining emotional virtues	Developing and maintaining intellectual values	Developing and maintaining the notion of common interests
Humanitarian sensibility for goodness	Humanitarian concern with intrinsic fairness	Citizenship concern for extrinsic concern of common justness
Qualitative assessments of self behavior with heavenly rewarded expectations	Quantified assessment of self and others' behaviors with respect to human dignity	Quantified assessment of an individual's rights with human rights

They deserve careful attention in defining and applying these terms. We need to clarify moral as a matter of an individual's choice and ethics as a matter of cultural popular valuable force that determines what action is right or wrong. Furthermore, are morals and ethics culturally determined by an individual and/or by a group? Is there a universal morality to be applicable to all people in different places and times around the globe? For the clarity of these positions we need to define carefully the terms of morality, ethicality, and legality (see Table 2.3).

WHAT IS MORALITY?

Before we consider specifically what makes an action good or bad in a moral sense, we should have a precise picture of the notion of morality itself. How we can define morality? Ernest Hemingway (1932: 4) once said: "What is moral, is what you feel good after and what is immoral is what you feel bad after." In a narrow sense, morality refers to a particular personal judgment concerning right in contrast to wrong, conveying a strong sense of assertion or rejection. Frankena (1963: 6) defined morality as: "a social institution of (personal) life, but is one which promotes rational self-guidance or self-determination."

What is the basis of morality? Does morality have a distinctive foundation or is it merely a matter of social convention and tradition, or a matter of an individual's taste and opinion? Any moral definition or principle contains cognitive elements in conceiving and supporting reasoning. This is what we are dealing with. Moral reasoning is an appeal to establish moral principles. Both moral reasoning and moral principles are involved in determining moral character and action.

The term *morality* signifies primarily a certain relation of an individual's acts that have some ends, as to a standard or principal of action. Morality, therefore, is an abstract signifying the moral order of an individual's acts. Is morality considered as the same as prudence? The answer is no. Whately (1859: 68) defined prudence as whatever is done wholly and solely from motives of personal expediency (from calculation of individual loss or gain) is always accounted a matter of prudence, and not of morality. When someone submits himself/herself to the will of another person merely because it is in his or her interest, or because they dare not to resist, we never call it morality, but merely prudence. For example, if you were offered good wages for doing something in favor of your employer, and against your subordinates, you might think it expedient to accept the offer, but you would not account it as a moral duty. Newton and Schmidt (1996: 3) have defined morals or morality as: "The *rules* that govern our behavior as persons toward other persons; also, duties."

As indicated before, the term *moral* is derived from the Latin word *mores*. *Mores* means the embodiment of fundamental individual values. There are two main traditional fields of value inquiry: morals, which is concerned with the problems of truthfulness and falseness, worthiness and worthlessness, and goodness and badness, and they're bearing on moral conduct. Ethics is concerned with the problems of justness and unjustness, fairness and unfairness, and righteousness and wrongness and their bearing on societal ethical decisions and actions.

Morality means conformity to the rules of the universal right conducts. For example, the term honesty is a universal phenomenon. In all cultures, honesty means to be truthful. An honest individual has been praised in all cultures.

Therefore, there are some values among all people around the globe that are universal and these universal values are considered as the foundational principles of humaneness. In addition, if we are judging bribery as a moral term, we arrive at the same conclusion: bribery corrupts an individual's character, defects the group's cultural value systems, and is wrong. However, if bribery is common practice in a given culture, then is it proper to engage in bribery in that country? This raises questions about the distinction between ethics and morality.

Morality is a term used to manifest humanity's universal virtues. Virtues refer to the excellence of intellect and wisdom and to the disposition of cognizance of mind to perform effectively its proper function. The moral virtues concern the habitual choices of rational thoughts in accordance with the universal logical principles. The contemplation of absolute truthfulness and the discovery of the rational principles that ought to control everyday actions have given rise to the intellectual virtues. The distinction between goodness and badness, truthfulness and falseness, and worthiness and worthlessness is called moral considerations. For example, moral people may consider goodness if they habitually think, value, and act in accordance with their intellectual conscience.

Sincerity in continuity of moral thoughts and acts is the keynote for morality. In other words, the meaning of moral is one to which a moral individual aspires (De George, 1995). Morality denotes the total characteristics of intellect and wisdom of an individual. The maxim of the intellect and wisdom is a careful calculation of virtues in the mind or description of the essential features of righteousness, truthfulness, and goodness in the character of a human being. Thus, when we speak of morality, we refer to a human's personal virtue through their intellectually excellent choices.

As human beings, we can make a distinction between true and false, and right and wrong. Therefore, we can make a distinction between the end results of morality and ethics. Morality's end result through intellectual truthfulness, righteousness, and goodness of thoughts and actions is revelation and happiness.

Wisdom and intellectual ability of mind and passionate activities of body that can be considered right or wrong is the main contextual domain of morality. The rules that govern an individual's thoughts, and the values that are embedded in intellectual and rational virtues are the subject of morality. Therefore, morality is a universal, general, and intellectual characteristic of humanity.

Distinct from both the real (natural) order of existing things and the logical (intellectual) order formed by human reason is the moral order. Both orders are caused by reason. It is within this context that the term morality is introduced as understanding formally in an orderly thought which wisdom has established a rational reason in human acts. However, an individual's tendencies toward pleasure can change such a rationalized thought and behavior and divert them into passionate desires.

An individual's passion depends on a variety of circumstances and conclusive end-results. *Passion* is a motivational principle and tendentious operational factor in an individual's daily behavior. We act because of joy or sorrow, love or hatred, and success or failure. It is obvious that an individual's behavioral consequences are accompanied by pleasure or pain, joy or sorrow, happiness or unhappiness, and courage or fear. All of these consequential motives are related to our intentional and tendentious attainment of personal objectives.

For behavior to be an ethical and moral, the individuals need to strive for excellence. Excellence in behavior is a virtue. Virtue is a positive derivative of the power of the mind toward happiness. Virtue is neither a passion nor a power. It is an extreme of excellence, rising above the excess and effect. Virtue regulates behavioral pleasure. It is the disposition of the intention toward good actions in a regular manner. For example, when we avoid good behavior pain follows, or when we strive for happiness, a satisfactory end-result follows.

What is morality, given that it occupies such an unchallengeable place in our "mind." Simply stated morality consists of those family virtues to enhance all family members' activities. Such enhancements are boundaries of sacrifice, tolerable efforts of children's security, and guarantee prosperous happiness for their future. Whatever it may be, morality is at least the following characteristics.

The Nature of Morality

Morality Is Defined: Morality is a means to cope with surrounding defected social behavior by providing enhanced advisable methods for understanding and behaving toward a virtuous end. When moralists try to define morality, they include all excellent human characteristics toward a happy life. The ultimate objective of morality is achieving excellence in mind, and behavior, in an individual's societal life, and revelation after an individual's death.

Morality Is a Conscientious Living Phenomenon: Our primary percept of morality is based on self-trial within an individual's intellectual mind-body court system with the presiding of our conscience. It is an individual's defense to decide for himself or herself what is true and what is false, what is right and what is wrong, what is worth and what is worthless.

Morality Is What One Learns: Morality is not genetic or biological, it is relatively perceived as foundational learning objectives and as permanent virtuous objectives in an individual's thinking and behavior resulting from understanding and experiencing what is happiness. Most moralists agree that human beings are moral in nature because they inherited intellectual wisdom from the human species. The most widely studies determinates of human intellect is biological, social, and cultural understanding. Biology influences certain intellectual characteristics in a number of ways. Our genes help determine many physical righteousness characteristics, and these may in turn affect our intellectuality. It is very difficult to separate "nature" from "nurture." The term "nature" denotes all genetic characteristics that people acquire from their parents and environments through their physical identity. The term *nurture* means all parental affection, protection, and convictions towards happiness for themselves and their children. Children learn from their parents how to value, how to believe, and how to behave towards themselves and others. Although learning from parents does not necessarily imply a positive or negative attribution in an individual's behavior, you may learn, for example, through your family behavior to be a "straight-faced truthful person or a strait-faced liar," or a "pathological altruistic person or selfish liar." The changes resulting from family moral orientation is viewed as a long life process.

Morality Is Not Accidental: Morality is a continuous intellectual deliberation concerning achievement of the state of excellence. It is not what one does that count for but what one does *conscientiously* in thinking and behaving towards excellence. Promoting an individual's excellence by mistake is not being moral. Giving money through corrupted people to charity is not charity. It is deception.

Morality Requires Intellectual Deliberation: Judgmental perceptions on successful or unsuccessful conclusions within the environmental conditions without intellectual deliberation on life events are not sufficient. Conscientious experimental trials can provide people with virtuous solutions. We all are born as unreflective thinkers, fundamentally unaware of the role that intellectual thinking is playing in our lives. Gradually, we learn how to think and act. Paul and Elder (2002: 47) believe that development of thinking is a gradual process requiring plateaus of learning and hard work. They believe thinkers should start their life-long journey through six stages (see Figure 2.3):

- The Unreflective Thinking: we are unaware of significant problems in our thinking.
- The Challenged Thinking: we become aware of problems in our thinking.
- The Beginning Thinking: we try to improve, but without regular practice.
- The Practicing Thinking: we recognize the necessity of regular practice.
- The Advanced Thinking: we advance in accordance with our practice.
- The Master Thinking: skilled and insightful thinking becomes second nature.

Morality Is a Manifestation of Self-Identity: We are living in a cryptomoral environment in which some groups of people admire smart criminals and charming cons or corrupted persons for fun not only in movies, but also, on TV news shows. In addition, we are tempted to be attracted to people who break the virtuous rules. People should know consciously what is going on in their personal lives and surroundings. To be moral is an unquestioned good. What makes our moral identity is the line between purity

PRAGMATIC ETHICAL KNOWLEDGE

Let us view the second ordination *pragmatic knowledge*. In pragmatic ordination, we are faced with major problems through the examination of knowable ethical, moral, and legal information. What is knowable depends on the different ways in which people can make their intentional and behavioral means and ends known. Adding to this problem is the fact that moral virtues, ethical values, and legal principles in different locations around the world are different. Hence practical knowledge is an operative dynamic action; therefore, intentions and manners of knowing will be pragmatic phenomena. Thomas Hobbes's moral philosophy is related to his psychological theory, in which he constructs his mechanistic conception of motivation. He opposed the prevailing notion of his time that the mind and body are different substances, maintaining that mental phenomena are nothing but physical motions. He believed that any action is traced to predispositions to that act in a certain direction. Desires move one to pursue objects, and aversions move one to avoid objects (Albert, Denise, and Peterfreund, 1984: 128).

The question arises here, what type of moral life does an individual prefer? Most moral and ethical issues are the result of more attention being paid to the knowable means and ends of an action. In some cases, they are more than conventions and consensus. They are arbitrary decisions and actions. Legal decisions and actions are known as the result of logical tests of consistency either through consensus or by some logic of relationship. Therefore, pragmatic knowledge is the result of some historical, experiential, or deliberated tests. While morality and ethics cannot tell you how to act at a given time and in particular circumstances, legal principles mandate you in all situations what should you do because law is a practical knowing of what to do in defined situations and conditions. Nevertheless, moral and ethical ordinations provide you knowledge that will serve you as general guidelines for actions.

SELF-LIMITATIONS ON MORAL BEHAVIOR

The Limit of Self-Interest and Moral Character

We all know that all people to some extent are egocentric. They seriously pursue objectively their lives. In the domain of survival, there are two connotations: *selfishness* and *prudence*. Since selfishness is defined as one who acts solely with a view to the self- advantage without due regard to the interest of others, prudence is not same as selfishness. A prudent person is not necessarily selfish, and neither is a selfish person necessarily prudent. However, selfishness always involves reference to self-interest, self-needs, self-wishes or self-desires. Prudence involves the self as well as the interests of a person or an organization that an individual is representing. However, it should be noted that prudence is the exercise of self-intelligence or self-forethought with respect to the mutual interest of self and others. To act imprudently is to think and act stupidly or irrationally from the mutual point of view of self and others. Finally, prudence is thinking and acting with more rational or enlightened self-interest. Selfishness is immoral, while prudence is ethical. If we want to examine selfishness and prudence in relation to an arbitrary judgment, we must consider their effects on the agent and others. For example, suppose two professors that apply for promotion and tenure in a university system, are concurrently serving as members of the promotion and tenure committee. Also suppose one of these professors is highly qualified and the other is unqualified. At the time of deliberation and judgment, the unqualified professor casts his/her vote in favor of the qualified professor, and in return, the qualified professor casts his/her vote as abstain (neither in favor nor against) the unqualified professor. Such a judgment is called prudence. It should be noted that there is a distinction between prudence and morality. Such a distinction makes a borderline between prudence and morality. Morality by all means and ends relates individual's judgments to the truth and denies selfishness and prudence. Prudence in return relates judgments to the pluralistic-interest of a group of professional specialists.

In order to fulfill the maximum of the self-interest, an individual needs to benefit self and may injure other(s). This means that survival is like playing a game. If you do not try hard to compete, you will be soon as a loser. There are two types of competition: fair and unfair. A fair competition is based on an equal opportunity at the beginning of the race with impartial judgment by the referees. Competitors inevitably need to express and manifest their volitions to the point of equilibrium, and then they accelerate them to exceed from that point to the ultimate succession. In doing so in moral competition, parties achieve three objectives:

- Competitors need to exercise their legitimate power in a way that competition proceeds with perfectly equal rights.
- They maximize the utility of their inherent power to lead other parties to confess their weaknesses and relinquish voluntarily their interest.
- They bring about these achievements in a way that parties respect the right of the free consent.

Since people's behavior is based on voluntary or involuntary intentions, their achievement is also based on good and evil consequences. However, both good and evil actions are related to moral, ethical, and legal intentions and consequences.

Evaluating competitors' objects and behaviors as good or evil depends upon no other basis than desires and aversions. One of the most moral duties is the duty to self. An individual carries the burden of two duties: to oneself and to others. It is a moral duty to preserve one's own life and self-respect. It is a moral duty to preserve others-respect within the obligatory context of the self-respect.

This is especially true of moral virtue.

A moral virtues is the kind of personal habit whose proper means and ends are consistent with choosing alternatives as a means between two extremes: (1) duty to self and (2) duty to others. This is precisely what we mean by an act of choice or force. We are now in a position to distinguish choice from force. Indeed, moral intentions and actions of an individual depend more upon what a person chooses than upon any other type of act they perform. Let us begin with self-interest perceptions and choices. While every forced action is involuntary, every voluntary action is strictly a free action of choice. Therefore, every act of choice refers to one specific kind of action performed and controlled by the will.

Egocentrism refers to an individual's inability to take of perspective other than his or her own. When personal objectives, motives, derives, and strongly held attitudes get in the way of the systematic analysis of causes, the attributive biases is known as a self-serving bias. This means that people tend to take credit for their success while denying responsibility for their failures. Self-serving biases are quite robust, occurring in many situations for most people and even across cultures (Flecher and Ward, 1988: 230).

The Limit of Self-Control: One of the issues of today's business is *promise*. A promise is a self- obligatory intention to fulfill duties on a specific short or long period of time. A promise carries two sides of moral and ethical obligatory duties: (1) to oneself, and (2) to others. Can one promise oneself to do something? Promises to oneself would be considered a form of self-control which one could release oneself at will. The language here must be metaphorical. For example, to say: I have promised myself not to gamble any more is to say: I have strongly resolved my greedy appetite by not gambling any more. Self-control is the stream of expression and action that is needed to resolve or settle an immoral and unethical habit. Although a promise to oneself is in some respect like a promise, it is not a genuine, or in any literal sense, a promise. To promise oneself to do something is to just be intentionally resolved to do it.

Promise to others is characterized by duties arising out of both written and oral contracts. In ethical contracts parties promise to each other to fulfill their reciprocal duties during a specific period of time with specific terms of intentions and actions. If parties do not fulfill their obligatory contracts, then one or both are in default. This rigid rule sometimes fails when the contract is not in writing with specific reciprocal obligatory duties. Then, conflict and dispute arises between parties whose expectations of each other are not fulfilled. One such equitable concept in the law of contract is called promissory, equitable, and estoppels duty. The ethical doctrine of oral promissory duty is based upon an individual's cultural value systems within the boundary of self-moral control. Halbert and Ingulli (2000: 19) stated:

> In order for a promise to be enforceable under the concept of promissory estoppels, there must be:

1. A promise that the promisor should reasonably have expected to induce action of a definite and substantial character on the part of the promise.
2. Which in fact produced reliance or forbearance of that nature.
3. In circumstances such that the promise must be enforced if injustice is to be avoided.

The Limit of Self-Discipline: Perhaps most fundamentally, self-discipline has given way to ethical, moral, and legal consciousness of an individual's interrelatedness of behavior with others. Self-discipline is a cognitive controlled prudent intention and action through intellectual reasoning. It maintains self-dignity and integrity and prevents contradictions, frustrations, disappointment, and anger. Self-discipline, however, is important for a number of reasons: not only to manifest self-respect, but also to set the standard that certain behaviors are expected from others. Self-discipline for a manager ensures that all employees must receive consistent treatment for similar infractions. Research has provided us sufficient guidelines about the most effective ways to discipline self and others.

One of the immoral, unethical, and illegal problems threatening most organizations is sexual harassment in the workplace. Under federal law, sexual harassment includes such activities as posting pornographic posters, cartoons, and drawings at work, requesting sexual favors, unwanted sex, lewd remarks, unwanted hugs, touches and kisses, and retaliating against anyone who complains about sexual harassment. The Equal Employment Opportunity Commission initiated a guideline on sexual harassment as of the following:

Unwelcome sexual advance, request for sexual favors, and other verbal or physical conduct of a sexual nature constitute sexual harassment when:

> Submission to such conduct is made either explicitly or implicitly a term or condition of an individual's employment, Submission to or rejection of such conduct by an individual is used as the basis for employment decisions affecting such individual, or Such conduct has the purpose or effect of unreasonably interfering with an individual's work performance or creating an intimidating, hostile, or offensive working environment [The EEOC Guideline on Sexual Harassment, 29 CFR 1604.11(a)].

Traditionally, most organizations had been influenced by masculine power (Steiner and Steiner, 1988: 592). Men and women have considered their opposite gender's identity within two different emotional and submissive perceptions: In some cases, men perceived women (1) as enjoyable immoral and unethical lovers and lovely legal wives; (2) as virtuous and respectable mothers, sisters, and daughters. In return, women have considered men (1) as immoral and unethical pleasurable lovers and faithful legal husbands; (2) as virtuous fathers, brothers, and sons. Within the domain of moral virtues, ethical faithfulness, and legal doctrine, women have found themselves in such settings a dilemma of harassment. In return, men could find themselves in another kind of sensational and emotional dilemma. For example, if men praise a young female coworker's beauty and her dressing style, some women unconsciously feel pleasure and consciously doubtful and suspicious about those comments. If men adopt masculine behaviors towards women, they may be scorned as unfeminine. In order for both genders to be treated equitably, men and women need to consider emotional and sensational limits. Both genders, through moral, ethical, and legal expectations, need to behave professionally. It has been observed in the case of Price Waterhouse Company a female accountant won the top contract but was denied promotion to partnership by male partners who, in written reviews, described her as macho and suggested that she overcompensated for being a woman. The company's representative who was assigned to inform the cause of rejection was a man. The man advised her: "To walk more femininely, talk more femininely, dress more femininely, wear make-up, have her hair styled, and wear jewelry" (*Price Waterhouse vs. Ann B. Hopkins*, 618 F. Supp. At 1117,57 LW at 4471, 1989).

Today's organizational environments have been dramatically changed. Federal law has defined two types of sexual harassment: *quid pro quo*, and *hostile work environment*. *Quid pro quo* means that sexual favors are a requirement or appear to be a requirement for advancement in the workplace. *Hostile work environment* means that a worker has been made to feel uncomfortable because of unwelcome actions or comments relating to sexuality (Trevino and Nelson, 1995: 52). Barton (1995: 109) indicated that three primary requites must met for a claim of sexual harassment to be successful:

o   The action must be sexual in nature, the place in a hostile environment, and be unwelcome.
o   The victim's clothing style, age, and position are irrelevant.
o   Any statement, suggestion, or conduct (including physical, verbal, or visual activities) could be subject to a claim, including activities that one party considers to be merely playful, but others consider degrading.

Of course harassment is more than just sexual, financial, and legal issues. It is also a moral one.

WHAT IS ETHICS?

Thus far we have defined morality in terms of an individual's pursuing self-interest and/or searching for self-egoism towards excellence, but we have not seen what is excellence in terms of collective socio-cultural value systems. Ethics could be defined as both social habits as well as responses to perceived extraordinary necessitated prudence in specific situations. In a conventional social behavior, ethics is defined as excellent cultural behavioral values as fits customs and traditions. In a narrow sense, ethics refers to an excellent particular social behavior. It refers to a societal benchmark or instrument of society as a whole for the guidance of good social behavior for individuals and groups. Nevertheless, ethics in social behavior differs in that it is coordinated with, but different from, science, technology, art, law, convention, and religion. All of the above phenomena may be related to ethics, but they are not ethics. Ethics in this sense is a social enterprise in which an individual or groups are inducted. What is significant to note is the individualistic aspect of the social enterprise; we have called it ethics. Nevertheless, morality is defined as personal rational self-guidance and ethics is defined as a social guided enterprise (Park and Barron, 1977: 3-23).

Ethics involves critical analysis of cultural values to determine the validity of their vigorous rightness or wrongness in terms of two major criteria: truth and justice. Ethics is examining the relation of an individual to society, to the nature, and/or to God. How do people make ethical decisions? They are influenced by how they perceive themselves in relation to goodness and/or excellence.

In this section we will define ethics as a purely theoretical treatment of moral virtues in terms of speculative and practical collective cultural value systems. In speculative and practical knowledge of goodness, righteousness, and worthiness, we are concerned with cultural value systems that are operable, either with intending to do something or actually doing something in the realm of goodness. Now, through these two alternatives, it might seem to define what ethical life should be, a manner of reflection in which it will indicate that it is not the kind of intending or knowing goodness, but it is the complete practical execution of goodness through the pluralistic behavior of a group of people.

The term *ethics* is derived from the Greek word *ethos*. In the Oxford English Dictionary (1963) ethos means the "genius" of an institution or system. Also, it defines "ethics" as the science of morals and the department of study concerned with the principles of human duty. Ethics concerns itself with human societal conduct, activity, and behavior such that they are done knowingly and to a large extent, deliberately and willingly. Ethics is concerned with the construction of a societal rational system through application of moral principles (virtues) by a group of people in a society.

Ethics is concerned with psychosocial actions and it can deal with good deeds in a society. Philosophers have identified ethics with one or the other of these extremes. Some have understood ethics to be speculative and demonstrative good of thoughts and behavior (deontological) and others have tended to identify ethics with completely the practical good end-results (teleological).

In the homogenous European and American cultures, the meaning of ethics is related to "The Love of God," and to "The Love of Wisdom." In the Greek tradition, ethics was conceived as relating to the "social niceties." Social niceties could be considered as custom, convention, and courtesy. In Chinese's culture, the word of ethics has been used as the word of etiquette, *li,* which originally meant to sacrifice. It refers to the fact that Chinese people should follow legally sanctioned etiquette, not to mention knowledge of hundreds of correct forms of behavior. The Chinese eventually came to believe that their behavior was the only correct etiquette in the universe, that all who did not follow the same meticulous rules of conduct were uncivilized barbarians (De Mente, 1989: 27-28).

Later, on a quite different orientation was introduced by the Judo-Christian ethics. In this tradition, the ideals of righteousness before God and the love of God and neighbor, not the happy or pleasant life, constitute the substance of ethical behavior.

As far as the term morality is related with deliberation of an individual's intellectual characteristics through their conscientiousness awareness, ethics is the pluralistic social conscious awareness of a group of people. Thus, morality is related to the individual virtues, and ethics is related to the cultural value systems (society's fairness, justness, and worthiness as excellence). Hence, morality is the foundation of an ethical society, it also relates to the existence of moral people who make the collective distinction of right judgments from wrong and good behavior from bad. Ethics generally mandates people to behave in accordance with valuable norms and standards in excellence that they accept and to which they and the rest of society hold others.

Ethics then can be defined as a systematic pluralistic attempt of social well-being in a society in order to make sense of our individual security and societal peaceful efforts in such a way to determine the rules that ought to govern human social conduct, the values worth pursuing, and the character traits deserving development in life. In his foundation of the metaphysics of morals the German philosopher Immanuel Kant (1785) stated: "Act only in accordance to that maxim by which you can at the same time will that it should become a universal law." In other words, human beings cannot adopt ethical principles of social actions unless they can do it with consistency, and it has to be adopted by everyone else. Without an accepted universal morality (virtues) there would be no stabilized ethical society to keep the world in peace and security. Beliefs and faiths are important ingredients in the ethical behavior. Different beliefs and faiths about moral and intellectual virtues can lead us to differences in what is described as ethical relativism.

The Nature of Ethics

Ethics Promotes Humaneness: As mentioned before, the nature of human beings is viewed with dual characteristics. Humanity's potentialities are multiple. Philosopher Sidney Hook (1946) stated that a human is like the egg which might develop into a chicken, but which might also, among other things, become an egg sandwich. Human objectives are plural, and they may conflict with each other or even with themselves in different situations. Why is such a complexity inherited in human nature? The answer indicates that when a choice has to be made between an individual and a group need, different people will weigh values differently. People may agree about a word but the word may have different meanings for different individuals. Such a general disagreement is rooted in the nature of egoism and selfishness of people.

Generally, people search for happiness and pleasure through excessive acquisition of power, wealth, reputation, sexual enjoyment, and luxurious life style. Such an excessive acquisition is the result of *appetite* and *greed*. There are two important connotations in regard to conscience awareness and cognitive perceptions: *appetite* and *greed*. *Appetite* in a physiological term is an intrinsic desire to supply any bodily want or craving. However, *appetite* in a psychosocial term is an inner drive or propensity to satisfy a want on the basis of acquired extrinsic demand. Appetite through physiological capacity contains limitation, but through psychosocial experience is unlimited. These issues manifest moral, ethical, and legal commitments of human behavior. *Greed* is an inordinate and rapacious desire, especially for wealth, power, sex, and reputation. It is denoted as an excessive and extreme desire for something, often more than an individual's rational share. Also, greed means avid desire for unethical, immoral, and illegal gain or wealth. Greedy intentions and actions are rapacious, ravenous, voracious, and gluttonous. Greed is simply what individuals want, then they excessively try to have them. Both appetite and greed are highly associated with an individual's intellectual, emotional, and sensational powers.

Appetite and greed are highly influential in the field of business. Before explaining conscience awareness and cognitive perceptions, let us illustrate by means of a chart the relationships between the different psychosocial characteristics of an individual.

Ethics Harnesses Power: *Power* is almost a dirty word. It may be associated with competence, strength, and perhaps with legitimate authority. Much of the writings of philosophers, political scientists, and researchers in business are concerned with the definition of power and with distinguishing among its types. Power stems from the Latin word *potere,* which means to be able. Benn (1967: 424) defined power as "the ability to get someone to do something that he/she otherwise would not do." Emerson (1962:31) emphasizes the application of power: "Its operationalization rests on the interaction of two factors: dependence and goals." French and Raven (1959) within the bound of power relationships, indicated several types of power: (1) coercive power, (2) reward power, (3) referent power, and (4) legitimate lower.

Within the domain of business power, there are other kinds of power: (1) money power, (2) sexual power, (3) charismatic power, (4) expert power, (5) authoritative power, (6) abusive power, (7) oppressive power, (7) corrupted power, and (8) corporate power.

Each of the above kinds of power has with specific consequences. For example coercive power often combines selfish interest with some types of threatening consequences such as fear, wrath, retaliation, domination, and intimidation. Ethical principles can harness the above kinds of power.

Ethics Promotes Intellectual Choice and Prohibits Mandatory Force: When we speak of an ethical decision, we imply two different alternatives for its execution: (1) free or voluntary choice (2) mandatory force. Equally obvious, however, is that the distinction between choice and force is the degree of coercion. Ethics promotes intellectual voluntary choices to comply with power. In the field of business, financial rewards and penalties are frequent kinds of coercion.

Choice and Definite Means and Ends: There are two different behavioral directions within an individual's body-mind interaction: desire and will. Desires are emotional and sensational pleasing appeals which meditate an individual to achieve an end-result (moral, immoral, or amoral). Desires pursue pleasure and enjoyment for favorable self oriented end-results and avoid pain and misery. The origin of desires is a mixture of emotional and sensational end-results but not assessment of their causes. On the other hand a will, in its intellectual sense, is a dynamic moving drive that guides an individual to be aware of the particular circumstance of the means and ends relationships. But the origin of a will is in its efficient and effective means and ends assessment (cause and effect assessment). A will is a conscience-deliberated awareness of a choice. A moral and ethical individual tends to choose pleasure or pain not merely because of pleasure or pain but because of achieving a good end-result or an evil to be avoided. Sometimes, individuals choose what is painful, not because it is painful but because of some good end-results that can be achieved through painful experiences. Therefore, people choose their intentional objectives as conscious expected ends in terms of good or evil rather than pleasure or pain. Being a self-willed individual means that what is, as being very intent on getting what is seeking. Acts of simple desires are not acts of choices. They are unconscious and in most occasions habitual behaviors. But the act of emotional feelings spring from sensational will. Since a desire is always associated with pleasure, an intellectual choice is not necessarily connected with pleasure and/or enjoyment. It is related to happiness and satisfaction.

We have now distinguished desire, will, and choice in relation to means and ends or intentions and actions. We still need to understand more of the nature of choice and to analyze precisely what the intention and act of choice is in an individual's mind-body relations. Also, we must realize how an intention in the action of choice takes place in the mind. A choice is a presupposed act of decisive deliberation. Just as the emotional and sensational desires follow upon an individual's feelings, so a specific act of the choice follows upon a specific act of the intellect. Therefore, the act of choice is following upon the intention of intellectual deliberation.

Deliberation is the essence of intellectual reasoning for making a preference of the final choices. Deliberation is the process of evaluating reasons for or against doing something. Consequently, deliberation is a conscience analysis about good and evil means. In moral and ethical reasoning, we cannot exercise a choice unless we deliberate the means of an action in terms of good and evil.

Command of Execution of Choice: How deliberated moral choices that can be good or bad, fair and unfair, just and unjust, and right and wrong in actions could be assessed? It is the subject of the execution of decisions. Execution of moral choices depends on reasoning and circumstances. They signify primarily certain cause-effect orders. We simply need to discover these orders, observe them, analyze them, formulate them, plan them, and execute them. There are several orders in an individual's life (e.g., moral order, ethical order, legal order, scientific order, systematic order, historical order, etc). All these orders are viewed as real and logical. All orders are caused by reasons and reasons are the efficient causes of effects. Reasons construct choices to be implemented in actions by the will in seeking an end. In studying the command of execution of choices, we need to analyze the will and expected consequential results of actions. Evidence suggests that a number of factors may need to be considered during the decision-making and implementation processes. It is has been frequently observed that managers mental representations of the world likely to be scientifically, culturally, and legally oriented rather than ethical and moral. When managers are faced with a totally new situation, they tend to immediately think about the future by looking at the present circumstances through a rear-view mirror. This mirror reflects their conscience awareness. In order to analyze the present circumstances and predict the future, managers need to go through a self-interrogatory process in order to discover the real choices and execute them. For clarifying this self-interrogatory process, you will find some guidelines below:

- *Why Should the Choice Be Executed?* This question concerns a holistic assessment in the mind of managers in executing decisions in action. Managers need to ask themselves: why are they doing what they are doing? Are their decisions rightly executed? Are their operational techniques scientifically valid and viable in order to safely obtain organizational goals? Are there other right techniques? If yes, why are these techniques being used and not others? Are these executed actions meeting the managers☐ motives for acting? Are these executed techniques matching their ethical, moral, and legal intentions? Sometimes, one can have a certain intention in mind and at the same time the proceedings of actions will bring about the opposite of what one intends.

- *When Should the Choices Be Executed?* Moral virtues, ethical values, and legal principles are the basic foundational milestones of human actions. The timing of the execution of choices is the matter of finding appropriate circumstances. The circumstance of the execution of choices in terms of timing can be assessed before, during, or after transformation of the decision-making processes. This timing refers not only to dates and hours but also to special periods of time, such as day or night, weeks, months, seasons, or a time of war or peace. Timing could be managed through three periods: preliminary, concurrent, and post operations. Nevertheless, the length of time involved in an action may carry a relevant moral, ethical, and legal circumstance. For example, people are committed to consider religious sacred days or periods of time in doing or not doing something in the public. In Moslem countries and Israel, there are specific fasting days during which people are prohibited to drink or eat in public areas.

- *Where Should the Choices Be Executed*? People behave differently when they are situated in different places. Sometimes people are doing some actions that are morally right in privacy, but the same action is considered immoral while done in public. The place of the act can change the nature of moral to immoral, ethical to unethical, and legal to illegal. The distinction between private and public is sometimes a relevant moral, ethical, and legal circumstance. For example, nudity in a religious place during a sermon can be considered as a sin, nudity on the stage of a theater during a play a shameful exposure, in a classroom during a lecture an unethical and illegal action, and in the bedroom a moral, ethical, and legal act. Therefore, moral, ethical, and legal actions can be practiced in a way that leads to harmony rather than disharmony with places.

- *By What means Should the Choice Be Executed*? It is proper to state that people need to pursue their objectives according to their intellectual reasoning. Reason is a powerful means to empower people's mind grasp what is good and what is evil. The moral and ethical choices are related to particular determinations between good and evil reasoning. These determinations are perceived as proceeding from what is right to what is wrong, what is fair to what is unfair, what is just to what is unjust, what is nice to what is nasty, and what is simple to what is complex. The measure of moral and ethical means consists in the conformity of the execution of the good choices. That measure needs to be correlated with a good faith in the sense that reason is rightly to be stated according to the order of execution of a decision. It also needs to measure what is meant by action. In moral and ethical decision-making processes managers need to decide from simple and ordinary reasonable experiences to the utility of complex multiplicity of organizational objectives. Therefore, moral and ethical reasoning consists of a correlated and integrated nature of good faith, good intention, and good means in action. The opposite, which is called evil, consists of departing from goodness to nastiness in reasoning and actions.

- *Should What Ends Execute the Choices*? It is the managers' responsibility to turn people potential into effective and efficient work. Effectiveness is the ability to set the right objectives and achieve them. In other words, effectiveness is the right way to do something.

Efficiency is doing things rightly. Productivity is also to do right things rightly. Efficiency is the relative amount of resources used to obtain effectiveness. Since effective and efficient people in production systems are viewed as good means to reach to good ends, they need to be constructively and productively motivated in order to be morally and ethically good. Therefore, to be moral and ethical in the workplace, employees and employers must behave reasonably well.

- *Who Should Execute the Choices?* Organizational decisions need to be implemented through appropriate formal channels by qualified agents. The agents need to be aware of what has been told and how to execute those commands. The agents should not be ignorant of selves and of who they are. The agents need to be professionally knowledgeable in executing decisions. The agents are accountable in wrongdoing. Inexcusable and inconvincible reasons cannot preclude the rights of customers. It is unethical, immoral, and illegal for an employer to hire unprofessional people to perform professional tasks. For example, the primary objective of a university is to render academic services to students by qualified professors. In some cases, it has been observed that because of financial savings, the university administrators combine graduate and undergraduate students in a classroom to be taught by a professor. In these circumstances, the instructors know that the level of instruction, the course contents, the breadth of knowledge, and the testing systems at both graduate and undergraduate levels are different. In the event that a conflict develops between the instructor's professional commitment and an administrator's responsibility for the institutional financial savings the conflict must be resolved morally and ethically for the student's welfare.

- *How Should the Choice Be Executed?* The manner of decision-makers can affect the nature and consequences of an action for better or worse. Managers should believe in establishing a healthy work environment. It is important for both employees and employers to respect human dignity and integrity in the workplace. Working in such an environment is a "social nicety." Morality and ethics are significantly more important than etiquette in fostering the mutuality of social niceties. Courtesy, convention, and respect are related to behavioral etiquette and to business ethics. All parties expect equitably to be treated well. For example, it is wise when firing an employee considers and implement moral, ethical, and legal mandates such as *careful consideration*, and *due process*. For the clarity of managerial responsibilities, several issues and procedures such as Employment-At-Will (EAW), Nepotism and Favoritism, Careful Consideration, and Due Process will be described as following.

ETHICS AND MANAGERIAL RESPONSIOBILITIES

Employment-At-Will

Traditionally, hiring and firing of employees is the prerogative decisions by managers. Employment-at-will is a relatively recent common law development in most developed nations. It gives employers unfettered power to dismiss their employees *at-will* for just cause, for good cause, or even for no cause (Halbert and Ingulli: 2000: 40). Historically, this concept is traced to the post-industrial revolution when it became advantageous for employers to have ability to hire or fire employees, depending on fluctuating demands of the marketplace. The reason behind such a connotation is cited in the United States' Legal System (*Adair v. United States*, 208 U. S. 161, 174-75, 1908) is: "The right of an employee to quit the service of the employer, for whatever reason, is the same as the right of the employer, for whatever reason, to dispense with the services of such employee," (Halbert & Ingulli, 2000: 40). As you see, the legal system is impartial and judgments arrive through equal causes, processes, and effects for all parties. Do you find any moral and ethical consideration in such a process? If your answer is no, then the legal bureaucracy is based on *amoral decisions and actions*. Therefore, in at-will decisions and actions morality and ethics cannot control causes, processes, and consequences of an adversary judgment. It should be noted that according to Mills (1989: 100) there are certain basic characteristics of legal processes:

- The law is a result of a process of historical evolution.
- The law is an often-paradoxical combination of unchanging principles and common sense adjustments to changing conditions (Holmes, Jr., 1981).
- The role of judges in making the law what it really is at any given time is very important.
- Legal thinking is essentially classification (i.e., a process of inclusion and exclusion) and analogy.
- Our system of law places considerable reliance on advocacy, or the adversary system, as a method of jurisprudence.
- Law may be divided into two categories: substantive and procedural.
- There are two broad standards in American law: (1) specific rules, and (2) equity (i.e., adherence to generally accepted principles).

Due Process

Due process is defined as the opportunity to defend oneself against alleged charges. Due process may include specific procedural steps in the grievance process, mediation process, preliminary discovery process, time limits, arbitration procedures, and providing based and just reasons for disciplinary penalties. The following questions should be asked about situations in which employees were granted due process.

Questions To Determine Whether Due Process Exists

- Through which channel of organizational authorities the does due process need to be initiated?
- Does the organization have a precedent process spelled out for administering the due process?
- Is the due process reasonable and fair for all involved parties?
- What type of careful consideration with the covenant of good faith and fair hearing exists in an organization?
- How should the process be preceded and what procedures should be followed?
- Has an employee properly and adequately been served with allegation of misconduct?
- Have the employees been offered an opportunity to freely represent themselves during a fair hearing?
- Have the employees been offered sufficient time in preparing their defense?
- Is there any protection for alleged employees who disclose facts to not be retaliated against?
- Is there an impartial committee to hear all parties during fair hearings and make decisions independent of the original management decision maker?
- Would all parties find reasonable ground and just cause(s) concerning the ultimate fair process, decision, and action?
- How will remedies be initiated and implemented and with what guidelines and time-lines?

Careful Consideration

Careful consideration is a common moral, ethical, and legal doctrine that states that employers should consider the employee's rights under a covenant of good faith and fair dealing. Managers should take care to see that all decisions and actions are made and executed properly, all organizational policies, procedures, and regulations are in order, and that all legal rights (employer-employees rights) are observed. For example, a landmark unethical, immoral, and illegal case is *Fortune v. National Cash Register Company (NCR)*. The case involved the firing of a salesman (Mr. Fortune) who had been with NCR for Twenty-Five years (*Fortune v. National Cash Register Co.*, 373, Mass. 96, 36 NE 2nd 1251, 1977). Mr. Fortune was dismissed shortly after selling a large order that would have earned him a big commission. The NCR without careful consideration of Fortune's rights intended to avoid paying him the commission.

Such a decision and action violated the covenant of good faith and careful consideration. According to one study, wrongful-discharge lawsuits cost an average of $80,000.00 to defend in the United States (Thorne, 1995: 28).

Nepotism and Favoritism

Nepotism is an irregular decision-making process by an organizational authority to provide and offer special privilege for relatives, friends, and associates that do not deserve to receive them. Examples include hiring, promoting, and rewarding monetary and non-monetary benefits largely to the above people because of the relationship, at the expense of more and/or equally qualified applicants or employees without just and good cause. Bierman and Fisher (1984: 634) pointed out that nepotism raises a number of moral and ethical concerns, among them disregard both of managerial responsibilities to the organization and of fairness to all other applicants. To deal with nepotism issues, many organizations, specifically public institutions, have adopted anti-nepotism policies of some sort. There are extreme policies: Some organizations prohibit the employment of relatives of an employee anywhere in the same organization. Less extreme policies prohibit the employment first related employee's relatives (husband and wife, mother or father, brother or sister, grandparents, nieces or nephews, and cousins) in the same department. The most unethical and immoral practice of nepotism is the assignment of a first-relative or an employee's spouse to the position of immediate and secondary supervisory or decision-making processes over another relative or spouse for hiring, job assignment, performance appraisal, and compensation. Most cases of conflict of interest are consequences of these types of irregular employment practices.

WHAT IS LEGALITY?

Since ethics is a behavioral ordination to harmonize conflicting psychosocial interest between an individual and other people, law is another practical and operative econo-political attempt to resolve the disputable issues between individuals and groups. Law is not viewed formally as an act of will. It is a practical reason that determines means in relation to some given ends. Oesterle (1957: 20) defined law as a certain ordination of reason for the common good, promulgated by one who has care of the community.

Law formalizes the socio-cultural and econo-political contracts under which the community limits the *harm* that members can do to other people. Also as Ahmed (1999: 113) states: "While it is recognized that the law is only setting the minimum standards for conduct, it is also assumed that competition shall keep raising that minimum level.". As we understand, law resembles ethics, in that both are social institutions that aim to improve human relations in various ways. However, law is an exterior principle of action in the sense that it establishes, in a universal and objective fashion, an order of action to be followed by people seeking a common end. If people do not comply with the law, fines, sentenced to jail and/or injunction, will penalize them.

Law, however, presents certain mandatory minimal standards of an individual's social conduct within the contextual boundary of group behavior. Legal standards regulate people's social actions with respect to what to do or what not to do. Also, law is a creative institution, and enactment of new statues of social general order. Of course, the law does not establish all expected standards of social orders and codes of conduct for a society. Therefore, law is an ordination pertaining to societal well-being reasons. It is the expression of what is reasonable to do under special circumstances and situations by all people.

Nevertheless, it should be noted that two major concerns might be added to the above definitions. The first is that by designation the common good as the necessary end of everything, we may distinguish a true law from so-called law laid down by a tyrant. Suppose an authoritative ruler who is in control of a state, claims that in reality he/she enacts laws for the political common good. Such ordinances are directed to maintain personal power in order to rule over the state and they are not true laws and do not properly carry an obligation to be obeyed by all people. Second, while the common good is the necessary end of every law, the common good needs to be directly effective for the benefits of the community as whole not as an egalitarian law for maintaining the interest of a partisan group.

The Nature of Law

Law Protects Individual and Group Rights: The law protects individual and group rights. A right is an entitlement and/or a privilege to act or have others act in a certain mandated fashion. The connection between legal rights and duties is that if you have a right to do something, the law mandates others to perform their duties in a certain way. One of the major issues in legality questions is: Why is legal compliance a must? Compliance follows the law, which is generally looking backward to past mandates. Compliance efforts reduce discretion, increase oversight, and tighten controls. Legal compliance has been viewed as a solid social floor for accepted behavior in a society. Since the law has to apply to everybody, therefore its standards are not so high as to inspire human excellence. It is ethics that inspires people to search for excellence.

Law Recovers Sustained Damages: Life is a challenge and people in their lifetime confront misfortunes. If people suffer misfortune, they need to put up with it and find sources and resources deal with it. If their misfortune is the fault of others, the law may step in and make violators pay damages. Through the civil law, the public steps in and demands punishment, fines, and imprisonment for offenses that are seriously enough to violate human rights. Law demands victims be compensated when offenders are found guilty of violating rules and regulations, ignore human rights, not perform legal duties, not comply with ordinances, breaching contracts, alleges negligence, proximate causes of injury, and possession illegal properties and substances.

Law Maintains the Promissory Contractual Statues of People: Law is a dynamic process to create peace and harmony among people. It cannot stand still, yet in certain ways it appears clear-cut. It provides a set of rules for peoples' behavior and organizational operations. The creation of law and the delivery of sanctions for rule breaking are contested processes. How law is made, how it is interpreted, and enforced is always debatable. We may disagree ethically and morally with laws, but we should understand and comply with them. Law instills expected behavioral standards and sets up a bureaucratic judiciary system for compliance with them. There is no free choice in legality. While ethics and morality provide us with a menu of options, legality mandates us to comply with those rules that are set in our society.

One of the issues in human socialization is compliance with rigid and technical rules of promissory contracts. The law has provided specific frameworks for buyers and sellers. As with other generalized legal mandates, these rigid rules sometimes fail us in our attempt to acquire justice. Fortunately in American culture our common law has evolved concepts of equity in order to pursue justice through a flexible judiciary system. This system is viewed as a true hallmark of fairness to do justice in such situations. Such an equitable concept in the civil law of contracts is the notion of promissory or equitability justice. Halbert and Igulli (2000:19) stated:

In order for a promise to be enforceable under the concept of promissory estoppel, there must be: A promise that the promisor should reasonably have expected to induce action of a definite and substantial character on the part of the promisee. Which in fact produced reliance or forbearance of that nature. In circumstances such that the promise must be enforced if injustice is to be avoided.

CHAPTER SUMMARY

The primary concern of this chapter was to study moral, ethical, and legal ordinations in terms of two fundamental distinctions: whether these phenomena are speculative understanding or pragmatic knowledge. Speculative understanding concerns a phenomenon and/or an object about which nothing is effective directly, and hence the phenomenon or object is placid. Pragmatic knowledge, on the contrary, is concerned precisely with a phenomenon and/or an object insofar as it is dynamic and tangible. There are three major behavioral *ordinations* of reasons for people who strive for achieving a common good: (1) constructive ideas, (2) valuable contents, and (3) decisive commitment. Ordination of reason signifies the establishment of cognitive and behavioral orders to search for proper ends through good means. Not all ordinations establish practical patterns of expected excellent behavior. One kind of ordination gives you constructive ideas, another kind offers you valuable contents, and the other one binds you with decisive commitments.

Etymologically, religious faiths, political ideologies, and cultural values are the three foundations of moral and ethical views among people. They have different meanings and perceptions concerning what are common good for individuals and groups. The term *morality* signifies primarily a certain relation of an individual's acts that have some ends, as to a standard or principal of action. Morality, therefore, is an abstract signifying the moral order of an individual's acts. Ethics is concerned with psychosocial actions and it can deal with good deeds in a society.

Philosophers have identified ethics with one or the other of these extremes. Some have understood ethics to be a speculative and demonstrative good thoughts and behavior (deontological) and others have tended to identify ethics with completely the practical good end-results (teleological). Law formalizes the socio-cultural and econo-political contracts under which the community limits the *harm* that members can do the social fabric.

Appetite in a physiological term is an intrinsic desire to supply any bodily want or craving. However, *appetite* in psychosocial term is an inner derive or propensity motive to satisfy a want on the basis of acquired extrinsic demand. Appetite through physiological capacity contains limitation, but through psychosocial experience is unlimited. These issues manifest moral, ethical, and legal commitments of human behavior. *Greed* is an inordinate and rapacious desire, especially for wealth, power, sex, and reputation. It is denoted as an excessive and extreme desire for something; often more than an individual's rational share.

QUESTIONS FOR DISCUSSION

- What is behavioral ordination?
- What is conscience awareness?
- What is cognitive judgment?
- What do we mean by constructive ideas?
- What do we mean by valuable contents of ideas?
- How can we cultivate a sense of commitment?
- Explain the distinction between speculative knowledge and practical knowledge.
- Why cannot ethics be purely speculative?
- What is the difference between ethics and morality?
- How do you define morality?
- How do you define legality?
- State and explain the definition of ethics.
- Why is the subject of morality viewed as absolute?
- Why is the subject matter of ethics variable?
- Are the principles of morality and ethics certain? Explain why.

- W hat is the first principle of morality and how do we arrive at it?
- Describe how the good, as an end, is a justified cause of personal judgment?
- What is the meaning of ultimate end in ethics?
- Is it possible to deny that there must be an absolute ultimate end?
- What is the difference between satisfaction and happiness?

CASE STUDY

ENRON: FAILING TO STOP ABUSE OF INDIAN PROTESTERS BY POLICE

In today's interconnected world where global corporations compete for finite cheaper resources including labor and raw materials, new markets, and prosperous profitable operations, human rights, and trade are increasingly intertwined. Through the pathway of industrialization of developing countries, oil, gas, and electricity firms, as the main sources of energy, have been embroiled in controversy because of their alleged involvement in abusing labor, violations of human rights, and destruction of natural habitat.   The United Nations lists the following in its Universal Declaration of Human Rights:

- The right to own property alone as well as in association with others
- The right to work, to free choice of employment, to just and favorable conditions of work, and to protection against unemployment
- The right to just and favorable remuneration ensuring for the worker and his family an existence worthy of human dignity
- The right to form and join trade unions
- The right to rest and leisure, including reasonable limitation of working hours and periodic holidays with pay

Kenneth Roth, (1999) the Executive Director of Human Rights Watch (HRW) reported:

Governments have a primary responsibility to make sure that human rights violations don't take place. But corporations can't look the other way when protesters are being beaten right outside their front gates. Enron has been shirking its responsibility to behave as a decent global citizen.

The Human Rights Watch's mission is to protect and advance human rights in all countries around the world. The HRW (1999) reports that some high-profile examples of human rights abusers are the Royal Dutch/Shell's operations in Nigeria; British Petroleum's development of the Cusiana-Cupiagua oil fields in Columbia; and alleged violations that occurred during Total and Unocal's construction of the Yadana gas pipeline in Burma and Thailand. Another energy company that warrants attention is the Enron Power Development Corporation, a subsidiary of the Houston-based Enron Corporation, which is one of the world's largest energy companies (http://www.hi w.org/hrw/teports/ 1999/enron/).

In 1985, the government of India announced that it was privatizing its energy sector. In the middle of 1985, the government of India announced that the Enron Corporation would build the largest electricity generating plant in the world for the state of Maharashtra at a cost of approximately $3 billion. The plant is known as the Dabhol Power Corporation (DPC) an international joint venture of three U.S. companies: the Enron Corporation, General Electric, and the Bechtel Corporation. Enron, initially, was the overseer of the company. Originally, Enron held 80 percent ownership, General Electric and Bechtel each held 10 percent. In November 1998, the Maharashtra government's Maharashtra State Electricity Board (MSEB) bought a 30 percent share of the DPC from Enron, reducing Enron's state to 50 percent.

The problems of this case are related to the responsibilities of the United Nations' affiliated organizations (e.g., International Labor Organization (ILO), World Health Organization (WHO), and the International Atomic Energy Agency (IAEA), the Government of India, the Government of the United States, the Enron management, the General Electric, the Bechtel Corporations, and the global private and public financial institutions that financed the Debhol Power project in India. The DPC agreement was condemned by Indian intellectuals, academics, trade unions, and surrounding inhabitants of the plant.

This case focuses on human rights violations of a subsidiary of the Enron Development Corporation in India: The Dabhol Power Corporation (DPC). Since its inception in 1992, the company has been accused of corruption, unfair acquisition of land from villagers, and environmental degradation. The corporation, as of February 4, 1999, shows the following financial status:

Return on Investment (ROI) 3.40%
Return on Equity (ROE) 11.49%
Return on Assets (ROA) 2.70%
Book Value Shares (BVS) $20.62 with an earning of $2.07)
Dividend Yield (DY) 1.55%
Long-term Debt/Equity was 1.22% for a total cash of $383,000,000.

Indian environmental activists and the nearby villagers who were opposed to the DPC's operation have been subjected to beatings and repeated short-term detention without court orders. During mass arrest at peaceful demonstrations in the villages surrounding the project site, protestors had been beaten with police canes (*lathis*) and in some cases sustained severe injuries. Through continuous investigation, the HRW found a systematic pattern of suppression of the freedom of expression and peaceful assembly coupled with arbitrary detentions, excessive use of force, and threats. A New York based rights organization stated that the arrests violate the internationally recognized rights of freedom of expression, assembly, movement, protection against unjust arrest and detention, and violation of these constitute human rights abuses.

Enron is responsible for assuming the cost of police protection of the power plant. Frank Wisner, former U.S. Ambassador to India, and now a member of the Board Director of Enron since 1997, stated that he had never seen any information on human rights violations related to the power plant. Also, in an interview with Enron spokeswoman Kelly Kimberly by the Wall Street reporter, Jonathan Karp, Kimberly stated that Enron had no control over the Indian police actions even though Enron assumed the cost of protection. She said Enron and its partners were still reviewing the Human Rights Watch report, but the company released a preliminary statement calling it out of context at best.

CASE QUESTIONS FOR DISCUSSION

- Do you find the Enron policy concerning the purchase of villagers' land commensurate with the United Nations Universal Declaration of Human Rights?
- Do you find any human rights violations in this case?
- If your answer to the second question is yes, then explain your rationale.
- Do you primarily find the human rights violations are the result of misbehavior of Enron?
- If your answer to the fourth question is yes, then explain your rational reasoning.
- Do you find any moral, ethical, and legal issues in this case? Explain them.

CASE SOURCES

Enron Oil & Gas Company, <http://www.eog.enron.com/main.htm>.

Human Rights Watch, "U.S. Corporation Complicated in Abuses in India," (January 1999).

NYSE, Market Guide, "The Benchmark of Quality Financial Information," <http://yahoo.marketguide.com/mgi/ratio/3052N.htm> (February 4, 1999).

The Asian Wall Street Journal, "Human-Rights Group Denounces Enron," (February 4, 1999), 11.

<http://www.hrw.org/hrw/press/1999/enr0124.hym>.

D. A. Zottoli, Jr., *Moody's*, (New York: Moodys Investors Service, Inc. 1999), 3210.

CHAPTER 3

MORAL THEORIES:

IDEALISTIC, REALISTIC, HEDONISTIC, EUDAEMONISTIC, AND AUTHENTIC

We cannot claim that sole happiness ends up with moral virtues,
unless we attain to the highest state of knowledge contemplation.

We cannot claim that all human beings search for intellectual reasoning,
unless they prove that they attend to the sole state of intellectual happiness.

We cannot claim that naturally all people express themselves rationally,
unless they are inspired by wisdom to be intellectual.

We cannot claim that the contemplation of truth is the highest good of human
beings,
unless we understand both the qualitative and quantitative value of a reasonable
life.

CHAPTER OBJECTIVE

When you have read this chapter you should be able to do the following:

- Uunderstand what we mean by a happy life.
- Aanalyze cultural influences on the moral character of individuals.
- Know what is the foundational basis of morality in human behavior by examining optimistic, pessimistic, and moderate views on morality.
- Know why people perceive morality differently.
- Develop conceptual skills to what extent is a general agreement on topics of pleasure and happiness.
- Establish foundational principles concerning how we perceive moral faith and beliefs.
- Develop a framework to examine different theoretical dimensions of moral theories.
- Establish a rational argument that places the components of morality into five major realms of deliberations: moral theories, moral principles, moral merits, moral intentions, and moral actions.
- Analyze moral theories in terms of their means and ends.
- Introduce general characteristics of moral theories.
- Conduct a comparative study among moral theories: moral idealism, moral realism, moral hedonism, and moral eudaemonism.
- Know what is the Platonic moral idealism.
- Know what is the Aquinasian moral idealism.
- Know what is the Hobbesian moral idealism.
- Know what is the Kantian moral realism.
- Know what is the Reidian moral realism.
- Know what is the Lockeian moral realism.
- Know what is the Spencerian hedonistic moral view.
- Know what are the eudaemonistic views of Jermey Bentham on morality.
- Compare hedonistic and eudaemonistic moral views.

THOUGHT STARTER

Today's international business transactions are characterized by fast-paced technological innovation and unremitting competition on a global scale. To survive in such a competitive environment, corporations need to focus on two major phenomena: (1) where are they now? (2) what directions are they moving? The challenge for businesses is to create a speedy and flexible path of development towards stabilization of their market positions and to successfully and continuously revitalize their innovative capabilities for synergizing their old businesses and energizing new ones. What these corporations need is a disciplinary approach to valuable innovations and search methods for opportunity finding strategies. These can lead to the proliferation of ethical statements, the creation of resounding corporate slogans, and programming their cultural value changes according to managerial moral commitments to their holistic stakeholders' profitability.

Profitability can be viewed from two different perspectives: (1) valuable profit maximization, (2) valuable profit optimization. Let us first qualitatively define what our valuable profits are, and as well as what we mean by quantities of valuable profits. The first qualitative meaning of valuable profits is the utility of our efforts in meeting our needs. The second quantitative meaning of valuable profits is the monetary worth of our efforts within a relative spectrum of our societal economic ordination.

Let us analyze both qualitative and quantitative value systems in conjunction with our moral convictions, ethical doctrines, and legal principles. Surely what we perceive valuable and what we value cannot be defined by money alone. They can be valued by what money can buy and what money can provide. Valuable money-power can be effective as a necessity for survival, but it is not the only sufficient phenomenon for having a happy life. Money alone does not guarantee a happy life because financial survival without happiness is like having millions of dollars in certified deposits (CDs) and living in a filthy and miserable environment. This perspective commends itself for being good business and having good business ethics because it originates directly within business theory and business transactions to move beyond bottom-line consideration of things not only as valuable profits for the continuity of production, but also as having inherent valuable utility in themselves (preserving personal integrity and valuable things).

Profitability is not, however, only a *quantitative* and/or accounting notion. There is also another inherent value system concerning profitability that carries an economic definition within a broader scope of references than quantitative and/or accounting assessment. Actually both profit maximization and profit optimization are almost identical in terms of quantities. However, they are different in terms of qualities.

Profitability is a societal contract between workers and capital holders, between producers and consumers, between buyers and sellers, and among nations. It is also a legitimate agreement between society and organizations, whose mandate and limits are set by ethical, moral, and legal systems. Actually, in profit maximization we define profits as the total *quantitative* revenues minus total costs in terms of the international money market values. Profit maximization shows the nominal values of a corporation's asset.

$$PM = TR - TC$$

We define profit optimization as a highly sophisticated total *qualitative* economic purchase power capability as total asset (equity and investment) minus total fixed costs, variable costs, and incidental costs.

$$PO = (TA) - (FC + VC + IC)$$

The inclusion of incidental costs within the decision-making processes opens the doors to a broader economic perspective. The broader perspective goes beyond monetary quantities and accounting numbers. Profit optimization requires knowing how profitable a real phenomenon is in terms of real values, not nominal values.

PLAN OF THIS CHAPTER

The primary concern of this chapter is to first define moral theories. Second is to identify moral theories in terms of two fundamental distinctions: Whether these theories are speculative idealistic understanding or realistic pragmatic knowledge. Speculative understanding concerns a phenomenon or an object about which nothing is effective directly, and hence the phenomenon or object is placid. Pragmatic knowledge, on the contrary, is concerned precisely with a phenomenon or an object insofar as it is dynamic and tangible. In addition, speculative understanding and pragmatic knowing are either, for the sake of simply, an individual's *conscience awareness* and *cognitive judgments* or for the sake of *formative* and *summative,* knowledge application to ordinate people's behavior or their societal interactions. We want to know what is a pleasurable life. What is a pleasant life? Are they the same through moral deliberations? How do different moralists view morality in terms of human beings' means and ends? How can morality influence business people to be receptive to moral principles in their decision-making processes and actions? These and other issues are the main objectives for this chapter.

VIRTUE, MORALITY, AND HAPPINESS

People commonly speak of having peace of mind and a happy life within contextual boundary of a sense of fulfillment of their wishes. The problem of what peace of mind and happiness consists of and how they can be attained proves difficult to perceive. Since all human activities are differentiated from reason (rational deliberations, emotional expressions, and sensational manifestations), a life style could be moral, or amoral, or immoral. Nevertheless, the law of reasoning indicates that happiness is greatly influenced and formed by extrinsic virtuous measure of moral beliefs and actions. Accordingly, we need to search for virtuous means and acts to be more fully oriented with virtue in general, in order to attain peace of mind and happiness.

One might observe that emotional and sensational people sometimes end up with miserable outcomes. To understand virtuous decisions and moral acts, we need to distinguish between voluntary and involuntary means and ends. Such considerations enable us to recognize precisely what intentions and acts are morally good and what are morally bad. Such recognitions need to be coherent with syllogism reasoning as the fundamental intrinsic manifestation of morality.

It is evident that not all humans can lead a virtuous life or act according to the spirit of happiness. Virtue is defined as the *excellence* of intellect. Searching for and solving the problems of humanity generates good in one's character. Since human beings psychologically do not live in a solitary fashion within and beyond themselves, they possess specific intrinsic relations within themselves and their conscientiousness. Such a quality in its perfect state presumes virtuous intellect and/or the pursuit of goodness in moral people.

As we have separated morality from ethics in Chapter 2, we defined *morality* as conformity to the universal right conducts. In addition, morality is a term used to manifest humanity's universal virtues. Virtues refer to the excellence of intellect and wisdom and to the disposition of the cognizance of mind to effectively perform its proper function. Moral virtues concern the habitual choices of rational thoughts in accordance with the universal logical principles. The contemplation of absolute truthfulness and the discovery of the rational principles that ought to control everyday actions have given rise to intellectual virtues. The distinction between goodness and badness, truthfulness and falseness, and worthiness and worthlessness is called moral considerations.

It is possible to divide the phenomenon of morality into five realms. Here the interest is in what the perceptual meaning of morality looks like, and how it functions within the cognitive conscientiousness awareness of an individual. Therefore, the first level is *moral theory*. As moralists and ethicists study it, it may, for our purposes, be taken as the foundational floor for humaneness. The second level appears in the realm of *moral principles*. The third level is the realm of *moral merits*. The fourth level manifests the *moral intention*. The fifth level comes into the realm of *moral actions*. In the following pages we will examine five major moral theories:

1. Idealism
2. Realism
3. Hedonism
4. Eudaemonism
5. Authenticism.

As you can see in Table 3-1, there are eight characteristics shared by five major moral theories within the contextual boundary of common moral sense. The common moral sense attributions are causal means, searching for ends, attributes, dimensional context, ideological views, prospective outcomes, psychosocial manifestations, and life-style orientations.

Through analytical perceptions concerning faith, beliefs, ideas, and opinions we need to identify specific characteristics of each. Since faith stands above beliefs, ideas, and opinions, it is an invisible power in the human mind concerning immortal certainties in existence. Faith is not concerned with the material world itself, which is an object of knowledge. Nevertheless, opinions are accompanied by doubt and fear, but faith is accompanied by certainty. Also, faith is firm and free from all hesitations, because it is a manifestation of spiritual power within the mind of an individual.

Table 3.1: Comparative Characteristics of Moral Theories

Common Sense	Idealism	Realism	Hedonism	Eudaemonism	Authenticism
Causal means	Ultimate cause: God	Ultimate cause: Government	Ultimate cause: Self	Ultimate cause: All creatures	Ultimate cause: Conscience
Searching for ends	Excellence	Values	Satisfaction	Happiness	Virtues
Attributes	Aesthetic	Conventional	Sensational	Rational	Humaneness
Dimensional context	Super-naturalistic	Intrinsic and extrinsic	Intrinsic	Holistic	Extrinsic
Ideological views	Utopianism	Materialism	Humanism	Naturalism	Spiritualism
Prospective outcomes	Exaggerated beautification	Desirable ownership	Standardized indoctrination	Objectiveity in oriented solutions	Intuitivism
Psychosocial manifestations	Faith	Beliefs	Ideas	Opinions	Wisdom
Life-style orientations	Religious	Econo-political	Sociocultural	Ecological	Peaceful and Harmonious

In all of the above moral theories we are concerned with the nature of goodness. How do we conceptualize goodness? With what courage and virtues? If we ask lay people on the street what is your moral ground, we are apt to gain an answer from a Judeo-Christian faith like: The Ten Commandments. From Confucianism faith the answer is to be obedient to the rule of harmonious goodness. From a Hinduism belief, the answer is tolerance of harsh conditions and search for peaceful solutions. From a Moslem's view, the answer is to submit yourself to God's will; *Ensha-Allah.*

The moralists see human behavior in relation to the intrinsic nature of conscientiousness and the extrinsic nature of God's authority (purposive excellent reason). The moralists define moral principles as a rule without exceptions. The moralists, finally, look at human's good intentions and actions in all levels of life. There are different perceptions concerning happiness. Some people claim that wealth produces happiness; others believe that wealth is identical with happiness, and there are some other people who seek wealth above everything including happiness. It is uncommon to find people who sacrifice their health, honor, and beyond for the sake of wealth. Such a different perceptual array of beliefs concerning happiness has dominated today's world. For the clarity of such an important issue, we need to analyze cultural and behavioral stratification.

CULTURAL AND BEHAVIORAL STRATIFICATION

The perceptual relation of an individual to nature is based upon life orientation. People place themselves and their possessions under the direction of the common natural and artificial value systems of their societies, and in return societies protect the rights and freedom of the individuals. People's qualities as individuals, their relationship to nature and to the world, their relationship to other people, and their orientation in time, place, and space are influenced by their moral virtues and cultural value systems. Adler (1986: 12) raises several questions regarding six dimensions:

- Who am I?
- How do I see the world?
- How do I relate to other people?
- What do I do?
- How do I use space and time?

In addition to the above questions, there are two other important questions:

- How much money is an individual seeking to gain as the primarily means in life?
- How can monies make an individual's life happy?

Responses to these and similar questions vary from culture to culture and/or person to person. Some cultures are more synergistic than others. Some cultures are more materialistic and others are more spiritualistic. Table 3.2 helps us to understand how some of these factors might influence the behavior of human beings (Moran and Harris, 1982: 19) It should be noted that human nature is either mutable or immutable. In relation to the above cultural value systems, we will look briefly at the three major cultural dimensions: (1) optimistic views, (2) moderate views, and (3) pessimistic views.

OPTIMISTIC VIEWS

How Do People Perceive the Nature of a Human Being?

Some people basically perceive themselves and others as good as reflected in a utopian cultural value system. There are some cultures that perceive human beings as the best products of nature or, in religious terms as the best of God's creatures on the earth compared to other creatures. They perceive good nature in human beings in order to trust each other with a great deal of reliance. In a highly respectful society, there is no secrecy about human affairs because people live in harmony with themselves and with environments. People are open-minded and individuals enjoy liberty. The judiciary philosophy of these cultures is based upon this connotation: People are considered innocent until proven guilty.

Table 3.2: Cultural Influences on Life Issues

Views	Pessimistic	Moderate	Optimistic
What is the character of human nature?	Human is evil	Human is a mixture of good and evil	Human is good
What is the relationship of human to nature?	Human is subject to nature	Human is in harmony with nature	Human is master of nature
What is the temporal focus of life?	To the past	To the present	To the future
What is the modality of human's activities?	A spontaneous expression in impulse and desires	Activity that emphasizes as a goal the development of all aspects of the self	Activity that is motivated primarily toward measurable accomplishments
What is the Relationship of human to other humans?	Lineal: Group goals are primary and an important goal is continuity through time	Collateral: Group goals are primary well regulated continuity of group relationships through time. They are not critical	Individual: The individual goals are most important

Sources: Adapted from Kluckhohn, F.R. and Strodtbeck, F.L. *Variation Value Orientations. Evanston.* Illinois: Row, Peterson and Company, (1961), 11. In Moran, R. T. and Harris, P.H. (1982). *Managing Cultural Synergy.* Houston: Gulf Publishing Company, (1982), 19.

People in a democratic society freely share their knowledge and experiences and help each other by all means and end. They are very sincere and friendly. In these societies change is permissible toward betterment and progress with good faith. For example, American society represents this type of cultural perception. The burden of proof is on the accuser. However, if we look at Spanish culture, we find that in such a society, people are suspicious of each other. For example, they believe they must constantly watch customers in stores. Shoplifting is a pattern of expected behavior in Spain.

What Are Individuals' Relationships to Their Institutions?

It is a general cultural pattern that indicates how people can dominate their social institutions and overcome obstacles. People perceive no real separation between institutional and individuals' boundaries. Their cultural beliefs allow them to live side by side with their institutions as their institutions are growing; they are developing their capabilities too. In an optimistic culture, policies and regulations have been mandated to alter the natural opportunities to the peoples' needs. People are allowed to alter and modify the nature of their institutions in order to enhance their lifestyles. Societal institutions help, guide, and assist people to search for better understanding. Change is possible because development, growth, and progress are the results of change.

What Are Primary Relationships of Individuals to Others?

Human beings are not born with ready-made relationships with others. Individuals create contacts and relationships with others. However, one cannot achieve this state of existence unless he/she is free. Human beings exist to create their positions and relationships with others. This indicates the reality that human beings attribute to their value systems.

What Are the Primary Modes of Human Activities?

Cultural value systems in a society reflect the differentiated relationships among people. People are oriented with the mode of "will-er." The "will-er culture" is more oriented to the prosperous moral activities. The psychological and sociological "will-ers" orientations speed up the process of change and they specify the direction of change to themselves and their environment. Progressive assessment of individuals' achievement is not perceived inherently by the nature of performers. The measurement is based upon the societal standards of expected moral behavior. Optimistic people are more motivated towards efficiency through hard working habits.

What Is the Temporal Focus of an Individual to the Society?

It is human perception that an individual should physically live in the present and metaphysically perceive the future. Future oriented cultures are more innovative in sciences and technologies. Conservative cultures prefer to maintain their traditional value systems. They hardly believe in drastic changes. They are very satisfied with the status quo. However, optimistic cultures evolve with new hopes and prosperity toward progress and development individually and collectively.

MODERATE VIEWS

Americans traditionally see people as a mixture of good and evil, capable of choosing one over the other. They are neither moral nor immoral. They are amoral. They believe in the possibility of improvement through change (Adler, 1986:13). This notion brings to mind the idea that American culture is a balanced culture. We will examine the same connotations through the moderate views as follows.

How Do People Perceive the Nature of a Human Being?

Although many people do not hold the extreme position of saying that individuals virtually "can do no wrong or no right" at all times, they believe that the individual nature of a human being is a dualistic function of mind and body. At one time, religiously, the soul of human beings existed in the world of pure spirit and enjoyed the highest bliss of pure contemplation. However, because of some contact with evil in a world of pure spirit, at the same time, the soul of a human being had been condemned and became a part of a body and formed an organic unit to live on the earth. Since the soul of a human being has formed an organic unit with the body, then it is subject to weaknesses. The end result of such dualistic functioning does not have a heavenly existence.

Plato stated that a human being's superior faculty is attributed to the soul (e.g. mind, logic, and reasoning) and inferior organic existence is attributed to the body (e.g. evil, change, corruption, and the like). People with such a cultural belief tend to categorize individuals into two major categories: (1) those people with the highest intellectual abilities who can be considered as rulers. Rulers must be intellectual authorities that should be perfectly educated, (2) Those people who have less intellectual ability and should be subordinated to the first group. If we consider the caste tradition in India, we see how Indian people conceptually make distinctive class stratifications among themselves on the basis of their cultural family heritage.

What Are Individuals' Relationships to Their Institutions?

There are some cultures that strongly believe that life is the essence of conscience. Individuals should live in harmony with their organizations and be loyal to their institutions. In return, organizations should provide them lifetime employment. There shouldn't be a separated view between employees and employers in such a society. Institutions should serve both organizational members and consumers as parts and as a whole.

What Are the Primary Relationships Between Individuals and Others?

Some cultures are more group oriented and strive to serve each other. In a general sense, while people share their views and help each other, individuals maintain and restore their privacy and independence. Mutual interest among professional groups facilitates harmony and helpfulness in these societies. These cultures are searching for and are proceeding toward unity through diversity. The surest path to the truth in these societies relies upon expert authorities and scientific findings. Lateral group membership includes all people who are currently part of an institution and provide opportunities for people who desire to join them. The prime criteria for recruitment of organizational members are trustworthiness, loyalty to the group, and comparability with other co-workers. For example, French culture is perceived to be more individualistic and less synergistic than other cultures. (Moran and Harris, 1982: 19).

What Are the Primary Modes of Human Activities?

Balancing organizational priorities in a moderate culture can provide each member with adequate opportunities for growth and development. Institutional authorities within the contextual boundaries of a moderate culture tend to develop loyalty and normative ethics in their employees in order to better coordinate different organizational factions. Under a moderate cultural view, institutions maintain more autonomy and responsibility toward organizational stakeholders.

What Is the Temporal Focus of an Individual to the Society?

Some cultures under the moderate view of cultural value systems prefer to perceive the use of time within the present outcomes. These people like to live in momentum fashion. They react to the short-term profits and make priorities to meet their short career path. In a general behavioral mode description, we call them "do-er" cultures.

PESSIMISTIC VIEWS

Although all human beings have distinctive cultural norms and values, it would be a mistake to judge any particular group and label them with a pessimistic value judgment. Geertz (1970: 47) indicates that: "We are, in sum, incomplete or unfinished animals who complete ourselves through culture." However, some cultures are more attached to past traditions, and others lean either to the present or future. By the same token, some cultures are more optimistically oriented and others are either more pessimistic or moderate. Pessimistic cultures view things with more emphasis on the negative and finally try to evolve positive outcomes. By viewing different studies of this direction, we can provide you with the following connotations regarding pessimistic views:

How Do People Perceive the Nature of a Human Being?

Some cultures function negatively. People tend to view others as basically evil. They are unethical and immoral in the real sense. They should not be trusted, because they are selfish. They are very capable to turn themselves to tyranny, savagery, atrocity, and inhumane feelings. They suspect and mistrust each other. People in daily behavioral interactions are very cautious. Doubt and suspicion are the main bedrock of such a society. They resolve not to be open to each other. People don't change voluntarily, because of their cultural orientation. They are controlled through very rigid value systems. In these cultures, interpersonal change within their personality is very difficult. In the event some mandatory change happens, the end results carry some degree of personality degradation. In these cultures, the judiciary philosophy is based upon this connotation: People are considered guilty until proven innocent. Suspicion, resistance, and disloyalty to the cultural authorities are very popular in these cultures.

What Are Individuals' Relationships to Their Institutions?

Cultural obedience is one of the distinctive manifestations of normative behaviors in pessimistic cultures. In these cultures people do not trust each other. However, they need to rely on some forms of authority. These cultures give more credit to the rulers' power and lose a sense of individual liberty. People are expected to be obedient to the rulers' wishes in order to be cared for doing thing at a time of necessity. All members of a pessimistic culture are virtually dominated by elite ruling groups. Within such a cultural environment power plays an important role. Like wealth, it is more a means than an end. One seeks political power not really for its sake but as a means for achieving pleasure, wealth, reputation or something else. Furthermore, it is evident that power can be used for good or evil, or happiness or misery.

What Are the Primary Relationships of Individuals to Others?

As indicated before, under the pessimistic cultural views, human beings are evil. They are not moral. Therefore, people under such conditions misbehave. People with this instinct behavior and this type of relationships with others should be constantly controlled. They believe that society should not provide maximum freedom for individuals, because if they are provided with liberty, they will revolt against authorities. Religiously, they stick with the cultural story of Adam and Eve who revolted against God in the Garden of Eden (Dupuios, 1985: 10). Therefore, organizational members should be obedient, silent, and ordered by authorities. Society should restrict individual freedom through rigid policies. High ranked authorities control societal members. They strongly believe in collectivistic judgment. If a member of the group is suspicious toward another, other members of the group without question adhere to such a belief. They believe that all others can trust organizational members, who are known by others or vice versa. Under pessimistic cultures, the process of policy is less flexible, because it is less time consuming.

What Are the Primary Modes of Human Activities?

Human perceptions under pessimistic cultural views tend to be more passive. They are more attached to their past experiences. They like to minimize their activities, because they believe that they will not enjoy adequate profits from their efforts. They tend to be motivated to work fewer hours, because they believe that the generation of wealth will not provide them with happiness. People believe major changes will happen at their own often slow-pace. They do not need to push or to be pushed to achieve long-term objectives. They believe everything and everybody is subject to the process of birth and death and that fate and destiny migrate from one authority to another sooner or later.

What Is the Temporal Focus of an Individual to the Society?

Under pessimistic cultural views, people perceive future life as the extension of past experiences. We call these types of people "be-ers." Under this view, all cultural value systems should be evaluated according to past experiences. Innovations and creativity should be justified according to the past experiences. For example, like most Asians, the Vietnamese have a more extended concept of time than most Americans. Americans measure time and react by the clock, Vietnamese by the monsoon. Vietnamese are suspicious of the need for urgency in making decisions or culminating a business deal. Traditional experiences of patience remain as the ultimate Confusion virtue in personal life as well as in business (Smith, and Pham, 1998: 174).

FOUNDATION OF MORAL THEORIES

Foundational Factual Problems in Morality

There are differences between moral and immoral intentions and actions. Those differences are related to means and ends in an individual's thoughts and behavior. There is an interest in having moral behaviors result in something constructive. Both moral and immoral people draw upon reasoning to justify their beliefs and actions. We cannot be immoral by accident, because it is a deliberative action. It is important that we stress here the possible problems that may be viewed by an individual as immoral. The moral opinions could be:

- The humans' biggest problems are themselves. Their natures are not certain, but in doubt (even about themselves).
- Morality inspires humans to be valuable in them as a criterion to measure all things. Therefore, they can be changed toward stages of good, better, and best and avoid worst, worse, and bad thoughts and actions.
- The primary purpose of morality is to create and maintain dignified conscientiousness awareness within the boundaries of reasoning power. Such a fundamental belief is based upon how an individual views autonomy, rationality, and impartiality in their judgmental perceptions.
- Some authority should not impose moral beliefs. They must be freely adhered to in order to be reasonable. Thus, morality is the product of reflective thinking.
- Individuals have the moral responsibilities to develop their moral characteristics and reform them through virtuous work experiences.
- Individuals have the moral obligation to develop and maintain virtuous power for developing their enhanced social behavior.
- The moral social reforms in an individual's moral character must genuinely move society towards goodness.
- Moralists should be the symbols of leading forces to teach other people the truth about construction and reconstruction of human personalities within the context of goodness.
- Reconstruction of morality in a society requires a virtuous doctrine based on behavioral excellence.
- Morality deals with human inner space, while ethics deals with outer human space.

Since the major theme of this chapter is moral theories, we will elaborate on this topic through reviewing different hypothetical assumptions of moral theories in the separate sections.

DIFFERENCES AMONG MORAL THEORIES

Socrates, the first great moral philosopher, stated the creed of reflective individuals and set the milestone of the task of moral theories. Since then most philosophers and writers have perceived and treated human beings in relation with morality and ethics. Some philosophers, whose views are oriented towards theological doctrines, appear to believe human beings are situated in the kingdom of God and they have to be obedient to Him and follow the Lord's orders in order to have revelation. On the other hand, non-theological philosophers such as existentialists, materialists, and naturalists conceive that human beings are situated within the general realm of nature with their own free choices and volitions. They believe that if human beings want comfort and peace they should not disturb or violate the rules of nature. The latter philosophers believed that human beings possess absolute control over their minds and actions and that is why solely themselves determine them. In such a path of life, existentialist philosophers believe that human beings, through their decisive virtues, can discover the worthy things concerning the right way of life.

Table 3.3: Comparative Analysis of Moral Theories

Theories	Causality	Deeds	Means	Ends
Idealistic Theologism	Ritual life and beyond earthly life	Spiritual virtues	Good intention	Revelation and eternal blessing
Realistic Naturalism	Stabilized earthly life	Intellectual virtues	Good choices and volitions	Mental and physiological comfort
Hedonistic Materialism	Material comfortable life	Self-interest decisions and actions	Good short-Term Decisions and actions	Appetitive pleasure and enjoyment through accumulated wealth and power
Eudaemonistic Existentialism	Continuity of a happily life	Necessitated virtues	Good long-term decisions	Personal happiness through enrichment of a meaningful life
Authentic Humanism	Altruistic life	Benevolent Heart	Helpfulness	Humaneness

Both groups of philosophers agree that, in the kingdom of God or in the realm of nature, human beings through their emotional fickleness and sensational infirmities are exposed to mysterious flaws of greed, bemoaning, revenge, fear, anger, savagery, cruelty, atrocity, and discrimination. However, both theoretical ethicality and morality focus their views on the nature of human beings. They perceive that humans possess means to overcome emotional and sensational unpleasant desires. These philosophers believe that human beings have to eradicate their sensational weakness, emotional absurdity, and dreadful desires. In Table 3.3 you will find the comparative characteristics of the different perceptions of moral theories.

In viewing and applying moral, intellectual, and necessitated virtues, many philosophers and researchers express their views through various types of reasoning. There are different schools of thought concerning moral theories such as idealism, realism, hedonism, and eudaemonism.

IDEALISTIC MORAL THEORY

Idealism moral theory includes all views that hold that there is an independent world that is mental or spiritual in nature. Idealists are usually religious or at least sympathetic with religious outlooks. Opponents to idealism morality are materialists or existentialists, or naturalists. The materialists consider that all reality consists of matter (money) and its manifestation for a comfortable life. They believe that even moral consciousness is a manifestation of material or bodily processes. We may distinguish three basic meanings of the terms of *ideals*:

- In the world of goodness, there are perfect ideals that can never be fully realized. Ideas are not static. Ideas are dynamic sources of urge. All ideas strive for self-identification and preservation. They struggle to rise to the threshold of consciousness. Thinking and willingness perceptions arise from the circle of intellectuality. Philosopher Herbart (1806) appeared to look at the goodness with favor in the so-called ideomotor theory of action that William James upheld. The theory of ideomotor action holds that ideas in the mind that have reference to action tend to produce actions. For example, we are inclined to think of perfect beauty in a physical term and excellence in character, not as attainable objectives, but as directions of aesthetic endeavors that can never be reached to their final objectives at least not in the form of earthly experiences.

- There is the ideal in the sense of something *excellence* which can be realized by wisdom and/or intellect. For example, when we speak of ideal weather, or ideal life, we perceived it as a balanced term neither severely cold nor very hot. Nevertheless, ideas are impulses. They are not separable from things. All ideas are impulsive. Morality involves approval and disapproval of judgments concerning those ideals. Aesthetics also, deals with judgments regarding the beautiful and the ugly judgments on appearances of things and phenomena. All moral judgments involve patterns of ideas judgments that bear certain relations to each other.

- Finally, there is an ideal in the derisive sense of something wholly visionary or quixotic. Within the contextual boundaries of the idealistic theory of morality, there are three basic moral ideas:

  o The ideas of intrinsic freedom and choice are viewed as a manifestation of moral judgments. These ideas state that the intellectual deliberative will of the individual is in harmony with an individual's inner conscientious convictions.

  o The ideas of extrinsic perfection and happiness are holistic in their nature. These ideas are harmonious relationships between the various striving powers of the self-will and the environmental-orderliness.

  o The ideas of benevolence and altruism are viewed as the final cause of happiness. These ideas mandate individuals help others in order to realize their worthwhile wills. For example, we are talking about businesses social responsibilities. This mandates mighty capital holders contribute their wealth for the goodness of society. Within such an ethical environment, not only do consumers live in peace and harmony with business entities, also, business owners receive appreciation from the public that they are service-oriented entities and server customer loyalty.

Principle Beliefs in Moral Idealism

This world is full of goodness and badness. It depends on how you perceive them. Avoidance of goodness may cause you sinful intentions (in religious terms) and dreadful actions (in miserable earthly-life terms). Human beings should try to stay in the kingdom of goodness. Nevertheless, separation of the human mind from the godly ideal of goodness is considered in terms of good intention and actions. It is the fear of bad intentions that tempts human beings to separate themselves from goodness and join badness. They need to solve this problem by copying, following or imitating knowledge. Like the installment plan of buying, copying, following, or imitating knowledge can solve problems:

We may distinguish three basic meanings of the term of moral idealism:

- There is an ideal in the sense of excellent behavior that can be realized, as when we speak of ideal friendship or of ideal weather. It is an idiom that states that: A friend indeed is a friend in deed. This is the surest state of human mind that should pursue heavenly life without corruption and defectiveness. People need to live in harmony with each other and with nature in order to maintain peace of minds.

- To search for goodness and beauty in our character not as attainable goals, but as a direction of our endeavor toward goodness. This direction can orient a human's mind towards goodness. This means that we need not only to think and talk about goodness, but also to attend in the pragmatic realm of goodness. Through mental goodness, we will be able to reach the gate of mental and moral health. Through the pragmatic realm of goodness, we will be able to apply spiritual virtues in our deeds.
- Finally, there is the ideal in the derisive sense of something holistically visionary to pursue goodness as happiness. Moral idealists believe in happiness through attending the process of goodness. They believe that we need to avoid blind-will, blind-fear, blind power, and blind-domination.

There is no doubt other than gifts of nature, such as intelligence, fortitude, courage, and perseverance are desirable, but they may be pernicious if the will directs them such that they are not good. For example, *loyalty* in its moral term within an organization is not impressive as a virtue when we consider the loyalty of an auditor to an embezzler. Such loyalty is based on blind-fear. *Courage* may further evil as well as good ends, as the case of the intrepid consumer abuser shows.

The global goodwill is not good purely good, because it may not achieve desirable consequences. The value of good will is based upon good means and good ends. Good will is reverence for duty and duty is founded on reason. Reasons seek universal principles for being ideally, physically, mentally, and socially good. There are three major schools of idealistic morality: Platonic, Aquinasian, and Hobbesian.

The Platonic Moral Idealism

Plato (427-347 B.C.) supposed that there are permanent good ideas that maintain their own existence irrespective of the existence or nonexistence of God(s). These good ideas require the minds of humans to give them reality by knowing them. Plato in his *Dialogues* (1892) found two basic beliefs relevant to morality:

- The doctrine of *teleology* in which everything in the universe has a proper function within a harmonious hierarchy of purposes. Thus, the ultimate of universal purposes have been explained in the nature of things. They are purposive rather than mechanistic. He is emphasized the why of an event rather than the how is happiness. This indicates that a human's purpose is relevant to their proper functions. Their proper purposive values, like that of everything else in the universe, depend upon their excellence in fulfilling those proper functions. The moral purposes of individuals in realizing their objectives are determined by the effective functioning of the basic constituents of the types of their personalities. The morally virtuous person is one who is in rational, biological, and emotional balance or in Platonic terms, one who is *wise, temperate, courageous,* and *just.*

- The doctrine of *ideas or forms* that refers to beliefs that general conceptions are not derived from experience but is logically prior to them. For example, each of us knows what is honesty. It is the truthful expression of an idea, reason, and/or motive. The idea of honesty is more real than the experiencing the truthful action. Plato culminated his account with the *Forms* or *Ideas* of the Good the conception through which he united the principle of teleology and the theory of *Ideas* or *Forms* with morality.

The Aquinasian Moral Idealism

Saint Thomas Aquinas (1225-1274) is known as one of the theological moral theorists who has offered us a Christianized version of Aristotle's moral theory. He adds the concept of the beatific vision of God as humanity's final goal, a special doctrine of free will, and a theory of natural law as the reflective divine order. Aquinas (1945) believed that there is a twofold perfection of rational or intellectual nature: (1) natural happiness, and (2) supernatural happiness (God 's image). Therefore, humans have two sources of truth rather one:

- Those truths with human faculties that provide us with virtues concerning our habitual choices of conduct. These choices are correct in outline but incomplete in details. Goodness involves choices, and choices include both appetitive and deliberative elements of moral conduct. A good character is constituted by habits of choices that are in accordance with appropriate principles. Identification of the will is the agency of good choices.
- The second types of truth are those truths that God reveals. He ascribed the source and authority of principles determining proper choices to the natural laws in which God makes them available to humans. These truths reveal God to be both creator of all good things and the determiner of their purposes in the state of existence. Nevertheless, each agent by its action intends an end.

As a result, Aquinas believed that the consequences of an individual's conduct are either foreseen or not. If they are foreseen, it is evident that they increase goodness or malice. But if the consequences are not foreseen, we must make a distinction. For if they follow from the nature of action, in the majority of cases, the consequences increase the goodness or malice of that action. On the other hand, if consequences follow by accident and seldom, then they do not increase the goodness or malice of the act.

Hobbesian Moral Idealism

Thomas Hobbes (1588-1679) is viewed as an idealistic materialist and as a highly pessimistic moralist. Hobbes's *Leviathan* (1839) presents a bleak picture of the innate qualities of human beings in the state of nature. Hobbes, like us, lived in a time of extreme violence and exploitation of human rights. Consequently, Hobbes contends that fear of violent death is the primary motive that causes people to create a political state by constructing to surrender their natural rights and to submit to the absolute authority of a sovereign.

Hobbes believes that competition is viewed as a war of every human being or group against every other one. The notions of justice or injustice, fairness or unfairness, rightness or wrongness have no place. Where there is no moral rule, there is no moral power; where no moral law, no justice. At the same time, he believed that exploitive forces such as fraud and corruption are in war with virtues. Justice or injustice, fairness or unfairness, rightness or wrongness are comparative valuable consequences of conditions that insure there is no propriety, no dominion, but only that every human being gets what he/she can get, for so long as he/she can keep it.

While human beings are in war with natural conditions, they cannot be successful unless they establish a covenant of mutual trust among themselves. Therefore, before the notions of justice or injustice appear, there must be some coercive power to compel human beings to perform in accordance with their mutual trust covenants. What is such a covenant mutual trust? It is a moral power to ensure the good of the commonwealth. Where there is no moral good commonwealth, there is nothing just or unjust.

A *commonwealth* goodness is said to be instituted when a multitude of people do agree, and covenant, every one, with everyone, that particular individuals, or assembly of individuals, shall be given by the major part the right to present the entire group as their representatives. With the establishment of the commonwealth goodness through the social contract, Hobbes tells us; the necessary and sufficient condition for morality is present.

Hobbes established the notion of civil authority and law as foundation of morality. He argued that morality requires *social authority, and law as the foundation of morality.* Nevertheless, Hobbes rejected the individual's consciousness awareness as the main source of morality. Morality, then, is based upon law the law of the absolute sovereignty of an individual, group, and/or nation. He assumed morality and legality pave in the same path of perceptual reasoning, because morality is a pluralistic phenomenon that turns out to be the dictation of reason through absolute civil power.

Conclusions

The idealism moralists, like others, deal with certain basic beliefs in morality. They are very impressed with the thought that the universe is ultimately something mental or spiritual. They are uncompromising opponents to materialism. They believe that spiritual belief in goodness is the main cause for existence. They believe that the states and activities of the self, as we experience them inwardly through our mental vision, are the only realities that we can know directly and incontrovertibly. They believe that our moral vision becomes the world of appearances. They believe that a valid universal morality is apprehended by the mind as perfectly clear and self-evident intuition of good faith, good will, and good act.

REALISTIC MORAL THEORY

The realistic moral theory is a more pragmatic, action-oriented view concerning morality. Moral realists hope to provide foundations for the moral guidance of mankind. The ideas of moral realists in the sphere of moral theory are varied and complex. A major problem for moral realists is how to cope with immoral actions and how we will be able to find remedies be that are compliant with definitions and standards of moral virtues. In other words, idealistic absolute goodness should how humans can achieve their moral objectives through intellectual wisdom and moral reasoning. In the realistic moral theory, we are trying to match our valuable practical behavior with our moral virtues.

A central difficulty of any moral theory is to do justice both to the absolute and to the relative aspects of moral values. By an absolute goodness, we need to know the statistical mean one that is intrinsically and always good in human intellectual wisdom and reasoning. However, by an extrinsic judgmental valuable perception concerning goodness, we may come out with several degrees of relative goodness with different comparative value systems. Since morally good will is an absolute good, many of the good things of life are *relative, not absolute.* We need to consider valuable moral behavior through excellence, best, better, and good, or conversely vice, worst, worse, and bad. Within such a magnitude, we may in practice find morality not as an absolute phenomenon, but as a relative one when compare to higher and lower qualities. There are numberless values that are relatively higher than others. As Montague (1930: 44) indicated: "No amount of happiness enjoyed by pigs can be equal to the happiness of Socrates."

Principle Beliefs in Moral Realism

How an individual's decisions and behaviors become good or bad depends on morality in a real pragmatic sense. Realism is old as existentialism, naturalism, and materialism. It deals with what actually exists. This indicates that an individual desires the ability to deny his/her past and present nature of existence. He/she desires to become something different and better than that he/she was in the past, or he/she now is. He/she desires to do what he/she desires in a practical sense. He/she desires freedom to determine his/her destiny.

Realism's philosophical assumptions are based on common sense. Realists try to conceptualize moral convictions of humans in nature within conditional and situational circumstances. They try to find contingent practical solutions for human problems and conflicts. There are specific moral principles that realists have found in their beliefs. These principles are as follows:

- Humans possess natural convictions concerning the extrinsic existence of power. This indicates that they are part of a highly orchestrated system of universal ordination.
- Humans possess convictions regarding the existence of moral truths. Moral truths existed before we discovered them. They will exist after we pass away. For example, honesty always has been viewed by all generations as goodness. It will remain the same in the moral sense, in future too.
- Humans possess convictions regarding the existence of spirituality in human nature. Attributes of moral virtues exist just as we know them, except for errors in our perceptions that are verifiable as mistakes. This indicates that life is a process of trial and error.
- Humans possess convictions regarding conscientious awareness not only of external objects, forces, and derivative powers, but also of the causal and multiple linkages among themselves.
- Moral behavior and experiences are the touchstones of what is real (seeing is believing).
- Such a knowable moral conviction shows us how material things as external manifests of nature are perceived as interdependent linkages among all elements in the universe.
- We are living in the midst of external realities that simply are what they are or they appear to be to our perceptions.
- Realism seeks to describe characters and their interrelated events as they really are without idealization, sentimentalization, and/or deception.

As we mentioned above, the term moral realism was to do with what actually exists (seeing is believing). Immanuel Kant called this empirical knowledgeable science. Kant believed in empirical moral knowledge (the application of realistic patterns of goodness and happiness in daily human life). He believed science is based on observation and direct exposure to knowledge. Knowledge always comes after the evidence found in the process.

In contrast to the moral idealists that believe in good will as the basic foundation of moral judgment, moral realists believe that good will or intentions alone are not sufficient to reach the pinnacle point of goodness. Good will should result in good-deeds. In addition, the application of moral realism principles in human mind and behavior can result in a stabilized life.

The Kantian Moral Realism

Within this breadth of real endeavor, we are examining Kant's views on morality that are based on goodwill as the means and ends of unconditionally good deeds. Immanuel Kant's (1724-1804) realistic morality is mainly set forth in his book *Fundamental Principles of Metaphysics of Morals* (1785). He sought an a priori principle that prescribes universal laws of conduct. He found two objectives in morality:

- *Goodwill as unconditionally good:* Kant concluded that the only thing in the world, which is good without limitation, is the good will to do one's duty. There are no other gifts of nature, such as intelligence, courage, and perseverance. These traits are desirable, but may be pernicious if the will that directs them is not good (Kant 1957: 539). He asked: What determines the nature of excellence? He answered to this question in his own way: The will is good when it is completely devoted to duty for the sake of duty.
- *Duty as the moral imperative:* The good will is not good unless it achieves excellent consequences. The value of good faith defines the nature of good will. For example, if a foolish person with his/her good faith does a foolish act, such an act is not perceived as moral because the foolish consequence does not carry any moral value. This means that moral acts need to have moral values along with good will in the agents' characters not only in means, but also in their ends. In the field of business, if a borrower gets a loan from a lender or a bank and spends it for charitable and/or for philanthropic purposes and then declares bankruptcy, such an act is viewed immoral, because the money was not his/her wealth. This gift to charity is wrong because it has violated the promissory contract between the lender and the debtor. In the field of business, it has been observed that many corporate managers have endowed huge monies of their corporations for social activities in their communities and then declared bankruptcy.

Just causes seek universal laws that are consistent or congruent with proper promissory conducts. Such a moral rule requires good faith in promises. To behave morally means to be able to properly *justify* self-conduct. In the Enron bankruptcy case, the CEO Ken Lay's actions with bad faith (not to be loyal to all stakeholders including employees and stockholders) contributed huge sums of money for philanthropic purposes in Houston. Consequently, he, by his good will, provided free-money for executives and political figures in the United States and provided his stockholders and shareowners that trusted him with nothing. What did Mr. Lay do? He resembled a robber who objected to being called a thief. He declared that all he did was to misappropriate property of Enron's employees' pension funds and the stockholders' trusts and appropriated them for some political groups and executives' interest and left nothing for his stakeholders. In addition, he donated millions of dollars to charities and community organizations with good will without the consent of his clients with good faith. This justification is scarcely less cogent than the logic of a political leader who establishes a dictatorship and then calls his/her act a democracy.

The formulation of categorical imperatives especially brings out the moral convictions held by realists in general that each individual has an intrinsic worth of consciousness in his/her conduct. We must not use all these worthy good faiths and good wills *merely* as means. We need to act within our community where each individual is at once ruler and subject. Kant (1898: 10) concluded that the only thing in the world, which is good without limitation, is the good will to do one's intellectual duty. Kant believes that a moral person needs to be experienced with the universal principles of goodness.

Moral experience is the touchstone of what is real. There are different perceptions in morality. These perceptions raise fundamental questions such as:

- What is the common sense of existence?
- What is an individual's intellectual sense of existence?
- Does morality answer to a universal sense of understanding?

To answer to these questions we will explain the realistic views of Thomas Reid and John Locke.

The Reidian Moral Realism

Thomas Reid (1710-1796) was the champion of the realism of common sense. His views are set in his *Inquiry into the Human Mind on the Principles of Common Sense* (1764). He held that an individual has dependable and immediate intuitive convictions regarding the existence of the external world, of moral truths, and of the existence of soul. He thought the universal conviction of human beings depends on moral truths. We have an immediate awareness, not only of external objects, but also of the causal and other relations between them. There are at least two main ways of conceiving universal moralism:

- We may regard universal moral laws as a set of separated principles that govern *forms* in truth. Forms follow the natural ordination. These forms are *mental* in their empirical nature.
- The moral laws of the nature do not govern natural processes, but only express specific *knowable* attributions to describe such

processes. These laws are the essence of common sense or, as Kant called it, science.

Reid believed that scientific empirical knowledge is based upon good choices and volitions in human mind and actions. This is the surest moral decision and action. We can call an employer a real moralist, because we mean that he/she never loses sight of the bitter taste of economic hardship. The realistic moral manager usually manages a corporation to achieve his/her moral objectives despite adverse circumstances. He never lies or deceives his/her stakeholders. These types of managers believe that if there are realities that cannot be altered, then the realist manager should alter himself/herself to suit them. For example, T. J. Watson, Jr. (1963: 15), Chairman of the Board of IBM, stated:

> The decision in 1914 led to the IBM policy on job security that has meant a great deal to our employees. From it has come our policy to build from within. We go to great lengths to develop our people, to retain them when job requirements change, and to give them another chance if we find them experiencing difficulties in the jobs they are in....But policies like these, we have found, help us to win the goodwill of most of our people.

With the same pattern of perceptions, managers in Japanese culture believe that in the time of economic recession, corporations should not layoff their excessive human resources because such an action will destroy laid off workers' normal life. Not only do Japanese corporations not retrench their operations, they accelerate their operational processes to produce more goods with lower costs in order to sell them with the lowest prices after the economic recession is over. Within this managerial culture, Japanese believe that they have served both employees and consumers with good-will, because employees will be able to continue their normal employment life with a lower pay and consumers will be able to appreciate their purchase power with lower prices. Therefore, Japanese business culture is based on a philosophy which indicates if everything is in their favor they enjoy it and if not, they adapt themselves to the reality of the economic life. They believed that all people should enjoy and/or endure on the basis of reality of life. Therefore, the realistic moral temper appears in all areas of realistic national culture. In sum, moral realists seek to describe the common sense of characters and events as they really are without idealization or sentimentalization.

Realistic Lockeian Morality

John Locke (1632-1704), whose moral theory influenced the American Founding Fathers, believed that every human is allowed to use what nature provides. Locke is known as a moral empiricist. People may make natural resources their own if they can use them and if others have as much, and as good, remaining for their use as well. The initial partition of the earth is a fact. Each person owns a portion of such partitions. The moral right of declaring ownership of natural resources is based on the fortunate condition of having been born in a country where resources exist.

Locke founded morality on religious authority, tempered with reasonableness. We are obligated to behave morally through God's commands. This is the ultimate sanction of morality. He believed that the truth in morality is not stabilized unless it is subject to periodical validation. There are numerous evidences in nature that demonstrates their validity to unbiased reasons.

Locke's realistic ideas on morality are further set forth in his *Treatise on Government* (1690). His views regarding moral behavior of citizens in a country is a diffused relationship between religion and government. Locke conceived an original state of nature provided by God where humans are entitled to such rights as freedom, justice, and the ownership of property. But humans violate these God-bestowed rights by seeking their own selfish ends and by robbing and enslaving each other.

Conclusions

Today, in a moral sense, we speak of human rights rather than natural rights. Human rights are rooted in law and protected by it. Natural rights are rooted in the sanctity of morality. In a just and moral society, legal rights are differentiated products of moral rights, and to some degree, they overlap to a considerable degree in pragmatism. Legal rights perform a negative function by telling people what is *forbidden*. A positive morality tells people what is permissible and what they *should* do.

Realistic moral theory is a doctrine that perceives goodness as a real means and ends to be properly linked in their right path of intellectual wisdom. Both good faith and good will require not the will of God, nor the might of nature, nor the edicts of society to make them better than they are. Pragmatic real good faith and good-will demands us that whichever of them is pragmatically relevant to a person's given good situation should be pursued. But demands are not commands. They should be congruent with possibilities of achieving good consequences.

HEDONISTIC MORAL THEORY

There are two other moral theories that whose principles we can apply as means and ends in examining our moral behavior. One is all *self-centric*: good behaviors endorse *hedonistic morality*; the view that pleasure is the only intrinsic goodness in life worth pursuing. Second is that the *egoist* people belief that both intrinsic and extrinsic values are not simply pleasurable which may differ in quality as well as quantity but creates *happiness*. This second view is called *eudaemonistic morality*. Since the basic value in terms of both assessments results in good ends, it is perceived as happiness, not pleasure. For clarity of meaning we describe pleasure through hedonistic moral theory and happiness through eudaemonistic moral theory as means and ends of morality (De George, 1995: 63).

The view that associates morality with self-interested decisions and actions believes that goodness is an intrinsic power can that manifest a pleasurable life as enjoyable life. The theory of morality that advocates a pleasurable life as the means and ends of goodness it is known as *hedonism*, a name taken from the Greek meaning pleasure. One question that surfaces in hedonistic moral objectives is: Is there some least common denominator in terms of which we can assess our perceptual goodness? The answer is yes. That is through the application of the moral theory of hedonism.

Principle Beliefs in Hedonistic Moral Theory

Hedonistic moral theory holds that basic human values should be oriented toward the promotion of pleasure and the avoidance of pain. According to this view, everything that people desire, want, or need, can be reduced in one way or another to pleasure or pain. Pleasure means the absence of pain.

The term of *pleasure*, in its strictest sense, is the immediate accomplishment of enjoyable sensational, emotional, and physical ends. Pleasure is the powerful dynamic motive that urges individuals to respond positively to their good need-dispositions. The immediacy and vehemence of sensational and emotional delightfulness would probably be the main reason for stability of human life and the survival of the human species. Therefore, all people need to enjoy their lives and avoid suffering.

Pleasure is the avoidance of experiencing depravation from need-dispositions. Pleasure is a search for gratification to be experienced with the fulfillment of physical, sensational, and emotional consequences. Depravation is a kind of momentary suffering from the stabilized states of deficiencies. Also, depravation is, culturally, assumed to be an aversive state that may involve withholding desired psychological tendencies. For example, in both Jewish and Moslem faiths, fasting, and in Buddhism and Hinduism, meditation, are considered conscious deprivation from such thing as eating and drinking in order to motivate people to appreciate and obtain fulfillment. The end-result is self-confidence and self-realization.

There is an idiom that states no pain, no gain. Pleasure can be considered two ways:

- As the end result of an action with a pleasurable memory.
- To the beginning of an action with the intention of pursuing a life-lasting enjoyment.

By analyzing these two processes, the interpretation of pleasure is different culture to culture. Some cultures conceive that pleasure, as the end-result is the last in execution, for it is the last thing to happen. But in other cultures, the end is the first, not in the order of execution, but in the order of intention. For example, some people believe in financial depravation by putting aside some income saving for the necessity of their future needs, while in other cultures people perceive pleasure on the basis of the immediate action of spending of their incomes to fulfill their immediate end-desires. This is the result of the complexity of human nature. There is no doubt that both types of cultures are striving for "goodness." One conceives pleasure in a long period of waiting time (as savings), while the other perceives it in a short period of time (as spending). In fact, the sense of pleasure is a trajectory state of excessive sensational and emotional enjoyment which turns an individual's behavior from depravation and suffering to the climax of enjoyment and fulfillment and then gradually turns it back to the original state of depravation and deficiency again. This is considered the momentum of the survival of the human race. In viewing the hedonistic theory, we will review Spencerian views.

Spencerian Hedonistic Moral Views

Herbert Spencer (1820-1903) was a hedonistic moralist who believed that *pleasure is the essence of the good*. Spencerian philosophy (1888) is a systematic thought, characterized by bringing various scientific thoughts into a systematic whole. To Spencer, pleasure has been defined as an individual's good experiences. Life approaches perfect goodness when it leads at once to present pleasure and remote pleasure. Spencer's hedonism also serves to define right and wrong decisions and actions. Conduct is right when it leads to pleasure for all. It is wrong when it entails avoidable pain and the depravation of pleasure. He believes that egotism must come before altruism. Since egotism is a product of determination, then human beings are capable of searching for pleasure more than pain. Society, therefore, exists in the service of individual members. The pleasure of the group exists in terms of the pleasure of its individual members. Nevertheless, egoism and altruism are complementary. But as the moral status of a society evolves, it will see that altruism becomes a mandatory moral objective to be achieved.

Spencer's hedonistic moral hypothetical assumption is based on a belief in the necessity of findings a scientific basis for the distinction between pleasure and happiness and for the general guidance of conduct. Toward this end, he considered it necessary to examine the linkage between nature and human desires. Also, Spencer regarded moral conduct as good to the extent that it makes life longer, richer, and happier for the individual, for his/her children, and for their social groups. He believed that hedonistic moral objectives are viewed as fulfillment in a society where there is durable peace and in which each individual achieves their desirable objectives and aids others in achieving theirs.

Conclusions

We may take into our considerations any kind of conscientious judgment concerning our conduct can be assessed by their end results of our self-conduct. Since a human being is a complex being, he/she possesses a vast range of intrinsic instinct, sensation, imagination, emotion, genetics, problem solving and innovation. Also, he/she possesses a sense of learning, memorization, and creation. He/she is a whole and unified being. He/she is searching for satisfaction within and beyond the self. This mandates him/her accomplish pleasurable objectives and avoid painful or dreadful consequences. For such reasons, he/she makes a priority of perceiving first pleasure in self and then in others. This characteristic in a moral sense is called hedonistic morality. Therefore, hedonistic moral theory is based upon these principles:

- Moral life is based on mitigation of pain and enhancement of pleasure first in self and then in others.
- Everything that people desire, want, or need, can be reduced in one way or another to pleasure or pain.
- Pleasure is an intrinsic process that can manifest and maintain a high egotistic status.
- Pleasure is the end result of self-satisfaction.
- Pleasure is an end in humans that manifests satisfaction.

To live well in the term of hedonistic moral philosophy is to live a life of pleasure. Hence, since the good life appears to consist of pleasurable activities and the good use of satisfaction, it seems to be very egoistical. Nevertheless, since the nature of human beings is to desire limitless pleasure, within such a contextual perception, they need to pursue goodness. In a closing, pleasure is viewed first and foremost as a state of interior well being, even by those who perceive it as an extrinsic objective for accumulating wealth because they enjoy the possession of the wealth.

EUDAEMONISTIC MORAL THEORY

As we mentioned above, there are two approaches in being moral: (1) hedonistic and (2) eudaemonistic. We have explained the hedonistic approach that is based on pleasurable and satisfactory means and ends. The advantage of the hedonistic approach has been challenged by another group of moralists who claim that not all intrinsically valuable good faith and good-will can be used to convert pain into pleasure or to unifies pleasure and pain in a balanced unity of existence. Also, eudaemonistic moralists maintain that pleasure is not the one and only thing that is good in itself; and hence, depending on the view that one adopts, that it is just one of a number of things that are good in this sense. Such a process is the result of our sensations and emotions. Since both sensation and emotion are differentiated from our feelings, then they may or may not establish a rational basis for being moral. What is intrinsically valuable in our conscientious is not simply pleasure but happiness (De George, 1995: 63).

The most serious defect of pleasure is that pleasure does not satisfy the whole ego of an individual person, nor even the best part of that person. People can share their pleasures with others through sensational and emotional enjoyments. Pleasure would not seem to provide the sort of happiness suitable to all people. Since pleasure does not create long range satisfaction for an individual and even the best intellectual values as Aristotle calls it the *moral virtue*, it would not seem to provide happiness suitable to an *intellectual virtue* because it is short-lived. It may be intense, but it never lasts. The magnitude of pleasure is derived from its own restriction and at best, it is limited to certain levels of goodness. This suggests that a certain type of moral egoism is typical of those who are concerned with avoiding harm to the self rather than gaining benefits for the self.

We should remember that eudaemonistic egoism is a doctrine that maintains the sanctity of human rationality and directs us to seek only our own happiness through intellectual virtues. Egoism contends that an action is morally right if and only if it best promotes the individual's long-term goodness. Within the mechanistic boundaries of morality, we need to identify the difference between *selfishness* and *egoism*. *Selfishness* is the inherent nature of emotional and sensational pleasurable goodness, while rational *egoism* is the inherent nature of moral happiness in terms of intellectual virtue. Therefore, we need to identify what is moral happiness.

What is Moral Happiness?

Eudaemonistic theorists believe that people use their best long-term advantages as the standard for measuring an action's rightness. If an action produces or is intended to produce a greater ratio of good to evil in the long run than any other alternatives, then that action is the right one to be performed or pursued. In such a case an individual should take that course of moral action to attain the state of happiness. Thus, we see how an eudaemonistic moral theorist perceives its means and ends on the basis of happiness.

We are now in a position to discuss what we mean by happiness. Within such a domain of inquiry, we need to face three distinctive questions:

- Can an individual attain moral happiness?
- Can an individual maintain moral happiness?
- Is such a moral happiness complete happiness for an individual's long-life process?

Again, let us recall what has been defined as moral happiness. Moral happiness is an ever-lasting process of having a good and clean life. All people agree that happiness is an ultimate state of end when conscientious awareness fulfills its proper mandates. In attempting to determine objectively what happiness consists of, we arrive in a state of life with virtue. The state of life with virtue is known as living according to moral reasoning, extending and concluding it with intrinsic and extrinsic excellent results. We will analyze the original questions concerning happiness and then outline the doctrine of eudaemonistic moral theory.

Principle Beliefs in Eudaemonistic Moral Theory

Eudaemonistic moralists believe that morality is primarily an individual's convictions toward excellence in term of intellectual virtue. If we perceive scientific endeavors as virtuous efforts that include science, understanding, wisdom, art, and prudence, then can we call them knowledge? If our attention is focused on knowledge, then we need to define what we mean by knowledge, science, data, information, and alertness as intellectual virtuous awareness.

In today's free market economy, the basic organizational resource is no longer material capital, labor, or natural resources, but knowledge-wealth. Knowledge is not the same thing as scientific formulas, data, or information, although it uses all these phenomena. Knowledge manifests a step further, beyond scientific boundaries. It is a conclusion drawn from the application of scientific formulas and information data after it is linked to other known and unknown phenomena and compared to what is already known. Scientific formulas direct us not only to be knowable about the functions of existence; also they direct us to know why something is true. This type of analysis is called syllogism.

Syllogism is a conclusive argument in which two premises and conclusions can be expressed either by demonstration or deduction. When we use scientific syllogistic formulas, we prove two domains of facts:

- The existence of logical truthfulness, demonstrated reasoning concerning a phenomenon, element, process, or dynamics of a synthesized membership functioning group.
- The possible deductive conclusion of a manifestation of premises that states why such formulas are true. For example, if a CEO is eligible to vote on the Board of Directors of a company, that CEO is a member of the Board of Directorates. Then the deductive result indicates that the board is a *codeterminative* one.

Science deals with human understanding concerning the discovery and formulation of the real world in which inherent properties of space, matter, energy, and their interactions can be perfectly scrutinized and predicted. Science is a rational convention related to the generalization of the expected environmental norms, expectations, and values. It is nothing more than the search for understanding of the fundamental reasoning of the real world.

Nevertheless, searching for discovers in the real world in practice is composed of ethical and unethical practices. Sometimes scientists ignore the rights of individuals or groups when reveals the real world. A successful scientific innovation needs to apply the pragmatic effective ones. The scientists' concern about innovativeness states that excellence needs a vision in order to be focused on the maximum prudence in achieving creative methods. This is the exact meaning of eudaemonistic moral practices. Such an edudaemonistic moral objective mandates that scientists question the answers of previous questions they wanted to answer, where the world of humanity is moving forward, to which path of discovery they need to be directed. For example, in biotechnology and biobusiness industry, how should scientists pursue the notion of happiness for humanity through cloning human beings? Within such an important scientific endeavor, how can human dignity and integrity be guarded? What bioscientists and bioethicists need to consider is to collect appropriate progenistic data through prodigical information systems in order to understand the consequences of cloning for the welfare of humanity.

Progenistic data are simple, absolute quantitative facts and figures that, in and of himself or herself, may be of little value or use. At this juncture, data is known as the raw facts, untouched by human minds. Nevertheless, we have more knowable data than we can tell. To be valuable and useful for humanity, data is processed into finished information by connecting parts with other data. Therefore, information is the end result of functioning membership of progenestic data processes that have been linked with other data and converted them into a workable and meaningful context for identification of specific right or wrong usage of data.

From another prodigical point of view, technological breakthroughs are known as integrated innovative systems which access through pragmatic processing of interlinked data, to both deep and broad domains of know-why, know-what, know-how, know-who, know-where, know-whose, and know-for cyberspace information systems in both corporations and industries as well as in modern societies.

By technological breakthroughs, we mean any consistent application of scientific discoveries about the natural world that is employed to achieve a purposive objective to modify the material world. Therefore, in a moral sense prodigical technology is purposive. It is applied to achieve both ethical and moral objectives. Technology differs from science. Science seeks knowledge while technology applies science for the manipulation of the natural world to achieve a goal (Marshal, 1999: 83). Within such a highly sophisticated cyberspace environment, cognivistic knowledge mapping, pragmatic operational designs of data gathering, and holistic processing of the interlinked distributive operational techniques can be potentially abusive systems.

Data processes and designed outputs can be easily misused by E-businesses in order to inflate the corporation's performance. Therefore, within the context of the real business world, we can claim that development of a technological civilization may not be evidence of progress from an ethical and moral point of view. However, technological developments are facts reflected in humanity's physical and intellectual abilities to affect and shape the natural environment and extend it to their desirable objectives (Parhizgar and Lunce, 1994: 55).

Under the above circumstances, the question of whether information can be assumed to be equivalent to, or at least possessing all the intellectual values when compared to knowledge, may be seen as a matter of logical reasoning. While the common practice has been to use the terms knowledge and information interchangeably, a number of differences between the two phenomena have been distinguished. Marshal (1997: 92) has described knowledge as inside the human mind and information as the knowledge outside the mind. Nevertheless, information may become knowledge when introduced into one's mental model.

Knowledge always contains a human intellectual valuable factor. E-sites, books, and pictures that contain nudity from the standpoint of biological sciences can be moral, ethical, and legal if they become knowledgeable sources of discovery only when scholars, researchers, and scientists absorb their real values and put them into scientific use. However, nude pictures, images, and the E-sites in advertising can be immoral, unethical, and illegal (pornographic magazines, books, and Internet E-sites) if children and adults are viewing them as a source of sexual pleasurable medium. Within such an analysis, through eudaemonistic moral approach, formation, illustration, and manifestation of nudity by scientists are moral because they are using them to discover the real valuable characteristics of human beings. However, pleasurable viewing by lay people is immoral.

Knowledge is perceived and applied to both means and ends. In its logical reasoning as a means, knowledge is information that can be used to secure valuable materials as cash or as abstract for the purpose of spiritual enhancement of the human mind. As an end, knowledge can be perceived as understanding logical reasoning or using it for contemplation or reflection of human enrichment. Knowing can be perceived as possession of knowledge, and learning as the process of the acquisition of knowledge. Training is viewed as the process of disseminating and contributing knowledge from a knowledgeable person to an interested intended audience in order to acquire wisdom. Knowledge languishes and fades if it is not cultivated by wisdom (intellectual virtue). Knowledge is not self-sustaining; it does not grow by itself. It has to be actively cultivated by scholars in order to remain alive.

Going back to our discussion concerning egoistic happiness, moralists distinguish between two kinds of egoism: personal and impersonal. Personal egoism holds that individuals should pursue their own best long-term goodness, but they do not say what others should do. Impersonal egoism holds that everyone should follow his/her best long-term goodness as a cultural value system. Egoism requires us to do whatever will best further our own interests and doing this sometimes requires us to advance the interests of others.

Several misconceptions haunt both versions of egoism. One criticism is that hedonistic moralists believe that people do only what they like, that they believe in eating, drinking, and be merry. Another misconception is that hedonism endorses self-interest and the view that since only pleasure is of intrinsic value; the only good in life worth pursuing is for self-pleasurable ends. This will promote selfishness. Selfishness corrupts human morality and turns people into savages. Therefore, by this reason eudaemonistic moralists believe in happiness not in pursuing pleasurable objectives. They believe that happiness is both intrinsic and extrinsic satisfaction. Eudaemonistic moral values spell out specific standards based upon the primacy of greatest value, which is known as liberty. Everyone should act to ensure greatest freedom of choices. Within the domain of business transactions, competitors should promote the marketplace for the sake of exchanging qualitative valuable commodities to be used as the essential happiness for the social welfare.

Jeremy Bentham's Eudaemonistic Morality

Within the domain of morality, Jeremy Bentham (1748-1832) is known as an eudaemonistic moralist who believed that morality is based on the principle that the objective of life is the promotion of the greatest happiness for all individual people. Also, Bentham (1823) is often thought of as the founder of utilitarianism ethics: "The school of philosophy that holds that the tendency of an act is mischievous when the consequences of it are mischievous; that is to say, either the certain consequences or probable." For our purposes within the boundaries of eudaemonistic morality, it is important to treat pleasure and happiness separately. Bentham's view on happiness is influenced by the principles of utility that specify the greatest amount of happiness is the purpose of life. In addition, he believed that the purpose of government is to foster the happiness of all individuals, and that the greatest happiness of the most people should be the goal of human existence.

Conclusions

Eudaemonistic moralists believe that there are multiple sources of happiness for individuals. People need to learn the right methods to choose the surest pathways in order to choose the best ones. They believe that the choice should be assessed by the greatest amount of prudence through intellectual virtue. Eudaemonistic moralists believe that standards are applied to both processes and consequences of self-volition or decision, the principle that everyone should act to generate the greatest benefits for the largest portion of human life. Moral standards are applied to the intent of actions or decisions; the principle that everyone should act independently to ensure that similar decisions would be reached by others, given similar circumstances for the purpose of happiness.

Eudaemonistic theory holds that the basic value in terms of moral behavior is a calculation of goodness and badness in terms of moral judgment. Some maintain that *happiness* is the essence of the right kind of thoughts, habits or behaviors. Happiness is more a means than an end.

(Happiness) = (Means of Goodness) > (Ends of Badness)

(H) = (MG) > (EB)

or

(Happiness) = (Good Faith + Goodwill)

(H) = (GF + GW)

Sometimes some people acquire wealth and power not really for their own sake but as a means of achieving something else and sometimes some people acquire wealth, power, pleasure, and reputation as an end. It should be noted that if the wealth and power have been accumulated for the sake of wealth and power, then the concentration of wealth and exertion of excessive power can produce either pleasure and misery. The accumulation of wealth and power can be used for good or evil. Therefore, it is perceived that happiness is an ultimate end when satisfaction and fulfillment of all intellectual desires are met.

As previously stated, in attempting to determine objectively what happiness is, it is primarily as Aristotle calls it intellectual virtues. Intellectual virtues make an individual's life in accordance with goodness of holistic healthy body and mind. There are two different ways to seek pleasure and happiness. The first is to search for feelings and experience practical values, and the second is to seek speculative cognitive knowledge in order to understand, either for the sake of simply knowing or for the sake of making decisions for conscientious actions. Nevertheless, if existence consists of both pleasure and happiness, decisions deserve specific attention:

- What do individuals conceive implicitly when they believe in goodness what does that say about pleasure and happiness?
- What can individuals learn from scientific values, which are the end results of scientific deliberations?

By completing goodness, we mean an individual seeking satisfaction and happiness as the ultimate end. Therefore, eudaemonistic moralists believe that happiness is the life-long objective for a moral person.

AUTHENTIC MORAL THEORY

People have always searched beyond their ages, probing the real and the universal image of their origin and prediction of their finality. The universal image of the origin of humans helps shed light on a variety of images in order to understand their nature and the entity in which they are living, perceiving, and proceeding. There are three major images concerning the nature of human beings: (1) unitarians, (2) binarians, and (3) trinitarians. Unitarians believe that the human is an independent agent beyond of the contextual premises of universe. Their spirits are subject to eternity. The Binarians believe that human nature is a composition of dual entity (e.g. matter and spirit; virtue and vice, good and bad; physical and metaphysical, etc.) within the context of the universal image. Their bodies are subject to defectiveness but their minds are subject to the evolutionary processes of development. The Trinitarians believe that human nature is a dependent agent within the context of *kinetic, kinesthetic,* and *telekinesis* derivative forces and power.

Kinetic forces and power exist on the surface of logic for the existence of human beings. Kinetic existence pays close attention to three domains of morality: (1) the positive imagery of the material need causes, (2) the realistic affinity of need quiddity causes, and (3) the positive conclusive need causes (Parhizgar, 2002: 124).

Kinesthetic forces and power represent the synthesis of *explicit* and *tacit* knowledge in the form of codified intelligence. It is the essence of sensational and rational movement within the brain. Explicit knowledge is a kind of intellectual wisdom that can be easily articulated and communicated. Tacit knowledge, in contrast, is knowledge that is not easily communicated because it is deeply rooted in the very in-depth of experience. Tacit knowledge is more valuable and likely to lead to sustainable competitive advantages than explicit knowledge, because it is much harder for competitors to imitate.

Telekinesis forces and power represent intuitive knowledge as the cognitive production of spiritual motion in the body without the application of material forces (mind). It is a power long claimed by spiritualists within the domain of human existence. This is viewed as the real essence of morality.

Within the context of the above viewpoints, we must now pay attention to another ethical theory that represents one rather extreme kind of psychosocial reaction to the traditional moral theories. This moral theory is known as the authentic theory of morality. This is the ethics which Freud (1949) calls the super-egoistic moralism. It should be noted, in a real sense authentic morality needs not be egotistic or even selfish.

The moral authentic theory is traced back to the views of Sigmund Freud (1856-1939). His ideas concerning psychodynamic theory of personality involve unconscious motivation and the development of personality structure. Freud viewed personality as the interactional processes among three elements within a person: the *id, ego,* and *superego*. Freud pictured a continuing challenge between two antagonistic parts of personality the *id* and the *superego* moderated by a third aspect of the self, the ego. He conceived the primitive and unconscious part of personality (the unleashed, raw, institutional drive struggling for gratification and pleasure) as the storehouse of personality. The id is governed by the *pleasure principle* the unregulated search for gratification. The ego is the reality-based aspect of the self that arbitrates the conflict between *id* impulses and *superego* demands. It represents reality. It, rationally, attempts to keep the impulsive *id* and the conscious of the superego in check, and represents an individual's personal view of physical and social reality (the conscience that provides the norms that enable the ego to determine what is right and what is wrong). There is an ongoing conflict between id and superego. The ego serves as a compromiser creating a balance between the id and the superego. However, when id and superego pressures intensity on an individual's personality, it becomes more difficult for the ego to work out optimal compromises.

The authentic morality binds an individual with conscientious judgment. This means it is not a pattern of action or trait of character, but it is compatible with being self-efficacy and unselfish in practice. Within a super-egoistic moral judgment, an individual does things along with an altruistic judgment within the boundaries of modesty and consideration for others. This moral ground mandates an individual to follow honesty, integrity, and dignity in his/her judgments. He/she needs to avoid being egotistic, egoistic, narcissistic, and selfish.

Principle Beliefs in Authentic Moral Theory

- Authentic moral theory is compatible with being self-effacing and unselfish in practice.
- An authentic moralist understands that goodness is not just the principle of judging as his/her own private maxim, but also, they must advance and/or advocate the notion of altruism to everyone else.
- An authentic moralist must be willing to see their principles of judgment actually adopted by other moralists who have the ability and intelligence to do so.
- An authentic moralists goes beyond his/her conscientious in the full sense of real understanding.
- The authentic moralists advocate the prudentialism as the whole foundation of judgment about their moral life.
- Since prudence is a virtue, the authentic moralists do have moral obligations to consider balancing self and others welfare in the time of judgment.

Conclusions

The principle of authentic moral theory is based the idea that the only factor relevant to whether the intentional, practical, and consequential result of a decision and/or an action is right or wrong is whether it is freely or authentically chosen by the person's superego (conscientiousness). The phrases "be true to yourself," "be a judge for your own behavior," and "do your own thing as your conscience commands you" suggest this sort of view. If these phrases were interpreted as meaning the one should do that which brings about the super conscience for oneself, then we would have an example not of eudaemonistic but of the restricted hedonistic theory of morality.

Valuable insights into an analysis of conscientious behavior may be obtained if we classify each of the individuals faced with moral values within three domains of self (superego, id, and ego). Such a classification within the self can solve moral conflicts within and beyond self (when you are in Rome, do as your conscientiousness commands you, not as Romans do).

The authentic moral theory is about human nature that claims that all moral values are ultimately differentiated from self-identity (humaneness). It claims to describe how people in fact ought to behave. Underneath such a theory is an altruistic judgment that binds humanity with goodness.

CHAPTER SUMMARY

People commonly speak of having peace of mind and a happy life within contextual sense of fulfillment of their wishes. The problem of what peace of mind and happiness consists of and how they can be attained proves difficult to perceive. It is seen that emotional and sensational people sometimes end up with miserable outcomes. It is evident that not all humans can lead a virtuous life or act according to the spirit of happiness. Virtue is defined as the excellence of intellect. Moral virtues concern the habitual choices of rational thoughts in accordance with the universal logical principles. The contemplation of absolute truthfulness and the discovery of the rational principles that ought to control everyday actions have given rise to the intellectual virtues. The distinction between goodness and badness, truthfulness and falseness, and worthiness and worthlessness is called moral considerations.

It is possible to divide the phenomenon of morality into five realms. Here the interest is in what the perceptual meaning of morality looks like, and how it functions within the cognitive conscientiousness awareness of an individual. Therefore, the first level is *moral theory*. As moralists and ethicists study it, it may, for our purposes, be taken to be the foundational floor for humanity. The second level comes the realm of *moral principles*. The third level is the realm of *moral merits*. The fourth level manifests the *moral intention*. The fifth level comes the realm of *moral actions*. In this chapter, we have examined five major moral theories: (1) idealism, (2) realism, (3) hedonism, (4) eudaemonism, and (5) authenticism.

Idealism moral theory includes all views that hold that there is an independent world that is mental or spiritual in nature. Idealists are usually religious or at least sympathetic to religious outlooks. Opponents to idealism morality are materialists, existentialists, or naturalists. The materialists consider all reality consists of matter (money) and its manifestation for comfortable life. They believe that even moral consciousness is a manifestation of material or bodily process. We may distinguish three basic meanings of the term *ideals*: (1) In the world of goodness there are ideals of perfect that can never be fully realized. Ideas are not static. Ideas are dynamic sources of urge. All ideas strive for self-identification and preservation. (2) There is ideal in the sense of something *of excellence* that can be realized by wisdom and/or intellect. (3) Finally, there is an ideal in the derisive sense of something wholly visionary or quixotic.

Both idealistic and realistic philosophers agree that, in the kingdom of God or in the realm of the nature, human beings through their emotional fickleness and sensational infirmities are exposed to mysterious flaws of greed, revenge, fear, anger, savagery, cruelty, atrocity, and discrimination. Within the contextual boundary of idealistic theory of morality, there are three basic moral ideas: The ideas of intrinsic freedom and choice are viewed as manifesting of moral judgments. The ideas of extrinsic perfection and happiness are holistic in their nature. The ideas of benevolence and altruism are viewed as the final cause of happiness.

This world is full of goodness and badness. It depends on how you perceive them. Avoiding a state of goodness may cause you sinful intentions (in religious terms) and dreadful actions (in miserable earthly-life terms). It is the fear of bad intentions that tempts human beings to separate themselves from goodness and join badness. They need to solve this problem by copying, following or imitating knowledge. Like the installment plan of buying, copying, following, or imitating knowledge can solve problems. Plato found two basic beliefs relevant to morality: The doctrine of teleology that means everything in the universe has proper functions within a harmonious hierarchy of purposes. The doctrine of Ideas or Forms refers to a belief that general conceptions are not derived from experience but they are logically prior to them. For example, each of us knows what is honesty. It is by means the truthful expression of an idea, reason, and/or motive.

Aquinas believed that there is a twofold perfection of rational or intellectual nature: (1) natural happiness, and (2) supernatural happiness (God's image). Therefore, humans have two sources of truth rather one: Those factual understandings with human faculties that provide us virtues concerning our habitual choices of conduct. In the second, those inspirational feelings that God reveals. He is ascribed as the source and authority of principles determining proper choices that of God that makes available to humans.

Hobbes believed that competition is a war of every human being or group against every other one. The notions of justice or injustice, fairness or unfairness, rightness or wrongness have no place. Where there is no moral rule, there is no moral power; where no moral law, no justice. The realistic moral theory is more action oriented. A major problem for the moral realists is how to cope with immoral actions and how we will be able to find remedies to be matched with definitions and standards of moral virtues. A central difficulty of any moral theory is to do justice both to the absolute and the relative aspects of moral values. By an absolute goodness, we need to know the statistical mean one that is intrinsically and always good in human intellectual wisdom and reasoning. However, by an extrinsic judgmental valuable perception concerning goodness, we may come out with relative degrees of goodness with different comparative values. Since morally good will is an absolute good, many of the good things of life are relative, not absolute. There are numberless values that are relatively higher than others. Realism philosophical assumptions are based on common sense. Realists try to conceptualize moral convictions of humans in nature. They try to find practical solutions for human problems and conflicts.

Kant sought a priori principles that prescribe universal laws of conduct. He found two objectives in morality: Good Will as Unconditionally Good and Duty as the Moral Imperative. Philosopher Thomas Reid (1710-1796) found in his philosophy at least two main ways of conceiving the universal moralism: We may regard universal moral laws as a set of separated principles that govern forms. Forms follow the natural ordination. These forms are mental in their empirical nature. The moral laws of the nature do not govern natural processes, but only express specific knowable attributions to describe such processes. These laws are the essence of common sense, or as Kant called it, science.

Locke is known as a moral empiricist. Locke founded his morality on religious authority tempered with reasonableness. We are obliged to behave morally by God's commands.

Realistic moral theory is the doctrine that perceives goodness as a real means and ends linked in their right path of intellectual wisdom. Both good faith and good will require not the will of God, nor the might of nature, nor the edicts of society to make them better than they are. There are two other moral theories whose principles we can apply as means and ends in examining our moral behavior. One is self-centric: good behaviors endorse hedonistic morality; the view that pleasure is the only intrinsic goodness in life worth pursuing. Second indicates that the egoists beliefs that both intrinsic and extrinsic values are not simply pleasurable which may differ in quality as well as quantity - but bring happiness. This second view is called eudaemonistic morality: since the basic value in terms of which assessment is made is happiness, not pleasure.

The authentic moral theory is about human nature that claims that all moral values are ultimately differentiated from self-identity (humaneness). It claims to describe how people in fact ought to behave. Underneath such a theory is altruistic judgment that binds humanity with goodness.

QUESTIONS FOR DISCUSSION

- What is essential human happiness?
- How much money should an individual seek in order to maintain happiness?
- How can money make an individual's life happy?
- What are the characteristics of human nature?
- What is the relationship of humans to nature?
- What is the modality of humans' activities?
- Explain the fundamental factual problems in morality.
- What we mean by morality?

- What is the difference between morality and ethicality?
- Why are moral theories different?
- What the difference between moral idealism theory and moral realism theory?
- What are the major differences between hedonistic and eudaemonistic moral theories?
- State why people usually search for pleasure not happiness.
- Explain the different views on moral idealism of platonic, Aquinasian, and Hobbesian morality.
- What are principle beliefs in moral realism?
- Explain the different views of moral realism of Kantian, Reidian, and Lockeian morality.
- What is the difference between selfishness and egoism?
- What is the foundational belief of hedonistic morality?
- What is the Spencerian hedonistic moral philosophy?
- What is the foundational belief of eudaemonistic morality?
- What is proportionate happiness? Can it be an ultimate end?
- Can human happiness in any way be considered complete happiness?
- What is relative human pleasure?
- Does human pleasure consist of a life of moral virtue?
- State the issue of contemplation vs. action.

CASE STUDY

THE ARTHUR ANDERSEN: DOING BAD IN THE NAME OF GOOD CORPORATE BOOK-COOKING STRATEGY

The demise of the energy giant, Enron is the largest bankruptcy case in U.S. business history for the year 2001. This action caught the world's attention. Enron's bankruptcy is the result of corporate deception and corruption. It is a story in which a group of unethical and immoral managers destroyed the public's trusts in America corporatism. At the end of Enron's reign, chief executive and financial officers destroyed corporate documents and sold their stocks to cover themselves and wiped out the life-time assets of Enron's employees and stockholders.

HISTORICAL BACKGROUND

In 1913, Arthur Edward Andersen founded the public accounting firm of Andersen, Delany & Company in Chicago. In 1917, his partner Mr. Delany left the company's partnership and since that time to the present day Andersen & Co. was formed. Since the inception of the company, Arthur Andersen recruited the brightest students, and then he turned them into thoroughly trained accountants who were able to go beyond their professional works by using unique scientific methodologies to improve corporate financial performances. After Arthur Andersen's death in 1947, the firm was almost dissolved, but Leonard Spacek was able to convince the company to remain active despite of its financial uncertainties.

Andersen Company, during Spacek's tenure, underwent a structural reorganization and developed a worldwide growth spurt, propelling revenues from U.S. $8 million in 1950 to $130 million just Twenty years later. This growth established Andersen Company as one of largest and most admired professional auditing services in the world. In the1970's, Harvey Kapnick succeeded Spacek. Andersen Co. operates over 300 offices worldwide. The company has two major operations: auditing and tax services, and consulting services. They are highly specialized in computer information accounting systems and business integration services. Arthur Andersen's market share is 20 percent of the international accounting firm market. Other international auditing corporations are KPMG with 20.4%, Ernest and Young with 18.4 percent,

Cooper and Lybrand with 17 percent Deloitte Touche Tohmaustu with 15.3 percent, and Price Waterhouse with 12.2 percent.

It was Harvey Kapnick's idea to convert Andersen Company from an auditing firm to an auditing-consulting firm. In 1980, Duane Kullberg replaced Kapnick and the consulting services remained, becoming the focus of the company. In the 1980s and 1990s, the company underwent several lawsuits brought by different bankrupt companies such as DeLorean Motors Company, American Savings and Loan, Deysdale Government Securities, and Resolution Trust Corporation, who claimed that Andersen had failed to inform the public of their findings and was of auditing guilty negligence. The company found legal loopholes to overcome all of these difficulties and continued its growth under the new leadership of Lawrence A. Weinbach.

In the year 2000, Andersen Company faced the same issues as in decades before. After Enron's bankruptcy, Andersen's business started to decline and many businesses terminated their auditing and consulting services with it.

PROBLEMS AND ISSUES OF THE CASE

Andersen has had a history of lawsuits for accounting malpractice. Its reputation has been damaged and it faces possible multimillion-dollar attorney fees and legal penalties. The worst-case scenario would be that the charges could trig insurance policies clauses and leave Andersen uncovered. Andersen has fraud accusation stemming from an audit on Houston-based Waste Management and paid a $7 million fine without admitting any wrongdoing. Andersen overstated earnings in the company's balancing sheet by $1.4 billion between 1992 and 1996.

Andersen has been involved in another lawsuit brought by Sunbeam Corporation. Andersen agreed to pay Sunbeam $15 million to settle a class action brought on behalf of shareholders of another client that had misstated its financial results during the 1990s. The client claimed that the CEO of Sunbeam Corporation had participated in the scheme of inflating earnings for the company.

Andersen could be liable for the bankruptcy of Enron. Enron's debt was omitted from the balance sheet and earnings were inflated since 1997 through 2001. Another allegation indicates that Andersen may face criminal charges if it is proven that its executives ordered the destruction of Enron's documents while being aware of a subpoena for them. CEO David Duncan was fired after he destroyed Enron's documents without authorization and the Security Exchange Commission (SEC) did not get a chance to look at any evidence of fraud. Mr. Duncan, ex-auditor of Enron, followed the instructions of an Andersen house-lawyer in handling documents. According to professional accounting practices, accounting firms should retain documents for several years.

Andersen CEO Joseph Bernardino declared that Nancy Temple, the lawyer at Enron from Andersen LLP, instructed accountants to save all-important documents and destroy everything else. The idea was to not leave any document behind except the most basic paper work.

ANALYSIS OF THE CASE

- Arthur Andersen and Enron are faced with unethical and illegal allegations for shredding documents.
- Arthur Andersen is liable for their part in the bankruptcy of Enron.
- Arthur Andersen has a history of class action file lawsuits for malpractice of accounts and incorrect reporting of balance sheets.
- Arthur Andersen has broken the professional public accountancy rules and code of ethics.
- Arthur Andersen has caused damage to the concept of independent auditing services.
- Arthur Andersen has covered up the misconduct and corruption of Enron's CEOs.
- Arthur Andersen misrepresented the balance sheet with inflated profits in order to mislead the stock market brokers to increase Enron's stock values.
- Arthur Andersen prevented the SEC from investigating Enron's financial wrongdoing.

CONCLUSION OF THE CASE

The malpractice of Arthur Andersen exposed by Enron's failure, is viewed as a professional deficiency in the profession of accountancy. It has caused doubt about whether the auditing industry will be able to hold onto its wholly self-regulatory and professionally independent framework.

CASE QUESTIONS FOR DISCUSSION

- What should be the role of an independent auditing firm?
- Do we need a new controlling agency to regularly audit auditing firms?
- What is the role of the Security Exchange Commission?
- What is the role of the corporate board of governance concerning fraud, corruption and deception?
- Who will protect the public against immoral, unethical, and illegal practices of CEOs?
- What is the side effect of corporate political financial contributions?
- What is the responsibility of mass media concerning corporate corruption, fraud, and deception?

CASE SOURCES

Arthur   Andersen,   "Red   Flag,   Averting   View   and   the   Restatement,"
<*www.andersen.com*> (February 20, 2002).

M.   L.   Cheffers,   "Lessons   From   Enron-Part   Four,"   <Arthur
Andersen.*www.andersen.com*> (January 18, 2002).

M. L. Cheffer, "Solving the Enron/Andersen Dilemma,"
<*www andersen.com* >(January 18, 2002).

CNN: "Enron," 2001,
<www.cnn.com/interactive/us/0201/enron.fall/key.players.html.>

J. Friedland, and R. Wartzman, "Look at Enron Figures Set to Testify Before
Congress Today," *The Wall Street Journal,* (Thursday, February 7, 2000).

D. McGinn, "The Ripple Effects," <*http://proquest umi.com*> *(Newsweek,* New
York: February 18, 2002).

M. E. Mullins, "Inside Enron's Partnership," (*USA Today,* January 22, 2002).

C. Woodyard, "Enron Accused of More Shredding," (*USA Today,* January 22,
2000).

CHAPTER 4

ETHICAL THEORIES: RELATIVISM, DEONTOLOGICALISM, TELEOLOGICALISM, AND UTILITARIANISM

Isn't it true that all good consequences of human acts are the results of their goodwill?
Also, isn't it true that goodwill is a differentiation of good faith?

Isn't it true that we do whatever we do as good because of what we perceive to be good?
Also, isn't it true that what we appreciate as a good thing, we apprehend as good?

Isn't it true that any good action begins with the intention of prospective good consequences?
Also, isn't it true that good consequences are the real intentions of good causes?

Isn't it true that the behavioral effects of someone are the end-results of their actions?
Also, isn't it true that the end-results are first, not in execution, but in the order of intention?

Isn't it true that all moral and ethical people seek goodness as the state of means and ends?
Also, isn't it true that all ethical and moral people should act to reach good means and ends?

CHAPTER OBJECTIVES

When you have read this chapter, you should be able to do the following:

- Know what is syllogistic reasoning.
- Know what we mean by Algebraic logic, Boolean logic, and Fuzzy logic.
- Know what is ethical theory.
- Know what we mean by ultimate means and ends.
- Know what we mean by pleasant and pleasurable needs.
- Know what is justness.
- Know what is fairness.
- Know what is righteousness.
- Be familiar with ethical relativism, deontologicalism, teleologicalism, and utilitarianism theories.
- Be able to understand the arguments for knowing principles of all ethical theories.
- Know different types of ethical theories.
- Know how to apply different types of ethical theories in managerial decision-making processes and actions.

STARTER THOUGHT

As the third millennium begins, the world's views through either syllogism or enthymeme reasoning on ethical and moral issues become more fragmented. Syllogism directs us to not only scientifically know what is true but also why it is true. Aristotle (384-322 B.C.), (1925) the original formulator of syllogism, conceded that syllogism is an artificial construct and on authentic method of reasoning concerning real life.

Enthymeme is a truncated form of syllogism, in which the rhetorical syllogism has been simplified for lay people in order to understand the importance of reasoning. Syllogistic reasoning contains several premises and conclusions. But enthymeme reasoning carries a promise and ends only with a conclusion. It represents the way in which ordinary people can understand deductive reasoning. Therefore, enthymeme is a shortened form of syllogism to facilitate quick decision-making processes. In the field of ethical reasoning, we must be capable of discriminating between the *quantity* and the *quality* of the means and ends. We must be concerned with the *truth* of the reasoning and the *validity* of the reasoning. *Truth* has to do with *content* of syllogism. *Validity* has to do with the *form* of syllogism.

The basic structure of syllogism involves three *premises* and three *terms*. The three premises are called the *major premises*, the *minor premises*, and the *conclusions*. The three *terms* that figure into syllogism is the *major terms*, the *middle* terms, and the *minor terms*. A premise is said to be impeachable:

- If it is false; or
- If it is in need of further defense before it can be accepted as true; or
- If it is meaning is not sufficiently determinate (i.e. very vague, or excessively ambiguous) that its truthful value can also not be unambiguously determined.

Premises that are not *impeachable* are referred to as *impeccable*. Implicit premises are very carefully selected statements that, when they are added to the premises of an invalid argument, convert them into valid ones. A term or expression is distributed if it refers to all the functioning members of its class. In addition a close synonym of *distributed term* is *universal term*. There are five rules of correctness and soundness for valid syllogism (Corbett, 1991: 24):

- There must be three functioning member premises and only three terms.
- The middle term must be distributed at least once in a natural summation.
- No term may be distributed in the conclusion of premises, if it was not distributed naturally in the premises.
- No conclusion may be drawn from either affirmative or negative of two particular homogeneous premises
- According to the first rule, syllogistic reasoning must involve three premises and three terms therefore less or more than three premises and/or less or more than three terms will lead to an invalid conclusion.

According to the above syllogistic rules we are examining three premises concerning the validity of different theories of ethicality, legality, and unethicality. As you see in the Figure 4.1 each of the above premises possesses specific boundaries.

Before we test the validity of a promise the logicality of the soundness of the reasoning we need to become acquainted with some further terminology associated with syllogism. First of all, we must be familiar with deductive determination in order to identify the *quantity* and the *quality* of the propositions in the so-called *categorical syllogism* or *functioning membership*.

Quantity reasoning is either *universal* or *particular*. If reasoning is universal and if its predication applies to *all* functioning members of a group of parameters, its reasoning is viewed as Boolean logic. The Boolean body of logic establishes a range of values with multiplicative identity in which every element is an idempotent. This means that when an element multiplies by 0 or 1, it remains unchanged (e.g., (0) multiply (1) = (0) or (1) multiply (1) = (1) or a truthful phenomenon multiplied by a truthful phenomenon then the result is equal to truth).

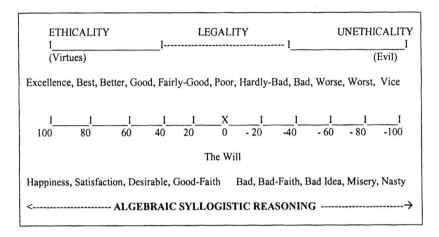

Figure 4.1: Syllogistic Appraisal of Reasoning Concerning Ethical, Legal,
and Unethical Judgments

If reasoning is particular, and if its predicate applies only to *some* functioning members of parameters, then, reasoning is viewed as algebraic logic. Quality reasoning is either *affirmative* or *negative*. When we see a pair of reasoning we understand that the course of reasoning is either affirmative or negative.

In order to decide why reasoning should be oriented toward discovering the truth, we must first ask: "Why is know-why logic the essential nature of inquiry?" This theme explicitly shows the essential continuous reasoning which should determine the nature and direction of reasoning in all places and times. Know-why logic signifies the rational reasoning that represents the essential nature of truth. Truth can be perceived through three major causes: formal cause, material cause, and efficient cause. Within a matrix of the truth, there are three levels of logical reasoning:

- Necessity in reasoning
- Sufficiency in reasoning
- Vitality of reasoning, including quiddity and equilibrium logic

Discovering the truth requires relentless holistic rational efforts to be expressed concerning the truth. Know-why logic is the embodiment of examination of our implicit conceptions, explicit perceptions, and deductive judgmental reasoning concerning the complex domain of truthfulness and falseness of inquiries.

PLAN OF THIS CHAPTER

There are different views on business ethics. Typically, ethical approaches are divided in two broad categories of philosophical reasoning: causal and consequential. Causal theories measure the ethics or correctness of any ethical act by the amount of good intention, decision, and action. Consequential theories, on the other hand, are unconcerned with intentions, decisions, and actions, but with the consequences of such a holistic process, and judge its ethicality, instead, on the bases of the duty or obligation out of which the impulse to act arises. The usual approaches to analyze foundational beliefs in ethical theories are to present in greater detail on causal means or consequential ends or the content of motives and practices of ethics.

This chapter will present various approaches, including the generally accepted strengths and weaknesses of each theory within a multicultural context. It will summarize key concepts of each theory and their positions to be considered to enhance the free flow of international business commodities and services and avoid moral and ethical dilemmas. It also discusses impasses to which these theories give rise. This kind of discussion and analysis will provide appropriate knowledge for judging the validity of grasping the significant reasoning for applying each theory. It will be shown how ethical theories can build a foundation in managerial perceptions to examine means and ends of business transactions.

To assist you in responding to the following and other inquiries we will provide you with a theoretical basis for ethical beliefs from different cultural perspectives.

- Without some comprehensive understanding of ethical theories, how can we judge which theory is appropriate to be applied in a given situation?
- What rationale is behind managerial decisions and actions? What guidelines are we to use in applying these different theories and approaches?
- What fundamental criteria for appraising business ethics to be used in order to determine which theory is best for a given problem, and what do we do if the application of different theories results in totally different means and ends?

In this chapter we will review four major ethical theories or approaches. These theories are:

- Relativism
- Deontologicalism
- Teleologicalism
- Utilitarianism.

INTRODUCTION

Since an individual's enriched moral and ethical conviction depends upon daily cause-effect relationships of all good and bad factors, we need to begin with consideration of the first principle of ethics. The first principle of pragmatic ethicality is related to good faith that can be originated in the realms of good-intention and good will. This principle manifests that not all individual actions or directions can be concluded into a streamline of good-means or good-ends because some individuals do not know really what is "good." The meaning of "good" as we perceive it in ethics signifies everything that intellectually appears pleasant and worthy of appreciation. Therefore, we do not appreciate whatever we do because we are afraid of what we emotionally or sensationally desire. We do appreciate what we do because of what we intellectually ought to do.

In arriving at a conclusive result concerning cause and effect of a good action, we need to analyze both intentions and consequences. When we say that all of an individual's actions should be directed toward some good consequences, we first need to associate our intentions with goodwill and second with good-ends. The meaning of good will in ethics is very broad. It signifies consequential results that appear desirable to us. Whatever is good, consequently, can be recognized with whatever is desirable. This recognition is confirmed in our ordinary daily experiences. Judging a decision or action either by causality or consequentiality requires a very broad understanding of the ethical problems in the field of business. Hosmer (1987: 12) has found five different views on the characteristics of ethical problems in management:

- Most ethical decisions have extended consequences.
- Most ethical decisions have multiple alternatives.
- Most ethical decisions have mixed ethical choices.
- Most ethical decisions have uncertain consequences.
- Most ethical decisions have personal implications.

On the basis of our discussion in Chapter 2, we assume at this point the two views of morality and ethicality are two separated compartments of goodness in human behavior. One of these compartments is related to an individual's moral goodness, the other one is concerned with societal group goodness. As we mentioned before, morality is more focused on an individual's cardinal virtues, hence ethicality is related to societal pluralistic cultivation of benevolent and altruistic life. We need to identify what is good than what is determining evil. We have defined the meaning of "good" with "desirable means and ends." The objection to such a definition raises an important difficulty, not about the nature of goodness as the first principle in ethics, but about interpretation and application of goodness to each individual as a desirable end. Therefore, since a desirable end is viewed as the result of emotional, sensational, and rational means of an individual, all people cannot generalize it. In order to examine all related views within the contextual boundary of ethics, we need to study different perceptions, positions, and directions of ethicists. We may now begin our review in the area of what is ethics.

THE THEORETICAL BASIS OF ETHICS

Ethics Defined

In Chapter 2 of this text, we have defined morality in terms of an individual's pursuit of self-interest and/or search for self-egoism of goodness, but we have not seen what is goodness in terms of a collective socio-cultural value system. We need to search for such a discovery through understanding the real meaning of ethicality.

Ethics involves critical analysis of cultural values to determine the validity of their rightness or wrongness of human group behavior and their organizations in terms of three major criteria: truthfulness, fairness, and justness. Ethics examines the relations of an individual to societal members and their groups, to nature, and to God through consciousness awareness. How an individual makes an ethical decision is influenced by the way they perceive themselves in relation to goodness. Ethics is a purely theoretical treatment of moral virtues in terms of speculative and practical collective cultural value systems. In speculative and practical knowledge of goodness, righteousness, and worthiness, we are concerned with cultural value systems that are operable, either with intending to do something or actually doing something in the realm of goodness. Although these two alternatives might seem to define what an ethical life should be, it is not the kind of intending or knowing goodness, but it is the complete practical execution of goodness through the collective behavior of a group of people.

Ethics is concerned with psychosocial intentions and actions and it can deal with good deeds in a society. Ethicists have identified ethics with one or other of these extremes. Some have understood ethics to be speculative and demonstrate good thoughts and behavior (deontological) and others have tended to define it as a complete practical good end-results (teleological).

As far as the term morality is related with the deliberation of an individual's intellectual characteristics through his/her conscientiousness awareness, ethics is the collective social conscious awareness of a group of people. Thus, morality is related to the individual virtues (excellence) and ethics is related to the society's fairness, justness, and worthiness (goodness). Hence, morality is the foundation of an ethical society. It also relates to the existence of moral people who make the collective distinction between right and wrong judgments and good behavior from bad. Ethics generally mandates people behave in accordance with valuable norms and standards in excellence that they accept and to which they and the rest of society hold others.

Ethics then can be defined as a systematic collective attempt at social well-being in a society in order to make sense of our individual security and social peace in such a way as to determine the rules that ought to govern human social conduct, the values worth pursuing, and the characteristic traits deserving development in life.

THE ULTIMATE MEANS AND ENDS OF ETHICS

In arriving at a final conclusion in individual's daily moral organizational life, an employee must analyze his/her activities within the end-result of goodness. The meaning of "goodness" is that to attract our tendencies or desires positively for the efficacy of our energy toward more legitimate organizational productivity. Since the first principle of morality is the realization of the self-evidence of good faith, all moral desires needed to be decided by goodwill. The goodness that we strive for is whatever we do because we perceive ourselves what we desire as goodness, and what we desire as goodness we appreciate our desires as good-ends. The most valuable outcome of an employee's contribution towards organizational productivity is stewardship (see Figure 4. 2).

MORALISM	AMORALISM
We-ism	Me-is
Principle-ism	Relativism
Right-ism	Duty-ism
Rationalism	Appetitive-ism
Egoism	Selfish-ism
Creative-ism	Imitate-ism
Effective-ism	Efficient-ism
Happy-ism	Pleasant-ism
Adventure-ism	Stable-ism
Productive-ism	Formal-ism
Survival-ism	Patriot-ism
STEWARDSHIP	

Figure 4.2:   Moral and Amoral Perceptions of Employees' End Results

There is no doubt that everyone desires a *pleasurable* and/or *pleasant* life (see Table 4.1). The problem is what constitutes pleasurable and/or pleasant life as two major components of goodness. People are the major operators for goodness and badness. Making legitimate profit and having money could be considered a moral goodness. The question is: Is there any intrinsic value of goodness in a piece of paper called money? The answer is no. What is the value of that piece of paper? The answer is: the intrinsic and extrinsic money-power value of that piece of paper which can be considered as *clean or dirty money* with which we can buy our desirable goods.

Dirty money has been viewed as the result of conducting illegitimate and unethical profitable businesses. It is in some specific cases illegal activities such as selling and buying drugs, body, pornographic films and tools, gambling, and the like are unethical and in some communities, they may be legal through licensing.

Clean money is considered money to be earned through legitimized, honest, and hard- working habits. Therefore, the extrinsic value-power of money carries valuable ends, while the intrinsic value-power carries valuable means. The more profit that we generate, the more goods (extrinsically) we can buy. There are two sets of needs: pleasurable and pleasant (see Table 4.1).

Table 4.1: Pleasurable and Pleasant Needs

PLEASURABLE NEEDS	PLEASANT NEEDS
Sex	Survival
Domination	Nurture
Attention	Escape
Adventure	Comfort
Egress	Goodness
Selfishness	Egoism
Greed	Honesty
Autonomy	Affiliation
Ambition	Guidance
Beautification	Aesthetic
Imitation	Innovation
Accomplishment	Achievement
Materialism	Spirituality
Freedom	Liberty

Wealth can be used either as means or as ends. It depends on how we appreciate its value. There are two conceptions concerning money. One is that people like money because they believe in survival to "eat, drink, be merry, etc" as we stated before. Fulfilling our needs through these behavioral activities can result in having a pleasant life. Another one is that people like money for the sake of money. Their life objectives are oriented towards the collection of money through savings. It is observed that this for group of people with very huge savings, having big savings is the source of pleasurable life. Usually, these people very stingy in some odd situations they suffer when spending money.

COMPONENTS OF ETHICAL BEHAVIOR

Everyone is familiar, to some extent, with ethical behavior in relation to justness, fairness, and righteousness in decision-making processes and real action. Since ethical decisions and judgments are based on cultural value systems in a society, there are certain ambiguities that are concealed in the signification of these cultural value systems. For example, in the field of business, we speak of a just cause; fair price, right wage, and these meanings are closely related to each other. Nevertheless they are not wholly the same. Let us begin, therefore, with the broadest meaning of ethics as a cultural value system. It contains justness, fairness, and righteousness.

What Is Justness?

The proper object of justness is right, that which is just. The proper Latin word for right is *jus,* and hence "right" is only another name for the just. From an ethical point of view, justness has had three clarifications: The first is that the source of justness is the natural law. Natural law is a generalized principle for an individual action inclining his/her feelings toward what is goodness in nature. The second point is related to his/her extrinsic cultural reasoning that is related to econo-political and sociocultural value systems for a happy life. These value systems are called civil rights in relation to and their consequential effects upon end-results of goodness. The third point is related to an individual's intrinsic cognitive conception concerning human rights either as pleasurable or pleasant or both life experiences.

An individual's main concern is about happiness regarding consequences of the common goodness. It is based upon individual liberty as the pleasant means and ends of a justified decisions and actions. Individual liberty is the most important pleasant moral order. Therefore, in a moral sense, we can say we are free to do we have a right to do. In the fields of domestic and international management operations, a manager needs to consider all above rights in the time of ethical decision-making processes and actions.

What Is Fairness?

We divide our ethical fairness concerning holistic sensational, emotional, and rational judgments into three great deals of prudence in regarding of being free from bias and dishonesty:

- Prudence is a careful unbiased consideration that comes from special relations between duties and obligations (impartiality).
- Prudence is viewed as those obligations that come from particular causes for right or wrong actions (straightforwardness).
- Prudence is viewed as those obligations that come from the particular rationalized means of actions (legitimacy).

A manager needs to make a fair judgment on the basis of impartiality, straightforwardness, and legitimacy.

What Is Righteousness?

Righteousness means that what everybody does should be suitable to what is or that judgments should be in conformity with facts, reasons, standards or principles. From an ethical point of view any decision or judgment could be weakened or deviate from the right course of action by too little or too much. An obvious instance is found in our daily attachment to special habits, tendencies, or extravagancy such as workaholism, alcoholism, sexism and others. A manager needs to reason rightly at the time of expressing judgments and decisions according to the speculative order of knowledge. The right reason is true knowledge of ethical principles.

IMPORTANCE OF FACTUAL ETHICAL KNOWLEDGE AND CONCEPTUAL CLARITY

It is very puzzling when we analyze moral consciousness and ethical judgments concerning what an individual should do in a certain situation. What one needs, is not really any ethical instruction, but simply either more factual knowledge or greater conceptual clarity of the nature of means and ends. Certainly, a large part of the debate about what to do concerning an ethical issue arises because we are ignorant of much of what bears on those problems. In the field of business ethics, much of our difficulty about decisions on trade transactions and producer-consumer relationships is due to unclear facts about the rights and duties of buyers and sellers. We stress these points because we think that ethical principles cannot overstress the importance of factual knowledge and conceptual clarity for the solution of moral and ethical social problems. To understand an ethical life and/or society, we need to review different views on theories of ethics.

THEORIES OF ETHICS

There is two core assumptions of ethical perceptions: (1) the atomistic universal of moral laws (intellect, wisdom, and knowledge) and (2) the cultural value systems (family, organizational, and national). Nevertheless, through our intellectual cognizance of value systems, the most fundamental agent is the universal self. All people are subject to a universal equitability regardless of the separation of contextual value systems in which they exist. Perhaps the most significant reasoning for such a declaration in ethics is its isomorphic nature of human beings. Human beings are not different in nature; however, their characteristics and behaviors are different -- personal and universal. The second core assumption attributes to the atomistic self. Personal behavior is rooted in personal traits and value judgments. It is the starting point of our intellect and wisdom and it is part of our ontological makeup as human beings. In the realm of our ethical reasoning and moral decisions and/or intentions, there is no consultation with other agents we consult nothing outside of ourselves we consult with our conscientious. However, in ethical decisions and actions we follow the cultural value systems. Thus, manifestation of ethical intellect and wisdom is the deliberation of extracted thoughts and actions from our immediate intellectual cultural context.

In spite of the implication and chained value systems of both morality and ethics, there are two major approaches in the realm of value systems: (1) Either that *objective* moral values are the universal beliefs of humanity or (2) that *subjective* ethical values are the products of societal valued cultures in the form of cultural choices.

When we speak of ethics, we refer to our cultural value systems concerning collective judgments of right and wrong and good and bad behavior. However, in multinational cultures there are different perceptions concerning what is right or wrong and good or bad. This variation has come from personal gains and lifestyles of individuals. In a small book like this, however, we must confine ourselves to working out fairly general theories about what is right. Two major dimensions can achieve judging what are right and wrong decisions and actions: consequential end-results, and nonconsequential or causal reasoning. In fact, the best way for us to proceed in working out such an endeavor with a deliberated breath is to review some of the main theories of ethics that have been proposed. These theories are: (1) relativism, (2) deontological, (3) teleological, and (4) utilitarian.

ETHICAL RELATIVISM THEORY

There is a basic question concerning: What is ethics in relation to absolutism or relativism logic?" That question raises another question: Are there objective universal principles of the human race upon which one can construct an ethical system of cultural valuable belief, religious faith, and political ideology that would be applicable to all groups in all cultures at all times?

The answer is no. The negative answer is not related to different ethical values, faiths, and beliefs that exist among nations. It is related to all experiences that we confirm as facts in our behavior. There is no doubt that there are certain common phenomena in all societies that are the same. What are these commonalities? They are those in which people do have faiths, beliefs, and values. With what degree is the matter of relativity? If all ethical beliefs in all societies are equally valid, then there is no variety of moral judgments concerning individual behavior. We believe in one faith. Then, there is one faith in all cultures that all people believe and behave in the same manner. Such a presumption is far from reality. There is no doubt that all people should be socially responsible for their acts. All people should work together in order to make their lives happy. The question is to what degree? With minimum, or medium, or maximum sacrifices? This creates different judgments in different societies. Such a fact establishes ethical relativism.

Ethical relativism is not a fact, but a theory that attempts to account for this fact. This theory arises from a failure to distinguish universal moral rules, and particular moral judgments, from moral principles. It involves a failure to distinguish the invariant moral principles from the variable conditions that, in accordance with these universal principles, require a variety of different rules and practices. Through ethical practices and principles we assume that ethical behavior may be relative. It does not follow universal principles around the world. Yet ethical relativism theory supposes that it does with different interpretations and applications of reasoning. It should be obvious that ethical principles do not require any uniformity of practice in different cultures, for they do not require any uniformity of practices in different circumstances.

Some people maintain that ethicality just does not boil down to religious faiths. Others have argued that the doctrine of ethical relativism indicates that right and wrong are only a function of what a particular society takes to be right and wrong. Thus, for the ethical relativists there is no absolute ethical standard. It is dependent upon religious and/or cultural contextual faith and beliefs. There is no universal criterion of right and wrong by which to judge other than that of particular societies (Shaw, 1996: 11).

Principles of the Ethical Relativism

Since some ethicists believe that ethics is largely a matter of perspective on what is worth doing and not worth doing, what is worth of knowing and not worth of knowing (e.g., sex education), and what is worth wanting and having, and what is not worth wanting and having, therefore, the objective of good living and a good life is different culture to culture. Some cultures believe in depravation for an appreciation of a pleasurable life, others believe in preparation and enhancement as the pleasurable fullness of life. Because of such diverse views on ethics, some ethicists believe that ethicality is a matter of relativism. There are some ethical principles concerning relativism as follows:

- For the ethical relativists there is no absolute ethical standard.
- Multicultural diversity value systems are the main cause of ethical relativism theory.
- Because of multicultural differences among nations what is right in one cultural context of circumstances may not be right in another one.
- Right and wrong are viewed only as a function of what a particular society takes to be right and wrong.
- The only ethical standard for judging an action is the ethical system of one society in which the act occurs.
- Ethical relativism depends on religious and/or cultural contexts, not on criteria for right and wrong by which to judge other than that of particular societies.

- Ethical relativism holds that no universal standards or rules can be used to guide or appraise an ethical decision or action.

Arguments

Ethical relativism theory holds that since people are different in terms of their religious faiths, cultural value systems, and econo-political ideologies, naturally, their ethical standards for judging their decisions and actions will be different too. The only societal group interests, political ideologies, and cultural value systems that are relevant for judging about the ethical status of their societies are their own. Throughout history, what one group of people assumed to be right, fair, or just, many others believed it was wrong or evil. For example, the Supreme Court of the United States on April 14, 2002, ruled that restrictions on businesses involved in the selling of the children pornographic tapes, pictures, images, sound, and the Internet shows are illegal. The Supreme Court of the United States ruled that such censorship is against first amendment of free speech. At the same time such businesses in religious oriented societies are viewed as immoral, unethical, and illegal. Therefore, the point behind any ethical standards or principles is that pluralistic ethical standards are the basis of ethical authority and people should follow them. Relativists content that the ethical answer depends on sociocultural and econopolitical situations.

The logic of ethical relativism extends to cumulative religious-cultural perceptions on goodness. Religious faiths and cultural beliefs mandate people follow the rule of the society. It argues that: "When you are in Rome, do as the Romans do." Religious-cultural relativists would argue that businesses should implement the ethical value systems of the host countries, while they are operating in those countries. In addition, ethical relativists claim that when any two individuals or two cultures hold different ethical views of a sociocultural value systems, both can be right on the basis of circumstances of time, place, and their own people's beliefs.

Different ethical views are products of religious faiths, cultural beliefs, and political ideologies. Thus, a mode or trend of behavior can be right for a person or one society, and the same action, taken in the same way, may be wrong for another person or society, and yet the two persons or societies are equally correct. For example, some members of our society believe that the business of abortion is immoral and unethical because viewed as murder and it is a sinful action. Others who are pro-choice believe that abortion is morally and ethically permissible because it is purely related to a woman's choice and desire to have or not have a child. The differences are rooted in their religious faiths, econo-political ideological beliefs, and sociocultural value systems. These differences are examples of transcultural, multicultural, and intracultural relativism.

Another example, in a culture with a religious pro-family value system like Moslem nations and Mormons in the United States with many socially advantaged men and economically disadvantaged women will probably look on monogamy as an ethical behavior while in other nations with equal econo-political opportunities for both men and women with approximately equal number of men and women perceive it as an unethical behavior. However, in the Moslem communities adultery is a greatest sin, which God never forgives the sinner, while in other cultures it is forgivable through confession to religious authorities. Therefore, judgment on adultery could be related to the religious faiths.

Different Types of Ethical Relativism

Many people express their judgment on the basis of their rational reasoning. In some cultures an action or judgment may be right for one person or society, and the same action or judgment, taken in the same manner, may be wrong for another person or society. What is exactly meant by these claims? Frankena (1973: 109) stated:

> We must distinguish at least three forms of ethical relativism First, there is what may be called *descriptive relativism*. When careful, it does not say merely that ethical judgments of different people and societies are different. ... Second, there is *meta-ethical relativism,* which is the view we must consider. It holds that, in the case of basic ethical judgments, there is no objectivity valid, rational way of justifying one against another; consequently, two conflicting basic judgments may be equally valid. The third form is *normative relativism* While descriptive relativism makes an anthropological or sociological assertion and meta-ethical relativism a meta-ethical one, this form of relativism puts forward a normative relativism a meta-ethical one, ... of relativism puts forward a normative principle: what is right or good for one individual or society is not right or good for another...

Therefore, ethical relativism theory has some unpleasant implications. First, sometimes it may ignore universal humanitarian value systems. Second, ethical relativists believe that ethical development and progress exist. Thus, we cannot say that our codes of ethics today will be viable for tomorrow; because we will be changed, our society will be changed, consequently, our codes of ethics ought to be changed too.

Pros and Cons For Relativism Business Ethics

The beliefs concerning ethical relativism reasoning reflect many dimensions in the field of business. Buchholz and Rosenthal (1988: 5) indicated that proponents of ethical relativism theory believe that:

> (1) Business must accommodate itself to social change if it expects to survive; (2) business must take a long-run or enlightened view of self-interest and help solve social problems in order to create a better environment for itself; (3) business can gain a better public image by being socially responsible; (4) government regulation can be avoided if business can meet the changing social

expectations of society before the issues become politicized; (5) business has enormous resources that would be useful in solving social problems; (6) social problems can be turned into profitable business opportunities; and (7) business has a moral obligation to help solve social problems that it has created or at least perpetuated.

Conclusions

Since ethics deals with theories of justice and injustice, the meaning of fairness and unfairness, worthiness and unworthiness, rightness and wrongness depend on operative judgments in certain situations. Through reviewing the historical cultural value systems around the world, no attempt is made to pass judgments on the basis of superiority or inferiority of these various ethical reasoning. Therefore, ethical relativists hold that the matter of ethics is a conditional operative one in different parts of the world or in different institutions. Consequently they believe that this type of reasoning is neutral because it does not advocate one set of ethical values over another it depends on specific circumstances.

DEONTOLOGICAL ETHICAL THEORY

Deontos in Greek means obligations or duties. The foundation of deontological ethical theory is based on reasoning on the basis of duties or obligations to self and others. Deontologicalists believe in standardization of prevailing moral principles. For example, if you believe honesty is a moral principle, and then nobody should interpret it differently (honesty is honesty). In the field of business, buyers and sellers are obligated to be truthful to each other in terms of their trading contractual conditions. Deontologicalists reject having different alternative choices in interpretation of specified rational reasoning for moral and ethical decisions and actions if just causes are clearly known for all parties.

Deontologicalists believe that application of different principles in similar cases for moral and ethical judgments can cause mixed outcomes (double standards). Through an ethical belief, harming self and others is immoral and unethical. They insist that an individual must always avoid harming self and others, whereas teleologicalists assume that harming self and/or others will sometimes be necessary to proceed for consequential goodness.

Deontological ethical theory is known as causal or nonconsequential ethics. Many ethicists have argued that the moral rightness of a decision and an action is determined by means but not solely by its ends. They believe that if the means of a decision and an action are good, then the ends will be good. If they are bad, the ends will be wrong. Ethicists who adopted this approach are therefore called deontologicalists or causalists. They believe that the right act is the one that initiates and applies the right principles, to precede it in the right direction, and to conclude it with the right ends.

Philosopher Joseph Butler (1692-1752), (1949: 45) who is known as one of the proponents of deontological ethics states:

> Any plain honest man, before he engages in any course of action, asks himself, is this I am going about right, or is it wrong? ... I do not in the least doubt but that this question would be answered agreeably to truth and virtue, by almost any fair man in almost any circumstance [without any general rule].

In addition, Butler in his philosophical reasoning holds that the ground for morality is "conscience." In his ethical deontological theory, conscience is conceived as a reflective or rational faculty that discerns the moral characteristics of actions. Consequently, he is not a defender of the popular votes in a society concerning the rightness or wrongness of a conduct. His conception of ethics is closer to this view that to the one in which conscience is understood as a name for mere reasoning of approval or disapproval due to psychological and social conditioning. For him, the judgments of conscience are not based on sensational or emotional feelings, but on moral reason.

Principles of Deontological Ethical Theory

There are certain fundamental ethical means by application of deontological theory of ethics. These principles are as follows:

- Deontologicalists believe that an ethical individual should be sincere in his/her faith and reasonableness in judgments.
- Deontological ethical theory is known as a causal or nonconsequential ethics.
- Deontologists argue that the moral rightness of a decision and an action is determined by the means but not solely by their ends.
- Deontologicalists contend that more than the likely consequences of an action determines right and wrong decisions and actions.
- Deontological theory of ethics maintains that we must act on the bases of truthful principles of morality regardless of what the consequential results will emerge.
- Deontologicalists view ethics as manifestation of causal reasoning for the truthfulness, righteousness, and goodness of decisions and judgments.
- Deontologicalists believe in three characteristics that are considered to be usually associated with good judgments. First, ethical judgments about the righteousness or wrongness of an action are held to be universally applicable. Second, being truthful and honest can be logically derived from the basic principles of all ethical systems. Third, mutual understanding concerning rules or principles that govern decisions and actions should be observed by all involved parties.

- Much of deontological theory is also termed universalism. The first duty of universalism is to treat others as means and not as ends. Other people should be seen as valuable ends in themselves, worthy of dignity and respect, and not as impersonal means to achieve our own ends.

Arguments

Deontologicalists contend that more than the likelihood of consequences of actions determines right and wrong actions. They do not necessarily deny that consequences are morally significant, but they believe that other factors including intentions with good faith and good-will are also relevant to the ethical decision-making processes and actions. They hold that there are some principles for distinguishing right judgments and/or actions from wrong. For example, a CEO of a corporation should not deceive his/her stakeholders by showering them with falsified profitability reporting figures and urge them to keep their stock options and then give away a portion and/or all of their stakeholders' assets for charity purposes (good-will). In this case, he/she has violated the principles of trust and obligation regardless of the consequential good end-results of his/her actions. Executive Ken Lay from Enron Corporation had been educated in very good schools and knew many econo-political authorities. He knew where to shop and always looked for the best deal. But he encouraged his employees to buy Enron's stock while he and other Enron executives sold their own stocks around $80.00 per share as the best price and then declared bankruptcy for Enron with $ 0.20 per share for Enron's employees and stockholders. This indicates not only how corporate corruption and deception in the American business environment contaminated giant businesses, but also manifests a vice and degradation of managerial action within corporate professional management systems.

Deontological theory of ethics maintains that we must act on the basis of truthful principles of morality regardless consequential results. We must judge ethical issues in our society regardless of a group's interests or majority and minority votes of people. We need to look at what really promotes the greatest goodness for oneself and the world of humanity.

There are two deontological philosophers whose views are related to obligatory principles of right, ought, and duty. These philosophers are George Edward Moore (1873-1958) and William David Ross (1877-1971). Moore (1948: vii) stated in his *Principa Ethica*:

> It appears to me that Ethics, as in all other philosophical studies, the difficulties and disagreements, of which its history is full, are mainly due to a very simple cause: namely to the attempt to answer questions, without first discovering precisely *what* question it is which you desire to answer. I do not know how far this source of error would be done away, if philosophers would *try* to discover what question they were asking, before they set about to answer it; for the work of analysis and discussion is often very difficult: we may often fail to make the necessary discovery, even though we make a definite attempt to do so. But I am

inclined to think that in many cases, a resolute attempt would be sufficient to ensure success; so that, if only this attempt were made, many of the most glaring difficulties and disagreements in philosophy would disappear.

In addition, Moore found, upon his analysis, "What is intrinsically good?" that, is, what is good unconditionally and invariable? He found that the question is in fact two questions, namely: "How is good to be defined?" and "What things are good?" Moore (1922: 273) insisted: "We must analyze the former before we address ourselves to the latter." He concludes that *good* is *indefinable*, but the term good refers to a property of things. He explains that the term *good* refers to a quality that is analogous in some ways to sensory qualities. The principle objective of goodness consists in its being intrinsic, that is, it is unchanging and absolute. When anything possesses it, it would necessary, under all circumstances, possess it in exactly the same manner. In sum, Moore determined that the ethical characteristics of human perception and behavior depend upon either self-evidence or external-evidence.

The deontological views of William David Ross resemble that of G. E. Moore in terms of intrinsic goodness to be defined as the quality of things. There is a decisive difference between them concerning the concept of obligation: In Moore's views the concept of obligations indicate rights, oughts, and duties that are linked to maximizing intrinsic goodness. In Ross's views there is no such linkage. Ross contents that rightness is a distinct and identifiable characteristic of an act and is generally independent of whatever good may result from their occurrence.

In Ross's arguments for ethical intuitionism, he insisted that the difference between what he termed prima facie (first appearance at the first glance), and *actual* duties make all difference. For example, if in the field of business, I promise to a customer to deliver specific merchandise on a certain time and date, I thereby create an ethical obligatory claim on myself in that customer. I know immediately within the boundary of my ethical principle, I ought to keep that promise and that I ought to reciprocate in some way. Ross perceived such an act which has the characteristic of generating ethical claims as prima facie duty. Therefore, deontological ethicists believe that our *prima facie* duties do not arise in prearranged harmony of ranked priority and/or nor do they occur singly. Nevertheless, some *prima facie* duties have a greater claim on us than others. As Ross (1930: 41) insists, in his book *The Right and the Good*: "A great deal of stringency belongs to the duties of 'perfect obligation' the duties of keeping our promises, of repairing wrongs we have done, and of returning the equivalent of services we have received." Thus, there are circumstances in which beneficence takes precedence over all other considerations. Ross's deontological views on obligations conclude that the following:

- All other ethical theories fail to recognize the complex relations involved in circumstances of obligations.
- The basic concept of *prima facie* includes a catalogue of many types of duty.
  - Some duties rest on previous acts of ourselves: implicit

- promises and duty of fidelity.
  - Some rest on previous acts of others: duties of gratitude.
  - Some rest on the fact or responsibility of a distribution of pleasure or pleasant: duties of justice.
  - Some rest on the mere fact that there are other beings in the world whose condition we can make better in respect of goodness: duties of beneficence.
  - Some rest on the fact that we can improve our own condition in respect of goodness or intelligence; duties of self-improvement.
- It is a mistake to regard every dutiful act as being for one and the same reason We need to make a distinction between prima facie and actual duty.

Deontologicalists believe in specific conditional characteristics that are considered to be usually associated with good judgments. First, ethical judgments about the righteousness or wrongness of an action are held to be universally applicable. Through the conscious intellectual cognizance of an individual, if an action is right for an individual, it should also be right for anyone else in the same manner. If it is wrong for everybody, it is also wrong for anyone else in similar occasions. They hold that general ethical principles can be applied on the basis of particular similar cases and may then be useful in determining what should be done on later occasions. However, it cannot be allowed that a causal principle rule may ever supersede a well-taken particular judgment as to what should be done.

Pros and Cons of Deontological Business Ethics

In the field of international business, the universal ethical rule says that it is wrong to bribe or to promote bribery for gaining an illegitimate interest or profit. It is a universal factual principle, because it corrupts the dignity and integrity of humanity and such unethical and corruptive action may apply to everyone anywhere else. Therefore, there are some universal principles that are central parts of an ethical marketing campaign. De George (1995: 256) states:

> The deontological approach to managerial ethics is the This universal truthfulness of ethical principles in advertising is: the immorality of untruthful, misleading, or deceptive advertising, the immorality of manipulation and coercion through advertising, the immorality of preventing some kinds of advertising, and the allocation and distribution of moral responsibility with respect to advertising.

reverse of teleological theory. Deontological ethical theory states that the moral worth of a decision and an action cannot be dependent upon the outcomes because those outcomes are so indefinite and uncertain at the time the decision to act is made. Instead the moral worth of an action has to depend upon the intentions of the person making the decision or performing the act. Another deontological approach is from the perspective of religion. If I wish the best for others, then my moral actions are praiseworthy, even though I happen to be an ineffectual and clumsy individual who always seems to be breaking something or hurting someone.

Personal intentions can be translated into personal duties or obligations because, if we truly wish the best for others, then we always will act in certain ways to ensure beneficial results. It is our duty to tell the truth. It is our duty to adhere to the terms of contracts. It is our duty not to take property that belongs to others. Truthfulness and honesty can be logically derived from the basic principles of all ethical systems. Within the principle context of deontological theory, there are some duties that we owe to others, while in teleological theory they are the actions that bring the greatest benefits to others. Deontological system is based on rules or principles that govern decisions and actions. In this formalistic view of ethics, the rightness of an act depends little on the results of the act.

Different Types of Deontological Ethical Theory

Deontological ethics emphasizes on decisions rather than intuitions. This, also, is the view of most existentialist philosophers. Existentialists, led by the famed Jean-Paul Sartre (1905-1980), believe standards of conduct cannot be rationally justified and no actions are inherently right or wrong. This view finds its roots in the notion that humans are only what we will ourselves to be. Sartre's famous interpretation of existence describes existence before essence. Sartre (1947: 27) stated:

> If existence really does precede essence; there are no explaining things away by reference to a fixed and given human nature. In other words, there is no determinism, man is free, and man is freedom. ... So in the bright realm of values, we have no excuse behind us, nor justification before us. We are alone, with no existence.

Thus, existentialism holds that what people are, is a function of the choices they make, not that the choices they make are function of what they are. Each of us is free, with no rules to turn to guidance. Just as we all choose our own nature, so must we choose our own ethical percepts? Therefore, each person may reach his/her own choice about ethical principles. In less extreme form, there are two types of deontologicalism: (1) rule deontologicalism, and (2) act deontologicalism.

Rule Deontologicalism: In choosing and judging on every ethical issue according to rule deontologicalism, one is at least able to first establish mechanical principles and reasoning rules. This suggests that in similar ethical circumstances applying the rules and principles is a viable foundation for the treatment of self and others similarly. Usually, rule deontologicalism holds that the expected ethical principles and rules consist of a number of rather specific criteria like those of telling the truth or keeping promises as always to act in such a certain kind of action.

Rule deontologists hold that the standard of right and wrong consists of one or more rules. We ought to tell the truth. It cannot be right for A to treat B in a manner in which it would be wrong for B to treat A, merely on the ground that they are two different individuals, and without there being any difference between the natures or circumstances of the two which can be stated as reasonable ground for difference of treatment.

Act Deontologicalism: Act deontologicalism holds that ethical behavior must follow ethical rules. The main point about act deontologicalism is that it does offer us expected intellectual standards concerning the recognition of right or wrong intentions and decisions in particular circumstances. It spells out particular ethical judgments concerning similar cases that are basic and general rules that are to be derived from them, not the other way around. Rule deontologicalism provides people with actual pragmatic standards to be followed. In the case that there are no ethical rules then we need to act on the basis of the rule of thumb (moral conscience).

Conclusions

In sum, deontological views of ethics are concerned about causal reasoning for the truthfulness, righteousness, and goodness of decisions and judgments:

- They are not concerned about the applicability of consequential results in pre-judgments about right or wrong actions. These ethicists focus their attention on the right causes regardless of consequences. For example, shoplifting is viewed as an unethical, immoral, and illegal action by all means and ends. It is a wrong action regardless the motive or circumstances of the shoplifter.
- Ethics is a cultural value judgment and overrides other considerations. We are ethically bound to do what sometimes we may not want to do.
- Ethical judgments should properly direct the individual's behavior towards morally right actions, and moral blame can properly accompany acting immorally. Therefore, while morality is considered a personal goodness of an individual, ethics is the collective intellectual goodness of a cultural value system of a group of people.

Since moral theories provide us with freedom of choice based upon consciousness judgments, they indicate that all moral convictions seem to vary from person to person. The most serious objection, perhaps, is the fact that the ethical rules of a society may be good or bad, moral or immoral, right or wrong, just or unjust, fair or unfair, and enhancing or impoverishing of human life. Through moral rules, we have agreed on one ground or another that the moral standards have offered us with alternative choices. In general, these choices have been two sorts: (1) deontological and (2) teleological. We already have analyzed the deontological ethical theory, now we will turn to the teleological analysis in the next pages.

TELEOLOGICAL ETHICAL THEORY

Telos in Greek means goals or results. As defined by the Roman Stoic philosopher Epicurus (336-264 B.C.), (1866) ethics deals with those things to be sought and those things to be avoided, with ways of life and with the *telos*. *Telos* is the chief aim or end in life. It measures the outcome or result of a course of decisions and actions in human activities.

Teleological ethicists hold that the position of moral ground and ethical worth of managers is solely related to the consequences of their behavior. This means, if a decision and an action are right, then their results should be right too, and if decisions and actions were right but the outcomes were wrong then such a managerial discourse can not be ethically right. For example, the Enron CEOs' behavior (as inside traders) in selling their own stocks on time and making huge profits as a consequence of a conspiracy and fraudulent acts by the auditing firm Arthur Andersen, was right on the basis of moral egoism for the CEOs, but from the perspective of the employees' pension funds was unethical. Such managerial behavior described above is rarely defended publicly. People reluctance are to be publicly identified with such a dishonest managerial decision and action given the widespread negative feelings about selfishness and chauvinism in our society, because while it may be legal, it is unethical.

Teleological ethicists are unconcerned with intentions, decisions, and actions, but they are severely sensitive to the consequences of such a holistic process. They judge the ethicality, on the basis of the duty or obligation out of which the impulse to act arises. In sum, teleological ethicists hold that the rightness or wrongness of an ethical issue is determined by the results that these processes produce.

Principles of Teleological Ethical Theory

Teleological theory indicates that the basic or ultimate criterion or standard of what is ethically right, wrong, obligatory, etc., is the ethical and unethical norms that are brought into being by decision makers and operators with their final end-results. The final appeal, directly or indirectly, must be to the comparative amount of good produced, or rather to the comparative balance of good over evil produced the ethical worth of a managerial behavior based on the consequences of the integrated intentions, decisions, and actions. Thus, an act is right for a manager if it meets the following criteria:

- They produce some good results for all involved parties.

- The end-result is based on the extension of corporate social responsibility to discover legitimate opportunities through usage of its resources in order to increase quality of products along side of its profits. It is ethical if a manager continues an action as long as he/she stays within the honest rule of competition without greed, deception, and fraud.
- It does not corrupt the public image and ruthlessly rub out honest businesses.
- The elementary canons of face-to-face managerial civility (honesty, good-faith, good-will, and good-ends) are observed.
- Anti-fraud, anti-deception, anti-force, anti-corruption, and anti-pollution are valued in the course of any and all contractual agreements between traders and buyers and sellers.
- Open and free competition on the basis of win and win strategies between buyers and sellers through profit optimization strategy are promoted.
- The corporation is legally known not only as an artificial person, but also has a social conscience to provide effective employment, eliminate discrimination, avoid pollution, and respect the laborer's rights.

In sum, a business relies on the ideal that what we see, we believe.

Arguments

The usual approach to analyze foundational beliefs in ethical theories is to present greater detail on causal means or consequential ends or the content of motives and practices of ethics. The teleological approach in managerial ethics places complete emphasis upon the basis of practical measurable consequences of decision-making processes and actions, not the intent and/or decisions of an action by managers about. According to the teleological ethical theory, managers should be concerned with these questions:

- What sort of consequences is relevant to determining right and wrong actions?
- What consequences are they seeking for whom?

Let us look at this latter question first. Suppose for a moment that we have agreed that a CEO's objective is to make profit. Then the question becomes: Whose profit is it that determines whether the CEO's behavior is ethically right or wrong? Managers may give two basically different kinds of answers to this question:

- Mutual profits for all statekeholders in a corporation
- Profits for the personal benefit of the CEOs and their affiliated interest

groups

The teleologicalists would hold that every stakeholder interest is relevant to others according to the ethical principles. In contrast to this, the other kind of consequences, which might be called, restricted profits, which would be unethical. The teleological ethicists hold that every stakeholder profit is relevant to each other.

The teleological ethical theory assesses the general public opinion concerning ethical and unethical business transactions through the results of the Gallup Poll, which surveys the public's opinions of the ethics of major corporations in the United States. Survey data from the fall 2000 Gallop Poll on Honest/Ethics in the Professions reveals that the honesty of American executives are thought to be high by only 22 percent of those surveyed. Over the past decade, this percentage has fluctuated between a low of 17 percent in 1996 and a high of 22 percent in 2000. It will be interesting to see the data after the collapse of two giant corporations: Enron and Kmart. The Gallop Poll shows specific groups of businesspeople rank even lower than the general category of business executives. Among those specific groups are real estate agents, stockbrokers, advertising practitioners, insurance salespeople, and car salespeople (Carroll and Buchholtz, 2003: 167).

The above survey result of the Gallop Poll is not surprising because as we mentioned before, the American business system functions on the basis of amorality to express a portion of truth not the whole. Nevertheless, the survey reveals the troubling fact that a majority of consumers have lost their faith in the integrity of businesspeople and expect businesses to observe ethics.

From the standpoint of ethicists a specific question will arise: How can the magnitude of the business ethics problem be more detectable today that it once was before? To answer this question, one must assess the consequences of both "descriptive business ethics" and "prescriptive business ethics" through the value judgments by people have made about the practice or behavior of corporate executive officers (CEOs). We need to know what we mean by consequentialist business ethics.

Teleological business ethics assesses the consequences of managerial decisions and actions as they have been observed and evaluated. This theory does not rely on what a corporation is saying in its mission. Instead, they examine what a corporation is doing. For example, the mission statement of Johnson & Johnson Company (http://www.jni.com/who_is_jnj/cr_usa.html) addresses its corporate beliefs about principles of responsibility to:

The doctors, nurses, and patients, to parents and all others who use our products and services ... to our employees, the men and women who work with us ... to communities in which we live and work and to the world community as well.

In practice, by evaluating Johnson & Johnson's operation, we have found that there is a discrepancy in what they believe and in what they operate.

Johnson & Johnson is under investigation by the Security Exchange Commission for possible "book-cooking" of profit in order to maintain its value of stocks very high.

The Multinational Monitor (1996) reported that approximately 17 percent of the corporate executives who attended the White House Conference on Corporate Citizenship in May 1996 were CEOs of corporations with criminal records corporations that have been convicted of everything from price-fixing to pollution, from procurement fraud to obstruction of justice. Among them was Johnson & Johnson's CEO Ralph Larsen. In January 1995, Johnson & Johnson's Ortho Pharmaceutical Corp. unit pled guilty to ten counts of obstruction of justice and destruction of documents in connection with a federal probe of the company's marketing of an anti-acne cream. This indicates how some corporations violate their mission for the sake of greed.

Conclusion

The teleological ethical theory focuses on the result of what a corporation has done in practice. In sum, teleological business ethics relies on what we see, we believe. In other words, how do we get from what is to what ought to be? Or what makes a business issue ethically right is the good that is produced by the outcomes of intentions, decisions, and actions, not the sole nature of the declared mission. Teleological ethical managerial approach appraises the net consequences of decisions and actions, not the individual's or group's intentions.

The teleological ethicists do not hold that intentional, decisional, and operational processes possess intrinsic values in and of themselves, but all processes must be evaluated in terms of their consequential values and vices, or good and bad consequences that they produce. The teleological ethicists hold that rules have to be followed not because of acknowledged obligations but because of the fear of punishment for breaking those rules. They are concerned with avoiding harm to the self rather than gaining benefits for self. These people believe that since cultural values are varied from culture to culture, then it is relevant to judge an ethical value system based on their outcomes in relationship to the cultural and religious standards.

The origin of an ethical action -- its efficiency, not its final cause -- is based on choice, and that choice is a desire to rationalize its ends. Ethically, the primary ethical act of a good choice and good will is *devotion*. *Devotion* is promptness to do whatever pertains to the manifestation of a good end via a good choice. An act of devotion is the most important end of the behavior of intellectual virtues. This is why good and right choices cannot exist either without wisdom and intellect or without a purified emotional state of harmony between mind and body. Good decisions and actions cannot exist without a combination of intellect and character. Intellect and wisdom themselves, however, move nothing, but only the wisdom and intellect which aim at an end through the human sensational and emotional body dynamics are practical movements through the synergistic combination of personal and social embodiment of cultural value systems.

Teleological ethical theorists reject the absolute universal ethical commitments because they believe that there are exceptional circumstances that can reverse a good action to bad or vice versa. For example, in the field of business, shoplifting is not moral, ethical, or legal. However, there are some people who believe that if a hungry person who really does not have any income to buy some foods such as fruits and bread and the like is subject to special circumstances, and if he/she consumes food in a grocery store without money, such an action is not viewed as shoplifting. It is viewed as sampling not from packages, but from open shelves of fruits and nuts. In addition, teleologicalists believe that in all circumstances means cannot justify ends. Therefore, ethical judgments should be focused on the end-results. As deontologicalists are pro-absolutism, teleologicalists are pro-relativism.

UTILITARIAN ETHICAL THEORY

In analyzing different logical arguments concerning ethical theories, we already have reviewed three theories: relativism, deontologicalism, and teleologicalism. Now we are turning to another ethical theory known as utilitarnianism. For those that value costs/benefits assessments within holistic intentional motives, decision-making processes, pragmatic operations, and measurable consequences they may appreciate the utility of having good things in their businesses. Speaking briefly, the relativism theorists focus on a variety of principles that indicate that there is no absolute ethical standard for having a happy life. Having a happy life depends on variable perceptions within multicultural value systems. Multiculturalism identifies a variety of reasons to believe in diversity among nations. This indicates what is right in one cultural context may not be right in another one. From another perspective, the teleological ethical theorists focus upon the net consequences of ethical means and ends. They believe that business ethics needs to be concern only with the net profit.

The deontologicalists focus upon application of ethical principles during decision-making processes and actions. Deontologicalists believe in standardization of prevailing moral principles. For example, if you believe honesty is a moral principle, and then nobody should interpret it differently (honesty is honesty).

Utilitarianism ethical theorists believe that all three ethical theories, relativism, deontologicalism, and teleologicalism, do not take the promotion of good businesses seriously enough. Also, utilitarianism eliminates the problem of possible conflict of basic ethical principles. They question: "What could be more plausible than the right to promote the general good for the greatest number of people?" They answer to this question with such a reasoning: The major point is that an act may be made right or wrong by the facts surrounding it, rather than the amount of good or evil it produces. This indicates that an act is not only moral or immoral it may be amoral. This argument opens new doors to the field of business that a manager's job in a competitive marketplace is not to reveal all corporate secrets to the public. Nevertheless, this does not mean that he/she should lie or deceive people. But he/she may act amorally to disclose a portion of the truth not the whole. This is the exact meaning of utilitarianism business ethics.

Principles of Utilitarianism Ethical theory

Philosopher Jeremy Bentham was motivated by the idea that "the Public Good" ought to be the object of the legislator General Utility ought to be the foundation of reasoning. McCollum (1998: A28) states:

> Bentham is often thought of as the founder of utilitarianism. The school of philosophy that holds that the purpose of government is to foster the happiness of the individual, and that the greatest happiness of the most people should be the goal of human existence.

To implement this social and political ideal, people need to measure pleasures and pains. In this way good and bad acts can be evaluated in terms of such factors as intensity, duration, and extent. Bentham (1838: 16) composed the following verse to aid the student in remembering the criteria of utilitarian measurement:

Intense, long, certain, speedy, fruitful, pure
Such marks in pleasures and pains endure.
Such pleasures seek, the private be thy end:
If it be public, wide let them extend.
Such pains avoid, whichever be thy view:
If pains must come, let them extend to few.

Utilitarianism ethicists such as Jeremy Bentham (1838) and John Stuart Mill tried (1806-1873), (1897) to work out an algebraic assessment in assessing pleasure and pain by using nine principles as follows:

- *Intensity* means vehement thoughts and feelings towards extreme degree of pleasure and avoidance of pain (but not disappearance of pain).
- *Duration* means continuance in time for having pleasurable time.
- *Certainty* means having confidence and assurance without doubt concerning the whole assessment of pleasure and pain. Such a course of judgment can establish further truthful and indisputable basis for goodness.
- *Propinquity* means appreciation of the nearness or proximity of pleasurable experiences for experiencing continuous goodness.
- *Fecundity* means the quality of producing a great number of pleasurable experiences and minimizing the greatest number of

painful ones.

- *Purity* means the condition of being free of evil and the freedom from extraneous matter or quality of pleasure that can enhance our spirit.
- *Extent* means the space or degree to which a pleasurable act to be continued.

Another utilitarianism ethicist John Stuart Mill added two more dimensions into assessments of pleasures and pains as follows:

- *Quality* means the extreme usefulness and utility of a pleasurable judgment with respect towards excellence.
- *Quantity* means identification of an infinite great amount of pleasurable judgments or actions accordance with a set of defined consistent rules.

Therefore, utilitarian ethicists hold that what is ethically right or wrong is ultimately to be wholly judged quantitatively by looking to see what promotes the greatest general balance of good over evil.

Utilitarian Business Ethics

A utilitarian approach in business ethics can be extremely helpful in thinking through an ethical dilemma. In sum, utilitarian ethicists believe in the following principles:

- The greatest virtuous values over vices.
- The greatest balance of pleasure over pain.
- The greatest good for the greatest number of the population.
- The greatest profits over costs.
- The greatest benefits for the greatest number of employees.
- Whatever satisfies the principle of utility also satisfies the requirements of justice, since justice is built into the principle of utility.
- The greatest net amount of happiness over misery.
- Actions affect people to different degrees with different circumstances.
- To maximize happiness not immediately but in the long run.
- The most certain likelihood of happiness over as great a number as possible.
- No personal or societal issue will be remained unsolved, because in practice, utilitarianism provides some formulating and testing judgments.
- Utilitarianism provides an objective and attractive way of resolving conflicts of self-interest.
- Utilitarianism concerns itself with the total happiness produced over miserable means and consequences.

- Utilitarianism searches for sacrificing minority happiness over majority happiness.

Therefore, what the preceding suggests is that perhaps we should recognize two basic principles of obligation: the principle of utility and some principle of justice.

Arguments

The utilitarianism that is the essence of the thoughts of Jeremy Bentham is derived from the word *utility*. A utility value denotes that things are good because of their usefulness for some purposes. Hosmer (1987: 98) states:

> Such a perception has come from the eighteenth-century meaning that referred to the degree of usefulness of a household object or a domestic animal; that is, a horse could be said to have a utility for plowing beyond the cost of its upkeep. *Utility* has this same meaning, and this same derivation in microeconomic theory. It measures our degree of performance for a given good or service relative to price.

Therefore, utilities in reality should be assessed by cost/benefit analysis for both sellers and buyers, and have to be computed equitably for everyone. This means that in the field of business ethics, the seller's satisfaction cannot be considered to be more important in some way that the buyer's satisfactions. What is more important than the interests of buyers and sellers is the decisional-rule that is then followed to produce the greatest net benefit for society.

Utilitarianism holds that an act is right if, and only if, it produces the greatest net benefit for society over any other act possible under any circumstances. Utilitarianism differs from the economic concept of cost/benefit analysis in that the distribution of the costs and benefits has to be included as well. That is, these are net benefits to society, and each individual within the society has to be considered equitably in the decision-making processes and operations, and also needs to be treated equitably in the distribution of goodness.

Utilitarianism holds that the sole standard of right, wrong, and obligation is an observation of the principle of utility. It dictates quite strictly that the ethical means and ends to be sought in all courses of transactions should be based upon the greatest possible balance of good over evil or the least possible balance of evil over good as a whole. Utilitarianism lies in its promise to provide for the humane, tough-minded individual a way of resolving complex moral problems and disagreements by rational means. With such a perception, another question appears: "How within the context of ethics we can include the least evil?" The answer is whatever the good and the bad are, they are capable of being measured and balanced against each other in some quantitative or at least in an algebraic perceptual assessment.

Application of Utilitarianism in the Field of Business

There are two major views to be analyzed when utilitarian ethical objectives are considered: (1) obligations and (2) values. These two views assess: "Are means more important than ends or vice versa?" First, utilitarian ethicists hold that when we are faced with two dissimilar facts concerning the utility of a decision and/or an action, or in other words, by trying to see which decision and/or action is likely to produce the greatest balance of good over evil, then that decision and/or action will be ethical. This kind of judgment is called "*pragmatic act utilitarianism.*

For example, suppose you are a manager of a large corporation and faced with sudden economic hardship. You need to lay off some of your excess employees with "rightsizing," "turnaround," "cutback," or "downsizing" strategies on the basis of an assessment of balancing loses and gains. You need to decide which groups or individuals of employees with what general characteristics should be laid off. Such an assessment could be based upon "seniority" or "merit" and or both rankings. Lying off people is not good for an individual because he/she will probably be without income for a period of time. From the other side, if you assess this matter on the basis of keeping these employees on the corporations' pay-role system and instead decide to keep the corporation's profitability low, you are going to wipe out the interest of your stakeholders. According to the utilitarian principles, you may decide either to keep them or to lay them off whichever one will carry the better choice. In such a situation there are two emotional and rational principles. These two are sympathy and antipathy. A holder of these principles approves or disapproves of particular actions not because of their consequences, but simply because of whatever feelings of approval or disapproval the person happens to find in him or herself. Such feelings in themselves are claimed to be sufficient reasons for one's moral judgment. In the event that managers express that they base their ethical judgments upon the common sense of the fitness of things, intentions, decisions, or actions, they are usually basing their convictions on mere subjective feelings. Some people perceive that using such a common sense could be dangerous in a rational way. Perhaps they may lead to vicious consequences in the long term.

Conclusion

Application of the utilitarianism ethical theory remains particularly important in the field of business for a variety of reasons. First, utilitarian thinking underlies much of the business transactions on the basis of risk assessments C to gain or to lose. Second, the balance of cost/benefit assessments may hurt very badly a minority group. Consequently, there is always the possibility of justifying benefits for the greatest majority of population by imposing sacrifices or penalties on minorities. This may not violate the civil rights or the human rights of minorities, but will violate their natural rights.

Another difficulty with utilitarianism business ethics is that the rights of a minority group can easily be sacrificed for the benefit of the majority.

Through the utilitarian philosophy of social goodness, *economic-class*, ruling-class, and *lay-class* are three major terms that make ethical issues contentious. These concepts immediately put *money-power* and *elite-power* on guard. The idea of economically well-endowed and privileged classes of people may dominate the ruling-class and/or the lay-class and may go against the ethical grain of a society. Then, through the application of the utilitarian principles of the greatest good for the greatest number, we may face difficulty. To avoid such a difficulty it is necessary to establish and lodge constitutionally checks and balances against the ruling-class or power-elite class.

In addition to the above problems, it is often difficult to obtain the information required to evaluate all of the cost/benefit assessments for all individuals who may be directly or indirectly affected by an action or decision. Then our judgments may not be right or wrong.

Within the context of utilitarian costs/benefits analysis and the greatest profits for the greatest number, we will be exposed to variety of judgments such as: best, right, proper, suitable and beneficial. Managers should keep the following guidelines in their mind when they are handling cases of conflicting ideals, causes, processes, and effects:

- When two or more ideals conflict, honor is the best one.
- When two or more causes conflict, choose the right one.
- When two or more rival processes conflict, choose the proper one.
- When two or more effects conflict, choose the suitable one.
- When two or more obligations conflict with consequences, honor the more beneficial one (see Figure 4.3).

Nevertheless, the selection of one of the above attributes would make our judgments more difficult.

Best	Right	Proper	Suitable	Beneficial
I_____I_____I_____I_____I				

Figure 4.3: Different Attributions of Goodness

As a decision maker, a manager needs to be knowledgeable about all direct and indirect attributions related to an ethical issue. If after he/she makes a mistake, his/her excuses will not be convincing. Some managers who are not atoned to with ethical and moral problems, in order to get away from conscientious guilt, may claim that they did not know. It would sound innocent to present the claims that "I didn't intend that to happen," or "I honestly didn't consider that alternative," or "I just didn't know." Such claims are not acceptable within the context of utilitarian cost/benefit assessments. Plato, in the *Republic*, claimed that ignorance is an aspect of evil since it is the opposite of "being" (Plato: *Apology*). Using Plato's line of thoughts, the right to act ethically implies a responsibility not to speak and/or act from ignorance.

CHAPTER SUMMARY

Judging right and wrong decisions and actions can be assessed through two major dimensions: consequential end-results, and non-consequential or causal reasoning. In fact, the best way for us to proceed in working out such an endeavor with a deliberated breath is to review some of the main theories of ethics that have been proposed. Therefore, we have explained different theoretical platforms of ethicists concerning four major theories of ethics. These theories are: (1) relativism, (2) deontologicalism, (3) teleologicalism, and (4) utilitarianism.

A basic question is: "What is ethics in relation to absolutism or relativism logic?" That question raises another question: "Are there objective universal principles in the human race upon which one can construct an ethical system of cultural valuable belief, religious faith, and political ideology that would be applicable to all groups in all cultures at all times?" The answer is no.

Ethical relativism is not a fact, but a theory that attempts to prove fact. This theory arises from a failure to distinguish between universal moral rules, and particular moral judgments, from moral principles. Some people maintain that ethicality just does not boil down to the religious faiths. Others have argued that the doctrine of ethical relativism indicates that right and wrong are only a function of what a particular society takes to be right and wrong. There are some ethical principles concerning relativism: For the ethical relativists, there is no absolute ethical standard. Multicultural diversity value systems are the main causes for having ethical relativism theory. Because of multicultural differences among nations what is right in one cultural context may not be right in another one. The right and wrong are viewed only as a function of what a particular society takes to be right and wrong. The only ethical standard for judging an action is the ethical system of one society in which the act occurs. Ethical relativism depends on religious and/or cultural contexts, not on criteria for right and wrong by which to judge other than that of particular societies. Ethical relativism holds that no universal standards or rules can be used to guide or appraise an ethical decision or action.

Deontos in Greek means obligations or duties. The foundation of deontological ethical theory is based on reasoning on the basis of duties or obligations to self and others. Deontologicalists believe in the standardization of prevailing moral principles. Deontologicalists believe that application of different principles in similar cases for moral and ethical judgments can cause mixed outcomes (double standards). Through an ethical belief, harming self and others is immoral and unethical. They insist that an individual must always avoid harming self and others, whereas teleologicalists assume that harming self and/or others will sometimes be necessary to proceed for consequential goodness. There are certain fundamental ethical means by application of deontological theory of ethics. These principles are: Deontologicalists believe that an ethical individual should be sincere in his/her faith and reasonable in judgments. Deontological ethical theory is known as a causal or nonconsequential ethics. Deontologicalits argue that the moral rightness of a decision is determined by the means but not solely by their ends. Deontologicalists contend that more than the likely consequences of an action determines right and wrong decisions and actions. Deontological theory of ethics maintains that we must act on the bases of truthful principles of morality regardless of what the consequential results will emerge. Deontologicalists view ethics as a manifestation of causal reasoning for the truthfulness, righteousness, and goodness of decisions and judgments. They believe in three characteristics that are considered to be usually associated with good judgments. First, ethical judgments about the righteousness or wrongness of an action are held to be universally applicable. Second, being truthful and honest can be logically derived from the basic principles of all ethical systems. Third, mutual understanding concerning rules or principles that govern decisions and actions should be observed by all involved parties. Much of deontological theory is also termed with universalism. The first duty of universalism is to treat others as ends and not as means. Other people should be seen as valuable ends in themselves, worthy of dignity and respect, and not as impersonal means to achieve our own ends.

Telos in Greek means goals or results. Teleological ethicists have held that the position of moral ground and the ethical worth of managers are solely related to the consequences of their behavior. This means, if a decision and an action are right, then their results should be right too, and if decisions and actions were right but the outcomes were wrong then such a managerial discourse can not be ethically right. Teleological theory indicates that the basic or ultimate criterion or standard of what is ethically right, wrong, obligatory, etc., is the ethical and unethical norms that are brought into being by decision makers and operators with their final end-results. The final appeal, directly or indirectly, must be to the comparative amount of good produced, or rather to the comparative balance of good over evil produced. Thus, an act is right for a manager and ethically right or acceptable if they produce some good results for all parties. The ethical worth of managerial behavior is based on the consequences of the integrated intentions, decisions, and actions. If the end-result is based on the extension of corporate social responsibility to discover legitimate opportunities through usage of its resources in order to increase quality of products along side of its profits, then it is ethical. A manager's action is ethical as long as he/she stays within the honest rule of competition without greed, deception, or fraud. Immoral and unethical lines of businesses corrupt the public image and ruthlessly rub out honest businesses. Therefore, a corporation has a major ethical objective to obey the elementary canons of face-to-face managerial civility (honesty, good-faith, good-will, and good-ends). To be ethical a corporation must value anti-fraud, anti-deception, anti-force, anti-corruption, and anti-pollution in the course of any and all contractual agreements between buyers and sellers. It must promote open and free competition on the basis of win -- win strategies between buyers and sellers through profit optimization. A corporation should be legally known as an "artificial person," and in addition it has a "social conscience" to provide effective employment, eliminate discrimination, avoid pollution, and respect the laborer's rights. In sum, a business relies on what we see it and what we believe it.

Utilitarianism ethical theorists believe that all three ethical theories, relativism, deontologicalism, and teleologicalism, do not take the promotion of good businesses seriously enough. Also, utilitarianism eliminates the problem of possible conflicts of basic ethical principles. They question: "What could be more plausible than the right to promote the general good for the greatest number of people?" They answer to this question with such a reasoning: "The major point is that an act may be made right or wrong by the facts surrounding it rather than the amount of good or evil it produces." This indicates that an act is not only moral or immoral; it may be it could be amoral. This argument opens new doors to the field of business that a manager's job in a competitive marketplace is not to reveal all corporate secrets to the public. Nevertheless, this does not mean that he/she should lie or deceive people. But he/she may act amorally to disclose a portion of the truth not the whole. This is the exact meaning of utilitarianism business ethics.

Utilitarianism ethicists tried to work out an algebraic assessment in assessing pleasure and pain by using nine principles as: *Intensity* means vehement thoughts and feelings towards extreme degree of pleasure and avoidance of pain (but not disappearance of pain).

Duration means continuance in time for having pleasurable time. *Certainty* means having confidence and assurance without doubt concerning the whole assessment of pleasure and pain. Such a course of judgment can establish further truthful and indisputable basis for goodness. *Propinquity* means appreciation of the nearness or proximity of pleasurable experiences for experiencing continuous goodness.

Fecundity means the quality of producing a great number of pleasurable experiences and minimizing the greatest number of painful ones. *Purity* means the condition of being free of evil and the freedom from extraneous matter or quality of pleasure that can enhance our spirit. *Extent* means the space or degree to which a pleasurable acts to be continued.

Quality means the extreme usefulness and utility of a pleasurable judgment with respect towards excellence. *Quantity* mean identification of an infinite great amount of pleasurable judgments or actions according with a set of defined consistent rules.

In sum, utilitarian ethicists believe in the following principles: The greatest virtuous values over vices. The greatest balance of pleasure over pain results in the greatest good for the greatest number of population. The greatest profits over costs results it he greatest benefits for the greatest number of the employees. Whatever satisfies the principle of utility also satisfies the requirements of justice. Since justice is built into the principle of utility consequently the greatest net amount of happiness results over misery. Actions affect people to different degrees with different circumstances. To maximize happiness not immediately but in the long run. The most certain likelihood of happiness is viewed as great in numbers. No personal or societal issue will be remained unsolved, because in practice, utilitarianism provides some formulating and testing judgments. Utilitarianism provides an objective and attractive way of resolving conflicts of self-interest. Utilitarianism concerns itself with the total happiness produced over miserable means and consequences.

QUESTIONS FOR DISCUSSION

- Is there any ethical theory to be single objectively oriented toward the ultimate end that is human happiness? Explain.
- What is the hierarchical ordering rank of happiness according to the utilitarianism ethical theory?
- What are the bases for being ethical according to the ethical theory of deontologicalism?
- What is the major reasoning for constituting the relativism ethical theory concerning goodness?
- Is there any evil action in the utilitarianism ethical theory? If yes, what is it?
- Are there any evil intentions and/or actions in teleological ethical theory? If yes, what are they?
- What is teleological human happiness?
- What is utilitarian ethical happiness?
- Which theory suggests that human ethicality cannot be completed?
- Explain the difference between morality and ethics according to each ethical theory.
- According to the utilitarian ethical theory, what is the proportionate ultimate end of ethicality?
- Which ethical theory is based upon absolutism ethical perceptions?
- Which ethical theory is pursuing its perceptual path towards having holistic good faith, good will, and good-end?
- Summarize the content of the ethical theory of teleological.
- How does the order of ethical treatment in deontologicalism differ from teleologicalism?
- In relation to ethical ideal, show how the meaning of happiness is analogical.
- Give arguments opposing the position of utilitarianism concerning absolutism of ethical means and ends.

- Give a criticism argument against utilitarian ethical theory concerning the happiness of majority and minority populations.
- Give a criticism argument against teleological ethical theory concerning evil means.
- Is there any ultimate evil end in any ethical theory? If yes, explain in which one.

CASE STUDY

NIKE: BATTLING BACKLASH FROM OVERSEAS SWEATSHOPS

Nike, Inc. is a multinational corporation. Its headquarter is located in Beaverton, Oregon. Nike is a manufacturer of footware, apparel, equipment, and accessory products. Nike, from its inception in 1964, has positioned itself as a world leader in the high-end athletic apparel and equipment business. Through athletic superstar endorsements, Nike has claimed that its products are made for champions. The euphoric feeling that overcomes the consumer when Nike is worn bolsters Nike's high quality image.

In 1998 Nike's image of coolness became bleak. The cool image was having difficulty thriving amidst criticism from the public and media. Fallen sales and record losses were indicatives of unethical labor practices in Asia. Several corrective measures needed to be taken in order to rebound from its slump in the marketplace, specifically in the United States.

Nike's products are sold in 110 countries worldwide through retail stores, independent distributors, licenses, and subsidiaries. Although Nike sells its products through various distributive channels around the world, its assembly and production plants primarily have been located outside of the United States. Asia is a key location for assembly and manufacturing processes because of economic advantages. It has been observed that Nike's strategic low-cost plants and high brand-equity make it the world's largest Shoe and Apparel Company. The company has also been able to maintain a stock rating of A1 due to its stabilized corporation's strategic management system. Nike's strong corporate image has allowed Nike to remain profitable despite some ethical and moral criticisms.

PROBLEMS OF THE CASE

The inherent ethical problems of Nike have occurred at its overseas assembly and production plants due to unfair labor practices. They are viewed as unethical practices in the United States. These unethical practices are ignoring minimum age requirements and minimum wage requirements, inadequate safety in the workplace, and the lack of maintaining industry standards.

MAJOR ROLE PLAYERS OF THE CASE

The major role players of this case are Nike's CEO Phil Knight, Asian workers, the International Labor Organization affiliated with the United Nations, the American stockholders, and the media. Each party has been concerned with its own agenda. For example, Asian workers had financial concerns in addition to their employment. Because of the low level of wages, Asian workers had to agree to certain levels of minimum wages in order to maintain a minimum living standard. Yet the public has been appalled by Nike's substandard labor practices and it's retaliating through its product boycotts. The media echoes the sentiment of unfair labor practices.

ANALYSIS OF THE CASE

Nike has been practicing with a different set of labor standards for its Asian assembly and production plants. For years, the Nike name conjured up heroic images. The Swoosh made people feel as if they were winners in sport games. That Nike cachet has been clouded by a new image of Asian workers in hot, noisy factories, stitching together shoes for as little as 80 cents a day. As a result of these varying unfair practices, Nike has had to defend its position to such an extent that its officials have said the company pays the minimum wage or industry standard in whatever country they operate in. Unlike the United States, it is socially acceptable to pay factory workers meager wages per day in Asia. As a result of Asian labor practices Nike paid workers the industry standard in the country of operations. The consequences of Nike's wage policy indicate that workers should continue to live in poverty and struggle to reach a minimum living standard. With such a wage policy, Nike could obtain competitive advantages to beat its competitors in the international market. However, social and economic improvements in the host countries are not attainable by their workers. Nevertheless, as reporter William McCall (1998) indicates:

Nike Chairman, Phil Knight, who acknowledged he has been described as >the perfect corporate villain for these times,' took direct aim at the criticism in May with plans for reforms. Knight promised to raise the minimum age for workers at Nike's contract plants in Asia to 18, improve factory air quality, allow independent monitoring and provide free education for workers.

CASE QUESTIONS FOR DISCUSSION

- Do you believe the International Labor Organization does exercise its mission in the third world countries?
- If no explain the major reasons for their negligence.

- Do you believe media and consumer criticisms create crises for businesses as usual or serious breakdowns in a company's system? Why?
- Which of the ethical theories describes Nike's unethical behavior?
- After investigating Nike's unethical labor practices in Asian countries, identify some ways these crises could have been (1) avoided and (2) managed more responsibility after they occurred.
- Do you believe the conventional ethic and social contract views are realistic with large multinational corporations like Nike? Why or why not? Explain.

CASE SOURCES

W. McCall, "Nike Battles Backlash From Overseas Sweatshops," *Marketing News,* (November 9 1998), 32: 23, American Marketing Association.

CHAPTER 5

PHILOSOPHICAL MEANS AND ENDS IN MORAL, ETHICAL, AND LEGAL BUSINESS RESPONSIBILITIES

There are always four *bodies* in our mind:
Everybody, Somebody, Anybody, and Nobody.

There are some means and ends in Everybody's mind,
Nobody thinks that Anybody can detect them.

When there is a doubt in Somebody's mind,
Nobody thinks that Everybody would realize it.

When there is a moral commitment to be observed,
Somebody expects that Everybody should consider it.

When there is a common sense of ethical responsibility,
Everybody can understand it, but Somebody cares about it.

When there are some conscientious people who care about good-will,
Somebody thinks that it is Everybody's responsibility.

When there is a job to be done by Somebody,
Everybody thinks that Anybody can do it but Everybody blames Somebody else.

CHAPTER OBJECTIVES

When you have read this chapter you should be able to the following:

- Develop conceptual skills in order to analyze global business ethics.
- Develop a framework of analysis to enable you to discuss how to ethically manage international organizations.
- Define business ethics, morality, and legality.
- Understand the importance of ethical, moral, and legal behavior in the workplace.
- Understand the complexity of international business transactions.
- Analyze the religious and secular motives of humanity.
- Grasp the magnitude of today's global business responsibilities.
- Review the historical and contemporary ethical, moral, and legal business dilemmas.
- Analyze the contemporary dimensions of international economic value systems.
- Confirm your relative strength of ethical beliefs.

THOUGHT STARTER

Global businesses today are quite concerned with issues of moral, ethical, and legal responsibilities because of pressures from the public, from media coverage, and from legal and governmental regulatory agencies. Opinion polls of the American public show doubts about the ethical standards of businesspeople at all levels. Hueber, (1990: 23) in his survey found that only three percent of the public believed that business executives had very high ethical standards. Another 22 percent rated them high. In another survey, Jackson and Collingwood (1987) found that the Harris Poll showed 49 percent of the public felt that white-crime was very common in businesses. White crimes are crimes such as money laundering, embezzling, fraud, bribery, corruption, deception, and perjury. Unfortunately, moral commitments and ethical responsibilities are not subject to an accurate aggregated measure. Steiner and Steiner (1994: 180) have found two basic views on business ethics: (1) the theory of amorality and (2) the theory of moral unity. The theory of amorality holds that since a businessperson's behavior is related to the selfishness of a profit-making appetite, therefore the application of moral principles is not relevant in any business transaction. On the other hand, the theory of moral unity holds that since businesses carry some social responsibilities, they should be judged by the socio-cultural moral standards of people.

Conceptions of business responsibilities are tied to the ethical and moral nature of profitability. Over the years most academicians expressed their views in this field as the following:

- Business obligations to pursue profitability is conditional on making those decisions, or following those lines of action which are desirable in terms of the objectives and values of our society (Brown, 1953:6).
- The businessperson's decisions and actions are taken for reasons at least partially beyond the firm's direct economic or technical interest (Davis, 1960: 70).
- The social responsibility of businesses encompasses the economic, legal, ethical, and discretionary expectations placed on organizations by society at a given point in time (Carroll, 1989: 30).

There are three-dimensional views concerning global business ethics: philosophy of responsiveness, social responsibility categories, and social issues involved. Philosophy of ethical responsiveness includes proaction, accommodation, defense, and reaction (Carroll, 1989: 4). For example, many people believe that global corporations should use their capital, skills, and power to play a *proactive* role in handling worldwide ethical, social, economical, and environmental problems. Others believe that global corporations should have a positive impact on all nations by *accommodating* investment, joint-venturing partnership, and transferring sophisticated technologies to all countries.

Social issues of global corporations include moral, ethical, and legal responsibilities. Global businesses should anticipate and try to solve problems in societies. They are responsible for prevailing social expectations concerning environmental and social costs of their actions (Schwartz, 1991: 47). Social responsibilities for businesses include consumerism, environmentalism, occupational safety, and stakeholders' interest.

PLAN OF THIS CHAPTER

The theme of this chapter concentrates on human rights, privacy rights, and business enterprises rights. In other words this chapter analyzes the clash among moral values, ethical rights, and legal duties that shape people's societal responsibilities. Most specifically, in the following pages, we define the key components of moral, ethical, and legal commitments of global businesses that make up a holistic and synthetic philosophy on causes, means, and ends in business peoples' perceptions and behaviors. Furthermore, in this chapter you will find pros and cons concerning the different ethical philosophical views on business responsibilities through defining libertarianism, conservatism, competition, oligopoly, and monopoly. In addition, in this chapter you will find hedonistic and eudaemonistic characteristics of businesspeople. Finally, this chapter highlights the conflict between the power to access to knowledge and technology and privacy rights.

MANAGERIAL BELIEFS AND PRIVACY

Charles Dickens, the famous English writer, stated:

> A wonderful fact to reflect upon, that every human creature is constituted to be that profound secret and mystery to every other. A solemn consideration, when I enter a great city by night, that every one of those darkly clustered houses encloses its own secret; that every room in every one of them encloses its own secret; that in every beating heart in the hundreds of thousands of breasts there is, in some of its imaginings, a secret to the heart nearest to it!

Charles Dickens's remarks are not unique ideas anymore because today's detectors can implant bugs in the bedrooms of people. Organizations own and use employees' E-mails as their property rights. Credit bureaus collect all financial records of people. Health insurance companies have access to patients' medical histories and genetic profiles. Employers push to exercise control over off-the-job behavior of present and former employees. Biotech enterprises through the application of the human genome the *Book of Life* can have access to the deep sources of genetic mysteries of individuals. Biotechnology has already manipulated the genes of animals and human beings, through gene therapy, to clone them. All these and other similar actions and operations raise tensions between moral, ethical, and legal privacy rights and the need to know information.

One of the most striking issues commonly related to a corporate success is the senior manager's deep and enduring commitment to the corporation's moral values and ethical beliefs in *humanity*. Humanity is the notion that any person has an equal natural right to have full *particularity* of his/her character to be taken into account by those who enter into relations with him/her. Humanity is an individual's natural right to be treated equitably, without deceit or violence. From another point of view, the primary driving force of planet-scale change in humanity is attention to be paid to prevent the growing numbers and increasingly disruptive activities based on biased perceptions with extreme appetite of personal greed. Major global-scale changes include ozone depletion, species extinctions, and global warming (Kempton et al., 1995: 1). These global-scale changes eventually may harm humanity.

Managers should respect human dignity and integrity. What is also evident is that commitments of managers, in order to be effective, efficient, and productive, require more than just formulating institutional codes of ethics and business strategies. A businessperson can easily learn how to disobey the law and ignore moral and ethical commitments and how to compromise with everyone on everything through a bargaining process for the sake of financial gain. Morality and ethics, however, do not work by compromises or plea-bargaining. Morality and ethics, by their inherent natures, are associated with goodness, justness, fairness, and rightness. They cannot compromise either with deception and violence or with evil ideas and vicious actions. A businessperson needs to be alert against greedy appetites of self-interest and evil acts. In such a competitive business environment, greed is like a passion, which always wins in the short run and loses at the ends. The good can win only by being morally and ethically consistent with good will, good faith, and good humor.

BUSINESS RESPONSIBILITIES

Society expects a lot from today's global businesses. Business responsibilities are inescapable facts. It is not only the manager's responsibility to investigate how a business can be built and run, but they also must get people to face up to their socio-ethical and environmental responsibilities now and offer future generations some opportunities by not depleting material resources. The natural world is constantly changing. But today's multiple simultaneous changes are unprecedented and potentially catastrophic. Business responsibilities include honesty in the corporation's financial reports, observing product safety, scientific discoveries, industry voluntary regulation, and government environmental protection and conservation policies.

Why Do Businesses Need an Ethical Philosophy?

Philosophically, a business could not be considered a selfish phenomenon. It is a moral and ethical endeavor that balances the level of corporate profitability with suitability of the consumer's efficacy. Should a generation of businesspeople live for themselves, or should they care and maintain their work integrity for something or some generations beyond themselves? This and other similar questions create the business philosophy. A business philosophy tries to answer to some questions:

- How to innovate a new way of life by knowing how does we know it?
- How value things not by pricing products and services but by valuing and maintaining our moral and ethical responsibilities to do the right things?
- How to build an achievable future in order to know what is there?
- How to achieve industry leadership in niche markets by doing what should be done?

In E-commerce today, to build and maintain a monopolistic Internet system as the main frame of technological memory is as dangerous as the "Library of Alexandria, which was burned to ashes during the Roman Civil War of 272AD." Today, computer hackers can easily destroy all saved information through spreading universal viruses (e.g., "I love you," "Joke," "Mother's Day," " LIFE-STAGES. TXT. SHS., susitikim shi vakara kavos puodukui, or E-mails with attachment "vbx," AWOBBLER: through "Win a Holiday," and "Melissa. Is it possible for medical, commercial, and financial institutions to be trusted to migrate their digital customer's profile and data into every new format as it comes along when formats are changing every ten years? What are the moral, ethical, and legal responsibilities of these and other institutions in saving customer information profiles? These and other similar questions can identify means and ends of businesses and how they may affect generations to come and how to maintain their ethical and moral responsibilities intact.

Why Do Businesses Need a Moral Philosophy?

There are holistic perceptions about periodic views on certain questions:

- What is humanity?
- What is a good life?
- What is happiness? What is enjoyment?
- What is the means of enjoyment?
- What is the end of happiness?
- Who are the greatest victims of today's greed?
- Who are the most denounced and vilified group of people on the earth?

Paikoff (1999: 9) believes that the only possible answer to these questions is related to business people who are denounced for one sin, because they are the epitome of *profitability*. They seek to make profit; the greatest profit possible by selling at the highest price the market will bear while buying at the lowest price. However, it should be noted that moral businesspeople are making profit by being the best they can be in their work, by innovating new images, by the creation of effective goods or a higher quality of services that consumers and customers can appreciate. Such business peoples' profitability is not either fraud, selfishness, immoral, or unethical.

The term business to businesspeople relationship denotes to the capabilities of people and organizations. The existences of businesses are not made by Mother Nature, but by the efforts of people. Businesspeople deserve to make a profit. Therefore, profitability, in the field of business, leads employers to the magnificent growth of businesses and prosperity in happiness.

Multicultural values are viewed as a necessary basis for global business transactions, even though they may not be sufficient by themselves. A community and its culture(s) present a dozen or more structural design forms of cultural behavior. They identify the distinctive cultural components that make a society different from others, and conclude by considering the different effects of cultural orientation in international business transactions. Successful and valuable businesspeople have to be lead by the intellectual people. It is sad that many people believe that the accumulation of wealth and power is a product of material things. However, wealth and power are primarily products of the human mind. It is the power of business peoples' mind that they synergize material things through the management of knowledge-wealth. Figure 5.1 illustrates five major valuable domains of global enterprises:

- Individuals' Moral, Ethical, and Legal Commitments.

- Cultural Values.
- Religious Virtues.
- Political Doctrines.
- Economical and Commercial Systems.

In the following chapters, you will find analytical discussions related to the above issues.

ETHICAL PHILOSOPHIES AND ETHICAL PROBLEMS IN GLOBAL BUSINESS MARKETS

Ethical Philosophies of Global Business Responsibilities

There are many moral and ethical problems in today's global business transactions. Global markets are not perfectly competitive and multinational corporations do not function, as ethical theories would have us believe. Six repositories of ethical value systems influence every businessperson: material inheritance and gains, religious faiths, cultural beliefs, political and legal doctrines, ecological experiences, and philosophies of life. These systems exert varying degrees of influence over individuals and over the society that they are living in. A common contradictory theme that includes the ideas of altruism, populism, reciprocitism, and individualism, is found in all of these value systems. The functions of these ideas bind individuals into a synergistic whole, which is the central purpose of all ethical ideas.

Altruism: *Altruism* could be defined as the principle or practice of unselfish concern for or devotion to the welfare of others. Altruism is opposed to egoism. Or in other words, the opposite of selfishness is altruism. Altruism is a philosophical term coined by Auguste Comte (1798-1857) who based it on the Latin word *alters*, meaning "others." Literally, altruism means "otherism." Comte defined altruism as "placing others above onself as the basic rule of life" (Edwards, 1967:173). Altruism is a kind of morality that inspires economists to dream up ethical societal justness. John Ridpath (1980: 14) observed altruism as the reason why:

> The altruist ideal of unrewarded service to others motivated the acceptance of the perfect competition model and its use as a standard of antitrust...The model appeals to altruists because it describes a world in which everyone is acting to best serve the interest of the consuming public.

Populism: *Populism* is defined as placing restriction of ownership on accumulation of wealth by monopolies. Populism is directly associated with democracy. It sides with the majority of the population against a minority of the wealthiest class of people. Populists believe that the ethical standard for judging competition should be based on social justice. Antitrust law puts the majority legal forces on the side of the majority of people. Hayek (1948: 114) claims that private property is often an undesirable and harmful privilege. He believes that free enterprise and competitive order do not necessarily designate the same resulting system, and it is the system described by the second that we want. In any form of free market economy, major businesses tend to be concentrated in the hands of a few who become rich and powerful, which could result in a monopoly or oligopoly. If they succeed, they can prevent free competitive entry into the industry.

Reciprocitism: Reciprocitism means mutual exchange of values between two parties (e.g., sellers and buyers). In the global business context, reciprocitism refers to mutual relationship or policy in commercial dealing between countries, by which corresponding advantages or privileges are granted, by each country, to the citizens of the other. Beside home and host countries' laws and regulations, ethical values may be beneficial to both producers and consumers. In addition, reciprocal interests between employers and employees may energize parties into pursuit of mutual profitability and suitability

Individualism: *Individualism* refers to personhood and selfhood of the atomic (ego, superego, and id) nature of an individual that exists and has moral claims apart from any associations except those that they have been chosen to form for the purpose of professional identity. This view is the position linked to John Locke's (1632-1704) social contract theory, which is embedded in the position of realism. Locke (1924) limited social contracts to *constitutional forms of government.* He believed that free people could not sensibly set up a despotic government which might take away all of their individual rights and give little or nothing in return. Furthermore, Locke (1924) founded morality on religious authority tempered with reasonableness. He stated that we are under obligation to behave morally through God's command. This is the ultimate sanction of morality.

The view of atomistic selfhood is also found in the theory of utilitarian ethics; the community is a collection of atomic individuals, and moral decisions are justifiable by their means and ends for their collective whole. In addition, the atomicity of personhood or selfhood is the common basis for positions as diverse as interest-group liberalism constraints such as government regulations. The terms individuals, or selves, and persons are examples of individualism. In the field of business ethics, the most important question concerning individualism is whether the self is an isolated, discrete entity, or is, by its very nature, part of a social process. Nevertheless, selfhood or personhood comes about through awareness of one's role in a social context. Since the nature of all businesses is fulfilling the selfish desire of businesspeople, namely profitability, therefore, they must appropriately be regulated either voluntarily by themselves, or by their governments. Individuals monopolize production systems, restrict competition, and financially or physically may harm consumers. Under constitutional rights and duties, individuals must give something back to the community and respect the public interest.

ETHICAL PROBLEMS WITH
THE GLOBAL MARKETS

There are numerous problems in global competition concerning ethical behavior by businesspeople. Globally, markets are not perfectly competitive, because sustainable competitive advantages may be likely. Most domestic businesses are faced with heavy foreign competition. They have experienced unjust competition by foreign rivals to inroad into their markets by unethical and in most cases by illegal entries. One of the key determinants of sustain is whether a firm's products are costly to imitate in non-regulated markets. Imitation without permission of the copyright owner and/or a patent holder is an unethical act. A sustaining framework, therefore, might focus on different market types where product imitation is largely or rapidly shielded (Williams, 1992: 29).

Competitive global markets could be described as slow-cycle, fast-cycle, and standard-cycle markets. Products in slow-cycle markets reflect strongly shielded resources positions where competitive pressures do not readily penetrate the firm's market position of strategic competitiveness. This is often characterized in economics as *monopolistic* positions. Monopolies are able to restrain trade and free enterprises in the areas they dominate. Monopolies are able to set specific conditions for transactions and fixed pricing systems for commodities. On the other hand, standard-cycle markets reflect moderately shielded resource positions where competitive interaction penetrates a firm's market position. However, they progress with improvement of their capabilities. The competitive firms may be able to sustain a competitive advantage. As such, they are labeled standard-cycle markets, often described as *oligopolistic* (Day, 1997: 48). Oligopolistic firms adjust prices in response to changing conditions or changes introduced by rivals in the same industry (Buchholz and Rosenthal, 1998:111). In the fast-cycle markets, a competitive advantage cannot be sustained; firms attempt to gain temporary competitive advantage by strategically disrupting the market (Hitt et al., 1999:186-191). The idea of disruption is to create a counterattack before the advantage is eroded. This tactic harms consumers, because they face discontinuity of services, parts, and maintenance of operative products after sales. The idea of disruption actually leads to cannibalizing the firm's products through the next stage of product evolution and entry (Conner, 1995: 209). Therefore, conducting a business in the global markets contains three major forms: Competition, Oligopoly, and Monopoly. It is a popular strategy for the MNCs, by competing in an industry, to be involved with a number of competitive actions and competitive counteractions.

Competition

Competition refers to the rivalry between two or more business enterprises to secure the patronage of prospective buyers. Competition depends very much on how their rivals are expected to react. Rivalry becomes competitive asymmetry, because the principle of competitive asymmetry exists when firms differ from one another in terms of their resources, capabilities, core competencies, opportunities, and threats in their industry and competitive markets.

Real competition occurs when markets are highly segmented, sales are highly fragmented, and products are highly differentiated by the size and quality on the basis of consumer demands, not producer desires. In reality, however, in the pragmatic competitive market, qualities are competitive by mixed pricing systems. In such competitive markets, competition is shifting from supply and demand to the allocation of resources in the most efficient manner to respond to the demand of the markets. In real fragmented competitive markets, buyers and sellers are so small that they have no influence over the markets, but qualities of products are competitive. In such competitive markets, consumers may find appropriate opportunities to make their choices.

Oligopoly

Oligopoly means there are few sellers or producers in a marketplace. By definition, pure oligopoly in an industry is composed of so few firms in an industry that each has to look over its shoulder. If your rival brings out a new model of a product, your market share might shrink unless you counter with a new model or lower prices on your current models. The point is that decision-making under oligopoly involves strategies. From an ethical point of view, like monopolies, oligopolies try to establish sufficient barriers to new firms in order to prevent them from entering the market. Both technical and strategic barriers can exist. Many oligopolies are also the result of mergers and acquisitions. For example, the major market share of the domestic carmakers in the United States belongs to General Motors, Ford, and Chrysler Companies. Oligopoly is a term used in the field of business when competition in an industry is never perfectly balanced. It contains a few large corporations to dominate the market and their actions influence rivals. In imbalanced competition, a few firms will eventually come to dominate their industries because they are the better competitors in the right place, at the right time, with the right products. Thus, most global industries in today's global economy are oligopolies. In an oligopolistic system, firms deal with each other more or less directly and take into account the effect of their actions on each other. They depend very much on how their rivals are expected to react. Oligopolies adjust prices in response to changing market conditions or to changes introduced by rivals in the same industry. In the oligopolistic markets, consumers are exposed to oligopolies' collective discretionary decisions and actions.

To coordinate the oligopolistic pricing system in an industry, some oligopolies recognize one firm as the industry's price leader (Markham, 1951: 891). Each firm tacitly agrees to set its price system around the levels announced by the price leader, knowing that all other firms will also follow its price leadership. Whether prices in an oligopolistic market are set by explicit agreements or by implicit understanding, it raises some moral and ethical issues concerning the price fixing. Price fixing by oligopolies in a market is considered a conspiracy against consumers and consequently decreases competition. Consumers, therefore, must pay the unjust prices of the oligopolies, and the freedom of both consumers and potential competitors diminishes (Velasquez, 1998: 201). For example, on December 5, 2001, Alfered Taubman, 76 years old, former Sothebay's Chairman, faced up to three years in jail after being convicted in New York of conspiring with rival auction house Christie's to fix commissions paid by sellers of fine arts (*Financial Times*, 2001: 1).

Monopoly

Monopoly refers to the exclusive control of commodities or services in a particular market by an individual and/or by a corporation. By definition, monopolists have no competitors. It is a type of control to manipulate the pricing system by the producer or seller's discretion. Also, a monopoly is simply defined to mean any large market share and product position held by an industry's leading company. In other words, monopoly is defined as a single-seller forcing all other competitors out of business. Monopoly means restriction on competition by establishing entry barriers, restricting consumers free choice, harming the community by a lack of respect for the public interest, conspiring against ethical, moral, and legal principles by price fixing, and rewarding the selfish appetite of a monopoly's greedy profitability. In a general term monopolistic markets are those in which a single firm is the only seller in the market and which new sellers are barred from entry because of high entry barriers, quantity below equilibrium, and prices above equilibrium and supply curve.

Monopsony

The term *monopsoy* refers to a type of marketplace condition that exists when there is one buyer (customer or consumer). Either the physical product can be varied in quality, or style, or the manufacturers can be varied. The only buyer sees differences in sellers' products and will pay different prices for them. A buyer in a monopsonistic market, therefore, can control the prices of the available goods. For example, there very few corporations that deal with NASA in the United States for the Space Agency.

PRIVACY AND INTELLECTUAL PROPERTY RIGHTS

Privacy refers to that sphere of life where one's behavior, thoughts, feelings, and so on are unknown to others and are not available for their scrutiny. Privacy has been defined as the state of being free from intrusion or disturbance in one's private life or affairs. One's private life is considered to be that which is not of an official or public character, that solitary or secluded part of life that does not include the presence of others. The private part of life is the most intimate and personal part of life, for whatever reason, that is not exposed to the public or available to outsiders (Buchholz and Rosenthal, 1998: 401). Privacy rights could be natural or possessive. The natural rights are anything due to another that is based ultimately on the natural moral law. Both rights cannot be abolished. For example, the consent of a male and a female being by nature is related to each other's rights for the production of their offspring. Therefore, it is the natural right of a couple to marry and have children. The possessive rights are dependent upon certain conditions in particular circumstances. The term of private property rights includes the ownership of land. It is also viewed as a natural right. Nevertheless, the private possessive rights are not absolute, while the marriage life is an absolute right, because the property rights are under certain conditions and for some significant use.

One of the major issues in international trade is the protection of intellectual property rights. Although *intellectual property right* is an abstract term for an abstract concept, it is, nonetheless, familiar to virtually everyone. Morally, ethically, and legally, stealing is wrong. In addition, misappropriation of other's property without the owner's knowledge and/or consent, either by deception or force, is viewed as an act of *usurpation*. There has been an almost wholesale pirating of American videos, compact discs, and cassettes abroad. American computer and software companies have seen their products copied and sold without payment of royalties throughout the world. For example, in 1995, the United States and China resolved a bitter dispute when the latter agreed to establish at least twenty-two task forces to oversee an anti-piracy campaign (Jackson et. al., 1997: 195). Copyrights, patents, trademarks, shop rights, trade secrets, inside information, inside trading, formula, brand, retail store brand, and counterfeiting are viewed as forms of intellectual property issues.

Types of Intellectual Property Rights

Copyright: Copyright is a legal term that is defined as the exclusive right to display or reproduce a literary, audio, or visual work by an author and/or by an institution. The copyright covers the actual form of the writing or the composition of a piece of music or an illustration of fine arts rather than the more general ideas on which the works are based (Punnett and Ricks, 1992: 237). A copyright, in essence, protects the expression of an idea in a specific term. American and Japanese legal systems protect particular forms of copyrights that an idea is expressed but not the underlying idea. Under both systems, the works must be original and fall within the broad realms of literature, science, fine arts, or music to be eligible for legal protection. Generally, U.S. law gave works created on or after January 1, 1978, copyrights protection for the life of the author, plus 50 years after the author's death. For example, IBM first sought U.S. copyrights for its operating system software in 1978 (Stewart, 1996: 281).

Patent: Patent is an exclusive monopolistic legal right for protection of a technological breakthrough to be given to an inventor, innovator, or substantially improved products or processes to a patent holder for a certain period of time. Patents, in essence, protect intellectual property ownership rights for a patent holder. The patent holder, by law, is responsible to develop the process of invention and/or breakthrough, as well as material products within a specific period of time. The period for filing the patent application to the production in of the object in the United States is 20-months on average and in Japan is six years on average (Stewart, 1996: 282).

Trademark: A trademark is a distinctive and unique commercial and/or institutional sign to represent a particular company or organization. Without acquisition of formal permission from the trademark owner that sign cannot be used by another organization or commercial entity A trademark is an exclusive right which carries some legal particularity for the trademark holder. Licensees and/or franchisees under special contracts and/or agreements for paying fees to licensors or franchisers in a certain period of time can use trademarks.

Shop Rights: *Shop rights* are exclusive legal rights for a company to use inventions, technological breakthroughs, or information of its scientists and/or researchers for the benefit of its organizational ends. However, scientists or researchers who have used a company's technologies, time, and resources do not have the right to take that knowledge, information, and/or formula with them and use them either for their own self-interest or for the benefit of their new employers. It is a typical practice in the United States that people who work in very sensitive scientific and technological areas for a company and/or for governmental organizations sign a contract to waive their individual exclusive rights for the benefits of their employers during and after separation from their organizations. There is an ethical issue in regard of the shop rights. That is related to the abusive and exploitation of human rights. Human right abuses occur when the contract violates an employee's civil rights by imposing unreasonable limitation an employee's freedom in terms of his/her personal knowledge repository. The right of a company to be the first to use and make profit from a scientist and/or a technologist who has used all company's resources is nonetheless defensible. This, however, does not mean that the company has the exclusive right to own the scientists' repository brain knowledge forever, because there are moral and ethical principles that govern the *idea that right to know is the right to act*. Know-how information is neither viewed as an exclusive right for a company or for an employee. It is viewed as public knowledge or information from which a society at large should benefit.

Freelancer's Rights: *Freelancer's rights* are those special intellectual property rights of an independent writer that by law are protected. On Monday, June 26, 2001, for the first time the United States Supreme Court issued it's ruling on vexing questions of the rights of copyright owners in the world of digital production. Justices ruled that publishers violate freelance writers' copyright when they put their articles in electronic databases without their permission. That means publishers must pay extra for their works or remove them from the database (Waldmeir, 2001: 4). This means that if a publisher such as *The New York Times* received an article free of charge from a freelancer (independent writer) and publishes it in the newspaper; *The New York Times* cannot include that article in its Website without the freelancers' permission. In addition, if *The New York Times* receives a royalty from users, then The New York Times needs to pay the appropriate loyalties to the freelancers.

Trade Secrets: *Trade secrets* are defined as any formula, pattern, device, or compilation of information used in one's business. These provide employers with opportunities to obtain advantages over competitors who do not know or use them (Epstein, 1989: 3). Trade secrets include customer or client profiles, research data, chemical formulas, engineering designs and techniques, manufacturing and processing procedures, surgical procedures, and machinery patterns. There are some moral and ethical issues concerning the selling of client or customer names and addresses to other businesses. Everyday, people receive much mail from different businesses without their request. This raises questions concerning privacy rights. By law, businesses and public institutions can sell their customer or client profiles to other businesses and make a profit out on them.

Brand Name: Most manufacturing firms practice several options available when considering product brand strategies. They might sell all their products (1) under one national brand, (2) under several national brands (a family of brands), (3) under private brand names, or both under national and private brand names. The most ethical problem in an industry is related to the channels of distribution for a dual national/private brand strategy. Examples of such strategies are (1) not selling both national and private brand versions of the products to the same channels of distribution members, (2) selling the national and private brand versions of the product in different geographical territories in order that they are less likely to compete in the same market areas, and (3) making the products physically different enough so that even if the first two kinds of distribution are not feasible, the direct competition between the national and private brand versions of the product will be minimized (Rosenbloom, 1999:336). Within such a brand strategic policy, consumers will be fooled because in reality the original functions of all these products are one but under different names. Such a marketing practice is *amoral*.

Ethical Issues Affecting Intellectual Property Rights

Insider Trading: Insider trading has been the subject of business ethics since the beginning of the Twentieth century, specifically during the 1980s, when so called criminal commercial geniuses such as Michael Milken, Ivan Boseky, Martin Seigel, and Dennis Levine made huge profits. These and others were caught in insider trading scandals. Although there is no precise definition for insider trading, it can be defined as buying or selling securities at specific times through access to the sensitive trading information such as mergers, buyouts, declaration of bankruptcy, and hostile take over before appropriate information to be announced to the public. Insider trading information about one's own company by an employee and/or by brokers, bankers, and legal firms can be used for buying and/or selling the stocks of those companies by informants before the information is disclosed to the public. These insider traders, most of the time, make huge profits. For example, recently a federal jury convicted James J. McDermott Jr., former Chief Executive of Keefe Bruyette and Woods, on charges of leaking inside information about banking mergers to his mistress, an actress who performed in adult movies under the name Marilyn Star. The case marks the first time a Wall Street chief executive has been charged and convicted of insider trading, said the Security Exchange Commissioner (Financial Times, April 28, 2000).

Insider Information: Using *insider information* for the purpose of personal profit making by an individual or a group of employees is ethically and morally wrong. In addition, insider information puts people who are outside the firm at an unfair disadvantage when they unknowingly transact business with an insider who is using information that is not available to others and actually belongs to the firm. Recent court decisions have held that it is illegal for an employee to use material insider information when investing in securities (Sethi, 1982: 288).

Disclosure of information by an employer to an employee is for the purpose of a company's profit making, not for the sake of an employee's personal self-interest. Some criteria related to deciding whether or not insider information is *proprietary* are set forth in a treatise entitled the Restatement of Torts that regards this type of information unethical and illegal (Buchholz and Rosenthal, 1998: 396). According to Spanner (1986: 10), these criteria include the following:

- The extent to which the information is known outside of the business

- The extent to which the information is known by those involved in the business
- The nature and extent of measures taken to protect the secrecy of the information
- The value of the information
- The amount of time, effort, and money extended in the development of the information
- The degree of difficulty with which the information could be properly acquired or duplicated by others

These issues surface whenever employees leave their companies and join a new one, and/or establish a similar business in the same industry. In these circumstances, application and/or disclosure of insider information of that company to the new one is prohibited and may expose employees to the possibility of lawsuits.

Counterfeiting: The term *counterfeiting* is used to describe the production of brand name products without the consent of the company holding the patent, trademark, or copyright. Sometimes consumers a fake product that is admittedly not of high quality and that fools no one as being genuine. For example, a hundred Nigerian children died from a cough medicine, and talcum powder was found in an anti-ulcer drug sold in Europe (*The Economist*, 1992: 85).

Privacy: The term *piracy* refers to the production of products by copying the original, without the consent of the company and/or individuals that are holding patent, trademark, or copyright. Reports of lost sales due to piracy vary substantially. It is very popular to pirate music CDs to be played through Internet Websites without the permission of the copyright holder before its release.

For example, the World Health Organization (WHO) estimates that 5 percent of prescription drug trade is counterfeit, and the figure is 70 percent for drugs used in developing countries. Pirated software sales probably exceed $15 billion a year and account for more than 70 percent of the market in the Middle East, Africa, and Latin America (Chaudhry and Walsh, 1995: 80).

There are several moral and ethical issues related to piracy. Cashing in on massive advertising of well-marketed patents, trademarks, and copyrights of products and formulas, with high quality outcomes tempts, greedy people to pirate them. Pirated products and formulas are not costly in production. Naturally, the price of pirated products is very low. When many countries and consumers realize that they cannot afford to buy the original brand of a product, but they need the product, they look for pirated products. In addition, many people see nothing morally wrong in buying counterfeit goods. For example, third world countries cannot financially afford to buy ATZ, for treatment of

AIDS, because with the $100.00 GNP per capita, individuals cannot afford the drug at 1,000.00 per month.

Price Fixing: The term *price fixing* refers to secretly arranging prices at a fixed artificially high level within a market either by monopolies or oligopolies. If ethical, moral, and legal justness and social utility exists in a society, then it is crucial that monopolies and oligopolies should refrain from engaging in such practices that diminish competition among rivals and free choices for consumers. Price fixing is an unethical and immoral intention. According to the philosophy of the free market economy, both competitors and consumers should have free choices in production and consumption. For example, the European Commission has imposed record fines totaling $747 million on pharmaceutical companies Roche of Switzerland, BASF of Germany, and several others for a nine-year conspiracy to control the market for vitamins. Both Roche and BASF companies played important roles in a cartel to fix the price for some of the most popular vitamins. In the United States, the antitrust authorities led to $500 million for Roche and a $225 million penalty for BASF. In addition, a former Roche executive was also jailed for four month and fined $100,000 (Guerrera and Jennen, 2001: 1).

Price Discrimination: *Price discrimination* refers to charging different prices for a specific product to different types of customers according to the buyer's characteristics such as race, ethnicity, religion, color, age, gender, and nationality. This is a popular practice in Third World Countries. Ethically and morally, price differences should be based on true differences in the cost of manufacturing, packaging, marketing, advertising, logistics, taxation, and tariffs, not on the basis of the type and socio-economic class of consumers. Price discrimination is different from the price discount.

Exclusive Dealing Bargaining: In an *exclusive dealing agreement*, a seller's firm institutes an exclusive dealing condition for a buyer that they should not purchase any similar products from certain sellers. This type of condition hooks the buyer to the seller's will. Ethically, this type of arrangement makes the buyer a captive one. For example, soft drink companies, Coca Cola and PepsiCo, restrict their buyer restaurants and airlines to having only their products. Buyer companies can only to choose one. This type of business diminishes the consumer's free choice and the real competition in a marketplace.

Tying Arrangements: In some international trade protocols, contracts, and agreements, sellers put buyers in contingency situations to agree to buy their supplies with package deal arrangements. The buyer enters into a *tying arrangement* where the seller to get its supply with the condition that they purchase certain other commodities from the seller's firm mandates it. In small business deals, buyers do not have the choice to choose their high qualitative supplies. Buyers need to purchase their supplies ranging from low, medium, and high qualities (mixed products). In addition, in the international trade agreements, tying arrangements force buyers to pay for products, maintenance, parts, services beyond sale, and training programs.

Manipulation of Supply: In oligopolistic markets, licensees and franchisees agree to keep their quantitative product numbers low in order to keep the price high. In the *monopolized supplying* chain industry, buyers agree to limit their supplies with frequent delivery arrangement so that prices rise to the highest level as compared to what would result from free competition. The artificial manipulation of supply can create a black market.

Bribery: The term *bribe* is referred to any valuable and favorable consideration given or promised to somebody for corrupt behavior in the performance of an official, public duty, and/or to obtain special arrangements for personal gain between two or more parties. A bribe in the field of business is defined as a payout to get something done to which the company is not entitled. *Bribery* is an act that is in any form immoral, unethical, and illegal. It involves giving and receiving money and other valuable things for a discriminatory treatment against a group of people and in the favor of others. Bribery is a remunerative intention and act for doing a favor that is inconsistent with the work contract or the nature of the work one has been hired to perform. The remuneration can be money, gifts, entertainment, or preferential treatment (Shaw and Barry, 1998: 283).

In the field of international business, the universal ethical rule says that it is wrong to bribe or to promote bribery for gaining an illegitimate interest. As William Daley, the U.S. Commerce Secretary (2000: 4), in the convention of the Organization for Economic Co-Operation and Development reported:

> The government estimated that 353 foreign contracts were "affected by bribes" between May 1994 and April 2000, and that U.S. businesses lost 92 of these contracts, worth about $26 billion...Progress on the international convention which outlaws the use of bribery to win foreign contracts, with the number of countries ratifying it increasing from 15 to 21 over the past year... The U.S. government had "varying degrees of concern" about the adequacy of anti-bribery legislation in countries including UK and Japan. The United Kingdom was severely criticized by OEDC members for its failure to implement the bribery convention.

Payola: The term *payola* is a secret or abusive pre-payment bribery to the influential and key decision-makers of a buyer's country and/or a company for selling a single brand or model of a product or a unique kind of service. Payola is viewed as an unethical and immoral payment for promotion of a single product. Payola creates dependency and continuity of customer loyalty to a single product. For example: in 1972, Carl Kotchian, Lockheed's President, went to Japan to sell the firm's new Tristar passenger planes to a Japanese airline. However, he found that his Japanese partners kept asking for large amounts of money under the guise of standard practice, and Kotchain was under subtle pressure to continue payola or lose the sale of the Tristar airplane model. These payola monies apparently wound up in the office of the Japanese prime minister. The story eventually came out, and the actions of Lockheed, Kotchian, and the involved Japanese officials were condemned as immoral acts (Newton and Ford, 1990).

Extortion: *Extortion* means to wrest money or information from a person by violence or intimidation, under the cover of office, when none or not so much is due. A business is a legal entity that is protected by law and by law enforcement officers. What should a company do when its operation abroad is threatened with destruction if a substantial extortionate money payment is not made to corrupted government authorities or law enforcement officers? Or the security of a plant and safety of personnel are threatened unless money is paid? Should that company close its plant because of these unethical and immoral demands? There is no doubt that such foreign companies are considered victims of extortionists. These and other questions raise serious ethical and moral issues. There is no doubt that in any case extortionate payments could be legitimate. Multinational companies should assess moral and ethical cultural beliefs and practices in the host countries before their entry. For example, in 1977, an importing company imported bananas from South America to Iran. The importer refused to bribe customs officers to release them as soon as possible. The customs officers apparently did not want to do a favor for this importer, because they reasoned that they were violating the law and the rights of other importers who were before him. Consequently, the ship remained in the port for three weeks and all bananas rotted. Then the government of Iran did not let the ship go into the Persian Gulf with rotten bananas. The ship had to leave the port with rotten bananas and dumped then in the Indian Ocean.

Kickbacks or Overt Bribe: The terms *kickbacks* and *overt bribes* are defined as improper and immoral percentage of secret income regularly given to a person in a position of power or influence as payment for having made the income possible. For example, in the medical profession, some doctors commit unprofessional actions in their practices by referring patients to specific laboratories and X-Ray institutions for the purposes of self-interest and in return they get their shares as percentages of receivable charges. How do the doctors keep the track of their orders? They can be informed when patients bring back the results to doctors.

Grease Money, Sweet Money, and Speed Money: *Grease money* or *speed money* is a kind of special payment paid to low ranking government officials to expedite the company's bureaucratic red-taped paper works. When there is a recognized expediter and when the amount of the payment is insignificant, is called grease money. Or when it is an accepted local cultural practice to pay low ranked government employees, it is called *sweet money*. Grease money could be illegal but not unethical or immoral. Grease money or speed money is different than *sweet money*. In Persian culture sweet money is called s*hirini*. *Shirini* means sweet. Sweet money is not viewed as intimidation, force, or as an in-front payment promises. It is a kind of voluntary appreciative payment, through the public eyes, and it is also viewed in the American culture as a tip. Of course grease money, and speed money are illegal in any form to be paid to any government employee either to the civilians or the law enforcement personnel. For example, Mr. Robert Stuart, the Chief Executive Officer of Quaker Oats indicated a statement to Quaker stockholders on November 10, 1976 as the following:

> There had been numerous requests for payoffs to minor government officials in order to obtain action to which we were legally entitled anyway and had been refused, resulting in one instance in physical abuse of a plant manager and, in several instances, in arbitrary delays in the processing of paper work necessary to clear already justifies governmental approvals.... Just to show you how frustrating a problem this really is.... One of the demands refused was from a customs official in connection with the movement of an employee's furniture. As a consequence of our manager's refusal to pay, the furniture was stored in the open in a rainy climate and was ruined. When it became apparent that no grease money would be forthcoming, the furniture, though now ruined, was taxed at its original high value (in Walton, 1977: 182).

Gift: A *gift* is defined as a present offered to somebody voluntarily without charge. A gift could be viewed as a donation, contribution, offering, benefaction, endowment, bounty, gratuity, tip, allowance, subsidy, or bequest. Different cultures view gift offering differently. For example, in many countries people culturally view a gift as a time-honed tradition to be offered to someone when a person retires, or when an individual is promoted to a higher position. Friends and sometimes-new subordinates offer their congratulations through offering that promoted person with individual and/or group gifts as a demonstration of respect and wishing him/her happiness and success. In different cultures the amount of the gift is limited. When the gift exceeds the permitted level, the person who has received the gift needs to return that gift to the organization.

PHILOSOPHIES OF SELFLESSNESS AND SELFISHNESS

The state of global business ethics is not easy to assess. It is very complex because it ranges within a continuum of selflessness and selfishness. Through the philosophy of ethics, there is two major thoughts concerning the global free market economy: Libertarianism and Conservatism. Since in practice, all global business transactions are intertwined between the poles of selflessness and selfishness, we can distinguish the difference of the two major factors such as socio-cultural and econo-political interactions. For the purposes of analysis, let us briefly consider libertarianism and conservatism in regulating the global free market economy.

Libertarianism and Regulatory Authorities

Libertarianism ideology envisions profit seeking as a personal ethical value. People are free to use their property, choose their occupation, and strive for economic gain in any legitimate way they choose. People in a democratic society should establish the image of self-made destiny by perceiving the notion of self-interest. This means that individuals have the right to live for their own sake, maintain personal interests, and strive for happiness. They should pursue their own goals independently, by their own work, and respect every other individuals' right to do the same for themselves and others. Governments should not interfere in people's private life, because self-interest is an individual concept. The government does not provide self-interest. If someone else defines self-interest, then the concept would have no meaning for anybody. According to the libertarianism philosophy, self-interest would oppose any type of illegitimate restriction.

The Declaration of Independence in the United States of America states that all men have an inalienable right to life, liberty, and the pursuit of happiness. What does the pursuit of happiness mean? Thomas Jefferson believed in:

The concept of man as being sovereign unto himself, rather than a subdivision of the sovereignty of a king, emperor, or state. In a free society, man exercises his rights to sustain his own life by producing economic values in the form of goods and services that he is, or should be, free to exchange with other men who are similarly free to trade with him... A wise and frugal government, which shall restrain men from injury one another, which shall leave them otherwise free to regulate their own pursuits (Norton et al., 1990: 215).

In most countries, businesspeople are not interested in political positions as a means to structure their own constituents. What they are interested is in staying in social power to influence politics. Businesspeople also form coalitions to create associations that lobby against laws. The distinguishing belief of libertarianism is pertinent to the ownership of the means of production for achieving the ends of self-interest. Employers and employees working hard for one objective is self-achievement.

Conservative and Regulatory Authorities

Frank Knight (1921), a founder of Chicago School of Anti-Trust doctrine, first spelled out the ideal of perfect competition in 1921. His doctrine was based on altruism. He believed that the ethical standard for judging competition is social justice. According to the conservatism doctrine, the only justification for business success is that the most productive systems are encouraged to make the greatest possible addition to the total social dividend. Laws must preserve those who lose in what Knight derisively called the game of business.

Conservatism doctrine indicates that competitive rivalry exists when multinational (MNCs) and multidomestic corporations (MDCs) establish an equitable balance between consumers' efficacy and producers' profitability. It is a popular practice that MNCs and MDCs enshrine property rights at the expense of human rights to the safety of products. The ideal form of competition is pure rivalry, where the industry is not heavily concentrated by a few nations, where there are no significant barriers to entry, and no product differentiations exist. In this kind of rivalry, both MNCs and MDCs have no other choice but to meet the competitive advantages by lowering production costs.

INDIVIDUALS' MORAL, ETHICAL, AND LEGAL QUALITY OF LIFE

Philosophically, intellectual businesspeople interact, as they ought, not as long as they can. Businesspeople always reflect their ends through their means. They reflect their image concerning the quality, and not the quantity of their wealth. Moral, ethical, and legal ordinations reflect how to optimize happiness and minimize suffering. Some contend that the loss of *quantitative* values is dividing the line between a good quality of life and a poor one. Others conceive that the *qualitative* values of life are based upon the cognitive functioning of personal characteristics. We formulate the quality of life as of the following:

Quality of Life (QL) = Individual's Natural and Social Endowment of Intellect (INSEE)

(INSEEI) . (Happiness [H] – Suffering [S])

According to the above formula, every human being is of equal rights, but not every life. As much as natural and social endowment intelligence becomes higher, the quality of life is higher and life becomes more meaningful.

Today, organizations are becoming borderless global institutions, through the free flow of information. Personal appearances are no longer the only way to be associated with others. People can communicate and close their deals through E-images, E-mails, and E-commerce. Accordingly, individuals possess two types of *selves:* (1) *real* and (2) *imagery. Self-imaginary* is a manifestation of an individual's characteristics in accordance with the integration of intelligence and feelings. It is a holistic behavioral representation of self-concept. The *real self* of an individual is related to the own-image and the *imagery self* is related to the others' judgments and perceptions. Self represents the total characteristics of an individual. It is a critical component of individual differences. The ecological, psychological, sociocultural, and behavioral traits and characteristics distinguish one individual from another.

As shown in the Figure 5.1, the first cluster includes variables for expressing self. This cluster includes variables that reflect the heredity and/or genetic identity of an individual. It manifests the physiological genetic characteristics such as weight, height, hair color, eye color, body shape, gender, sensation, race, ethnicity, and appearance of lifestyle.

The second cluster includes psychological variables that reflect past experiences that somehow prepare an individual cognitively and emotionally for perceiving self. This cluster is concerned with psychosocial factors such as feelings, needs, motives, attitudes, perceptions, traits, ability, potentials, faith, and learning styles. Also, this cluster represents feelings of competence, trust, confidence, abilities, and intellectual potential.

The third cluster includes sociocultural variables that are related to the level of valuable socialization and past dynamic group learning experiences. This cluster shows the type of personality, conceptions, attributions, beliefs, values, family, ideology, wealth, expectations, and lifestyle.

The fourth cluster concerns behavior. This cluster identifies the type of behavior such as self-image, self-esteem, self-concept, self-monitoring, self-efficacy, self-absorption, self-reliance, self-interest, self-serving, self-actualization, self-achievement, and self-management.

Self is a whole and a unified entity that owns an extraordinary variety of characteristics in an individual. Self possesses instinctive sensation, emotion, imagination, intellect, information, knowledge, problem-solving abilities, and genetic characteristics. Therefore, we easily gain the impression that self is so complex that it cannot easily be analyzed. Discussion related to self is traced back to the views of Sigmund Freud (1856-1939). As previously indicated, Freud viewed self as the interactional processes among three elements of personality: the id, ego, and superego. It was Sigmund Freud (1889) who first perceived that people were often not aware of the causal effect relationships influencing problems of human behavior. From this view, Freud concluded that unconscious mental processes motivate much of human behavior. He conceived in these processes that the id, as the primitive and unconscious part of self, is the storehouse of personality. The id is an unleashed, raw, and institutional drive struggling for gratification and pleasure. The ego is the conscious, logical portion that associates with reality. The ego represents reality, and it rationally attempts to keep the impulsive id and the conscious of the superego in check, and represents an individual's personal view of physical and social reality. The ego is the conscious and logical portion of an individual's reasoning that associates with reality.

NATURAL AND SOCIAL INTELLIGENT ENDOWMENT ↓			
Representative Ecological Differences	Representative Psychological Differences	Representative Socio-cultural Differences	Representative Behavioral Differences
Weight Height Hair color Eye color Body shape Gender Sensation Race Ethnicity Appearance style	Self Needs Motives Attitudes Perceptions Traits Ability Potentials Faith Learning style	Personality Conception Attributions Beliefs Values Family Ideology Wealth Expectations Life style	Self-Image Self-Esteem Self-Concept Self-monitoring Self-efficacy Self absorption Self-reliance Self-achievement Self-interest Self Serving Self-actualization Self management

↓ Family-Related Status	↓ Job-Related Status
↓ Ability and skill efficiency	↓ Work-related efficiency

↓ Moral Character

Figure 5.1: Variables Influencing an Individual's Moral Character

The superego is the conscience that provides the norms that enable the ego to determine what is right and what is wrong. The superego is the storehouse of values, including moral attitudes learned from society. There is an ongoing conflict between the id and superego. The ego serves as a compromiser to make a balance between the id and superego. However, when id and superego pressures become intensified, the result becomes more difficult for the ego to work out optimal compromises.

Moral, ethical, and legal ordinations promote a higher quality of life. These are concerned with seeking a good and meaningful life. More broadly, in searching for the good life. An individual needs to search for excellence in character. Good may be viewed as intrinsic: good in themselves, or viewed as an extrinsic instrumental good that serves as the means for achieving ends usually higher levels of good which could be perceived as excellence. For example, honesty is an intrinsic goodness, because honesty is good in its real pragmatic meaning and action. The quest for the greatest goodness in a hierarchy of goodness is the quest for rational thoughts with good intentions. What is quality as well as quantity. This type of goodness is called *eudaemonism*. As De George (1995: 63) indicates, this position maintains that what has to be calculated is not pleasure or happiness but all intrinsically valuable things, which include friendship, knowledge, and a host of other valuable behavior and good will in themselves.

MORAL REASONING CONCERNING THE MEANS

People are not aimless. Whatever the aim is, they make good and bad choices. People do whatever they intend to do and behave in that manner. What they intend to do is whatever they deliberate on selves and others' reasoning for achieving good and/or evil ends. It is true, in one sense, that an end is last in execution, for it is the last thing to happen. But in another sense the end is first, not in the order of execution, but in the order of intention (Oesterle 1957: 17).

Deliberation is a pragmatic and possible workout of reason. We consider and evaluate reasons for or against doing something. We still need to understand the nature of a choice itself because the act of choice may cause a misunderstanding. Morally, a right choice should be based on good will. It should follow the intellectual reasoning for specifying the right ends through the right means. A manager without intellectual deliberation and good choices cannot succeed at creating an everlasting goodness. Good managers morally need to establish in their character sufficient good will, useful knowledge, and reliable information in order to make good choices and to take good actions.

EUDAEMONISTIC MEANS AND ENDS

Through *eudeimonistic goodness* an individual's moral, ethical, and legal ordinations can be characterized by observing conscience, conscientiousness, integrity, dignity, honesty, rightness, discipline, orders, rights, duties, responsibility, accountability, respectfulness, politeness, courage, prudence, truthfulness, trustfulness, fairness, justness, fortitude, patience, good will, good faith, magnanimity, perseverance, sincerity, and loyalty.

Conscience: An individual possesses a sense of *self-love*. According to English Philosopher Joseph Butler (1672-1752) self-love is the effective regulative principle that operates when individuals organize their desires to promote their own best interests. When they control their *appetites* to further the public good, the operative principle is that of *benevolence*. Yet, Butler tells us, there is no guarantee that these regulative principles of self-love and benevolence will always reinforce and complement one another. Under these circumstances, conflicts between personal and social interests are frequently resolved by a regulative principle of a higher order, namely, the conscience.

Table 5.1: Analysis of *Positive* Perceptual Attributions Concerning Religious Faith, Moral Judgments, Ethical Behavior, and Legal Ordinations

PERCEPTUAL ATTRIBUTIONS	POSITIVE ATTITUDES	EARTHLY EXPECTED CONSEQUENCES	HEAVENLY EXPECTED EENDS
Religious Faith: (Behaviors) Individualistic Orientations	Virtuous Intentions	Conscience Awareness	Spiritual Revelation
Moral Judgments: (Conducts) Individualistic Orientations	Conscience Normative Conceptions	Syllogistic Reasoning For Philanthropic Helps	Universal Order For Goodness and Peaceful Solutions
Ethical Values: (Professional) Pluralistic Orientations	Conscientious Cognitive Perceptions	Social Praiseworthy and Honorable Reception	Blessing Wishes and Solemn Ritualistic Happiness
Legal Ordinations: (Mandated Compliance) Collectivistic Orientations	Meritocratic Compliance and Jurist Prudence	Material Usefulness, Advocacy For Justness and Right Decisions	XXX

The conscience is the functioning of reason that at times acts as the arbiter of conflicting interests between self-love and benevolence. It is the commander of our moral obligations to convince us to perform our moral duties (Butler, 1849). Therefore, conscience is the knowledge of right and the self-evidence of conviction within an individual's personal judgmental perception.

Conscientiousness: *Conscientiousness* is a moral cognitive conviction by an individual who controls his/her decisions and actions according to their conscience. It is a dynamic movement agent in an individual's moral mind that manifests the final self-assessment. As indicated in the above definition, conscientiousness is the self-assessment from which there can be no appeal to any higher moral or ethical principle. It is the supreme ultimate end in an individual's moral character. That is, the state of excellence in the mind and judgment.

Table 5.2: Analysis of *Negative* Perceptual Attributions Concerning Religious Faith, Moral Judgments, Ethical Behavior, and Legal Ordinations

PERCEPTUAL ATTRIBUTIONS	POSITIVE ATTITUDES	EARTHLY EXPECTED CONSEQUENCES	HEAVENLY EXPECTED ENDS
Antagonistic Beliefs (Disbelievers)	Sinful and Filthy Intentions	Conscious Guilt and Condemned Intentions	Godly Dissatisfaction and Forbidden Intentions
Immoral Judgments and Actions	Shameful, Improbable, and Faulty Actions	Dampened Reactionary and Filthy Actions	Exonerated Punishment Extortion
Unethical Behavior and Malevolent Conduct	Blameworthy and Condemned Reactions	Social Hatred and Abhorrent Abomination	Psychosocial Distressful and Miserable Lifestyle
Illegal Intentions and Actions	Chaotic Anarchy and Terrorist Mentality	Punishment, Impoverishment, Savagery, and Thoughtlessness	XXX

Integrity: *Integrity* means soundness of and adherence to the ultimate state of moral character; excellence. Moral and ethical principles mandate people to preserve their honest thoughts and express their intellectual ideas without fear of retaliation. The German philosopher Friedrich Nietzsche (1844-1900) believed that a moral person needs to be independent in thought and strong in conviction, even in the face of group pressure and government authority (Nietzsche, 1917). Martin Heidigger (1889-1927), another German existentialist philosopher expressed his ideal of nobility and thoughts for the importance of resolutive conviction to personal integrity rather than succumbing to socio-political pressures to conform. He believed personal integrity means that one cannot coexist with everyone who is not ethical, so it is incumbent on each person to choose individual lifestyles and commitments carefully.

Businesses are particularly relevant examples of group-pressure that can potentially damage individual integrity and dignity (Heidigger, 1962). *Dignity* is closely related to self-consideration in relation to the manifestation of self-identity. Dignity means self-respect gained by the conformity of excellence in an individuals' moral character. It is a base for suitable character traits for a person. Individuals with a high quality of integrity try to elevate their moral character to the highest standard of morality and ethics. For an individual self-respect is normally extended to the consideration for oneself as an independent agent. Self-respect is the opposite of self-contempt. Thus, integrity is an ultimate tendency to represent a favorable opinion of self-image according to the highest state of intellectual excellence.

Dignity: *Dignity* is closely related to the degree of excellence in relation to the manifestation of self-identity. Dignity means qualitative self-respect to the conformity of excellence in an individuals' moral character. It is an honorable worthiness for suitable and sustainable character traits for a person. An individual with a high quality of dignity tries to elevate their moral behavior to the highest standard of morality and ethics. For an individual, self-respect is normally extended to the consideration for oneself as an independent dynamic agent. Self-respect is the opposite of self-contempt. Thus, dignity is the highest honorable behavioral tendency to represent a favorable manifestation of self, based on a comparison of one's own worth comparing with that of others.

Honesty: *Honesty* means an individual is a straightforward and trustworthy in dealing with the discovery of truth and expression of the truthful judgments concerning self and others. An honest person does not withhold one's own feelings, ideas, and knowledge relevant to realization and expression of the whole truth. A *moral* person reveals, by all means and ends, the whole truth, only the truth, and not beyond the truth, while an *amoral* person reveals only a portion of the truth.

Rightness: Moral and ethical decisions and actions are nothing less than the full awareness of what one ought to be according to their religious faith and cultural value systems. Thinking about revealing the truth in business is no more than acknowledging that one has taken into account and is willing to be righteously responsible for their effectiveness and efficiency. *Rightness* in management is a mandated self-conviction for attesting to justness and being decisive to attest the rightful judgment on the basis of three "Cs":

- The need for *careful consideration* of the rightful principles to be applied. This considers causes, means, ends, consequences, and such specific concerns as justness.
- The need for prompt rightness of *contributions* to the well being of a society through the value and quality of the usefulness of judgments.
- The need to be *committed* to carefully viewing the impartial consequences of the usefulness of judgments in relation to the intentional and unintended reputation of self, one's own company, and industry.

To set the image of rightness straight, there are some amoral problems in American enterprises. Shaw and Barry (1998: 36) state:

Half of American businesses is family business: 50% of the GNP; 50% of the employees. Some of these family businesses are among the Fortune 500. Others are Mom and Pop groceries and Sally and Lou's Restaurant. But it is essential to remember that however much our focus may be on corporations and corporate life, business in America is not monolithic, inhumane enterprise.

Discipline: *Discipline* is an intrinsic precision of one's own mind through behavior to act in accordance to rules of self-conscience conduct and/or organizational mandated beliefs. It is an orderly behavior in accordance with the maintenance of self-integrity and dignity. Obedience to the intellectual conscientiousness or to the mission (the legitimate reason for the existence) of a corporation is a matter of discipline. There are several personal attributions related directly to discipline such as appearance, respect, politeness, punctuality, dependability, efficiency, and cooperation. Although disciplinary actions in organizations are considered as desirable and necessary for orderliness, they raise concerns about fairness, justness, and rightness for the individuals in the way they are treated.

Orderliness: *Orderliness* is an extrinsic precision of one's surrounding belongings and/or atmospheric environment. It is a purity of neatness and putting in a sequence of arrangement all things on the basis of necessitated arrangements. Orderly people do not live in a messy and filthy environment. We need to avoid living in a mess. Ethical and moral people need to keep their environments clean. Many businesses are observed to be in love with making profits, either by carelessness or by negligence in destroying the habitats. They destroy habitats by clearing land for farming, grazing, and settlements; by draining and filling wetlands; and by poor land management they may lead their ecological life toward destruction. They also destroy species by pollution and by introducing new species that overtake native species (Kempton et al., 1995: 27). For example, one corporate disaster is the Exxon Valdez Oil Spill in Prince William Bay, Alaska, which destroyed the habitat of the living things around that region.

Rights: *Rights* are legitimate claims which one person has or can make on another. A right defines a freedom of choice and action. Rights are moral entitlements or privileges that invoke corresponding duties on the part of others. A right to own material objects is a free choice of the use to which those objects will be managed. A right to a specific action, such as free speech, is the freedom to engage in that activity without repression or prosecution. The connection between rights and duties is that if someone has a right to own something, then someone else has a correlative duty to act in certain ways. We have moral rights derived from specific relationships, roles, or circumstances in which we ought to be. For example, as individuals, we have the right to survive and others have the duty to respect it. Rights are divided into two classes: (1) natural rights, and (2) other rights.

Natural Rights: Natural rights are those rights that are created by nature. Natural rights are those entitlements that morally constrain social orders. Natural rights ought to be developed through a mandatory process. Natural rights are self-evidence of coexistence. All men and women view them equally. In modern days, natural rights, through the Charter of the United Nations, are called *human rights*.

Other Rights: The other rights are societal agreements and/or entitlements (e.g., parental rights, civil rights, collective bargaining contracts rights, etc.) concerning social privileges for individuals and institutions. For example, Title VII of the Civil Rights Act of 1964 in the United States with the Equal Employment Opportunity Commission (EECO) protects employment rights against discrimination. Also, the *Human Development Report of the United Nations* (2000), in terms of human rights, indicates that having access to income and education is an example of competing claims on resources, not rights. In addition, it indicates that the rule of social rights is not only vital to protect the interests of domestic and foreign investors, it is also essential for all domestic citizens, above all the powerless (*Financial Times*, 2000: 12). Or in the United States to have access to medical facilities is viewed as a privilege not as a right. This means that if an institution that provides you with health care insurance employs you, you will be able to manage your health and medical care costs. Otherwise you will have difficulty in supporting your medical costs. Also the Act of 1978 prohibits discrimination against pregnant women. The 1967 Age Discrimination in Employment Act extends protection to people 40 years of age and older. The Americans with Disabilities Act (ADA) of 1990 extends protection to the private sector by requiring all companies with more than 15 employees to make reasonable accommodations in order to employ workers with disabilities. Also, HIV infection (AIDS) is considered a disability and the ADA law protects people who have it.

Duties: *Duties* are those self-mandatory commitments to conform to natural and societal rights. Duties are what one is morally required to do to self and others. Duties are conscientious determinations of a person either to do or to refrain from performing certain acts. British scholar W. D. Ross (1930: 42) divides duties into seven basic types:

- Duties of fidelity: that is, to respect explicit and implicit promises to deal with people, to create expectations, reliance, and trust.
- Duties of reparation: that is, for previous wrongful acts.
- Duties of gratitude: that is being grateful or thankful for receiving favors.

- Duties of justice: that is, by the quality that a person is virtuous in all respects.
- Duties of beneficence: that is, to make the condition of others better.
- Duties of self-improvement: that is, to drive a person progressively to become what one is capable of becoming.
- Duties to not injure others: that is, to avoid vicious decisions and actions.

Responsibility: *Responsibility* is closely related with rights, duties, and obligations. Responsibility is the self-conviction to comply with a just cause. An individual has a responsibility, in the moral sense, to do those things that are mandated by moral duty. For example, managers have four major moral and ethical responsibilities:

- They are trustees of various stakeholders.
- They are powerful agents for the wise execution of organizational policies and procedures.
- They have the obligation to balance the interests of the main constituents of an organization.
- They are coordinators of all employees' duties and activities.
- These four interrelated responsibilities (trusteeship, executive, balancing of interests, and coordination) are the main ethical and moral responsibilities of contemporary managers.

Accountability: *Accountability* is closely related to several other concepts besides duties and responsibilities, obligatory and mandatory commitments, possibilities and capabilities in doing something, and finally making alternative choices for doing right or wrong actions. Accountability means the acceptance of the consequential results of self-conducts, and the willingness to answer to higher authorities. It is the obligation to give an account of our decisions and actions to higher authorities and/or society. Accountability is conditional. A person needs to be accountable, if causes and consequences can clearly justify reasonability, appropriateness, correctness, and prudence in his/her decisions and actions. Accountability includes liability in intentional and consequential outcomes within the boundary of self-mandated behavior.

There are many attributions attached to accountability such as: praise and pride, blame and condemnation, and shame and remorse. *Liability* for one's actions means that one can rightly pay a compensatory price for the adverse effects of one's own actions on others. There are moral and legal liabilities. For example, the Superintendent of the Corpus Christi School District was found accountable for buying liquor with the school district's money. According to the records, he lost his jobs over a 1995 receipt that included a glass of wine in his lunch, paid with taxpayers' money. Taxpayer's money should be spent for educational purposes, not for personal pleasure (*Laredo Morning Times*, 2000: 10A).

Magnanimity: *Magnanimity* means being generous in mind. The word magnanimity is made up of two Latin words: *magna*, means signifying great and *anima*, means signifying the soul. Therefore, the nominal meaning of this value is to be generous in mind. For example, for a manager, magnanimity means to have deliberated with good reasoning by the demonstration of great efforts, regardless of cost and benefit analysis, for an important qualitative decision or action. Magnanimity is the breath of qualitative intention and action toward building and maintaining conformity in high qualitative character.

Perseverance: *Perseverance* is another moral virtue where an individual is persistent to achieve specific legitimate objectives regardless of obstacles and annoyances. A manager perseveres in the virtuous sense, if he/she reasonably persists in achieving a difficult action, even though the length of time necessary to complete that action is long and laborious. For example, strategists need to develop the virtue of perseverance in their thoughts and behaviors because they have to wait to achieve their strategic objectives over a long period of time with continual efforts.

Courage: *Courage* means the high quality of mind in decisions and an action that enables one withstand facing with difficulty, danger, and pain as the result of standing against unethical and immoral people. In the field of management, some managers need to stand firmly and without fear against unjust and unfair decisions and actions. Courageous people tend to be fearless in expression of their rational reasoning with acceptance of possible retaliatory actions. Courageous decisions and actions are very risky.

Prudence: *Prudence* is an intellectual manner of careful consideration when an individual is faced with problems and issues and acting or reacting with care. Prudence is a careful moral obligation toward particular decisions and actions for achieving good-ends through good-means without risk. A manager needs to carefully assess the circumstances of a decision or an action in order to understand what should or shouldn't In addition, managers need to make sure that a decision or an action should have an assent to suitable means and ends. A manager needs to avoid inconsistency in his/her intentions and negligence in actions. We should not give credit to a foolish manager with good intentions who does the wrong thing. Crisis management needs courageous people to solve problems. All managers should know prudent decisions and actions, and all employees should be expected to act accordingly. However, prudence may be either good or evil.

Truthfulness: *Truthfulness* means conformity with causal fact or reality. An individual's moral and ethical conduct is based upon truthfulness, and validity of causes and reasoning in decision- making processes and actions. Sometimes reasoning is based upon sensational and emotional attachment of an individual to pleasure and enjoyment (to enjoy for a logical success or to enjoy with unjust reasoning of failure of others as a sign of revenge), and sometimes it is the result of intellectual deliberation on factual logical reasoning for actuality of existence. To say that a statement is true is to make the claim that it accurately manifests the signs of reality for the factual existence of an object or a state of affairs. *Validity*, on the other hand, is only our assessment of the existence of reality with the structure of reasoning regardless of just causes.

The truthful ethical decisions and actions in a corporation depend on how consistent a manager is with the ethics of knowledge. He/she should answer the following questions:

- Is it true that the concept of scientific thoughts and statements and those of ethics and values belong to different worlds?
- Is it true that the world of scientific thoughts and actions are subject to tests?
- Is it true that the world of *what* is subject to test, and the world of *what ought to be* subject to no tests? Is it true that the power of intellect differs from the power of willingness and from the power of desire?

To know something well through reason is to know something as true. Truthfulness, therefore, is the reasoning of intellect to perceive facts or reality. For example, a manager's intention in discharging an employee without just cause is a faulty intention, but the validity of the discharge hearing and processes could correctly be observed. In another words, all our statements of allegations may be false, but the procedural reasoning will be correct. Truthfulness in decision-making processes and actions should be based on three conditions:

- Correctness of the just cause
- Soundness of structural reasoning
- Validity of information and data

Truthfulness: *Trustfulness* is the reliance on the dignity, integrity, and confidence in a moral and ethical character. Trust is fragile. It takes a long time to build. It takes a short time to break. It is hard to regain (Sonnenberg, 1993: 22). Recent research by Schindler and Thomas (1993: 563) identified five dimensions that underlay the concept of trust:

- Integrity
- Competence
- Consistency

- Loyalty
- Openness (see Figure 5-1).

They found that importance of these five dimensions is relatively constant:

Integrity > Competence > Loyalty > Consistency > Openness

Moreover, integrity and competence are the most critical characteristics that an individual looks for in determining another's trustworthiness. They found that integrity seems to be rated highest because without a perception of the other's "moral character" and "basic honesty," other dimensions of trust were meaningless (Butler and Cantrell, 1984: 19-28).

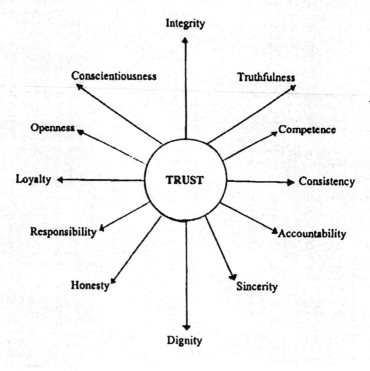

Figure 5.1: The Sunshine of Trust

Fairness: *Fairness* is a moral characteristic and ethical obligation of an individual to judge about self and others' behavior free from bias, discrimination, dishonesty, and inappropriate comments. A decision or an action is fair if all involved parties engage in the process freely, without coercion. If all parties have adequate and appreciative knowledge of the relevant aspects of an issue, then the deliberative judgment can be fair. If one of the parties misrepresents the criteria, hides relevant information in some way, or intimidates the other party, then the procedural and consequential result of judgment would be unfair. Fairness is a meaningful word to be considered in the policy of an organization. When we talk about fairness, we are not talking about equality; we are doing something equitably, reciprocally, and impartially. In the field of business, usually transactions are ethically fair; unless a seller hides principle valuable information from buyers coerce them by intimidation, deception, and threats to buy their products.

Justness: The proper object of *justness* is right, that which is just. The proper Latin word for right is *jus*, and hence right is only another name for the just. Through an ethical point of view, justness does have three clarifications: The first is that the source of justness is natural law. Natural law is a generalized principle for an individual action inclining feelings toward what is good in nature. The second point is related to an individual's extrinsic cultural reasoning, which is related to econo-political and sociocultural value systems. These value systems are called rights, in relation to and consequences upon the end-results of goodness. The third point is related to an individual's intrinsic cognitive conception concerning human rights. Individuals are concerned about themselves regardless of the consequences for the common good.

Justice is a matter that essentially dissolves serious disputes between parties. Justice is based on an individual's moral rights. Justice is essentially comparative. Justice becomes an issue when parties unevenly compete with each other, when benefits and treatments are not equitably distributed, and when rules and laws are discriminatory administered. The moral right of an individual entitles that person to be justly treated like others. Justness depends on the idea that benefits or penalties should be distributed equitably for all. In other words, the moral rights of some individuals cannot be ignored or sacrificed merely in order to guarantee a somewhat better distribution of benefits for others. If we think that exploitation of children by some multinational corporations in the Third World Countries is unjust, then such an action is immoral and unethical. We then condemn a corporation that exercises exploitation, even if exploitation makes those children economically stronger. The greatest benefits for some economically deprived children in a country cannot justify injustice for all children around the world. Philosophically, standards of justice do not override the moral rights of individuals. For example, if a manager's decision or action is unjust for his/her subordinates, then we normally condemn that manager of unjustness. There are three types of justness:

- *Distributive justness:* That is concerned with the fair distribution of benefits and related burdens on all.
- *Retributive justness*: That is concerned with the imposition of

punishments, penalties, and fines upon those who do wrong.

- *Compensatory justness*: That is concerned with the just remedies for those people who lost some rights when others wronged them.

Righteousness: *Righteousness* means an individual is suitable to what they are supposed to do, or that a judgment should be suitable to what is in conformity with facts, reasons, standards or principles. From an ethical point of view any decision or judgment could stay with the right course of action by too little or too much. An obvious instance is found in our daily attachment to special habits, tendencies, or extravagancy such as workaholic, alcoholism, sexism, prejudices, and others. A manager needs to reason correctly when it comes time to expressing causes of judgments and decisions according to a speculative order of knowledge. The right reason is true knowledge of ethical principles.

Fortitude: *Fortitude* is a blending behavioral mode of endurance during expected emotional fear and intellectual expression of boldness in making the right decision. People possess different levels of fortitude. These levels are the potential strengths in their minds that enable them to endure adverse events with courageous actions. Fortitude is clearly an admirable intellectual virtue that an individual can create through a high quality in thinking, strong positioning power in choices, and positive attitudes in progressive actions. A manager needs to have the best-known intelligible attitudes toward successful and useful means and ends of self-conduct. Fortitude is not equivalent to courage. Fortitude brings out more accomplishment in intellectual deliberations, whereas courage is sometimes applied to an emotional or sensational action without assurance of the final possibility of positive consequences.

Patience: *Patience* is a virtue that moderates behavioral frustration during various hasty decisions and actions. Patience promotes and develops cheerfulness and principally tranquility of the state of the generous mind despite great injuries and other subversive actions. Fortitude is closely related to the extent of endurance and tolerance. Patience in times of miserable situations prevents morale breakdown. It releases grief and sorrow. A manager needs to be patient because he/she is behaving as a thoughtful leader who has the responsibility of leading their subordinates. In contrast, impatience often promotes selfishness, hastiness, greediness, anguish, fear, frustration, and anger.

Sincerity: *Sincerity* denotes a moral charter who possesses a sense of justness free from deceit, hypocrisy, or falseness. A manager needs to be sincere in his/her mind and action. Sometimes people say something but act differently. These people are not judged as sincere people.

Loyalty: Loyalty means willingness to promote and respect the interest of someone to whom an individual has an obligation or commitment. Loyalty is associated with fidelity. Loyalty is a reciprocal obligation of two parties to each other (e.g., husband and wife; employers and employees). According to the American Idealist, Josiah Royce (1916: 16-17):

> Loyalty is the willingness and practical commitment through-going devotion of a person to a cause. A man is loyal when, first, he has some cause to which he is loyal; secondly, he willingly and thoroughly devotes himself to this cause; and when, thirdly, he expresses his devotion in some sustained and practical way, by acting steadily in the service of cause.

However, loyalty is not ethical and moral when we notice the loyalty of a thief to another thief.

Biologists are celebrating a historic achievement with the announcement of drafting the first human genome the *Book of Life* that provides our biochemical blueprint in 3 billion genetic "letters" (*Financial Times*, 2000: 16). Since, half of each individual's DNA is inherited from each parent, traditionally, a DNA paternity client was an angry mother trying to pin responsibility on her ex-lover to support his or her children. This action has been changed. Today, in the field of biotechnolgy men are now turning to DNA labs to identify their partners' fidelity. Male insecurity about their partners' fidelity is creating a massive new client base for DNA experts, fueling an expansion in the testing industry (Adiga, 2000: 16).

The Goodwill: Choice and deliberation are two major component parts of a *will*. We need to understand the nature of moral obligations -- *the good will* -- in order to make a right choice. An individual can make a choice on the basis of either emotional or intellectual reasoning. Emotional choices can end with pleasure (appropriate sensational and feeling enjoyment) or pain (excessive sensational and emotional deprivation). In contrast, intellectual choices can end with happiness (appropriate usage of intellect) and avoidance of misery (inappropriate and/or no usage of wisdom). Simple emotional acts of desire are not choices of an individual's will. Emotional desires are acts of tendencies for pleasure. An individual's will is an intellectual satisfactory intention in reasoning. Intellectual choices are not necessarily connected with pleasure or pain, but with happiness and satisfaction. Also, intellectual choices are associated with self-volition, that is, as being very intent on getting what people seek. Therefore, managers need to act on the basis of their will, especially, the good will.

What determines the goodness of good will? Kant (1724-1804) answered this by saying that the will is good when it is completely devoted to duty for the sake of duty. As for duty, it is prescribed by the moral imperatives. Thus, the good will is reverence for the duty and duty is founded on reason.

The Good Faith: The *good faith* is considered as reaching to the perfect stage of human moral power. It attains whatever is the good of a power. The good faith differs from the power of willingness and from the power of desire. Both of these powers are appetitive powers. However, abuse of power happens, has always happened, and will always happen. Whereas the faith is a cognitive power, greedy power is an emotional power. The good faith consists of grasping things in a rational and reasonable mode of assurance. To know something is good because it is good to know something as true. For example, in an assembling line of production, a production manager's decision to rework a defected product with good faith is considered as moral decision to treat customers with good faith. It also makes workers be conscious of doing what is right even with more costs and efforts.

The Good Humor: Dooley (1941: 37) states:

> *Humor* is an attitude toward an event, situation, or to a life that makes what otherwise would appear sad and terrible seem insignificant and amusing (or at least tolerable). It rather tends constantly to turn aside suffering to create happiness.

Freud (1960) stated that humor is one of the highest psychic functions enjoying the special favor of thinkers. He describes humor as the vehicle that lets energy that has built up in certain psychic channels be used or discharged in spite of the usual censoring by the superego. This energy may be discharged or cathetered in a language or behavior that is funny. Good humor is viewed as a brake in a serious situation. It helps to curb expanding energy on feelings. Turning psychic suffering, pain, and pleasure into energy, which is felt as humorous pleasure, is efficient (Buchman, 1980: 1715). Laughing truly takes less energy and time than crying, and we feel better. We can be in pain for extended periods of time but we cannot keep on laughing for long. Freud (1928: 2) states: "Like jokes and the comic, humor has something liberating, about it; but it is also has something of grandeur and elevation, which is lacking in the other two ways of obtaining pleasure from intellectual activity." Good humor is different from bad language. In good humor, people consider moral and ethical behavior, while in bad language; people use dirty jokes and unethical or immoral slang.

Grotjahn (1956) speaks of four humorous moral or immoral or ethical and unethical behaviors:

- The *Kidder,* a derivative of the word "like a child," is, like a child, in a position of humility and passive endurance. This humor style mocks playfully, yet with an element of cruelty. Usually, women do not kid, as it is socially unacceptable. Instead, they tease.
- The *practical joker* is an eternal adolescent. As a style of humor that employs cruelty, practical joking falls halfway between an intended aggression and its intended witty, verbal, and nonverbal expression.
- The *wit* is a person whose humorous personality style is formed by destiny, not by choice. When angry, he/she uses his/her natural talent

as a weapon. The *clown* has his origins in his costume and acting funny things out.

Coser (1960) studied humor as a communication facilitator among colleagues. It is known as an equalizing function, which reduces distances between people. Salameh (1983) classifies humor into four levels:

- Destructive humor
- Minimally helpful humor
- Very helpful humor
- Outstanding behavioral humor

Serenity: *Serenity* means the desire for quality in making peaceful and tranquil discoveries of relationship with good will. It is a moral characteristic in which an individual creates an honorable, respectful, and reverent social atmosphere by using good and polite words in communication. Serenity is not only respecting others, it is also related to showing dignity in self-identity.

Politeness: *Politeness* means showing good manners and courteous respect toward others in the forms of verbal and written communication, body language, and behavior.

HEDONISTIC MEANS AND ENDS

Sometimes for some people the denominator of goodness is based on their emotional, sensational, pleasurable, and enjoyable ends. These good faith, good will, and good deeds are called *hedonistic*. Hedonism holds that the basic values of goodness are the differentiation power between pleasure and pain. According to this type of view, everything that people pursue or demand should be directed toward enjoyment or simply as the absence of pain. This view contains selfishness. Just as a healthy body cannot compromise with the filthy and vicious mind, intrinsic moral goodness not work by compromising between vicious and rational intentions. The goodness comes from the healthy mind and the healthy mind comes from the healthy body. If not, then evil ideas and vicious actions are giving rise to the greedy means of appetitive selfishness to win evil ends. Through hedonistic perceptions an individual's behavior may be exposed to evil means and vicious ends such as: cynicism, nepotism, favoritism, cruelty, filthiness, felony, slitting, greediness, heartlessness, falsification, viciousness, revengefulness, cheating, stealing, plagiarism, gossip, rudeness, dishonesty, egoistic, incompetence, offensiveness, reproachful, fraudulent, negligence, deception, harmfulness, harassment, intimidation, influencing, falsification, bribery, kickbacks, payola, overcharging, corruption, scandals, price gauging, unfairness, unjustness, and wrong doing, exploitation, discrimination, false advertising, and breach the contract. In order to understand in depth these human characteristics, we will define them as following.

Cynicism: *Cynicism* is a pessimistic mental characteristic of an individual who doubts or denies the goodness of human motives and who often displays attitudes by sarcasm. It is a bad habit that manifests in a contemptuous mistrust of scientists, politicians, religious, and business leaders, (Olasky, 1985). The classic studies of business ethics conducted by Baumhart (1961: 6) and Brenner and Molander (1977: 57) in 1950s -1970s, found that corporate CEOs have repeatedly reported their own cynicism. They expressed the pressure that they felt to compromise their personal ethical standards on the job. They were even more cynical about their peers' ethics than their own (Carroll, 1975: 4).

Cruelty: *Cruelty* means letting nothing stand in one's own way and using any methods and all means and ends to wipe them out. Cruelty is an extreme degree of selfishness by a person willfully and knowingly causing pain and harm to others. Such an emotional motive is derived from the lack of kindness, gentleness, and compassion. Usually, this type of manager is very harsh and brutal. Cruel managers behave with atrocity, barbarity, and inhumanity. There is no mercy in their characters. Cruelty is the result of savagery and jealousy. Unfortunately, in the field of global business, there are unfair practices of ruthlessness with greedy appetite. Some businesspeople are motivated by eradicating extradite competitors. Also, cruelty is a tool to exploit people.

Filthiness: In the field of ethics a *filthy* character means having moral impurity, corruption, and obscenity in an individual's mind and action. Usually, those people who do not observe politeness in their daily communications treat other people impolitely. They use vulgar or obscene words, sentences, and metaphoric slang of foul words and languages to offend others.

Felony: The term *felony* means committing any various vicious actions that, by law, are prohibited. This malicious and treacherous characteristic converts people into savagery. Misdemeanor character is the pure immoral, unethical, and illegal characteristic of a felon who deserves to be severely punished. Unfortunately, there are many examples of this horrible immoral characteristic in today's field of business. For example, recently there was an English physician, Dr. Harold Shipman, who murdered 215 patients in England (CNN.2002). In another similar case, recently a registered nurse killed 30 patients in the state of Kentucky by injecting over dosage lethal substances into the vein of hospital patients serial killers.

Greediness: *Greediness* is an excessive, inordinate, and rapacious desire and appetite for accumulation of wealth and power beyond the legitimate share. We can identify greedy businesses from a moral point of view, how they behave through hostile takeovers, junk bonds, and greenmail. Greed is viewed as an infectious psychological disease, not only to motivate the greedy people to acquire soft money, but also, it motivates others to be absorbed into such a trap. Pernicious greed is nonproductive and its only aim is quick acquisition by almost any means of personal gain as their justified ends.

Churning: *Churning* is a special greed in which a selfish person pushes other people to use their rights, assets, and/or reputation for achieving his/her own self-interests as ends in themselves. Eichenwald (1993: C1) indicates in his article entitled "Commissions Are Many, Profits Few," in the stock market, when brokers encourage unnecessarily their clients to buy and/or sell their stocks in order to reap a commission. This action is not based on moral trust, but it is based on greed and selfishness churning. The brokers' targets in a churning process are to make deals in order to get their commissions regardless of the client's interests. Likewise, Kant would object to churning in the field of medicine. Churning means when a physician uses patients and/or their specimens such as sperms, eggs, ovaries tissues, stem cells, and blood as subjects in a medical experiment without the patients' consent. Even though great social benefit might result, the researchers would intentionally use the patients as a means to the researchers' own goals and thus fail to respect the patient's basic humanity (Shaw, 1996: 61).

Heartlessness: Human experiences are conveyed into emotional expressions that allow us to center the perspective of other human beings. Personal feelings take shape within a culture and articulate the experiences of a given life into a more or less meaningful whole. *Heartlessness* means unfeeling and unsympathetic ways of judging others with dysfunctional or fragmented feelings. As long as we behave inhumanely, we ignore our moral and ethical commitments to self and others. Such a cold feeling of unjustness and unfairness motivates heartlessness people to view their business behaviors as a sole milking customer to the last purchase power abilities.

Revengefulness: *Revengefulness* refers to a type of punishment or injury inflicted in return for one received. It is a bitter experience to be carried out to injure another person for a wrong doing to one or to those who are felt to be like one. Different cultural beliefs and religious faiths have different ideas concerning revengefulness. Some believe in forgiveness and forgetfulness (e.g., Christianity) while others believe in an eye for an eye (e. g., Jewish and Moslem cultures). Nevertheless, revengefulness constructs a chain of sequential aggression and ruthlessness.

Rudeness: *Rudeness* refers to deliberated roughness in behavior and language (oral, written, body, and sign languages) with harsh intentions to insult others by *words and bodily symbolic sings*. These types of behaviors and communications can turn people into enemies. A manager needs to be gentle in character and polite in communication during conversation with others in order to be able to properly function in their leadership role.

Viciousness: *Viciousness* refers to grossly immoral intention and action to give or to be readily disposed to evil. Such immoral and unethical means and ends characterize a personality of a person by faults and defects. Viciousness may be the most hatred characteristic of inhumane behavior. For example, it has been observed that some mechanics in towns spread sharp nails in the nearby parking lots in order to give drivers flat tires. Then, they will create a very crowded customer profile in their mechanic shops.

Falsification: *Falsification* is a form of faithlessness. It is a form of deceit that so clearly identifiable that it has its own name, faithlessness. It is a condition for someone being incorrect, untruthful, and treacherous to testify against innocent people.

Deception: *Deception* means any various kinds of concealing, acting, or a statement of fraud in a misrepresentation or conversion of a fact. Deception is an attempt to wrongly persuade somebody to buy a defected product as non-defected one with a regular price. It exploits customers with ambiguity, concealing the facts, and exaggerating the superficial usefulness of products. For example, deceptive ads dominate the global business environments. They jingle, rhyme, build, and attract images of consumers. Ads are trying to persuade consumers to buy a company's defected products. It is true that when ads are ambiguous, they can be deceiving. It is unethical and immoral for someone to use deceitful psychological appeals in the field of business to pressure customers to buy their inferior products with the maximum price.

Fraud: *Fraud* means breaching the confidence to gain some unfair or dishonest advantage over somebody. Fraud is viewed as an evil act. It is unethical, immoral, and illegal for someone who makes deceitful statements to gain illegitimate self-interest. Fraud, in the field of business, is a deliberated use of deception to cause the loss of some value to either one of the buyers or sellers' advantages. In any case of buying or selling products or providing services, there is an obligation on the part of buyers and sellers to take reasonable care that the exchange is one of equitable values. For example, if a seller morally injures a buyer with deception, then the seller has committed fraud. In such a case, the seller practices fraud by knowing that the product is defective and does not carry any discount in its price accordingly or does not inform the buyer of the effectiveness.

Cheating: *Cheating* is a deliberated act of violation of moral and ethical principles. In a legal term, it is viewed as a violation of the rules and regulations of the society. It refers to the use of fraud deliberately to hoodwink someone or to obtain an unfair advantage over another. For example, a seller may cheat customers by selling short in number or in weight. On the other hand, morally, ethically, and legally, if a buyer practices fraud by a known fact that the seller is ignorant of the true value of a product, he/she takes advantage of the fact and does not pay the seller with the appropriate true value. Buyers also may cheat the sellers if they take deliberated advantage of an error in calculation on the part of the sellers or if the seller inadvertently gives back more change to buyers than is due to him/her.

Stealing: *Stealing* means to take property of others without permission or right, secretly, or by force. Stealing is the vice of taking unjustly what belongs to others. Shoplifting, money laundering, robbery, pick pocketing, and embezzling are vices of unjustly taking money and/or merchandise that are belonged to others. The above injustices are all committed by *deed*. There are other injustices such as an inappropriate act of copyright, patent, trademarks, and piracy. These are committed by *words*. Most of the above injustices not only are immoral and unethical, but also they deserve to be exposed to lawsuits and trials in the courtrooms.

Usury: *Usury* is a vice of charging excessive interest on a loan of money. This meaning of usury is a modern one. In some cultures, by their religious faiths (e.g., Islamic Faith), usury is observed as a sin and prohibited because money is conceived to have only one essential use, to be properly spent. However, today money is employed for investments as capital in order to develop wealth without human efforts. As long as the borrower is taking advantage of the money, therefore the lender has the right to share an appropriate portion of that profit. At the present time, therefore, usury is understood to consist of a charging a rate of interest that is excessive, i. e., beyond a rate usually determined by law (Oesterle, 1957: 156).

Egoistic Habit: An *egoistic habit* pertains to being self-centered and preoccupied with self-desires. It is a habit of valuing only interference to oneself personal interest. In an immoral behavior, an egoistic habit is that each person regards his or her own welfare as the supreme end of action beyond the contextual boundary of the public conscientiousness.

CHAPTER SUMMARY

In this chapter you have found pros and cons concerning the different ethical philosophical views on business responsibilities through defining libertarianism, conservatism, competition, oligopoly, and monopoly. In addition, in this chapter you have been exposed to hedonistic and eudaemonistic characteristics of businesspeople. Business responsibilities include observing product safety, scientific discoveries, industry voluntary regulation, and government environmental protection and conservation policies.

Philosophically, a business should not be considered a selfish phenomenon. It is a moral and ethical endeavor that balances the level of corporate's profitability with suitability of the consumer's efficacy. Profitability, in the field of business, leads employers to the magnificent growth of businesses and prosperity in happiness.

Altruism could be defined as the principle or practice of unselfish concern for or devotion to the welfare of others. Altruism is opposed to egoism. *Populism* is defined as placing restriction of ownership on accumulation of wealth by monopolies. *Reciprocitism* means mutual exchange of values between two parties (e.g., sellers and buyers). *Individualism* refers to personhood and selfhood of the atomic (ego, superego, and id) nature of an individual that exists and has moral claims apart from any associations except those that they have been chosen to form for the purpose of professional identity.

Competitive global markets could be described as slow-cycle, fast-cycle, and standard-cycle markets. Products in slow-cycle markets reflect strongly shielded resources positions where competitive pressures do not readily penetrate the firm's market position of strategic competitiveness. *Competition* refers to the rivalry between two or more business enterprises to secure the patronage of prospective buyers. Competition depends very much on how their rivals are expected to react. Rivalry becomes competitive asymmetry, when firms differ from one another in terms of their resources, capabilities, core competencies, opportunities, and threats in their industry and competitive markets.

Oligopoly means there are few sellers or producers existing in a market. Oligopoly is a term used in the field of business when competition in an industry is never perfectly balanced. It contains a few large corporations that dominate the markets and their actions influence rivals. *Monopoly* refers to the exclusive control of commodities or services in a particular market by a corporation. It is a type of control in order to manipulate the pricing system by the producer's discretion.

One of the major issues in international trade is protection of intellectual property rights. Although *intellectual property right* is an abstract term for an abstract concept, it is, nonetheless, familiar to virtually everyone. Morally, ethically, and legally, stealing is wrong. In addition, misappropriation of other's property without the owner's knowledge and/or their consent, either by deception or force, is viewed as an act of *usurpation*.

Privacy refers to that sphere of life where one's behavior, thoughts, feelings, and so on are unknown to others and are not available for their scrutiny. *Copyright* is a legal term that is defined as the exclusive rights to display or reproduce a literary, audio, or visual work by an author and/or by an institution. *Patent* is an exclusive monopolistic legal right for protection of a technological breakthrough to be given to an inventor, innovator, or substantially improved products or processes to a patent holder for a certain period of time. Patents, in essence, protect intellectual property ownership rights for a patent holder. A *trademark* is a distinctive and unique commercial and/or institutional sign to represent a particular product, company, and organization. *Shop rights* are exclusive legal rights for a company to use inventions, technological breakthroughs, or information of its scientists and/or researchers for the benefit of its organizational ends. However, scientists or researchers who have used a company's technologies, time, and other resources do not have the right to take that knowledge, information, and/or formula with them and use them either for their own self-interest or for the benefit of their new employers. The term *counterfeiting* is used to describe production without authorization and/or the consent of the company holding the patent, trademark, or copyright. The term *piracy* refers to the production of products by copying the original without the consent or permission of the copyright holding company and/or individuals that are holding patent, trademark, or copyrights. The term *price fixing* refers to secretly arranging prices in a fixed artificial high level within a market either by monopolies or oligopolies.

The term *bribe* refers to any valuable and favorable consideration given or promised to somebody for corrupt behavior in the performance of an official, public duty, and/or to obtain special arrangements for the personal gains between two or more parties. *Payola* is a secret or abusive pre-payment bribe to influential and key decision-makers of a buyer's country and/or a company for selling a single brand or model of a product or a unique kind of service. Payola is viewed as an unethical and immoral payment for promotion of a single product. *Extortion* means to wrest money or information from a person by violence or intimidation, under the cover of office, when none or not so much is due. A business is a legal entity that is protected by law and by law enforcement officers.

The terms *kickbacks* and overt *bribes* are defined as improper and immoral percentage of secret income regularly given to a person in a position of power or influence as payment for having made the income possible. *Grease money* or *speed money* is a kind of special payment paid to low ranked government officials to expedite the company's bureaucratic red taped paper work. When there is a recognized expediter and when the amount of the payment is insignificant it is called grease money. A *gift* is defined as a present to be offered to somebody voluntarily without charge. A gift could be viewed as a donation, contribution, offering, benefaction, endowment, bounty, gratuity, tip, allowance, subsidy, or bequest. Ethically, morally, and legally, different cultures view the gift offering differently.

Through *eudaemonistic goodness,* an individual's moral, ethical, and legal ordinations can be characterized by observing conscience, conscientiousness, integrity, dignity, honesty, rightness, discipline, orders, rights, duties, responsibility, accountability, respectfulness, politeness, courage, prudence, truthfulness, trustfulness, fairness, justness, fortitude, patience, good will, good faith, magnanimity, perseverance, sincerity, and loyalty. Sometimes for some people the denominator of goodness is based on their emotional, sensational, pleasurable, and enjoyable ends. These types of goodness are called *hedonistic*. Hedonism holds that the basic values of goodness are the differentiation power between pleasure and pain. According to this type of view, everything that people pursue or demand should be directed toward enjoyment or simply as the absence of pain. This view contains selfishness. Just as a healthy body cannot compromise with the filthy and vicious mind, intrinsic moral goodness does not work by compromising emotional and rational intentions. The goodness comes from the healthy mind and the healthy mind comes from the healthy body. If not, then evil ideas and vicious actions give rise to the greedy means of appetitive selfishness to win the evil ends. Through hedonistic perceptions an individual's behavior may be exposed to evil means and ends such as: cynicism, nepotism, favoritism, cruelty, filthiness, felony, greediness, heartlessness, falsification, viciousness, revengefulness, cheating, steeling, plagiarism, gossip, rudeness, dishonesty, egoistic, incompetence, offensiveness, reproachful, fraudulence, negligence, deception, harmfulness, harassing, intimidation, influencing, falsification, bribery, kickbacks, payola, overcharging, corruption, scandals, price gauging, unfairness, unjustness, wrong doing, exploitation, discrimination, false advertising, and breach of contract.

QUESTIONS FOR DISCUSSION

- What are business responsibilities in multinational and domestic corporations?
- Why do businesses need ethical philosophy?
- Why do managers need moral philosophy?
- What do we mean by populism and individualism? Explain their differences.
- What is reciprocitism in the field of business?
- What is competition?
- What is the difference between oligopoly and monopoly?
- What are different types of property ownership?
- Describe what are the differences between copyrights and patents.
- What is shop right?
- What is the difference between a brand name and a counterfeit product?
- What is wrong with insider information and privacy?
- What are differences between price fixing and price discrimination?
- What is the difference between price fixing and tying arrangements?
- What is the difference between bribery and payola?
- Are grease money, sweet money, and speed money moral and ethical?
- What is the difference between selflessness and selfishness?
- What are the principles of libertarianism?
- What are the principles of conservatism?
- What are eudaemonistic principles of ethics?
- What are hedonistic means and ends in ethical justifications?

- What are the ethical and moral differences between eudaemonistic and hedonistic moral principles?
- What is the difference between dignity and integrity?
- What are the differences between discipline and order?
- What are different rights?

CASE STUDY

HILLSDALE COLLEGE' S PRESIDENT: ACADEMIC ADMINISTRATIVE DIGNITY AND INTEGRITY

The daughter-in-law of the president of Hillsdale College committed suicide on campus after it was alleging that she had been having an affair with the college president. As a result, the result, the president resigned his position because of immoral, unethical, and illegal behavior. Hillsdale College is a liberal-arts college two hours west of Detroit. The president took office in 1971 and served for 28 years. The president was very successful in fund raising from the private sector, and received federal aid and financial assistance for students. He appealed to the rapidly growing conservative ethical, moral, and cultural values to help and preserve the college's independence. During his 28 years tenure, the president raised $325-million for Hillsdale. The president got what he worked for and managed to convince the board of trustees to pay him an annual salary of $448,000.00.

This is the irony: While conservative cultural values are based upon ethical and moral behaviors, and believe that people ought to be held accountable for their conduct, the board of trustees evidently did not wish to hold the president responsible for his misconduct for many years. Of course, conservatives sometimes avoid exposing their own immoral and unethical behaviors because they fear of public condemnation. Conservatives are not the only ones who sometimes find themselves living in opposition to their cultural and religious value systems.

The alleged misconduct of the president came, therefore, as a shock when two conservative magazines, *The National Review* and *The Weekly Standard* reported an allegation that the cause of the suicide of the president's daughter-in-law was directly related to his sexual misconduct. The magazines alleged that the president had carried on a long-term sexual affair with his son's wife, the mother of his grandchild. Not only that they said, he had also had affairs with other women (Wolfe, 1999). Also, a monthly newsletter of conservative thought, *Imprimis*, is published by the college and sent to nearly one million readers. The president's daughter-in-law was managing the *Imprimis* and the Hillsdale College Press.

The Chronicle of Higher Education under the Michigan Freedom of Information Act obtained some documents indicating that the president's daughter-in-law had resigned her job on September 8, 1999. She gave few details as to why she was leaving but said:

You know me, I hate to be the object of attention. I have been such an object in the college community for many years now. I just want this to be as private as possible and, most of all, I don't want to have to answer any questions.

Her resignation came just days after the president announced that he planned to remarry. He had divorced his first wife, who had cancer, five months earlier (Van Der Werf, 1999).

When the President's immoral, unethical, and illegal behavior surfaced, he resigned from his position and requested that the board honor him with early retirement. The board of trustees announced that the president's request for early retirement had been granted. In addition, only after widespread publicity did the college say it would investigate the allegations.

How, then, should people respond to such an important ethical and moral issue. It is fair to question moralists and ethicists, who preach moral virtues, family values, and sexual restraint, yet act irresponsibly by ignoring moral principles?

According to critics, the president consistently acted as if he were above restraint including ethical and moral restraints and he seemed to have had as much respect for his son as he did for dissenting faculty members, students, and the community at large. According to some dissent faculty members, the president was an autocrat whose leadership style was authoritarian in the extreme. The president allegedly treated faculty members (at least those who dared to challenge him) as non-persons. According to the American Association of University Professors, since 1988, after dismissing a history professor (the AAUP report criticized the college for not protecting faculty members from the improper exercise of administrative power) the president did have such a leadership style and the trustees were aware of these facts (Wolfe, 1999).

CASE QUESTIONS FOR DISCUSSION

- In theory, the trustees have ultimate responsibility for moral, ethical, and legal soundness of an institution of higher education, because the president serves on their behalf. If ever there is a reason to believe that trustees owe their integrity and dignity to the moral and ethical cause of an institution of higher education, not to the person who runs, then should they be accountable to their clients (the public)?
- Whatever the implications of this development on the public accountability of the universities, the principal ethical and moral responsibilities of universities comprise discrete constituents that prototypically function in unison and strive to achieve goals that are individually sought but collectively achieved. Within a university, theoretically speaking, in this effort both faculty and staff are accountable to the administration, and administration is accountable to

the board of trustees. Therefore, isn't it within the objective of accountability to maintain a pattern of continuing and/or periodic evaluation of the president's ethical, moral, legal, and professional behavior?

- Since an institution of higher education is not a linear hierarchy that subordinates the faculty to the administration alone, isn't it a network of shared responsibility in which every node is reciprocally accountable to another?
- With the installation of the post-tenure administrative review process, it is safe to say that the president of a college/university is virtually in a state of permanent evaluation?
- Since university presidents, or chancellors receive no regular annual evaluation by way of faculty and student inputs, is it the right way presidents or chancellors tend to formulate their relationships with their trustees on the basis of personal chemistry, subjective rapport, or political considerations unrelated to the performance of their ethical, moral, and professional responsibilities?
- Isn't it immoral and unethical for a president who is an academic leader to break the moral and intellectual virtues by sexual temptation and tendency to have affairs with his daughter-in-law and other women in a campus?

CASE SOURCES

Alan Wolfe, "The Hillsdale Tragedy Holds Lessons for Colleges Everywhere: Point of View," *The Chronicle of Higher Education.*. XLVI, no. 15 (December 3, 1999), A72.

Martin Van Der Werf, "Police Rule Death at Hillsdale College a Suicide," *The Chronicle of Higher Education.* XLVI, no. 16 (December 10, 1999), A42.

CHAPTER 6

ETHICS OF BUSINESS KNOWLEDGE MANAGEMENT

There is no useful moral knowledge,
if it is not somehow applied to some practical means and ends.

There is no ethical knowledge to be sought,
if it is not in someway applied sooner or later.

There is no legal knowledge to be examined,
if it is not somewhat practical to some extent.

There is no analytical knowledge to be viewed merely for it's own sake,
if it is not effective in solving problems somewhere to reveal the truth.

There is no scientific knowledge to be questioned,
if it is not pertaining to questioning answers rather than in answering questions.

CHAPTER OBJECTIVES

When you have read this chapter you should be able to do the following:

- Analyze and further explore the factors that inhibit managerial responsiveness to organizational ethical changes.
- Know whether ethics is adequate as science or as a holistic knowledge.
- Analyze different types of business philosophies and their relationship to business operations.
- Identify crucial societal factors that influence business profitability in the long run.
- Identify both dimensions of material and non-material cultures in relationship to the importance of ethical values in evaluating, financing, and accumulating wealth.
- Describe why ethics must be a practical science.
- Know the meaning of practical ethics.
- Know how ethics is both a process and a conclusion of a business event.
- Know not only that what type of event is true but also precisely why it is true.
- Know how an individual who is intellectually well informed of doing well and evil can be characterized.

THOUGHT STARTER

The research literature has manifested the real face of knowledge management is multi-variable and multidimensional. Such peculiar characteristics can lead managers to successful objectives if they adequately understand the magnitude of these variables and dimensions and adequately respond to environmental changes. This is true for a number of reasons.

First, since some managers simply target business profitability as their sole objective by all means and ends, they may fail to notice the ethical and legal changes in their environment.

Second, research has also shown that managers can be aware of their immoral, unethical, and illegal operations, but may fail to make adequate responses to correct them. After getting caught in a controversial situation, they may then underestimate the importance of business ethics in a long-term business operation. For example, disgraced financier Robert E. Brennan, who became nationally known in the 1980s as "Penny Stock" by appearing on TV commercials for his First Jersey Securities Inc. to urge investors to buy penny stocks, was labeled a cheater in 1990s by federal regulators. He declared bankruptcy in 1995, when a federal judge in New

York ruled that he cheated First Jersey investors and ordered him to pay $78 million to the Securities and Exchange Commission (SEC). The SEC charged that Bernnan employed "boiler room" tactics to manipulate the market in low-cost, high-risk shares of little-known companies to fleece people who were pursued by a high-pressure sale force. The government charged Bernnan with improperly shielding assets to keep them from being used to pay off $45 million he agreed to pay to aggrieved investors. In 1995 he declared bankruptcy and hid his assets. Finally, he was arrested in August 2000 for bankruptcy fraud when he cashed $500,000 worth of chips at the Mirage casino in Las Vegas (Gold, 2000: 2E). How Mr. Bernnan misled stock traders is an example lacking sufficient knowledge about small companies' operations.

PLAN OF THIS CHAPTER

Scientific formulas, technological innovations, and knowledge-based information systems are essential components of money-power or material-objects in the business world. However, at the same time, these variables can serve people either through right or wrong directions; depending on the appetite of money-power holders. Nevertheless, scientific formulas, technological breakthroughs, and information systems are a practical reality. They should be used in order to increase the wisdom of human beings. Practical reality is thus a truth of ethical action, not a truth of theoretical knowledge. What kind of business knowledge (theoretical or practical) is business ethics? The perception of practical knowledge refers to the fact that business ethics is a holistic embodiment of scientific formulas, technological breakthroughs, and information systems that should direct businesses on the right direction. This holistic embodiment is known as paradigm of knowledge management. An ethical paradigm of knowledge management system brings organizational constituencies together along with a humanitarian conviction. It links the organizational mission to its legitimate practical operational and conclusive commitments.

This chapter examines the evolution of scientific advancements, technological developments, informational prodigies, and business strategies and their attributes in relation to synergistic knowledge management systems. It discusses how knowledge management can provide moral, ethical, and legal strategic advantages through the examination of the ways they affect organizational operations, vertical and horizontal organizational structural design, and interorganizational relationships. Thus, we shall seek to know, what is a paradigm, what is a paradigm of knowledge management, and what is a paradigm of business ethics.

MORAL CONVENTIONS AND ETHICAL COMMITMENTS OF SCIENTISTS AND TECHNOLOGISTS

As the third millennium begins, the world's evolutionary paradigm of knowledge management is being reshaped in as fundamental a manner as at any other time in human civilization. In our modern society, the level of reliable knowledge about the world has increasingly developed. By any measure these scientific advancements and technological breakthroughs are extraordinary achievements, unmatched in history. Just to give an idea of the rate of expansion of our knowledge since 1900, the number of research papers published in the field of chemistry was of the order of thousands; 100 years later, the equivalent number stands at more than 500,000 conference papers and professional journal articles a year (*Financial Times*, 2001: 11). Nevertheless, with all of these progressive scientific and technological efforts, people feel that the world is becoming an increasingly uncertain and dangerous place to live. The main reason for such a pessimistic impression lies not on the neutrality of science and technology, but rests on the intention and objectives of some scientists and technologists who morally, ethically, and legally abuse their discoveries, or provide ample opportunities for immoral and unethical professionals to abuse scientific discoveries and misuse technological breakthroughs for the purpose of evil acts.

One primary objective for international business today is to make efforts to manage and leverage humanely the organizational knowledge management system. Having greater access to scientific formulas, technological breakthroughs, and information systems is useless unless the corporate knowledge management system is put to use to further legitimate and ethical operational processes. Knowledge management neutrality should lead and be equated with ethical virtuous neutrality for professionals. The former is acceptable as a condition of personal career and the latter is acceptable as a condition of social justice. The quest for ultimate ethical valuable knowledge management systems is one side of the equation between money-power and humanity-power. Those professionals who use money-power knowledge management merely increase the distance between what is possible and what is desirable. To exert money-power or material-objects without aiming toward humanitarian moral imperatives is to exert money-power without moral responsibilities This chapter examines the evolution of scientific advancements, technological developments, informational prodigies, and business strategies and their attributes in relation to knowledge management systems. As we mentioned before, it discusses how knowledge management can provide moral, ethical, and legal strategic advantages through examination of the ways they affect organizational operations, vertical and horizontal organizational structural design, and interorganizational relationships. Thus, we shall seek to know, for example, what is a paradigm, what is a paradigm of knowledge management, and what is a paradigm of business ethics.

UNDERSTANDING BUSINESS PARADIGMS

What Is a Paradigm?

It is useful before discussing what is a paradigm of knowledge management, to know first what we mean by a "paradigm." A paradigm is a basic framework through which we conceive and perceive the world, giving shape and meaning to all our knowledge, and experiences, providing a basis for interpreting and organizing both our conceptions and perceptions (Palmer, 1989: 15). A paradigm is more than a theory because it is a holistic synthesized essence of our mind and actions within the historical events of our culture. A paradigm is a fundamental asserted belief that sometimes isn't even articulated until brought into question by someone else's new competing paradigm. Since the paradigm of science, technology, and information systems has been implemented in the various international markets with different applications of means and ends, in reality that paradigm is faced with serious moral, ethical, legal challenges and critical conclusions.

In today's cyberspace stock market, we need to know what is the real function of the E-stock trading systems. How it is designed and who is operating, and what international regulatory agencies control it. This and other similar scenarios have to find new moral, ethical, and legal solutions for survival and continuity of E-commerce. Money-power through domestic political ideologies, of course does not have to be universally liked to be successful. Some multinational corporate managers define money-power in terms of politic: victory and defeat, and others perceive it as a process of honesty to serve customers with legitimate level of profitability. The most important perceptual judgments customers can make about a corporate CEO's performance are essentially about his/her character. It is not what CEOs declare, or even what they do. The thing that really counts is the intangible perception of who the professional managers are. Can they be traced? What are the values and character that inform their decisions and operations? For example, money laundering is one of the major unethical and illegal issues in the international E-banking industry. For the first time a group of 11 of the world's leading international private banks have stepped up to fight against organized crime and corruption by agreeing on anti-money laundering practices. These banks are Citibank, UBS in Switzerland, ABN Amoro, Brarclays Bank, Banco Santander Central Hispano, Chase Manhatan Private Bank, Credit Suisse Group, Deutsche Bank, HSBC, J.P.

Morgan and Societe Generale (Hall, 2000: 10). Therefore, one of the solutions for the international E-commerce is to establish a new path of global conceptual and perceptual view concerning the operations of traders on the basis of "Multiethical Paradigm Knowledge Management Model (MPKMM)."

What Is a Business Ethics Paradigm?

Corporate responsibilities mandate a business entity to be accountable for its economic, legal, ethical, and discretionary commitments to its stakeholders. This provides a synergistic paradigm for its stability, survival, and profitability.

In order to harmonize economic, legal, ethical, and moral discretionary responsibilities of a firm, managers must first be trustworthy. Managers need to be professionally committed to safeguarding and balancing the interests of all stakeholders including society at large without violating their personal dignity and integrity. They need to generate direct enduring relationships with their stakeholders. Corporate responsibilities without accountability cause mistrust and cynicism among stakeholders.

Responsibility, therefore, not only includes "what must we do?" and "what ought we do?" it also spells out "what we should do?" and "what might we do?" Carroll (1979: 499) suggested that to the extent business corporations fail to acknowledge discretionary or ethical responsibilities, society, through government, would act, making them legal responsibilities. Government may do this, moreover, without regard to a firm's economic responsibilities. A firm can fulfill it ethical responsibilities by fulfilling its commitments to each group of stakeholders. As we are aware of corporate corruption among many CEOs through "book cooking" by auditing firms, the government of the United States legislated a sever punishment for these corrupted managers. Since the Enron scandal, there are other corruptions in which have gone under government investigation by SEC. These corporations are WorldCom.Inc., American Online (AOL) as a subsidiary of Time Warner, Johnson & Johnson, Adelphia Cable Co., Xerox, Tyco International, Imclone Co., Martha Stewart Co. and others.

In viewing a corporation's paradigm of business responsibilities and accountabilities, we first need to define what are definitions of a business through different perceptions of stakeholders. In general, a corporation's business definition conveys: "What is most important about a company concerning economic, legal, ethical, and moral responsibilities and accountabilities of that company?" Also, how those specifications can distinguish that company from its competitors. Business diffusions provide firms with specific identities that describe what is "central, distinctive, and enduring" about them (Albert and Whetten, 1985: 263). Business definitions spell out managerial beliefs and faiths concerning their personal professional commitments and their expected ethical behavior in an industry related both to their strategic decisions and processes. Table 6.1 illustrates the paradigm of business definitions concerning responsibilities and accountabilities of a firm through the interests of different groups of stakeholders.

Business entities recognize the importance of their market size and product positions within the industry's competitive environments. In order to survive in such competitive environments, business need periodically to redefine their missions due to contingent circumstances of the industry's innovative changes and to accelerate the shifts of customers demographics and demands to their outlets by providing higher qualitative products and/or services with an optimized pricing policy. As a result, managers must define their strategies through three key issues facing the corporation as a whole. These key issues are *innovative strategies, directional strategies,* and *parenting strategies.*

Emerging Strategic Knowledge Management: Emerging strategic knowledge management through active participation of specialists and skillful scientists and technologists. Appropriation of sufficient funds for research and development (R&D) facilitates innovativeness and technovativeness in acquisition of new technologies and substitution of new products and/or services (innovative strategies). Within such a domain of strategic operation, maintaining the corporation's ethical values, moral principles, and legal mandates provides safe opportunities for stabilization, survival, and profitability of the firm.

Directional Strategies: The firm's overall orientation towards prudent directional strategies. A business is primarily concerned about strategic choices and directions. This is true of small and large companies, a one-product line company or a conglomerate (multi-heterogeneous businesses) one, and a domestic company or multinational one.

Parenting Strategies: The comprehensive integration of managerial ethical moral, and legal style in which CEOs coordinate their corporation's decisions, actions, information, deployment of resources, and cultivation of product lines and strategic business units (SBUs) *parenting strategies*. *Parenting strategies* are specific kinds of supervision of all divisions for the purpose of fitness through a paternalistic managerial style. It provides holistic harmony among corporate constituencies to live together as a family through resource sharing and development.

Table 6.1: Paradigm of Business Definition Through Perceptions of
Different Groups of Stakeholders

STAKEHOLDERS	BUSINESS DEFINITION	GROUP'S INTEREST
ORGANIZATION	What products and/or services will the firm offer with what expected rate of profitability?	Firm's stability, survival, and continuous high rate of profitability
CUSTOMERS AND CONSUMERS	Suitability, efficacy, and safety of the firm's products and/or services for their consumerable needs	The equitable fairness between consumers' utility purchase power and the fair price for products and/or services quality
STOCKHOLDERS AND SHAREOWNERS	How much do they know about their investments with what expected rate of their investments' security and profitability or losses?	Expected rates from receivable return on their investments through earning per share and the return on their assets
BOARD OF DIRECTORS	Soundness in strategic decision-making processes and operations. Concerns for maintaining personal interests	Expected safeguarding shareholders' interests through controlling, monitoring, and supervising top management behavior in relationships to strategic objectives through reviewing ROA, ROI, ROE, EPS, and financial leverage
MANAGEMENT	Soundness in decision-making processes and operations through strategic measuring efficiency, effectiveness, and productivity Concerns for maintaining their personal profit sharing and reputation	Expected high salary and benefits through articulation of strategic vision, leadership, and accomplishment of the firm's objectives
EMPLOYEES	Safety and security of the workplace, continued employment, and sufficient earnings as wages, salaries, benefits, commissions,, and acquisition expertise through pragmatic learning objectives	Expected incomes to fulfill their demanded financial obligations. To balance their net earnings with their family purchasing power
GOVERNMENT	Expected compliance with law and promoting the national economy through innovative hardworking habits	To receive taxes from earnings, capital gains, sales, interests, and trade tariffs to meet the national expenditures
COMMUNITY	To develop progressive trends in economic growth and development and enhancement of the societal welfare of citizens	To increase both national GDP and GNP per capita

WHAT IS A PARADIGM OF KNOWLEDGE MANAGEMENT?

In today's free market economy, the basic organizational resources are no longer material capital, labor, or natural resources, but knowledge-wealth. Knowledge is not the same thing as scientific formulas, data banks, and information systems, although it uses all of these phenomena. Knowledge manifests itself a step further beyond scientific boundaries. It is a conclusion drawn from the application of scientific formulas, technological breakthroughs, and information systems after it is linked to other known and unknown phenomena and compared to what is really known and what we should know.

Within the contextual domain of knowledge inquiry, our initial concern is to state precisely how we view the paradigm of knowledge management as an integrative system of scientific, informational, and knowledge-based endeavor. In terms of the fundamental distinction, first, we can question whether this paradigm is a tacit knowledge or explicit. Second, whether the paradigm of knowledge focuses on intellectual capital and captures measurement of the intellectual intangible asset. Third, whether this paradigm of knowledge is concerned with the optimization of knowledge creation and its smooth flow into organizational life or if it is viewed as a transformation of knowledge into practices. The proceeding ethical remarks lead us to the methods that are operational to the scientific, technological, and informational success. To aid the following discussion, I will define several terms associated with the paradigm of knowledge management.

We may perceive that since the objective of qualitative life is to discover the new path toward excellence, therefore, the paradigm of knowledge management is to deal with those acts that proceed from the deliberative good-will in the field of business. Nevertheless, the extent of the nature of scientific goodness is highly variable and to some extent, it is controversial. For example, in the industry of transportation, scientific discoveries facilitated more quick movements of population and commodities; however it created more pollution to harm the environment and people.

What Is Knowledge?

Knowledge always contains a human intellectual valuable factor. Knowledge is distinguished from science, data, and information. Knowledge has been perceived through different perceptions and outcomes. Peter Drucker (1993: 5) coined the term *knowledge-work* in the early 1960s. Knowledge-work involves the creation of a new understanding of nature, multidisciplinary effective functioning of integrated parts of problem solving, structural summation of synthesized organs, and application of science, information, and aesthetics in innovation. This new paradigm needs to be examined in terms of moral, ethical, and legal implications. In the 1990s corporate managers begun to recognize knowledge as an important resource that, like other organizational resources, should be managed. In traditional organizational paradigm management systems, managers usually concentrated on cash flow, human resources, or acquisition of raw materials and component parts. In the modern technological era, managers have begun to capitalize in knowledge ventures, specifically for companies that are striving for managing knowledge-wealth.

Knowledge-wealth is an intangible resource which synergizes an organization to effectively acquire, create, apply, and transfer know-what, know-how, and know-why across the company and modify their activities to reflect new knowledge and insights (Garvin, 1998: 47). Buchholz and Rosenthal (1998: 60) state:

Within pragmatic process philosophy, all knowledge is understood as fallible, to be tested by ongoing consequences in experience. And knowledge emerges through intelligent reflection on experience within nature. Our experience within nature undergoes continual change, and while some aspects of experience are relatively stable, other aspects are unstable.

Also, Zack (1999: 45) states:

Organizations are being advised that to remain competitive, they must efficiently and effectively create, locate, capture, and share their organization's knowledge and expertise, and have the ability to bring that knowledge to bear on problems and opportunities.

Knowledge management is a modern form of E-business that organizes scientific, technological, and informational intellectual and creative properties. It refers to the efforts to systematically search for, find, organize, establish, and make available an organizational intellectual capital for more productivity. It is a continuous intellectual effort through knowledge discovering, sharing, and applying innovativeness toward more profitable outcomes. Also, knowledge is a phenomenon in which achievable synergistic outcomes can be obtained through prodigy.

The synergistic organizational knowledge paradigm system is the sum of its scientific discoveries, technological innovativeness, informational databased processing, experimental testing, and understandable reasoning. A comprehensive paradigm of knowledge management system includes capturing, processing, storing, and disseminating knowledge, but also fosters knowledge learning through an organization.

Intellectual reflection on knowledge acquisition has been pursued for about as long as records of human intellectual activity are available.

Traditional epistemology identifies three distinctive kinds of knowledge: (1) knowledge of things and objects, (2) knowledge of how to do things, and (3) knowledge of statements or propositions. Lundvall (1996) has identified four categories of knowledge:

- *Know-what-knowledge*: facts that can be broken down into bits and easily codified
- *Know-why-knowledge*: principles and laws
- *Know-how-skills*: the capability to undertake a given task successfully
- *Know-who-information*: who knows what and who knows how to do what

Collins (1993: 95) has made a clear distinction between codified and non-codified knowledge. He proposed four categories of knowledge:

- *Symbolic-type knowledge* that can be transferred without loss in a codified form   (e.g., e-books and floppy disks)
- *Embodied knowledge* held within the body of a human (e.g., how to play golf; the knowledge is internalized, but not easily communicated)
- *Embrained knowledge* held within the physical matter of the brain (e.g., certain cognitive abilities are related to the physical structure of the brain)
- *Encultured knowledge* that is linked to social groups and society

Miller and Quintas (1997: 399) expressed their views on the basis of Collins' four categories of knowledge that distinguishes between "knowledge of information and contextual knowledge" and made another type of categorization of knowledge as:

- *Catalogue knowledge* known as "know-what"
- *Explanatory knowledge* known as "know-why"
- *Process knowledge*: that is known as "know-how"
- *Social knowledge* known as "know-who"

Blackler (1995: 1021) has proposed five categories of knowledge:

- *Embrained knowledge* or *abstract knowledge*: This depends on conceptual skills and cognitive skills, generally conflated with scientific knowledge and accorded superior status.
- *Embodied knowledge* or *action-oriented knowledge*. It is likely to be only partly explicit: transmission requires face-to-face contact,

sentient and sensory information and physical clues, acquired by doing and context-dependent.

- *Encultured knowledge* or related to the process of achieving shared understanding. Embedded in cultural systems, likely to depend strongly on language, and hence to be clearly socially constructed and open to negotiations.
- *Embedded knowledge* or knowledge that resides in systemic routine: It relies on the interplay of relationships and material resources; may be embedded in technology, practices, or explicit routine and procedures.
- Encoded knowledge or knowledge recorded in signs and symbols, such as books, manuals, codes of practice, and electronic records. Encoding requires the distillation of abstract codified knowledge from other richer forms of knowledge.

Flack (1997: 383) has developed a categorization scheme that also attempts to encompass knowledge source and storage as follows:

- *Formal knowledge*: It is embodied in codified theories, formulas and usually encoded in written or diagrammatic forms in which they are acquired through formal learning.
- *Instrumentalities*: It is embodied in tool and instrumental use. It requires other components informal, tacit and contingent for effective use. It may be learned through demonstration and practice.
- *Informal knowledge*: It is embodied in verbal interaction, rules of thumb, tricks of the trade, held in verbal and sometimes in written forms (e.g., manuals, guidebooks). It is a pattern of learnt interaction within a specific milieu.
- *Contingent knowledge*: It is embodied in specific contextual distributed fashion. It is apparently trivial information specific to particular context. It is sometimes available as data that can be looked up or acquired by on-the-spot learning endeavor.
- *Tacit knowledge*: It is embodied in people and rooted in practice and experience. It is transmitted by apprenticeship and training.
- *Meta-knowledge*: It is embodied in the organizational cultural pattern. It is viewed as general organizational saga and philosophical assumptions concerning values and beliefs. It can be local or cosmopolitan acquired through socialization.

SIX THEORIES OF ACQUISITION OF KNOWLEDGE

There are six theories of understanding things: (Weber, 1960: 13-14):

1. *Revelation Theory*: This view holds that the final test of the truth of assertions is their consonance with the revelations of authority.

2. *Coherence Theory*: This theory says that a statement is true if it is consistent with other statements accepted as true. Statements, of course, must be "true" to the particulars to which they refer, just as revelations accepted as valid in religion are not necessarily extended to other areas of beliefs.

3. *Preventative Theory*: This view holds that reality as presented to the mind in perception is known directly and without alteration. Errors of perceptions occur, but further observation is able to detect and explain them.

4. *Representative Theory*: This view, again favored by certain realities, holds that our perceptions of objects are not identical with them. This differs from the presentative view sketched above which goes the length of saying that when we perceive truly, our perception is identical with the object perceived. This implies that the object perceived literally enters the mind that perceives it -- a rather startling conclusion. The representative realist tries to be more cautious on this point. What we see when we look at a tree is only its image. The tree cannot be identical with this image. The image is in one's mind, and the mind is somehow located in the brain; if the tree is fifty feet high there is not enough room, (physically), in one's brain to accommodate it.

5. *Pragmatic Theory*: This view holds that statements are true if they work successfully in practice. If an idea or principle is effective in organizing knowledge or in the practical affairs of life then it is true. The belief of the pragmatist that the function of knowledge is to guide through and action successfully is at the root of the important development in American education known as the progressive movement.

6. *Intuitive Theory*: This view varies so much in its definition that it sometimes becomes identical with some of the other theories

sketched above. At one extreme, intuition refers to a mysterious and immediate inner source of knowledge apart from both perceptual observation and reasoning. At the other extreme the term intuition has been used to designate generally accredited and immediate ways of knowing, such as immediate sensation, or the immediate awareness we may have of self-evident or axiomatic truth.

What Is Moral Knowledge?

It is worthwhile to define moral knowledge as it refers to the excellence of intellect and wisdom and to the disposition of cognizance of mind to perform effectively its proper function. Also, it is worthwhile to define morality as seeking knowledge either for the sake of simply knowing or for the sake of doing or making something excellent. In addition, it is worthwhile to define legal knowledge as an ordination of a practical reasoning to signify the establishment of an order to attain a given proper end. As we stated before, therefore, morality is related to the personal knowable beliefs and faith, ethics is related to the acceptable societal group's valuable perceptions, and legality is concerned with formulating peace and order by a mandated practical reasoning concerning doing or avoiding an action or operation. For the clarity of these branches of knowing we first will define science, second, technology, and third information.

MULTIETHICAL PARADIGM OF KNOWLEDGE MANAGEMENT SYSTEM

At the heart of the evolutionary multiethical paradigm of knowledge management system (MPKMS) lie four related forces:

1. Advancement of science
2. Convergence of technological breakthroughs into computing, communication, and information systems
3. Explosion of knowledge
4. Assertion on validity and viability of progenistic knowledge for the conclusive operational result of innovative outcomes

This new integrated membership functioning system of know-why fuzzy logic, know-what structures, know-where information, and know-how knowledge is now generally manifested in the composition of global business ethics. For the clarity of these attributes, I will analyze each one within their contextual boundaries as follows.

Know-Why Fuzzy Logic

In order to decide why knowledge should be oriented toward discovering the truth, we must first ask: "Why is know-why logic the essential nature of inquiry?" This theme explicitly shows the essential continuous reasoning which should determine the nature and direction of knowledge in all places and times. Know-why logic signifies the rational reasoning that represents the essential nature of truth. Truth can be perceived through three major causes: formal cause, material cause, and efficient cause. Within a matrix of the truth, there are three levels of logical reasoning: (1) necessity of reasoning, (2) sufficiency of reasoning, and (3) vitality of reasoning including quiddity and equilibrium logic (Parhizgar, 2000: 51).

CAUSES AND REASONING	FORMAL CAUSE	MATERIAL CAUSE	EFFICIENT CAUSE
NECESSITED REASONING	Logical truth	Scientific truth	Generalized truth
SUFFICIENT REASONING	Syllogistic truth	Technological truth	Prodigical truth
VALIDITY OF REASONING	Deductive truth	Observable truth	Synergistic truth
NETURE OF TRUTH	Conventional truth	Pragmatic truth	Progenistic truth

Figure 6.1: The Matrix Structure of the Essential Truth

By looking at Figure6.1, you will find three cause-effect consequences of different types of truth. These consequential functioning truths are conventional, pragmatic, and productive truths. Each type of truth provides you with different judgments concerning decision-making processes in the field of business management. For example, through conventional "moral" truth, corporate managers are viewed as trustworthy people whose responsibilities rely on their personal dignity and integrity. Through pragmatic "amoral" truth, corporate managers are viewed as successful management scientists whose responsibilities rely on quiddity and equilibrium of cost-profit analysis. Through productive "legal" truth, corporate managers are viewed as energetic leaders whose responsibilities rely on the synergistic functioning of holistic outcomes of a corporation to boost its capabilities and potential within the quantitative analysis of corporate performance.

Discovering the truth requires relentless holistic rational efforts to be expressed concerning the truth. Know-why logic is the embodiment of the examination of our implicit conceptions, explicit perceptions, and deductive judgmental reasoning concerning the complex domain of truthfulness and falseness of inquiries. Within the contextual boundaries of know-why logic, there are two extreme opposite poles: (1) truthfulness and (2) falseness.

```
TRUTHFULNESS-----------------------50%-----------------------FALSENESS
                X X   XXXXX   X      XX      XX
                      XXX                    X
                      XX
```

Figure 6.2: Syllogistic Reasoning Proximity for Truthful Assertion
in Fuzzy Functioning Membership Logic

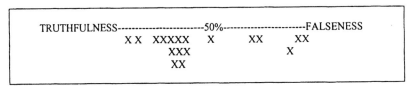

```
TRUTHFULNESS-----------------------50%---------------------FALSENESS
              X     X       XX      XXXXX
                 X                  XXX
              XX         XX      XX      XX
```

Figure 6.3: Syllogistic Reasoning Proximity for Falsehood
Assertion in Fuzzy Functioning Membership Logic

By looking at Figures 6.2 and 6.3, we may find that if something is true, therefore, it cannot be false or vice versa. However, there are some "membership functions" of parameters and events within a business system that indicate some functioning membership groups are partially true and others are partially false. Such a conclusive result manifests the degree of relativity. For example, if you look at the balance sheet of a corporation you may find that a corporation has achieved its business objectives by showing 4% profit (nominal profit). Viewing this percentage of growth through "amoral" pragmatic truth, we find that nominally such a *quantitative* figure has increased its assets with annual 4% of profitability. But if you view it through productive *qualitative* truth, you may find that this corporation has not made any real profit because 4% of profits will mach with the annual 2% inflationary rate and 2% depreciation of machineries, tools, and equipments (real profit). In reality, therefore, such a corporation is not a profitable one. In other words, we can identify these membership functioning facts to be either leaning toward truthfulness or falseness. The relativity of a compounded component membership functioning fact depends on the location, the volume, and the size of characteristics of the membership functioning groups and their holistic proximity assessment between the magnitude of truthfulness and falseness and their more proximity towards one side of the magnitude of truthfulness and falseness.

From another perspective, since religious faiths and cultural values of some membership functioning groups are differentiations of moral and ethical perceptions of specific groups and groups are periodically refunctioning, then they may not be considered as pure true or false connotations. This is the major argument concerning absolutism and relativism of moral and ethical judgments. This type of reasoning is known as fuzzy logic. Therefore, fuzzy logic specifies billions of probabilities and possibilities of integrated membership functioning systems between the poles of truthfulness and falseness. In order to analyze such a complex task, we need to identify the magnitude of the truth from the standpoint of fuzzy logic. For example, let A be the event that a decision selected is of economical type, and let B be the event that another decision selected is of ecological type; if we ask a mathematician, a manager, and a lawyer:

For the result of $P(A \cap B)$, we get these responses:
A mathematician using the multiplicative
rule of probability replies with: $P(A \cap B) = P(A) \cdot P(B)$, assuming that A and B are independent events.

A manager in search of synergy replies with: $P(A \cap B) = \mu > P(A) \cdot P(B)$, assuming that A and B are correlated fuzzy events.

A lawyer considering divorced events replies with: $P(A \cap B) = 0$, assuming that A and B are disjoint or mutually exclusive events.

This assumes $P(\bullet)$ is a probability function with domain A (an algebra of events) and counterdomain the interval $[0,1]$ which satisfies the axioms of probability theory; and on the other hand μ represents a fuzzy membership function associated to the probability of the intersection ($\cap$) of A and B.

The meaning of "synergy" effect ($\Delta H = H_S - H_T$) can be clarified by using the annual rate of return (H) for all n independent products in a product line, $H_T = (S_T - O_T)/I_T$, where S_T represents.

The total sales of the firm for all their unrelated products ($S_T = \sum S_T$),

similarly for operating costs $O_T = \sum O_i$ and investments $I_T = \sum I_T$.

$S_S = S_T$, but if $O_S < O_T$ and $I_S < I_T$, therefore $H_S > H_T$, where subscript S denotes the respective quantities for an integrated firm, while subscript T is the sum for independent enterprises. The synergy effect can produce a combined return on the firm's resources greater than the sum of its parts. In other words when companies are splitting the synergy will be lost. When companies are merging the synergy then the synergy is emerging.

Fuzzy logic embraces gray areas and partial truths (amoral). Fuzzy logic was introduced by Lotfi Zadeh (1965: 338) as a means to model the uncertainty of natural phenomena. The process of fuzzyfication, as a methodology, generalizes any specific theory from a crisp (discrete) to a continuous (fuzzy) form. Fuzzy logic is a way to deal with the uncertainties and reasoning we have as human beings. Fuzzy know-why logic is a kind of reasoning that speculates answers in favor of more complex explanations. The end result of fuzzy logic is progenistic innovation.

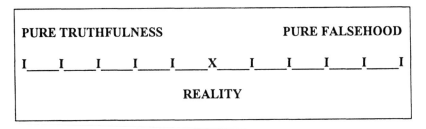

Figure 6.4: The Domain of Fuzzy Logic Reasoning

A progenistic innovation is a creative mindset of novel things. It is a new way to think about everything. Innovation is best described as pervasive creativity that perceives drastic change beyond the present and creates a future vision. According to moral and ethical judgments concerning good or bad, just or unjust, fair or unfair, and right or wrong, people constantly change their positions and express their views differently. This type of judgment is related to fuzzy know-why logic.

Fuzzy logic is a superset of conventional (Boolean) deductive logical system that has been extended to handle the concept of partial truth truthful values between "completely true" and "completely false." As previously stated the Boolean body of logic establishes a range of values with multiplicative identities in which every element is an idempotent. This means that when an element multiplies by 0 or 1, it remains unchanged [e.g., (0) • (1) = (0) or (1) • (1) = (1)] or when a truthful phenomenon multiplied by a truthful phenomenon then the result equals to the truth).

Sometimes in fuzzy logic we cannot classify and specify some effects in terms of just black and white. According to fuzzy know-why knowledge, people are constantly reengineering, restructuring, reorganizing, and reexamining their views about life events. Therefore, fuzzy thinking, fuzzy logic, and fuzzy future are the essence of human rationalization of reasoning. Fuzzy future confuses community with networking, joy with stimulation, and meaning with matter. Fuzzy future logic is really the best we can hope for sometimes it asserts truthfulness and sometimes overrides falseness. For example, according to moral and logical fuzzy knowledge there are three major domains of reasoning: (1) algebraic logic, and (2) boolean logic, and (3) fuzzy logic.

Algebraic Logic	Boolean Logic	Fuzzy Logic
$R \cdot R = R^2$	$R*R = R$	$R \otimes R = \mu_{R \otimes R}$
$R \cdot W = W \cdot R$	$R*W = W \cdot R$	$R \otimes W = \mu_{R \otimes W}$
$W \cdot W = W^2$	$W*W = W$	$W \otimes W = \mu_{W \otimes W}$

R represents an event of take a right action, and W is the event of take a wrong action, while   represents a fuzzy membership function of the product of two events. If we look at the above equations through Algebraic logic, Boolean logic, and Fuzzy logic we will find different outcomes of reasoning when we compare them to each other. We know that R $\neq W$, but if we let R = 1, and W = -1, thus $W^2 = R^2$, then for example, if something becomes wrong in a society for all citizens then according to algebraic logic that wrong thing will be perceived as good for all. If a tyrant behaves equally to all citizens, then according to Algebraic logic that behavior is perceived as justice. But in Boolean logic and Fuzzy logic the result of wrong things is wrong and it does not follow the algebraic rule.

The comparative results indicate that there are three types of moral and ethical cultural reasoning among nations as follows:

- Those nations that believe and assert that everything, by its inherent nature can be either good or bad and we cannot change good to bad or bad to good because good is good and bad is bad. In some of the Middle Eastern cultures, their religious logical perception is constructed based on Boolean logic. For example, Shiate' Moslems believe that the twelfth Imam (Saint) is alive and his representatives, as Ayatollahs, will function on behalf of him the Jurist Prudence Philosophy.

- Those nations that believe and assert that everything could be good and bad; and depends on our perception fuzzy logic (e.g., Japanese culture that perceives everything on the basis relativity could be good or bad).

- Those nations that believe and assert that survival is not related to good and bad and we should not use such distinctions in our life. Survival is a mandate. Survival is an *amoral* phenomenon — algebraic logic (e.g., some European and American cultures). It is logical to follow law rather than moral and ethical principles in our daily life. For example, merit pay is one of the major issues in employee's motivation and organizational productivity. There are two types of logic to be perceived in practice in such a process (1) causal and (2) consequential. Some managers justify their decisions on the basis of "gross pay" merit pay increased regardless of the actual "net pay income." Others may perceive it on the basis of consequential dimension as "net pay income." Through causal dimension, managers focus on "gross income" instead of "net income." It has been observed that sometimes through increased percentage of merit pay, the tax classification of employees' income will change. Despite the increased rate of merit pay, the result will be lower than the "net income" as compared to the previous years.

Is it moral and ethical to practice the second merit pay system? The answer will be based on causal or consequential perceptions of managers. Through moral and ethical perceptions, a merit pay needs to increase the purchase power of employees comparing it to the previous year(s). However, through a legal perception, the merit pay is based on the "gross pay," not on the basis of the net pay. Employers view their merit pay systems on the basis of equitable and fair balance among employees' productivity not on the basis of tax brackets. Some employees who have more dependents enjoy more tax break rather than those who do not have.

Know-What Structure

One of the first problems for global business ethics is know-what structuring of the international value systems between home and host countries. This is viewed as establishing a bridge between two countries for further diplomatic dialogues and commercial transactions. In such a domain of inquiry, several questions should be addressed:

- Should multinational corporations define and then classify the political, economical, sociological, psychological, and religious beliefs and ideologies of their home countries and express them to the host countries?
- Should multinational corporations identify and then select preferred value systems in the host countries?
- Should both home and host countries come to a mutual ordination of shared-value systems of mutual importance?

If the answer is yes to one of the above propositions, then the ordering value systems need to be responsive to know-what principles to be considered for both home and host countries. Thus, the main foundation for structuring mutual agreements between home and host countries is based on identification of mutual moral principles and ethical valuable background.

Then, both parties need to identify their agreed liability and accountability to such causes and effects.

In structuring the know-what management paradigm system of global business ethics, identification of the boundaries of the moral, ethical, and legal value systems should be closely related to the distinctions of three domains: (1) cognitive, (2) affective, and (3) effective transactions.

The Cognitive Transactions: To deal with cognitive transactions, managers often practice selective perceptions by making conscious or subconscience beliefs and opinions on some issues as to which facets of societal values on which they are going to base their ethical behavior. This identifies the basic foundation of normative morality.

Normative morality is based upon personal self-discipliniary and societal-discretionary ordered value systems. Normative morality manifests a manager's moral principles, beliefs, and expectations to justify their behavior on which they base their judgments and actions. The ethical societal norms identify distinct sets of socio-cultural value systems including legal rules for behavior. These ethical normative rules provide various sources including family and friends, the local community opinions, national beliefs, religious indoctrination and faith, econo-political platforms, the workplace attitudes, and of course, civil law and international human rights. In addition, the cognitive domain includes those objectives that deal with the recall or recognition of knowable problems concerning defective products and services. This requires the establishment of a research center to collect and compile all data as the main source of know-how knowledge concerning both producers and consumers. Then an exchange of information between parties must be established. This is the domain in which it is central to the continuity of work together in order to improve quality of products and services.

The Affective Transactions: The second part of know-what is concerned with the "affective" domain of knowledge. It includes structuring mutual objectives that describe changes in reengineering the product or services by producers and reconstructing interest, attitudes, values, and development of appreciations and adequate adjustments to new products and services. Know-what objectives in this domain should be stated very precisely?

The Affective Transactions: The third domain is the manipulative restructuring of the know-what business ethical knowledge. Although managers recognize the existence of this domain, sometimes they do not believe in development and appreciation of these objectives. Ethical effectiveness should be purely descriptive. This indicates that the value systems or quality of one class of value as compared with another should not be established. This means that managers should avoid partiality to one view of morality, ethics, and legality as opposed to another. They need to attempt implicitly to avoid biased judgments and actions. Another way of saying this is that valuable moral, ethical, and legal objectives that describe intended behavior should be included in the paradigm of knowledge management system. For example, one of the home or host countries may have efficiency in their value systems on quantitative product development; others may have qualitative product improvement. The end result is the emergence of a combination of both qualitative and quantitative value systems. Both cases need to be effectively functional.

Know-Where Information

Know-where information in an organization is a matter of actual operational knowledge. A firm's information knowledge consists of several levels of hierarchies. Virtually all-organizational levels can be depicted in terms of their information dimension. In its simplest form it can be drawn as a line, a continuum from individual-based to corporate-wide and to industry-based information.

Know-How Knowledge

Now that we have analyzed multiethical know-why, know-what, and know-where logical reasoning concerning structuring a corporate knowledge wealth, we want to describe how this dynamic knowledge management paradigm system can be used in a global firm. Although the MPKMS suggests that the knowledge-wealth of a firm can be analyzed along four dimensions:

- Corporation's ethical reasoning (the why dimension)
- Products and services (the what dimension)
- Customers (the whose dimension)
- Information (the where dimension)

We are focusing now on technologies (the "know-how" dimension). Know-how knowledge includes personal computers, Internet service, software, high technological components (such as microprocessors), other hardware components, workstations, minicomputers and mainframes, and information technology consultation services. By including such a broad range of know-how knowledge and devices and also by labeling the various firms that produce and provide these products and services, the users can quickly get an understanding of how a line of production system has evolved and which portions of the product or service dimension are more "crowded" than others. Through conducting some further research, firms can get a feel for the relative size of various product and service markets.

Analysis of know-how knowledge contains focusing on three cognitive mapping of the corporate's operational direction: (1) job shop, (2) mass production, and (3) flexible manufacturing systems.

The Job Shop System: Job-Shop know-how knowledge is viewed as a vital source for strategic decisions and actions that crystallizes the establishment of a continuous regular production system on the basis of the "know-whose" dimension. Organizational knowledge can reside wholly within an expert, or can be shared within a professional group, or the firm's managerial system. In all of the above cases organizational knowledge-wealth maintenance is a complex and dynamic valuable commodity. This is related to retention of experts and specialized employees. Brawn and Woodman (1999: 175) state:

> Essvac is a vaccine manufacturing company wholly owned by Archer Pharmaceuticals Ltd (AP)... AP has declared its interest in product development (vaccines) in its mission statement and has research and development (R&D) division as part of its structure. Henry Black is the only member of that division with both theoretical and practical experience of vaccine R&D. He is due to retire in 18 months' time and, whilst there is talk of him being missed, both for his knowledge and his contacts, there are currently no plans to replace him. No other mechanisms exist within the organization to retain his knowledge for the Group Henry needs to disseminate his knowledge to new employees.

This peculiar trend is viewed as preserving the Job-Shop knowledge within AP. It was internalized by recipient and used as a component part of the organizational knowledge-wealth. Ethical questions might be raised:

- What is Mr. Black's intellectual freedom concerning being hired by another pharmaceutical company to produce the same type of vaccine?
- Is he free to do so, or is he under moral obligation to the "shop-right" not to take the company's secrets to other competitors?

Another example of the Job-Shop is the Rolls-Royce Company that rigorously concentrates its know-how knowledge by making all component parts and assembled products through its own shop. The Job-Shop know-how knowledge seeks to stabilize its actions, despite the characteristics of the rapid production-life-cycle of the auto industry.

The Mass Production System: Mass-Production know-how knowledge concentrates on formulating a firm's operational strategy through adopting continuous changes including irregularities, with frequent discontinuities and wide swings in its rate of change. For example, Chrysler Company by swinging from modern to old models, and from old models to new models of its illustrates that it is outsourcing nearly all its manufacturing components and focusing on final assembling objectives. There is an ethical question in regard to manufacturing Chrysler's old designs and models within the new assembled product-lines. In this case the question is: "Is it safe to produce new cars with 1940s designs?" The answer is not clear. It needs to be tested in the marketplace to assess its viability.

The Flexible Manufacturing System: Flexible-Manufacturing know-how knowledge can be assessed through *versatility* of using three key functioning members of indicators: effectiveness, efficiency, and productivity. Effectiveness relates to the degree to which the know-how knowledge meets the scientific structuring of the manufacturing system. Efficiency is defined as an assessment of know-how knowledge used with consideration of cost-benefit analysis for a given output to implement such a manufacturing knowledge in practice. Productivity is defined in which know-how knowledge, as a viable scientific formula, is by experts with embedded information in order to be converted into embodied knowledge for the purpose of coetaneous profitability.

Know-Whose Knowledge

The primary task of syllogistic knowledge management system is to discover members of scientific and scholarly professions. These professionals are citizens of their own large societies to which they have, by virtue of their elaborated stock of rigorously tacit knowledge. An occupation requires a more than ordinary amount of tacit knowledge. Also, it is an acquired tacit and explicit knowledge by persistent and systematic study and authoritatively certified knowledge. The primary task of a knowable person is the acquisition and transmission of knowledge and its logical reasoning application to solve complex problems. Within this contextual boundary, there are different types of people such as academicians, technologists, informationalists, and sophists.

Academicians acquire, discover, and assimilate knowledge by scientific methodological studies, interpret them logically, and transmit them to learners. Academicians transmit knowledge about the methods of discovery especially the validation of knowledge in problem solving. Academicians do not apply the technological knowledge themselves. They discover and transmit the principles and techniques of the application of knowledge and their rules or methods governing their application.

Technologists apply the explicit knowledge which academicians taught them in practice. Technologists examine what scientific formulas are known about particular phenomena and how to dispel error, confusion, and misunderstanding of pragmatic application of knowledge. Informationalists seek large stocks of complex and imitative knowledge that have not been mastered by the laity of their clients, to whom the professions address themselves. This paradoxical acquisition of knowledge gives to the infomationalists large opportunities to abuse the position of acquired information.

Sophists' possession of syllogistic logical reasoning requires greater intellectual breadth in amount and intensity of fundamental criticized and tested reasoning than scientists, technologists, and informationalists. These differences in the amount of and quality of holistic knowledge possessed by sophists are ultimately the grounds for the exploration of innovative reasoning and predictable solutions. Nevertheless, scientists are reputed to not only have specialized knowledge and the inclination of objectively considering alternatives, but also are reputed to have scholarly, detached, and dispassionate judgment.

KNOWLEDGE-BASED INTEGRATION OF PHILOSOPHY, SCIENCES, ARTS, AND TECHNOLOGY

Knowledge-based understanding relies on the synergistic integration of philosophy, technology, arts, and sciences. The main reason for applying the interdisciplinary approach is based on a holistic view of the concept of peoples' culture, which includes all human made-knowledge. Among some of the special features of knowledge-based understanding is active participatory observation of the moral consciousness, the emic view on cultural values, the fundamental value orientation of ethical relativism, the synergistic pragmatic end results, and the holistic cultural relativism.

The moral approach holds that the universal truth is essentially a generalized principle that holds the sanctity of humanity. Labor forces and customers around the globe, particularly in the United States are becoming more diverse in terms of national origin, race, religion, gender, predominant age categories, and personal preferences.

The world is shrinking rapidly. Multinational corporate assignments are becoming a standard part of a sounded business. Cross-cultural understanding and behavioral skills are a necessity. As the result the traditional management knowledge that has been highly fragmented and uncompleted is not effective any more. With an eye toward educating tomorrow's global managers, we need to think and behave globally.

Today, multinational organizations are faced with unsolved potential problems and issues. The main reason is a misunderstanding of multicultural value systems. It is necessary to move from "tolerance" to "appreciation" when managing multicultural organizations. The main challenge of today's and especially tomorrow's managers is to be aware of specific multicultural changes, along with the factors contributing to the organizational synergy.

Table 6.2: Holistic Interdisciplinary Relationships Between Academic Philosophy, Sciences, and Technology

KNOWLEDGE BRANCHES	PRIMARY DIVISIONS	SUB-DIVISIONS
PHILOSOPHY	Metaphysics	Cosmology, Ontology, Theology, Causalogy
	Epistemology	
	Axiology	Morality, Ethics
	Phenomenology, Aesthetics, Humanities, and Arts	Literature, Music, Dances, Movies, Theatrical drama
SCIENCES	Observable Sciences	Astronomy, Geology, Physics, Chemistry, Mathematics, Statistics, Science of Logic, and Scientific Quantitative Methods
	Natural Sciences	Zoology (Animals), Botany (Plants), Protistology (One-Celled Organisms), Biorheology, Biology, Physiology, Microbiology, Immunology, Ecology and Evolution, Molecular and Cellular Biology
	Social Sciences	Economics, Geography, History, Political Sciences, and Demography
	Behavioral Sciences	Anthropology (Physical Anthropology, Cultural Anthropology, Archaeology, Anthropological Linguistics, Ethnology/Ethnography), Demography, Sociology, Psychology, and Social-Psychology
TECHNOLOGY	Traditional Technologies	Eolithic, Neolithic, Monolithic, Craftsmanship, and Synthetic
	Modern Technologies	Mechanistic, Automotive Robotics, Cybernetic, Cyber-Robotics, Micro-Technology, Nano-Technology, and Cyber-Space Technology

A successful scientific innovation needs to apply the practical effective ones. Scientists concerning innovativeness have stated that excellence needs a vision to be focused on the maximum achievement of innovativeness. This objective mandates scientists to question the answers of what they want to be, where the world of humanity is going, which the path of discovery in which will assist in the maintenance of human dignity and integrity. Scientific endeavor requires a single scientific project, no matter what its history, to have more accomplishments. In order to understand the holistic knowledge-based integration of means and ends of all actions and dynamic movements, we need to define branches of knowledge: philosophy, science, and technology (see Table 6.2).

WHAT IS PHILOSOPHY?

Philosophy is a basic foundation of conceptual understanding of human's life for the examination of cause and effect of existence. In a traditional conception, philosophy endeavors to integrate all human knowledge. Inquiries such as the following domains of knowledge have shaped philosophy:

- Was there a beginning of time?
- Will there be an end?
- Is the universe infinite or does it have boundaries?
- Is the universe developing or is it shrinking?
- Or could be it both finite and without boundaries?

On viewing these conceptions and others, the current problems of philosophers still relate to three areas of inquiry: metaphysics, epistemology, and axiology. Thus, philosophy is the integration of all human knowledge and erects a systematic view of the nature and the place of human beings in it. In an attempt to study multicultural behavior of different groups of people, we should try to understand the three above modes of arriving at knowledge.

Metaphysics

This concerns issues of the nature of reality, and humanity place in it:

- What is the matter in its essence? How does it form the vast material cosmos ordered in time and place (Cosmology)?
- What about the existence and the nature of a super power God (Theologically)?

- What does it mean to exist? What is the criterion of existing (Ontology)? (Ontology refers to the knowledge of the nature of the world around us).
- What are the ultimate causes of things being what they are
- (Causalogy)?
- What are the ultimate effects of things being what they will be (Consequentiallogy)?

Epistemology: This has to do with the problem of knowledge:

- We have knowledge.
- How is this possible?
- What does knowledge mean?
- Can all knowledge be traced to the greatest gateways of our senses (to the senses plus activity of reasoning, or to the means and ends of reasoning)?
- Do feelings render knowledge wordless but true?
- Does true knowledge ever come in the form of immediate intuition?
- How can we identify different branches of knowledge?

Axiology: This is concerned with the problems of value. There are three main traditional fields of value inquiries: (1) Phenomenology, (2) Morality, (3) Ethics, and (4) Aesthetics.

Phenomenology: What is the essential nature of the mind and/or soul (Phenomenology)? Phenomenology stresses careful descriptive value systems through an appearance or immediate object of awareness in human experience. Phenomenology is a qualitative conceptual awareness that can be manifested constructively by quantitative value judgments in the human mind. Rational decision-making processes in the field of business consist essentially of starting with certain axioms or assumptions, stated as principles of applicability of successful experiences and knowledge to the world of business experience.

Morality: The term *moral* is derived from the Latin word *mores*. In the *Oxford English Dictionary* (1963) "moral" means habits to right and wrong conduct," to "good and bad virtuous or vicious," to "right or wrong in relation to actions and conducts," and in an etymological sense, it means "pertaining to the individual's manner and custom of judgments." Morality is the term used to manifest the individual's virtue. Morality also has to do with an individual's character, and the type of behaviors that emanate from that valuable character. Virtue refers to the excellence of intellect and wisdom. Morality's end result through intellectual truthfulness, righteousness and goodness of thoughts and conducts is happiness. Conscience is a base for moral acts. It is the ability to reason about self-conduct, together with a set of values, feelings and dispositions to do or to avoid conceiving and perceiving actions. While morality is viewed as telling the whole truth, amorality is telling a partial truth. Individuals are morally obligated to develop an objectively correct conscience; but their own judgmental behavior usually is in accordance with their conscience. Failure to fulfill one's moral commitment can lead not only to blame and shame, but also to remorse (De George, 1995: 119).

Ethics: The term *ethics* is derived from the Greek word *ethos*. Ethos means the "genius" of an institution or system. Also, it refers to the science of morals and the department of study concerned with the principles of human duty. Ethics concerns itself with human societal conduct, activity, and behavior that are manifested through knowledge and deliberated behavior. Ethics is the collective societal conscious awareness of a group of people. Ethical end results through societal conscious understanding of fairness, justness, and worthiness can lead human beings towards social justice and peaceful behavior.

Aesthetics: Of particular interest to the human concepts are the formal aspects of art, color, and form, because of the symbolic meanings they convey. Aesthetics pertains to a culture's sense of beauty and good taste and is expressed in arts, drama, music, folklore, and dances (Ball and McCulloch, Jr., 1988: 269).

Aesthetics pertains to a culture's sense of beauty, excellent thought, and illustrative elegant visual tastes. It is the reflection of human expression in humanities: arts, music, dances, movies and theatrical drama. Of particular interest to multicultural behaviorism is artistic combination of humanities: arts, colors, and forms specifically in exhibitor conceptions and perceptions; because each group conveys symbolic meanings and values in human cultural taste.

Humanities: Humanities are those branches of knowledge that are concerned with human thoughts, beauties, and values. Humanities mean art, history, and literature. Humanities are the branch of learning regarded as having primarily a cultural character and usually including languages, literature, and arts.

- *Arts*: Arts are the productions or expressions of what is beautiful, appealing, and/or of what is more than ordinary significant. Arts are the establishment of human unity in variety, similarity, proximity, and connectivity in bounded perceptions. Arts are expository detailed modes of creativity of novel things. Art manifests compositions of an individual and/or a group of human beings' emotional, sensational feelings, and thoughts to explain or manifest something in specific causal forms. Artists manifest the interrelations, tendencies and/or values of human beings with their environments. Such behavioral modes represent the interpretation of cultural facts, conditions, concepts, theories, beliefs and relationships between the individual's diametrical conception and the cultural circumferences of the human's life cycle. Artists try to explain human's inner motivations at a particular time and place.

- *Music and Dances*: Music is an art of sound in time that expresses ideas and emotions in significant forms through the elements of rhythm melody, harmony, and color. Dances are rhythmical movement of one's feet, body, or both in a pattern of steps.

- *Movies and Theatrical Drama*: Movies are motion pictures. They are a genre of art or entertainment. Movies are selling specific motion pictures of ideas, body movements, fashion, sex, history, political ideologies, sociocultural values, and industrial life-styles (Parhizgar, 1996: 309).

WHAT IS SCIENCE?

In a general term we can define "science" as simply the empirical process that can form the generalized inquiry by which viable understanding is obtained. Science deals with humanity's understanding concerning the discovery and formulation of the real world. Science can tell us how to act at a given time and in particular circumstances in order to succeed an end. Science is the opposite of opinion because it formulates generalization of deductive understanding. Therefore, science is defined as the conclusion of the good intellectual habit. It is the knowledge of true promises. It contains certain conclusions following necessarily from premises. Science deals with the humanity's understanding concerning the discovery and formulation of the real world in which inherent properties of space, matter, energy, and their interactions can be perfectly scrutinized and predicted. Science is a rational convention related to the generalization of the expected environmental norms, expectations, and values. It is nothing more than the search for understanding of the real world. Nevertheless, the real world in practice is composed of ethical and unethical phenomena. Therefore, scientific discoveries reveal these attributions. That is the main reason that scientists believe that science is a neutral phenomenon. To use it or not depends on the moral convictions, ethical values, and legal commitments of the users in practice.

In the field of scientific inquiry, a scientist uses analytical scientific methodologies to discover valuable alternatives for generalized problem solving techniques. Therefore, scientific findings are reliable and validated to further problem-solving alternatives. For a scientist, mathematics is a tool for building models and theories that can describe and, eventually, explain the operation of the world be it the world of material objects (Physics and Chemistry), living things (Biology), human beings (Social or Behaviors Sciences), the human mind (Cognitive Science), or human truthfulness, justness and fairness (Cognititive Science). Therefore, science is the manifestation of positivistic conception of inquiry and has provided an acceptable understanding of the nature. The distinction between science (normal science) and non-science or quasi-science (pseudo-science) is therefore blurred.

Berelson and Steiner, (1964: 16-17) indicate that organizational behavioral researchers strive to attain the following hallmarks of science:

- The procedures are public.
- The definitions are precise.
- The data collection is objective.
- The findings are replicable.
- The approach is systematic and cumulative.
- The purposes are explanation, understanding, and prediction.

Several frameworks help explain observed objects and phenomena: basic research, applied research, development research, and accelerated research.

- *Basic research* focuses on theoretical problem areas in order to innovate new techniques and methods as final products of a group of scientists' innovativeness and invention (e.g., cloning human beings or animals). The basic research results in with patents, copyrights, and shop-rights.

- *Applied research* has two objectives: (1) to explain enhanced interrelationships between material objects and/or phenomena and (2) to compliment the theoretical frameworks for such an explanation. Applied research tends to diversity scientific techniques to be varied as a product along with its product life cycles (PLCs).

- *Development research* focuses on versatility of a product and/or phenomenon in terms of more discovery of new characteristic and applicability of a product and or phenomenon. (e. g., the PhD syndrome glorifies development research for its own sake; or the baking soda can be used for taking odors of refrigerators). From this perspective, something useful may flow from basic research, but what matters is the applicability of knowledge itself.

- *Accelerated research* focuses on speeding up the process of maturity of previous research systems in order to reach to their final products within a very short timetable to milk the market niches' opportunities (e.g., the Cash Cow). Accelerated research is very important because of the product's physical attributes and capabilities most effect on the financial performance of a firm. Accelerated research focuses on progenistic entrepreneurial aspects of products and infopreneurial of databases.

Taxonomy of Sciences

Acquisition of knowledge refers to an individual's perceptual and practical capabilities that typically take in information via the senses through scientific methodology. They are most comfortable when containing the details of any feasible situation in a quantified understanding process. Sciences generally can be classified into four major categories:

1. Observational sciences
2. Natural sciences
3. Social sciences
4. Behavioral sciences

Observational Sciences: Observational sciences include Astronomy, Geology, Physics, and Chemistry. The primary aim of these sciences is to describe a cause-and-effect relationship between material things. The observational sciences offer the best possibility of accomplishing this goal simply through manipulation of independent variables to measure their effect on, or the change in, the dependent variables.

Natural sciences: Natural Sciences include Zoology (Animals), Botany (Plants), Protistology (One-Celled Organisms), Biorheology (Deformation and Deterioration), and Biology (Physiology, Microbiology, Immunology, Ecology and Evolution, and Molecular and Cellular Biology). Natural sciences identify real characteristics of causes, functions and structures of all material things.

Biology concentrates on with the study of all living things. Biology examines such topics as origins, structures, functions, productions, reproductions, growth, development, behavior, and evolution of the different organisms. For an international manager, familiarity with both biological and ecological conditions of the working place is a must. In most cases, both endemic and epidemic diseases are the most organizational interruptive problems in multinational organizations. Many organizations are annually losing a portion of their budget because of tardiness and absenteeism.

Social Sciences: Social Sciences include Economics, Political Sciences, Demography, History, and Geography. Economics is the study of the production, distribution, and consumption of goods and services. Social sciences are concerned with areas of the labor market, capital intensity, synergistic dynamic of human resources planning and forecasting, accessibility, scarcity, and suitability of productive resources, and assessment of profitability concerning economic development and growth through cost-benefit analysis.

The mainstream of thought for modern civilized societies through history is concerned with power, politics, people, and public policy. Politics in all societies is a fact that has made our modern life very complex. Politics is considered to be the fundamental concern in today's international diplomacy (Parhizgar, 1994: 110). Politics has been defined in number of ways. A common theme running through politics is behaviors aimed at exercising influence through the exertion of power (Meyes and Allen, 1977: 672-678). The study of diplomatic behavior: decision-making, conflict resolution, focusing on interest objectives of groups, coalition formation, preservation of classes of power, power-distance, and rulership.

Demography is the science of bio-statistics and quantitative statistics of populations: as of births, deaths, diseases, marriages, numbers, means, percentages all both material and non-material value systems, etc.

History is a branch of scientific analytic knowledge dealing with past events. It is a continuous, systematic narrative of chronological order of past characteristics of human civilizations as relating to particular people, country, period, and person.

Geography is the science dealing with the real differentiation of the earth's surface, as shown in the character, arrangement, and interrelations over the world of such elements as climate, elevation, soil, vegetation, population density, land use, industries, or states.

Behavioral Sciences: Behavioral Sciences include Anthropology (Physical Anthropology, Cultural Anthropology, Archaeology,

Anthropological Linguistics, and Ethnology/Ethnography), Sociology, and Psychology.

Anthropology is the science of human. Anthropology is literally defined as the science of human generations with the interactions between generations and environments, particularly their cultural environments.

Physical Anthropology is the study of the human condition from a biological perspective. Essentially, it is concerned with the restructuring the evolutionary record of the human species and to deal with how and why the physical traits of contemporary human populations vary across the world.

Cultural anthropology deals with human beings learned behavior as influenced by their cultures and vice versa. In a general form and term, cultural anthropology studies the origins and history of human cultures, their creation, evolution, development, structure, and their interactive functions in every place and time (Beals and Hijer, 1959: 9). Cultural anthropology deals with humanity's conceived and perceived behavior as influenced by their culture, and vice versa. Since the definition of a total culture is usually beyond the scope of a single specialist, anthropologists have developed specialization of this science into: Psychological Anthropology, Economic Anthropology, Urban Anthropology, Educational Anthropology, Medical Anthropology, Rural Anthropology, and Applied Anthropology. In sum as Harvey and Allard (1995: 11) indicate: "An anthropologist takes the role of an observer from a culture more developed than our own and describes features of our civilization in the same manner as we describe cultures we view as primitive."

Archaeology is the study of the lifestyles of people from the past as determined by excavating and analyzing the sites, artifacts and written records. Archaeologists reconstruct the cultures of people who are no longer living. Archaeologists deal mainly with three basic components of culture: material culture, ideas and behavior patterns.

Anthropological Linguistics is the study of human speech and language. This branch of knowledge is divided into four distinctive branches: historical linguistics, sociolinguistic, descriptive linguistics, and ethnolinguistic.

Ethnography deals with the study of specific contemporary cultures and *ethnology* deals with more general underlying patterns of human culture derived through cultural comparison. Cultural anthropologists provide insights into questions such as: How have traditions, habits, orientations, and customs relating to a group of people emerged? How are marriage customs, and kinship systems operated? In what ways do people believe in supernatural power? How do migration and urbanization affect each other?

Sociology is traditionally defined as science of society. Psychology is the science of behavior. It generally includes animal as well as human behavior. Sociology is traditionally defined as the science of society, for searching and solving social problems within the context of its dynamic processes, purposes, and goals. Sociology is the science of human groups and is characterized by rigorous methodology with an empirical emphasis and conceptual consciousness (Luthans, 1985: 36). Sociology is the study of social systems like families, occupational classes, mobs, and organizations. The overall focus of sociology is on social behavior in societies, institutional behavioral patterns, organizational structures, and group dynamics.

Psychology has been defined as the science of behavior. Psychologists study the behavior of human beings and their perceptions in both industrial and/or agricultural organizational ecology. Psychologists study the behavior of people in organizational settings. There are many formative schools of thought in the field of psychology. The most widely known are structuralism, functionalism, behaviorism, Gestalt psychology, and psychoanalysis.

Wilhelm Wundt founded structuralism theory of psychology in 1879 in Germany. He had established a laboratory for studying human psychology. The theory revolved around conscious experience and attempted to build the science of mind. This theory applies to a structural division of the human mind into units of mental states such as sensation, memory, imagery, and feelings.

Functionalism was developed by American Psychologist William James (1842-1910) and philosopher John Dewey (1859-1925). This theory of psychology is based upon the function of mind. Emphasis is mainly placed on humanity's adaptation and adjustment to the ecological environment. This theory of the mind is emphasizes human sensory experience such as learning, forgetting, motivation, and adaptability to a new situation. Morgan and King (1966: 22) state: "Functionalism had two chief characteristics; the study of the total behavior and experience of an individual, and an interest in the adaptive functions served by the things an individual does."

The foundation of the behaviorism theory is based upon the connectivity of the human mind toward behavior. Behaviorism was influenced by the Russian Psychologist Ivan Pavlov (1849-1936). Since the structuralists were only concerned with the mind, and functionalists emphasized both mind and behavior, behaviorists focused on consequential results of such a connectivity in relations with observance, objective behavior, and the significant outcomes of human mind and body movements.

Psychoanalysis psychology has come from Sigmund Freud (1856-1939). His theory is about unconscious motivation and the development and structure of personality and his treatment techniques.

Social psychology is academically interdisciplinary. It consists of an eclectic mixture of sciences and arts (Luthans, 1985: 30-38). Social Psychology is generally a synthesized scientific theory of psychology and sociology. If social psychology emphasizes on individual behavior, its close tie is with psychology. Also, it is equated with behavioral science. From the standpoint of emphasis on sociology, social psychology is the study of an individual behavior within relation to the groups (group emphasis).

WHAT IS TECHNOLOGY?

Terpstra and David (1991: 136) state:

Technology is a cultural system concerned with the relationships between humans and their natural environment. A society is well adapted to its environment when its technological system is: (1) environmentally feasible, (2) stable, (3) resilient, and (4) open to revision.

Technology focuses on a system of ideas to be reflected in physical and non-physical material or cyberspace things such as matter, machine, waves, time, light, and movement.

From another point of view, technological breakthroughs are known as integrated innovative systems which have discovered how to access through processing both deep and broad domains of know-why, know-what, know-how, and know-where cyberspace information in both corporations and industries as well as in modern societies. Within such a highly sophisticated cyberspace environment, cognivistic mapping, pragmatistic operational designs of data gathering, and holistic distributive operational techniques can be potentially abusive systems. Data processes and designed outputs can be easily misused by E-businesses to inflate the corporation's performance. Therefore, within the context of the real business world, we can claim that development of technological civilization may not be evidence of progress from an ethical and moral point of view. However, technological developments are facts reflected in humanity's physical and intellectual abilities to affect and shape the natural environment and extend it to their desirable objectives (Parhizgar and Lunce, 1996: 394).

In today's free market economy, the basic organizational resource is no longer material capital, or labor, or natural resources, but knowledge. Knowledge is not the same thing as scientific *formulas, data* or *information,* although it uses all. Knowledge manifests a step further beyond scientific boundaries; it is a conclusion drawn form of application of scientific formulas and information after it is linked to other known and unknown phenomena and compared to what is already known.

Scientific formulas direct us not only to know what is something true but also why it is true. This type of scientific knowing is called syllogism. Syllogism is a conclusive argument in which two premises and conclusions can be expressed either by demonstration or deduction. When we use scientific syllogistic formulas, we prove two domains of facts:

- The existence of logical truthfulness of demonstrative reasoning concerning a phenomenon, an element, and a process, or dynamics of a synthesized group.
- The possible deductive conclusion is the manifestation of politics that states why such formulas are true. For example, if a CEO is eligible to vote in the Board of Directors of a company, that CEO is a member of that Board of Directors. Then the deductive result indicates that the Board of Directors is a codeterminative one.

Data are simple, absolute quantitative facts and figures, that, in and themselves, may be of little value use. Data represent observable or factual quantitative incidents or figures out of a context. Data are not directly meaningful. To be valuable and useful to the organization, the data are processed into finished information by connecting parts with other data. Data should be placed within some meaningful contextual boundary of an event in order to be meaningful. Therefore, information is data that have been linked with other data and converted into a meaningful and workable context for specific right or wrong use. Therefore, knowledge is the essence of codified meaningful information to be believed and valued based on the workable organized accumulation of information through cognitive experience, communication or inference.

MORAL, ETHICAL, AND LEGAL GLOBAL INTELLECTUAL PROPERTY RIGHTS

As we stated in the previous chapter, the term intellectual property generally covers patents, copyrights, shop rights, surgical procedural rights, trademarks, and trade secrets. The international ethical and legal debate is whether such items should be considered as commercial private rights for owners and if they should be protected by the international community on a global scale, and, if so, to what extent. Some countries, specifically developing countries, are against monopoly of knowledge and technology. They believe that scientific discoveries and technological breakthroughs are non-commercial phenomena. Therefore, they view them as a kind of "public domain" not "public property" to be transferable to them without payment to the discoverers. These countries believe that developed countries, through holding the copyrights, patents, trademarks, shop rights, trade secret, and surgical procedural rights, manipulate their progressive scientific movements and can cause them to be more retarded. They argue that intellectual property rights should be based on socio-ethical legitimization toward enhancement of human rights rather than econo-political privileges for a specific group's advantages. Also, developing countries believe that knowledge should not be monopolized. They believe that knowledge is an integral part of international "public domain." The main argument between developed and developing countries emerges from the discussion that what counts as property concerning "knowledge ownership," and "knowledge property," and globally to what extent may copyrighters and patent holders claim exclusive rights over them.

The debate concerning intellectual property rights is about two different subject matters: (1) tangible and intangible properties as well as (2) ownership, lease, and rent of these properties. Let us first to define property and then analyze the inherent exclusive rights for copyrighers and patent holders. In a general term, property is defined as a tangible and recognizable dynamic reality both in the form of goods and lands. Property is an essential or distinctive attribute or quality of a "thing or a phenomenon." Ownership is defined as a legal right or privilege of possession of something. Ownership refers to possession of property of any kind that has been or is capable of being handed down to descendants or disposed of otherwise in a will (e.g., estate, money, valuables, securities, chattels, land, and buildings).

The intellectual property such as ideas, information, data banks, and technological breakthroughs are very new developments in human culture. Culturally, scientific discoveries have been treated as part of the "public domain." Such an international public domain was handed down generation by generation. Historically, no individual or groups ever claimed possession of sciences, traditional technologies, or discoveries. Nevertheless, in the late 20th century when the application of scientific formulas was implemented to create material things, such as nuclear plants, machines, and computers, then the idea of intellectual property emerged. Consequently, discoveries of scientific formulas and technological breakthroughs emerged as copyrights and patents. The philosophy behind the patents and copyrights is based on the political ideology of capitalism philosophy. All human efforts, including their intellectual deliberations, are subject to the exclusive rights to their respective writing and discoveries. Such exclusive rights contain the monetary claims as rights and privileges.

This political platform has created different perceptions among different cultures. Accordingly, different cultures perceive knowledge as the main source of economic development and growth. Then the value of knowledge is subject to the free market economy based on demand and supply. Is it moral and ethical to perceive knowledge as a commodity? Answering this question varies culture to culture.

In the European and American capitalism systems visualization of the flow of knowledge and manufacturing products are substantially sheltered from the direct impact of econo-social forces. This culture focuses on the primacy of added economic value systems through application of knowledge in material things. This concept depicts the application of scientific advancements and technological breakthroughs as one of the foundations of business transactions. Scientific formulas and technological procedures could be viewed as commodities to be bought or sold, because they are the main sources of economic advantages. These business transactions exist within a market environment and influence the added market values of knowledge and technology. These economical added value systems have shaped commercialization of these phenomena by impinging economical and political forces. Through intellectual property rights and exclusive technological privileges, a capitalistic society can maintain both ownership power-manipulation and power-exploitation of knowledge distribution among nations. Also, it can be used as leverage for balancing the distribution of wealth among nations.

Regardless of the nature of intellectual property rights and ownership, each nation possesses its own value and belief systems concerning the self-interest of copyrighters and patent holders and the public interest. The end result is that while intellectual property rights are subject to global issues, it is difficult to establish a global consensus basis for their legitimization (see Table 6.3).

For example, in the Islamic cultures, which stretch from Africa to Asia and accounts for almost a quarter of the world's population, Moslems articulate a coherent, sophisticated, and distinctively non-Western view on intellectual property rights (Behdad, 1989:185). In a general philosophical indoctrination, Moslems believe that the owner of all things is God, and we, as human beings, are tenants of God who have the opportunity to temporally possess these things. Therefore, morally and ethically Moslems believed that they need to take care of all properties including their intellectual deliberations. Moslems through their religious principles (Zakot) do not believe in pure ownership. They believe that in any form of personal ownership, there is a voluntary moral and ethical obligation to give away a portion of their wealth for the welfare of society beside of mandated taxation systems. Moslems are not only obligated to accumulate wealth, they are also committed to pay 2.1/2% of their cash balance and any other liquid assets such as gold, silver, bonds, etc. per year to impoverished and unemployed people (Awadudi, 1989: 121). This type of religious obligation provides society with a fair economic distributive system. In the West, such a policy has been initiated by governmental inflationary system.

Buddhism also possesses a long tradition regarding economics and property rights. Shintoism views the need to have ownership as a family obligation. They need to synergize the family wealth. Japanese do not consider the need to work either as an individual nor a social obligation. They consider it a family obligation. Therefore, accumulation of wealth in this culture is bound to certain cultural patterns of expectations from family members.

The argument in the domain of intellectual deliberation is about whether scientific discoveries or technological breakthroughs are counted as properties. Furthermore, the terms property and ownership through the history of mankind have changed dramatically. For example, in the 19th century slaves were represented socially and legally properties of masters and in the 20th century in most Moslem countries such as Afghanistan, Iran,

Saudi Arabia and others many women are considered the property of men. For example, Iranian married

Table 6.3: The Need to Work and the Beliefs to Distribute Wealth Among Three Religions.

ATTRIBUTIONS	EUROPEAN AND AMERICAN SOCIETIES	FAR EASTERN SOCIETY	MIDDLE AND NEAR EASTERN SOCIETIES
RELIGION	Protestantism	Shintoism	Islamism
PERSPECTIVE	Individualism	Famialism	Brotherhood
GOAL	To accumulate wealth for the time of individual necessity	To accumulate and distribute wealth only among family members	To accumulate and distribute wealth among family members and Islamic societies

women (not single ones) without written permission of their husbands are not allowed to leave their country. In the Western culture, human body parts are pantentable. To this date, there have been more than five hundred patents registered by the U.S. Office of Patents on behalf of biotech corporations. The developed countries believe that intellectual property rights provide incentives for future innovations and to the competitive profitability of companies that spend money on research (Steidlmeier, 1993: 157).

CHAPTER SUMMARY

This chapter examines the evolution of scientific advancements, technological developments, informational prodigies, and business strategies and their attributes in relation to knowledge management systems. It discusses how knowledge management can provide moral, ethical, and legal strategic advantages through an examination of the ways they affect organizational operations, vertical and horizontal organizational structural design, and interorganizational relationships.

One primary objective for international business today is to make efforts to manage and leverage humanely the organizational knowledge management system. Having greater access to scientific formulas, technological breakthroughs, and information systems is useless unless the corporate knowledge management system is put to use to further legitimate and ethical operational processes. Knowledge management neutrality should lead and be equated with ethical virtuous neutrality for professionals. The former is acceptable as a condition of personal career and the latter is acceptable as a condition of social justice. A paradigm is a basic framework through which we conceive and perceive the world, giving shape and meaning to all our knowledge and experiences, providing a basis for interpreting and organizing both our conceptions and perceptions. A paradigm is more than a theory because it is a holistic synthesized essence of our mind and actions within the historical events of our culture. A paradigm is a holistic fundamental asserted belief that sometimes isn't even articulated until brought into question by someone else's new competing paradigm.

Knowledge is not the same thing as scientific formulas, data banks, and information systems, although it uses all of these phenomena. Knowledge manifests itself as a step beyond scientific boundaries. It is a conclusion drawn from the application of scientific formulas, technological breakthroughs, and information systems after it is linked to other known and unknown phenomena and compared to what is already known. Knowledge always contains a human intellectual valuable factor. Knowledge is distinguished from science, data, and information. Knowledge has been perceived through different perceptions and outcomes. Knowledge-wealth is an intangible resource which synergizes an organization to effectively acquire, create, apply, and transform know-what, know-how, and know-why across the company and modify activities to reflect new knowledge and insights. Applying knowledge for problem solving is a new path of prodigy. Traditional epistemology identifies three distinctive kinds of knowledge: (1) knowledge of things and objects, (2) knowledge of how to do things, and (3) knowledge of statements or propositions.

It is worthwhile to define "moral knowledge" as it refers to the state of excellence of intellect and wisdom and to the disposition of cognizance of mind to effectively perform its proper function.

At the heart of the evolutionary MPKMS lie four related forces:

- Advancement of science
- Convergence of technological breakthroughs into computing, communication, and information systems
- Explosion of knowledge
- Assertion of validity and viability of progenistic knowledge for the conclusive operational result of innovative outcomes.

In order to decide why knowledge should be oriented toward discovering the truth, we must first ask: "Why is know-why logic the essential nature of inquiry?" Know-why logic signifies the rational reasoning that represents the essential nature of truth. Truth can be perceived through three major causes: formal cause, material cause, and efficient cause. Within a matrix of the truth, there are three levels of logical reasoning: (1) necessity of reasoning, (2) sufficiency of reasoning, and (3) vitality of reasoning including quiddity and equilibrium logic.

One of the first problems for global business ethics is know-what structuring of the international value systems between home and host countries. In structuring the know-what management paradigm system of global business ethics, identification of the boundaries of moral, ethical, and legal value systems should be closely related to the distinctions of three domains: (1) cognitive, (2) affective, and (3) effective transactions.

Normative morality is based upon personal self-disciplinary and societal ordered value systems. Normative morality manifests managers' moral principles, beliefs, and expectations to justify their behavior on which they base their judgments and actions. Know-what is concerned with the "affective" domain of knowledge. It includes structuring mutual objectives that describe changes in reengineering the product or services by producers and reconstructing interest, attitudes, values, and development of appreciation and adequate adjustment to new products and services. Ethical "effectiveness" should be purely descriptive. This indicates that the value systems or quality of one class of value as compared with another should not be established. This means that managers should avoid partiality to one view of morality, ethics, and legality as opposed to another.

Know-where information in an organization is a matter of actual operational knowledge. A firm's information knowledge consists of several levels of hierarchies. Virtually all-organizational levels can be depicted in terms of their information dimension.

Now that we have analyzed multiethical know-why, know-what, and know-where logical reasoning concerning structuring a corporate knowledge wealth, we want to describe how this dynamic knowledge management paradigm system can be used in a global firm. Although the MPKMS suggests that the knowledge-wealth of a firm can be analyzed along four dimensions corporation's ethical reasoning (the "why" dimension), products and services (the "what" dimension), customers (the "whose" dimension), and information (the "where" dimension) we are focusing now on technologies (the "know-how" dimension). Know-how knowledge includes personal computers, Internet sites, software, high technological components (such as microprocessors), other hardware components, workstations, minicomputers and mainframes, and information technology consultation services. Analysis of know-how knowledge focuses on three cognitive mappings of the corporation's operational direction: (1) job shop, (2) mass production, and (3) Flexible manufacturing systems.

Job-Shop know-how knowledge is viewed as a vital source for strategic decisions and actions that crystallize the establishment of a continuous regular production system on the basis of the "know-whose" dimension. Organizational knowledge can reside wholly within an expert, or can be shared within a professional group, or the firm's managerial system.

Mass-Production of know-how knowledge concentrates on formulating a firm's operational strategy through adopting continuous changes including irregularities, with frequent discontinuities and wide swings in its rate of change.

Flexible-Manufacturing know-how knowledge can be assessed through the versatility of three key indicators: effectiveness, efficiency, and productivity. Effectiveness relates to the degree to which the know-how knowledge meets the scientific structuring of the manufacturing system. Efficiency is defined as an assessment of know-how knowledge used with consideration of cost-benefit analysis for a given output to implement such knowledge in practice. Productivity is defined such that know-how knowledge, as a viable scientific formula, is used by experts and comes out with embedded information in order to be converted into embodied knowledge for the purpose of more profitability. The primary task of syllogistic knowledge management system is to discover members of scientific and scholarly professions. An occupation requires more than the ordinary amount of tacit knowledge. Phenomenology stresses careful descriptive value systems through an appearance or immediate object of awareness in human experience. Phenomenology is a qualitative conceptual awareness that can be manifested constructively by quantitative value judgments in the human mind.

QUESTIONS FOR DISCUSSION

- What is a paradigm?
- What is a business ethics paradigm?
- What are different definitions of a business through stakeholders' perceptions?
- What is paradigm of knowledge management?
- How do you define knowledge?
- What are differences between explicit knowledge and tacit knowledge?
- What are differences among theories of knowledge? Explain.
- What is moral knowledge?
- What is fuzzy logic?
- What is know-what structure?
- What are differences among cognitive, affective, and effective transactions? Explain.
- What we mean by job-shop and shop-right?
- How do you define science, technology, art, and philosophy? Explain.
- Are Ethics and morality parts of philosophy? Explain how.
- What are differences among phenomenology, epistemology, and axiology? Explain.

- What is aesthetics?
- Is business ethics as an observational science? If yes or no explain.
- What is the difference between science and technology? Explain.
- What are differences between copyrights and patents? Explain.
- What we mean by property rights through moral, ethical, and legal interpretation?

CASE STUDY

AMERICAN CORPORATE CEO'S SCANDALS AND THEIR LAVISH LIFESTYLE AFTER BANKRUPTCY: A FEW BAD APPLES IN A BOX

Today, there is a battle line draw between honesty and dishonesty in corporate America.   There are three types of managers in corporate America:

Honest managers perceive their business leadership role as "heroes." Their ethical and moral convictions are based on: "what can I give you from my personal knowledge, talents, and experience," because you have trusted me to take care of your investment? This type of managers is "altruistic" in mind and behavior. They praise honest employees and honest auditing companies who ascribe another's success to superior work ethics, self-discipline, or luck just being in the right place at right time and possessing the right professional skills.

Dishonest managers perceive their business leadership role as "hoodwinkers." They like to hide by establishing a close unethical connection and immoral relations with politicians and crooks in the marketplace in order to fulfill their selfish objectives. They conclude that the honest world is diseased. It rewards the wrong doers, the wrong people, and the wrong abilities. Then a hoodwinker's managerial lifestyle is based on "what can you give me?" or "how can I deceive you to give me your money?" and "who cares what I give you in return?" They strive to find loopholes in order to cheat their clients. They hire very powerful law firms to keep them off the hook. If they are caught for wrong doing, they will bribe authorities, mislead the public, share illegitimate wealth with auditing companies, acquire loans through greedy bankers with the highest interest rate, deal with illegal traders, and make a contract with the soulless dealmakers who crawled through cellars of honest cultures and infect them with their immoral and unethical habits and practices. These hoodwinkers are closely connected with unprofessional "Wall Street, Main Street, and State Street power brokers." If they find that they are scrutinized in an investigation, they immediately resign, liquidate their assets, and hide or transfer them to their relatives or other countries. Finally, if they can't hide their shame, they may commit suicide.

Amoral managers perceive their business leadership role as "camouflaged swingers." They are living on the borderline between honest and dishonest managers. The camouflaged swingers are viewed as people who grab money, and capital. They like to "grab huge sum of money as wages, benefits, stock options, and cash them in before scandals surface, they run." These managers are not immoral or unethical. They don't lie and they don't tell the whole truth. They reveal a partial truth (amoral). They like to gain, gain, and gain money through very high salaries, very high stock options without restrictions, and live a lavish lifestyle. They are searching for pleasure and gain with their legitimate wealth.

MAJOR ROLE PLAYERS OF THE CASE

In the beginning of the 21st century, the infectious disease of greed and the corporate epidemic of dishonesty spread among some of the giant corporations in America. Such an infectious disease caused some corporations to declare bankruptcy. Consequently many honest hardworking families, including corporate employees and stockholders, lost their life savings because of unethical and immoral behaviors of the corporate boards of governance and chief executive officers of these corrupted corporations. Among these greedy board chairmen and/or CEOs are the former CEO of Enron, Kenneth Lay; the former Enron CFO Andrew Fastow; the ex-Southeby's chairman of the governing board Alfred Taubman; the former CEO of WorldCom Inc., Bernard Ebbers; the former WorldCom Inc. CFO Scott Sullivan; and the former CEO of Tyco International Company, Dennis Kozlowski.

ANALYSIS OF THE CASE

Many corporate executives have continued to live with a lavish lifestyle even as the value their company's stocks have plummeted amid corporate scandals including bankruptcy. Ross (2002) reports:

The home under the most scrutiny at the moment is a 7,000 square foot mansion owned by Dennis Kozlowski, former CEO of Tyco International. ... The former WorldCom CFO Scott Sullivan is building an enormous mansion in Florida. WorldCom of cooking the books, leading to the company's bankruptcy, accuses Sullivan. Sullivan says everything he did was legal. ...Up in New York State, construction has continued on the country estate owned by Martha Stewart, who is under investigation for inside trading...In Bell Air, workers are still busy on the $98 million, 8-

acre, 50-room estate owned by Gary Winnick, the former chairman of Global Crossing, which filed for bankruptcy in January

Most of these former CEOs and corporate board members have found a legal loophole in some states like Florida, so that the principle places of their residence are essentially untouchable. They are safe from civil lawsuits and creditors.

Each of the above former CEOs or CFOs are accused of possible business fraud, corruption, and deception. Some of these managers like Ex-Sotheby's chairman of the governance board, Alfred Taubman got very light sentences compared to their illegitimate gains and crimes. Federal judge George Daniels sentenced Alfred Taubman to one year in prison and fined him $7.5 million for leading a six-year price fixing conspiracy between the world's dominant auction houses (Chaffin, 2002: 7).

One of the outrageous incidents is related to the Tyco's CEO Dennis Kozlowski and CFO Mark Swartz's larceny case that had looted the company out of $600 million. During his tenure at Tyco, Kowzlowski invited a few people to the party for his second wife's fortieth birthday on Sardinia Island, which cost $2 million. Tyco footed about half the bill for that party. Jurors on October 24,2003 saw the 30-minute video of that party. They watched how Kozlowski welcoming guests, toasting his wife, and dancing to a performance by singer Jimmy Buffett who was paid $250.000. The tape also showed guests wearing togas and tight briefs. Also the video showed gladiators, chariots, and dancing around the pool. Kozlowski watched the video in the court, and he was smiling and nodding his head at several different points. Finally, Kozlowski said: "It was a nice party, with nice people." (*CNN News*, 2003).

CASE QUESTIONS FOR DISCUSSION

- Do you believe corporate America's missions are ethical and moral? Explain.
- Do you believe the private sector in a capitalistic society should or shouldn't be controlled by regulatory governmental agencies? Explain how.
- Do you believe that the CEO's principal residential estates should or shouldn't be touchable by law when they declare bankruptcy? Provide pros and cons.
- Do you believe that bankrupted corporate CEOs deserve to keep their salaries, benefits, and stock option profits as "a merit pay?"
- Do you believe the government is able to control the financial states of corporate America?

- Do you believe college and university professors and researchers are the best professionals to audit corporate America's financial books? If no, what other professional groups should audit them?
- What should be the role of Wall Street, Main Street, and lay people to control all social organizations including governmental agencies, private sectors, and non-profit organizations?
- Do you believe the American judiciary system is capable of fighting against corporate crimes?
- What should be the aggressive role of the Security Exchange Commission (SEC) to control all business organizations and auditing companies?
- In a capitalistic society like America who is responsible for inside trading irregularities?
- Should the SEC take an aggressive role and try to control all business organizations and auditing companies?

CASE SOURCES

J. Chaffin, "Ex-Sotheby's Chief Jailed For a Year and Fined $7.5 Million," *Financial Times,* (Tuesday April 23, 2002), 7.

CNN News. (2003),
<Http://money.cnn.com/2003/10/28/news/companies/tyco_
party/index.htm?cnn+yes>.

B. Ross, "Places For Corporate Princes Executives Keep Building Mansions Despite Scandals."< *abcNEWS com*> (2002).

<wysiwyg://10/http://www.abcnews.go.com/...metime/DailyNews/exec_ho
mes_020725.html>.

CHAPTER 7

MORAL VIRTUES, ETHICAL VALUES, AND THE CORPORATE STAKEHOLDERS' CONVICTIONS

We do not like some people, because they may be nasty,
but we dignify them, because they are human beings.

We do not praise some people, because they may be greedy,
but we blame them, because they may be selfish.

We do not respect some people, because they may be dishonest,
but we condemn them, because they may be corrupted.

We do not love some people, because we may perceive them as ugly,
but we respect them, because they may be beautiful inside.

We do not honor some people because they may be rich or poor,
but we do honor them, because they may be compassionate.

We find some people do not act wisely, because they may be ignorant,
but we find them honest, because they may be simple-minded people.

CHAPTER OBJECTIVES

When you have read this chapter you should be able to do the following:

- Define moral virtues and ethical value systems.
- Develop conceptual skills to determine to what extent there is a general agreement about moral character.
- Develop an understanding about ethical value systems and their relation to the problem of amoral behavior.
- Develop a comprehensive understanding of the nature of virtue and why are there two principal kinds of virtue.
- Develop a framework of analysis in order to enable you to discuss what is the difference between moral virtue and ethical value systems.
- Establish a framework in order to realize what is the immediate purpose of virtue.
- Analyze the efficient cause of intellectual value systems.
- Analyze the efficient cause of moral virtue.
- Know how virtue is maintained once it is acquired.
- Explain how and why moral virtue and ethical values can enhance means and ends of human behavior.
- Explain the concept of a social contract related to the concept of stakeholders.
- Know how stakeholder groups affect each other.
- Understand how the environment can be a stakeholder, when the environment is not human.
- Critically analyze global environmental forces in order grasp the real meaning of how a corporation can potentially take account of the global moral, ethical, and legal mandates.
- Know why the concept of stakeholder analysis is necessary before stakeholder management principles can be developed.

THOUGHT STARTER

Supposedly, you are working in an institution that many of your peers and associates believe that they have been nasty, unfair, and unjust to their institutions, to their clients, and to their community. You are realizing that you are associated with a group of people to whom conspiracy, plotting, corruption, and selfishness are the main activities of their daily lives. You do not have any opportunity to leave that place, because you are assume that everywhere that you go will be the same. Therefore, you are convicted to stay and work in such an environment. Through your cognitive judgment, you are classifying your peers and associates into three groups and labeled these groups as:

- Unethical, selfish, and pathological liars, majority groups
- Moral, altruistic, and truthful people, minority groups
- Amoral, political, and opportunistic, they are belonged to the bellowing wind party, partisan groups

Supposedly, you are trying to be a good person, a professional colleague, and an impartial person. Supposed you are doing your duty, as you consciously perceive it and seeking to do what is good for yourself and your associates. Furthermore, you are not silent. You are expressing your honest views without fear of retaliation by corrupt superiors. Supposed, also, that the first group dislikes you because you are not submitting your volition to their evil wishes. What are you doing is based on your moral virtues and ethical values? Supposedly, you find an opportunity to be the executive officer of your institution with one condition: to change your moral conviction and submit yourself to the will of unethical majority of your colleagues and associates and implement their unjust wishes in order to gain very high salary and lay a foundation for a better job in another similar organization in the near future. Should you take that opportunity?

Considering the above scenario, you are exposed to three alternative choices:

- To deny the proposed opportunity and maintain your personal moral conviction and ethical values and be faithful to your personal dignity and integrity
- To accept the new proposed opportunity and change your moral conviction and ethical values and submit yourself to the will of unethical and immoral associates and peers and keep your promise.
- To accept the new proposed opportunity and promise to adhere your will to the wishes of corrupted associates and peers before election, and when you get to the office, denounce the majority's unethical and immoral wishes and get rid of the majority people and replace them with good and professional people.

By choosing one of the above alternatives, you put yourself in an ethical and moral trial and question yourself about basic principles if you have good reasoning for your choice.

PLAN OF THIS CHAPTER

We believe that people learn best when they understand means and ends of their decisions, actions, and behaviors. These attributes represent their moral characters, ethical commitments, and intellectual potentials. Aristotle analyzes human personality into three elements: passions, faculties, and states of character. Since passions (anger and fear), and faculties (wisdom and intellect which recognize fear from anger) are not in and of themselves blameworthy or praiseworthy, virtue must be a state of character (Albert, Denise, and Peterfreund, 1984: 40). In this chapter, we focus on the important characteristics of a businessperson concerning behavioral virtues, values, norms, and beliefs. Furthermore, in this chapter, we will explain the profit motive in its proper perspective through analyzing moral, ethical, and legal responsibilities of stakeholders. While making profit is the only way for a business to survive, to what extent a corporation should strive for legitimate profitability is a worthy question?

HUMANENESS AND COMPETITION

Some people believe that all human beings have basic drives toward self-respect and self-actualization. These characteristics are the quest to be all we can be. These people believe in the state of humaneness in order to foster the notion of individual growth, improvement, and progress in personality. Humaneness is the distinctive idealistic good side of people that is centered on promoting spirituality among people. The focus of humaneness is on the self rather than on the nature of activities or jobs themselves, the group in which these activities function, or the leisure activities these people pursue. Activities are not only inescapable necessities for these people, but also involve liberation from nature and innovation in a social and independent entity. Nevertheless, when all humanity is expected to develop and grow their conscious awareness, then a real sense of competition appears. This is the beautiful side of humaneness because it promotes growth and development for all members of a society. However, there is a problem with the ultimate ends of competition. That problem stems from the notion of emphasizing self as more materialistically productive rather than spiritually searching for growth and development. Then, humaneness converts itself into material gains in order to fulfill the ultimate material needs.

Philosophically, businesses through humanistic doctrine must serve people by fulfilling the balance between material and spiritual goodness -- not by depriving people of natural goodness. Businesses should respect social activities and natural resource endowments to an extent that will provide people with work not as an end in it, but as an end in providing consumers with a high quality of goods and/or services. Also, they should respect social activities to an extent that will provide people with work not as an end in it, but also as a means within the context of an enriched life. Humanists and ethicists believe that working hard is a valuable habit not only for valuing the nature of work, but also for valuing its social commitments. Work should be valuable in terms of what it contributes to the individual's personal growth and development.

Humanists believe that working hard is not a valuable habit for valuing the nature of work by its own sake, but it should be valued in terms of what it contributes to the individual's personal and societal growth and development. In another words, businesses should not be separated from society. They are inseparable parts of society and enjoy reciprocal relationships with their environments. Corporations are like highly sophisticated machines that logically resist any attempt to place moral and ethical responsibilities on them. A car does not realize that is hitting a human being, an animal, or a bunch of paper. It is the operators or drivers that use or misuse such machines for their immoral personal objectives. For example, Enron with more than 21,000 employees around the world, had revenues over $100 billion dollars in the year 2000. Enron has won a string of awards, including *Fortune*'s America's Most Innovative Company award for an unprecedented six years between 1966 and 2001. In the year 2000, Enron won the *Financial Times*' Energy Company of the Year award and Boldest Successful Investment Decision (*BBC News*, 2002). Suddenly, such a giant corporation with such an extraordinary financial operation collapsed. Within the international stock market, most media and assessment organizations lost their reputations. People will not trust promotional news concerning companies. People lost trust in managers, because Enron's management team, with unprofessional help of the auditing company Arthur Andersen cheated stockholders. Danley (1990: 165-170) said: "Just as one cannot blame the automobile in a drunk driving accident, to ascribe responsibility to such machines [as corporations] ... is tantamount to mistaking the created for the creator."

Today, individuals within contextual econo-political and psychosocial boundaries of their environments have a set of virtues, values, norms, and beliefs that together form their moral characters and ethical commitments and make them what they are. Virtues, of course, are intellectual deliberative judgments on the matter of have to, must be, and ought to be in their distinctively moral sense. Virtues are highly attached to the psychosocial characteristics of human beings. Values are periodical assessments with evaluations of judgments concerning the quality, worth, or desirability of activities, situations, consequences, or institutions in relation to what should be. Values can be expressed by saying that something is or is not valuable, desirable, or good. Norms are established criteria to be within the contextual boundary of specific domain of expected behavior. Moral, ethical, and cultural norms are not punishable, but violators of law are punishable. Beliefs are emotional and sensational judgments concerning an establishment of ideas and feelings. Beliefs are emotional and sensational judgments concerning established ideas and feelings. Beliefs are viewed as criteria for judgments. Beliefs are individual's expected judgments that people think about given concepts. For example, we believe in a participatory, not in a representative, democracy, because you know that you are capable of making the right decision by electing qualified representatives.

Virtues, values, norms, and beliefs are principles of judgments that individuals expect all people to consider them accordingly when they think and act, when faced with a given similar situation. There are distinctions between moral judgments and value judgments.

Moral Judgments

Moral judgments are based on absolute moral virtuous principles in an individual's mind (conscience). Value judgments are based on relative societal pluralistic value principles (societal conscientiousness). People use both judgments in their daily behavior. Nevertheless, distinction between moral judgments and value judgments is important. Moral judgments are based on holistic intellectual deliberation of excellent, effective, and qualitative conscience choices. They are viewed as the maximum outcome of well cared and for prudent decisions and actions. Within moral judgments, there are no more alternatives beyond these choices.

Value judgments

Value judgments are based on relative mixed sociable assessments of cultural behavior that can range from excellent, best, and better to good for making the right decisions and taking correct actions. Also, value judgments could be concerned about wrong decisions and actions that could range from vice, worst, and worse to bad decisions and actions. Managers should look at virtues, values, norms, and beliefs as much as possible on the bases of morality and ethics, when they are confronted with some dilemmas. In ethical and moral terms, value judgments should not be only based upon legal mandates. They should be based upon moral virtues and ethical values. When a manager is confronted with some dilemmas, he/she has plenty of choices between the magnitudes of excellence over vice. Making managerial judgments is based on choices within the domain of the above magnitudes. For the sake of clarity, we will define virtues and values first, then we will analyze their inherent consequences and operations.

WHAT IS VIRTUE?

Let us begin with formulating a framework for investigating virtue and value. *Virtue* refers to an aesthetic representation of the state of a sober mind that allows an individual to interpret the beauty of an observable moral character. Virtue generates excellent inferences of humaneness. This concept derives from prior lifetime moral and ethical studies of intellectual deliberations on learning, perceiving, and problem solving. In the process of intellectual deliberation, people do not just add new information to describe accumulated facts concerning their happiness, they also, like scientists and ethicists, construct their intellectual models of moral character on the basis of what people value. Thus, virtues are the good of intellect. What do we mean by the good of the intellect? Oesterle (1957: 172) states: "In order that there be intellectual virtue there must be some good realizable in the intellect, for virtue always implies a perfection of human power, which is to say, it attains whatever is the good of a power."

The word *virtue* is translation of a Greek word *arete*. Peters (1967: 25) indicates that the meaning of virtue cannot only be moral virtue but also excellence in a broad sense. Virtue is the disposition of intellectual deliberation to act well in an exceptional manner. Virtue cultivates specific characteristics in the human mind such as honesty, generosity, kindness, politeness, forgiveness, courage, gratitude, considerateness, and conscientious. Virtues need to be learned by teaching and practicing to be excellent, or perhaps by grace. Virtue possesses three component parts in its meaning:

- Searching for the excellence in the process of intellectual deliberation of an individual's mind as an utmost sign of humaneness.
- Searching for effectiveness of discovered excellence in an individual's intention and action in order to fulfill moral ends-convictions
- Searching for creation of innovative norms of values toward qualitative end- results.

Aristotle believed that for every kind of activity, there is a state of excellence. Accordingly, we seek excellence in personal relations as well as in business relations. A key word for Aristotle concerning humanity is virtue. Human minds operate well or badly and either for good or evil. Through a moral conviction, our immediate concern is the effective causes of virtues. Virtuous decisions and actions derive their merit only from virtuous motives. Good action is the immediate purpose of virtue. Plato found four cardinal virtues: wisdom, courage, temperance, and justice.

Intellectual virtues lead a human to live well. Intellectual virtues are the products of excellence in mind. They generate and increase personal integrity and dignity through exceptional qualitative effective learning. The means and ends of virtues vary culture-to-culture and/or religion-to-religion. For example, Confucian moral virtue remains the bedrock of Chinese thought and behavior throughout Asia. Virtuous traits as espoused by Confucius are based on three principles:

- Eespect for human dignity
- Fairness in judgment (what is unfair to one is unfair to all)
- Reversibility (willingness to be the recipient of one's own manners and actions), (De Mente, 1990: 21)

Christianity regarded virtue as having seven cardinal characteristics. Three theological virtues "faith, hope, and love" and four human virtues "prudence, fortitude, temperance, and justice." This was essentially St. Thomas Aquinas's view on virtue. Since St. Augustine regarded the last four as forms of love, only the first three were really cardinal for him (Frankena, 1973: 64).

Moslems view virtues as having excellence in harmonized faith, knowledge, action, dignity, integrity, chastity, generosity, courage, forgiveness, politeness, tolerance, patience, and truthfulness in human mind and behavior (Mawdudi, 1986: 61).

Intellectual virtue is ordered by knowledge, for we need to think well in order to acquire knowledge. The surest means of acquiring knowledge is by one who has knowledge. Nevertheless, possession of knowledge by a scientist does not guarantee that a scientist can be a virtuous person. In the history of mankind, there are many scientists who committed crimes or have been used as instruments in crimes against humanity. Therefore, virtue is a state of excellence that a person needs to learn it, attend, and continuously apply in his/her mind and behavior.

People from their childhood need to learn virtuous thoughts and behavior. It is easier to teach people how to properly do right things than try to change their behavior after they have learned a pattern of behavior. Therefore, if we are right about this assumption, virtue is a required cognitive perception for the realization of a happy life. By understanding the meaning of virtue more precisely, we shall be better able to understand what is a happy life. Finally, we should understand the fact that jealousy is an ignoble motive and benevolence is a virtue.

What are Different Kinds of Virtue?

Aristotle found virtue to be an excellence or very high quality of humaneness of two types. One type of excellence you can learn by instruction: how to think intellectually. This, Aristotle called intellectual virtue. The other virtues can only be obtained through critical, habitual thinking. This, Aristotle called wisdom. Wisdom is perceived as the foundation of moral virtues. Aristotle argued that we develop virtues by engaging in moral activities. Moral virtue is the way of securing moral excellence. We are tempted to think that morality is the expression of personal preferences, as McIntyre (1984: 6) calls it as emotivism.

From another rational angle, there are two principal kinds of virtue. One kind is a perfect causation for the power of reason itself. This virtue is based on the deductive power of the intellect (intellectual virtue). The other kind of virtue is a development of the appetitive power of knowledge that is rational by participation in the domain of virtue (wisdom or moral virtue). Wisdom or moral virtue is a virtue in the primary meaning of the word for the ability to express reasoning, while intellectual virtue is a virtue that only in a secondary sense can create innovativeness toward perfection or excellence. We must take into account the distinction between intellectual virtue and wise virtues, for the efficient cause of each one. We have wise virtue in mind, and this usage is conforms to the intent to have common practices in behavior. From the standpoint of final cause, the purpose of wise virtue is to pre-dispose us to act more perfectly and in a distinctively humane manner.

When business leaders talk about the need for total quality management (TQM) or total circle quality control (TCQC), they claim that quality is job number one. Or when a company declares in that its mission its trademark is the mark of excellence, these all are viewed as references to the same concept Aristotle captured in virtue. Business leaders do speak of their commitments to quality and excellence of their products and/or services, and these two words are close to what Aristotle meant by values. Both quality and excellence in a final virtuous result should be effective. In today's business world, there are two groups of business people: Moneymakers and Money-Appropriators (Rand: 1999: 30).

Moneymakers: Moral and ethical successful business people who are men and women of intellect could legitimately accumulate their wealth through application of their wisdom. These people could be called moneymakers. These people believe that they should fight for the political ideology of capitalism, not as an economic issue, but with the most convicted moral pride, as an ethical issue. They believe that material and knowledge wealth are primarily products of not physical factors, but of the human intellect. They believe that both material and knowledge wealth are tools of exchange and they are products of the human mind. They believe that wealth should not grow in nature; it has to be produced by the wisdom of people. The best evidence is related to the tumbling of the stock market. Specifically, the stock market crashes in 1998 and 2002. In 1998, the stock market fell 25 percent down. Stock traders did not learn a lesson from such a crash and continued to be by the fooled exaggeration of corporate reports, flaws that caused the crash.

Again, on Friday July 19, 2002, the stock market fell to it lowest rate: DJI lost 390.20 and reached to the lowest level of 7,629.00; NASDAQ lost 37.80 and reached 1,281.35; and S&P lost 33.81 and reached 813.94 (*abcNEWS.com*, 2002). What was the main reason for such crashes? It was highly related to the perceptions of stock traders who lost confidence in corporate reports because they found that some of these financial reports were unethical and illegal. Some auditing companies like Arthur Anderson practiced unprofessional accountancy by book-cooking practices. Book-cooking practice is viewed as an immoral and unethical auditing system. Instead of telling the truth, they provided wrong information to exaggerate the performance of a company. As long as the auditing figure accuracy has not been challenging, the corporation could have obtain very good stock market values. As long as the acts of auditing fraud, deception, and corruption were discovered, the company will be exposed to mistrust and drastic loses its in stock values.

Ethicists believe that people are independent entities who possess inalienable rights to their own lives a type of right derived from their intellectual nature. These people believe that each individual holds that people are ends in themselves, not the means to the ends for others.

Money-Appropriators: There are other types of businesspeople who believe in amoral successful business transactions. These people are men and women who believe in exploiting resources, including human beings. They are looking for the green fields of a cheap labor market. These people are *money-appropriators, and* are not innovators (they are exploiters). Money-appropriators try to acquire unearned wealth through the efforts of scientists and technologists who discover new knowledge wealth. Since scientists and technologists need to be employed in order to survive, money-appropriators exploit them. Money-appropriators manipulate the market not by their intellectual efforts, but by emphasizing public ads that show maneuvering strategy to empty the pockets of good-faith believers and transfer them into their own pockets. These people believe they should fight for the political ideology of a political system, on the basis of econ-political gains.

Do you find any moral virtue or ethical value in the personality of money-appropriators? For example, Steven Madden, founder of the Eponymous New York Shoe Design Company and retailer was charged with securities fraud and was convicted and ordered to pay $7.8 million in penalties for insider trading and stock manipulation. In addition, Mr. Madden faced a potential 41 to 51-month jail term on the criminal charges. Also, he was barred for seven years from serving as an officer or director of any public company (Labate: 2001: 15).

Virtuous and Non-Virtuous Senses of Excellence

As we have indicated in Chapter 2, morality is viewed as an individual's internal nature of good character. Within such a philosophical perception, morality has to be expressed in the form, being this, not in the form, doing this. Virtue is an inherent characteristic of the civility of mind that should have sufficient capacity to maintain goodness in a human mind. Those who advocate this view perceive moral virtues as being excellence, in opposition to a moral duty, or doing excellence. The notion of a moral virtue is worth looking at here. This indicates that some CEOs who have possessed moral virtue in their characters are able to exert moral power in their organizations. They believe in a moral and ethical workplace. For those CEOs who mandate themselves to do moral and ethical actions, they may not inherently possess moral virtue. These CEOs orally say that they should be moral and ethical, but in actuality they are doing immoral and unethical actions. Therefore, believing in being moral and ethical is viewed as a syllogistic moral conviction to be good and also a reason why one must do good things.

Moral virtuous must be distinguished, not only from moral obligation of goodness, but also from voluntary goodness. We must, therefore, identify different sorts of inherent goodness or badness in the nature of agents: persons, groups of persons, phenomena, things, actions, behaviors, emotions, motives, and intentions. In a general sense, according to the existentialist philosophy, everything in nature is good and there is no bad thing in the universe. It is the ill intention and action of human beings that make good things bad. If people do not use materials and phenomena within their appropriated domain of goodness, then they turn good things into bad things.

Consider the expressions being a good life, and having a good life. In the first case we emphasize the nature of goodness to prevail for everybody as "be-ers" to be effective, qualitative, and excellent, while in the second sentence, we perceive a good life on the basis of "do-ers," which are viewed as differentiated characteristics of individual human uniqueness. For example, in the field of biotechnology, providing sufficient proteins for livestock can produce more beef. In this case, there are two systems: vegetarian fodder and cannibalism fodder. For more in-depth analysis, we will explain the case of Mad Cow Disease in the following pages.

At the beginning of the 20th century, biologists in Britain found a new method to change the natural vegetarian feeding chain system of livestock to cannibalism, the meat and bone meal (MBM), in order to provide cattle extra protein. After World War I, the British government became so enthusiastic that made it obligatory for all livestock feed to contain MBM. This innovative scientific method caused most European farmers and ranchers to save money and make extra profit. For the last five decades Britain has exported several thousands livestock, and millions of tones of beef and MBM for cattle to foreign countries including France, Germany, Spain, Italy, Poland, Canada, Korea, and others. However, after a few decades there was a deadly virus outbreak among European cannibalized cattle. In 1986 the British government initiated a task force to conduct a research project in order to discover causes of such a catastrophe (Parhizgar, Parhizgar, and Parhizgar, 2001).

That research project was conducted under the auspice of Lord Phillips. On October 2000 the Britain's bovine spongiform encephalopathy (BSE) inquiry report came out through Lord Phillips and scientists at the UK government Central Veterinary Laboratory (CVL). They recognized mad cow disease as a serious international disease. The report recognized that MBM was a kind of cannibalism disease among cattle. In addition, the British scientists, in 1996, discovered the first cases of variant Creutzfeldt-Jakob disease (nvCJD) or the human BSE. Consequently, after fourteen years of investigation, the UK government banned the cannibalism feeding system for livestock (Cookson, 2000: 11). Cohen (2002) reports:

> A woman in Florida has less than three months to live as she wastes away from deadly mad cow disease; the first known human case of the disease in the United States, according to the Center for Disease Control and Prevention.

Researchers confirm that the BSE outbreak in Britain has reached around 100,000 infected cattle. In the past few years, sales of beef have fallen by 27 percent in the EU: by 40 percent in Italy, and by more than 50 percent in Germany. However, while systematic testing is under way in the Netherlands and Denmark, sales of beef face an uphill struggle in Spain, Italy, and France (Jonquieres and Bilefsky, 2001: 14). Since November 14, 2000, German cows have tested positive for the BSE disease. The possibility of contamination of 400,000 older cattle with BSE is very high and the German government is more likely to slaughter and destroy all old cattle (Atkins, 2001: 2). The Belgian Federal Agency for Food Safety asserts that the test results on some suspected rate of infection of cattle are five times higher than expected. They discovered 14 suspected cases of BSE among 2,700 animals tested in the first week of the measures (Sullivan, 2001: 26).

Also, the international panic over mad cow disease may be about to claim unlikely victims such as Canada and the United States. In 1993, Canada discovered an infected cow with BSE. In 1993 a Canadian farmer, Darrel Archer imported 19 water buffalo from Denmark, at the beginning of this year, at a cost of $130,320, to set up a dairy operation on his Vancouver Island farm. Consequently, the Canada's federal food inspection agency ordered Mr. Archer to remove or destroy the herd. Canada has banned imports of susceptible animals or animal products from any country in which BSE has been detected. Since a case involving an animal imported from the UK in 1987, Canadian authorities have ordered the slaughter or return of all cattle imported from the UK since 1982. Canada now permits imports of cattle or beef from five countries that the government has determined to be free of BSE: the United States, Australia, New Zealand, Argentina, and Finland (Morrison, 2000: 3). In the United States, on January 25, 2001, regulators had placed some cattle in Texas under quarantine as a precaution while officials probed into whether a feed mill violated rules designed to keep mad cow disease out of the food supply. A spokesperson on behalf of the Food and Drug Administration (FDA) announced that: "To date, no cases of (mad cow disease) have been confirmed in the U. S. Consequently, shares of fast-food giant McDonald's Corp closed more than 4 percent lower" (Reuters, 2001).

The BSE epidemic catastrophe forced most European nations to slaughter their cattle and through precautious mandatory laws, banned all import and export of livestock and sales of contaminated beef in the European Union's supermarkets. The financial losses in the UK have been estimated between $5 to $6 billion over the last five years, of which 40 percent was paid by the European Union (*Financial Times*, 2000: 14).

Rarely in the recent living memory of the European Union and North America have all nations plunged so rapidly into a scientific turmoil. The international panic over mad cow disease may be about to claim that a scientific man-made mistake of changing the natural vegetarian system of feeding livestock has changed trustful perceptions of laymen to suspicion. Scientists are not immune to make scientific historical mistakes because science is based on conventional trial and error.

The emergence of infectious proteins within the neurons and cells of the human body can cause neurodegenerative diseases. Nascent prions can be created either spontaneously by mutation of a host protein or by exposure to an exogenous source. By the decade of the 1980s, experts suspected the recycling of animal waste and dead cow caused the generation of bovine spongiform encephalopathy (BSE) in livestock. Many scientists found that the main cause for the cow's brain damage was a slow virus, called a prion an infectious deadly protein molecule that can be alive in the ashes of incinerated bodies of animals. The prion theory was very controversial when first proposed in 1982 by Stanley Prusiner (1997: 13363), a biologist at the University of California, San Francisco. Nevertheless, prions finally achieved full scientific respectability in 1997 when Prusiner won the Noble medical prize (Cookson, 2000: 11).

Prusiner and his research teams through their research discovered that prions are composed largely of a modified form of the prion protein (PrP) designated PrPSc. Prions do not have a nucleic acid genome to direct the synthesis of their progeny. A post-translational, conformational change features in conversion of the cellular PrP (PrPc) into PrPSc during which alpha helices are transformed into beta-sheets. Prion diseases can be both inherited and infectious. Investigations of prion strains have led to the conclusion that variations in disease phenotype are determined by conformation of PrPSc.

From 1982 to 1996, most European governments, farmers, and beef industries continued to feed their livestock with MBM. However, health authorities confirmed that up to this date, according to Smith (2000b: 2) more than 80 people in the United Kingdom and two in France have died from the fatal disease of nvCJD the brain-wasting disorder linked to BSE. At the other extreme, if the incubation period is very long, there could be more than 1,000,000 victims over the next few decades. This is the beginning of this fatal virus.

In the 1990s most European countries made it totally illegal to feed livestock with MBM (Wrong, 2000: 6). This man-made catastrophic and scientific mistake has cost most European countries because of the need to slaughter and destroy million of tones of contaminated beef. Sweden was among the European countries that quickly banned the use of such a mistaken scientific technique. Soon after, in 1987, Swedish farmers themselves introduced a voluntary ban on the use of all meat and fish products in nearly all-animal fodder, with a total ban becoming law in 1991. The Swedish Farmers Association (SFA) declared that: "For ethical reasons we stopped giving ruminants meat. They (livestock) are vegetarians and should stay so" (George, 2000: 2).

Finally, in the United Kingdom in October 2000, Lord Phillips through his scientific report revealed that BSE was an entirely new man-made disease that had started with a chance mutation in the brain of a single cow. The mutation would have reshaped a normal protein, called prion precursor protein or PrP, into a prion. The role of PrP in the healthy brain is not yet known. However, recent research suggests that PrP is involved in signaling between brain cells (Atkins, 2000: 2). Once a prion is present in the brain, it converts PrP into more prions through a slow but deadly biochemical chain reaction. Several studies are directed at elucidating the structure of PrPSc: (1) synthetic PrP peptides carrying pathologic mutation, (2) small redacted PrP molecules supporting PrPSc formation, (3) EM image analysis of 2-D paracrystalline arrays of PrPSc, and (4) epitope mapping of PrPSc using numerous recombinant antibody fragments (Prusiner, 1997; Viles et al., 1999; Supattapone et al., 1999; Liu et al., 1999). In addition, nervous tissues of contaminated cattle contain the highest concentrations of prions. It is necessary to remove SRM from beef entering the human and animal food chain. Specifically, the spinal cord, skull, tonsils and ileum of contaminated livestock contain prions.

The European Union's effort to stop the spread of BSE or mad cow disease is very expensive, because it mandates an overhaul of the European commission's food safety mechanisms and the trade of livestock among European countries. The shake up was prompted by wide spread criticism of Brussels' handling of the BSE epidemic that erupted in Britain in 1988, and was given added impetus by growth of the disease in France. There have been four major issues at the stake:

- The government's ban on MBM has led farmers to ask the government to subsidize more agricultural financial support. This issue may violate the General Agreement on Trade (GAT).
- The ban on MBM may reopen trade disputes with the United States over imports of soybeans to compensate the shortage of protein for livestock.
- The increase of BSE in Europe can create some animosity toward destruction of the cattle industry around the world.
- The effects of the BSE can be spread over the sausage, hot dogs, and fast food industry.
- There is a possibility on the evidence that milk might be effected by BSE, and nobody can rule it out.
- The remaining ashes of the incinerated cows can contaminate the environment and cause ecological effects on plants, animals, and humans.
- The BSE has inflated subsidies to farmers either by the governments and/or by creating a chain reaction cycle of international trade disputes among nations to compensate their losses.
- Nobody knows just how serious the problem is, or how long it will last.

Despite constructing incinerators for destroying slaughtered contaminated cattle in England and France, and converting of the existing plant in Scunthrope, only 60 percent of MBM livestock will have been incinerated by 2002. The problem is that prion can survive in the ashes of incinerated mad cows. The incinerated cow ashes that contain prion are harmful to the environment. International agricultural traders are being warned by scientists that the U. S. and Argentine soy and rape brought in for animal feed is now genetically modified and could be contaminated (Smith 2000 b: 6).

Another costly preventive measure by the European governments is the testing of all cattle that are more than thirty months old. In January 2001, the European Union introduced tough measures to reveal cases of BSE in all member countries. They made a decision to test all European cattle including bulls against BSE. In the Bull Breeder Industry, bull owners decided to withdraw their bulls after Bull Fighting Shows from slaughters houses and incinerate them instead. In Spain the custom is that once fighting bulls have completed their career, they are sent to the slaughterhouse and butchered for human consumption. At the premier bullfighting fiestas C such as Feria de San Isidro, which is held in Madrid, Spain, in May of every year, breeders can expect to earn two prizes:

- A monetary value of equivalent to $11,000 for offering their finest specimens to the ring
- To earn more money when the beasts are sent to the slaughterhouses.

According to statistical figures in Spain, bullfighting entertainment companies put 11,000 bulls into the rings and gain very good financial outcomes from their shows. After the shows they send them to slaughterhouse for their meats and bones to be consumed by people or recycle them as the MBM to feed cattle (Crawford: 2001: 1).

WHAT IS VALUE?

Before one can build a classification scheme concerning a moral and ethical hierarchy of values, it must be clear what ideas, factors, principles, and beliefs are those that are to be preferred or praised. This is not much of a problem when one is valuing the nature of material things, because people value material things on the basis of the utility of their effectiveness related to their needs. But such a value assessment will be difficult to use in assessing beliefs and ideas concerning non-material needs of life (e.g., love and hate, fair and unfair, honesty and dishonesty, moral and amoral).
From a materialistic standpoint Woolf (1981) defines value: "First, as a fair return or equivalent in goods, services, or money for something exchanged, and the second is the monetary worth of something: marketable price." Patrick Primeaux (2002: 244) defines value as:

A relative worth, utility, or importance, and ... is a numerical quantity assigned or computed. These definitions not only provide answers to our questions, but lead us to conclude that who and what we value, as well as our value, are defined primarily in economic terms: money, utility, numerical quantity. Not only is money an object, it is an object that can be quantified numerically. Its utility, its usefulness, is also quantified numerically.

According to these views values are relative and bounded within a spectrum of best and worst (see Figure 7.1).

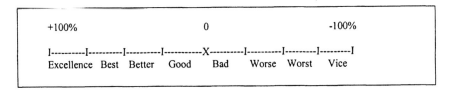

Figure 7.1: Assessment of Relative Values Within the Boundary of a
Spectrum of Excellence and Vice.

As moralists or ethicists, we are concerned with changes produced in
individuals as a result of a dynamic life cycle of incidents or necessities. Global
or universal statements or experiences may represent such changes. Or they may
be represented by the actual description of a holistic life philosophy of a group
of people as the result of their religious faiths, cultural values, political
ideologies, and scientific and technological experiences. Nevertheless, since all
people possess an inherent mandated cause to fulfill their lively objectives, they
may be inferred from the conscientious moral and ethical tasks, problems, and
observations used to test or valuate their valuable material and non-material
things. Although the objective-oriented life cycle perceptions of an individual
are bound through testing the effectiveness of materials and techniques, they
may be in an almost unlimited number of valuing things. Therefore, it is
assumed that a business leader needs to value the holistic processes of his/her
activities with intended outcomes of his/her decisions and actions.

Values are enduring beliefs that people hold about morals, equality,
freedom, democracy, patriotism, and so on (Steiner and Steiner, 1994: 29).
Rokeach (1973) defines value as fundamental, relatively stable, and prescriptive
beliefs that a specific behavior or aim of existence is preferred to a different
mode of behavior or aim. Values offer us a sense of right and wrong, good and
bad. Values, thus, are general good guidelines that people use to make decisions
and appraise the results of their actions taken by themselves and by their societal
institutions.

Values are enduring beliefs that specific modes of thought, behavior, and
conduct or end state of existence are personally or socially preferable to an
opposite or converse modes of thought, behavior, or conduct or end state of
existence (Rokeach, 1973). They are powerful motives for people and
institutions to bind different perceptions together. Individuals learn values as
they grow and mature. Values emerge within the context of the interactions of
humans with nature. Values do not change very easily, but over time they do
change.

From a moral and ethical standpoint, values are defined as an intellectual
deliberative pattern of norms to be programmed by moral virtues and cultural
beliefs. The heart of scientific wisdom is the belief in a value system. Values
need to be implemented in human behavior. There are different value domains in
people's perceptions: religious, philosophical, aesthetic, scientific, and

ideological. Values provide a template or blueprint for people in their personal and social life processes. Values classify people's perceptions concerning surrounding things much as genetic systems provide such a template for the organization of organic processes (Geertz, 1964: 62).

Social values are not something that individuals can experience in isolation. Social values are not merely the sum of a group's values, but are the sum of cultural values through generation to generation. Social values are reflected changes in ideas and perceptions of a community that constantly value things. For this reason, values are social experiences. The experience of value emerges from both shared and unique experiences. Our social values must constantly be reevaluated, if we desire to survive. We need not only to evaluate what we value, but, also, we need to question why we value.

In the field of business we need to constantly value things and events in order to hold or release some values. Is it worthy to do so? The answer is yes. Since values could be subjective, therefore, they can be arbitrary. Arbitrary reality emerges from this view of value, as value is then a highly individualistic judgment. Some people assert that values are not subjective. They believe values are objective, because our judgment is driven from observation or experience. We object in nature, because experience desires to fulfill or appeal in nature. Nevertheless, people can validate their judgmental testing value systems along with their intelligent capabilities.

Two Types of Value

There are two types of value: theoretical and pragmatic. Theoretical values stem from philosophical perceptions concerning the life-style and experiences of individuals. Theoretical values are deductive impressions from the insight conception of how to value life and, to some people, after life. This contains a dual perception between peaceful or chaotic life-cycle incidents, moral and immoral character, ethical and unethical behavior, material and spiritual attachments, and finally earthly and heavenly lives.

The pragmatic values are based on the utility of science and the methods of pure reasoning or intuition by which values are grasped. Thus, one way to grasp value is to assert that there are absolute and unchanging values for all to know if they know things properly. The other way is a sense of value in which individuals think or feel that they are valuable. Each individual and each society has a set of norms, beliefs, and values that together form their cultural values. Norms are expected criteria for behavior and beliefs are inferences made by and observed about underlying states of expectancy. Beliefs seem to form the core conceptual ideas and opinions concerning the acceptability of something or to be denominated by some faiths. Sproul (1981: 204) defines: "A belief is understanding that represents credible relationships between objects, properties, and ideas." Beliefs are imbued with powerful emotional feelings. The fervor with which people hold their religious or dogmatic ideologies is good examples.

Beliefs are viewed as confidence in truth or existence of something not immediately susceptible to rigorous proof (Parhizgar, 2002: 40).

Foundations of Value Systems

Values exist at the deepest level in an individual's conscientious mind or in the ideological doctrine of a community. Values are general and basic determinant criteria for classifying things and ideas in some ways in an arbitrary manner. There could be an almost infinite number of ways of valuing things and ideas. To guide us in our selection of criteria for the purpose of establishing a value system classification and to make the result more readily understood and used, we need to establish certain guiding principles.

It is very important to understand the influence of culture on values. Doing business in a global marketplace often means that managers encounter a clash of values between different cultures. Take the value of loyalty, for example. Japanese are completely loyal to their families. Accordingly, Japanese workers are loyal to their employers and *vise versa*. In contrast, in the United States, corporate loyalty is not important, because both employers and employees value opportunities to leave each other.

Values also affect individuals' views of what constitutes authority. For example, French managers value authority as a right of office and rank. Their behavior reflects this value, as they tend to use power based on their position in the organization. In contrast, managers from the Netherlands and Scandinavian value group inputs to decisions and expect their decisions to be challenged and discussed by employees (Neale and Mindel, 1992: 27).

Another example, gift exchanging is one of the ethical problems in the field of business. These gifts begin with a cycle of future favoritism to be exchanged between parties. What a culture may consider payoffs and bribes may be considered legitimate ways of doing business in other countries. We may be prone to judge the value systems of others, but we should resist the temptation to do so.

Value differences between cultures must be acknowledged in today's global economy. Tolerating multicultural values can help us understand other cultures. Within the contextual boundaries of international business relationship we need to learn more about home and host countries' value systems. We need to learn how promises are value as moral, traditional, and practical practices of your business. We need to avoid prejudgments of the host countries' customs as immoral or corrupt. We need to assume that the host country's value systems are legitimate unless proven otherwise. We should refuse to do business when stakeholder actions violate or corrupt moral and ethical values of both home and host countries. We should conduct our business relationship as openly as possible.

Instrumental and Terminal Values

Rokeach (1973) distinguishes between two types of values: instrumental and terminal. Instrumental values are defined as reflective values that are assumed in the means to achieve objectives. That is why they represent the acceptable behaviors to be used in achieving some ends. Instrumental values identified by Rokeach include ambition, honesty, self-sufficiency, and courageousness. Terminal values, in contrast, represent the objectives or the end state of goodness to be achieved. He identifies terminal values as happiness, love, pleasure, self-respect, and freedom among terminal values (see Tables 7.1 and 7.2). We are classifying instrumental and terminal value characteristic as follows:

Table 7.1: Instrumental and Terminal Values

INSTRUMENTAL VALUES	TERMINAL VALUES
Honesty	Trustfulness
Conscience	Conscientiousness
Hopefulness	Cheerfulness
Helpfulness	Powerfulness
Righteousness	Happiness
Orderliness	Accurateness
Forgiveness	Compassion
Open-Mindedness	Universality
Dignity	Integrity
Discipline	Achievement
Responsibility	Accountability
Magnanimity	Perseverance
Prudence	Confidence
Politeness	Self-Respect
Courage	Fearfulness
Fairness	Humaneness
Justness	Equitableness
Patience	Temperance
Sincerity	Serenity
Good-Faith	Goodwill
Good-Humor	Enjoyment
Loyalty	Obedience
Intellect	Wisdom
Imagination	Independence
Knowledge	Competence
Prosperousness	Successfulness
Indulgence	Gratification
Self-Control	Devotion
Affection	Likeliness
Sensibility	Liability

Table 7.2: Instrumental and Terminal Invaluable Characteristics

INSTRUMENTAL INVALUABLENESS	TERMINAL INVALUABLENESS
Cynicism	Pessimism
Bigotry	Prejudice
Cruelty	Atrocity
Felony	Villain
Heartlessness	Tyranny
Revengefulness	Violence
Rudeness	Confrontation
Viciousness	Hostility
Deceit	Dishonesty
Fraud	Deception
Cheating	Laziness
Stealing	Chaos
Bribery	Corruption
Embezzlement	Mistrust
Piracy	Destruction

Value Orientation

Change is viewed as a sign of progress or retardation. When values change, their impacts can be felt in the ways in which moral, ethical, and legal systems operate. Value orientation means change and change agents continuously interact with each other effectively. Kluckhohn and Strodtbeck (1961: 11) suggest:

Value orientations are complex but definitely patterned (rank ordered) principles, resulting from the transactional interplay of three analytically distinguishable elements of the valuable process of the cognitive, the affective, and the directive elements which give order and direction to the ever-flowing stream of human acts and thoughts as these relate to the solution of common human problems. The variation in value orientations in any society results in the co-occurrence of *dominant and variant* value orientations.

Kluckhohn and Strodtbeck's fivefold classification of value orientations associated with the five common human problems and the range of variation postulated for each is presented in Table 7.3. Five problems indicated by Kluckhohn and Stradtbeck (1961: 11) are as follows:

• What is the character of innate human nature?

- What is the relation of man to nature?
- What is the temporal focus of human life?
- What is the modality of human activity?
- What is the modality of man's relationship to other men?

Table 7.3: The Five Value Orientations and the Range of Variations
            Postulated For Each

ORIENTATION	Human Characteristics	Human Characteristics	Human Characteristics
HUMAN NATURE	Evil	Natural Mixture of Good and Evil	Good
HUMAN AND NATURE	Subjective to nature	Harmony with nature	Mastery over nature
TIME	Past	Present	Future
ACTIVITY	Being (be-er)	Doing (do-er)	Becoming (will-er)
RATIONAL	Linearity	Colaterality	Individuality

Source: Adapted from Kluckhohn, F.R. and Strodtbeck, F. L. *Variation in
Value Orientations*. New York: Row and Peterson, (1961), 12.

From this vantage point, multiculturalism value is one of the domains that
are proportionately shared in all three characteristics of the human race
(morality, ethics, and legality). These three domains are analytically
distinguishable variables in human life. Morality, in its normative dimension,
comprises the individual's hidden or silent valuable characteristic of a person
with survival conditions. It encompasses the most moral compartmentalization
of an individual's value system. Ethics, in its social-structural component,
consists of a social value symbol's status-sets in which all members in their
capabilities are role occupants outside of their moral boundaries of the focal
ordination of their society. Ethics is considered the social valuable sphere of a
society. The ethical status-set profiles of all people in a society are crucial for
their role performance within a focal ordination of a community. This is
especially true of what Parsons (1960:59) calls institutional personnel, who are
concerned with the overall ethical mentality of a society. The third component
part of societal compartmentalization is the legal system. This system legitimizes
mobilization of resources and the distribution of wealth among citizens.

How the above three-component part of a community function is the most proximate and affective factors in valuing the societal principles of belicf in a nation. From a nation's micro-economic perspective, the degree of harmonization among moral, ethical, and legal value systems identifies how people cope with uncertainties. How these three component parts of value systems interrelate is an intricate theoretical and empirical problem that may be depicted in a concentric system.

THE CONCEPT OF STAKEHOLDER

Although a managers' sole responsibility is to respond competitively to global business challenges by delivering qualitative products and services to their customers with lower prices, they also have to be loyal to their stakeholders by preserving their legitimate rights. For the last half of a century, each scholar has defined the concept of stakeholder differently somewhat. Each definition generally stands for a shared idea, namely, that a firm should heed the needs, interests, and influence of those affected by their policies and operations (Frederick, 1992: 5). Abrams (1951: 29) is usually credited with sharing his views about stakeholders in the field of business. His theme followed by Freeman (1984). Freeman developed the stakeholder concept to be defined, described, and analyzed as a business's the main cause of existence. He believed that a business is not an isolated, segmented part of a society. A firm has a direct relationship with society.

The concept of stakeholder is defined as any entity or group of people that has a stake, or interest. Traditionally, in the field of business, the most important stakeholder groups of a corporation have been recognized as the shareowners or stockholders, namely investors. Today, such a concept has dramatically been changed to include all interest groups to a company is intrinsically and extrinsically linked. The most important groups include: stockholders or shareholders, the boards of governance, consumers, employees, management, labor unions, community, and government. Shareholders and stockholders' financial responsibility is limited to the value of their shares in a firm. The power of stakeholders is limited. Today, with the expansion of corporate power in the free market economy, the individual stockholder or shareowner's power is very limited. For such a reason, shareholders have established shareholder activists.

Shareholder Activists

Today, some investors are facing corruption through the immoral, unethical, and to some extent illegal tactics of some managers. Jackson, Miller, and Miller (1997: 61) indicate:

Investors are beginning to pressure corporations with tactics such as media exposure and government attention. Some have formed a class of corporate owners called *shareholder activists*. These groups of shareholders pressure companies to boost profits and dividends, link executive pay to performance, and oust inefficient management.

In the 1990s dissatisfied stockholders expelled a number of CEOs from major corporations such as General Motors, IBM, Apple, and Eastman Kodak (Fabrikant, G. 1995: 9). There are several issues and interest groups' objectives that should be analyzed in this section. These issues are: consumerism, individualism, collectivism, and protectionism.

Consumerism

Consumerism is a latent value system between the sellers of goods and services as producers or providers, and buyers as customers and consumers. It is also a movement in which the maintenance of the rights of consumers as an important part of a corporation's stakeholder is seriously considered. The protest of the consumerism movement echoes against the immoral and unethical behavior of some corporations that practice discrimination against specific groups, unfair treatment of different genders, and illegal actions against consumers. Consumerism is mainly concerned with having certain rights to make their own choices at the time of consumption. They need to be able to use their intelligence to be able to make free choices in the marketplace and not be deceived. Consumers are concerned about having intelligent choices and free decisions, not mandatory forces, on spending their monies. They are concerned about having the right to accurate information, fair prices, and sufficient qualitative products and services that they have paid for.

Consumerism is a movement designed to maintain an equitable balance between the rights and powers of consumers in relation to the rights and powers of sellers of products and services. Steiner and Steiner (1980: 273) indicate: "Consumerism does not mean that *caveat emptor* let the buyer beware is replaced by *caveat venditor* let the seller beware."

Peters and Waterman Jr. (1982) *In Search of Excellence· Lessons from America's Best-Run Companies* provoked widespread managerial thinking about the importance of consumers as the major stakeholders. They sent a strong voice concerning consumer interests as an instrumental tool in a corporation's successful operation. Consumerism is a phenomenon that identifies honest business people from dishonest. Honesty is a virtue because it is necessary in order for a businessperson to conduct his/her business successfully in a normal competitive marketplace. A businessperson needs to have a sense of honesty in his/her mind to seek values and to voluntarily trade them with others. The moment the latent value of honesty is taken away by greed and selfishness, the business is doom to fail.

Individualism

Some times specific terms we use quite frequently are so much taken for granted that we never stop to consider what they really mean. The terms *Individuals* and *individualism* are examples of these phenomena. However, the recognition of the term of *self-survival* indicates that there are serious implications relating to moral, ethical, and legal issues. The moral basis of individualism is based on rational selfishness. What is rational selfishness? It depends who perceives: the hammer or the nail. It holds that each individual is free to choose his/her lifestyle, respecting the legal right of all others to do likewise. Since legal rights promote equal privileges, then there is no possibility in representation of the altruistic ethics of self-sacrifice in such a society.

The best place to begin with the identity of an individual is with understanding of the individual and the community that is contained in reality. Politically, some nations defined and perceive selves as rational beings. They perceive their roles as survival and achieving their wellbeing by using their intelligence. They produce valuable things that can be effective in their lives. Since an individual inherently does not possess all elements of self-sufficiency, he/she needs to be linked to others in order to fulfill his/her survival needs. In such an event, self-achievement raises the issue whether the self is an isolatable atomic and discrete entity, or is by its very nature part of a social process (Buchholz and Rosenthal, 1998: 56).

The moral views of some American and French philosophers indicate that atomic individuals exist in an independent sphere of thought except those individuals who choose to form their own purposeful valuable groups. Such a view stems from John Locke's (1632-1704) *social contract*. Locke believed that the basis for understanding the nature of a corporation is a voluntary association of investors who have established an entity to pursue their individual objectives. These objectives link investors together. These bonds cannot root them in any ongoing endeavor that is more than the sum of their separate selves (synergies). Nevertheless, each individual separately possesses separate wills and separate egoistic desires. Each individual is entitled to inalienable rights to such things as freedom, equality, property ownership, and justice. Through individualism ideology, individuals have authority over their own personal conscience and moral choices.

Individualists hold that an individual's gain is another individual's gain, because morally these individuals are bounded to their reciprocal contracts. Within the contextual boundary of such a voluntary contract individuals can maintain their own dignity and integrity. Individualists hold that the ability of a person is an added value to all other peoples' performances. In other words, if an innovative product can effectively be marketed itself, this indicates that all individuals who are attached or linked to that product can proportionately enjoy some gains.

Collectivism

Collectivism ideology regards human beings as rational brutes whose interests are conflicted. People are selfish. They need to struggle in order to survive. The entire primacy of their struggle for survival is to overcome barriers. This indicates that they need to eliminate others in order to provide sufficient room to grow, develop, and progress. Morally and ethically, what do they need? Do they need to get rid of selfishness? All people are brothers and sisters. They are producers and consumers. They equitably need to share their joyful and sorrowful experiences. People need to be judged on the basis of their altruistic will. They believe in social justice, not in individual justice. They believe all people from certain racial groups, economic classes, colors or nationalities should have equitable share for enjoying their lives. They need to consider the best for all, not for parts.

The term *collectivism* is an ethical belief that mandates all people not only to produce equitably, but also to consume equitably too. This is one of the crucial problems with such an ideology. Nevertheless, collectivism in practice eventually ends up with either patriotism or chauvinism. Another side effect of collectivism is protectionism. Protectionism is a result of collectivism perception. Protectionism makes people lazy. Protectionism prevents people from exercising their free will in order to decide what to produce and how and prevents from thinking about possible bankruptcy when they are faced with abler competitors. Collectivism retards competition.

Collectivism criticizes individualism in that in a free market economy, an individual's gain is another individual's loss (e.g., the function of the stock market). They also criticize individualism ideology in that it can promote fraud under the bankruptcy laws. They raise this question: Can you find any means and ends of freedom in these societies? They answer no, because they believe that individuals cannot rely on their own power, they are dominated by the differentiated power of a hidden invisible econo-political power. They are servants for masters. Who are their masters? Those people who hold the hidden invisible power, the street stockholders. Within such an ideology, individuals cannot rise as far as their abilities would take them, because periodically the invisible power-holders, with the assistant of econo-political brokers and corrupted managers, make drastic changes to trim their accumulated wealth and power. Within a lawless and corrupt private business sector, individuals lose their freedom, choices, and rights through reckless practices of boards of governance and CEOs that artificially drive up stock prices for their own gain. In the long run, these private corporations destroy company assets, the pensions of employees, and the workers' jobs.

Protectionism

It is very important to recognize that the activity of a business is not like a game or a sport to entertain an investor's egoism. The objective is to manufacture valuable products and/or render effective services that can serve the utility of consumers' life. In such a competitive environment, it is not fair to protect some businesses by providing them with incentives in order that their investors enjoy free gains. Protectionism is an ethical doctrine designed to evaluate actions that have good and evil consequences.

In a free market economy, to initiate the policy of free trade can enhance domestic production system. It helps producers improve the quality of their products and/or services, and also, helps consumers access better qualitative products with lower prices. In such a situation, domestic businesses feel heavy pressure from foreign competitors with better products and lower prices. They may request the government protect them from foreign competitors. In this situation, the real loser group is consumers. From a general point of view, economic growth is the result of no restriction on trade, not only among individuals, but also among cities, states, and indeed nations. It is not ethical to provide incentives for some domestic investors without just cause and betray customers or society at large with lower quality, and higher prices of products and/or services.

Garrett (1966: 8) indicates that managers are ethically responsible for their actions in situations where both good and evil effects might occur. They are ethically permitted to risk predictable consequences, but unwilled negative impacts on people or society if they carefully consider and balance five factors:

- Managers must assess the type of good and evil involved, distinguishing between major and minor forms.
- They should calculate the urgency of the situation.
- They must assess the probability that both good and evil effects will occur. If good effects are certain and risks of serious harm are small or remote, the situation is favorable
- The intensity of influence over effects must be considered.
- The availability of alternative methods must be considered.

Classification of Stakeholders

In all human psychosocial and econo-political groups, there are interest groups who are identified as stakeholders. It is helpful to classify them according to specific criteria. Each stakeholder, either individuals or groups, plays an important role in a corporation. Each stakeholder has different levels of power over that corporation. An understanding of these ethical and moral factors is integral part in analyzing stakeholder classification. As shown in Table 7.4, stakeholder groups are classified based on:

- Those individuals and/or groups with sole ownership of shares and/or stocks in a corporation.
- Those individuals and/or groups with business relationship with a corporation.
- Those individuals and/or groups with their socio-cultural and political values shared by a corporation.

Table 7.4: Classification of Stakeholder Individuals and Groups and Their Ethical, Moral, and Legal Values, Interests, and Stakes

STAKEHOLDERS	VALUES, INTERERSTS, STAKES, AND RELATIONSHIPS
Shareowners, shareholders, and stockholders	The financial value system of a corporation has a direct impact on these groups' wealth and life-style.
Manager	The survival value system of a corporation has a direct impact on managers' employment and their future professional and promotional statues.
Employees	The continuity of the corporation's manufacturing and/or service operations can economically be related to the workers' employment, their daily earnings and pension funds.
Ecological environmental factors	The environmental and ecological stakeholders are silent and do not have the ability to raise their voices against destructive operations of a corporation. Nevertheless, within an accumulated extensive time of consumption, the corporate problems and issues surface in a society in which all citizens and residents of that community will be affected.
Community	These stakeholders are not directly linked to the corporation's operation but have some social, economical, and political interest in the continuity of the corporation's operational processes Community is very sensitive to the managerial decision-making processes and actions concerning moral, ethical, and legal ordinations concerning the welfare of the community.
Governmental agencies	The corporation's financial donations, contributions, and fund raising plans for supporting public figures in governmental agencies are of interest to politicians Antitrust laws and, environmental regulatory agencies protect the public against selfish desires of business people.
Consumers and customers	The qualitative and quantitative production, distribution, and sales of goods and rendering of services are directly related to the consumers' utility demands and their either satisfaction or dissatisfaction.

- Those individuals and/or groups with their ecological and environmental issues related to a corporation.

All of the above stakeholders rely on the integrity of the management team of a corporation to uphold society's values and expectations. For the clarity of the above attributions, we will analyze stakeholders' ethical, moral, and legal responsibilities in the following pages.

Shareowners as Stockholders

Capital investors in a corporation are mainly known as two groups: shareholders and stockholders. In addition to these groups, creditors and lenders could be included in such a category. In theory both groups of shareholders and stockholders can play crucial roles for survival of a corporation. In reality and to some extent in practice, except in small companies, power has shifted away from both groups to managers. Critics express their concern about excessive managerial autonomy and secrecy in their decision-making processes and operations. In practice, it has been observed that today's large corporations need greater stockholder democracy. In addition, they need to be represented by an ethical and legitimate board of governance. In pursuit of such objectives, investors are requesting to receive more truthful information in order to make wisely decisions on their investments. Reformers argue that many issues of interest to stakeholders cannot survive the thicket of Securities and Exchange Commission (SEC) because sometimes most shareholders (specifically employees' stocks as pension fund options) are locked within their corporations and do not have the liberty to exchange them. It should be noted that by law, managers have been offered such a liberty to exchange their stocks but such a privilege is prohibited for employees. For example, all senior managers of the Enron Corporation by law have had a golden opportunity to sell their stocks before the announcement of bankruptcy, while employees were unable to sell their pension fund stocks. Consequently, all employees lost their pension funds.

Managers as Stakeholders

The views that a corporation has to take into account the entire ethical, moral, and a legal mandate depends on the managerial truthfulness in decisions and actions. What should managers do as a group of stakeholders? Clearly they have to take ethical decisions and legal actions. Managers can only do this by reference to a moral code. What are the main moral codes that can be accepted throughout a corporation's lifetime and what are their sincere beliefs on honesty? There are two extreme alternatives: (1) cynical egoism, (2) secular altruism.

Cynical Egoism: Cynical egoism asserts that managers should do whatever they feel like to safeguard the corporation's profitability. They reject assuming any objective standard for the good. The good means gratify their profitability desires, maximizing their personal utilities, and indulging their emotional bindings. Such an amoral belief is based on cost-benefit analysis. Within the contextual amoral domain of cynical egoism, managers calculate the honest and dishonest routes in their decision-making processes and then value the outcome on the basis of each outcome that would occur. Finally, they estimate consciously or unconsciously combined (honest and dishonest) alternatives to be chosen.

Secular Altruism: Secular altruism asserts that managers are in a position of trust and they must consider all stakeholders' profits as the corporation's beneficiaries. They should sacrifice their own personal desires for the balanced benefits of stakeholders. Nevertheless, secular altruism does not have a firm stand against dishonesty if decisions and actions would be beneficial to the manager's country. In other words, within the global market place secular altruism management ethics does not have a firm stand against dishonesty by multinational corporations.

Employees' Stock-Ownership as Stakeholders

The philosophical reasoning behind the employees' ownership of stocks states that employers may establish trust funds on behalf of worker's pension funds. In addition to receiving their wages and benefits, employees enjoy profits from the dividends and potential appropriation of their company's stocks. Some corporations provide employees a greater stake in the outcomes of the organization through profit-making methods, gain-sharing privileges such as linking pay to performance, stock contribution options, and retirement plans. This is reasoned to motivate employees to increase their productivity, loyalty to the corporation, reduce tardiness and absenteeism, and work closely with management.

Historically, employees have been viewed as workers to be hired to perform assigned tasks and receive specific wage or salary. After forty years of legislation, employees today enjoy many other privileges. These include the right to object to immoral and unethical or illegal work requirements, the right to freedom of choices in decisions made outside the work place, and the limited right to privacy. Nevertheless, employers have retained one key right: *employment at will.* This right legally allows employers to lay off employees for any economic reason when necessary. This has been a general rule with industrialized society. As O'Reilly (1994: 44) indicates employers state to workers that:

> There will never be job security. We will employ you as long as you add value to the organization, and you are continuously responsible for finding ways to add values. In return, you have the right to demand interesting and important work, the freedom and resources to perform it well, the pay that

reflects your contribution, and the experience and training needed to be employable here or elsewhere.

Consumers as Stakeholders

Historically, consumers have had one basic right to be observed by businesses. That right is to guarantee the utility and safety of products that they have purchased. Within this kind of expected situation trust forms a basis for successful market place transactions and is the most important ethical and legal issue with respect to maintenance integrity between sellers and buyers. Consumers as stakeholders in the market place should have some basic level of trust that the products they buy are safe to be used as indicated in writing on the labels, or orally expressed by sellers and will give them effective utility value that they expect. Without that trust between producers and consumers and/or sellers and buyers, the market place will not function very efficiently. It is obvious that the maintenance of consumer trust is the most important objective within the forces of competition.

Ethically, consumers expect that businesses should not violate their rights by deception, fraud, or greed. From an ethical point of view, several advocates based on the beliefs that extending rights to consumers and building protection of these rights into a societal ordination will establish trust between buyers and sellers have taken a right-based approach. Trust between sellers and a buyer enables the marketplace to function more effectively and create a healthy competitive environment. Consumers as stakeholders within a marketplace are concerned about moral issues that keep recurring: issues of rights and obligations; individual and group rights and their obligations. The pragmatic ethical, moral, and legal rights and duties developed in chapter six need to be kept in mind here. As was seen in that chapter, sellers and/or buyers rights and duties are not something absolute, such that group rights are an automatic infringement upon an individual's natural freedom. Rights emerge in the ongoing process of community adjustments, and in the very ethical, moral, and legal rights one has as obligations.

Governmental Agencies as Stakeholders

Governments and businesses have a symbiotic relationship. Governmental agencies at all levels local, state, and federal are stakeholders of the corporate world. Not does only government set standards for businesses, but also, it buys hundreds of billions of dollars of goods and services from private companies. Steiner and Steiner (1994: 5) define:

> Government encompasses a wide range of activities and institutions throughout the country... Government may be defined as the structure and processes through which public policies, programs, and rules are authoritatively made for society.

There are three major philosophical foundations for the establishment of a government: utilitarian, egalitarian, and universalism (Parhizgar, 2002: 73).

Government is found in serving:

- The greatest good for the greatest number, and the greatest misery for the smallest number of poor citizens, not the smallest number of wealthy citizens (utilitarianism).
- The greatest good for the smallest advantaged or disadvantaged number, and the greatest misery for the greatest number (egalitarianism).
- A balancing of various principles of fairness for all (universalism).

McCollum (1998: A28) states:

> Jeremy Bentham, English philosopher is often thought as the founder of *utilitarianism*, the school of philosophy that holds that the purpose of government is to foster the happiness of the individual, and that the greatest happiness of the most people should be the goal of human existence

This type of philosophy can be found in representative democracies.

In practice, there is another popular philosophy that is perceived as *egalitarianism*. It holds the maximum role of a government is to prevail justice in duty and rights among individuals, and inequality is justified only if its existence causes all, especially the favored (advantaged or disadvantaged classes of people) to benefit. This type of government can be found in authoritarian governments.

The third philosophy is the *universalization* of the role of the government as it can also be called *intuitionism*. It is not to prevail happiness only for a majority or for a minority group of people (advantaged or disadvantaged). It should be for all. The role of a government cannot contradict the happiness of another group of people within a nation. The government's role is commanded to do what is right for all not for a part. Intuitionism government is perceived as accommodation of several multi-principles of justice, including liberty, property rights, and human equal rights for all. This type of philosophy can be found in participatory democracies; it is very idealistic.

As indicated above, any type of government as a stakeholder in the free market economy is concerned about concentration of wealth in the hands of a few people. Because of such a fear, governments interfere in businesses. One of these interferences is limiting the market size of a corporation to less than 50 percent in order to prevent monopoly. As Salsman (1999:191) indicates:

> Antitrust theory stems partly from the conservatives' unwillingness to identify capitalism's essential nature as the only social system protecting man's right to live rationally and selfishly. ... Instead, conservatives define capitalism as the system of competition. Thus, they observe any lessening of competition as an open invitation to socialism.

One of the moral, ethical, and legal issues of governmental intervention in the business world is the fear of monopoly by big businesses in a capitalistic society. Thomas E. Sullivan (1991: 13) quoting of Republican Senator Sherman of Ohio concerning inequality and concentrations of capital said: "He conceded that big business did lower prices, but complained that this saving of cost goes to the pockets of the producers. He warned that the popular mind is agitated with problems that may disturb the social order." Ridpath (1999: 169) indicates:

> Unlike most statistic measures adopted in this country (America), antitrust laws were not a European import. They were originated and fostered by Americans; predominantly, by American *conservatives In particular, the conceptual underpinnings* of American antitrust were supplied by... the founder of the Chicago School of economist Frank H. Knight.

Nevertheless, antitrust was born in the late nineteenth century, with the passage of Interstate Commerce Act (1887) and the Sherman Act (1890).

Today's American ethicists are primarily altruistic. They are asking government to cut taxes in order to stimulate the economy. They are looking forward to provide equal opportunities for working class people in order to be employed not for businesses or the wealthy people, but to pursue their individuals' life enrichments.

Community as Stakeholder

The relationships between business and society on local, state, national, and global levels are based on four fundamental elements:

- Material things such as goods and/or non-material things such as services to meet the necessities of community
- Monetary-added values to the community wealth such as economic development and growth and technological innovativeness.
- National wealth and societal enhancement through manufacturing, commercial, trade, and other economic activities of both individuals and institutions.
- Financial help through collection of taxes to support community's public expenditures.

Businesses provide communities with employment to fulfill family cohesiveness. In return, communities are expected to safeguard and respect companies' properties. Ethically, it is not fair for businesses to be hurt by the public. Communities need to support businesses in order to be able to strengthening their economic and social wellbeing.

ECOLOGICAL CORPORATIONS' ETHICAL CONVICTIONS

The global ecological corporate stakeholders' convictions are especially concerned with global environmental changes, because the causes of damage are disconnected in time and space from those who are harmed. Based on moral, ethical, and legal convictions of a corporation, we may conclude that ecological values derive from three major sources:

- *Anthropocentric* (**human-centered**): Econo-political values are predominantly utilitarian and are concerned with only those financial environmental changes that effect human's welfare. On the basis of the utilitarian theory of ethics, for example, if we cut down all trees and dry out all of the wetlands, then we are going to lose out not only nutritional resources but also we are going to be exposed to the scarcity of chemicals, drugs, paper, wood, and other valuable resources. Therefore, because of such a humanitarian philosophy, people should not harm the environment. Nevertheless, they are convicted by their moral obligations to stop the destruction of nature. These people believe that humanity is an infestation on nature analogous to an illness. This implies a moral duty to reduce both the size and impact of the human pollution.

- *Theocentric* (**God-centered**): Socio-religious values are predominantly deontological and are concerned with qualitative spiritual desirability in life and after life and more abstract feelings towards goodness for satisfaction of God and harmony within the realm of God's kingdom. On the basis of deontological theory of ethics, for example, theocentrists state that environmental protection for survival of all creatures is a human duty because God created all species with specific purposes. Therefore, it is the corporate's duty to safeguard the kingdom of God.

- *Ecocentric* (both biocentric): living-things centered and envirocentric: non-living things-centered): environmental values grant nature itself intrinsic rights to function naturally. These values grant species the right to continue to exist and function within the contextual natural circumstances of survival. On the basis of ecocentric theory of ethics, for example, biocenterists argue that the nature has intrinsic functional worth, apart from its human use. Each element in the universe functions according to its intrinsic nature. Therefore, businesses need to properly function with nature.

All of the above categories overlap and encompass each other, because in reality they are highly dependent on each other. To look at the manuscripts of major religions, we may find different ethical and moral convictions for human beings towards the nature. The Judeo-Christian view of creation is intrinsically anthropocentric. It states that humanity has a transcendence of, and rightful mastery over nature. For example, an exploitative view is expressed in Genesis:

> And God said unto them,
> Be fruitful and multiply, and replenish the earth, and subdue it;
> and have dominion over the fish of the sea, and over the fowl of the air,
> and over living things that moveth upon the earth (Gen. 1:28).

Within the Judeo-Christian faith as Paikoff (1999: 66) indicates:

> All life, including human life, is struggle against nature. Nature, to a living organism, is adversary to be conquered. It is not a god to be worshiped. Man's ascent from the cave began with the recognition that nature must be turned into a means to our ends, and the end is our life.... Life is action, not stillness, aggressive self-preservation, not passivity. Everywhere we see life battling with nature, i.e., with the given.

The question of human control over the nature can be separated into two parts:

- Whether humans have a superior right to control nature compared to other universal creatures and elements?
- Or are humans able to do so?

According to the European and American industrialization philosophical reasoning, the establishment and operational processes of a factory means intervening in nature. A factory does not regard or consider nature to be preserved. It interferes in the soil to extract the chemicals and the water it needs for its operation survival. The same is true of animals. They eat trees and roots of trees and eat other animals to survive, and human beings eat most of them. If human beings respected and refrained from interfering with nature, they would starve and die. Again Paikoff (1999: 67) states:

> Consider what life is like in the underdeveloping nations. These nations are underdeveloped precisely because they respect nature. They don't interfere... They don't use fertilizers or pesticides. They have no industrial pollution; only natural filth and dung. They have no oil drilling. They have nothing. Just unending natural toil, mass disease and starvation.

Therefore, interfering and changing the nature of the nature for good and/or bad is considered as a survival mandate for the Western civilization. Nevertheless, we should understand that the nature of human beings who are intelligent, rational, and thoughtful planners inspire them to keep their environment clean. Nevertheless, human beings should do what all life does, but with intelligence and foresighted vision.

In contrast to the Western philosophical reasoning, one of the most important claims made by the Islamic faith is the obligation of human beings to respect nature as the kingdom of God. Proponents of such an opinion argue that species should be protected because God created them. Within this faith, the theocentric value statements derive from the assertion that humans are parts of nature and therefore have the same fundamental capabilities and are subject to the same ethics. For example, with a guardian view on the Islamic scripture, Koran has indicated:

> He to whom belongs
> The dominion of the heaven
> All things that are
> Has He begotten: nor has He
> A partner in His dominion:
> It is He who created
> All things, and ordered them
> In due proportions
> (Koran: Surat Al-Furqan, Ayat 2)

> Sees thou not that
> To Allah (God) prostrate
> All things that are
> In the heavens and on earth
> The sun, the moon, the stars;
> The hills, the trees, the animals;
> And a great number among
> Mankind? But a great number
> Are (also) such as
> Unto whom the
> Chastisement is justly due.
> (Koran: Surat: Al Hajj, Ayat 18).

Within the Islamic faith, to respect the means in the nature of good is to regard or consider for something, and thus to refrain from not to interfere with it. Consider the difference between respecting nature, and interfering with nature. Respecting nature means respecting reality. Reality is the world considered as unchangeable, as something outside humanity's power to alter. For example, the law of gravity around the earth is a law of nature. You have to respect that law otherwise you will die if you leap from the top of a building. Since you are living on the earth, you should respect it and you should not be worry about gravity. You do not have to worry about interfering with gravity because you do not have such a power to interfere with it. In the Islamic faith, respect for preservation and conservation of natural resources is considered a religious mandate. Nature should be clean, and you have to live accordingly within such a condition.

Within the Chinese Confucianism beliefs, harmony between *feng shui* or wind water is an essential part of life. Chinese believe that wind and water are earth forces that can cause success or failure. *Feng shui* reflects the belief that people and their activities are affected by the layout and orientation of their environmental conditions. Europeans and Americans want to control nature whereas the Chinese want to be harmonized with it. Adler (1986:18) states:

> Perhaps the contrasting relationships become clearer in the saying of three societies:
>
> 1. *Ayorama;* it can't be helped (Inuit - Canada) reflects subjugation.
> 2. *En Sha Allah, if* God is willing (Moslem - Arabic) reflects harmony with nature and submission to God.
> 3. *Can Do,* all will do it (American) reflects dominance.

EVALUATION OF ENVIRONMENTAL ETHICS

What is the proper relationship between business and nature? In the European and American utilitarian cultural philosophy, nature has been regarded as an adversary to be exploited and conquered. Utilitarianism, the greatest good for the greatest number, provided ethical justification for economic development even when it causes environmental damage. Within the ideological philosophy of capitalism, all economic values that stress productivity and largely ignore environmental damages have been perceived as an ethical principle. Capitalism through utilitarian argument proves that although pollution is harmful to nature, the economic gains benefit though jobs, products, taxes, and economic development and growth.

Eastern civilizations, from Islamic faith, to Buddhism and Taoism have placed a greater emphasis upon the ethical and moral convictions of business people and nature. They portray a more humble and less domineering role for humanity vis-à-vis nature. Aldo Leopold (1970: 239) is known as an expanded environmental ethic. He states:

> All ethics so far evolved rest upon a single promise: that the individual is a member of a community of interdependent parts... That land ethic simply enlarges the boundaries of the community to include soils, waters, plants, and animals, or collectively: the land... In short, a land ethic changes the role of *Homo sapiens* from conqueror of the land-community to plain member and citizen of it. It implies respect for his fellow members and also respect for the community as such.

Leopold argues that the conventional concept of an ethical society, or the area of human existence in which ethical duties existed, was too narrow.

The ecological stakeholders are silent entities who do not have sufficient voices in business circles. Ecological changes are occurring to many natural systems, on local, continental, and global scales. Within the domain of business ethics, there are five major global changes which effect not on today's environment, but also generations to come. Unlike local ecological problems, environmental issues typically do not damage immediate local area. These five areas are:

- Habitat destruction and species extinction
- Global warming and greenhouse gases-- monoxide emissions from automobiles and factories
- Toxic wastes released to deserts, rivers, streams, and oceans
- Ozone-depleting cholorofluorocarbons (CFCs)
- Noise pollution

Other emissions of pollutants into the atmosphere have threatened the balance of nature. Solutions to ecological problems must overcome the disconnection between business causes and the environmental effect. Within the structural foundation of financial investments in the global free markets, people are causing the ecological problems. These causes are often remote from the people or other creatures suffering effects. For example, in the large metropolitan areas, people who drive cars or conduct unhealthy businesses who operate polluting equipments may not be the same people who suffer from asthma or other pollution-related health effects. It is one of the critical problems of industrialized nations which industrial processes are damaging to the environments. The cumulative impact of industrialization and mechanized farming has been to cause serious local, regional, and global deterioration. It is immoral and unethical for these patients to bear the health care costs and provide opportunities to those people who conduct their businesses by greed to pollute the environment and enjoy profits.

Habitat Destruction and Species Extinction

Both industrialization and commercialization of natural resources can cause drastic changes in nature. It is more difficult to see how species are lost when construction of dams, shopping centers, housing projects, mining, and other activities shrink some habitat below a critical size. Both industrialization and commercialization of natural resources can destroy habitats by clearing land for farming, grazing, settlement, and commercial centers; by draining and filling wetlands; and by poor land management which causes the desertification. Also, they destroy or to some extent extinct endemic species and replace them with new species that overtake native species for the main purpose of capital gain.

Habitat extinctions occur naturally, at an estimated background rate without human intervention; of less than one per year. With human-caused changes, the rates of extinction to be somewhere between four thousand and twenty-seven thousand per year (Wilson, 1989: 108; World Resources Institute, 1992: 128; Peters and Lovejoy, 1990: 353).

Global Warming and Greenhouse Gases: Monoxide Emissions from Automobiles, Airplanes, and Factories

The earth's atmosphere is like a greenhouse building that creates a natural greenhouse condition for plants, animals, and humans to survive. It traps the sun's heat and keeps it warmer inside. Visible light passes through the atmosphere, striking the earth's surface and heating it. This surface heat radiates back up as infrared light. Naturally occurring greenhouse gases absorb part of the infrared in the lower atmosphere, thus keeping the earth warmer.

Figure 7.2: The Greenhouse Effect Absorbs Infrared (Heat) and Keeps
the Earth Warmer

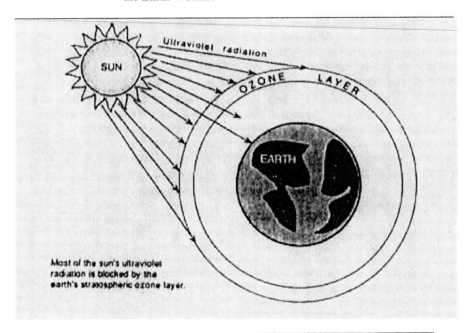

Source: Adapted From W. Kempton, J. S. Boster, and J. A Hartley,
Environmental Values in American Culture, (Cambridge,
Massachusetts: The MIT Press, 1995), 31.

The primary natural greenhouse gases are water vapor (in clouds), carbon dioxide (CO_2), methane, nitrous oxide, and tropospheric ozone. In addition to the above natural gases, humans have also introduced new greenhouse gases such as chlofluorocarbons (CFCs) and other halocarbons that do not occur naturally and cause ozone depletion as well as greenhouse warming. Major greenhouse gases are shown in the Figure 7-2. Within the field of business, these gases are ranked by their effect on increasing radioactive forces. The effect column in the table is an assessment of the Office of Technology Assessment (OTA) during the eighties (1991: 45) and the research of Calderia and Kasting (1993: 251).

Table 7.5: Major Anthropogenic Greenhouse Gases

GREENHOUSE GASES	EFFECT	LIFETIME (YEARS)	ACTIVITIES CAUSING EMISSIONS	INDUSTRY
Carbon Dioxide (CO_2)	55%	1000	Primary fossil fuel burning, secondary deformation	Auto industry, factories, and logging industry
Chloroflourocabons (CFCs)	24%	100	Refrigerators, foam insulation cans packing, previously spray cans; now banned	Chemical industry
Methane (CH_4)	15%	10	Rice paddies, ruminant animals Coal mining, natural gas leaks, landfills, and biomass burning	Food industry, mining, and municipal waste management
Nitrous Oxide (N_2O)	6%	150	Nitrogenous fertilizers, burning fossil fuels, and biomass	Mechanized agriculture and plants

Sources: Partially adapted from Office of Technology Assessment (OTA), *Changing by Degrees: Steps to Reduce Greenhouse Gases,* OTA-O – 482, (Washington, D.C.: U.S. Government Printing Office, February 1991), 45.

K. Caldeira, and J. F. Kasting, "Insensitivity of Global Warming Potentials to Carbon Dioxide Emission Scnarios," *Nature.* 366, (November 18, 1993), 251-253.

Within the context of ethical and moral discussions concerning human-made greenhouse gases, there are two contradictory theories: 1) Deotological Prevention Theory (DPT), and 2) Utilitarian Adaptation Theory (UAT).

Deontological Preventive Theory: The proponents of DPT believe that it is the responsibility of human species through application of ethical and moral convictions to solve all environmental problems. If a human and or an industry caused an environmental problem, a preventive approach would either modify or stop the activity so that the problem would not occur. As long as businesses are causing problems, they are responsible for solving those problems. Businesses should put aside a percentage of their profits to research how to clean up the environment. Citizens of a country are not responsible for paying the clean up costs.

Utilitarian Adaptive Theory: By contrast, proponents of the UAT believe that life is a challenging process and we need to proceed with innovative methods and techniques in order to grow, develop, and progress. Within the context of growth, development, and progress, there are some risks that producers and consumers should take. *Adaptation* is the decision to find ways to live with a changing environment without trying to postpone our growth, development, and progress. Change is the nature of human nature and we should not prevent changes in our society, because progress is the consequence of change. It is not ethical and moral to put barriers on the way of businesses and prevent them from growing, because survival of a business is based on growth. For example, if inhabitants of a polluted city are suffering from smog, they need to wear masks in order to inhale clean air, or to buy purified and non-toxic drinking water. Such operations provide many employment opportunities and economic incentives for its citizens.

Toxic Wastes Released to Deserts, Streams, Rivers, Lakes, and Oceans: The major sources of water pollution are industrial, municipal, and agricultural. Pollutant substances entering streams, rivers, lakes and oceans include organic wastes, heated water, sediments from soil run-off, nutrients such as fertilizers, detergents, and human and animal wastes, toxic chemicals, oil spill, pesticides, herbicides, oil and gas products, lead, atomic wastes, and particulate (particles of solid or liquid substances produced by stationary fuel combustion, and industrial processes). Most of the toxic wastes have irreversible affects on the ecological condition of the earth.

Ozone-Depleting Cholorofluorocarbons (CFCs): Ozone (O3), a gas molecule made up of three oxygen atoms, is formed naturally in the stratosphere C the earth's upper atmosphere. This stratospheric ozone, along with clouds and particles, shields humans and other species from the sun's ultraviolet radiation. To understand ozone depletion, we must start with the sun. The part of the sun's light that humans can see is compose of a spectrum of colors, as can be seen in a rainbow. In addition to this visible light, the sun gives off other forms of light not visible to our naked eyes. On either side of the sun's visible light spectrum are *ultraviolet light* (UV) and *infrared light*, also called radiant heat. Ozone depletion involves ultraviolet and the greenhouse effect involves visible light and infrared. Ozone depletion lets more ultraviolet through the atmosphere to hit us. The ozone layer is being thinned by human-made chemicals called chlorofluorocarbons (CFCs) used for refrigerators, air conditioners, foam insulation, and many other things and to a lesser extent by haloes that are used in fire extinguishers. The critical state of ozone depletion is obvious in Antarctica, where chemical reactions occur more quickly in cold air. UV levels will increase human skin cancers worldwide and damage other species.

Figure 7.3: The Ozone Layer Prevents Harmful Ultraviolet Light From Reaching Earth's Surface

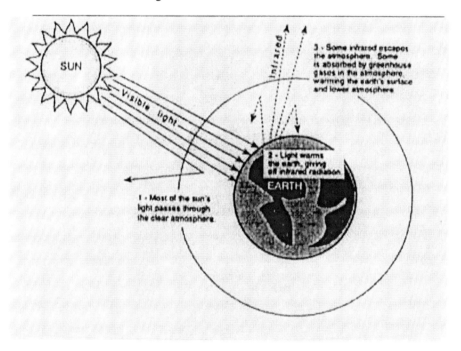

Source: Adapted From W. Kempton, J. S. Boster, and J. A. Hartley. *Environmental Values in American Culture*, (Cambridge, Massachusetts: The MIT Press, 1995), 30.

The U. S. Environmental Protection Agency (EPA) estimates that the elimination of CFCs by an international treaty will prevent 27 million deaths that otherwise would occurred from skin cancer during the next century. The usually fatal term of skin cancer, which is called melanoma. When one also includes nonmelanoma cancers are the more common and treatable forms, a total of 132 million skin cancers are estimated to be averted by this treaty (Shabecoff, 1987: A1.).

Noise pollution: One of the problems of the industrial and mechanized agricultural countries is noise emission. Usually, business people and farmers use some types of machinery and animals in their production operations that make excessive noise. Both businesses and farmers need to protect the public health and welfare. The sources of noise pollution are varied and range from transportation vehicles (cars, airplanes, ships, trains, metro), chain saws, loading, and unloading steel, stereos, and the like. Researchers within the Occupational Safety and Health Administration (OSHA) indicate that adequate protection should be provided for the ears of workers and surrounding industrialized inhabitants who are exposed to noise levels of 85 decibels or greater for 8 hours. For example, the decibel level of a lawn mover is 80 and 96, a motorcycle can reach 110, and a vacuum cleaner hovers between 70 and 85 (Bahadori and Bohne, 1993: 12).

CHAPTER SUMMARY

Some people believe that all human beings have basic derives toward self-respect and self-actualization. These characteristics are the quests to be all we can be. These people believe in humanity to foster the notion of individual growth, improvement, and progress in personality. Humaneness is the distinctive idealistic good side of people that is centered to promote spirituality among people. The focus of humanity is on the self rather than on the nature of activities or jobs of themselves, the group in which these activities function, or on the leisure activities these people pursue.

Today, individuals within contextual econo-political and psychosocial boundaries of their environments have a set of virtues, values, norms, and beliefs that together form their moral characters and ethical commitments. Virtues, of course, are intellectual deliberative judgments on the matter of have to do, must do, and ought to do in their distinctively moral sense. Virtues are highly attached to the psychosocial characteristics of human beings.

Values are periodical assessments with evaluations of judgments concerning the quality, worth, or desirability of activities, situations, consequences, or institutions. Values can be expressed by saying that something is or is not valuable, desirable, or good. There are two types of judgments: moral judgments and value judgments.

The concept of stakeholder is defined as any entity or group of people has a stake, or interest. Traditionally, in the field of business the most important stakeholder groups of a corporation have been recognized as the shareowners or stockholders; namely investors. Today, such a concept has dramatically been changed to include all interest groups that a company intrinsically and extrinsically is linked. There are a number of groups with whom a business is intricately linked. The most important groups include: stockholders or shareholders, the boards of governance, consumers, employees, management, labor unions, community, and government.

Consumerism is a latent value system between the sellers of goods and services as producers or providers, and buyers as customers and consumers exchange them between each other. It is also a movement in which the maintenance of the rights of consumers as an important part of a corporation's stakeholder is seriously considered.

The terms of *individuals* and *individualism* are examples of these phenomena. However, the recognition of the term of *self-survival* indicates that there are serious implications relating to moral, ethical, and legal issues. The moral basis of individualism is based on rational selfishness. What is rational selfishness? It depends who perceives to be a hammer or a nail. It holds that each individual is free to choose his/her lifestyle, respecting the legal right of all others to do likewise.

Collectivism ideology regards human beings as rational brutes whose interests' conflict. People are selfish. They need to struggle in order to survive. The entire primacy of their struggle for survival is to overcome barriers. This indicates that they need to eliminate others in order to provide sufficient room to grow, develop, and progress. Morally and ethically what do they need? Do they need to get rid of selfishness?

Ethically, consumers expect that businesses should not violate their rights by deception, fraud, or greed. From an ethical point of view, several advocates based on the belief that extending rights to consumers and building protection of these rights into a societal ordination will establish trust between buyers and sellers have taken a right-based approach. Trust between sellers and buyers enable a marketplace to function more effectively. Consumers as stakeholders within a market place are concerned about moral issues that keep recurring: issues of rights and obligations; individual and group rights and their obligations.

Governments and businesses have a symbiotic relationship. Governmental agencies at all levels, local, state, and federal, are stakeholders of the corporate world. Not only do governments set standards for businesses, but also buy hundreds of billions of dollars of goods and services from private companies.

The global ecological corporate stakeholders' convictions are especially concerned with global environmental changes, because the causes of damage are disconnected in time and space from those who are harmed. Based on moral, ethical, and legal convictions of a corporation, we may conclude that ecological values derive from three major sources: (1) *Anthropocentric* (human-centered), econo-political values are predominantly utilitarian and are concerned with only those financial environmental changes that effect human's welfare. These people believe that humanity is an infestation analogous to an illness. This implies a moral duty to reduce both the size and impact of the human pollution. (2) *Theocentric* (God-centered): Socio-religious values are predominantly deontological and are concerned with qualitative spiritual desirability in life and after life and more abstract feelings towards goodness for satisfaction of God and harmony with His realm of kingdom. On the basis of deontological theory of ethics, for example, theocentrists state that environmental protection for survival of all creatures is a human duty because God created all species with specific purposes. Therefore, it is the corporate's duty to safeguard the kingdom of God. (3) *Ecocentric* (both biocentric: living-thing centered and envirocentric: non-living thing-centered): environmental values grant nature itself intrinsic rights to function naturally. These values grant species the right to continue to exist and function within the contextual natural circumstances of survival. Each element in the universe functions according to its intrinsic nature. Therefore, businesses need to properly function with nature.

QUESTIONS FOR DISCUSSION

- How do you define virtues and values?
- What are differences between virtues and values?
- What are two principal kinds of values?
- Does virtue mean the same means and ends in the two principal kinds of values?
- What is the efficient cause of virtue?
- What extrinsic influential forces such as religion, education, and politics can help to develop virtue in a person?
- Explain and analyze how and why virtue consists in a mean not in an end.
- Explain and analyze how and why value consists in an end of an intention or an action.
- Distinguish between a virtuous objective as a mean and a relative value as an end.
- Who are stakeholders in the field of business?
- What is the concept of social contract related to the concept of stakeholders?
- How do stakeholder groups affect each other?
- How can the environment be a part of stakeholders, when the environment is not human?
- Analyze global environmental forces in order grasp the real meaning of how a corporation can possibly take account of the global moral, ethical, and legal mandates.
- Why is the concept of stakeholder analysis necessary before moral, ethical, and legal stakeholder management principles be developed?
- What are the side effects of business pollution on the human race?
- What we mean by Utilitarian Adaptive Environmental Theory?
- What we mean by Deontological Preventive Environmental Theory?
- What is the green house effect?
- What is the ozone layer?

CASE STUDY

PEOPLE DIDN'T HAVE TO DIE: SARA LEE'S TAINTED HOT DOGS

Between August and December1998, tainted hot dogs manufactured by a Sara Lee plant in Zeeland, Michigan, carried a bacterium called *Listeria monocytogenes*, killing 9 people, causing three women to have miscarriages, and seriously sickening at least 79 people in 12 states. Sara Lee closed parts of the plant and recalled 30 million pounds of hot dogs and deli meats, which cost the company $50 to $70 million. The recall involved meats manufactured between July and December 1998, sold under brand names such as Ball Park, Hygrade and Bil Mar (*Conlin, 1999: 54*).

Sara Lee Corporation is a conglomerate global and marketer entity. Sara Lee Corporation was founded in 1939 when Canadian entrepreneur Nathan Cummings purchased the C. D. Kenny Company, a small distributor of wholesale sugar, coffee and tea in Baltimore, Maryland. Cummings's strategy was based on relentless growth and development of his corporation through application of novel management techniques and acquisition of many interrelated businesses. In 1979, Sara Lee Corporation took the initiative strategy by its Chairman of the board of governance and CEO within the globalization (in 58 countries and markets branded products in more than 180 nations) and diversification of its products into five distinctive lines of businesses: (1) Sara Lee Food, (2) Coffee and Tea, (3) Household and Body Care, (4) Food Services, and (5) Branded Apparel. Sara Lee Annual Corporate Report indicates its annual revenue was more than $20 billion, having 141,500 employees, and 89,000 stockholders. Sara Lee operated in more than 58 countries and made a wide range of products in more than 180 nations. Its management style was based on decentralization principles. Each plant or line of business was led by an operating executive with a high degree of autonomy and accountability for the performance of that business line.

Sara Lee Corporation's Mission:

> Sara Lee Corporation will build leadership brands in three highly focused global businesses: Food and Beverage, Intimates and Underwear, and Household Products. Our primary purpose is to create long-term shareholder value.

PROBLEMS AND ISSUES

Why, in the highest scientific and technological advanced nation like the United States, are hot dogs and deli meats hazardous? The answer lies in how people process meats. The USDA authorities in 17 states identified the vehicle for contaminated hot dogs and possibly deli meats produced under many brand names by one manufacturer: Bil Mar Foods. Neither the health departments nor the company recalled the Bil Mar Foods products until December 1998 five months after contamination. If they had made an ethical and moral decision concerning their consumers, people did not have to die and/or others did not have to become sick. Greed, negligence, and carelessness by the company's managers, delays by governmental regulatory agencies, and insufficient governmental inspectors cost innocent people their lives.

Contamination of hot dogs and deli meats took place in one of the Sara Lee meat processing plant in Zeeland, Michigan. Such a criminal action took place in operational lines due to the luck of hygienic procedures. Nevertheless, Sara Lee corporate responsibility and accountability resulted in questioning complex issues such as legal and ethical questions. In addition to the above issues, Sara Lee was faced with its technological capabilities in order to make meat safer as the result of irradiation, freezing, and defrosting hot dogs and deli meats.

CASE ROLE PLAYERS

The Sara Lee CEO, the Zeeland plant's operation executives and its employees, and the packaging, distribution, and grocery stores are part of such an incident. However, Sara Lee's members of the board of governance, the artificial persons, who had committed crime and whom the legal authorities held accountable. The food poisoning victims, who had weakened immune systems, including pregnant women, infants, and elderly or people with chronic digestive diseases, are among the victims of such an event of negligence. In addition to meat processors and packers, FDA and USDA are accountable for such an incident.

ANALYSIS OF THE CASE

Generally, there are three types of products that consumers buy: (1) foods and drugs, (2) materialized products that they use them and then dispose them, (3) non-material products such as services which are related to their psychosocial wellbeing. The first groups of products are directly related to the physical survival status of consumers. As mentioned above, this case involves various ethical and legal dimensions of processed and packaged meat businesses. Within a meat-processing plant, there are several procedures concerning sanitation and radiation of meats and their processing equipments. In addition, workers' hygiene is the number one issue, because they have direct contact with meats. There different chained responsibilities for food producing concerning health: breeding, butchering, processing, packaging, transporting, refrigerating, storing, consumption of expiration dates, selling, defrosting, cooking, serving, eating, and keeping leftovers in refrigerators. Within such a chained processing system, consumers have to be interrelated with different businesses and people.

One thing is evident. If the plant manager had taken serious actions after the evidence of listeria used been formed during the plant's environmental testing, they could have detected contaminated areas and clean them. Such negligence caused both Sara Lee and customers to suffer. Sara Lee lost around $50-$70 million and customers lost their health and even their lives. Furthermore, Sara Lee's financial loses and damages may not end here, as the corporation was faced with heavy lawsuit costs and possible penalties.

Sara Lee has lost its reputation for having safe nutritional products. Consumers are paying more attention in choosing hot dogs and deli packaged meats. Thus, not only the reputation of the company directly was damaged, but also other companies in the meat industry suffered. Consider all losses and damages resulting from such negligence. The food industry is exposed to more regulation. Indifference of to the health and safety of nutritional and pharmaceutical products is a direct violation of moral and ethical principles, even though law does not require any preventive actions.

CASE QUESTIONS FOR DISCISSION

- Do you find any difference between raw meat and cooked meat regulatory systems?
- Do you find in the Sara Lee's corporate mission statement any ethical and moral convictions?
- Who are the stakeholders of this corporation?
- How do they value their consumers?
- What is the major problem for FDA and USDA concerning the implementation of food safety?
- How should the members of board of directors of Sara Lee Corporation deal with its CEOs and SBUs?
- How can technology help or hurt Sara Lee Corporation concerning the safest of its products?
- Do you think is it morally and ethically the positions of CEO's and the board of directors' chairmanship to be concerned about safety and security of their customers?
- Do you feel Sara Lee's negligence in recalling contaminated ground beef is justified? Explain why.
- Do you find any spirit of humaneness in Sara Lee Corporation concerning protecting the natural rights of children, elderly, and pregnant women?

CASE SOURCES

M. Conlin, "These People Didn't Have to Die," *Forbes,* (February, 8, 1999), 54-55.

Sara Lee Corporation Website:
<wysiwyg://5/http://www.saralee.com/corporate_overview/index.html.>.

CHAPTER 8

TRUST, RIGHTS, AND DUTIES

We do not trust all people, because they may be jealous,
but we can trust them, if they are benevolent.

We do not trust all people through their utterance,
but we can trust them, if they are honest in their hearts.

We do not trust all people, because they may break their promises,
but we can trust them, if they are sincere in their intentions.

We do not trust some politicians, because we are afraid to be traded,
but we can trust them, if they prove that they have moral and ethical convictions.

We do not trust the wondering world, because we are afraid of being eliminated,
but we trust it, because we are able to find solutions to maintain our survival.

We do not trust the effectiveness of all inventors, because we are in the process
of progress,
but we can trust them, because we may have assurance on how can things be
improved.

We do not trust the intensity of natural forces, because we are not in control of
power,
but we can trust it, because we may have competence to know how to deal with
the existence.

CHAPTER OBJECTIVES

When you have read this chapter you should be able to do the following:

- Develop conceptual skills in defining trust, rights, and duties.
- Develop a framework of analysis to enable you to understand the differences between rights and duties.
- Define what is a common good.
- Understand the importance of ethical, moral, and legal obligations in socialization.
- Understand the complexity and differences between positive and negative rights.
- Analyze the holistic characteristics surrounding trust by reviewing moral virtues, ethical values, and cultural beliefs.
- Define and analyze components of moral values: dignity, integrity, self-confidence, self-reliance, and conscientious alertness.
- Define and analyze ethical values: courage, altruism, nobility-in-mind, generosity, and conscious awareness.
- Define and analyze cultural beliefs: truthfulness, consistency, responsibility, good faith, and continency.
- Know what are relationships between sellers and buyers in terms of producers and consumers' rights and duties.
- Grasp the magnitude of today's global business responsibilities.
- Understand how managers can manipulate organizational entities to acquire personal profit.
- Know how managers can make false data to deceive the public.
- Know how a judiciary system treats criminal CEOs.
- Know how managers can make free-money through their trustworthy professional duties and how they can be corrupted in their behavior to cheat their stakeholders.

THOUGHT STARTER

In the preceding chapters, we listed, defined, and analyzed a variety of moral characteristics, ethical trends, and legal principles on what constitutes goodness and justness in human nature. In a humanistic term, we can claim that the somatic nature of human beings is a metabolic function to precede life with continuity of growth and promising a prosperous reproductive outcome. Human beings are mandated to maintain their lives as they are supposed to be in the kinds of lives they have. Also, human beings possess other forms of lives; intellectual lives. This mandates them to be able to effectively communicate with each other and establish specific relationships with their associates. It is sufficient for the purpose of moral and ethical objectives to state that human beings are living with reason, and their lives are guided by reason. Therefore, human societal life is based on activity of thinking.

Since individuals possess unique characteristics of thoughts, therefore, their reasoning and living objectives are different. Nevertheless, all human being are subject to natural selection. This mandates them to understand their natural and social orders. Accordingly, they properly function within their specific social clusters. Within the natural order, all human beings are subject to the same destiny: birth, life, and death. But within the social cluster, human beings are mandated to follow the natural reason in a general term and at the same time to be the master of their own lives with their intellectual will. The will is the centerpiece of human life. Moral and ethical problems can arise from apprehension of the intellectual will. Morally, the intellectual will should provide people with the state of interior excellence. This mandate can fulfill an individual's objectives to live happily. Even those who pursue an external object like material-wealth or knowledge-wealth, pursue them primarily because of the satisfying results from the possession of such wealth.

Within such a variable contextual cluster, people's objectives differ from each other according to their special somatic natures. Many characteristics and traits of human beings are considerably different from each other and illustrate varying aspects about human life. Some characteristics and traits are individually related to their learning experiences and some are socially oriented for projecting their future. Within such a variable environment, the question will arise: should there be some basic functions or characteristics which belong to all people by virtue of which they act distinctively as human beings? If people perform such functions and/or construct such characteristics well, would they achieve their moral and ethical objectives? If the answer is yes, then what phenomena constitute the cohesiveness of human beings? In other words, we are asking what are the characteristic structures, functions, and relationships of human beings with society. Isn't it a fact that human beings are living in a society that could be characterized as a social setting?

It is a fact that the nature of human beings is very complex. Their characteristics range over a vast area of sensibility, emotionality, rationality, and artistic creativity. We conclude that the natures of human beings are so complex in a structural, functional, and social forms, they should not be analyzed just as one sort of being. In some ways, human beings are distinctive from others, and in other ways, they share similar characteristics with others.

Clearly, they are the whole and unified individuals. The terms individual, or self or a person are examples of a whole and a unified human being. Consequently, these terms have serious implications for many issues relating to morality and ethics.

PLAN OF THIS CHAPTER

Throughout the first seven chapters of this text, we emphasized the point that egoism, selfishness, and conflict of interest on the one hand, and power, reputation, and monies on the other, come closest to the center of what ethics is all about. In a broad sense, ethics can resolve and harmonize conflicts of interest through maintenance of trust, consideration of human rights, and performance of duties. Therefore, this chapter deals with the most contentious issues of today's life: trust, rights, and duties. This chapter provides general behavioral characteristics about people who feel morally and think and act according to their conscience. Also, this chapter provides you with information about being caught between one's conscientious judgment and the greedy appetite of immoral and unethical managers. In this discussion, it should become clear the way that this rethinking of managerial responsibilities moves beyond traditional assumptions, tensions, and dilemmas. Furthermore, this chapter begins with definitions and explanations of trust, rights, and duties within the moral sense that offers managers a broad vision to be responsible to the convictions of self and others. In addition, it highlights the conflict between the power of access and rights and duties. Finally, it will discuss excusable, convincible, and inconvincible conditions for moral and ethical duties.

INTRODUCTION

Let us begin with the broadest meanings of trust, rights, and duties, and then take up the more specific meanings and attributes of these terms. What is trust and what can trust make for a society to be moral and ethical? What are rights, and what rights do people have? What is duty, and what does a duty in a moral and ethical sense for humanity? At least a few characteristics are always found in humanity that everyone would regard as moral and ethical convictions of human beings. One of these characteristics is that the natural rights of human beings are universal. By this we mean that any human being is entitled by the principles of humanity to obey natural law. In addition, human beings by their natures have established different moral, ethical, and legal principles in order to advance and pursue their common good. Nevertheless, some people deliberately seek to go against the common good through egoism, selfishness, and greediness C in a world, by being lawless. Lawlessness is, thus, one of the characteristics of today's civilized and uncivilized societies. Through greediness, some human beings ignore the rights of self and others and desire to attain more than they deserve. They pursue egoistic motives in order to have access to illegitimate power and ignore moral, ethical, and legal principles at the expense of others in any and all ways possible. For example, look at the epidemic greediness of CEOs of large corporations in American business. Irresponsible and greedy managers have converted the interest of public corporations to their personal gain (e.g., Enron, WorldCom., Quest, Global Crossing, Dynegy, Tyco, Xirox, Adelphia, AOL Time Warner, Johnson and Johnson).

Trust is the most characteristic of human socialization. Trust is, therefore, a foundation for humaneness that signifies moral, ethical, and legal order to achieve peace and harmony on earth. A right is an entitlement to act or have others act in a certain standardized way. Duty is the notion of completeness of moral, ethical, and legal obligations. Duty is a constraint on the scope of permissible actions, but not all constraints are duties. The connection between rights and duties is that, generally if you have a right to do something, then you and/or others have a correlative duty to act in a certain specific way.

Every society, if it is to survive, must possess a social order to be transmitting from one generation to another. Thus, all generations and societies have some systems of socialization. We may speak first of the order of a society by defining and analyzing the term socialization within the context of civilization, then, we will discuss trust, rights, and duties among these civilized people. Distinct from both the real order of socialization and individualization assumed by human reason are the moral, ethical, and legal orders. All societal moral, ethical, and legal orders are caused by reason, although the causality is of a different kind in each domain. In the moral order, reason is the inherent cause, in the ethical order reason is the formal cause, and in the legal order reason is the intellectual cause. In studying these orders, therefore, we start with social order B socialization.

SOCIALIZATION

Within societal life processes, the words trust, duties, and rights are familiar enough to all of us. Human life is the essence of an individual's social interaction with surrounding, people, things, and phenomena. Life is a long process of shaping an individual's patterns of virtues, values, standards, skills, attitudes, motives, and knowledge to conform to those reliable and desirable objectives. In an individual's societal life cycle, many groups of people are involved: family members, friends, teachers, peers, professionals, social institutions, religious organizations, and political and legal agencies. These people exert pressure on individuals to conform to socially approved virtues, values, and attitudes and to motivate or sometimes to force them to comply with given standards of expected behavior. These expected behavioral standards mandate individuals to internalize their social values to cooperative, honest, and responsible outcomes. In return, society provides a reliable sense of trust among its members to guarantee their rights. Therefore, trust is considered as the foundation of socialization.

Socialization is the result of two dynamic processes: (1) cooperation, and (2) competition. Cooperation is defined as psychosocial readiness to work synergistically together with other people in order to achieve specific societal objectives. Within such a dynamic environment, every member of society is entitled to specific expected rights and duties and interrelationships with others based on trustworthy moral and ethical obligations to achieve altruistic synergistic results. Within the life cycle cooperation, the relative win-win synergy is the ultimate result for all parties (see Figure 8.1).

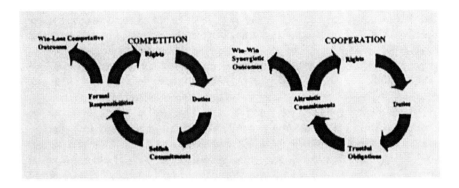

Figure 8.1: Moral and Ethical Cooperation and Legal Competition

On the other hand, not only do people cooperate with each other to a certain level of socialization, also they compete with each other to have access to valuable scarce resources. Competition is defined as the best set of potential forces or capabilities that allows individuals, groups, and institutions to consistently outperform their rivals. The moral, ethical, and legal competition is to outperform rivals' objectives with an honest qualitative rivalry. It is not merely matching the performance of others, but also, it is ceasing the race of performance with sustainable competitive advantage. In other words, in a fair competitive environment, competitors possess equal societal rights and duties to be responsible and accountable to their markets for racing their efforts to gain more profits. The end result of competition is the ability to enjoy consistently high level of performance year after year. Such a sustainable result creates an environment for those capable rivals to survive and incapable ones to be diminished (see Figure 8.2).

As you may notice, while the end result of competition is based on selfish desires to achieve individualistic objectives, the cooperative efforts of altruistic societies end up with win-win synergies in which all parties enjoy a fair share of benefits. It is very sad that in recent years American business environments have had unethical and immoral managers who have robbed the trust of the public under the shelter of free competition. Pope (2002) through his research has discovered that one in six chief financial officers (CFOs) of American corporations report that they have been pressured by their chief executive officers (CEOs) to *misprint* their corporate financial reports and violate professional accounting rules and codes of ethics.

Socialization is a process by which individuals learn about religious virtues, cultural values, social beliefs, economical norms and trends, political ideologies, and legal standards of expected social behavior. Individuals through their social experiences learn how to establish relationships with others on the basis of trust, rights, and duties. This process provides individuals with formal and informal information through different cultural orientations.

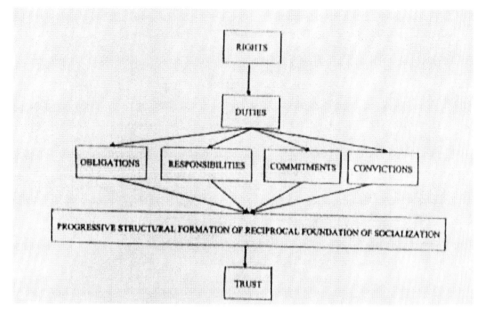

Figure 8.2: Contextual Cluster of Socialization

Trust can establish the basis of social confidence in people, products, services, and material things. Without trust, people would not work together efficiently. In addition, individuals go through formal orientations by societal institutions such as families, schools, professional organizations, religious institutions (e.g., scriptures, churches, alters, mosques, and temples), and governmental legal agencies in order to learn how to adapt themselves to societal rules and regulations (See Figure 8. 2). According to Terpstra and David (1991: 55):

> Socialization is the (process of) cultural learning. This instruction in what
> is socially defined as normal, right, effective, and efficient limits the range
> of variation of potential human actions. Some socialization is manifest. ...
> Other socialization is latent.

According to Piaget (1977), there are two basic processes at work in human socialization: *assimilation* and *accommodation*. In assimilation, the new patterns of values are changed to fit the known values. Assimilation modifies new environmental information to fit into what is already known. In accommodation, the current known values are changed to fit the new emerging values. Accommodation restructures or modifies the existing schemes so that new information can fit in better ways. As a general rule, when people learn how to be individualized within the context of the rules of socialization, they are at the same time internalizing their moral and ethical necessities to obey them. In order to understand better the elements of socialization, we will define and analyze trust, rights, and duties in more depth in the following pages.

WHAT IS TRUST?

Trust is defined as relying on the solemn confidence of integrity, dignity, and justice in self and/or others concerning decision-making processes and actions. It is a characteristic of high-reliance on an individual or an institution where people believe in their trustworthiness of characters, abilities, and operations. Also, it is related to the confidence in the ability or intention of an individual to pay attention to the worthiness and truthfulness of their commitments to some future promises for good. Trust is the state of one to whom something is entrusted. It illustrates an obligation or responsibility imposed on one in whom confidence or authority is delegated. For example, a CEO of a company is in trust by shareholders to take care of their investments with careful consideration.

In the field of business, there is a reciprocal trustworthiness among producers and consumers concerning the appropriate declaration of trust between the quality and quantity of a product and their denominated monetary values. Through principles of socialization, consumers have confidence in producers that their products can facilitate an easier life for them. Therefore, trust is the centerpiece of a good relationship between consumers and producers. Jack Welch, the Chief Executive Officer of General Electric (1993: 86) states:

> Trust is enormously powerful in a corporation. People won't do their best unless they believe they'll be treated fairly.... The only way I know to create that kind of trust is by laying out your values and then walking the talk.

It is obvious that maintenance of trust is not inherent in the marketplace itself, as the forces of competition do not automatically maintain it. Trust-based business relationships can provide assurance between traders to perform their duties. In some cultures, business deals are based on a handshake seals a deal, and a business partner's word is considered to be a contract (e.g., oral or written contracts).

Trust is thought of as having a conscientious self-guidance or self-reliance in an individual's good-faith personality. Also, a trustworthy individual is a person whose perception is based on an optimistic view that people have good faith, and positive attitudes toward self and others. Conversely, bad-faith is defined, as Jean-Paul Sartre expresses, for human self-deception in which we blame others for actions that we have freely chosen.

The central feature of bad-faith is that the deceiver and the deceived are one and the same (Stewart, 1996: 297). Individuals need to build self-reliance and self-confidence in their personalities in order to establish a trustworthy relationship with self and others. Trust could be taken on the basis of a face value. This characteristic means that some people are very open, direct and spontaneous. Trustworthiness can lead people by competence, not by formality in relationships with others, and by establishing sensible moral and ethical commitments in people's conduct.

The most elusive belief in business ethics is trust. Although it is difficult to document or assert the process of trust between producers and consumers, trust possesses a moral virtue and ethical values. Having a trust in somebody or an organization saves a great deal of time and energy in maintaining good relationships with others. Trustworthiness exhibits and acknowledges the truthful commitment of an authority faced with difficulties through the expression of courageous remarks and dignified ideas without fear of retaliation. Trustworthiness is the core concept of a moral character and ethical behavior to keep intellectual promises. Trust promotes a feeling of self-confidence, self-reliance and security among partners, friends, and even marriage without checking up on daily behavior.

Pillars of Trust

Before we proceed to describe dimensional views concerning trust, we are providing you with three pillars of trust: (1) moral virtues, (2) ethical values, and (3) cultural beliefs (see Table 8.3). We will summarize these views through a matrix of characteristics as follows:

Table 8.1: Holistic Characteristics Surrounding Trust

ATTRIBUTIONS	SUBCHARACTERISTIC
MORAL VIRTUES	Dignity Integrity Self-Confidence Self-Reliance Conscience Alertness
ETHICAL VALUES	Courage Altruism Nobility in Mind Generosity Conscientious Awareness
CULTURAL BELIEFS	Truthfulness Consistency Responsibility Good Faith Continency

Moral Virtues

As we indicated in the previous chapter, virtues are intellectual deliberative judgments on the matters of have to do, must do, and ought to do in their distinctively moral sense towards excellence. Virtues generate novel excellent inferences and solve problems of humanity. This concept derives from prior moral and ethical studies of intellectual deliberations on learning, perceiving, and problem solving to achieve happiness. Within the domain of this concept, there are five moral inherent characteristics which companies make the soundness of moral character. These characteristics are dignity, integrity, self-confidence, self-reliance, and conscientious alertness.

Dignity: *Dignity* is closely related to self-consideration in relation to manifestation of the good side of self-identity. Kant (1898: 12-14) defined dignity as a respect for a value without price and thought that such a dignified attitude is essential for recognizing the moral worth of a person. He then proceeded to explain the relationship between goodwill and duty: a good will is one that acts for the sake of duty. Indeed, human actions have inner moral worth only if they are performed from duty. Actions that result from inclination or self-interest may be praiseworthy if they happen, for whatever reason, to accord with duty, but they have no inner worth. For example, a woman who preserves her life in routine conformity to duty is acting from an inclination that is according to duty, but not from duty. On the other hand, to preserve dignified life when it has become a burden, only because duty requires it, is morally correct. Dignity means self-respect to the conformity of excellence in an individuals' moral character. It is viewed as a base for suitable characteristic traits for a person. Individuals with the quality of dignity try to elevate their moral characters to the highest standard of morality and ethics. For individuals self-respect is normally extended to the consideration for oneself as an independent agent. Self-respect is the opposite of self-contempt. Thus, dignity is a tendency to represent a favorable opinion of self in conjunction with others based on a comparison of one's own worth with that of others. Managers need to dignify their identity by respecting their intellectual decisions and actions.
The relationship of integrity with a multinational corporation that may operate in different countries needs to have special attention. A MNC needs to adjust itself to the host country's cultural value system. Nevertheless, preservation of its identity would be a crucial matter for maintenance of its reputation in the international markets.

Integrity: *Integrity* means soundness of and adherence to moral character (excellence). Moral virtues and ethical values mandate people to preserve their honest thoughts and express their intellectual ideas without fear of retaliation. Corporate excellence is not identical with managers' moral excellence, because there are several legal mandates that apply to corporations but not to managers.

It is doubtful that a firm's excellence is compatible with organizational members immoral decisions and actions. Also, a firm's excellence is the valuable compatibility of that organization with the cultural beliefs of people who condone it employees to behave either immorally or act unethically or amorally in the performance of their duties for the operational benefit. Integrity prevents an individual from committing any malicious actions.

Self-Confidence: *Self-confidence* is defined as a strong belief in self-trustworthiness. An individual can have assurance about himself/herself concerning positive or negative judgments in stating reasoning. This moral characteristic encompasses the ability, desire, and tendency to interact and develop very strong relationship with others on the basis of having knowledge and expertise. Many researchers have found that having self-confidence and retention of intellectual mental health in one's own ability allows one to deal with unforeseen cross-cultural occurrences. They are critical when adjusting to new environmental conditions. One example is the work of Hawes and Kealey (1981: 239), who studied 160 technical advisors and 90 spouses working on 26 projects in six countries. Their data revealed that participants' self-confidence in technical competence had a significant effect on whether they were comfortable and productive in the overseas assignment. Those managers who have strong feelings of self-confidence concerning their own knowledge can make better conscious decisions within and beyond of the scope of the surface levels of those decisions.

Self-Reliance: *Self-reliance* is defined as consistency in expressing intellectual reasoning on the basis of reliable sources and/or scientific methods. Self-reliance creates a disciplined prosperous foundation within the individuals' personality to achieve moral objectives through the application of ethical principles. Self-reliance can help an individual avoid an adversarial evasion of factual events during a crisis. When self-reliance becomes effective, self-trust and public-trust can be merited and secured. When self-reliance fails, self-identity, self-dignity, and self-integrity will be lost. Therefore, trust and self-confidence are viewed as knowledge-based conscious awareness for being honest and truthful. Furthermore, trust establishes ethical standards beyond the requirements of the law. Trust creates a comprehensive self-awareness within the mind of an individual in order to be faithful to his/her conscious judgments during decision-making processes and actions.

Conscience Alertness: *Conscience alertness* is defined as being intellectually reliable, dependable, and careful in decision-making processes and actions. We have all felt the pangs of conscience, but what exactly is conscientious alertness and how reliable a guide is it? Conscientiousness is not literally a little voice inside human beings. Our conscientious alertness evolves as our internalized moral instructions guide us from different viable sources (e.g., religious faiths, scientific values, legal mandates, and cultural beliefs). It is an ethical characteristic that motivates people to tell the truth, and be honest in order to be praised by self and others. Conscientious awareness is a sense of self-approval concerning having done what it is supposed to be done. In addition, conscientiousness refers to a general characteristic of an individual who has good work habits, preserving know-how knowledge, and achieving prosperous objectives. Research findings indicate that conscientious alertness is related to work-related behaviors and performance (Botwin and Buss, 1989: 988). How reliable is conscientious alertness? People often say: "Follow your conscientious," or "You should never go against your conscience." One should be honest, fair, right, and just during a course of judgment. The point here is not that we should ignore our conscience, but that the voice of conscience is itself something that can be critically examined. A pang of conscience is like a warning. When you realize it, you should definitely stop thinking and doing wrong things and reflect on the rightness, justness, and fairness of what you are doing (Shaw, 1996:18)

Ethical Values

Throughout the history of free enterprises, there has been a primary notion in ethical value systems: the subjective utility of cynical egoism. It is a product of our emotions. Emotions are not primaries of our moral and ethical premises (virtues, values, and beliefs). They truly are our momentary pleasurable self-interest toward egoism. Nevertheless, only intellectual deliberative long-range guidance can provide us happiness whether on a desert island or in the domain of humanity. The business person who thinks and behaves according to subjectivity of the utility of cynical egoism, not only cultivates a sense of valuable understanding, but also calculates strengths and weaknesses and opportunities and threats on the basis of two routes: 1) The honest route and 2) The dishonest route. Then, either consciously or subconsciously, he/she makes the final decision with the highest net obtainable value in profit making.

In the honest route, the businessperson calculates all moral, ethical, and legal attributes to his/her decision-making processes and operations. In the dishonest route, he/she might be well articulated in the legal terms, but fails in moral and ethical dimensions. In the latter case, he/she may succeed, and the likelihood of getting caught is low. Nevertheless, if he/she is caught, he/she will pay a very heavy price. This doctrine has been attacked through the ages for being an inadequate reason to guide a businessperson's moral action. In order to be moral and ethical, we will analyze the attributes of courage, altruism, nobility-in-mind, generosity, and conscience awareness as component parts of ethical value systems.

Courage: *Courage* is defined as a quality of mind that enables an individual to encounter difficulties without fear. Courage is clearly an admirable and praiseworthy quality for an individual to have. Within the contextual domain of morality and ethics, there are two praiseworthy qualities: *courage* and *fortitude.* Within the domain of courage, there two qualities: *altruism* and *praiseworthiness*. It is necessary to make distinction between the two. We know that fortitude is highly linked to intellectual prudence and courage is linked to emotional braveness. Fortitude is an appetite that is based on good reasoning. Fortitude eliminates any possibility of unpleasant and threatening consequences. But courage eliminates fear through boldness in expressing an intellectual reasoning to express justness. Courage is fear-free. Fear is perhaps the emotion that comes to mind of a courageous person when exposed to a situation where he/she puts himself/herself at risk for the benefit of others. A courageous person is viewed as an altruistic person who has an attachment to buy retaliatory consequences. On the other hand, fortitude is a prudential moral characteristic in which self-survival is considered as the finality of a rational challenging process.

By looking at the Figure 8.4, it is evident that fear and bravery are opposite emotions in the human nature. We act or react either with fear or without fear. In both cases, there is a risk- taking emotion. Keep in mind that one who courageously deals with truth are a trustworthy and honest person.

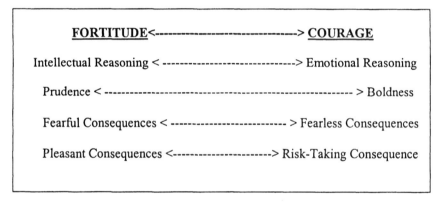

Figure 8.4: The Magnitude Consequences Between Fortitude and Courage

Altruism: *Altruism* could be defined as the principle or practice of unselfishness by providing goodness for the welfare of all people including self. Altruism is opposed to egoism. Or in another words, the opposite of selfishness is altruism. As members of society, all people are concerned about their interdependent and interconnected societal life affairs. They need to trust each other in order to survive. With such an assumption, all of us have moral convictions and ethical commitments as well as economic self-interest concerns. Within such a broad vision, people are motivated by both economic and humanity concerns. By this token, we can categorize people into two groups: selfish and altruistic. Some people are very selfish in economic terms. They work hard and earn legitimate incomes solely to fulfill their own desires. On the hand, there are some people who also work very hard and earn legitimate money for the welfare of self, as well as sharing their humanitarian happiness through economic contributions for the welfare of others. People judge the second group as trustworthy altruistic people. Nevertheless, sometimes you can find some people who pretend that they are altruistic, but in reality they are very egoistic. For example, the United Way is a humanitarian and philanthropic organization. Morally, ethically, and legally, this organization is supposed to be altruistic. In 1992, the United Way's reputation as a trustworthy organization was tainted by immoral, unethical, and illegal actions of its president. President William Aramony resigned amid charges of mistrust, nepotism, and misuse of the agency's funds. President Aramony betrayed the good will of donators by using them to support his selfish, lavish lifestyle. Since that scandal, the United Way has been struggling to regain public trust. For United Way, doing business differently is now seen as a matter of the organization's survival (Segal and Del Valle, 1993: 68). This indicates that when you lose your moral and ethical reputation in your business, it is very difficult to regain it, because you have lost the public trust.

Nobility-in-Mind: Nobility is defined as the state or quality of mind for being exalted to moral excellence. It is a mental power to elevate the human mind and feelings to the utmost stages of dignified and glorified of humanity. In order to reach to such a stage, Plato believed that humans have purposes or proper functions. Their values, like that of everything else in the universe, depend upon their effectiveness in fulfilling these functions. The nobility in a human's mind is within his/her rational, biological, and emotional balance, or in Platonic terms, one who is *wise, temperate, courageous*, and *just* can be trustworthy (Albert, Denise, and Peterfreund, 1984:10).

We should try to know the state of a mind or feelings, as it really *is* for only this reveals what it *ought* to be. George Wilhelm Hegel (1770-1831) declared that: AThe history of the world is the world's court of justice,@ (Loewenberg, 1929: 468). The foundation and outcomes of such a world's court of justice is based on human virtues. In sum, everyday all human beings are attending the world's court of justice. Some of them who possess nobility in their mind can attain happiness, while others struggle with miseries. Nobility-in-mind In the field of business means to conduct an effective business in order to be beneficial to both producers and consumers. Of course this notion is very idealistic, but not impossible by serving them well and/or providing them with equitable product quality and appropriate pricing system with profitability.

Generosity: *Generosity* is defined as readiness of an individual or a group to contribute to material wealth and knowledge wealth for the societal good-cause of an action or an operation. Generosity is based on combination of material and non-material or ethical and practical considerations. Capable or wealthy people have a moral duty to consider society's wellbeing when they are making decisions about how to donate time, money, and other resources for just societal causes of actions or operations. Accompanying this attitude, in the field of business, is the practical wisdom that you can't make profit, if your customers are poor. In a moral sense, if upper class people feel a moral duty to aid unfortunate people, then they will not be criticized or condemned for antisocial or unethical behavior. Generosity promotes charitable principle C the expectation of giving to needy people. In addition, royalty has consistently been expected to give to needy people. Charitable contributions of businesses in many nations can be a supplementary safety net to help governments for those citizens and/or institutions in need. Within the international markets, such a charitable action provides trust among nations in the time of natural disasters.

Conscience Awareness: *Conscience* is defined as the internal cognitive source of awareness to recognize right and wrong concerning one's own intentions and actions. Conscience is not literally a little voice inside a human being. People often believe that they should follow their conscience in critical judgments, or they should never go against their conscience. Under specific circumstances, conflict between egoism and public-good are frequently resolved by a regulative principle, namely, the conscience. Conscience is the reasoning which functions at times as the arbiter of conflicting interest of egoism and benevolence among people. When businesses control their financial appetite and not gain improper profits, this operative principle is called benevolence. Conscience is the authoritative conviction for our moral obligations. Conscience motivates us to perform our moral duties. In sum, conscience is a judgment of the practical intellect and the knowledge of right within us that makes us moral agents.

CULTURAL BELIEFS

We have now completed our treatment of moral virtues and ethical values, and we have seen how virtues and values, as good habits, can establish a sense of trust among people. As we now begin to treat cultural beliefs, we must keep in mind that enhanced cultural traditions, customs, and attitudes of a group of people can signify the establishment of trust among people. Within the domain of cultural beliefs, we now define and analyze principles of beliefs as truthfulness, consistency, responsibility, good faith, and continency.

Truthfulness: One of the most important issues in all cultures is the distinction between truthfulness and falseness of an idea, a decision, an action, or an operation. Philosophers capture this distinction in terms of reasoning. Scientists capture this distinction on the basis of validated pragmatic experiences. Nevertheless, both philosophers and scientists agree on two principles to be used for finding the truth: (1) one distinction is when our reasoning is based on correct data or observable experiences. 2) the other distinction is when our reasoning and experiences themselves are faulty. With such distinctions, both the real order of existing things and the reasoning order of formal deductive judgments by intellect are called moral order. This means that sometimes, all our statements are true, but our reasoning is incorrect or *vice versa* -- all our statements may be false, but the reasoning is correct. For example, in the field of business, we may state that our business made a profit by looking at the corporation's financial data such Return on Investment (ROI), Return on Assets (ROA), Return on Equity (ROE), and Financial Leverage (FL). This statement can be true, if investors gain an appropriate earning per share (EPS). This statement can be false, if investors have not received any EPS and/or lost their principal assets. In such a case, a firm made profit but because of heavy inflationary rate, taxation, intensive competition, very high management salary and stock options, and/or financial book cooking, shareholders did not make any interest on their investments. Is it moral in this case for a CEO to announce that his/her corporation made profit? The truthful answer relies on the positive or negative outcomes of an EPS.

Dewey (1929: 260) defined truth as a reflective thinking that is a satisfactory method of problem solving. One is guided to a solution by both past experience and creative ideas. Truth can thereby transform an obscure condition into a situation that is clear, coherent, settled, and harmonious. The pragmatic criterion of truth is directly related to the outcomes of the reflective process of an operation (e.g., EPS). Those ideas that are successful in resolving problematic situations are true, whereas those that do not lead to satisfactory adjustments are false. Therefore, truthfulness is based on a holistic picture and judgment of an idea or an operation from the beginning to the end result. Those managers who rely on the whole process and conclusions of an organization are Amoral@ people, and those that portray the positive portion of an operation and hide the negative side of the outcomes are amoral.

Consistency: *Consistency* is defined as an informational cue indicating the truthful frequency of an idea, operation, or a behavior over time. Also, consistency, in a moral sense, is the characteristic of following the same doctrine, value or principle, given the same circumstances, at all times. Within the domain of consistency, there should be two forms of truthful cues:

- *Distinction* refers to the degree to which an individual behaves, or a firm operates the same way in other situations, places, and times.
- *Consensus* refers to the extent to which other people in the same situation, place, and time behave or operate the same way.

We judge our and other's behavior on the basis of holistic correlated and integrated experiences not in a short period of time, but in a long one. We form our cultural beliefs based on whether these cues are true or false. As an example of analyzing a corporation's cultural value system, supposed you have received several complaints from customers regarding one of your products' safeties. You have not received complaints about other products. Upon reviewing that specific product, you note that engineers previously indicated a defect on the same product, but you have ignored it (e.g., Ford Company's products: Ford Pinto and

Ford Explorer). In this case, you would most likely conclude that the complaints must stem from unethical and immoral behavior of the Ford's company's culture. Consequently, some customers have lost their trust in the Ford Explorer model to such an extent that Ford Company had to stop manufacturing that model.

Responsibility: *Responsibility* is defined as an obligation or duty to do something with the expectation of achieving some expected structured ends. Responsibilities and duties are closely related to each other. We have a duty to fulfill our responsibilities, and we are obligated to fulfill our duties. Yet responsibilities and duties are not the same. Responsibility is a formal mandate to be committed to perform those duties that a person or an institution is supposed to do. Duties are those binding moral obligations that an individual or institutions are morally and ethically committed to fulfill. Duties refer to what one feels bound to do. The feeling of personal responsibility is a prerequisite for moral duties. Moral responsibilities should be done knowingly and willingly. Moral responsibilities are viewed as acceptance of causal duties. This means that if an individual is responsible to do something, he/she is entitled to do it and he/she does it because it is their duty.

There are two attributes related to responsibility: (1) knowingly and (2) willingly. Instead of saying that an individual has the duty to do it knowingly and willingly, we may say intentionally. The important point is that within the context of responsibility there is a self-voluntary intention by self-choice not by other's force. Individuals who assume full responsibility for their actions are frequently called responsible people. When such an attribution to be attached to personality of an individual, then other people believe that these people are trustworthy.

Good Faith: What is *good*? and what is *good faith*? are the major questions concerning the moral character of an individual. Are these goods unconditionally and invariably? Philosopher George Edward Moore (1873-1958), (1922: 273) found two different connotations concerning good: (1) how is good to be defined? (2) what things are good? He insisted that we must deal with the former before we address ourselves to the latter. He defined the term of good, as referring to a simple property of things. It is a primitive and irreducible quality. When we say that all moral and ethical not legal actions are directed to some good, we intend to associate the world good with the word end. This means that the term of good refers to a quality that is analogous in some way to our cultural value systems.

The meaning of good, as we use it in morality and ethics, is very broad. It signifies the desirability to reach the means and ends of happiness. We do whatever we do, because of what we desire to be good and what we desire to be good, we have assurance that it is good. Believing in goodness means believing in good faith and attending the course of goodness means having good will. Nevertheless, good faith and good will are two different domains of perceptions.

This means that we may intellectually, intentionally, deliberately, and willingly strive for reaching goodness or sometimes we may emotionally desire to reach goodness but we never do. Nevertheless, in both cases, we have good intention that justifies our good faith. Philosopher, Immanuel Kant (1724-1804), (1898: 1st Sec.: 10) stated that good faith and good will can be good even if they are unable to attain the ends they seek, they would still be good in themselves and have a higher worth than the superficial things gained by immoral actions.

Continency: The term of *continency* means self-restraint against excessive passion, pleasure, and greed. An individual who seeks continency through his/her choice is searching for moral virtues. Conversely, the term *incontinency* means to pursue an excess of passion, pleasure, and greed. This person knows that the excess is wrong, but he/she succumbs to the strong impulse of passion, pleasure, and greed and experiences no repentance. People behave differently in different ages, situations, times, and places. People's behavior is not static; it is dynamic. Such a dynamic phenomenon falls between two extremes of virtues and vices. In a moral sense, the magnitude between *virtue* and *vice* is the subject of moral life, because virtue and vice are the extremes of goodness and badness. *Virtue* is considered the foundation of excellence and it is an extreme of perfect. *Vice* is considered the foundation of corruption and self-destruction and it is an extreme of imperfectness. Nevertheless, we are living and working in a highly sophisticated technological era in which ethical dilemmas have increased. A truth phone, currently on the market, a monitor telephone conversations and detects sub-audible microtremors associated with stress and lying. Video cameras are hidden in pencil sharpeners. Wristwatch cameras offer ever-increasing detection of unethical behavior. A laser device can hear conversations a half mile away by measuring sound vibrations in an office window (Dutka, 1999: 18). Radio waves can be used to read the images on a computer monitor several blocks away by a helicopter or a small single engine airplane, using trespassing in your home space. In Tampa, Florida, all public places are equipped with cameras to control people's behavior and detect criminals on the streets. All these technological devices often address legal rather than ethical issues. The major ethical issue is penetration of human rights by artificial intelligence to reduce liberty and increase controlling systems to limit people's freedom.

Those individuals who desire to have a moral life attempt to attend the virtuous courses of perfection (perfectionists). Conversely, those people who desire to respond to their excessive passion, pleasure, and greed attend the worst kind of courses of viciousness -- destructionists.

Passion is defined as any kind of instant feeling or vehement emotion to fulfill sensational desires (e.g., she broke into a passion of joys). *Pleasure* is defined as the state of feeling pleased. It is the state of enjoyment derived from an individual's gratification. *Greed* is excessive desire to acquire or possess more than reasonable and permissible things; specifically reprehensible acquisitiveness and insatiable desire for wealth. Most people's life styles are between virtuousness and viciousness. Those that lean more toward virtuousness have a tendency toward *continence*. They possess a high rate of self-restrain. Conversely, those people whose desires are conquered by viciousness possess a rate of incontinence.

It is necessary, therefore, to find out the general cultural attitudes of a nation or a group of people in relation to virtues and vices. Since most people are continent rather than virtuous, and incontinent rather than vicious, we need to elaborate on these characteristics. Before analyzing the terms of continence and incontinence, we need to identify specific moral and immoral attributions in relationship with the two through describing happiness and pleasure.

Happiness and pleasure are viewed as two extreme states of human life. Happiness shapes the whole moral character in congruence with continence, while pleasure only responses to the parts of satisfactory desires. Since pleasure is short-lived, it may be intense, but never lasts. We strive to achieve happiness, because we believe in attaining something that will be continual and ever lasting not transitory and intermittent. Specifically, happiness resists vehement passion in relation to the sense of pleasure. Since happiness is the finality of moral excellence, in practice, continence as the mean of happiness leads us to virtue. However, the finality of continence is moral *temperance*. Therefore, it is necessary first to achieve the attitude of temperance, and then attain continency. In a general term, temperance is the starting point of moral life through continence. Conversely, pleasure is the most obvious characteristic of human sensuality that immediately attracts us.

Because pleasure is an inherent part of our nature, moral convictions raise a question: what do we do to be moral in relationship with pleasure? Pleasure in a moral sense can be divided into two courses of enjoyments: (1) necessary enjoyments, and (2) desirable enjoyments. Necessary enjoyments provide us with a sense of survival. It is a logical term that implies our inner consistency of existence. But desirable enjoyments can provide us with excessive or overwhelmingly enjoyments. Within the domain of such enjoyments, a sense of restraint can safeguard us against self-destruction and corruption.

BUILDING TRUST IN AN ORGANIZATION

The moral character and the institutions of ethics concerning trust affect stakeholders of a business. From the standpoint of employee-employer relationships, these principles affect a number of factors in an organization is daily operation and in an employee's daily life. The ruling theory of trust within a corporation distinguishes a number of moral and ethical factors concerning mutual respect and loyalty among employees and an employer, or among shareowners and executive officers. The justification for such a mutual loyalty and respect lies partly in a view of the rights of ownership to control the process of investment between the decision-making processes by top management as rights of ownership and as agents of shareholders on the one hand, and other stakeholders' duties of loyalty and obedience on the other hand. The mechanisms for establishing reciprocal trust between an employer and employees vary as widely as do the potential issues. These mechanisms vary both in terms of issues concerning the inside and outside of a corporation and in terms of actual power-sharing positions. For instance, some perceive employees as commodities to be bought and sold by employers with a specific pricing system range in order to carry specific immoral and unethical operations in the marketplace. If employees are caught through legal auditing systems, then employers back off and ignore their rights or loyalty. Such mechanisms are essentially external to the particular international business operations in which bribery and/or payola are involved. Participation of employees in bribery and payola processes on one hand manifests loyalty of employees to employers, and disloyalty and disrespect for employees to their individual integrity and dignity.

As previously stated, the value of an organization is based on the trust that stakeholders have established among themselves. Stakeholders are loners or people who want to be recognized for their motives. Producers strive to establish confidence in consumers for the effectiveness of their products or services. Consumers strive to establish confidence in producers to motivate them to continue their services for their effective consumption. Shareholders strive for effective investments to serve their financial interests as well as meet the interest of consumers. Nevertheless, trust is a reciprocal phenomenon between two parties. The following ways can help you to build trust in an organization:

- Demonstrate that you have self-integrity, self-confidence, and self-reliance. Demonstrate that you are striving to preserve the rights of others as well as your own.
- Demonstrate that you are conscientiously striving for honesty and truth.
- Demonstrate that your judgment is free of prejudice and discrimination against people, institutions, and countries.
- Demonstrate that your consistency in applying moral values and ethical principles in guiding your decision-making processes is your truthful conviction for justice.
- Demonstrate that you strive to maintain consumer confidence.
- Demonstrate that certain forms of virtuous beliefs and valuable norms in conducting your business are the main cause of your organizational mission.
- Demonstrate that the dual implications of producer's interest and consumer's benefit are based on conscientious reasoning for the maintenance and continuity of mutual respect.
- Demonstrate that self-disciplinary rules, principles, ideals, virtues, and values are the main convictions of your organization in order to serve its stakeholders.
- Demonstrate that certain learned and inherent ways of feeling that accompany your organizational's ideals, beliefs, and rules should help you act in accordance to your self-conscious conviction.

- Demonstrate that certain sanctions of motivation that you express in your verbal communication, namely, praising, should not be used as blaming others.

WHAT ARE RIGHTS?

What are *rights*? and what rights *do* people have? are the broad topics of morality, ethics, and law. Broadly defined, a *right* is an individual's attachment to, affiliation with, entitlement to, and privileged of having possession of something. Also rights legitimate entitlements that invoke corresponding duties on the part of others. It is an entitlement to act or have others act in a certain way. If something is mine, I have the right to protect it, to keep it, to sell it, to use it, and, in rare cases, to abandon it. Rights can be defined in terms of moral, ethical, and legal duties either by an individual or by groups. The question of rights can, therefore, be put in terms of natural as well as societal entitlements.

Naturally, human beings are entitled to intellect, memory, communication, innovation, liberty, and socialization. This means that all human beings should have the right to think critically, to remember past experiences, and have the right to express them without fear. They have the right to liberty and free association with others and to share their innovative ideas and opinions with others without any limitation. Since human beings are purposive agents, they must be entitled by natural rights to liberty. Also, since freedom and liberty are the necessary conditions for purposive action, then they should strive for maintaining and enhancing freedom and liberty. But what is liberty? Is it a natural right of entitlement to a maximum or minimum standard of liberty? Both libertarian and fatalism philosophies believe that freedom and liberty depend on the scarcity of resources.

Human beings through their natural rights are individuals of profound self-esteem. They are entitled to the competence of their own mind to deal with the problems of existence. They look at the natural habitat and at the world of humanity, wondering:

- What are their natural individual rights?
- What are their pluralistic societal rights?
- What ought to be done to respect them?
- How can these rights be maintained or preserved?

Nevertheless, the most important natural rights for human beings is the assurance of continuity of their species through natural selection of generations to come. On the other hand, pluralistic societal rights are not like natural inherent rights. People do not wait to be given or wait for somebody to give them a chance to be entitled to these conventional, legal, and contractual rights. They make and take their own rights. Pluralistic societal rights are not like natural rights. People set them not by nature. Pluralistic societal rights are not set by chances. They are set by choices. People calculate how to safeguard them against those who attempt to bypass or deny them.

Positive and Negative Rights

As indicated above, entitlements to, attachment to, affiliated with, possession of, and privileged with bestowed rights can be either from natural norms and principles that specify all human beings are permitted or empowered to do something or are entitled to have something done for them (e.g., human rights). Natural rights primarily have been established in a universal form by precise ordering of just causes for the existence. Human beings do not make them. Human beings try to discover them. But human beings through specific institutionalization of reasoning make moral, civil, property, and criminal rights. Natural rights are not limited to a particular jurisdiction. Also, a natural right can be derived either from a cultural value system within or beyond a political arena (e.g., religious rights or denominations) or from a specific ideological doctrine (e.g., conservative or libertarian belief, or leftist and rightist). Entitlements can also be derived from a system of religious faith independent of any cultural value system or from a particular legal denominated system. Nevertheless, all rights are attributed to some intentions and actions. For example, legal rights are limited to the particular jurisdiction within which the legal system is in force. The legal entitlements permit or empower a person to act in a specific way or require others to act in certain ways toward that person (Velasquez, 1992: 59).

Rights inherently have double faces: positive and negative. Also, rights could be perceived as specific attributive entitlements either to positive or negative duties. Positive rights reflect the vital entitlements of all human beings in receiving certain benefits. For example, the right to be educated, to be diagnosed and treated, to have equal employment opportunity, to have equitable pays or wages and so on are positive rights. Positive rights are rights to obtain privileged opportunities and/or certain kinds of equal treatments. Negative rights are those entitlements to be free to hold and practice religious beliefs, professional privileges, political ideologies, and cultural customs and traditions without outside interference. Negative rights protect human dignity and integrity without enforcement by governments, or radical and partisan groups. Negative rights reflect the vital entitlements that all human beings have in being free from outside interference such as freedom of speech, assembly, religion, and so on.

Correlated with these rights are duties that indicate all human beings should not interfere with others' pursuit of happiness. There are two philosophical schools in relationships of human beings to God, to themselves, to other human beings, and to nature. In sum, there are two schools of philosophies concerning positive and negative rights: (1) *libertarianism,* and (2) *fatalism.*

Libertarian Philosophy of Rights: *Libertarian* philosophy of rights emphasizes all rights as the finality of human nature. Within this philosophical ideology, libertarians believe that all human beings are the architectures of their own destiny. These rights provide them with autonomy in their free will to pursue their survival objectives. No other forces have any right to interfere in their personal destiny and make any decision on behalf of them, because human beings are free to act according to their will, purposes, and faiths. However, within this idealistic ideology, there are inclusive negative exceptional rights for children, elderly, sick, and insane people. This right needs to be respected by each individual, other people, and as well as the institutions of society.

Moral rights limit the validity of appeals to social benefits and to the numbers of people. If a person has a right to do something, then it is not the right of others to do it, even though a large number of people might gain much m

Fatalism Philosophy of Rights: *Fatalism* is a doctrine that people believe in destiny. They believe all events are subject to fate or inevitable pre-determination by God. They accept all things and events as they are. This type of moral doctrine is based on a belief that all things that are existed are subject to the universal order for their own sake with specific universal purposes. They are bound to consider as the chief quality in everything that that is most useful to them. Furthermore, they believe that they are bound to form abstract notions for explanation of the nature of things, such as goodness, badness, order, confusion, beauty, and deformity. Those who understand the mystery for the causes of existence firmly believe that there is an eternal cause or order in all things. These mysteries will never be revealed to mankind.

Foundational Arguments For Rights

The notion of rights has received a great deal of attention in civilized societies. Various causes of rights have appeared to be pressed for individuals and groups, such as human rights, civil rights, women's rights, consumer rights, patients' rights, students' rights, academicians' rights, investors' rights, the right to live, the right to die, and the rights of unborn children are examples. Where do these rights come from and what gives rise to the above kinds of rights? These are the main issues in this section of our deliberation.

Throughout history, people established new forms of cultural, social, political, and economic power in order to maintain their own identity. Since all of us are human beings, therefore we are living in the state of humanity. Accordingly, there is a claim that all human beings are subject to the same rights. Some advocates believe that just as God created laws of nature that transcend different cultures and religions, so God created laws of morality and ethics which are available to human reasoning.   Therefore, each society functions according to priorities for its social class-stratification. This means the rights of individuals is based on who you know, but not on what do you know C connections. One important difference between the societies of the world according to Max Weber (1946) is the recognition of the rights of individuals and groups in relationships to their wealth, power, and prestige. First, the rights of individuals are stemmed from one another by the extent to which they have accumulated economic resources, or in other words, their wealth. Second, the rights of individuals rooted in acquisition of power, which Weber defined as the ability to exert it to achieve one's own goals and objectives even against the rights and wills of others. The right to have power can be manipulated and be used at will. Power may be evil. This is expressed in Lord Acton's celebrated dictum that: "Power tends to corrupt and absolute power corrupts absolutely" (Steiner and Steiner, 1994: 47). Third, the rights of individuals are formulated according to their prestige or reputation, which Weber defines as the social esteem, respect, or admiration that a society confers on people. Accordingly, to one degree or another, all people are socially differentiated on the basis of assuming criteria for profession, education, ideology, age, sex, and possession of political and money power. In addition, according to Morton Fried (1967), societies are classified according to their rights into three types:

- Egalitarian societies who have few or no groups that have greatest access to the greatest volume of wealth, power, or prestige.
- Rank societies who have unequal access to prestige or status but not unequal access to wealth or power. In rank societies, there are a fixed number of high-status societal positions, which only certain individuals because of their skills, wisdom, industriousness, or family linked to power or other personal traits have access to those rights.
- Stratified societies are characterized by considerable inequality in all forms of societal rights; wealth, power, and prestige. As a general rule, the greater the role specialization, the more complex the justice system of stratification.

Social scientists, generally, recognize two different types of stratified societies in regard of rights: (1) *class*, and (2) *caste*. In *class* systems, a certain amount of status mobility of both upward and downward variables exists (i.e., American culture). In contrast, societies based on *caste* rank the entitlements of rights according to birth. They believe membership in castes is unchangeable. Therefore, in caste systems upward and downward social mobility is virtually nonexistent (i.e., Anglo, Indian, Kuwaitian, and Saudi Arabian cultures; racial supremacy).

All these rights are tightly correlated with duties. A person, a group, and a nation can only exercise their rights to something if sufficient justifications exist. For clarity of this subject matter, it is sufficient to analyze the foundational arguments concerning the rights. In this section, we will divide our arguments into two sections: (1) the international human rights, and (2) the National bill of rights.

THE INTERNATIONAL ANALYSIS OF HUMAN RIGHTS

The connection between natural rights and duties is that, generally speaking, if an individual has a right to live, then others have a correlated duty to act in certain ways to respect that right. In addition to natural rights, we also have moral and ethical rights; human rights. Human rights are universal. Everyone has natural rights, just by virtue of being human, not because they live within the boundary of a certain sociocultural or political-legal system. If the natural right to life is a human right, then everyone, everywhere at all times, has the right to survive. Therefore, human rights are equal rights. Also, human rights are not transferable either by giving or lending them to other people. That is what is meant when human rights such as life, liberty, and the pursuit of happiness are viewed as human rights; nobody should deny it.

Human rights are based on the natural duties, not in the sense that they can be derived from a study of human nature but in the sense that they do not depend on ideological beliefs of religious, racial and/or political-legal systems. A right to self-preservation is an example of one such right. Since happiness is the virtuous finality of human dignity, rights are the valuable finality of humanity. All human beings are entitled to natural rights regardless of their pluralistic and/or collectivistic political or social institutions. A right to self-preservation is an example of one such right. As previously indicated, an individual can only exercise a right to something, if they can prove that they are entitled to the existence of sufficient justifications, that is, that a right has overriding status.

Table 8.2: United Nations Universal Declaration of Human Rights

UNITED NATIONS UNIVERSAL DECLARATION OF HUMAN RIGHTS
• The right to own property alone as well as in association with others • The right to work, to free choice of employment, to just and favorable conditions of work, and to protection against unemployment. • The right to just and favorable remuneration ensuring for the worker and his family an existence worthy of human dignity. • The right to form and join trade unions. • The right to rest and leisure, including reasonable limitation of working hours and periodic holidays with pay
Source: R. A Buchholz and S. B. Rosenthal, *Business Ethics: The Pragmatic Path Beyond Principles to Process*. New York: McGraw-Hill Book Company (1998), 30.

Table 8.3: Protections Guaranteed By the Bill of Rights

PROTECTIONS GUARANTEED BY THE BILL OF RIGHTS

First Amendment: Guarantees the freedom of religion, speech, and press and the rights to assemble peaceably and to petition the government.

Second Amendment: Guarantees the right to keep and bear arms.

Third Amendment: Prohibits, in peacetime, the lodging of soldiers in any house without the owner's consent.

Fourth Amendment: Prohibits unreasonable searches and seizures of persons or property.

Fifth Amendment: Guarantees the rights to indictment by grand jury, to due process of law, and to fair payment by grand jury, to due process of law, and to fair payment when private property is taken for public use, prohibits compulsory self-incrimination and double jeopardy (trial for the same crime twice if the first trial ends in acquittal or conviction).

Sixth Amendment: Guarantees the accused in a criminal case the right to a speedy and public trial by an impartial jury and with counsel. The accused has the right to cross-examine witnesses against him or her and to solicit testimony from witnesses in his or her favor.

Seventh Amendment: Guarantees the right to a trial by jury in a civil case involving at least twenty dollars.*

Eight Amendment: Prohibits excessive bail and fines, as well as cruel and unusual punishment.

Ninth Amendment: Establishes that people have rights in addition to those specified in the Constitution.

Tenth Amendment: Establishes that those powers neither delegated to the federal government nor denied to the states are reserved for the states.

* Twenty dollars was forty day's pay for the average person when the Bill of Rights was written.

THE CONSUMER BILL OF RIGHTS

In 1962, President John F. Kennedy delivered a special message to Congress calling for a broad range of legislative and administrative action to guarantee the rights of consumers. In addition, President Kennedy enunciated what has since come to be called the Consumer Bill of Rights (see Table 8.4).

Table 8.4: Consumer Bill of Rights

CONSUMER BILL OF RIGHTS
• The Right to Safety: The consumer has right to be protected from dangerous products and/or services that might cause injury or illness and from the thoughtless actions of other consumers. • The Right to a Choice: The consumer has the right to be able to select products from a range of alternatives offered by competing firms. • The Right to Know: The consumer must have access to readily available, relevant, and accurate information to use in making purchase decisions. • The Right to Be Heard: The consumer must be able to find someone who will respond to legitimate complaints about abuses taking place in the market and products that do not meet expectations. • The Right to Recourse and Redress: The consumer has a right to expect full compensation for injuries or damages suffered as a result of unsafe products or abuses in the marketplace. • The Right to Full Value: The consumer has a right to expect a product to perform as advertised and meet expectations that were created so that full value is received for the money spent. • The Right to Education: The consumer must have access to educational programs that help them understand and use the information available in the marketplace to make rational purchase decisions. • The Right to Representation and Participation: The consumer interests must be represented on policy-making bodies that deal with issues related to the marketplace.
Source: R. A. Buchholz and S. B. Rosenthal, *Business Ethics: The Pragmatic Path Beyond Principles to Process.* Upper Saddle River, NJ: Prentice Hal, (1998), 297.

Kennedy's Consumer Bill of Rights was a political, not a legal mandate, because it did not have the force of law. President John F. Kennedy first listed four rights:

- The right to safety
- The right to a choice
- The right to know
- The right to be heard

These rights were latter on supported by Presidents Linden B. Johnson and Richard Nixon. They added to the above rights four more rights.

Donadlson (1989: 81) considered a pioneer in the field of international ethics. He has expressed his own list of fundamental international rights (see Table 8.5).

The Foundation of Property Rights

Within the contextual boundaries of business ethics, rights may be moral and ethical as well as legal. The moral rights are those entitlements in which all characteristics of the world of humanity are shared by all people regardless of their genders, colors, ethnicities, races, religious, political, cultural, social, and economical characteristics (e.g., goodness, truthfulness, justness, fairness, worthiness, and beauties). Moral rights are important and justifiable claims or entitlements. Moral rights of either kind are tightly correlated with conscientious duties.

Table 8.5: Donaldson's Fundamental International Rights

DONALDSON'S FUNDAMENTAL INTERNATIONAL RIGHTS
• The right to freedom of physical movement. • The right to ownership of property. • The right to freedom from torture. • The right to a fair trial. • The right to nondiscriminatory treatment. • The right to physical security. • The right to freedom of speech and association. • The right to minimal education. • The right to political participation. • The right to sustenance.

Source: T Donaldson *The Ethics of International Business* New York: Oxford University Press, (1989), 81

Legal rights can be put in terms of the entitlements to intellectual properties or to material things. Intellectual property rights are similar to liberty rights, copyrights, shop rights, freelancers' rights, and patent rights. Material property rights are similar to ownership of land, buildings, business outlets, investments, and the like. In both intellectual and material entitlements, the following question can be raised in terms of ethical as well as legal production and usage endeavors: Who owns nature and what are the legal and ethical attributive rights attached to these ownerships?

John Locke (1632-1704), the British philosopher, whose theory influenced *Christian capitalism*, argued that the Christian capitalism ideology has two gospels, the Bible, and the capitalistic state (Meiklejohn: 1942: 57). There are several issues concerning natural rights and state rights. According to Meiklejohn (1942: 83), the trouble is that people confuse conscience with prudence. People are notoriously deceiving themselves and others regarding their own and other's rights. He states that individuals who wish to be religious on all days of the week can accept the urges of prudence as the voice of conscience. Another way of living in the Christian-capitalism society is to serve conscience and God on Sundays and be a rugged individualist on other weekdays on the grounds that it is not wrong to do what the state does not forbid.

Locke (1924) held that God created the universe and created mankind. When God created human beings, He endowed them with eternal, inalienable rights to such things as freedom, equality, and humanity. God had authority over conscience and moral law. But God *did not create the state*. Before people created the state, people were living in a *state of nature* in which they were not fully able to enjoy the rights God had bestowed upon them. This was because the rights of human beings were violated by the selfish actions of other mighty human beings. Violations and cruelties of people to each other caused people to organize themselves into statehood and consequently initiated the *social contract*.

The social contract is dictated by people's moral prudence and maintained by legal enforcement. Accordingly, human beings became subject to two types of rights: 1) conscience and 2) prudence. Through the moral contract, the citizens of a state become responsible to God in matters of conscience, but in matters of prudence, they found it wise to keep an armed truce with other states, respecting their contractual rights so that they could respect their own (Weber, 1960: 29).

According to political ideologies, the notion of *state capitalism* in each nation possesses its own characteristics. These characteristics establish the foundations of rights for individuals and groups. For example, the American economy is dominated by a relative handful of large corporations and their domestic retail stores. These corporations are linked in a variety of ways to each other in order to create the notion of *corporate America*. The American statehood capitalism ideology has stemmed from the *Christian capitalism*. This religious and econo-political ideology has created two types of capitalism: (1) people's capitalism and (2) family capitalism.

People Capitalism: The ideological foundation of people's capitalism has stemmed from constitutional rights. Within such a pluralistic society no one group has overwhelming power over all others and each may have direct or indirect impact on others. In people capitalism power is diffused, because decentralization of power makes less tyranny and the exploitation of a few people or groups by others less possible. American capitalism is permeated by the competitive value of quality that encourages pluralism.

The Constitution encourages pluralism in different ways. It guarantees of rights to protect one's liberty and freedom for individuals to pursue their interests. In addition, the Constitution diffuses political power through several independent branches of governmental power. If individuals and groups influence one branch of government, the other branches can diffuse it. The democratic representation of people's power has established its own cultural value systems through different groups. These group representatives are political parties, governmental agencies and bureaucrats, social interest groups and lobbyists, managers and executives, scientists and technologists as experts and technocrats, working class people as labor unions, and auditors and researchers as think-tank consultants. The people's capitalist power imposes immediate close boundaries on the discretionary exercise of business power, because their power will be restricted and shared with the family capitalists.

Family Capitalism: Most sectors of American economy are dominated by relatively small groups of Family Capitalists. These groups include private Federal Reserve System, private corporations, commercial banks, investment banks, law firms, family offices, boards of governance, holding companies, medical and pharmaceutical companies, foundations, charitable organizations, and political donations.

Having access to resources from the state of nature needs to be ruled by strength. Nevertheless, without a state, no property can be held on legal grounds. In a state of nature there is no justice, because there is no legal law except the moral law. However, in the state of nature, there is an ethical shared law that is sustained by the general good will. Then the question is: By what right do certain people possess the exclusive claims to natural resources simply because they were fortunate enough to have been born in the country where the resources existed? Do some people have a right to control resources and monopolize them? Or are the natural resources of the world, such as crude oil, are for the benefit of all people not just for the lucky few? The answer requires not only legal reasoning but also moral reasoning and arguments. The main issues concerning resources rights are as followings:

- Scarcity of resources
- Availability of scientific potential and technological capabilities

- Accessibility to material resources
- Durability of resources
- Efficacy of resources to meet necessary needs
- Flexibility of the state laws
- Suitability of resources for production systems
- Profitability on economical values of resources
- Cost-benefit analysis of the alternative resources
- Consistency in continuity of availability of resources

WHAT ARE DUTIES?

It is clear that all rights establish some sorts of duties. Rights would be of little value as an ordering principle of human acts without duties. Let us investigate what is meant by duties in the moral, ethical, and legal senses. Duties are viewed as notions of completeness. Oral and/or written entitlements to any type of rights for an individual establish specific bases for obligatory binding duties for that individual and others in order to put it in practice. When we speak of a duty, we mean an action that we are obligated to undertake or to refrain from regardless of whether we find it in our interest to do so or not. Duty is a constraint on the scope of permissible actions, but not all constraints are duties.

Moral duties are distinct from legal duties, and the necessary conditions of each are distinct too. A necessary condition of the validity of duties is the validity of the procedure by which the moral duty imposing them is enacted to those duties. Duties, to begin with, apply directly only to actions. To make the issue clear, we must say that what is meant is a duty that we would have to discharge by doing what results are found in our rights. Duties are the result of four types of necessities.

The Necessity of the Obligatory Act in Relation to the Necessity of Causes: This duty needs to be done top reserve the rights of self and/or others. Since moral duties are based upon conscientious cognitive virtues, they are bound with the intellectual will in the sense that there is a necessary relation between causes and affects. Such a duty will not destroy the liberty for acting or not acting. It demonstrates a necessity for the existence of good or just causes. We are speaking here primarily of moral obligations in relation to natural rights C existence. Since we have defined morality as an individual's desire toward goodness, then others cannot impose morality or moral obligations on us. We are the only ones who can recognize such a necessity to be imposed on ourselves. If we desire to exist and survive, then we need to understand the real causes for being.

For example, in the field of business, it is understood that in order to exist and survive, we need to establish an order between producers and consumers and/or among competitors. This order should be based on appropriate rational obligatory causes. In this case, the causes of necessity are found in human species and among them. Therefore, the moral duties at their highest general level state that a cause needs to be rational and the related courses of actions to that cause must be morally good not vicious. Consequently, the moral duties spell out the boundary of obligations, but do not spell out the contents of those duties. Therefore, such reasoning is called a *formalistic moral approach*. In a formalistic moral obligation, Hegel's dialectic reasoning as *thesis* and *antithesis* are combined to form a *synthesis,* used to understand causes, processes, and effects of duties.

The Necessity of the Act in Relation to the Necessity of the Means: This duty must be done as necessarily leading to the achievement of common good. This obligation applies in an analogous manner to humanity. With respect to human rights, asking usually states the question of ethical obligation whether human rights bind us with our conscience. In answering this question, we must recognize that human rights are justified through the doctrine of humanity. The doctrine of humanity's finality is relied on to insure the validity of reasoning in defending a logical statement or an action for the goodness of humanity. It is a feature of deductive discourse in which the relation between premises and conclusions is such that if the premises are true (thesis), then the content of pros and cons (antithesis) is rationalized, and consequently the conclusive results (synthesis) could not be false. It should be true. Since the means of humanity is good, the ends, therefore, should be good too.

Sometimes parts of law are not based on moral or ethical law; they are based on *categorical imperatives*. Categorical imperatives provide us with choices to follow or not, depending on whether we wish to attend the moral and ethical philosophy of humanity and to achieve it or not. Kant provides us with three formulations of Categorical Imperative:

- For a necessary action to be moral, it must be amenable to being made consistently universal.
- It must respect rational beings as ends in themselves.
- It must form and respect the autonomy of rational beings.

Are these possible in humanity? Are these possible in all socio-cultural, psychosocial, and econo-political arguments? By analyzing the following example are find the answer is no. In the field of business, sellers, buyers, and traders need to make their deals on the basis of their necessities. This statement is universal. Sellers, buyers, and traders need to have autonomy in production and conditions of sales within the domain of their legal binding rights. This will be true according to the second principle. The problem arises from the third principle between parties, because within international market, sellers, buyers, and traders may not respect each other. Then many transactions would not be morally or ethically valid according to this doctrine. In E-commerce, selling sexual images through the Internet is legal, but considered unethical in some societies. The universal moral code in humanity binds us unconditionally to our duties by not providing pornographic ads or images through the Internet.

The Necessity of the Act in Relation to the Necessity of the Ends: In responding to this statement specifically, we must recall that the notion of humanity is not the final cause of civil law in all societies. Civil law is either just or unjust. It depends on political ideologies and fiduciary philosophies. If we assume that the final end of law is happiness for all human beings and it is just, then it needs to have the power of binding with conscience. This duty must be done as necessary leading to the given ends; the power derived from natural law, through natural law, and to the eternal law. Then the necessity of the act in relation to the necessity of ends must aim at the common good of humanity.

Institutionalization of Duties

One common way to institutionalize moral, ethical, and legal concepts of duties is to define those obligatory considerations and actions which control peoples' conduct is to divide the duties into four categories: (1) the required, (2) the permissible, (3) the forbidden, and (4) the contractual. These widely accepted fourfold classification is used in different societies differently.

The Required Duties: The *required* actions are duties, and these are the only actions that have moral merit. The required actions must be obeyed under penalty of punishment in a legal term, or under condemnation in an ethical term, or under blaming in a moral sense. The act in question must be one that an agent may intentionally choose to do it regardless of the merit of its moral, ethical, and legal senses.

The Permissible Duties: The *permissible* actions are merely all-right duties in which an individual in certain conditions and situations is obligated to do. The permissible actions are associated with risk. Cairncross (1991: 56) indicates:

Familiar risks are less frightening than the unfamiliar; visible risks less scary than the invisible sort. People clearly feel more frightened by the remote risk of a large catastrophe than by the greater risk of an equivalent number of deaths spread out over a long period.

The Formidable Duties: The *forbidden* actions are those wrong actions that an individual is obligated to avoid. The forbidden actions must be obeyed under penalty of sin, punishment, condemnation, and blame. This means that those who wish to lead not simply morally adequate, but morally perfect lives, need to avoid forbidden actions such as stealing, embezzlement, perjury, corruption, fraud, cheating, etc.

Contractual Duties: The *contractual* duties justify obligations by consent to the rule imposing duty on the part of the agent to whom it applies. The point of contractual justification of duty is to address the problems that arise from justifications of a duty by appealing to the aggregated benefits of complying with them. The contractual duty denies the legitimacy of duties that require the sacrifice of one person simply for the good of others.

Moral duties do not presuppose the validity of any legal procedure. An agent might find that a legal duty contradicts a moral duty, unless conformity with moral duty is among the criteria of legitimacy of the legal enactments. A legally enforceable contract requires three elements:

- An offer: A party that has indicated to another party a desire to enter into an agreement under specific committed terms has made an offer
- Acceptance of the offer: When the other party has stated a willingness to accept the proposed transaction under the same terms, there is an acceptance of the offer.
- Consideration of offer: Consideration is a legal mandatory term of art that refers to anything of value that the parties exchange as a result of rights and duties of the agreement. To say that one has an actual duty to do a certain thing is to suppose that he/she possesses an available option to do it. It must be something that a person is capable of doing and there must not be special circumstances that prevent him/her from exercising that capacity.

For further analysis of this subject matter, we will analyze imperfect duties and exceptional excusable conditions in the following pages.

Imperfect Duties and Excusable Conditions

A duty needs to be carried out by a capable and qualified person. In some cases, the exceptional excusable conditions and circumstances may diminish moral obligations. By conditions and circumstances, we mean the singular conditions of human acts to be effective either positively or negatively. A circumstance becomes morally obligatory to the degree that it affects directly the goodness or badness of the action done. These are known as imperfect duties with excusable conditions. Imperfect duties emerge from wishy-washy rights, and excusable conditions arise from impossibility in the nature of performing an action. These conditions provide the reasons for weakening or canceling duties. Imperfect duties and excusable conditions fall into one of the three categories:

- Imperfect duties and excusable conditions may or may not correlate with a right on someone's part to demand its performance. A duty must clearly correspond to a specific right held by a specific person. Also, duties need to correspond to appropriate related rights. A duty to act kindly may not be grounded in anyone's right to your kindness. A duty is a rational mandate to do something. It is not an emotional mandate to be carried out by personal emotional discretion.

- Duty and the exertion of power must be in your control and be possible to be executed. If a person has a duty to perform a job, then the performance of that job must be possible. We cannot be morally, ethically, and legally responsible if we are not entitled fully to specific rights and duties. We are excused from moral responsibilities as De George (1995: 113) states:

If (a) the action in question is an impossible one to perform, (b) we do not have the ability required in the given case, (c) the opportunity for our performing the action is absent, or (d) the circumstances are beyond our control.

For instance, assume you are operating a transportation company and you have signed a contract with a company as to have responsibility for carriage of goods and deliver them to its customers overseas. It is a fact that application of the content of contract puts a commitment to your carriage to do all its duties. At the end of the contract there are some excusable rules and exceptional phrases to be applied to a list of per package or per unit of cargo as limited liability. These excusable liabilities include acts of God, acts of war, acts of public enemies, riots and civil commotions, inherent vice or defect, and insufficiency of packing or missing marks. What about those excusable conditions that you did not include in the contract, but are not in your control such as terrorist actions in the sea? or the crash of a cargo jet due to cumulous clouds? Are you liable on the sea for such terrorist or environmental actions and conditions? To some extent the answer is yes, if your customer has bought a comprehensive insurance. If not, you are not responsible.

- Duties are excusable if you have lack of knowledge. Lack of knowledge is known as ignorance. Ignorance can make an action involuntary. The broad meaning of ignorance is equated with non-knowing of any kind. For instance, one often says: "I would not have done it in that way, if I knew better at that time." As a responsible agent, you acted out of ignorance; it seems evident enough that ignorance can cause acts to be involuntary. In addition, ignorance in the moral context is the lack of knowledge about practical affairs, not speculative knowledge. With respect to knowledge, there are two excusable moral conditions: (1) *excusable ignorance*, and (2) *invincible ignorance*.

Excusable Ignorance: Excusable ignorance makes a responsible person free of duties. In a moral sense, it is because of knowledge that we seek ethics, and it is ignorance that we wish to avoid immoral and unethical behavior. If we do not have sufficient knowledge to predict the consequences of an action, then we are ignorant of the future consequences. Our lack of knowledge makes it impossible for us to achieve goodness. In this case, if we do it, then we have the fear of failure not to succeed. This type of obligation is excusable.

Invincible Ignorance: If someone has a duty to perform a certain act, the duty is present regardless of his/her desire to perform. He/she cannot escape the basic moral obligation of finding out how to know. Ignorance in this way can happen to us by negligence. Acts of refusing to know and of being ignorant spring from our will that we do not want to know those things that we are supposed to know. In this case, it is not excusable. But if someone cannot overcome specific situational conditions and it is evident that he/she has exhausted all possible alternatives, then he/she will have no blame, because he/she cannot be expected to know what is impossible to know. This is called invincible ignorance.

Duties are excusable if an act is involuntary. The question we wish to consider in this case, therefore, is the following one. When does a condition make an act involuntary? This question can be answered primarily by diminishing *consequent* ignorance and *antecedent* ignorance. The conditions of consequent ignorance and antecedent ignorance happen when there is a lack of interrelatedness between a state of ignorance and the act of willingness. In such a condition, we are not knowledgeable about the past, and we will not be able to predict the future. If the act of ignorance is a differentiation of the act of willingness, then such ignorance is voluntary. Morally, it is not subject to excusable circumstances. In reality, these types of excuses are simply to deceive others or us. Antecedent ignorance indicates that a state of ignorance prior to an act of willing may cause conditions to be excusable, because knowledge was absent. Such an action may be excusable, if the responsible person willingly tried all possible alternatives, but he/she failed. This act is excusable because that individual made that act involuntary.

Duties are excusable if the required freedom is diminished. In such an excusing condition one has to do with impairment or impediments to our free will and action in question. Distinguishing the diminishing required freedom may be a result of the lack of possible conditions or the lack of control over the direction or the course of controlling systems. In such excusable conditions, we are not able to go through four functional areas of controlling systems: inspection, detection of problem areas, prevention of possible deviated actions, and correction of deviated actions. The lack of control over the above controlling functions may be a result of the existence of intrinsic, extrinsic, and/or coercive excusable conditions.

Seller-Buyer and Traders as a Two-Parties' Duties

A two party business deal denotes exchange of products and/or services either with equitable values of monetary currency or with equitable valuable goods and services within a contextual binding pricing system. A binding contract composes a recognizable statement of an existed agreement, the signature of party against whom enforcement should be sought, and general and/or the specifications of quality and quantity of sold goods should be indicated The primary difficulties concerning duties stem from reciprocal obligations based on binding promises. A secondary problem comes from reference and context concerning quantities and qualities of products and services and monetary currencies. This mutual promissory deal is called a consensual contract between sellers and buyers or traders. In modern days, in addition to buyers and sellers or traders' duties, other promissory consensual mediums appeared as creditors and debtors, and guarantors and insurance companies to facilitate their financial transactions. Furthermore, other principles such as interest, insurance, guaranty, warranty, and liability appeared in the field of business. Under these new moral, ethical, and legal principles, there appeared new obligations such as the mandatory will-duty, and the free-will obligation, creating contractual relations equal to the promises.

Within the contextual obligatory duties between sellers and buyers or traders, there are certain principles that can confirm mutual agreements between parties. These obligatory principles are: (1) consentaneity, (2) reciprocity, (3) bargaining, (4) exchange, (5) transferability, and (6) inspectorships.

Consentaneity: *Consentaneity* denotes voluntary contractual agreements between two points as parties to make a deal on mutual equitable valuable objectives (e.g., the seller's objective is to sell the product or render a service and receive the price, and the buyer's objective is to receive the product or service to be used effectively without any fraud, defection, or deception and to pay the price).

Reciprocity: *Reciprocity* denotes a mutual obligatory movement between co-related contractual points of symmetrical objectives (e.g., the free will to sell and the free will to buy, or the free will for exchange).

Bargaining: *Bargaining* denotes both negotiating qualitative and quantitative valuable movements between co-relative points of symmetrical objectives towards the center by both parties (e.g., to move from the higher demand of a seller for the price, and the lower offer of payment by a buyer to a consensus point of mutual satisfaction).

Exchanging: *Exchange* denotes a *quid pro quo* movement between parties on the promissory contract to take place between the hands of sellers and buyers in the market place.

Transferability: *Transferability* denotes an obligatory changes of the title from a seller to a buyer after reciprocal deceleration of the receipts of the price by the seller and delivery of the product or rendering of the service by the buyer.

Inspectorships: *Inspectorships* denote both parties compare the specification of representations, specifications, conditions, qualities, fitness, warrantee, real liens, pay price, damages or rescission of contract misrepresentation, return arrangement, and replacement or refund.
It should be noted when a contract term is not met, the contract is breached. A breach may render the entire contract to be voided – contract default. Because of the breaching contract, parties may claim monetary damages, expectation damages, and reliance damages.

CHAPTER SUMMARY

Trust is the most pervasive characteristic of human socialization. Trust is, therefore, a foundation for humanity that signifies moral, ethical, and legal ordinations to achieve peace and harmony on the earth. A right is an entitlement to act or have others act in a certain way. Duty is the notion of completeness of moral, ethical, and legal obligations. Duty is a constraint on the scope of permissible actions, but not all constraints are duties. The connection between rights and duties is that generally, if you have a right to do something, then you and/or others have a correlative duty to act in a certain way.

Socialization is cultural learning. Socialization is a process by which individuals learn about cultural values, beliefs, norms, and standards of expected social behavior. Individuals, through their social experiences, learn how to establish relationships with others on the basis of trust, rights, and duties. This process provides individuals with formal and informal information through different cultural orientations. There are two basic processes at work in human socialization: *assimilation* and *accommodation*. In *assimilation*, the new patterns of values are changed to fit the known values. Assimilation modifies new environmental information to fit into what is already known. In *accommodation*, the current known values are changed to fit the new values.

Trust is defined as relying on the solemn confidence of integrity, dignity, and justice in decision-making processes and actions. Trust promotes a feeling of self-confidence, self-reliance, and security among partners, friends, and within a marriage without checking up on daily behavior. *Dignity* is closely related to self-consideration in relation to the manifestation of the good side of self-identity. *Integrity* means soundness of and adherence to a moral character; excellence. *Self-confidence* is defined as having a strong belief in self-trustworthiness. *Self-reliance* is defined as having consistency in expressing intellectual reasoning on the basis of reliable sources and/or scientific methods. *Conscientious-Alertness* is defined as being intellectually reliable, dependable, and being careful in the decision-making processes and actions. *Courage* is defined as a quality of mind that enables an individual to encounter difficulties without fear. *Altruism* could be defined as the principle or practice of unselfishness by providing goodness for the welfare of self and others. Altruism is opposed to egoism. *Nobility* is defined as the state or quality of mind exalted to moral excellence. *Generosity* is defined as readiness of an individual or a group's intention in contributing wealth for the societal good cause of an action or an operation. *Conscience* is defined as the internal cognitive source of awareness to recognize right and wrong concerning one's own intentions and actions. *Truthfulness* is based on a holistic picture and judgment of an idea or an operation from the beginning to the end result. *Consistency* is defined as an informational cue indicating the truthful frequency of an idea, an operation, or a behavior over time. Within the domain of consistency, there should be two forms of truthful cues: *Distinction* refers to the degree to which an individual behaves, or a firm operates the same way in other situations, places, and times. *Consensus* refers to the extent to which other people in the same situation, place, and time behave or operate the same way as we expected. *Responsibility* is defined as an obligation to do something with expectation of achieving some ends. Responsibilities and duties are closely related to each other but are not the same. We have a duty to fulfill our responsibilities, and we are obligated to fulfill our duties. Yet responsibilities and duties are not the same.

People behave differently in different ages, situations, times, and places. People's behavior is not static. It is dynamic. Such a dynamic phenomenon falls between two extreme axes of virtues and vices. In a moral sense, the magnitude between *virtue* and *vice* is the subject of moral life, because virtue and vice are the extremes of goodness and badness. *Virtue* is considered the foundation of excellence and it is an extreme of perfect. *Vice* is considered the foundation of corruption and self-destruction and it is an extreme of imperfectness. *Passion* is defined as any kind of instant feeling or vehement emotion to fulfill sensational desires (e.g., she broke into a passion of joys). *Pleasure* is defined as the state of feeling pleased. It is the state of enjoyment derived from an individual's gratification. *Greed* is excessive desire to acquire or possess more than reasonable and permissible things; specifically reprehensible acquisitiveness and insatiable desire for wealth.

What are *rights*? and what rights *do* people have? are the broad topics of morality, ethics, and law. Broadly defined, a *right* is an individual's attachment to, affiliation with, entitlement to, and privilege of having possession of something. Duties are viewed as notions of completeness. Oral and/or written entitlements to any type of rights for an individual establish bases for obligatory binding duties for that individual and others in order to put it in practice. Moral duties are distinct from legal duties, and the necessary conditions of each are distinct. A necessary condition of the validity of duties is the validity of the procedure by which the moral duty imposing them is enacted.

Imperfect duties and excusable conditions fall into one of the three categories: Imperfect duties and excusable conditions may or may not correlate person free of duties. In a moral sense, it is because of knowledge that we seek ethics, and it is ignorance that we wish to avoid immoral and unethical behavior. *Invincible Ignorance* means if someone cannot overcome the situation and it is evident that he/she has exhausted all possible alternatives, and then he/she will have no blame, because he/she cannot be expected to know what is impossible to know. This is called invincible ignorance.

Within the contextual obligatory duties between sellers and buyers or traders, there are certain principles that can cause mutual agreements between parties. These obligatory principles are: *Consentaneity* which denotes to voluntary agreeing between two points as parties to make a deal on mutual equitable valuable objectives. *Reciprocity* denotes a mutual obligatory movement between co-related contractual points of symmetrical objectives between two parties. *Bargaining* denotes both negotiating qualitative and quantitative valuable movements between co-relative points of symmetrical objectives towards the center by both parties for the sake of mutual agreement. *Exchange* denotes a *quid pro quo* movement between parties on the promissory contract to take place between the hands of sellers and buyers in the market place. *Transferability* denotes an obligatory change in the title from a seller to a buyer after reciprocal deceleration of the receipt of the price by the seller and delivery of the product or rendering services by the buyer. *Inspectorships* denote to both parties to compare the specification of representations, specifications, conditions, qualities, fitness, warrantee, real liens, pay price, damages or rescission of contract misrepresentation, return arrangement, and replacement or refund.

QUESTIONS FOR DISCUSSION

- What is the difference between voluntary and non-voluntary decisions and actions?
- What is an act of compulsion? Explain.
- What is trust and to what extend does trust solve human socialization?
- What do we mean by social and cultural assimilation and accommodation?
- What is the difference between rights and duties? Explain.
- What are differences among required, permissible, forbidden, and contractual duties?
- What is the meaning of excusable ignorance and invincible ignorance in ethics?
- What is a circumstance that causes an act to be excusable? Explain.
- Distinguish differences between antecedent and consequent ignorance.
- List the different kinds of moral circumstances and explain each with an illustration.
- What is the definition of a voluntary duty?

CASE STUDY

THE CORRUPTED FALLING LEADER IN COMMUNICATION: WORDCOM. INC.

The Website of WorldCom, Inc. (2002) indicates:

> From everyday phone calls to advanced networks running over the Internet, WorldCom services underpin the success of tens of thousands of businesses around the globe. We are a digital communications company made up of thousands of people from all over the world, the kind of people who live for technology. The kind of people who like working for a company that has one of the largest, wholly owned IP (Internet Protocol) networks on earth. And offers every data service under the sun. Our services range from telephone and fax to Frame Relay and ATM data services, to advanced solutions like IP Virtual Private Networks (IP VPNs) and Web Hosting.

In 1983 cofounders Bernie Ebbers, Bill Fields, David Singleton, and Murray Waldron worked out details for establishing a company in communications in a coffee shop in Hattiesburg, Miss. A waitress as LDDS, or Long Distance Discount Service suggested the company's name. In 1984 LDDS sold its first minute of long distance to the University of Southern Mississippi. Between 1988 and 1994, LDDS acquired more than a half-dozen communication companies and expanded its reach through out the United States. In 1994 LDDS acquired an international company IDB WorldCom. In 1995 LDDS changed its name to WorldCom Inc., and Mr. Ebbers became as CEO of the company. In 1996 WorldCom Inc. acquired UUNET Technologies Inc. through merger on November 10, 1997 WorldCom and MCI announced $37 billion merger. In 1998 WorldCom acquired Brooks Fiber Properties and CompuServe. On June 21, 1999 the value of the WorldCom's stock reached its peak of $64.50 per stock.

In 1999 WorldCom and Sprint announced a $115 billion merger agreement. It was called off in June 2000. In 2000 WorldCom's sagging stock price forced CEO Ebbers to sell 3 million shares of the firm to pay off debts. In February 28, 2001 WorldCom laid off about 6,000 employees nationwide. On April 29, 2002 CEO Ebbers resigned and John Sidgmore was appointed as the new CEO. On June 14, 2002 Sidgmore announced WorldCom would lay off 17,000 employees. On June 24, 2002 WorldCom admitted to the public that its financial officers inflated earnings by $3.8 billion. Such book cooking caused stockholders to lose their assets and the value of each stock fell to 20 cents per stock. On June 26, 2002, the Security Exchanged Commission filed fraud charges against

WorldCom Inc. On July 21, 2002 WorldCom Inc. filed for Chapter 11 bankruptcy protection. In August 1, 2002, the FBI arrested former top WorldCom chief financial officer Scott Sullivan, and former WorldCom Controller David Myers with criminal charges in Manhattan.

CASE ROLE PLAYERS

The CEO's personal loans for $408 million were dumped into the company's debt. Arthur Andersen was the auditing and consulting agency for WorldCom Inc. Arthur Andersen's unprofessional practices have deceived stockholders with their book cooking strategy. Five U.S. Congressmen were among major shareholders of this company. Illegal, unethical, and immoral practices of financial and accounting divisions of the WorldCom caused 20,000 employees to be laid off. Key managerial offices were pushed to be silent concerning bad news. Employees who were complaining concerning customer complaints were fired. Many computer analysts and information systems of the firm caused to program faulty programs with errors for customers. Where are the former shareholders of companies who dumped their corporate debts into WorldCom and goat very good price for their own stock. Do you think WorldCom employed many white criminals in the field of international business?

ANALYSIS OF THE CASE

The July 2002 publication of the New York Stock Exchange's *Your Market* reports that three co-chairmen discussed recommendations to the New York Security Exchange's corporate accountability and listing standards committee to help investors restore their trust. One of these three commissioners is Leon Panetta, director of the Panetta Institute for Public Policy and White House Chief of Staff under former president Bill Clinton. He believes that honesty in legislation concerning the dynamic forces of the market place and economic system should not concern the NYSE.

Mr. Gerald Levin, retired CEO of AOL Time Warner expressed his own view concerning the accountability of corporate America. Mr. Levin stated (2002: 4):

> It's a question of finding the right balance in mandating more requirements that will improve the system of checks and balances, transparency and disclosure that we already have. In response, Mr. Panetta states: Yet at the same time to make sure those steps don't undermine the great dynamic forces that make our markets and economic system the greatest and strongest in the world. You can't legislate honesty, but at the same time that doesn't mean you can't improve the checks and balances in the process.

How can you justify honesty in the stock market by such a political mentality?

When you read opinions of these influential authorities concerning honesty, truthfulness, and justness in the marketplace, you will be disappointed by how these policy makers ignore ethical, moral, and legal mandates of our society. It is a fact that people have lost their trust. Entering investors back to the market is one of the greatest tasks of corporate America today. What is the role of American legislative, judiciary, and executive powers to eradicate corruption, deception, and fraud from public corporations? What do you think?

CASE QUESTIONS FOR DISCUSSION

- What are the main issues concerning business ethics in this case?
- What are the opinions of authorities concerning reforming corporate America?
- What is the trend of conspiracy against stockholders in the stock market?
- What is the role of the SEC in controlling publicly owned private corporations' corruption, deception, and fraud?
- Why should people trust CEOs and CFOs of publicly owned private corporations?
- Do you find negligence of corporate governance by Wordcom.Inc.'s board of governance?
- Do you believe the chief executive officers of a company should be the same as the members of the board of governance?
- Who is responsible for loses of stockholders?
- How can the American court system compensate stockholders?
- Should government or professional agencies play active roles to regulate publicly owned private companies against fraud, deception, and corruption?

CASE SOURCES

WorldCom. US· (2002), < *wysiwyg://27///http //www1.worldcom com/us/about*>

CBS News/Former WorldCom ExecsFace Charges/ July 25,2002,
<*wysiwyg·//3/http.//www cbsnews com/stories/2002/07/15national/main515106.shtml*>

L. Penetta, "Where Do We Stand? Your Market," (New York Stock Exchange Inc. In Conjunction With Time Inc, Custom Publishing, July, 2002), 4.

ABCNEWS.com· Ex-WorldCom Execs Surrender to Feds (2002)'
<*wysiwyg //4//http //abcnews go.com/sections/business/DailyNews/WorldCom_020801 h tml*>

CHAPTER 9

GLOBAL BUSINESS ETHICS AND ECONO-POLITICAL IDEOLOGIES: CAPITALISM, SOCIALISM, COMMUNISM, HUMANISM, AND IMPERIALISM

We cannot afford to live with ignorance and fear,
unless we learn how to be very well educated.

We cannot be hide-bound with prejudice, if we go through our lives,
unless to be informed at the end as we were at the beginning.

We cannot live without what is really valuable in our lives,
unless we understand what is truly valuable in our minds.

We cannot predict the bottom-line of an econo-political ideology,
unless we examine it by analyzing its whole practical outcomes.

We cannot be moral and ethical going through our lives,
unless to be knowledgeable within the boundary of our life process.

We cannot live without knowing the process of our lives,
unless we realize that the finality of human life.

CHAPTER OBJECTIVES

When you have read this chapter you should be able to do the following:

- Develop conceptual skills in analyzing ethical and moral attributions in four major global econo-political ideologies: capitalism, socialism, communism, humanism, and imperialism.
- Develop a framework of critical analysis to enable you to understand the differences between popular global econo-political ideologies.
- Define different types of businesses from the standpoint of moral, ethical, and legal value systems.
- Understand global econo-political implications and visible and invisible power players in the international free market economy.
- Understand the complexity of the global financier alliances strategies and how they maintain their financial power in the global markets.
- Analyze the holistic characteristics of political alliances and how they pursue their profitability objectives.
- Define global financial derivatives and their impacts on the global stock market.
- Define and analyze the seven types of global business categories: honest businesses, camouflaged businesses, *multi-fin-pol* businesses, *multi-corp-mag* businesses, hoodlum businesses, hoodwink businesses, and business rings.
- Know how global financiers can manipulate the international economy through their affiliated political arms.
- Critically analyze global financial environmental forces in order to grasp the real meaning of amoral mandates.

THOUGHT STARTER

In the earliest days of our ancestral life, there was no clear definition and sign of econo-political ideologies on the earth. Life was very simple. It was a dynamic process from birth, development, growth, and aging towards the final stage of death. To our ancestral mind the earth seemed to be the whole flat floor of the universe; the sky was presumed to be a dome above it across which the sun, moon, and stars passed and passed again. Space was assumed, for the most part, to be emptiness. For a long time, because of ignorance, humans did not realize the motion of planets. There were periodic changes punctuated by fluctuations between cold and heat at great intervals in that emptiness. There were flaring centers of heat and light. People did not know that the center of the earth has been hot from the beginning of its creation to this day and they felt nothing of that internal heat on the surface. The internal heat was not been perceptible the surface, except for volcanoes and hot springs. Also, there have been periods of a great wetness and dryness throughout the earth.

Conditions of natural life depend upon astronomical and terrestrial fluctuations of extremity into which we will not enter here. Three hundred years ago, the imagination of our race had a background of six thousand years. Now that curtain has risen and humans looked back to a past of scores and hundreds of millions of years. Our world today seems to be emerging with fluctuations from a prolonged phase of adversity and extreme conditions. The oil and natural gases are considered fossilized fuel today; in the past they consisted of great tree ferns, gigantic equisetums, cycad ferns, and vegetation. Many of these plants took the form of huge-stemmed trees, of which great multitudes of trunks survive fossilized to this day. Some of these fossilized trees and cycad ferns changed their shapes. Those that were hundred feet high now are subject to old historical orders and classes. Their original images and size vanished from the earth. Nevertheless, ignorance remains because ignorance was the first and still is the foremost disease that can deny some humans the right to live on the earth.

Today peoples' lives are not only subject to all forms of econo-political power; they are subject to religious-political ideologies. Also, their existence and their societal life styles are subject to the effective outcomes of global econo-political ideologies. Everything has been changed except the law of nature. Natural human life is a dynamic process from stages of birth to development, from development to growth, and from growth to aging. But societal life doesn't follow such an order. Some people are very lucky from the time of birth to the date of death, and some are not — it depends on their family's societal status, geographical and ecological locations of their birth, religious creeds, cultural value systems, material and non-material wealth, and finally econo-political ideologies.

Dynamic natural growth is viewed as an increasing movement toward existence. Modern social lives depend on econo-political ideologies of nations to provide privileges for specific groups of people and deprive others. The modern societal life of some groups around the world are not in congruence with their natural needs. Some may enjoy the best and others may suffer the most. It depends where you are born, where you are educated, and to what group you are affiliated or linked. Nevertheless, with all these differences human beings are subject to natural rules: birth, development, growth, aging, and death.

PLAN OF THIS CHAPTER

This chapter attempts to identify some socio-economic and political problems and moral and ethical implications of five major ideologies: global capitalism, socialism, communism, humanism, and imperialism. It provides some basic philosophical and perceptual categories for understanding the inherent characteristics of each ideology within global business environments. In particular, this chapter addresses the following topics:

- The philosophical reasoning for each ideology and their major historical views
- The key ideological and pragmatic features of each ideology
- Different justifications and reasoning of each theory concerning moral virtues and ethical values in the global business environments
- Fundamental criticism and praiseworthiness of each ideology; in particular, concerning natural and societal rights and duties
- The rise of global conglomeration of oligopolies and oligarchies and the shortcoming in the application of each ideology concerning competition, alliances, and joint venturing partnerships among global multinational and multicultural corporations

INTRODUCTION

Throughout history, people, power, public policies, and above all political ideologies have been the mainstreams of thought for modern societies. Specifically, global class-power coalition, class-intersecting alliances, and cross-class agreements mutually can reinforce each class of people within a nation or beyond. One of the complexities of the global financial market understands the rule of reasoning concerning changes. Every incident tends to become a test of strength or weakness between global classes of people or among nations. Within such a complex global competitive marketplace, there are visible and invisible derivatives that manifest when a class or nation has lost opportunities or gained some financial power not only in a specific deal, but also in subsequent greater purport that would arise in the future. Each financial derivative class power-coalition feels that it must stand by its allies whatever specific issue arises.

THE GLOBAL FINANCIAL ELITE ALLIANCES

The global financial elite alliances are defined as a partnership of two or more corporations or business units to achieve strategically significant financial objectives that are mutually beneficial. Alliances between companies or strategic business units (SBUs) have become a fact of financial life in modern businesses. Wheelen and Hunger (2002:130) indicate that more than 20,000 alliances occurred between 1992 and 1997, quadruple the total five years earlier. Some alliances only last a short term, allowing only one of the partners to be successful. Between 30 percent and 50 percent of all alliances are unsuccessful due to conflicts and control among the partners. For example, the successful global alliances between Chrysler & Benz corporations led to full merger.

The reasons for global alliances are: to obtain technology and/or manufacturing capabilities, to obtain access to specific markets, to reduce financial risk, to reduce political risk, to achieve or ensure a competitive advantage, and to create strategic synergy through prodigy. *Prodigy* means manifestation of manipulated integrated scientific advancement and technological breakthroughs into an extraordinary power for creating functional productivity through enhancement in size, amount, extent, and degree forces among business cells. For example, Kodoma (1992: 70) states that prodigy will have a great impact within the biological and chemical industries, which will create a fourth generation of materials. He claims that: "The fourth generation will allow engineers [bioengineers] to custom design new materials [organs] by manipulating atoms and electrons." One product that is being considered for this category is carbon fibers, which are being used to make airplanes; the next in biotechnology is cloning (Parhizgar, 2002: 71).

The structural and operational components of the global econo-political elite alliances are always found embedded in the historical cultural and political ideologies of colonialism, communism, and capitalism. Global colonialism can be defined as a distinctive political ideology in which within its boundary an elite culture exploits popular cultures of foreign lands. Global class-financier coalition is known as imperialism. They expand their econo-political appetite beyond their national territories. They are expansionists. Also, within the ideological colonized popular cultures, the colonial elite culture is not perceived exactly the same as the culture of the rich and well to do, nor is the popular culture limited to the general will and run of the colonized people.

Historically, colonial powers were limited to a few European nations with a given range of interests from accumulation of wealth to econo-political power and social status. They have enforced a fashion of patronage and connoisseurship in the arts and discovery in technological resources and scientific advancements at home and host nations. Those colonial elite cultures dominated the colonized popular cultures. Those born in popular colonized cultures could not share in the culture of the global cross-coalition elites, at least not without transforming themselves through wealth and marriage which could occur only in exceptional cases or to operate their businesses within one of the compartmentalization of business rings. There are two historical contradictory arguments concerning global elite coalition: Smithian and Marxism.

The classical dialogue between these two ideologies addresses the issue of can capitalism lead to human happiness? Smithians answer yes and Marxism answers no. Smithians follow the ideology of Adam Smith (1723-1790) and believe that if self-interested people are left alone to seek their own economic advantage, the result, unintended by any one of them, will be greater advantage for all; synergy. They believe that government interference is not necessary to protect the general welfare (Smith, 1869). Marxism argues that if people are left to their own self-interested devices, those who own the means of production and political power will rapidly reduce everyone else to virtual slaves. Although the few may be fabulously happy, all others would live in misery.

As a natural result of free competition in a free market economy, quality will improve and costs-prices will decline without limit. Such a notion will raise the real standard of living of every buyer. Sellers, in order to maintain their profitability, need to protect their interests by forcing themselves to innovate new technologies and/or products within a new marketplace. Smithians believe that the end-result of such a trend is raising the real wealth of the nation as a whole. Therefore, with such an ideological platform, technologies will be developed without limit, quality of products will improve without limit, wealth will increase without limit, and society will prosper without limit.

On the other hand, the eighteenth century of Marx's theory of historical materialism accounted for the theory of epochal changing transition from feudalism to capitalism. Marx called it the "home territory" of the theory of history (Miller, 1984: 237). Marx focused not on the making of wealth but on how wealth is distributed. He was concerned about who gets wealth and who gets to enjoy it when specific people have generated it. Marx was resentful of the capabilities of the super-capable people. He argued that the welfare of citizens in a society as a whole would be vastly improved by balanced distribution of wealth among employers and employees through profit sharing. The central focus of Marxism historical materialism is an epochal changing transition based on the dynamic movement of the feudal mode of local production system into a global cross-class alliances system in the financial markets. Such an idea has ignored the intellectual super-capabilities of elite people in production – namely innovativeness.

Nevertheless, in the late Twentieth century, the role of markets in promoting global free market economy has been based on dissolving the national economy and establishing globalization of financial alliances. The main motive for capable people is the lack of internal prime mover capable of explaining its historical evolution. On this view, conversion of colonialism into global capitalism as Cohen (1988: 84) states is the fundamental cause of social evolution: "In an autonomous tendency for the productive forces to develop. ... The nature of the production relations of a society is explained by the level of development of its productive forces." Cohn maintains that global capitalist relations of production arose when and because they are most apt to promote economic growth, given the existing level of economic development, and social progress of the forces of production. Nations should explore mechanical and procedural methods to refine their political ideologies in order to minimize the chances of disruption and cope with economic crises. While each society organizes its econo-political infrastructure on the basis of its own terms of faiths, beliefs, and ideologies, the degree of separation or unification of these perceptual phenomena are considerably varied from one society to another. Nations differ in their societal life structure based on three important dimensions:

- The extent to which political ideologies are distinct from cultural beliefs and religious faiths. In some societies there is separation of church and state (e.g., The United States of America). In other societies there is unification among cultural beliefs, religious faith, and political ideologies (e.g., The Islamic Republic of Iran). Between these two extreme zones of societal hierarchical structures, there are other nations in which either they are more oriented toward combination of religious faiths and political ideologies, or cultural beliefs and econo-political ideologies or less oriented towards those combinations.

- The extent to which wealth, power, and reputation are concentrated into specific social groups or castes (e.g., the economic and/or political elite groups or castes) can be conceived as the prime mover of the wealth in a nation.

- The level of econo-political integration of the size of the religious faiths, cultural beliefs, and econo-political ideologies as the final cause for their existence can be assessed as the real reasoning.

Although societies do not all fit neatly into one of the above categories, these threefold schemes are useful to help us understand how different societies administer and interrelate themselves to others. Nevertheless, business ethics ultimately rests on a base of political ideology, economic doctrine, and cultural philosophy. In developing countries, the basis for determining the legitimate relations between producers and consumers from an ethical point of view is contained with exploitation of national resources through authoritarian governments. The global capable alliances develop mini dominated powers in developing nations within the contextual realm boundary of the global alliances ideology. Within such a contextual domain of ideology, the global elite capital holders establish amoral relationships with the third world governments, but not with their people. Consequently, national governments' moral and ethical commitments to their people will be based upon the means and ends of governments and global alliances, but not based on relationships of people and governments. Such governments establish loose moral and ethical relationships between domestic businesses and governments in order to allow governments a great deal of secrecy.

The most important characteristic of the global elite alliances is vested in a tendency for free trade among nations, competitive regional market economy, and a shared global market-type system in which all capital holders can easily convert their investments into different international currencies. Such a global free market system is not controlled either by governments or by any national capital holding individuals or groups. Within this system, the national governments do not set the price of goods and the rate of profitability. The governments control neither prices nor wages. Also, the governments do not control their domestic production systems. At the national level, the governments do not control and intervene in business operations. However, at the global level, the international alliances may monopolize production and sale systems through their inclusive ownership or control of supply; or through global conglomerated oligopolies by fixing and controlling the price systems.

In conclusion, global alliances claim that they expand entrepreneurial reproduction systems in two possible ways. First, wage and commission earners in trade, advertising, marketing, and sales who are considered to be unproductive workers increase the number of people belonging to the new middle strata.

These workers are not working in the lines of manufacturing systems and do not increase the economy's value while their consumption vitalizes the market (Moszkowska, 1935: 97). These service-oriented workers, who are known as non-productive labor forces, are sideliners of over consumption. Second, the massive over consumption of commodities through military expenditures by governments provides lucrative opportunities for global alliances to make more profit. We can argue that the following eight major ethical critiques of the global elite alliances can monopolize the global financial markets. Therefore, we can conclude that the global elite alliances is inherently amoral because:

- It cannot operate under a universal moral and ethical system.
- It can establish international worker exploitation for lowering costs and maximizing shareholder profit.
- It promotes the vested interest of the few giant conglomerated oligopolies and/or oligarchies.
- It retards developing nations from domestic competitive operational production systems.
- It creates more economic gaps among people and less achievement in improving a better, more just, and more equitable society at the domestic market level.
- It dominates the national political democracy and consequently, giant global corporations will exploit the nation.
- It eliminates the national sovereignty of small businesses of developing nations and deepens the international debts.
- It adjusts the historical system of colonialism into a modern form of global plutocracy.

WHAT IS FINANCIAL DERIVATIVE POWER?

One of the most important environmental changes is a financial derivative. Why have those derivatives grown rapidly over the last three decades? The answer is based on customization and satisfaction of the important business needs of the private sector and/or national economies of alliances. Since global financial markets are risk-oriented, businesses tend to gain or to lose money through those derivatives. Gains or loses of international businesses are based on right or wrong managerial decision-making processes and derivative deals, just as they always have been in deals in stock and real estate markets. Nevertheless, all global financial derivative outcomes depend on major sociocultural and econo-political cracks and crashes in one or more of the domestic and/or continental financial markets.

Global financial major cracks or crashes are viewed as natural incidents that cause the global financial market to revive itself and flow. How these financial cracks or crashes happen and how often they happen depends on several honest relationships and dishonest linkages among global alliances game-players.

Crashes or cracks in global financial markets are not exogenous calamities like earthquakes. They are real disastrous facts, tracing back not only to business transactions between parties, but also to the deliberatively national central bank's deflationary operations or governmental inflationary policy to overreact to their previous financial judgmental errors or governmental economic ill-fated decisions and actions in other directions. As Miller (1997) indicates, global financial derivatives come these days basically with three different flavors.

Derivatives Exchange-Traded Futures and Options

These derivatives are traced back to Holland and Japan in the seventeenth century. Modern financial derivatives in the United States were booming in the early 1970s. The derivatives futures and options are based on the conditions of *credit quality*. For example, in any financial market, nobody will deal with you if you cannot convince him or her that you have adequate capital or substantial collateral to make a financial deal. Who are credit quality rating agencies? Within the global alliances market, there are some agencies like Moody's International and Standard & Poors who do credit analysis in the private sector and the U. S. governmental affiliated agencies such as Securities and Exchange Commission - SEC.

Derivative Financial Swaps

Derivatives financial swaps are known as contracts in which two counterparties exchange payment streams, typically a floating short interest-rate stream for establishing a long-term fixed-interest rate streams, or a stream in dollar for a stream in Euro or Yen. These derivatives could be based on raising short-term interest rates by the Federal Reserve System (U.S.) or by central banks in other countries in order to stabilize the long-term anti-inflationary rates from rising.

Derivatives Structured Notes

Derivative structured notes operate based on a customized structured deal. These derivatives sometimes create situations a bit bizarre for some parties involved in those deals. For example, a French firm borrows money from a Japanese bank at a rate of 5.567 percent in U.S. dollars plus the amount by which the returns on the French stock market exceeds that on the Brazilian market.

When considering the complexity of the above derivatives, the questions may best be raised as:

- In a global free market economy, who are the major *visible* and/or *invisible* regulatory forces?

- Are these visible and/or invisible forces bankers, politicians, economists, capital-holders, business-owners, the Wall Street financial analysts, public accounting and consulting firms, global econo-political journalists and/or consumers at large or combinations of all?
- Who will protect the public interest for the common good?

These and other moral, ethical, and legal issues are the major themes within the global contextual econo-political boundaries of this chapter.

POLITICAL IDEOLOGIES

As a factual belief, human beings are living within two integrated environments: (1) the natural (we can identify it as ecology), and (2) the artificial (we can identify it as a culture). From the standpoint of a material view, the ecological environment provides all organic elements including human beings, animals, plants, and other substances like the air and water with appropriate conditions to survive. However, the artificial environment (culture) provides specific human-made social conditions to survive. Those conditions that are an authoritatively approved set of political ideas are ideologies. Thus, the specificity of conditions could be called ideologies.

A political ideology is a set of political ideas; a formalized belief system that explains and justifies a preferred political order for society. Ideologies offer a socio-political and cultural strategy (processes, institutional arrangements, programs, and hierarchical power) for their attainment (Mullins, 1972: 498-511). For example, Lane (1962: 3-15) in his *Political Ideology* undertook to discover the latent political ideology of the American urban common man through in-depth interviews with fifteen American males. He describes ideologies as "group beliefs that individuals borrow."

As Marger (1985: 16) indicates: "Ideologies comprise beliefs that, through constant articulation, become accepted as descriptions of the true state of affairs." Ideologies are worldviews, which are built upon and reinforced by a set of powerful dominant class of beliefs and values in societal interactions. For example, the idea of progress, which has been a defining ideology in traditional Western civilization, was built on a set of beliefs about capitalism. Capitalist ideology includes economic efficiency, self-interest as a major motivator, and exploitation of resources through impersonal market mechanism. Such an ideology creates enormous inequalities of wealth and opportunities among citizens of capitalistic societies. On the other hand in the modern American democracy, beliefs and practices of the ideology of democracy is a combination of popular sovereignty, political equality, and majority ruling. American culture continuously seeks to reconcile these competing beliefs and values.

Barrett (1991: 194) has found six notions in defining ideology and explained as:

- The opposite of material reality (illusory)
- A sublimate of material life-processes serving class interests (class-bounded)
- An expression of the dominant material relationships (superstructure)
- A terrain of struggle resulting from material transformations (revolution)
- A mediation between classes as a postponement of class rule (Bonapartism)
- Reification or mystification (fetishism of commodities)

In a multicultural analysis, in all the above approaches, an ideology implies to a thoughtful reality that concludes subjectivity of the world in which we live. There are two types of persons: (1) natural persons, and (2) Artificial Persons. Natural persons are defined as dynamic creatures whose existence is subject to the ecological personalized law. Artificial persons are those formalized entities that operate under the societal law (e.g., families, groups, organizations, corporations, communities, cities, states, and nations). In the field of business, we are concerned with corporations.

Political ideologies in all societies are facts that have made our modern lives very complex. As used here, Holbrook (1994: 21) states:

> Politics involves the active pursuit of success awarded by others. In other words, it entails the use of one's own products or consumption experiences as a means to the other-oriented ends of achieving a favorable response from someone else.

Politics is considered to be a fundamental concern in today's global economy. Nevertheless, there is a danger that contaminates the moral and ethical convictions of human beings. That danger is personal greed and corporate corruption. Greed destroys human dignity and corruption destroys societal trust. Trust within a citizenship and among nations has been defined as mutual confidence that no party to an exchange will behave opportunistically and exploit another's vulnerabilities. Also, greed and corruption defect the real sense of democracy. Greed needs to be harnessed and corruption needs to be prevented. Democracy has provided the public with a second power system, an alternative power system that can be used to counterbalance economic power. For example, the collapse of giant corporations like Enron, WorldCom, Adelphia and others is a new manifestation of corrupted relationships between political authorities (as recipients of corporate soft money for their election) and the corporate interest groups such as their executives. Groups, politicians and executives made irregular fortunes at the right time at the expense of employees' pension fund options and against the interest of stockholders' trust and good faith in Enron's managerial and accounting auditing system (Arthur Andersen Accounting Corporation).

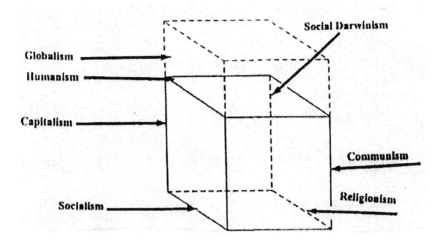

Figure 9.1: Development of Sociocultural and Econo-Political
Ideologies Within the Context of Globalization

Within the contextual domain of the global free market economy, political
ideologies play important roles in the distribution of wealth among nations and
within a nation. Likert (1973) through his research, found four types of
government power: (1) exploitable-authoritarian, (2) benevolent-authoritarian,
(3) consultative-inquiry power, and (4) participatory democracy. His ideal
system was participatory democracy, where all people actively are involved in
decision-making policies. Nevertheless, none of these theories considered
humanism as the core concept for their practical outcomes. Regardless of the
type of government and their human sensitivity, all of the above systems are
concerned with five major issues in the global market economy:

- How much should people produce and with what efforts and with what
  type of arrangements for profit sharing? Ideally, all citizens of a nation
  should be productive with effective utility of production factors in order
  to enjoy high standard of living. There should be some mechanisms to
  assess the equilibrium between employers and employees concerning
  issues of profit sharing by investors' dream and individuals' fair share
  of productivity contributions.
- What type of society's scarce resources should be consumed?
- Who should own those resources?
- With what limitations for the purposes of consumption, preservation,
  and conservation and with what competitive cost-benefit mechanisms?

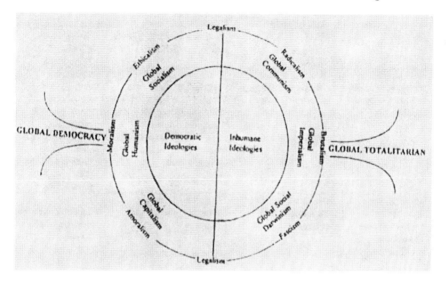

Figure 9.2: Development of Global Political, Ethical, and Moral
Ideologies and Unethical, Immoral, and Inhumane
Ideologies

There are varieties of methods to produce finished or usable products. Nevertheless, all material resources and methods of production systems are subject to the rules of scarcity, rarity, availability, usability, suitability, accessibility, durability, flexibility, limitability, transferability, productivity, accuracy, quality, and profitability. Somehow, in some way, holistic decisions must be made as to the above attributes and to all variable inputs. The methods of all production elements and processes as throughputs need to be constructed and organized, and holistically their outputs should be assessed at particular time, places, and markets.

- Why does the present generation not feel a commitment to future generations for consumption, preservation, conservation of raw material resources, and sanitation of toxic wastes?
- What type of mechanisms exists with what type of expectations?

These mechanisms must exist in order to preserve a fair share of consumption of resources for the present and future generations. For example, the most precious elements in human life are biospheric elements such as air, water, and food. The following issues and problems should be analyzed:

- Are we polluting our planet and its sphere with toxic wastes, emission, carbon monoxide, global warming, ozone depletion, and food contamination for the sake of profit making?
- For whom will it be produced?

RIGHTS AND DUTIES	BENEFICENCE: PROMOTING HUMAN'S WELFARE	JUSTICE: ACHKNOWLEDGING HUMAN RIGHTS	RESPECT FOR INDIVIDUALS: FREEDOM AND CIVIL LIBERTY
Basic moral and ethical facts about human that ground the rights and duties.	Humans are isolated, independent animals with vulnerable somatic needs, cap[able of survival and adjustment.	Humans are social dependent entities who must live in communities and therefore must adopt social structures to maintain peace and harmony in their communities.	Humans are intellectuals with rational free wills; able to make their own choices, predict their future, assess consequences, and accept responsibilities.
Moral virtuous principles and ethical valuable preferences.	Human welfare and satisfactory end results.	Equitable happiness based on justness and fairness.	Searching for intellectual choices, respecting for individual's freedom and striving for maintaining civil liberty.
Application of moral and ethical theories.	Deontological reasoning for coexistence.	Utilitarian reasoning for establishing just societies.	Bureaucratic amorality. Categorical imperative. Cognitive reasoning in formalizing human rights and duties in order to be innovative.
Samples of formulating business legitimate rights and implementing business responsibilities.	Providing employment opportunities for employees, maintaining safe, secure, and pleasant working conditions, and responding positively to the community's high quality of lifestyle.	Compliance with law, enforcing civil rights, avoiding discrimination, preventing perjury, deception, , corruption, and fraud, abolishing favoritism, prohibiting nepotism, crashing monopolies, and offering credit where credit is due.	Promoting competition through respecting competitive efforts and rights, treating consumers with high quality of products and/or services, accumulating legitimate wealth as a moral duty, protecting and conserving natural resources, treating employees as human beings, not just as tools of production, and respecting different regroup faith and intellects.

Figure 9.3: Fundamental Sociocultural and Econo-Political Principles of Rights and Duties

- Once a commodity is produced, who has the right to get it?
- Is it based on consumers' purchase power or desirability of distributive systems to provide some markets with economical incentives and deprive others by political injunctions. For example, the World Health Organization (WHO) has estimated that, of the 26 millions Africans with HIV, 5 millions would be suitable for immediate treatment with anti-retroviral therapy (Pilling, 2001: 4).
- Should we assume that essential drugs are ordinary commodities to follow the global market economy mechanisms -- the demand-supply rule? In order to have access to Azidothymide or ATZ or other compatible drugs, African AIDS patients should have sufficient economic capabilities and income in order to be able to acquire them. The Burroughs-Wellcome Company has been the center of ethical and moral controversy over this drug for establishing a very high price. The moral and ethical question then is what mechanism is there to distribute products with what pricing system among the Least Developing Countries (LDCs) comparatively to the developed countries? Is it moral or ethical to abandon African's AIDS patients, because they cannot afford to spend $800.00 or $1,000.00 a month per patient to be provided with their drugs? The reality indicates that most African patients cannot afford to spend between $5 to $10 a year per patient's prescription. How determine these drugs be manufactured and distributed throughout the global free market economy? As Griffith (2001: 3) reports:

A US-based AIDS organization plans to give 20 percent of the profits from a promising new HIV drug to the South Pacific island state of Samoa, a move aimed to improve relations between pharmaceutical companies and developing countries.

The business ethics and society teaches us from the issue upward, rather than from the principle downward. For references, a brief overview of the sociocultural and econo-political principles and forms of reasoning most used in this text is found in Figure 9. 3.

RELIGIOUS FAITHS, CULTURAL BELIEFS, AND POLITICAL IDEOLOGIES

As mentioned in the discussion of global moral, ethical, and legal ordinations in Chapter Two, all societies; if they are to remain viable over time, must maintain social order through peaceful solutions during the time of conflict. All societies must develop good will to resolve their disputes and regulate the immoral, unethical, and illegal behavior of its members. Within such a domain of argument, business ethics ultimately rests on a base of political ideology, economic doctrine, and cultural philosophy. In order to understand the terms and meanings of religious faiths, cultural beliefs, and political ideologies, we will describe them in the following pages.

Religious Faith

A faith is an emotional enforcement for believing in *ritual* reality. There is a tendency among some people that emphasizes the belief aspects of a religion and overlook ritual elements of a religious behavior. This may be a result of the frequently observed falling away from the practice of many traditional rites. A faith is a meaningful reliance on a strong intention that psychologically can be used as reinforcement for expression of an idea or an opinion. A faith eradicates anxieties, quits self-doubt, and makes an idea or an opinion in congruence with truthfulness, worthiness, and righteousness. A faith is a presumable ritual enforcement of the attitudes that peace and revelation (the reduction of fear, misery, and inferiority feelings) are the only ends for a human being. Finally, a religious faith is an emotional and sensational fidelity and loyalty to a spiritual phenomenon, person, promise, and/or oath. Failure to fulfill the obligation would be breaking the faith. In connection with having a distinction between a faith and a belief, we are inclined to say: Look for ritual first, then for beliefs connected with them. For example, in the ritual pantheists (the doctrine that God is the transcendent reality of the material universe and human beings are only creatures who can perceive God everywhere) see God in the trees and the birds and the very air. Or in the Moslem faith, people perceive that business people are "God's favorites." Therefore, business people need to consider God's order in their business transactions and behavior. It is a tradition in the Moslem business world to assume that business people have established a partnership with God in their line of businesses. This is a ritual faith for paying annually a certain percentage of their profits (*Zakot*) to charities for the public good in addition to taxes. Or in the faith of Christianity, the benevolent hearted people give away a portion of their material things and wealth for the goodness of their communities.

Cultural Beliefs

Beliefs are inferences made by and observed about underlying states of expectancy. Beliefs seem to form the core conceptual ideas and opinions concerning the acceptability of something or to be denominated by some faiths. Sproul (1981: 204) defines: "A belief is understanding that represents credible relationships between objects, properties, and ideas." Beliefs are imbued with powerful rational feelings. The fervor with which people hold their cultural value systems is good examples. Beliefs are viewed as confidence in truth or existence of something not immediately susceptible to rigorous proof. For example, the global ecological corporate convictions are especially concerned with global environmental changes, because the causes of damage are disconnected in time and space from those who are harmed.

Parhizgar and Parhizgar (2002: 826) state:

> Based on moral, ethical, and legal convictions of a corporation, we may conclude that ecological values are derived from three major sources of beliefs: (1) Anthropocentric (human-centered), (2) Theocentric (God's-centered), and (3) Ecocentric (biocentric).

Anthropocentric: *Anthropocentric* beliefs concentrate on econo-political values. They are predominantly "utilitarian" and are concerned with only those financial environmental changes that effect human welfare. In the utilitarian theory of ethics, for example, if we cut down all trees and dry out all of the wetlands, then we are going to lose not only nutritional resources, but also, we are going to be exposed to the scarcity of chemicals, drugs, paper, wood, and other valuable resources. Therefore, based on such a humanitarian philosophy, people should not harm the environment, because they are convicted by their moral obligations to stop the destruction of nature. These people believe that humanity is an infestation on nature analogous to an illness. This implies a moral duty to reduce both the size and impact of the human pollution.

Theocentric: Socio-religious values are predominantly deontological and are concerned with qualitative spiritual desirability in life and after life and more abstract feelings towards goodness for the satisfaction of God and harmony with His kingdom. On the basis of deontological theory of ethics, for example, theocentrists state that environmental protection for the survival of all creatures is a human obligation because God created all species with specific purposes. Therefore, it is the corporation's obligation to safeguard the kingdom of God.

Ecocentric: Both biocentric living-thing centered and envirocentric non-living thing-centered is the major targets in ecocentric beliefs. Environmental values grant nature itself intrinsic rights to naturally function. These values grant species the right to continue to exist and function within the contextual natural circumstances of survival. On the basis of ecocentric theory of ethics, for example, biocenterists argue that nature has intrinsic functional worth, apart from its human use. Each element in the universe functions according to its intrinsic nature. Therefore, businesses need to properly function with nature.

WHAT IS A CORPORATION IN TERM OF POLITICAL IDEOLOGY?

A corporation is a legal entity in which its own artificial personal identity conducts a business operation. It carries certain legal rights and duties. The corporation substitutes itself for the individual shareholders or stockholders in operating a business and incurring liability. Its authority to act and the liability for its operations are separate and apart from the individual investors who own it (Jeffcut, 1994: 225). Corporations are assumed to be functioning entities within the context of a political-legal system. It is not possible to analyze all related economic and political theories that govern today's global free market economy. In any business environment today Parhizgar, Wil'man, and Parhizgar (2002: 363) found seven major business sectors (see Figure 9. 4).

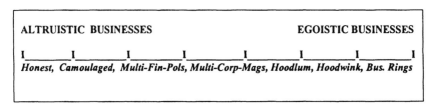

Figure 9.4: Seven Types of Businesses: Very Ethical To Unethical

Honest Businesses: The *Honest Businesses* cater their operational activities to respond to the consumption demand of the masses. They provide consumers with their everyday necessary commodities and services. These corporations could be small or large. At any size, they are providing tangible, effective products and services for customers (e.g., bakeries, grocery stores, airlines, hospitals, technomedical and pharmaceutical corporations, etc.).

Honest businesses are committed to establish an ethical and moral relationship between corporations and their environmental forces. This type of business promotes understanding realistic interrelationship of business units with other forces in society. Owners, managers, and employees of an honest corporation are energized by ethical, moral, and legal inputs of various kinds. These inputs, which have desirable consequences for all parties establish mutual trust between producers and consumers. All parties are highly integrated and each party as a part of the whole system is oriented toward preserving itself, maintaining the integrity of its boundaries, and increasing its survival opportunities. On the basis of genuine integrity of all parties, the business systems creates products and/or provides services and take actions that affect all areas of society. The impacts influence different individuals, groups, institutions, and nations and lead them to a better world to live. What conclusions can be reached about the honest businesses in society?

- Honest businesses clearly manifest their moral and ethical commitments to maintain their integrity and integrate their corporate cultural value systems into the society.
- An honest business is not basically hierarchical or dominated by a greedy and corrupted small group but is a moral and ethical interacting agency to influence and maintain the integrity of society. Any stakeholder group may have potential influence on business

transactions, but they never lose their commitments to the corrupted interest of partisan groups.

- An honest business's mission is to stabilize its market size and product positions in order to receive the support of consumer loyalty for its survival.

- The basic objective of an honest business is recognized by the essential application of moral virtues (excellence) and cultural values (qualities) to the continued survival of that entity. Through such a system, an honest business system coexists with coetaneous responses to the wellbeing of a society.

An honest business creates a positive impact on its customers.

Camouflaged Businesses: *Camouflaged businesses* are commercial entities that are playing the role of *trustees* in legitimate and legal fronting businesses. *Trustees* are individuals and/or institutions with integrity. They avoid cruelty, greediness, or more than commonly experienced hypercritic or enviousness. They are in trust to act on behalf of investors to put their monies in a special place or in an honorable and legal business or to keep them scrumptiously unmingled with their own property and assets. They hold social self-regulative advantage over most other people who care about other people's interest. Trustees operate like an airport's traffic controllers who know how to provide sufficient information and directions for taking off and landing of airplanes in the airports and direct aircraft against natural barriers and air collisions in the air.

The moral and ethical trusteeship view of a business was developed more than fifty years ago by Frank W. Abrams (1951: 29-35), when he put forth the ten-revolutionary concept that corporate executives should have their own version of the physicians' Hippocratic Oath:

> Business firms are man-made instruments of society. They can be made to achieve their social usefulness; and thus their future can be best assured when management succeeds in finding a harmonious balance amongst the claims of the various interested groups... Management, as a good citizen, and because it cannot properly function in an acrimonious and contentious atmosphere, has the positive duty to work for peaceful relations and understanding among men; for restoration of men in each other in all walks of life.

Trustees hold the title to property for the benefit of another. The trustees then make decisions with respect to setting prices, controlling production, and determining the control of exclusive geographical markets for all of the people in trust. It became apparent that the trust wielded so much economic power that corporations outside the trust could not compete effectively. A *trust company* is a business entity organization to exercise the functions of a trustee, but usually occupied also with banking and other financial activities. First let us define a trust company and then we will analyze the inherent ethical and moral conditions of these companies. *Trust* is a fiduciary relationship in which one person (the trustee) holds the title to property (the trust estate or trust property) for the benefit of another (the beneficiary). It will be helpful to recall in this connection the division of money-power as *vegetative, sensitive,* and *rational* entities within a trust company.

Multi-Fin-Pols Businesses: The *multi-fin-pols Businesses* are specialized large multinational networking corporations with very huge volume of financial assets in their respective operational holdings. Lundberg (1968: 305) has called these invisible hands *fin-pols* (financial politicians). They operate under a diversity of ways to move money around the world avoiding conventional channels. Some property dealers, photocopying bureau, carpet traders, fairground operators, computer memory chip suppliers, E-stock traders and brokers, accounting firms, and mobile telephone importers are among the modern *multi-fin-pols* criminals and corrupted politicians use to hide cash and money flights around the globe. These corporations operate with very large sums of money and extensive channels of distribution. Sometimes these assets and operations are partially known to the public and partially anonymous. Specifically, these *multi-fin-pols* are giant corporations that influence the daily life-style of all global citizens.

Historically, these *pols* have been belonged to different social classes: baronies and dukedoms, feudal and landlords, the *Templers, Shriners,* or *priesthood* systems, and *kings* and *presidents.* Some times these *multi-fin pols* cooperation fall apart. In their overlapping aspects, governments and *finpolities* and *corp-magies* are almost identical. The International Monetary Fund estimates that global crime and corruption generates flows of as much as $1,500 billion a year. Some of this passes through offshore financial centers such as Switzerland, Luxemburg, the Channel Islands, and Small Caribbean nations that offer either strict banking secrecy or lax regulation (Willman, 2001: 16).

Another alternative of *multi-fin-pols'* financial operation is likely to appeal to international financial networks by *havalah* in the eastern world (in Moslem countries). In both Persian and Arabic languages *havalah* is a kind of financial and capital flight and informational money transmission system which allows payments to be made in one place in return for cash being provided in another -- for a fee without leaving any traceable written documentation. According to Willman (2001:16) "Mainstream financial centers such as London and New York are also used for money-laundering simply because it can be easier to conceal illicit funds in the enormous amounts that flow through daily."

The so-called defense industries are such an indispensable part of governments today as to have given rise to the concept of the Warfare States. The presidents' or kings' offices, Departments of Defense, Departments of Commerce, Departments of State, Secret Intelligence Agencies and the international arms dealers and brokers are the special big-board members of these corporations. For example, the United Kingdom is financial regulators discovered $4 billion from Nigeria under the late General Sani Bacha passed through London, often en route to other financial centers such as Jersey and Switzerland. In 1999 Citibank, part of Citigroup, transferred huge sums of money for Raul Salinas, brother of former Mexican President Salinas De Garde. Earlier in that year, Bank of New York was found to have handled more than $7 billion from Russia to the Bank of New York in the United States (Willman, 2001:16).

Multi-Corp-Mags: The *multi-corp-mags* (multi-corporation magnates) are known as small, elite groups of business-people and/or their brokers who are incorporated within the international econo-political systems and dominate the greatest mass of the ordinary population of the world. The chief instrument of *multi-corp-mags'* power is global and/or multinational corporations, more particularly the large financial and manufacturing institutions. These institutions run by corporate magnates with a mechanism to maximize profits constant with growth. From an internal point of view, *multi-corp-mags* do everything attract investors to trade their stocks. The *multi-corp-mags'* rationality is that to do everything they can in order to maximize profits. They employ deceptive advertising and products, produce below-par goods even for vital military and space agencies, evade taxes, abuse weights and measures, and engage in creating monopolies and monopsonies through creating high rates of price-fixing, and in general, do whatever they can, legal or illegal to maximize their market size and product positions. *Multi-corp-mags* perceive their international role as follows:

- They believe that the international free marketplace is highly hierarchical, and a small number of *multi-fin-pols* (multi financial politicians) should influence the marketplace.
- *Multi-corp-mags* are the major role players of the international economy, and should manipulate governmental agencies to increase their profitability.
- *Multi-corp-mags* believe that the international econo-political power should move down from the top elite groups of nations. Unlike democratic theory, which postulates that political leaders should serve the will of the people, the *multi-corp-mags* should dominate the world market for the benefit of a small group of business executives, politicians, and plutocrats.
- *Multi-corp-mags* believe that the United Nations' policies are dominated by the financial interests of businesses and wealthy nations and should be used as a tool to aggrandize the interests of these groups.
- *Multi-corp-mags* believe that the role of global and/or multinational corporations is paternalistic at best and exploitive at worst.

The global *multi-fin-polities* and *multi-corp-magnates* are more than large corporations. They are specific conglomerate entities in which they serve all governments around the world by the notion of "the know your customer rules." Their interests are not aligned with the interests of any single nation. They are bureaucratic organizations and as such they are organized primarily to increase their profits within a competitive environment. As a consequence, the particular values and aspirations of individual employees of those corporations have relatively minimal and transitory impact on the organization as a whole. The *multi-fin-pols* and *multi-corp-mags* are not confined to a single nation; they can easily escape the reach of the laws of any particular nation by simply moving their resources or operations out of one nation and transferring them to another nation. In addition, they are manipulating public politicians (*pub-pols*), religious politicians (*relige-pols*), law politicians (*law-pols*), and labor politicians (*labe-pols*) in order to control the marketplace. All of the above *pols* are sober politicians who primarily and exclusively are concerned with manipulating governmental agencies for controlling who should get or should not get — what, why, when, where, and how.

Hoodlum Businesses: *Hoodlum businesses* are those legitimate business people who are gaining control of a legitimate corporation and utilizing all their tricks to secure full advantageous power in order to divert the regular investment direction either into emulating investors with no gain, or merging with gangsters' hidden investors. Internationally, the *hoodlumers* are often unschooled or illiterate people. They are men and women of action, compulsiveness, and repetition in their business acquisitiveness. They are very specialized in detecting the loopholes of the legal systems to operate and achieve their illegitimate business objectives. They pretend that they are the most honest and reputed businesspersons with a sense of humor and etiquette. They show an inclination to be honest in small humanitarian donations and be devoted to societal prestige and status, self-confidence, and self-validation. However, they are money buyers and sellers rather than commodities and services (Lane, 1965: 106). They are looking for gigantic illegitimate and illegal business deals.

Hoodwink Businesses: *Hoodwink businesses* are those kinds of entities in which fraud, deception, and covering-up unethical, immoral, and illegal actions are extensive in their common daily business transactions. Corruption is viewed as the main outcomes of hoodwink businesses. *Hoodwinkers* are particularly interested in acquiring the federal, state, and municipal selling and buying contracts through corrupted governmental authorities. In most occasions hoodwinkers find appropriate power brokers in the governmental offices in order to facilitate their business deals. Hoodwinkers in the professions such as legal and medical fields cover up corrupt business deals with governmental corrupted authorities that are caught.

Business Rings: International ruthless gangsters called organized crime or corporate *business rings*. These organizations operate their businesses within different industries as follows:

- The distinctive role of organized illegal gambling, unlicensed alcoholic beverages, pornographic short and long movie making and distribution systems, the E-sex business sites, specific sex seller houses and their sex workers, and sex escort businesses as functions of legalized mass-consumption of sociable pleasure and greed. For example, on August 8, 2002, the United States Customs Service announced a despicable and repugnant international business ring that sexually used 45 children, including 37 in the United States, were molested by their own parents who put their pornographic pictures on Internet sites for making money. These sexually exploited children's parents have received money through pornographic E-sites. Parents included residents of seven states along with residents of Denmark, Switzerland, and the Netherlands (Brunker, 2002). In addition, specific business activities for selling addictive drugs which change the mentality and behavior of people and in some occasions criminals in order to provide legitimate and rational reasons for businesses related to the Department of Justice, namely jails and penitentiaries.

- White-collar crime functions under the global invisible underworld power and forces. They legitimize their businesses by legal front-businesses. They acquire their business legitimization by corrupted politicians; especially in the banking industry for money laundering, motels, hotels chains, and nightclubs in diverse pleasurable resorts and commercial areas.

- Legal importing and exporting businesses to cover up bootlegging, smuggling, narcotics traffic, embezzling funds, committing insurance fraud, stealing, and reselling stolen merchandises in black markets. They regularly pay bribes, payola, kickbacks, and grease-money to authorities and insider-trader informants. They give away under-the-table money to governmental regulatory authorities for human trafficking such as slavery trades on behalf of the sweatshops, and cheating in E-casinos and gambling tables and also in slot machines. They create specific satellite teamsters and mobsters to govern businesses. These *business-rings* turn the happy and honest global business world into a jungle. They demoralize the society in order to have access to free-money, free-sex, free-power, and apparent pleasurable and entertainment times. For example, as Williams (2002: 5) reports:

Lax management at the United Nations refugee agency permitted a criminal gang to extort millions of dollars from desperate refugees in Kenya seeking resettlement in the west... the UN's anti-fraud office in New York said about 70 people were involved in the crime ring.

DIMOND DEALERS IN THE INTERNATIONAL BLACK MARKETS

Investigations of various researchers and mass media on business corruption in different nations indicate that the immoral and unethical practices in business transactions have been widespread. *Multi-fin-pols* and *multi-corp-mags* as well as domestic and international *hoodlum, hoodwink,* and *business rings* have made payments to officials in developed and as well as in developing countries. Table 8 illustrates the ranking of 54 countries according to the severity of international corruption.

Table 9.1: International Corruption: A survey of Business Perceptions

Rank	Country	Score 1996 (max = 10.00)	Score 1995	Rank	Country	Score 1996 (max = 10.00)	Score 1995
1	New Zealand	9.43	9.55	28	Greece	5.01	4.04
2	Denmark	9.33	9.32	29	Taiwan	4.98	5.08
3	Sweden	9.08	8.87	30	Jordan	4.89	—
4	Finland	9.05	9.12	31	Hungary	4.86	4.12
5	Canada	8.96	8.87	32	Spain	4.31	4.35
6	Norway	8.87	8.61	33	Turkey	3.54	4.10
7	Singapore	8.80	9.26	34	Italy	3.42	2.99
8	Switzerland	8.76	8.76	35	Argentina	3.41	3.24
9	Netherlands	8.71	8.69	36	Bolivia	3.40	—
10	Australia	8.60	8.80	37	Thailand	3.33	2.79
11	Ireland	8.45	8.57	38	Mexico	3.30	3.18
12	UK	8.44	8.57	39	Ecuador	3.19	—
13	Germany	8.27	8.14	40	Brazil	2.96	2.70
14	Israel	7.71	—	41	Egypt	2.84	—
15	USA	7.66	7.79	42	Colombia	2.73	3.44
16	Austria	7.59	7.13	43	Uganda	2.71	—
17	Japan	7.09	6.72	44	Philippines	2.69	2.77
18	Hong Kong	7.01	7.12	45	Indonesia	2.65	1.94
19	France	6.96	7.00	46	India	2.63	2.78
20	Belgium	6.84	6.85	47	Russia	2.58	—
21	Chile	6.80	7.94	48	Venezuela	2.50	2.66
22	Portugal	6.53	5.56	49	Cameroon	2.46	—
23	South Africa	5.68	5.62	50	China	2.43	2.16
24	Poland	5.57	—	51	Bangladesh	2.29	—
25	Czech Rep	5.37	—	52	Kenya	2.21	—
26	Malaysia	5.32	5.28	53	Pakistan	1.00	2.25
27	South Korea	5.02	4.29	54	Nigeria	0.69	—

The rank relates solely to results drawn from a number of surveys and reflects only the perception of business people who participated in these surveys. A perfect 10.00 would be a totally corrupt-free country. Same methods, but fewer countries and surveys were used to arrive at 1995 score.

Source: Financial Times, July 26, 1996, p. 3 using data from the Transparency Corruption Perception Index 1996. Reprinted with permission of FT Pictures/Graphics.

GLOBAL BUSINESS ETHICS AND ECONO-POLITICAL IDEOLOGIES

Within the context of multicultural business ethics, we have provided general introductory information concerning global business transactions. In the following pages, we will provide a brief analysis of five major holistic socio-cultural and econo-political ideologies: (1) global capitalism, (2) global socialism, (3) global communism, (4) global humanism, and (5) global imperialism.

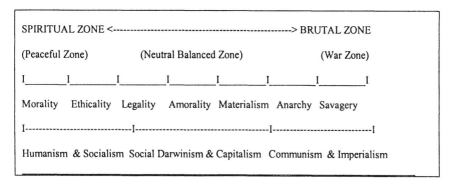

Figure 9. 5: Subsystems of Political Ideologies

By looking at Figure 9.5 the subsystems of econo-political ideologies, you will find two opposite zones concerning ethics: (1) spiritual and (2) savagery zones. Humanism functions in the spiritual zone and savagery functions in the opposite brutal zone. Humanism inspires people to move toward qualitative meanings of humaneness through constructive thoughts, innovative intentions, interdisciplinary norms, moral convictions, and ethical social behavior. The spiritual zone not only motivates and directs human beings to deal with patters of interactions and order within an individual's personality, it strives also for prevailing peace and harmony among all human beings. The brutal zone engulfs human selfishness with the savagery ideas of colonialism, feudalism, slavery, and imperialism.

Capitalistic ideology is a global economic system in which the economies of capitalistic forces are intricately interconnected through invisible global hands. Capitalism as we know it is the product of the thought of Adam Smith (1723-1790) and a group of philosophers and economists in Western civilization. The foundational concept and practice of capitalism is based on the *voluntary exchange*: two business parties of sound mind with clear purposes meet in marketplace, to which each party seeks to satisfy some felt needs. Capitalists hold that each has qualified resources that which will satisfy the other's needs; the housewife needs bread with a certain monetary purchase power, the bakery needs cash with specific rate of profitability; and they exchange at a price such that the exchange furthers the interest of each. Consequently, both parties walk away with the voluntary exchange with the hope of being richer. Adding to the value of the exchange is the notion of competition among dealers and buyers. Because there are many purveyors of each good in the marketplace, the customer is not forced to pay exorbitant prices for things needed. Nevertheless, in a capitalistic competitive marketplace, sellers and buyers win the competition through efficiency and producing the appropriate qualitative and quantitative goods at the lowest possible price or through allotting their scare resources toward the most valuable of choices presented to them. Meanwhile sellers and buyers alike must pay attention to the market as whole, periodically adjusting production and purchasing trends in order to take advantage of fluctuations in *supply and demand.*

Capitalistic *amoral* characteristics of Smithian philosophy within the system of free enterprise believe that sellers look for the best possible chance of finding for sale what they want to produce, and buyers look forward buying those goods that they need, in good quality and quantity with a reasonable price.

Smithian economists believe that capitalistic economy should not be concerned about benevolent and humanitarian notions of serving people, because this system is based on an *invisible hand* of enlightened self-interest to achieve common good, even as we think we are being most selfish. In order to be able to understand the real magnitude of global capitalism, we need first to explore it through different questions about processes and consequences. These questions are:

- What is the basic philosophy of global capitalism?
- What exactly is the practical nature of global capitalism?
- What have been the accomplishments and consequences of capitalism in relation to morality and ethics?
- What are the inherent prospective effects of global capitalism for humanity in the future?
- Is global capitalism moral or amoral?

We shall try to respond to the above questions in the following pages. Before defining capitalism ideology, it is appropriate to review some historical trends in the modern socio-cultural and econo-political endeavor. There are four important chronological dates in the modern history of global capitalism:

- The year 1616 is the date of the demand for land in Virginia, when colonists discovered tobacco as staple crop. The British mercantilism advantages became clear in Virginia to acquire tobacco from its own colony, rather than pay premium prices to foreign countries. For the first time Virginia planters purchased Africans when a Dutch ship brought twenty blacks to Virginia's shore. That was the beginning of slavery in America" (Ayers, Gould, Oshinsky, and Soderlund, 2001: 50).
- The year of 1717 is the date of establishment of the global Freemasonry socio-political movement. Further on, we will elaborate on this establishment in this chapter as the main influential global group to map the invisible power of capitalism.
- The year of 1818 is the date of establishing massive number of commercial banks (400) in the United State to provide credit for traders

and issuing notes that served as currency in cash-starved areas. Thomas Jefferson worried that: "Our citizens are clamoring for more banks, more banks" (Ayers, Gould, Oshinsky, and Soderlund, 2001: 299).

- The year of 1919 is the date of establishing the Council on Foreign Relations with headquarters in New York, London, and Hamburg to influence the econo-political mapping of global capitalism power. We will elaborate on this organization in this chapter.

GLOBAL CAPITALISM IS DEFINED

Global capitalism is defined as an international econo-political system in which the major portion of global investments, production systems, and distribution of goods and services is in the hands of the private sector of international business alliances. It operates under what is termed as profit-making systems. It seeks maximum profit. It allows no modification in terms of human needs. Through a moral and ethical dimension, there is nothing wrong with such a mandate, because in the field of business ethics, making profit is viewed as a legitimate contract between sellers and buyers or between producers/providers and consumers. Capitalism can function within a global free market economy freely to respond to the needs of all human beings. Jerry Mander, an advertising executive reads out a statement:

> The rising tide of the global economy will create many economic winners, but it will not lift all boats. [It will] span conflicts at home and abroad. ... [Its] evolution will be rocky, marked by chronic financial volatility and widening economic divides. [Those] left behind will face deepening economic stagnation, political instability, and cultural alienation. They will foster political, ethnic, ideological and religious extremism, along with the violence that often accompanies it (Harding, 2001: 4).

Pure global capitalism ideology is certainly about material inequality. That is the reason that you cannot apply morality and ethics in such an econo-political system. The real competitive deal is to identify a winner and a loser. Since today we are living in a global multicultural environment, there are varieties of moral and ethical value systems among nations. Sometimes these multicultural value systems are in contradiction or even confronting each other. For example, the advertising billboards of female sexuality in the Western and/or in Christian civilization are viewed as permissible exhibition of the natural beauty of females who are givers and guardians of life. In the Eastern civilization and Moslem faith, pictures of partly naked Western women advertising Hollywood movies, or tobacco are interpreted as a death cult of women's dignity. Moslems, through their religious scriptures, Koran, believe that those advertisements are not illustrating aesthetic sides of the natural beauty of women. Moslems believe that those billboards suggest sexual acts, intimate pleasure, and women's ubiquitous demand for the corruption of young male adults. From such a point of view, global capitalism cannot function under a unified system of morality and ethics. Thus, global capitalism needs to adjust itself to amorality.

Interactive combination of the above key features makes international capitalism very complex. The traditional means and ends of traditional capitalistic economy are different from the new global capitalism economy. The global capitalistic econo-political ideology operates under five basic laws:

- In a competitive free global market environment, the law of demand states that as the price of goods and services increases, the quantity demanded of those goods and services will fall. As the price of necessary goods and services falls, the quantity demanded of those goods and services will rise. This means that buyers' purchase power will be stronger and extended. Consequently buyers can obtain cheaper necessary goods and more savings.

- In a competitive free global market environment, the law of supply basically states that, as the price of necessary goods and services goes up, so does the quantity supplied (overconsumption of resources) — and, correspondingly, as these prices decrease, so does the quantity supplied (underconsumption). This means that sellers find golden opportunities through marketing niche to produce and sell more necessary goods. According to the Matrix assessment of the Boston Consulting Group (BCG), such a line of business will be emerged in the stage of Star.

- In a competitive free global market environment, the law of the conjunctural overproduction basically states that, as the production of capital (means of production -- resources) goes up, so does the position of the value of capital (profitability) increases the surplus qualitative value of the capital (overproductivity). In other words, it is only the overproductivity law that can validate and revive the constant value of the national wealth. This means that the capital needs constantly replenished through technological innovation or otherwise it will perish.

- In a long-term competitive financial survival process, the law of tendentially falling profit basically states that, as the real value of the national currency of assets (material wealth and knowledge wealth) is stabilized, the price of products and services goes up, consequently the quantity demanded of those goods and services will go up. As the result, the inflationary rate goes up, and the interest rate also goes up. It is this plurality of the value of capital relationship with the price that the class struggle as the absent cause of crisis appears.

- Economic crisis in a free market economy is not the result of a single, systematically acting cause, but it is the result of strengthening position of giant capital holders in the market place and the slow down of the cash-flow of small businesses and the weakening of the income and purchase power of the working class by sudden massive lay offs and bankruptcy of small and giant corporations. This principle provides an opportunity for the global capitalistic system to make a balance between overaccumulation of capital investments and overconsumption of commodities and/or services of consumers. According to the overaccumulation wealth, giant capital holders need to trim their overexpanded reproduction constituencies through application of turnaround, cutback, downsizing, and rightsizing strategies as a measure for establishing their immanently reproduced equilibrium status which is only temporarily interrupted by economic crisis. On the other hand, according to overconsumption theory, small businesses and working class people find themselves in critical economic crisis as the immanent disequilibrium between incomes and costs. Nevertheless, consumption is inevitably related in relation to employment as the main source of production. In such a case, retrenchment of reproduction forces is, therefore, occurs through the third parties (bankers and lenders) alien to producers and consumers. As a result, workers start to consume their savings up to the point of depleting their financial resources and to be hooked to the habit of credit overconsumption. Consequently, bankers and lenders can charge their clients with higher interest rates on their adjustable loans.

There are six fundamental key features in the global capitalism:

- Global competition
- Global and multinational companies
- Global alliances
- Profit motives
- Private overaccumulated ownership (oligopolies and/or oligarchies)
- Business amoral transactions

Through reviewing the following pages you will understand how global capitalism has merged and operated through the history of mankind. We will analyze the above key features of global capitalism in more detail in the following sections.

Global Competition: As you have noticed in the above laws, one of the most important key features of the global capitalism is competition. Competition creates unequal consequences in profit making processes. It is a sad economic fact that the consequential rule of competition in a capitalistic society ends up with a single merchant who could become unjustly rich and a starving person's effort necessary to acquire a loaf of bread becomes very high. Competition has two different correlated consequences on both sellers and buyers. Free competition among sellers is the market regulator that keeps a community activated only by self-interest from degeneration into a ruthless profiteers —

monopoly. Also, competition among the buyers (customers or consumers) makes sure that the available goods end up in the hands of those to whom they are worth the most -- not those that need them the most.

A duplication effort in resources consumption is a part of price competition. Free competition is the lifeblood of a global capitalistic system. In the free market economy, competition is more efficient than the government centralized planned economy. Also, competition in a capitalistic society provides a safe heaven for an individual or a group of investor alliances that try very hard to exploit resources and direct them toward their own self-interest motives. The global capitalistic system provides legal protections for investors in order to facilitate appropriate success toward more productivity. Also, competition is defined as providing adequate opportunities for individuals or groups of investors in order to establish a synergistic potential investment environment for concentration of wealth in a certain group of alliances. Eventually, such a concentric investment can be used effectively to seize the marketing edge in an industry. The concentric diffusion of synergistic wealth and production systems provides an individual or a firm with opportunities to conduct a business to pace the path of an entrepreneurial success in the right place at the right time with the right products. Also, it meets the demand of consumers. Thus, competition needs synergistic diffusion of wealth and production systems through very intense technological marketing prodigy.

Global competition directly links an individual and/or a group's marketing potential with appropriate demanding global chains of consumption. Such a synergistic capability causes it to beat the equilibrium of the marketplace. By competing in an intense marketplace, we mean not only to check the appetite for profit making through lowering prices, it also means to break the competitive pricing cycle with higher quality of commodities or services and more volume of sales. Successful competition keeps prices for desired goods or services stabilized through the escalation of self-correction toward controlling the pace of the marketplace.

Global and Multinational Corporations: As we mentioned in chapter one, a *Global Corporation* is a business entity that obtains the factors of production from all countries around the world without restriction and/or discrimination against by both home and host countries. Also, it markets its products and/or services around the globe for the purpose of making reasonable profit.

A *multinational corporation* is a highly developed conglomerate organization with a deep worldwide involvement in econo-political involvements for obtaining the factors of production from multiple specific countries around the world and manufactures its diverse products for specific markets. These corporations have gone through historical evolutionary stages and social responsibilities. In the nineteenth century, Chief Justice John Marshal defined a *corporation* as: "An artificial being, invisible, intangible, and existing only in the contemplation of law. Although a corporation is not something that can be seen or touched, it does have prescribed rights and legal obligations within the community," (Shaw and Barry, 1998:144).

The chief instrument of the goal of a global capitalistic economic power is the *G-pub-corp-pols* (Global-Public-Corporate-Polity). The *G-pub-corp-pols* are, at their best, completely rational mechanistic entities with a single overriding goal: the maximization of money-power as profits constant with steady growth. The irony is the notion of profit maximization that does not apply to the welfare of all global citizens.

Harding (2001: 4) reports that:

> A survey this summer in Le Monde, the French newspaper, showed 56 percent of people in France thought multinational corporations had been the beneficiaries of globalization. Just 1 percent thought consumers and citizens had benefited.

Usually, global capitalism alliances serve only the oligopolies and/or oligarchies of global capital holders. There are several moral and ethical issues concerning global capital holders. Can a global corporation suffer for violating ethical rules that restrict international enterprises for the sake of the common good (e.g., the cases of pharmaceutical companies concerning AIDS patients in Africa)? Sometimes the global or multinational corporations do everything that they can, including much that is amoral, to maximize their profits. They produce below-par goods, evade taxes, evade weights and measures, and engage in price fixing. To the outsiders, they do whatever they wish to maximize their profits.

GLOBAL ALLIANCES

History indicates that after World War II, industrialized nations experienced sudden economic growth. Industrialized nations started to look abroad for green field areas for natural resources, cheaper labor, mass production, and mass consumption for economic synergistic gains. As the result, traditional global econo-political alliances such as Illumitaties, Freemasons, the United Nations, the Council on Foreign Relations (CFR), and the Trilateral Commission emerged. Illuminaties and Freemasons are invisible and secret societies in all countries except in the United States. Because of limitation of this textbook, we will briefly introduce these global alliances in the following sections.

Illuminati: The *Illuminati* is a secret society that was established on May 1, 1776 (around the date of Industrial Revolution) in Ingolstad, Bavaria, Germany by Adam Weishaupt. The organization was an illuminated operation in which it was connected with the powerful Grand Orient Masonic Lodge of France. The order's name of illuminati had the meaning of the enlightened ones. The Illuminati was designed for one purpose: to carry out the plans of high Freemasonry to create a New World Order by gaining a foothold in the key policy-making positions of all nations. Roberts (1984) through his historical research found that Weishaupt expressed his opinion on Illuminaties' objectives as:

> By this plan we shall direct all mankind. In this manner, and by the simplest means, we shall set all in motion and in flames. The occupations must be so allocated and contrived, that we may, in secret, influence all political transactions.

On July 16, 1782, the Masonic congress of Wilhemsbad was held. Roberts (1984: 56) also indicates: "This meeting included representatives of all the Secret Societies: Illuminaties as well as Freemasons — which now number no less than three million members around the world." However, the Grand Orient Lodge of France and the network of illuminated Masonic Lodge have created the New World Order or New International Order.

Freemasons: The *Freemason*'s philosophy simply is based on the belief that God is the sum total of all that exists. They believe in God-force or life force. Such a force is reflected in all things — human beings, plants, animals, and all other things. Because of this philosophy, Masons believe in one-world humanity. They like to work together through enlightenment to create a New World Order. Most sources place the official birth of Freemasonry at 1717. Some researchers indicate that Freemasons are traced back to the old civilizations. Freemasonry is nothing more than an econo-political and social brotherhood organization. Its origin traces back to Knights Templar. The Knights Templar was a military and religious order in Jerusalem found by nine French Knights. Their stated mission was to protect pilgrims on their way to the Holy Land during crusades (Webster: 1924: 32). After the fall of Jerusalem in 1187, the order established its headquarters in Acre. The Templars were forced to relocate once again in 1291 when Acre fell to the Moslems. This time their headquarters were moved to the island of Cyprus.

> By then the Templars, through their enormous wealth and widespread brotherhood organization, had become the bankers of Europe, and the order was no longer primarily a military one. It was especially influential in Spain, France, and England, where commandeered of knights, men-at-arms, and chaplains were organized, each under its own superior, subordinate to the Grand Master of the Order (*Collier's Encyclopedia*, 1985).

Pike (1966: 816) states: "Their watchword was, to become wealthy in order to buy the world." Finally, the Knight Templars merged with stone mason guilds of Europe.

The difference between Masons and Freemasonry is that Masons are operative stone masonry and Freemasons are speculative Freemasons. The stonemasons were actually employed in the building profession. With their enormous wealth, they constructed scores of castles and cathedrals in Europe, mosques in Arab countries, and temples in Asian countries. They were known to conceal themselves at times under the name of Brethren Masons." (Pike, 1966). In the eighteenth century the "new order" expanded rapidly. Toward this end, a new ultra-secret society was formed. The members were the highest degrees of the Masonic Order. This Order within an Order is known as the Illuminati.

Paul Rich and Guillermo de los Reyes (1996: 20) indicate:

> Our knowledge is not confined to pictures of members or lodge rooms. Since a continuing emphasis is on fidelity to the original ceremonies, it is possible, notwithstanding the order's secrecy, to describe the actual initiations as performed a century and half ago. They are little changed today. Evidence that they were intended to cement ties among members abounds in the surviving transcripts.

Malcolm Duncan (1974: 42-47) indicates:

> In the Entered Apprentice or first degree, the following characteristic exchange occurs:
>
> Q. What came you here to do?
> A. To learn to subdue my passions and improve myself in masonry.
> Q. Then I presume you are a Mason?
> A. I am so taken and accepted among all brothers and fellows.
> Q. How do you know yourself to be a Mason?
> A. By having been often tried, never denied, and willing to be tried again.
> Q. How shall I know you to be a Mason?
> A. By certain signs, a token, a word, and the perfect points of my entrance.
> Q. What are signs?
> A. Right angles, horizontals, and perpendiculars.
> Q. What are tokens?
> A. Certain friendly or brotherly grips, by which one Mason, may know another in the dark as well as in the light ...
> Q. What were you next presented with?
> A. Three precious jewels.
> Q. What were they?
> A. A listening ear, a silent tongue, and a faithful heart.
> Q. What do they teach?
> A. A listening ear teaches me to listen to the instruction of the Worshipful Master, but more especially to the cries of worthy distressed brother. A silent tongue teaches me to be silent in the Lodge, that the peace and harmony thereof may not be disturbed, but more especially before the enemies of Masonry. A faithful heart, that I should be faithful and keep and conceal the secret of Masonry and those of a brother when delivered to me in charge as such, that they may remain as secure and inviolable in my breast as in his own, before being communicated to me.

> One of the most influential organizations in this respect has been
> Freemasonry, which has been successful in creating a popular belief that
> membership is a key to power and that it has inspired the founding
> fathers.... Thus a secret society derives some of its significance from being
> not so secret. The need for leaders to have a mysterious source of power,
> of having been anointed and set apart, surely has something to do with
> why political personalities became active Masons and bothered, along with
> all their other duties, with holding Masonic office.

Global Council on Foreign Relations: It is a fact that there could be no
international diplomatic understanding without active participation of the
world's governments in some forms of socio-political relations, specifically in
international trade and finance. History has taught nations that they need to
effectively communicate with each other. One of the most global agencies
before the establishment of the United Nations was the Council on Foreign
Relations (CFR). *The Council on Foreign Relations Handbook* of 1936 provides
the following statements concerning the philosophy and mission of CFR as
following:

> On May 30, 1919, several leading members of delegations to the Paris
> Peace Conference met at the Hotel Majestic in Paris to discuss setting up
> an international group that would advise their respective governments on
> international affairs.... It was decided at this meeting to call the proposed
> organization the Institute of International Affairs At a meeting on June 5,
> 1919, the planners decided, it would be best to have separate organizations
> cooperating with each other. Consequently, they organized the Council on
> Foreign Relations; with headquarter in New York, and a sister
> organization, the Royal Institute of International Affairs, in London, also
> known as the Chatham House Study Group, to advise the British
> Government. A subsidiary organization, the Institute of Pacific Relations,
> was set up to deal exclusively with Far Eastern Affairs. Other
> organizations were set up in Paris and Hamburg, the Hamburg branch
> being called the Institute Fur Auswartige Politik, and the Paris branch
> being known as Centre d'Etudes de Politicque Etrangere....(Mullins,
> 1985:33-34).

According to Epperson, (1985: 196), funding of the CFR was provided by
bankers, businessmen, and corporations including J. P. Morgan, Bernard Brauch,
Otto Kahn, Jacob Schiff, Paul Warburg, and John D. Rockefeller, among others.
Interestingly, these bankers and businessmen are among the same people
involved in the forming of the Federal Reserve.

In the decades of 1980s and 1990s, the CFR's financial supporters included
leading organizations and individuals including American Express Philanthropic
Program, Chemical Bank, Citibank/Citicorp, Rockefeller Brothers Fund,
Rockefeller Family and Associates, Rockefeller Foundation, David Rockefeller,
Morgan Guaranty Trust, John D. and Catherine T. MacArthur Foundation,
ARCO Foundation, British Petroleum American, Inc., Mercedes Benz of North

America, Inc., Seagram and Sons, Inc., Newsweek, Inc., Reader's Digest Foundation, Washington Post Company, the Asia Foundation, the Association of Radio and Television News Analysts, the Carnegie Corporation of New York, The Ford Foundation, The General Electric Foundation, The General Motors Corporation, The Hewlett Foundation, the Andrew W. Mellon Foundation, the Alfred P. Sloan Foundation, and Xerox Foundation (*CFR Annual Reports:* 1987: 104; and 1990: 141). Also, Roberts (1985: 203) indicates:

> The CFR is 'the establishment' not only does it have influence and power in key decision-making positions at the highest levels of government to apply pressure from above, but it also finances and uses individuals and groups to bring pressure from below.

The American CFR currently has 2,670 members, of whom 952 reside in New York City, 339 in Boston, and 730 in Washington DC. In addition to its headquarters in New York City, the CFR has thirty-eight affiliated organizations, known as Committees on Foreign Relations, located in major cities in the United States (*The CFR 1990 Annual Report*: 6).

The Global Bilderbergers: Another historical and influential public organization is *The Global Bilderbergers*. This organization consists of approximately one hundred power-elite groups from the nations of NATO (North Atlantic Treaty Organization), (Roberts, 1979: 185). This organization is interlocked with that of the CFR, and may therefore be accurately categorized as a CFR sister organization. In addition, the Aspen Institute is also a sister organization of CFR and the Global Bilderbergers. The Ford and Rockefeller Foundations fund the Aspen Institute. The Aspen Institute has been described as a training and orientation school for prospective world government administrators, (Roberts, 1979:189).

The Club of Rome: Another influential organization that has drawn its members from the Council on Foreign Relations (CFR) is the Club of Rome (COR). It is an informal organization of less than one hundred people who are scientists, educators, economists, humanists, industrialists, and national and international civil servants (Meadows, Meadows, Randers, and Behrens, 1974: 9). Mesarovic and Pestel's (1974: 203) study indicates that Aurilio Peccei, the Club's founder, states:

> Their world model, based on new developments of the multilevel hierarchical systems theory, divides the world into ten interdependent and mutually interacting regions of political, economic or environmental coherence. ... It will be recognized of course that these are still prototype models.

Mesarovic and Pestel (1974: 203) have assumed a Herculean task. The full implementation of their work will take many years.

Considering the entire above international alliance organizations, they are highly involved in establishing a global power to safeguard their individual and group interests. These global alliances conduct annual regular meetings in luxurious hotels and resorts. Because of such a type of socialization, we called them the *G-pub-pols*. The *G-pub-pols* are the actual front line and cutting edge of global capitalism. As long as they run a highly orchestrated global economy, they are in complete charge of the global economy.

Among the global front line *G-pub-pols* are the International Monetary Fund, and the Federal Reserve System or the Central Banks in all nations around the globe. For example, in the United States, the establishment of Federal Reserve System traces back to 1913. Roberts (1984: 56) indicates that contrary to public belief, the Federal Reserve is not a government institution. It is a privately held giant financial corporation owned by stockholders. Until a few years ago, however, the name of those who owned the Federal Reserve was one of the best kept secrets of international finance due to a provision of passage of the Federal Reserve Act agreeing that the identities of the Fed's Class "A" stockholders not be revealed. At the time the Federal Reserve Act was passed as Dalton (1985: 4) reports:

> This Act establishes the most gigantic trust on earth. When the President [Wilson] signs this bill the invisible government of the Monetary Power will be legalized...the worst legislative crime of the ages is perpetrated by this banking and currency bill.

Gary Kah (1991: 13) indicates:

> According to Mr. R. E. McMaster, the top eight stockholders are Rothschild Banks of London and Berlin; Lazard Brothers Banks of Paris; Israel Moses Seif Banks of Italy; Warburg Bank of Hamburg and Amsterdam; Lehman Brothers Bank of New York; Kuhn, Loeb Bank of New York; Chase Manhattan Bank of New York; and Goldman, Sachs Bank of New York. These interests own the Federal Reserve System through approximately three hundred stockholders, all of who are known to each other and are sometimes related to one another.

As it has been observed through the second half of the 20th century, it was the econo-political trend in the stock market when the Fed lowered the prime interest rate, the values of stocks and the stock volumes in exchange in the marketplace increased. Nevertheless, such a trend has not been effective anymore in the year 2001 after the terrorist attack in the World Trade Center in September 11, 2001. The Fed has decreased the interest rate repeatedly, and instead of stock market values rising, as expected, they went down. The major reason for such a sudden change is based on the financial dependency of the global and multinational corporations on the global plutocracy. Most corporations are no longer dependent on the American bank industry. They are dependent on the *G-pub-pols.*

The United Nations: Of the numerous global organizations, treaties, and agreements, the United Nations (UN) is one of the most global visible and extensive alliances. In 1945, at the UN's founding conference, forty-seven members of the CFR were in the United States delegation and chartered the establishment of the United Nations. In 1969 during a debate between Lt. Col. Archibald Roberts and Congressman Richard L. Otting, Director, United States Committee on the United Nations, Roberts (1986: 4) testified:

> In a letter to the President, Franklin D. Roosevelt, date 22 Dec. 1941, Secretary Hull, at the founding of a Presidential Advisory Committee on Post War Foreign Policy. This Post War Foreign Policy Committee was in fact the planning commission for the United Nations and its Charter.

The United Nations' purposes are the following:

- To maintain international peace and security
- To develop friendly relations among countries
- To achieve international cooperation in solving international problems of an economic, social, cultural, or humanitarian nature
- To be a center for harmonizing national efforts in these cases

The Trilateral Commission: The late 1960s and early 1970s are crucial periods of time during which large number of Americans became aware of the fact that major segments of U. S. industries were falling under the control of just a few multinational establishments. The global capitalists became involved to funnel the international capital from American and European countries to Japanese industrialists and Organization of Petroleum Exporting Countries — OPEC's magnates. The global capitalists have had assurance that the OPEC's magnates promptly invest their assets in the West and acquire Western companies and real estates in America. It was in such a period of time that the Islamic religious faith converted into a political force to such an extent that in 1973, the OPEC's Arab members put the oil embargo into effect against the West. In such a crucial economic crisis, the Shah of Iran increased the flow of oil to the West in order to moderate the Arab nations' embargo crisis. Nevertheless, the Iranian people in 1979 forced the Shah of Iran out of power and replaced him with Ayatollah Rouhollah Khomeini.

Parhizgar and Jesswein (1998: 141-150) indicate: "In the early 1970s, the world, industrialized nations and developing nations alike, paid about $2 a barrel for petroleum produced by the 13-member Organization of Petroleum Exporting Countries (OPEC). Over time, with high and increasing demand in the oil market, and control over its supply exerted by OPEC, the price of oil jumped to over $35 by 1981. As Exhibit # 9-8 below shows, changes in the price of oil over the past twenty years have been substantial.

Table 9.2: Compassion Debt Outstanding, 1970-89 (Percentage of Long-Term Debt)

	Debt from official sources			Debt from private sources			Debt at floating rate		
	1970-72	1980-82	1989	1970-72	1980-82	1989	1970-72	1980-82	1989
Argentina	12.6	9.0	18.6	87.4	91.0	81.1	6.6	29.2	80.4
Bolivia	58.2	49.3	81.8	41.8	50.7	18.3	7.3	28.4	24.2
Brazil	30.7	11.9	27.0	69.3	88.1	73.0	26.1	46.0	66.3
Chile	46.0	11.1	32.9	54.0	88.9	67.1	8.3	23.4	53.9
Colombia	68.1	46.1	52.6	31.9	53.9	47.4	5.4	33.7	42.2
Costa Rica	39.8	36.8	52.6	60.2	63.2	47.4	15.5	42.4	43.7
Ecuador	51.4	29.5	38.6	48.6	70.5	61.4	8.2	37.2	63.3
Guatemala	47.5	71.0	76.0	52.5	29.0	21.0	3.5	5.6	10.3
Honduras	73.8	62.6	81.4	26.3	37.4	18.6	1.8	18.9	19.0
Jamaica	7.4	68.3	83.9	92.6	31.7	16.1	4.7	17.3	23.8
Mexico	19.5	10.9	20.9	80.5	89.1	79.1	31.8	61.4	75.3
Nicaragua	65.3	58.0	82.3	34.7	42.0	17.7	44.2	42.1	18.4
Peru	15.6	39.4	46.7	84.4	60.6	53.3	16.1	22.9	28.7
Uruguay	44.2	21.1	23.2	55.8	78.9	76.8	10.1	28.5	70.4
Venezuela	30.8	3.6	3.2	69.2	96.4	96.8	17.2	57.8	73.9
India	95.1	83.9	53.9	4.9	16.1	40.7	0.0	3.0	16.7
Pakistan	90.5	92.6	93.9	9.5	7.4	6.1	0.0	3.2	10.6
Sri Lanka	81.6	79.5	85.1	18.4	20.5	14.9	0.0	12.9	3.5
Indonesia	72.3	51.7	61.0	27.7	48.3	39.0	4.9	15.1	27.8
Korea, Rep.	35.2	34.3	37.3	64.8	65.7	62.7	11.8	29.0	20.2
Malaysia	51.0	21.9	49.0	49.0	78.1	76.4	17.4	36.7	43.9
Papua New Gu·	6.1	23.4	34.8	93.8	76.6	65.2	0.0	22.9	16.4
The Philippines	22.6	31.4	53.0	77.4	68.6	47.0	7.2	24.1	41.6
Thailand	40.1	39.1	42.5	59.9	60.9	57.5	0.4	22.4	24.9
Cameroon	82.2	56.6	72.7	17.8	43.4	27.3	1.8	11.3	9.7
Congo, Peopl	86.5	45.3	58.4	13.5	54.7	41.6	0.0	15.1	31.7
Cote d'Ivoire	51.6	24.3	41.1	48.4	75.7	58.9	19.1	36.9	35.4
Ethiopia	87.3	90.9	87.5	12.7	9.1	12.5	1.5	2.1	5.2
Ghana	58.0	90.3	91.9	41.9	9.7	8.2	0.0	0.0	1.4
Kenya	58.3	54.8	72.5	41.7	45.2	27.5	2.1	10.1	3.7
Liberia	81.1	74.0	82.8	19.0	25.9	17.2	0.0	16.9	11.3
Malawi	85.8	72.2	95.1	14.2	27.8	4.9	2.3	21.9	3.7
Niger	97.0	41.0	73.9	2.9	59.0	26.1	0.0	13.4	7.7
Nigeria	68.8	15.1	47.6	31.2	84.9	52.4	0.7	48.0	37.8
Senegal	62.2	69.1	93.9	36.8	30.9	6.1	24.5	9.4	1.5
Sierra Leone	60.6	67.4	82.7	39.4	32.6	17.3	3.8	0.0	1.2
Sudan	86.9	75.1	78.4	13.1	24.9	21.6	2.2	9.6	14.2
Tanzania	61.0	75.5	94.5	39.0	24.5	5.5	0.4	0.3	2.4
Zaire	42.5	65.9	89.2	57.5	34.1	10.8	32.8	11.9	5.3
Zambia	22.0	69.7	86.1	78.0	30.3	14.0	20.7	10.2	14.3
Algeria	48.3	22.4	28.5	51.7	77.6	71.5	33.9	23.4	32.3
Egypt	70.9	82.4	82.3	29.1	17.6	17.7	2.1	2.5	8.9
Hungary	0.0	12.1	11.7	0.0	87.9	88.3	0.0	81.3	64.4
Morocco	79.1	55.9	76.6	20.9	44.1	23.4	2.7	27.2	39.7
Poland	9 23	36.6	68.5	7.7	63.4	31.5	11.3	47.0	64.0
Portugal	29.3	24.7	19.7	70.7	75.3	80.3	0.0	33.9	29.8
Tunisia	71.4	60.1	72.2	28.6	39.9	27.8	0.0	13.6	19.4
Turkey	92.2	63.3	46.8	7.8	36.7	53.2	0.8	23.0	29.8

Source: World Bank (1991), 191.

The skyrocketing price of energy had a traumatic impact on those nations that were dependent on foreign oil -- both the industrialized West and the developing Third World countries. The most obvious and immediate effect of the increase in oil prices was a redistribution of wealth among developed and developing nations to such a startling extent that the OPECs' economic might rose to reach the levels enjoyed by the larger, more-industrialized West. While in the 1970s many non-communist industrialized nations sank in economic recession, the OPEC countries suddenly were gorged with money. Developing nations not blessed with oil staggered under the new cost of fuels and fertilizers needed to lift them from poverty. With the transfer of wealth to some developing nations, a dramatic shift in economic power appeared. Not only did the major oil-producing states controlled a vital resource without which all Western economies would face collapse, they also had accumulated by the end of 1980 some $300 billion in foreign assets.

The oil exporting countries (OPEC) recycled their foreign exchange surpluses in three ways:

- By buying Western consumer goods, military hardware, industrial equipment, food and other commodities.
- By investing their funds in development projects at home or in foreign countries, especially in the United States and Western Europe.
- By lending or recycling the money through official and private channels, most notably the Euromarkets, to hard-pressed oil-importing nations in the Third World.

The security of the Middle East oil supplies had been in the forefront of U.S. foreign policy planning since the 1973 embargo and production cutbacks. This became even more pressing in 1979 with the change in government in Iran and the resulting destabilization of the oil market and the new apprehensions among Western industrialized nations dependent on the region's oil. In 1980 the trade surplus of the oil exporting nations reached $152.5 billion (compared with $82.6 billion in 1974). During that year, industrial nations and non-oil-exporting developing nations suffered record deficits in their trade balance of $125.3 billion and $102.0 billion, respectively. These figures represented a fifty percent increase over 1979 in both the oil exporting countries' surpluses and the industrial nations' deficits. The higher deficits in the industrialized world were due almost entirely to its trade imbalance with the oil-exporting nations (*Rivalry in the Persian Gulf*, 1981: 71-98).

The abundant inflows of financial resources to the developing countries came to an end in 1982. Falling oil prices shocked several economies that had become dependent on its continued rise, thus setting off the debt crisis. One of the consequences was the decrease in net capital flows to most developing countries. Many developing countries, burdened by internal debt, found themselves in economic difficulties and several multinational institutions became more fearful of defaults. The main source of the decrease in capital flows to the developing world came from the private sector. As a result of the debt crisis, increased private flows went primarily to meet the debt servicing needs of debtor countries and little additional capital was available for investment and sustained growth. The persistence of the debt crisis in the early 1980s caused the debtor countries to experience a reversal in resource transfer, lower investment and growth, and higher inflation. The severely indebted middle-income economies experienced an average growth of 2.3 percent from 1973-80 and 2.1 percent for the period 1980-1990 and the average annual percentage growth of debt of severely indebted middle-income economies declined from 25.2 percent for 1973-80 to 16.2 percent for the period 1980-90. (Kaminarides and Nissan, 1993:123-138).

The deep international economic recession of the late 1980s and early 1990s was coupled with high inflation and an increase in the values of hard currencies in the international market. Demand and prices for high technology and other manufactured imports by developing nations increased sharply. Developing nations have thus had to borrow heavily to finance their resultant trade deficits. These and other socio-political and economic factors have led to the inability of developing nations to offset their newly expanded indebtedness. However, this has also resulted in economic hardships for both lending and borrowing countries.

According to the United Nations' Economic Commission, developing nations were in the midst of socio-political and economic crisis. In the early 1980s, the major international development agencies concluded that trade and investment were the best strategies for achieving economic recovery and development in most developing countries (Patrick, 1994: 241). But such a strategy ended in 1982, when the abundant inflows of financial resources to the developing countries ended also. The decline in technological and economic assistance from industrialized nations was a major factor setting off the debt crisis. Many developing countries, burdened by internal debt, found themselves in economic difficulties and several multinational financial institutions were evermore fearful of defaults. Because of the crisis, private flows of capital escalated primarily to meet the debt servicing needs of debtor countries and to pay off the compounded interest with little additional capital available for investment and sustained growth World Bank *(World Bank Development Report* 1991: 125)

Simultaneously it was becoming painfully obvious that the developing nations were not able to maintain any competitiveness vis-à-vis the developed countries. During the 1980s we see in Exhibit 9-9 that total debt service for developing countries was rising by 35.8 percent. Yet Gross Domestic Product per capita raised a mere 8.6 percent. At the same time, GDP per capita for the developed world was growing at a rate of 46.5%. GDP per capita for developing countries grew from $682 in 1980 to $746 in 1990, while for the developed world it grew from $10,700 to $19,985 (World Bank *World Development Reports* for 1982 and 1992). Much of this disparity might be attributable to the growing debt burdens carried by the developing countries.

The increasingly global market economy prompts questions about the depth and persistence of knowledge-wealth (technology) and economic-wealth (international monetary). In the late 20th century the Arabic world had two major common factors that have been influenced during their modern political diplomacy: oil and Islamic faith. These two factors became political tools for European and American oil companies to be involved in political affairs of the Middle Eastern nations. At the same time the OPEC energy crisis had a direct effect on the Japanese industrial complex. In the 1980s, the Japanese auto industry found a golden opportunity to export compact cars to the global market. Global consumers were forced to cut back their energy consumption. At the same time the U. S. auto industry plunged into a deep recession from which they had to establish joint venturing partnerships with Japanese's companies. As it turned out a newly industrialized power — Japan — emerged. As a result, the new era of global economic interdependence emerged with the establishment of the Trilateral Commission. The Trilateral Commission (TC) was formed in 1973 (The *Trilateral Commission*: 1986: 2). Zbigniew Brzezinski,, who became President Jimmy Carter's National Security Advisor during the American hostage taking by Ayatollah Khomeini drafted the Trilateral Commission's charter and went on become the organization's first director (1973-1976), (Kah, 1991: 45).

In the 1970s, most multinational corporations realized that a major factor in whether a corporation is profitable or not was its multicultural management strategies. Of course, not all domestic and/or multinational corporations manage multiculturalism the same way, but when these relations become well managed these multinational corporations may have had considerable profit advantages. In the decade of 1970s the Arab Kings and Sheiks, and the Shah of Iran immediately funneled oil money from OPEC back into American and European countries. In addition, some of the Arab Sheiks became vice-presidents of some banks such as Chase Manhattan Bank in New York (Kah, 1991: 45).

Global Profit Motives: In a democratic society, business ethics and living standards of working families are intimately tied together for parents to work hard and earn honest money in order to raise their children. Such an ethical motive can reinforce societal wellbeing of any community. People can earn money through three types of motives:

- To be motivated to work either physically and/or intellectually for others and earn wages, salaries, and/or commissions.
- To be motivated to invest their savings in the financial markets such as depositing their cash money in a bank as Certified Deposits (CDs) and earn interest or to buy municipal bonds or stocks and earn interests and/or profits (loses).
- To be motivated to invest their savings and credits in a business for making a decent profit or a sudden loss.

It should be noted that in conducting a business, there are three major factors:

- The value and volume of profits/loses
- The value and volume of circulated money and products and/or services
- The value and volume of goods or services that should not be overlooked.
- In a free market economy, the value and volume of the profits, money, and goods or services are not predictable or controllable. Because of such an uncertainty, both employers and employees are prone to the variability and vulnerability of profit motives of their competitors

There are two major types of profit motives: (1) hard working profit and (2) soft working profit. Hard working profit is related to the relentless physical and intellectual efforts to be productive in a production system (e.g., privatized business sector). Soft working profit is related to the light bureaucratic working conditions in some non-profit organizations and/or not-for-profit-organizations (e.g., some public offices). Nevertheless, in both cases, if individuals are affiliated with or related to upper class people, they are the major decision makers. If they are belonged to the middle or lower classes, they need to adjust their situations to the will of the higher-class investors (*corp-mags*) and/or governmental authorities (*pub-corp-pols*). These people are called *finpolitan* and/ or *corppolitan* elite groups.

Global *finpolitan* or *corpolitan* elite groups make decisions relevant to tariffs, wages, prices, price controls, interest rates, employment policies, investment expansion or contraction, and supporting political figures to get to the governmental key positions. These global *finpolitan* or *corppolitan* elite groups are called global ruling class or *G-pub-corp-pols*. Their profit motives are crucial in making decisions about war and peace. Whether there is war or peace, they are ready to adjust their businesses to the evolving situations. Some clarification and analysis of the profit motives of three *pols (fin-pols, corp-mags,* and *G-pub-corp-pols*) seems appropriate here.

Business success in global capitalism is praised by maximization of stockholders' profit motives. The doctrine of financial success for the above three *pols* is based on the inner rules of the credit system game. Global citizens are born with credit debts in hospitals, they live with credit debt in their lives, and die are buried or cremated with the credit plastic card debts. Successful global citizens are those that have died without credit card debts. The competent global citizens are those individuals who could care for themselves and their family members; the self reliant and successful individuals.

Private Overaccumulated Ownership: Global capitalism as an econo-political derivative power is closely related to the private ownership either through individuals, or alliance groups. It is a system of financial investment for the purpose of making more money through money-power. Individuals, oligarchies, oligopolies, and global alliances purchase various means of production systems from all over the world in order to use them for manufacturing goods or providing services for the sake of making profits. The socialist critique of global *capitalist* inequality spotlights the qualitative differentiation of social locations captured by the concept of *class*, *(*Editorial Perspectives*: Science & Society,* 1994:131).

Hofstede (1980) indicates that cultural heterogeneity has been viewed as power-distance index in nations. It represents seven beliefs: (1) wealth, (2) economic growth, (3) geographic latitude, (4) population size, (5) population growth, (6) population density, and (7) HERMES (a Greek word for the god of commerce) in organizational innovation and investment. He found that social structure is most likely in power-distance countries where power, wealth, and prestige are used to reinforce social inequality. Cultural differences in the performance for social class hierarchy are important because Burn and Stalker (1961) found that inequality of prestige, rewards, and social power increase innovation. Innovation results from decentralization of power. Global capitalistic private ownership operates under various systems of economic class stratification such as *oligarchies, oligopolies,* and *alliances.*

THE CRITIQUE OF MORAL GLOBAL CAPITALISM

The structural and operational components of the global capitalism are always found embedded in the historical cultural and political ideology of colonialism. Global capitalism is a new adjusted product of the traditional form of colonialism. The eighteenth century of Marx's theory of historical materialism accounted for the theory of epochal changing transition from feudalism to capitalism. Marx called it the home territory of the theory of history (Miller, 1984: 237). The central focus of such an epochal changing transition is based on the dynamic movement of the feudal mode of local production into a global marketing system. The role of markets in promoting global capitalistic economy is based on dissolving the national economy, because national plutocrats lack internal prime movers capable of explaining its historical evolution.

In this view, conversion of colonialism to global capitalism as Cohen (1988: 84) states, is the fundamental cause of social evolution and it lies: "In an autonomous tendency for the productive forces to develop.... The nature of the production relations of a society is explained by the level of development of its productive forces." Cohn maintains that global capitalist relations of production arose when and because they are most apt to promote economic growth, given the existing level of economic development, and social progress of the forces of production.

In developing countries, the basis for determining the legitimate relations between producers and consumers from an ethical point of view is contained with exploitation of national resources through authoritarian governments. Global capitalism develops mini dominated powers in developing nations within the contextual realm boundary of global capitalism. Within such a contextual ethical domain of business, the global capital holders establish amoral relationships with the third world government not with their people. Consequently, national governments' moral and ethical commitments to their people will be based upon the means and ends of governments and global capitalists, not based on people and governments. It establishes a loose moral and ethical relationship between domestic businesses and governments in order to allow governments a great deal of secrecy. For example, in November 1986 revelations of a secret, unethical, and illegal scheme to fund freedom fighters in Nicaragua, where in the United States sold weapons through Israel's government to Ayatollah Khomeini who was considered as a sworn enemy of both the United States of America and Israel. The U. S. and Israel worked out a laundering scheme to have Israel give Iran missiles, and then for the U.S. to resupply Israel. The Iran-Contra scandal is one example of how politics operates in the post-industrialized world(http://libreray.thinkquest.org/17823/ data/ irancontra.html).

The most important characteristic of global capitalism is vested in a tendency for free trade among nations, competitive regional market economy, and a shared global market-type system in which all capital holders can easily convert their investments into different international currencies. Any national capital holder individuals or groups do not control either by governments or such a global free market system. Within this system, the national governments do not set the price of goods and the rate of profitability. The governments control neither prices nor wages. Also, the governments do not control their domestic production systems. At the national level, the governments do not control of intervene in the business operations. However, at the global level, the international alliances may monopolize production and sale forces through their inclusive ownership or control of supply; or through global oligopolies by fixing and controlling the price systems.

In conclusion, global capitalists claim that they expand entrepreneurial reproduction systems in two possible ways. First, wage and commission earners in trade, advertising, marketing, and sales are considered unproductive workers by increasing the number of people who belong to the new middle strata. These workers are not working in the lines of manufacturing systems and do not increase the economy's values while their consumption vitalizes the market (Moszkowska, 1935: 97). These service-oriented workers, who are known as non-productive labor forces, are side effects of overconsumption. Second, by the massive overconsumption of commodities through military expenditures by governments it provides lucrative opportunities for global capitalists to make more profits.

We have examined eight major ethical critiques of global capitalism. Global capitalism is inherently amoral because:

- It cannot operate under a universal moral and ethical system.
- It establishes international worker exploitation for lowering costs and maximizing profits.

- It promotes the vested interest of the few giant oligopolies and/or oligarchies.
- It retards developing nations from domestic competitive operational production systems.
- It creates more economic gaps among classes of people and less achievement in improving a better, more just, and more equitable society at the domestic market level.
- It dominates the national political democracy and consequently, giant global corporations will exploit the nation.
- It eliminates the national sovereignty of small businesses of developing nations and deepening them into the international debts.
- It adjusts the historical system of colonialism into a modern form of plutocracy.

ETHICAL AND MORAL ATTRIBUTIONS OF GLOBAL SOCIALISM IDEOLOGY

Global Socialism Ideology (GSI) generally illustrates that whoever control the means of production should hold power to determine how pluralistically people live. According to the GSI, this task is the responsibility of a democratic government. The state is a secular construct that facilitates an increase in moral virtues, cultural values, and legal doctrines as collective aims. Often democratic governments promote society in the path of freedom and justice. These labels for the national unity tend to encompass the whole society, or at least very large chunks of it. People expect to be ruled by trustworthy spiritual (not necessarily religious ones) leaders who seek to mediate between people and the divine world above. The leaders reject jurisprudence ideology. They believe their laws should come from divine revelation and humanism, but not be drawn up by jurists.

The government should initiate comprehensive tax policy and labor law to guarantee the basic public interest through human rights for all not for parts. The government is characterized as a public administration for operating the purposeful fulfillment or enforcement of public policy.

The government must be concerned with the uses and abuses of power and profound human tragedies. The government should prevent multinational corporate corruption and domestic business briberies through strict legal mandates not to lead them to unjust or immoral ends. Also, the government of this ultra-socialism ideology should find a way to overcome imported defected ideas that can pollute the integrity of national civilization. People in socialist countries believe that since imported corruptions are manipulative and deceptive, it is the role of the government to liberate their cultures from foreign corrupted and polluted cultural trends and purify their citizens' minds and ideas not by force, but by ethical and moral education. For example, the international child pornography business through free flow of videotape trade and/or the

Internet should be highly regulated. This type of socio-cultural perception can be named as liberalization in ethical and moral philosophical cleansing. The moral and ethical philosophical agents are known as mystical nativism. For example, the Japanese ethical and moral philosophy is rooted in the ethnic nationalism, Zen, and Shinto-based nativism. They believe that they were a world-historical race descended from gods, whose divine task was to lead all Orientals into a new age of Great Harmony. Their ethical and moral mysticism is not in any particular dominated orders such as materialism, liberalism, capitalism, communism, individualism, humanism, or rationalism.

It is very difficult to separate Global Socialism Ideology as an economic system from socialism as a political system, because they believe that moral and ethical power should be driven by the force of will of spirit and souls, not by the force of military power. It should be noted that since the Global Capitalism Ideology prohibits governments to operate any business for profit making purposes, the Global Socialism Ideology promotes governments' joint partnership with the private sector to service the community. The key characteristic of the Oriental ethics is based on self-devotion, sacrifice, discipline, austerity, and submission to the collectivistic goodness and a deep faith in the superiority of paternalistic ideology over other reasoning.

The GSI is based on a socio-cultural and econo-political belief that the government to some extent should involve in government-business ownership along with private sector. At the same time Global Socialism Ideology should not be identified with or confused with communism ideology, because communism ideology as a political mover, has never been achieved. In a communistic ideology, there is no divine faith as the source of lives and activities. Communism ideology is a political platform to manipulate and exploit the national endowed resources in order to promote a monopolistic elite group's interest. We will analyze the immoral and unethical of Communism Ideology latter on in more detail in this chapter. Although in the modern Japanese polity, there have been numerous unethical and immoral events, they were influenced by the Western cultures to defect Japanese spiritual beliefs and trade confusion (e.g., the Lockheed payola payments to the Japanese politicians in 1980s).

Principles of the Global Socialism Ideology

The Global Socialism Ideology is based on regulation of the economy toward the interest of social justice within the recognized context of familial loyalty, obedience, frugality, and hard working habits. Within such an ideological belief the government should strive for promotion of the general welfare of all global citizens regardless of their econo-social and political status. The Global Socialism Ideology should echo the public voice within the holistic contextual boundary of the modern scientific advancements and technological developments. The GSI should be characterized by four features, each of which parallels to some extent to the Global Capitalism Ideology with some differences. The four features of GSI are:

- The right to business income for natural persons (individuals) and artificial persons (commercial corporations and business firms) is based on providing appropriate equitable opportunities through allocation of resources to be granted, regulated, and enforced by government authorities. The key government authorities are viewed as representatives of all families who are given appropriate democratic rights to freely elect their representatives. There is a difference between the democratic capitalism ideological election procedures and the democratic participated socialism one. In the democratic capitalism election the voting rights are limited only to those types of eligible population who have reached the voting age with naturalization and immigration privileges. There is a question that arises from the nature of democracy. That question indicates that how in a democratic society minor children should be deprived from exercising their civil rights. The only answer would be through their parents and/or their legal guardians and legally be offered to cast their votes by their parents and/or legal guardians. If you find such a voting trend in a country, then you can name such a nation as a democratic socialized country.
- Natural and artificial persons typically have exclusive rights to moderate their consumption of resources that they can transform them into finished or usable products and trade them with the purpose of legitimate profit making objectives. They need to take into account conservation and protection of resources on the basis of the notion of pluralistic fairness and justness.
- The government has exclusive rights and authority to own, operate, and manage some of heavy industries and public services. Individuals have legitimate professional rights to own, operate, and having income from mass public services such as judiciary, educational, health, and medical services, shelter and housing, and family welfare or public services such as space, land, sea, and air transportation, heavy equipments, natural resources, and the like. Global socialized medicine, education, housing, public transportation, family welfare, and the like should be assigned to the "non-profit professional associations and not-for-profit organizations" as another alternative to enhance the social competitive spirit of a nation.
- The major form of production system should be focused on conservation and preservation of fossil energy. This means that the major problems of industrialization must be faced by the notion of pluralistic socialist economies -- businesses should be accountable for cleaning up the environment. If industries with their industrialization operations cause problems of waste and pollution, global warming, major anthropogenetic gases [Carbon dioxide (CO_2), chlorofluorocarbons (CFCs), Methane (CH_4), and Nitrous oxide (N_2O)],

they need to be accountable for cleaning up the environment.

- To respect the workers' integrity is a fundamental human right in industrialized socialized societies. Worker dissatisfaction, tedium and boredom at work, unfair manual and think wages and/or salaries, and unsafe and insecure working conditions should not be exercised in order to meet the greedy appetite of shareholders.

- Social ownership of the means of production systems does not deny the private ownership of production facilities, machineries, tools, and personal property ownership rights. It is viewed as a complementary reinforcement of public services in a market place. The form of ownership could be professional associations, unions, worker ownership, or joint venturing partnerships between these entities and multinational corporations.

- Social ownership means to own or to operate the major resources such as oil-reserved fields and other minerals as the result of nationalization of these resources either by government or their subcontractors. State ownership involves direct operational controlling systems by governments.

- In the global socialism ideological systems, governmental agencies are viewed as employees of citizens of nations. Their stakeholders are viewed as the worldwide community of human race. Therefore, governments should serve people; people should not serve their governmental authorities. The government should not exploit its people. The government should not take advantage of people by paying them less than the market value they produce in order to make profit. People should make profit not their governments. In such a philosophical view, equitability not equality would be the main thematic criterion for setting the implementation of meritocracy. Since people are different in their efficiency and effectiveness, naturally their productivity would be different too. Then individuals deserve to be treated equitably. Therefore, equality of opportunity is not necessarily guaranteed. On the other hand their quiddity needs should be weighed and to be treated fairly and equitably.

- The profit sharing between individuals and governments and or between executives and employees or between investors and workers is the central ethical question of global socialism. All individuals' patents and copyrights should have a special clause for paying a percentage as loyalty to their community. Society should be built on the basis of mutual profit sharing. Within the boundary of GSI the value of worker ownership of lifetime scientific and technological specialization and practical skills are assumed as potential valuable financial knowledge wealth. Professional specialized people expect their societies to value such a momentary privileged knowledge-wealth that deserves to be valued in investments and trades. In the capitalistic societies values of assets are limited to monetary wealth, but in the GSI in addition to the values of monetary wealth, there is another capital known as knowledge-wealth. Knowledge-wealth is viewed as a long time monetary investment in education for concluding professional specialization. Therefore, the GSI respects such an investment and gives credits to those specialization and skillful capital holders. This means that not only are professional workers viewed as employees of a corporation and are entitled to receive their wages or salaries, they are also viewed as a group of capital holders (knowledge-wealth) who are entitled to get fair returns on their educational investments as long as they are working for a corporation or a business. In conclusion, as the monetary capital carries interest for shareholders, knowledge-wealth carries monetary interest for professional specialization. What is evident in such a system is professional workers are viewed as workers and shareholders of a company.

In conclusion, through moral and ethical indoctrination of social virtuous justness and fairness, the GSI carries values for professional specialists to be credited with equivalent monetary value system for their long-life investments in their life-time educational investment as we have called it knowledge-wealth or knowledge-capital. In addition, the Global Socialism Ideology is an introduction to reach to the Global Humanism Ideology.

THE GLOBAL COMMUNISM IDEOLOGY: ETHICAL OR UNETHICAL?

What is perhaps best known of the principles of communistic ideology is an inspiration from Marx tradition *from each according to ability, to each according to need,* (Marx 1938).

For Marx, the equal relationships among production, appropriation, distribution, and consumption of material things are the major principles of the ideal communistic society. Such an ideology is radically different from the welfarism of a socialist and/or a capitalist ideology. For Marx, econo-political ideology has been viewed as the foundational relationships between human beings generation by generation. Among the relationships of production, appropriation, distribution, and consumption, Marx emphasized distributive justice.

One of the chief concepts of Marxian's concern is distributive justice ideology. What is an ideology? An ideology is a holistic multi-dimensional set of econo-political and psychosocial ordered ideas that explains and justifies a preferred mode of behavior within the mind-set of individuals in relationship with cultural value systems and militant fundamental beliefs in a society. It is either existing or proposed, and offers a synergistic strategic streamline of structural processes, institutional policies, indoctrination of plans, and programs for achieving its ultimate desired objectives.

The most important sensitive concept in communistic ideology is class. For any society to be stabilized and have survived over time, they need not only to produce to meet their own needs (in Marxism called necessary labor), but also a surplus. This is because, in any society some people will not be able to perform the labor necessary to meet their our needs. What they need to do is to consume the surplus of the labor. For instance, in order to survive, people must make appropriate provision for their infants and their infirmed. This is a fundamental argument that people need to enjoy from *distributive justice* and make their society classless. Marx argues that if those people who perform productive labor only meet their own needs, then other members of society who cannot, will not survive. Therefore, laborers not only need to be productive in order to meet their own needs, they need to be productive in a manner in which the social surplus should come into existence for the benefit of all.

This perception is somewhat open-ended to be used by ideologues to promise individual groups of races, ethnicities, and religions to embrace their prevailing ideological justice concept for forming classless society. Such a definition carries a message to be popularized by all types of people. In Marxism ideology the above definition includes material value systems. Burzenisky (1970: 72 and 83) reveals his views about the philosophies of Karl Marx by stating that:

> Marxism represents a further vital and creative stage in the maturing of mans's universal vision. Marxism is simultaneously a victory of the external, active man over the inner, passive man and a victory of reason over belief: it stresses man's capacity to shape his material destiny; finite and defined as man's only reality.... Marxism, disseminated on the popular level in the form of communism, represented a major advance in man's ability to conceptualize his relationship to his world.

Since the communistic ideology is more dominated by materialism ideology, it denies the other valuable dimension of ideology; spirituality. Within the communistic ideas and operations, an ideology arises as a reflection of the conditions of the material life of the society and of the interests of certain classes. The ideology of the working class and its party is Marxism-Leninism; the revolutionary weapon in the struggle for the overthrow of the exploitive system and the building of communism. As we will analyze the communistic ideology in more depth, you will be able to understand the historical background of that idea. A brief outline of some of the fundamental concepts of Marxism-Leninism-Maoism should be helpful in order to be familiar with such ideas.

Karl Marx's utopian ideological political-economy theory for classless societies primarily is based on his interpretation and understanding of the condition of the nineteenth century aristocratic-capitalism system in England. He theorized his views according to a dialectical process of two major views: (1) *Dialectical Materialism*, and (2) *Historical Materialism*. For Marx, Dialectical Materialism is viewed as a body of political thought, or guidance which is known as Scientific Communism, which deals, first, with the strategy of communist revolutions, second, the political problems of socialist states, and third, the official history of materialism. Generalization about human beings and society, past and present is called Historical Materialism. Marx believes that an economic-political materialism's interpretation of history is based on class struggle. As he puts it: "History of all hitherto existing societies is the history of class struggle." He believes that the laws of historical development move societies through successive stages from primitive communalism to slavery, to feudalism, to aristocratism, to capitalism, to socialism, and finally culminating the building of an ideal communistic society where the means of production belong to all and the laborers' work both for themselves and for society as a whole. Each of the stages prior to communism carries within itself a part of the dialectical process the seeds of its own destruction; its own inherent contradictions which will eventually destroy itself.

Interpretation of historical materialism is very complex. Within such a process the main antagonistic classes are the proletariat, or urban workers, and the bourgeoisie, or capital producers. Marx believed that in a capitalist state the exploitation of the former by the latter is the key dialectical element that would eventually lead to socialism, under which exploitation of man by man would cease (Barry and Barner-Barry, 1987: 25). Marx frequently uses the language of morality in describing the ills of capitalism as inherent contradictions within its system. Marx views all social changes follow the concept of dialectic arguments. The concept of dialectic, borrowed from German Philosopher Wilhelm Friedrich Hegel (1770-1831), refers to a process of disruption by which higher truth is reached by confronting the contradictions of a given statement: "Thesis confronted by antithesis produces synthesis or higher truth." Marx's adaptation of Hegel's concept of dialectical movement of society positioned the economic political factors as the key ingredients in class struggle. Communism ideology is a form of secular totalitarianism.

Philosophical Foundation of Communism Ideology

The distinguished philosophical characteristics of communistic ideology is said to be collective ownership of the means of production. Collective ownership of the means of production should not be confused with personal ownership of daily necessities for survival. These personal ownerships are not generally used for the production of commodities to be produced and sold as surplus products. However, sometimes lay-people may personally own those tools and produce in very small scale of personal surplus production. They may sell their personal surplus production in the black market. We need to identify the philosophical moral status of the communistic ideology through the following statements:

- The state ownership and control of virtually all econo-political and socio-cultural activities of the country is based on collectivistic ideology. Collectivism prohibits private property ownership. This means that any property that could be a basis for speculation or illegal economic gain by individuals is prohibited.

- Within the communistic ideological framework, there is no free market to be managed by the private sectors or small groups of investors. In a communistic country the government:
  - o Sets the price of goods and services.
  - o Sets the wages and salaries of all citizens including the minimum and maximum with their differentiating ranging tables.
  - o Sets a controlling production system, appropriation of funds, distribution channels, and sales on the basis of equal benefits for individuals and/or family members with a coupon system.
- Government exercises its econo-political and socio-cultural monopolies (exclusive ownership and control of supply) and monopsonies (exclusive control of demand (e.g., only by governmental bureaucracies).
- The personal property ownership is distinguished from private property ownership. Personal property ownership includes things used for personal consumption or enjoyment (e.g., books, computer, pen, shoes, car, etc.). The personal property ownership should not be used for the economic exploitation of other people.
- Atheism is a principle belief in historical materialism. In communistic ideology, there is no room for religious faith, because of material collectivism. No overt believer would be allowed to occupy a position in government bureaucracy.
- The Communist party is above criticism. It is not subject to any challenge for running the country.
- Within the contextual boundary of communistic ideology, the economical and political systems are virtually inseparable.
- In a communistic society, the political forces determine the courses of actions taken by centralized and planned economy.
- The long-life communistic political leadership (e.g., Lenin, Stalin, and Brezhnev in the former Soviet Union; Mao and Zhao Pang in China; Castro in Cuba; and Young in North Korea) and their associates have been guided by what Marx called a dictatorship of proletariat, the working and peasant class of people.
- Within the context of class processes there are three presumed systems as production, appropriation, and distribution of the social surplus:
  - o Production refers to the manner in which the economic surplus comes into existence by the working class. The government manages the surplus, because there is no private ownership for the working class labor and/or for peasants.
  - o Appropriation refers to the processes and mechanisms by which initial claims are made on this surplus by government.
  - o Distribution refers to the processes by which every member of

society is served equally with goods and services regardless of their needs.

Within the communistic society those who produce the surplus may oppose its appropriation by others. According to Marx's historical materialism, human history reveals that diverse class struggles and structures have caused societies to move from slavery, feudalism, capitalism, socialism, and communism. Nevertheless, absent here is any notion of equilibrium or social harmony.

The Communist Moral and Ethical Critiques

Along with the demise of the former Soviet Union's international power which disintegrated it into fifteen independent states and lost its communistic domination in the Eastern European countries, the historical materialism of Marxism lost it's predictable prophecy. Such a historical claim has proven that not only have socialistic nations not moved toward communism, but also they reversed themselves toward capitalism. One of the most fundamental managerial problems indicated that centralized economic planning failed to promote industrialized progress into an innovative one. In addition, the ideal of equality for all has caused individuals to be alienated from their own efforts. Since the Marxism historical materialism failed to link individuals to each other, it could not maintain the integrity of their surplus for the benefit of all. It promotes an autocratic system to exploit and manipulate their lay-people's efforts for the benefit of the lifetime political elite group — the communistic party.

Capitalism, for Marx, was a necessary stage of economic and social development, but a stage that was to be superseded by the higher stage of communism. Many Marx's followers have put this condemnation of capitalism into moral from and claim that capitalism is inherently immoral, because the wealth flows primarily to capitalist appropriators and to those most favorably positioned to receive distributed shares of the surplus — the corporate's board of governance and its executive agents. Nevertheless, capitalism ideology cannot be moral, but it can be amoral and legal.

We shall examine five major claims of these Marxists on the basis of moral and ethical perspectives: (1) class exploitation, (2) alienation of human dignity, (3) the vested interest of the "political elite group," (4) unjustified claimants on surplus to be managed by workers, and (5) elimination of the producers from the appropriators.

Class Exploitation: Communistic ideology dictates the legitimacy of a classless society through the notion of equality. However, it assesses the legitimacy of econo-political elite class ruling through the lens of justice. In another words, it creates two classes of people: rulers and lay-people. Then the notion of justice raises a question: "Do life-long political leaders believe in justice?" The answer in theory is yes but in practice is no. They believe that they are guardian angles to safeguard the interest of their community. They believe that the community at large is the agent of production. The community, past and present, is the repository of knowledge, skills, and capital that dictate a society's level of productivity and its ability to generate wealth. Within such a path of reasoning they believe justice as fairness requires that all citizens should be equally provided to all of society's distributive privileges. In reality, who are the initial receivers of surplus and by what legal rights are those who are in power? They are political power brokers and privileged social positions. Such a consequential result states that justice is for lay-people not for rulers. Therefore power-holders in practice exploit and manipulate masses in order to maintain their own power-position.

Alienation to Human Dignity: The second criticism of communistic ideology manifests a serious concern for ignoring human dignity. There is an alienated feeling among the ruling elite group to ignore the lay-people's dignity and integrity. There is a crucial question concerning alienation of lay-people. That question is: What constitutes the alienation of lay-people? Within the contextual boundary of communistic ideology lay-people are servants of the collectivistic econo-political system. They have to work to please governmental authorities. The work becomes a mandatory obligation of citizens to satisfy the ruling elite group in power. Within such a psychosocial boundary, citizens at their workplace have no feeling of belongings. Consequently, the end result is alienation.

The productive lay-people who are exploited and manipulated in their efforts toward the notion of collectivism become sole agents of authoritative government. The servants' productive outcomes become no longer the lay-people's own. The more powerful the authoritative communistic government, the more diminished the integrity and dignity of the lay-people. The *alienation* of productive lay-people in their socio-economic activities means not only do their efforts become an object outside themselves; it also alienates them from their own personal value system. The economic outcomes that lay-people offer to the authoritarian government will be used against their humanitarian welfare. Consequently, the communistic government becomes a hostile agent, creating more alienation to exploit them further.

In a communistic country the nature of work and its meaning become a separate phenomenon from the humanitarian nature of lay-people. The work is not a part of their inherent pride of personal value systems. The lay-people's working pride does not fulfill themselves in their work because their work carries unappreciated values. They feel misery rather than wellbeing.

It is a fact, when the work becomes alienated from the lay-people, they will not develop freely their mental and physical energies. Consequently, they will not be able to be creative and innovative in the work place. When people are at their workplace, they are looking to get to the end of the day. When they go home, their work becomes homeless in their workplace.

***The Vested Interest of the Ruling Elite Group*:** The third criticism of the communistic ideology is that the government is the protector of the ruling elite group at the expense of all members of society. If the government is not actually run by the ruling elite group, bureaucrats for the benefits of the ruling party run it. Within such a condition, the function of bureaucrats is to protect the vested interests of political power brokers against all members of society. Bureaucratic communistic system regulates the behavior of all citizens and dictates to them what they are allowed and not allowed to do in their daily lives. Whether or not this is the case, the aim of communistic government is to maintain the interests of lifetime political elite ruling class through red tape bureaucracy. Such a bureaucracy manipulates all functions of businesses including production, appropriation, distribution, sales, and consumption goods and services in a society.

ARE THERE ANY MORAL AND ETHICAL CONSIDERATIONS IN IMPERIALISM IDEOLOGY?

Imperialism is known as selfish compounded desires for a nation to abuse foreign lands and people through commercial, industrial, financial, scientific, political, journalistic, intellectual, and religious impulses. It is an out thrust of the whole expansionist ideology. It provides alienation to native lands to diffuse their inherited cultural value systems. In the historical trends of imperialism, some European countries such as the British government perceived the apartheid supremacy of the Whites over colors, the French of their *mission civiliasatrice*, and the German of diffusing *Kulture*. According to such an ideological belief within the boundary of the Social Darwinism, the White races have more fitter or gifted intelligence and talents than colors. Such an ideology has created barbaric culture in order to promote slavery, torture, famine, and filth in foreign lands in order to gain material opportunities.

All of the above unethical and immoral actions are obviously aligned with self-interest. For example, when we are talking about imperialism, usually we speak of people and their actions being immoral or unethical. We also describe an econo-political ideology or a system as legal system that has been shaped through one-sided interest. The irony about this argument is, if holding slaves is immoral and unethical, then there is a fundamental violation of human rights. If all nations believe that slavery is an ugly face of savagery then in practice they should not practice it through legality.

Slavery is ownership of other human beings. It is wrong to own other human beings and to fail to recognize them as ends in themselves. Slavery constitutes an econo-political system. We use the term slavery in two different senses. In the first sense we mean the practice of slavery. This defines a relation between people and a way of treating people differently. Then we need to analyze both the relation and the actions that follow as a result of the relation. In the second sense, by slavery we mean that economic system in which the slave relation is the fundamental productive relation for obtaining free wealth through the efforts of slaves for masters.

We characterize the system of imperialism by the productive system. It is an ownership by force, not by choice. The imperialism ideology in the international trade system that promotes disrespect for purchasing the ware brought by local merchants as produced by local methods. The imperialist is by no means content simply to purchase what local merchants provide them. They are demanding a kind or a quantity that pre-industrial handicraft methods could not supply. They invest capital in dominated countries, setting up mines, plantations, docks, warehouses, factories, river shipments, and banks. They build offices, homes, hotels, clubs, and resorts suitable for their expatriates. In an overall assessment, the imperialism power takes over the econo-political life of a dominated country, and transforms large elements of local population into the wage employees of foreign corporations.

The imperialism ideology seeks to operate both economically and politically in order to establish a manufacturing system in the colonized, protected, and/or influenced countries on the basis of cash-and-carry manufacturing systems with minimum costs and maximum profit. It also seeks the development of territorial claims and invested capital in order to import their own methods of production and management system to those countries. Nevertheless, imperialism is known as a power to promote mass-slavery in dominated nations.

We can recognize the economic system of mass-slavery in two different ways. One involves evaluation the morality of the fundamental economic relationship between imperialism power and dominated nations on which it is built. This is based on a *structural analysis.* It involves looking at the basic structures and practices of the system, because the system is defined by its structures and practices. The second way of evaluating economic system is *an end-state approach.* It involves looking at what the system as a whole does to the people affected by it.\

DO YOU FIND MORALITY AND ETHICS IN HUMANISM?

The sociocultural and econo-political ideologies of global capitalism, social Darwinism, communism, and imperialism have not given the priority of the principle form of welfarism in favor of humanity at large. Global capitalism is often obsessed with the ideology of international law and materialism ideology within the realm of the competitive global free market economy. Social Darwinism ideology is absorbed with the segmented profit-making habit for a privileged elite group of people under the notion of the law of physical nature: the survival of the fittest and demise of the sickest ones. Communism ideology is occupied with manipulation and exploitation of human rights within the notion of classless society and equal distribution of minimum necessities for all individuals regardless of the nature and level of their abilities and needs. Global imperialism is obsessed with expansionism by controlling over others through colonialism, physical and wage slavery, racism, sexism, colorism, and discrimination against specific denominated religious groups. Imperialism denies their dominated individuals and nations the freedom to make their own choices and undermines their individual human and civil rights and sovereignty. To some extent each of the above econo-political ideologies and motives refuse to treat all human beings around the globe subjectively. Humanism concerns about what is truly valuable in life. Most of the above econo-political ideologies to some extent do not pay attention to the realm of ethical and moral ultimate reality; humanism.

Humanism and Welfarism Ideologies

Global humanism and welfarism are viewed as the twofold proliferated ethical and moral convictions for survival of human species and humaneness. They are inspired by commitments to justice and compassion for all. Humanism and welfarism are against poverty, destitution, corruption, and injustice of every kind for the present and future generations.

Despite all scientific advancements and technological developments, human beings find their existence within a swinging domain of a radical magnitude zones that are composed of two extreme dual spiritual and brutal ideological characteristics. It is a moral conviction and ethical mandate for humanity to expect each one to have a *life* to live. Life is a natural gift not an econo-political privilege or a role to perform. That life must be *lived with dignity and integrity.* Through realization of an inherent conscientious worth of life each human being expects humanity to provide them with at least the minimum income and support necessary to "live *life* fully." This requires that all nations to be committed to the notion of lifelong moral and ethical convictions, educational and technological experiences, and employment connections. Such a humanitarian indoctrination can create a healthy environment in which the nature of humanity can flourish. Humanity can survive under the notion of global *welfarism.*

Global Welfarism as the First Cause and Final Effect of Humanism

Global welfarism in an econo-political term refers to the continuity of enhanced *life.* It avoids interruptive econo-political catastrophes for all human beings. In addition, global welfarism ideology promotes the notion of re-creation of humanity and societal re-ordination according to the new forms and conditions of environmental forces toward a progressive life style. Global welfarism is a social process that relentlessly strives for re-formulating the new pace of social progress. Welfarism takes immediate steps to perpetuate the species and also sustains those members of society whom it is in its capacity to save. Welfarism does not mean to provide material needs and services only for the third or economically disadvantaged classes of people. It provides happiness for all not for parts. Despite global capitalism, social Darwinism, communism, and imperialism ideologies which all operate under heavy competition to disintegrate societies, humanism re-creates innovative methods to cope with disruptive socio-economical lives.

Welfarism is an alterable milieu that entails all notions that the human life is in the continual process of being restructured as the result of natural catastrophes or human accidental ill-fated experiments to be repaired. Welfarism is the pure moral and ethical convictions of humanity to provide remedies for natural miseries and all other social illnesses. It does not try to institute specific privileges for a specific group or class of people. It refuses to rank or rate individuals in regards to their econo-political worth. It resents racism, sexism, and discrimination in all societies with the notion of humanism. In the economic and financial sphere, humanism is all about enhanced class-border connectivity. Nevertheless, humanism never denies the liberty and freedom of human beings. It promotes a dynamic ground for promoting both manifestation of spiritual and material worth in an incorporated mental and physical environment. Finally, welfarism provides appropriate opportunities for all individuals to achieve their ultimate dynamic state of happiness within a fruitful life.

Humanism and Justice

All modern econo-political ideologies encompass a small range of normative perspectives concerning the practical ethical and moral values of human beings. They state justice, fairness, and rightness according to their own interpretation of ideological indoctrinations. As it was mentioned before, universally, econo-political indoctrination is explicitly normative. It rejects the ideas of institutionalists that deny diversity of cultural value judgments. Institutionalists try to segment universal humanity according to their sociocultural and econo-political doctrines. Institutionalization of an econo-political ideology rejects the ideas that other socio-cultural and religious beliefs could possibly enhance their national value judgments. Institutional ideology refuses to treat human subjectivity in the manner prescribed by humanism's vision. In such an account, institutionalists envision that human nature is a malleable and largely should be shaped by econo-political ideologies not by multicultural milieu or spiritual values that individuals enter at birth with cultural and religious value systems. Nevertheless, humanism strives for expanding areas of integrity and dignity of the human race within the context of genuine spiritual choices. Such a genuine moral and ethical choice provides alternative options in choosing the best solution for miserable conditions. Social Darwinism Ideology (SDI) indicates the survival of the fittest and the demise of the weakest of the sickest. Humanism Ideology (HI) indicates the survival of all sickest, weakest, and fittest would be the main objective for humanity.

CHAPTER SUMMARY

Throughout history, people, power, public policies, and above all political ideologies have been the mainstreams of thoughts for modern societies. Specifically, global class-power coalition, class-intersecting alliances, and cross-class agreements mutually can reinforce each class of people within a nation or beyond. The global financial elite alliances are defined as a partnership of two or more corporations or business units to achieve strategically significant financial objectives that are mutually beneficial. The reasons for global alliances are: to obtain technology and/or manufacturing capabilities, to obtain access to specific markets, to reduce financial risk, to reduce political risk, to achieve or ensure a competitive advantage, and to create strategic synergy through prodigy. *Prodigy* means manifestation of manipulated integrated scientific advancement and technological breakthroughs into an extraordinary power for creating functional productivity through enhancement in size, amount, extent, and degree forces among business cells.

Nevertheless, business ethics ultimately rests on a base of political ideology, economic doctrine, and cultural philosophy. In developing countries, the basis for determining the legitimate relations between producers and consumers from an ethical point of view is contained with exploitation of national resources through authoritarian governments. The most important characteristic of the global elite alliances is vested in a tendency for free trades among nations, competitive regional market economy, and a shared global market-type system in which all capital holders can easily convert their investments into different international currencies. Any national capital holder individuals or groups do not control either by governments or such a global free market system.

Political ideologies in all societies are facts that have made our modern lives very complex. Politics involves the active pursuit of success awarded by others. In other words, it entails the use of one's own products or consumption experiences as a means to the other-oriented ends of achieving a favorable response from someone else. Politics is considered to be a fundamental concern in today's global economy. Nevertheless, there is a danger that contaminated the moral and ethical convictions of human beings. That danger is personal greed and corporate corruption. Greed destroys human dignity and corruption destroys societal trust. Trust within a citizens and among nations has been defined as mutual confidence that no party to an exchange will behave opportunistically and exploit another's vulnerabilities. Also, greed and corruption defect the real sense of democracy. Greed needs to be harnessed and corruption needs to be prevented. The function of democracy has been provided the public with a second power system, an alternative power system that can be used to counterbalance the economic power. A faith is an emotional enforcement for believing in *ritual* reality. There is a tendency among some people that emphasizes on belief aspects of a religion and overlook ritual elements in a religious behavior. This may be a result of the frequently observed falling away from the practice of many traditional rites. A faith is a meaningful reliance on a strong intention that psychologically can be used as reinforcement for expression of an idea or an opinion. A faith is eradicating anxieties, quits the self-doubt, and makes an idea or an opinion in congruence with truthfulness, worthiness, and righteousness. Beliefs are inferences made by and observed about underlying states of expectancy. Beliefs seem to form the core conceptual ideas and opinions concerning the acceptability of something or to be denominated by some faiths.

As a factual belief, human beings are living within two integrated environments: (1) the natural (we can identify it as ecology), and (2) the artificial (we can identify it as a culture). From the standpoint of a material view, the ecological environment provides all organic elements including human beings, animals, plants, and other substances like the air and water with appropriate conditions to survive. However, the artificial environment -- culture -- provides specific human made social conditions to survive. Those conditions that are authoritatively approved set of political ideas are ideologies. Thus, the specificity of conditions could be called ideologies. A political ideology is a set of political ideas; a formalized belief system that explains and justifies a preferred political order for society. Ideologies offer a socio-political and cultural strategy (processes, institutional arrangements, programs, and hierarchical power) for their attainment.

A corporation is a legal entity in which under its own artificial personal identity conducts a business operation. It carries certain legal rights and duties. The corporation substitutes itself for the individual shareholders or stockholders in operating a business and incurring liability.

The *honest businesses* cater their operational activities to respond to the consumption demand of masses. They provide consumers with their everyday's necessary commodities and services. The *camouflaged businesses* are commercial entities that are playing the role of *trustees* in legitimate and legal fronting businesses. *Trustees* are individuals and/or institutions with integrity. They avoid cruelty, greediness, or more than commonly hypocritical or enviousness. The *multi-fin-pols businesses* are specialized large multinational networking corporations with very huge volume of financial assets in their respective operational holdings. They operate under diversity of ways to move money around the world avoiding conventional channels. The *multi-corp-mags* (multi-corporation magnates) are known as elite small groups of business-people and/or their brokers who are incorporated within the international econo-political systems and dominated the greatest mass of ordinary population of the world. The chief instrument of *multi-corp-mags'* power is the global and/or multinational corporations, more particularly the large financial and manufacturing institutions. These institutions run by corporate magnates with a mechanism to maximize profits constant with growth. From an internal point of view, *multi-corp-mags* do everything about the successful international operations to attract investors to trade their stocks. The *hoodlum businesses* are those legitimate businesspeople who are gaining control of a legitimate corporation and utilizing all their tricks to secure full advantageous power in order to divert the regular investment direction either into emulating investors with no gain, or merging with gangsters' hidden investors. Internationally, the *hoodlumers* are often unschooled or illiterate people. The *hoodwink businesses* are those kinds of entities in which fraud, deception, and covering up unethical, immoral, and illegal actions are extensive in their common daily business transactions. Corruption is viewed as the main outcomes of hoodwink businesses. Hoodwinkers are particularly interested to acquire the federal, state, and municipal selling and buying contracts through corrupted governmental authorities. The *international ruthless gangsters called organized crime operate the Business Rings*.

QUESTIONS FOR DISCUSSION

- How do you conceptualize ethical and moral foundations of political ideologies?
- How do you define global financial elite alliances?
- What are the major views of Smithianism and Marxism econo-political ideologies?
- What are the important characteristics of global elite alliances?
- What are different types of financial derivatives?
- How do you define political ideology in relation to ethical and moral convictions?
- How do you define religious faith and its relation with ethics and morality?
- How do you perceive cultural beliefs concerning business ethics?
- How do you define a corporation in term of political ideology?
- What are the major characteristics of honest businesses?
- What are camouflaged businesses?
- What we mean by *multi-fin-pols* businesses?
- What are differences between Hoodlum businesses and hoodwink businesses?
- How do you assess business rings' characteristics concerning ethical, moral, and legal convictions?
- Do you find ethics and morality in global capitalism?
- How do you justify global socialism ideology concerning human welfarism?
- Do you find any ethical and moral convictions in communism?
- What we mean by ethical and moral global humanism?
- How do you assess global imperialism?
- Who are invisible global power alliances?

CASE STUDY

CONFLICTS OF CHILD LABOR, HUMAN RIGHTS, AND CIVIL RIGHTS IN CHINA: THE LEVI STRAUSS & CO. - LS & CO.

Levi Strauss & Co. - LS & CO. has set four core values in its mission: (1) empathy, (2) originality, (3) integrity, and (4) courage:

- Empathy begins with listening; understanding, appreciating, and meeting the needs of those they serve.
- Originality begins with on authentic and innovative American icon - known the world over.
- Integrity begins with doing the right thing; honesty and trustworthiness to do what we say we are going to do.
- Courage begins with standing up for what we believe; the willingness to challenge hierarchy, accepted practices and conventional wisdom.

THE LEVI STRAUSS'S PROFILE

Levi Strauss immigrated to New York in 1847. His original home was Bavaria. In 1853, he moved to the gold rush state - California. He was searching for wealth. He lived in San Francisco to sell dry goods to the gold rushers. Soon after, a prospector told Strauss of miners' trouble in finding strong and durable pants. Strauss made a pair out of canvas for the prospector. Word of quality of the rough pants spread quickly through the prospector's remarks. In 1854, Levi Strauss donated $5 to the San Francisco orphanage only one year after arriving in the city.

In 1873, Strauss and Jacob Davis created their first pair of waist-high overalls, which later became known as jeans. The pants soon became a necessity for lumberjacks, cowboys, railroad workers, oil drillers, and farmers. Strauss continued to construct his pants and work in the wholesaling business until he died in 1902. LS&CO. passed to his four nephews who continued their uncle's jeans business.

After World War II, Walter Hass and Peter Hass assumed leadership of LS&CO. In 1948, they suspended the company's wholesaling business in order to focus on manufacturing Levi's clothing. In the 1950s and 1960s, Levi's jeans became the international popular apparel for youth. The company went public in

1971, when Levi Strauss of Japan was recognized. By the mid-1980s, profits dropped. While marketing product-driven companies hurried into China, Hass pulled out to protest human rights abuse.

LS & CO. manufactures and sells its innovative branded jeans, sportswear, and pants through retail subcontractors and company-owned outlets in more than 100 countries. For the year 2001, 67 percent of total sales were from the Americas, 25 percent from Europe, and 8% percent from Asia Pacific. LS & CO is ranked number 383 in *Fortune 500*, and number 26 in *Forbes Private Fortune 500*. Its operating divisions include Asia Pacific, Europe, Middle East, and Africa. The Americas include Canada, Argentina, Brazil, Mexico, and U. S. A. The performance of LS&CO. in the decade of the 1990s declined drastically. In 1996, its sales reached $7.1 billion and went down to $5.1 billion in 1999. Its net income reached $735 million in 1995 and fell to $5 million in 1999. The company reported an income deficit in the first three months of the year 2000.

International competitors of LS&CO. are Abercrombie & Fitch, American Eagle Outfitter, Benetton, Calvin Kliein, Fruit of the Loom, Guess?, Haggar, JC Penny, Limited Brands, NIKE, Osh Kosh b'Gosh, Oxford Industries, Polo, The Gap, and Tommy Hilfiger.

PROBLEMS AND ISSUES OF THE CASE

One of the major problems for LS&CO. has been related to heavy competition in the jeans market. As the jeans market became more competitive, Levi's Strauss lost its focus. It failed to promptly respond to changing fashions. Consequently, LS & CO. had to close most of its plants and ended production in the United States. LS & CO. moved most manufacturing plants to those countries which had lower-wages including China. As April of 2002, LS & CO. named six U.S. manufacturing plants that will or have, by now, shut down as part of its shift away from manufacturing. This shift is due to the company's desire to focus more on being a marketing and product-driven organization rather than a manufacturer. Closing these manufacturing plants in the U.S. and lying off approximately 3,300 employees, about 20 percent of the workforce employed by LS&CO., will have significant socio-economic impact.

On the basis of its mission, LS & CO. was committed to balancing its social values with business success which maintaining its low cost operations. It should be noted that in 1993 LS & CO. closed its plants in China and in 1998 had to return back to China in order to maintain a marketing product-driven culture.

Moving plants to lower-wages foreign countries inevitably exposed LS & CO. to child labor, civil rights, and human rights violations. The government in China allowed for child and labor camps. Chinese employees whom were caught peacefully protesting were given the death sentence or were sent to slavery camps. Therefore, the implementation of human rights became extremely difficult to practice within the company's grounds. For such violations, LS & CO. had to decided to leave China or to be prepared to encountered severe pressure from human rights activists at home. In an assessment, LS & CO. found that if it wanted to operate in China, several issues regarding civil rights and human rights needed to be addressed and the company was taking the risk of losing consumer loyalty as a result of China issues.

On the other hand, heavy competition in the jeans market forced LS&CO. to remain in China. According to LS & CO.'s executives, staying in China will be more beneficial to the employees. In an attempt to ensure workers rights within the organization, LS & CO. designed and implemented the Business Partnership Term Engagement in China. This agreement required suppliers to comply with the company's codes of conduct in order for LS & CO. to do business with them.

ANALYSIS

LS & CO., from the time of its inception, has been one of the ethical corporations that served the community through its social commitments to goodness. In its value and vision, LS & CO. clearly states: "Our history is filled with relevant examples of paying attention to the world around us. We listen. We innovate. We responded." LS & CO. with such a social value and vision for more than two centuries was very successful. The problem started when it moved some plants into authoritarian and communistic countries such as China that created an unethical perception of LS & CO. among customers. As we mentioned before, LS & CO. found itself among heavy competition in the marketplace. Hass needed to find solutions to solve the company's problems. First, Hass decided to move to China that provided him with lower labor costs. This type of decision caused LS & CO. to convert the company's belief from stakeholder-driven culture to marketing product-driven culture. Second, Hass was confronted with human rights and civil rights advocates and he had to return back to the original company's cultural belief. Hass began reengineering and reinventing the company's strategy so that LS & CO. could be a receptive apparel company in the industry – cutting the time it took to get jeans to stores from three weeks to 72 hours. Through such a strategy, LS & CO. continued to believe in company patronage and social responsibility. In 1993 Hass decided to withdraw from China. After five years, Hass found that he had to change not only the company's cultural value systems and visions from the stakeholder-driven culture to marketing product-driven culture, but also to return back to China because of economic reasons.

As we mentioned before, LS & CO. declared plans to shut down 29 factories in North America and Europe and to clear out 16,310 jobs. Countering LS & Co.'s announcement, *Fuerza Unida,* a working class organization of women workers in San Antonio, Texas, evaluated calls for solidarity with its seven-year campaign for corporate responsibility at LS & CO.'s. The San Antonio workers challenged LA & CO. to offer them a comparable package. Workers created *Fuezra Unida* after the 1990 layoffs.

In the San Antonio factory, the new closing came just three years after UNITE entered a labor-management partnership with LS & CO. In 1994, to avoid plant closing, UNITE said that the 6,400 new layoffs were due to a decline in capacity for LS & CO.'s domestically, rather than an effort to move jobs to other countries with lower-wage workers. *Fuerza Unida* requested solidarity in boycotting Levi's products. The organization also called for community groups to reject money from Levi Straus Foundation.

In 1998, alluding to better labor conditions, LS & CO. announced it would step up its use of China subcontractors. Furthermore, Hass reorganized a third of its European plants to the closure list that year. By the time the U. S. Plants closed, LS & CO. provided laid off workers with three weeks full pay per year of service with the company and a continued payments of health insurance of up to eighteen months. This compensation, of course, applied to all lay off employees that worked for the company and not only for those who were unionized.

It should be indicated that according to an Amnesty International report, human rights abuses in China are worse than ever. The National Labor Committee referred to widespread occurrences of physical abuses, forced overtime, exhausting work hours from 10 to 15 hours shifts without overtime bounces, and wages as low as 13 cents an hour.

A company's social responsibility must be inherent in its strategic objectives, simply to aid the well being of society. Without bottom line concerns, a company's social responsibility cannot be implemented. When a business entity is making legitimate profit that company can claim social integrity in its mission. These days many business entities are proud of being philanthropic. According to LS & CO.'s chairman Robert Hass: "The organization needs to be an ethical creature – an organism capable of both reaping profits and making the world a better place to live." Now that the profit exists for LS & CO., one can imagine the Levi's can afford the practice of ethical concerns in their workplaces.

CONCLUSION

Executives at LS & CO. learned from experience that in order to remain competitive and profitable, meticulous attention must be paid to changing market trends along perceptions of customers. It is imperative for a business entity to identify and promptly adapt to changing fashions. LS & CO.'s executives set up a "code of conduct" that applies to the whole organization including suppliers. They initiated a "code of conduct" as follows:

- None of Levi's products are to be manufactured under forced labor.
- Workers will not be put at risk.
- Workers free to exercise their rights.
- No discrimination on any basis.
- Environmental responsible methods of production will be used.
- Suppliers and subcontractors shall prohibit child labor, and comply with

guidelines on minimum wage for employment with China's labor laws.

CASE QUESTIONS FOR DISCUSSION

- How do you assess LS & CO.'s commitments to human rights?
- How do you assess LS & CO.'s commitments to the American labor market?
- Do you believe that LS & CO.'s closing plants in America after two centuries of using American laborers is an ethical decision? Explain why.
- Do you believe exploitation of workers in China is a legitimate cause for making more profit? Explain why.
- Do you think conversion of the LS & CO.'s values from the stakeholder drive-value to the marketing product-value will help ethical and moral commitments of this company? Explain why.

CASE SOURCES

Benjamin Medea, "A Riveting Announcement: Clean Cloths Campaign," *San Francisco Bay Guardian*. June 10, 1998, < http://www.cleanclothes.org>.

<http://www.levistrauss.com,>, "Chairman of the Board: Levi Strauss & Co.," September 11, 2002.

<http://www.globalexchange.org>, October 16, 2002, "China: What It's All About, *Global Exchange."*

<http://www.citinv.it,,> "Fuerza Unida Renews Call For Solidarity Against Levi's, Labor Notes, January 1998.

P.   Humphrey,   "Levi   Strauss   Plans   a   Return   to   China." <http://www.expressindia.com,>, October 16, 2002.

≤http://www.citinv.it>>, "Levi Strauss Cuts Jobs in US, Europe," *ITFLWF Newsletter,* 1998.

R. Rapaport, R (1993), "What Happens If a Company's Global Reach Exceeds its Ethical Grasp?" *Prototype*. November 19, 1993), 19.

<http://www.levistrauss.com/about/vision/ >

CHAPTER 10

MORALITY AND ETHICS IN GLOBALBUSINESS SOCIAL DARWINISM

The "survival of the fittest and the demise of the weakest and the sickest" are different to a moral wondering person, to a wise experienced person, to a simple-minded person, to an adventurous person, to a greedy appetitive person, to a politically ambitious person, and to a wicked naked person.

The moral wondering person seeks to know the answers to questions and to question the answers.
The wise experienced person seeks the discovery of truth through intellectual deliberations.
The simple-minded person seeks the discovery of the survival of faith through praying.
The adventurous person seeks to know how to be innovative to discover nature.
The greedy appetitive person seeks the discovery of gold mines through dirt.
The politically ambitious person seeks to access power through popular persuasion.
The wicked naked person seeks to quench the thirst of lust through passionate pleasure.
The bottom line for all types of the above persons is how the values of life are sought.

CHAPTER OBJECTIVES

When you have read this chapter you should be able to do the following:

- Be familiar with the New World Order.
- Be familiar with evolutionary theory.
- Develop intellectual skills to understand the general agreement about Social Business Darwinism.
- Develop and understand the syllogism application of moral virtues and ethical values in the field of business.
- Develop a comprehensive reasoning concerning survival of the fittest.
- Establish analytical skills to know why international politics is dominated by business alliances.
- Know how humanity differs from practical Social Business Darwinism.
- Explain how and why moral and ethical values can enhance the "existence needs."
- Explain what is the competitive conceptual perception concerning: the "struggle to exist," "survival of the fittest," "natural selection," and the "most favored races."
- · Know the phases of neuron genesis evolutionary path of Social Business Darwinism ideology.
- Critically, analyze the nature of business systems, the locus of control, and the practical models of business transactions.
- Develop a comprehensive understanding concerning monopolies, monopsonies, oligopolies, oligarchies, and conglomeration in the field of international business.
- Criticize the practical processes of immoral, unethical, and illegal international business transactions.
- Analyze the impact of the Social Business Darwinism ideology in relationships between developed and developing countries.
- Know what is the relationship between business taxation and Social Business Darwinism ideology.

THOUGHT STERTER

Religious faiths and political ideologies have played important roles in socialization of modern societies. These phenomena conquered the hearts and minds of enlightened people and were held firmly until the widespread qualms of the 20th century. Scientific prosperity and technological capabilities of the 20th century favored developed nations to maintain their superiority in the econo-political diplomacy.

Our world today seems to be emerging from fluctuations of prolonged phases of adversity and extreme ideological challenges. Science and technology provided bedrock at the bottom of the whole movement of global industrialization. They become crucial tools to be used as wonders in daily life. Scientific and technological innovations multiplied in all developed countries faster than the world has ever seen. In the history of mankind, never had the rush of scientific innovativeness and technological inventions been so fundamentally structured; so structured to solve human problems, and at the same time raise new ideological conflicts among nations. A conflict of interest exists when a nation must make a decision whether to advance its national interests, or some other allied nation's. Conflict of interest arises when a nation desires to advance its selfish gains without just causes.

Scientific innovative technological challenges set forth more capabilities for the human race to synergize both mass-construction and mass-destruction. This is the new industrialized role of developed nations. At the present time, they have made plans for thousands of years ahead of time to meet the coming changes. One of the crucial impacts of pragmatic scientific discoveries came into academic circles with an emphasis upon biology and life sciences.

The greatest symbolic date of evolution is traced back to Charles Darwin's publication of The *Origin of Species* in 1859. Evolution, after Darwin, became the fundamental platform not only for natural sciences, but also it became a promising econo-political ideology for the New World Order:

- What is the New World Order?
- Where did it come from?
- Where does American econo-political ideology fit into the plan of such a hierarchy?

Reflecting on this matter, we need to analyze the groundwork of the early 1990s in which President George Bush made it clear in his State of the Union address on January 29, 1991. A portion of his speech indicates:

> For centuries, America has served the world as an inspiring example of freedom and democracy. For generations, America has led the struggle to preserve and extend the blessing of liberty. And today, in a rapidly changing world, American leadership is indispensable. Americans know that leadership brings burdens and sacrifices. But also, why the hopes of humanity turn to us. We are Americans; we have a unique responsibility to do the hard work of freedom.... We know why we're there (the Persian Gulf War). We are Americans: part of something larger than ourselves. ...What is at stake is more than one small country; it is a big idea: a "new world order," where diverse nations are drawn together in common cause to achieve the universal aspirations of mankind. The world can therefore seize this opportunity to fulfill the long-held promise of a "new world order". Yes the United States bears a major share of the leadership in this effort. Among the nations of the world, only the United States of America has had both the moral standing and the means to back it up (President George Bush, Congressional Quarterly: 1991: 308-310).

has had both the moral standing and the means to back it up (President George Bush, Congressional Quarterly: 1991: 308-310).

PLAN OF THIS CHAPTER

This chapter addresses two key factors in international joint venturing programs; namely, the venture's focal activities (i.e., the fundamental activities that drive the giant corporations into global alliances) and the key linkages between giant corporate networking to establish global oligopolies and oligarchic power as the fittest business entities to survive. The crucial variables that shape these two organizing decisions involve the degree to which the venture's investments, product, market, and technology are related to the international business alliances. Can we say that international business alliances operate in an intense competitive international environment and have moral obligations to contribute to the international common good? Our answer to this question will be based on practical observations from these business entities.

This chapter deals with the most fundamental capabilities of competitive forces within the international free market economy. As we defined in Chapter One, global, multinational, international, transnational, transactional, and foreign corporations have a number of well-known features with specific commercial objectives. They are artificial persons and as such they are organized primarily to increase their profits within a global competitive environment. In business terms, they are rational entities able to achieve their dominant ends. They are bureaucratic organizations, which are identified through fundamental structural mechanisms, the dominant profit-making objectives, while people who come and go run them. As a consequence, the particular moral and ethical aspirations of stakeholders have relatively minimal and transitory impact on their transactional operations as a whole. In addition, they operate within conglomerate structural mechanisms in several nations. This carries several implications for their survival. The more a venture is a conglomeration, the greater the challenges facing consumers. The more oligopolistic and/or oligarchic power is in a marketplace, the greater the monopolistic potential for capturing know-how knowledge.

Also, this chapter provides you with analytical reasoning concerning the most profound theory of continuous ethical and moral implications for survival of the fittest corporation. Furthermore, this chapter begins with definitions and illustration of ideological survival-power domination in nature and in the business community. In addition, it highlights the conflict between ethical and moral competition and corrupted power to maintain survival of the fittest.

INTRODUCTION

Discussion and analysis about moral and ethical decisions and actions in the field of business is concerned with intellectual deliberation and moral reasoning or with intellectual means and ends. Reason is peculiar ability of humans to organize ideas, opinions, beliefs, and faiths to discover new concepts, patterns, and realities. Humans, chiefly, concern with the operation of reason and either its exploration or exploitation to discover new verities. Reasoning through exploitation is a kind of blind force that ends up with selfishness, greed, ignorance, and cruelty. Reasoning through logical debated exploration is another kind of intellectual deliberation on the ground of moral convictions to exercise the power of choice, good choice, to move human mind towards rational development; evolution. Nevertheless, both exploitation and exploration of irrational and rational elements have had profound effect on contemporary civilization (Powell, 1967: 415).

Business practices are prime examples of this kind of discourse. A manager in this kind of discourse should try to maintain the integrity of stakeholders such that what they recommend or execute is the optimum way to achieve organizational legitimate objectives. In a competitive market, the managerial objectives may be to improve the quality of a product and, at the same time, to lower its costs; to refine a marketing policy and procedure to make it more efficient mark up; and to create an atmosphere for maintaining customer loyalty. Nevertheless, this kind of moral and ethical deliberation entails some considerations that are peculiar to the sanctity of managerial integrity. Specifically, in the international market, the idealistic objectives mandate global corporations to have moral obligations for preserving the sanctity of the common good. However, a realistic analysis holds that it is not possible to apply moral concepts and ethical principles to international activities, and ethical principles to international affairs because the popular application of "Social Business Darwinism Ideology." Do we find international common good within the domain of contextual boundaries of humanity in international business? Unfortunately the answer to this question will be in the negative.

Global business networking mapping is one of the major objectives of giant corporations. In order to establish a global business-networking mapping, a giant corporation needs to implement three major premises of the Social Business Darwinism:

- Developmental transformation leading to a primary repertoire
- Synaptic selection to yield a secondary repertoire
- Reentry to the foreign markets

For example, Microsoft Corporation from the time of its inception tried to initiate its activities through application of these principles. Microsoft's operating system licensing agreements required all personal computer producers to pay Microsoft a royalty on every computer they manufacture, even when no type of Microsoft item was installed in the machine. The Microsoft anti-competitive strategy forces the PC makers to use only the Microsoft operating system. They had no other alternative and were obligated to eventually become an automatic loyal consumer and distributor. Because many PC makers are small companies with limited capital, buying from both Microsoft and another companies for a different operating system is very expensive.

THE ENTHYMEME REASONING IN BUSINESS SOCIAL DARWINISM

One of the most special considerations in managerial decision-making processes and actions is the *humanitarian feasibility of causes-processes-effects of enthymeme*. Enthymeme represents the way in which ordinary people reason deductively. According to this view, in an enthymeme, instead of having two premises and a conclusion, one ends up with different conclusions. Lay people do not have the patience to follow all the steps of a full deductive reasoning. They need to hear simplified forms of deductive reasoning for making decisions and taking actions. Here is an example of how you or some one else might argue in the form of an enthymeme. As a manager, you may decide to compete with your competitors. Everyone agrees that something should be done or made to increase your corporate profitability (e.g., quality improvement, lowering costs, cheaper prices, more product efficacy, and so on). You cannot just assert that your decisions or actions can be made or done on the basis of greed. You must illustrate how it legally can be done and rationally convince your stakeholders that it can be done.

For example, the Ford Corporation's repetitive incidents of the Ford Pinto, and the Ford Explorer, are prime unethical and immoral decisions and actions of ill-fated executives choosing to ignore the safety of customers. Such actions may be legal in the industrial world, on the basis of relative weight between customer's purchase power and the unit costs plus productivity.

Another consideration that you may have to take care of in this kind of argument is the *plausibility* of your decisions and actions. You may very well be able to establish the feasibility of your decisions and actions, but if you cannot establish your policies and procedures that are likely to succeed, you probably will not be able to maintain the integrity of your corporation. Arthur Andersen's book-cooking and unprofessional decisions and actions to destroy all the Enron documents and E-mails for the sake of protecting former Enron executives and affiliated political authorities are prime examples of business greed and corporate corruption in the United States of America; exploitation. The executives' order to shred Enron's documents put Arthur Andersen in a high-risk situation such that most honest businesses lost their trust in that auditing accounting firm. Arthur Andersen cannot attract many clients any more. To many ethicists, the decisions and actions of executives of both Enron and Arthur Andersen illustrate how giant corporations can manipulate the stock market and how powerful corrupted interest groups can pocket huge sums of soft-money. How will small stockholders be able to get back their assets? The answer is related to the impossibility of such actions. Those almighty hoodwink and hoodlum businesspeople, with the assistance of capable lawyers, will be able to get away from the justice system. The question is: "To which pockets $ 2.4 billion were deposited as the asset of such a giant corporation?"

As with most other kinds of argumentative analysis, an ethical decision or action depends on the *credibility* of managers involved in the decision-making processes and actions. In order to do good businesses, investors have to trust corporate managerial capabilities and judgments. Managers have to establish themselves as reliable and viable authorities in the matter of being discussed or operated. What we are talking about here is the ethical conviction and moral appeal of decision-makers

The subtle manifestation of ethical and moral corporate credibility may emerge from the legal tone of the justice system in a country. This indicates that . if in a society there is a positive justice system, crooks cannot fool their clients. If the justice system is manipulated and/or influenced by unethical and immoral business authorities and powerful special interest groups, then the most almighty of fittest corrupted financial groups will survive and their businesses will continue to operate in a country and/or in the international marketplace very well. This system is known as an evolutionary business ideology; "Business of Social Darwinism." Within the international business market, there are many underground forces that facilitate very quick movement of capital and put them in the safe boxes. No authority will be able to detect them, because they are very influential in the international diplomacy.

THE IMPACT OF EVOLUTION

Evolution means that change whereby something becomes different as a result of modification of its own structure. In the conceptual reasoning of the theory of evolution, the new things are always related to something that existed before. As applied in biosciences, evolution attempts to explain the progressive development of more complex forms of life from simple ones. Nevertheless, the theory of evolution was never restricted to biosciences.

Evolutionary philosophies hold that the way to conceptualize anything is to understand a phenomenon's historical development. In reviewing the history of philosophy, Hegel (1770-1831) had introduced the evolutionary conception into metaphysics. To Hegel, it was evident that for people to enjoy freedom, order, or dignity they must possess a potent and independent state of intellectual deliberation. That state, for him, became the institutional embodiment of intellectual reason and liberty. He conceived of reality itself is a process which contained a trend towards development, having an inner logic and sequence of its *own*. He became a philosopher of unfolding change. To Hegel, the pattern of change requires one to be dialectic, or the mind's irresistible need to proceed by the creation of opposites. A given state of affairs (the thesis) would in this view inevitably produce the conception of an opposite state of affairs the antithesis, which would equally inevitably be followed by reconciliation and a fusion of the two (the synthesis). Those who deny that have accepted Hegel's dialectic of the moral virtue of dignified people ignorance is bliss.

Hegel argued that innocence (thesis) must encounter evil through temptation and agreed for an irrational expansion of power (antithesis) in order to rise to the tried and the virtue of innocence (synthesis). Loewenberg (1929: xiv) made this clear in an astute analysis by saying:

> His (Hegel's) logic, playing the double role of uniting opposites and of providing a negative mate for the synthesis issuing from such union, suffers no philosophy to escape from the fate it decrees. Hegel's own method decrees that his own system be ultimately jettisoned.

The unvarying hop-step and jump from thesis to antithesis to synthesis portrayed above seems appropriate in today's business world. Simplifying it as follows will increase the moral value of the concept of dialectic, especially for businesses. Dialectical development of moral thoughts is its movement in the direction of greater competence and accomplishments. All discrepancies among moral, immoral, and amoral business people arise because temptation, greed, and selfishness are unlimited. In any domain of profitability there are assertions and denials, which serve as theses and antitheses. Hegel never tried of pointing out individual's addiction to partial truth, narrow prejudice, and partisan views. The only hope of arriving at a survival conclusion between monopolized businesses and antitrust governments is to attain an ethical synthesis to prevail fuller justice of the whole (e.g., the antitrust settlement agreement between Microsoft and U. S. Government).

The idea of progress within the boundaries of the evolutionary processes of survival power have followed the Hegelian- dialectic philosophy, making people think of human affairs in terms of a time process. Such a philosophical foundation caused the rise of biology, geology, and social sciences and opened the door to evolutionary ideas.

Evolution was in its origins, a philosophical rather than a scientific concept. However, during the early nineteenth century, some natural scientists had begun to explore the possibilities of a theory of evolution as a reasoning explanation for the existence of so many different varieties of life on earth. Jean-Baptiste Lamark (1744-1829) and Charles Lyell (1797-1875) were pioneers in arguing that individual species changes in such a way that entirely no species come into existence. But it remained for Charles Darwin to expound a fully development theory of evolution in his *Origin of the Species* (1859), (Powell, 1967: 417).

Within such a historical trend, what Darwin did was to stamp evolution with the seal of science. In 1859, in his *"On the Origin of Species,"* Darwin applied the same hypotheses to human beings. This scientific theory maintained that evolution occurred because some species were able to adapt to changing environmental conditions and thereby to survive while those lest fit were destroyed. This "survival of the fittest" viewed the entire cycle of life from the view of the organism's essential needs to gather food and to protect themselves against their enemies.

By social evolution, Darwin meant that human beings are mutable. This means that no species is created to remain unchanged once and for all. All species of living organisms, plant, animal (including humans), microscopic or elephantine in dimensions, living or extinct, have developed by successive small changes from other species that went before them. All living things are interrelated and subject to the same law of evolutionary development. All evolutionary changes are viewed as the result of "necessity in needs" to be adjusted to the changing condition of the environment. The most fundamental characteristic of the existence needs is by the notion that all human beings are the most intelligent dynamic units in nature. They have intrinsic and extrinsic desires to meet their existence needs. Parhizgar (2002: 125) stated in the Kinetic Existence Needs Theory:

> *Existence needs* can be perceived through three major causes: formal causes, material causes, and efficient causes. Within a matrix context of existence, there are three levels of needs: (1) necessity causes, which have been perceived as initial causes: formal needs causes, material needs causes, (2) sufficient needs, which have been apperceived as evolutionary needs: spiritual needs, biological needs, and sociocultural needs, and (3) *vital* needs, which have been perceived as dynamic needs. The formal causes imply the holistic dimensional multiplicity of being.

Moreover, as Ayala (1994: 230) indicated, there are two major views concerning evolutionary theory:

- One concerns history. Some philosophers of science have claimed that evolutionary biology is a historical science that does not need to satisfy the requirements of the hypothetic-deductive method. The evolution of organisms, it is argued, is historical process that depends on unique and unpredictable events.
- The second kind concerns the elucidation of the mechanisms or processes that bring about evolutionary changes. This dimension deals with causal, rather than historical relationships.

Human beings and their organizations reproduce their new species. They give rise to other similar human beings and organizations either by growing through mutation, merges, or by joint venturing partnerships, and emergences. Reproduction is a characteristic of natural and artificial selections (e. g., sexless reproduction in the fertility clinics; and natural parental mutation in a family). No natural living thing goes on living forever. There seems to be a limit of artificial selections. No natural living thing goes on living forever. There seems to be a limit of growth for every kind of living thing, but societal institutions like governmental agencies or banks as the most fittest trends will last to the last bureaucratic social organizations that human beings invented them – regardless of their political ideologies.

Among very complex creatures like human beings, the reproduction system is not usually so simple. They grow up to a certain limit of size. Then, before they become unwieldy, their growth declines and stops. According to the evolutionary product life cycle (EPLC) law, all products start their lives by going through different stages of infancy, development, and growth. Products start their lives by going through different stages of infancy, development, growth, efficiency, maturity, effectiveness, productivity, profitability, saturation, and decline generation by generation (see Figure 10.1).

Figure 10.1: Evolutionary Product Life Cycle (EPLC)

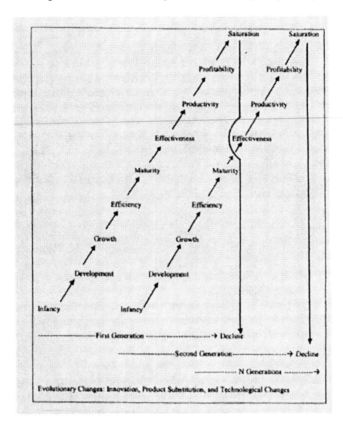

There are three major forces within the EPLC: innovativeness, product substitution, and technological changes. These forces can cause continuous changes. In addition to the complexity of human challenges, another troubling characteristic of many emerging environmental conditions are that evolutionary product life cycles may become very short. Usually, business opportunities through emerging technological innovativeness are characterized by an almost explosive growth in demand. However, it should be noticed that such emergency market opportunities have very short life cycles. Consequently, businesses need to introduce a new generation of technological innovativeness with new products in order to survive (e. g., Microsoft's products: Windows 95, 98, and 2000).

Humans are not exceptional to this evolutionary product life cycle law. After individuals have lived and produced offspring for some time, they age and die. This is the law of nature; a sort of necessity. Nevertheless, there is a practical limit to human life as well as to their growth. On the other hand non-living things, such as crystals emerge, but they have no set limits of growth and size. Crystals once formed may last unchanged for millions of years like diamonds. There is no reproduction for any crystal, but they are bound to fluctuations of their size and values in different markets. Diamond values depend on the size and purity. For human beings, living, growing, reproducing, and dying lead to some evolutionary consequences. One of the consequences is uniqueness of *individuality*.

There are always slight differences between parents and their children. According to evolutionary theory, every species changes all its individualities in each generation. Every species of living things is continually dying, and being replaced by a multitude of fresh individuals with new ecological characteristics. Some of the individuals will be stronger or sturdier or better suited to succeed in life in some way. Many individuals will be weaker or less suited and will perish sooner. In each generation there is, as it were, a picking over of a species.

The most unsuitable species are picked off, while preference is given to the strong and suitable ones. This process is called *"Natural Selection,"* or the *survival of the fittest.* Applying Darwin's evolutionary theory, to the societal continuity of a culture is called *"Social Darwinism.* This means that every favorable and stronger species survives and unfavorable ones die. Mutation will be seized upon and welcome by natural selection during the ages of friction and fraction. Then, there will be changes either in themselves or adaptation to new conditions generated by generation. These changes and adoptions are called the *modification of species.*

SCIENTIFIC MODIFICATION OF SPECIES

An individual is a living organism; and in one sense, everything that he/she will ever achieve has been coded in his/her genetic material. Parhizgar and Parhizgar (2000: 185) in their scientific research analysis found three major areas of concern that should be considered: *genotype, phenotype,* and *phylontype.*

Genotype in a physiological term represents the composition of DNA, RNA, and their fascinating interaction (see Figure 10.2). It corresponds, to the makeup identity of an individual for determination by the genetic contributions of each parent. Equally fundamental is the notion of *variation* in genotype, because of the huge number of genes contributed by each parent and the numerable ways in which they can be combined.

Figure 10.2: Biocybernetic Relationship Between Natural and Artificial
Characteristics of Human Beings

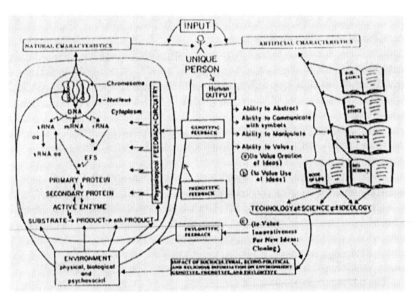

Phenotype is an intellectual term, which represents the individual's observable characteristics as expressed within a given cultural environment. An individual possesses extremely intellectual power that puts to large number all-purposeful information processing mechanisms and/or perhaps even an infinite number of their uses. Equally fundamental is the notion of *proclivity* in phenotype.

Proclivity manifests an individual's tendency to execute certain specifiable intellectual operations that can be centrally viewed, while proving incapable of performing other intellectual operations. The main reason for such a discrepancy is the extent to which different portions of the nervous system are committed to carry out particular intellectual functions, as opposed to being available for a wide range of operations. Therefore, each individual possesses certain inherent knowledge and skills in practicing and using their cognitive perceptions.

Phylontype represents characteristics of biological diversity through manipulation of genes within a planned biotechnological environment. The diversity of contemporary life reflects past episodes of speciation. Furthermore, when it comes to more complex human potentials such as capabilities to solve problems, to appreciate and create technology and music individuals still are unaware of their synergistic components and phenotypical expressions. Within this boundary in searching for evolutionary relationships among diverse characteristics of organisms, individuals need to identify functional mechanisms of their characteristics. These functional characteristics require synergetic taxonomy, identification and classification of human behaviors. The best-manipulated system of genes is known cloning through genetic engineering.

Taken together the synergistic powers of all genotype, phenotype, and phylontype would be considered as a foundation for identification of any individual's behavior, cultural orientation, and intellectual personhood profile. Through a bioanthropological view, human species have gone through both stages of genotypic and phenotypic of modification of species. In the late 20th century, bioscientists and biotechnologists discovered the *The Book of Life.* Such an evolutionary scientific integration and modification will result in breeding the third generation of human species through cloning-phylontype.

THE INTERNATIONAL BUSINESS SOCIAL DARWINISM

The monopolistic greedy appetite of some international commercial sharks can eradicate the domestic and international small business of the "fish population" as the main source of their nutrition. International commercial sharks without small business populations go hungry and soon or later tear apart their own species. In such a ruthless competitive environment, the end result is "survival of the fittest and the demise of the weakest ones." This follows from the doctrine of *Social Darwinism Ideology,* (SDI). In light of the global business competition, there are few critical issues to be considered about SDI. These issues are not primarily econo-political but macroethical or micromoral concerns about values in the free world of international enterprises. These issues are as follows:

1. Is it true that ethical and moral competition is possible in the free global business environments in respect to the rights of both large commercial corporations and small business firms?

2. Does SDI require a divorce between materialistic corporate power and qualitative value systems of societies' individual enriched lives?

3. Does SDI create oligopolistic giant international corporations to respond to the specific powerful elite groups' demands rather than to the needs of the public?

4. Does SDI serve those nations who are least well off in the international community or those nations that have power, money, and an appetite of greed?

5. Does SDI turn democratic nations into inhumane, powerful bureaucratic powers to dispose its own citizens' rights for the

sake of maintaining the interests of the elite groups? Within a
Social Darwinism competitive market place business decision
makers and operational managers do not observe holistic ethical
and moral mandates.

6.   Is it true that governmental or financial elite groups and/or
combinations of both sometimes make inhumane decisions in
order to maintain their own power?

Within a Social Business Darwinism competitive market place business
decision makers and operational managers do not observe holistic ethical and
moral mandates. They are looking for their own self-interest. They are pursuing
their business objectives to win. Social Business Darwinism competition is
viewed as a game. At the end of the game there are winners and losers. Winners
use all their resources to take advantages of market opportunities to such an
extent to drive weaker competitors or losers out of the marketplace for the
purpose of expanding their market size and extending their product positions.

Within a Social Darwinism competitive marketplace, if the strongest firms
eliminate their profit-making objectives, then the risk taking would be reduced,
and consumers would suffer. It is very usual for businesses to be motivated as
much by the fear of losing money as they are by the desire to make money. The
fear to losses indicates that resources could not be as highly valued as the same
resources might be in another industry. Within SDI there is no room for
governmental business protection or subsidies.

Social Darwinism business competition is progressive. Competitive
strategies that are achieved at one time may later fail because they are found to
be wrong. Then businesses need to strive for formulating new strategies in order
to survive in the market place. Furthermore, we would like to examine Social
Darwinism Ideology through moral convictions and ethical commitments by
responding to the above questions and issues.

PHILOSOPHICAL FOUNDATION OF SOCIAL DARWINISM IDEOLOGY

Any type of econo-political ideology including Social Darwinism Ideology
needs comprehensive cognitive understanding for structuring its own rational
power. Such a scientific idea can be traced back to the Darwinism Evolutionary
Theory. Darwin thought that evolutionary changes in species are not the result of
intelligent or purposeful activity in the organism, but essentially they are the
results of conditional chances. This means that individual organisms, through
their genetic heredity inherit slightly different characteristics in order to survive
in new conditions. This assumption may be true in Social Darwinism Business
Theory. Certain phrases, not all of them invented, by Darwin, sum up the
evolutionary theory.

Evolutionary theory is based on four major characteristics:

1. A struggle for existence
2. Resulting in the survival of the fittest; and the demise of the sickest and the weakest
3. Through natural selection the weakest will be manipulated by the strongest
4. Only the most favored races will survive

Races in this context mean not human races but the strains within a species. The struggle for existence refers to the fact that, in nature, individuals are born to live with a normal life span. The survival of the fittest refers to individuals who possess specific characteristics to survive in a competitive condition. Natural selection refers to the fittest survival without purpose in themselves. The favored *races* refer to the strains within a species having good survival powers. In examining the application of Social Business Darwinism, we employ three criteria:

1. The generation of individual monopolistic representation through licensing can cause unique responses to each different licensors but it creates stronger responses to be repeated by renewing agreements of the same conditions. This validates the more dependency of licensors to the giant corporation' s patent holder.
2. The generation of class representations of licensors in the interconnected networking systems results in having common class characteristics. This will be used as an expanded stem cell business for unifying a monopolistic business.
3. In a holistic system of a monopolized business, the individual licensors, and their class representatives are required to interact by reentering into given associative recall of different licensing agreements in a common class, the survival of the fittest. This common class synergizes the power of the patent holder or copyright owner.

ANALYSIS OF THE SOCIAL DARWINISM IDEOLOGICAL STRUCTURES

How can we reconcile the moral and ethical regulatory variability of a dynamic ideology during its development? Consideration of the general ethical principles of an ideology supports the view that a social ideological structure arises as a result of the complexity of primary developmental processes, econo-political competition, and commercial and business activities. Within the domain of such an ideological perception, nature is no longer viewed as in harmony. It is a scene of struggle. Nature is viewed as a world of tooth and claw. Within a competitive marketplace, struggle and elimination of the weakest is natural, and as means toward evolutionary development, such a struggle might even be considered good. There are no fixed species or perfected form of species. Change is everlasting, and everything seems merely relative to time, place, and environmental conditions. Within a competitive marketplace, there are no norms of good or bad. A good corporation is one that will survive and a bad one will die.

Table 10.1: Phases of Neurogenesis Evolutionary Path of Social
             Darwinism Ideology

1. Cells' (commercial corporations and business firms) proliferation.
2. Cells' (marketing and sale) global functioning migration.
3. Selective cells (commercial and business) aggregation.
4. Neuronal (global alliance financial and technological centers) cytodifferentiation.
5. Cells' (corporations' survival and firms' demises; expansions or bankruptcies) capabilities during developmental stages of commercial and business globalization.
6. Formation of channels of alliances' connectivity:
    a. Acquisition of financial and business informational positions including volume of assets, market size, and product positions.
    b. Axonal outgrowth and path finding of outsourcing resources.
    c. Target locus identification.
7. Center-periphery adjustments and interrelations of effective sources of power alliances.

Source: Partially adapted from W. M. Cowan, "Aspects of Neural Development," *Int. Rev. Physiol*, (1978, 17: no. 150), 90.

In sum, Social Darwinism actively applies the ideas of the struggle for existence and survival of the fittest of individuals, groups, and businesses. Many countries to show that some people or nations are superior to others have applied this doctrine. In practice, the fittest deserve blessings because they have proved themselves fitter than the shiftless poor; or the giant businesses in the marketplace must take over smaller ones; or the price war is morally a fine thing, proving virility and survival value of those corporations who competitively fought very hard for survival.

THE EVOLUTIONARY THEORY
OF BUSINESS DARWINISM

Darwinism evolutionary theory has provided insight into the analysis of global financial and business transactions. Evolutionary theory of Social Darwinism Ideology has undergone theoretical changes resulting in re-assessment of the nature of systems, the locus of changes in systems, and   the models by which change occurs within living systems (Svyantek and Hendrick, 1988: 243)

Within the philosophy of Social Darwinism Ideology, the survival responses of commercial corporations and business firms either to the economic development and growth or to a crisis of a particular type of socio-cultural and psycho-political event depend upon the inherent financial positions of those entities. The commercial corporations and business firms possess two throughputs allowing the inflow information to be processed toward alternative consequential outcomes: First, to acquire appropriate information in advance in order to adjust itself to the power-based conditions. Second, to utilize all resources and mobilize all power to diffuse unpleasant outcomes. Within such a complex evolutionary path of performance, some corporations become the principle change agents through their own innovative decision-making processes and actions, and others become dominated forces to be exposed to unexpected dynamic changes.

If we analyze the end result of such a competitive process, we will discover power based towards one of these competitive entities the fittest will survive and the weakest will demise. For example, a dramatic competitive technological shifting strategy within an industry through environmental forces would be to the advantage of a giant corporation and to the disadvantage of small ones. The major reason for such an end result indicates that a giant corporation is financially ready to adjust itself to the new technology, while the small ones are struggling to survive. Nevertheless, evolutionary signals will be effective on all types of commercial and business species; for some positive and for others negative. Evolutionary signals will reinforce the position of the leading giant corporations. Their side effects make small businesses shaky and force them to conduct their businesses in an inhibitory transitional system that blocks the unwanted pathway. After these events, the economic crisis can produce only one response to the favor of the fittest (see Figure 10.3).

For example, after September 11, 2001 terrorist attacks by hijackers on the World Trade Towers in New York and Pentagon Building in Washington D.C., the security of all American airports became a national political issue. The federal government of the United States decided to take over security checkpoints in American airports. Before September 11, private security firms managed most American airport security checkpoints and electronic devices. They neglected to perform their duties. Consequently, the U.S. federal government took over the responsibility.

They neglected to perform their duties. Consequently, the U.S. federal government took over the responsibility.

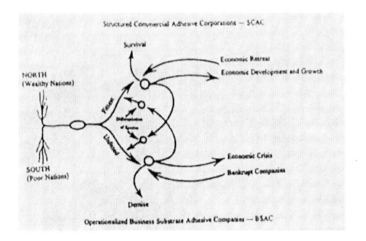

Figure 10.3: Pathological Analysis of Social Commercial and Business Darwinism Ideology

The twentieth century's condition of global enterprises has created two species: (1) giant commercial corporations (GCCs) and (2) small bussiness companies (SBCs). GCCs are in reality are known as those entities either directly absorbing small businesses through hostile take-over, acquisitions or mergers, or causing them to go bankrupt. Entering into a business with limited capital and resources in a global social Darwinism marketplace now and always has been a very risky affair. Many businesses start up their operations with a slow pace of development and patiently look forward to a promising economic prosperity. Many are called to merge; few are chosen to be faced with heavy lawsuits and/or mismanagement, and most who remain with the thinnest of survival margins have to constantly be financed by short-term commercial bank loans. "Milking" of small businesses goes on during bankruptcy proceedings in which unfit debtors will squeeze out with heavy losses. Nevertheless, those preferred or favored bankrupt companies go under reorganization proceedings and are restored to formal financial health, often under the same name (e.g., Chrysler Corporation in 1980). It should be clear that the term conglomeration is different from the giant corporations in more than mere size.

WHAT IS CONGLOMERATION?

Conglomeration of a corporation is one of the most important characteristics of giant corporations. When giant corporations perceive that some of their important; early entry seems to be a key to success when established corporations move into a young industry (Smith and Cooper, 1988: 111-121).

Conglomeration of giant corporations through acquisitions and mergers can lead global corporations to move into attractive industries without losing their regular market share and/or product positions. Conglomeration provides giant global corporations appropriate opportunities to survive – survival of the fittest. Giant global conglomerate corporations are supported by their massive financial reserves and they are protected by absolute guarantees against total risk and failure. They are like granite cliffs against the wave of the sea. Excessive competitive conglomeration leads to continual breakdowns in the marketplace. As these breakdowns have received more attention from the public, so has the idea that our competitive nature is somehow to blame. In light of the Social Darwinism Businesses, five questions can be used to reassess competition:

1. Is there true ethical competition possible in the field of international business? Social Darwinism theory argues that the free international market necessitates multinational competition to turn businesses into a jungle in which ethics are directed not by the rules of fair play but by "survival of the fittest." Businesses need to adapt their operations according to the rule of jungle.

2. Is it true that business ethics can regulate greed and selfishness of international businesses? Social Darwinism argues that according to the law of the jungle, survival competition becomes so keen that the market forces would eventually punish or destroy those companies that transgressed against society's rules.

3. Should the market place be regulated by governmental agencies? According to the law of intense competition, by the nature of "survival of the fittest," competitors in a marketplace become so vicious that many and/or occasionally all businesses are forced out of business, then so doing no good either for them or for the society they serve.

4. Does competition in Social Darwinism make a difference between work ethics and life ethics? In other words, does the intense nature of competitive fittest survival create a division between what one does for a living and one's life, leading to alienation and aggression in the marketplace? The answer is yes. The intense competition in the international marketplace creates a difference between home and host country's business ethics.

5. Does Social Darwinism serve those businesses that are worse off in the market place?

THE MORAL CONDITIONS OF SOCIAL DARWINISM IDEOLOGY

Following the path of Social Darwinism Ideology reasoning, the ultimate goal of the English philosopher Herbert Spencer's (1820-1903) objective on ethics was to find a scientific basis for the distinction between right and wrong and for the general guidance of conduct in humanity. Spencer, who popularized the doctrine of Social Darwinism Ideology, provided moral reasoning for the accumulation of large fortunes through economic operations. Spencer believed that life is a continuing process of adaptation to a harsh external environment. Accordingly, businesses should engage in a competitive struggle for survival in which the fittest survive. The stronger the competition, the more prosperous corporations can exist. Toward this end, Spencer examined the nature of the physical universe in which such conduct occurs. Spencer regarded his ethical philosophy as a synthetic one in the sense that it attempts to set forth a consistent set of universal principles that can be verified empirically by the separate sciences.

Spencer believed that people's knowledge is always relative. There are several problems with the ethical relativist position. First, there is an argument offered by Donaldson (1996: 49): "Ethical relativism is morally blind." There are fundamental virtues and values that are cross- cultural. Companies must respect those virtues and values (e.g., honesty). This argument counters ethical relativism through the existence of supra-international moral norms and virtues. Second, if the ethical relativists' credo, "When in Rome, do as the Romans do," holds, then such an ideology violates the code of ethics. Third, since ethical relativism is dominated by norms and rules within a society, it may have emerged through non-democratic means or through some power elite groups' interest. The distribution of power may be such that powerful elite groups may be oppressing other groups within their society (Steinmann and Scherer 1997: 77).

Spencer believed an individual's reasoning for survival is contingent. All survival reasoning depends on other things being true. Donaldson (1996) argued that the foundation for this position is absolutism. There are moral principles that are equally valid and applicable anywhere in the world regardless of their national cultural value systems and political ideological beliefs. Such principles are based on the notion that:

1. There is a single list of moral truths (e.g., honesty, honor, truthfulness).
2. Such truths are expressed only with one set of concepts (e.g., humanity not by savagery or slavery, and/or by tyranny).
3. Behaviors that follow such truths are dependent of the context (e.g., existence).

For example, theocracy and blind faith as fanatic fatalism have, through history, entreated true believers to uphold their beliefs, even by the sword or the club, against those of pagan and disbelievers (Iyre, 1999:9). Although Spencer was not an atheist, he was viewed as an agonist. Spencer concluded that absolutism requires all phenomena to follow a principle, power or force. It is conceivable that the colonial power of the second half of the second millennium emerged from such a policy. Colonial power has forced colonized nations to dismantle their economic infrastructures on the basis of the economic theory of factor endowment theory to concentrate wealth through absolute power. The historical colonial power to some extent has been converted to a new economic monopolistic power as global imperialism.

Hofstadter (1945) believed that Darwin's theory of evolution set forth in his *Origin of Species* (1859) had effects on social thought in Europe and America. Karl Marx in 1869 hailed the Darwinism theory as supporting his views concerning the class struggle in history. Marx (1867) addressed the global workers, to unite them against the bourgeois. He said: "You have nothing to lose because economically you are weak. You have nothing to lose except your chains."

Although Darwin had been talking about the struggle for survival among animals, his views also apply to militarists and plutocrats. There is no inconsistency in applying the Social Darwinism Ideology for a person, a corporation, or a nation. By the notions of survival values, Darwin meant biological survival values, which do not necessarily imply moral survival values. The ambiguity of terms appears when we assume that being able to survive is in fact the same thing as being worthy of survival (Weber, 1960: 252). Darwin, however, viewed intelligence as a rather late product of evolution. It develops gradually in a competent species in order to reach its most potent form in their society.

Social Darwinism Ideology is the major dynamic motive for application of the evolutionary theory in biological and social sciences. Darwin believed that scientific biological and social objectives grow out of experience; they do not direct all experiences without knowledge. Darwin held that societies, like animals, meet novel situations through natural variations and the only species that is able to survive is the fittest not the weakest and/or the sickest ones. Natural variation occurs as an unconscious variation of gene structure. Social variation occurs as a conscious awareness. If intellectuals neglect their moral convictions and ethical commitments in their scientific endeavors, society plunges into corruption. Nevertheless, it is a law of nature that societies meet novel situations not by waiting hopefully for a suitable natural variation. Intellectually, they exercise a reconstructive imagination that proceeds experimentally in discovering new adaptations to weed out corruption. Societies, unlike animals, have the conscious desire, not merely to survive, but to survive well societies have the desire of growth and progress.

According to this philosophy in the field of global business, Peter Drucker (1980: 11) indicated that businesses must strive to position their activities against inflation because with an inflationary situation, making profit is by its definition impossible and businesses gradually will vanish. In order to fight against inflation, corporations need to make adequate profit in order to survive in economic hardship. Inflation by its nature is an unethical phenomenon. Inflation is the systematic destruction of wealth. Businesses need to adjust sales, prices, inventory, receivables fixed assets, equities, their depreciation, and earnings in respect to inflation; not with total precision but within a reasonable range of probability. Therefore, according to the Global Social Darwinism Ideology, if a nation desires to survive, it must build a strong adjustable and reliable economic position because without this assumption it is impossible to survive the never-ending occurrence of the dynamic processes of evolutionary life.

CONTRADICTION IN SOCIAL DARWINISM

The universal Social Darwinism theory conceives that all animals engage in a perpetual struggle for existence, not merely against the nonliving environment, or against other species, but also against blood relatives. Accordingly, Spencer believed that there are two sets of ethics: (1) family ethics is based on the principle of charity and benevolent benefits they are apportioned without relation to merit. (2) State ethics is based on justice and benefits that are apportioned on the basis of competitive merit.

In the case that family ethics interjects into business or government by well-meaning people, it will be an inappropriate interference with the laws of nature and would slowly corrupt businesses and society (Spencer, 1888). However, it should be noted that Social Darwinism is sharply criticized by humanitarians as a cult of ruthless individualism, because they believe that Social Darwinism makes life longer richer, and happier for the fittest individuals, their children, and their affiliated powerful social groups who easily can monopolize the wealth and power in a society. At the other end of the international business life spectrum, poor nations could be dominated by rich nations. This is the amoral myth of global businesses. Along the line of this unethical perceptions, the survey by the United Kingdom's Ashrodge Centre for Business and Society found that human right issues had caused 36 percent of the biggest 500 companies to abandon a proposed investment project and 19 percent to disinvested from third world countries. The potential difficulties facing companies operating overseas have been highlighted by cases such as that of Shell in Nigeria and PepsiCo, which pulled out of Bunna in 1997 after intense pressure from human rights activists. Despite the growth of multinational companies' investment, the survey found that only 44 percent of international companies' codes of conduct made explicit reference to human rights. (Maitland, 2000: 3).

The ideological rationale for the Social Darwinism business theory is to play a business game with hit-and-run strategy in order to be able to survive. According to this philosophy, if an international firm is exposed to an economic recession in a market and it is faced with a quick profit-making opportunity, then the firm has to get in and as soon as possible get out, even if the getting in or getting out produces exploitation and misery for the abandoned consumers. Walton (1977: 9) stated: "The point is simple enough: practical ethics may produce results at the price of the innocent third parties; practical ethics calls for no substantial sacrifice; practical ethics is invariably self-serving." In supporting the above reasoning, the former Chairman of the Board of International Business Machines (IBM), Watson Jr. (1963: 5) believed that: "If an organization is to meet the challenges of a changing world, it must be prepared to change everything about itself except those beliefs as it moves through corporate life." In other words, survival and continuity of a firm is the most important objective of a corporation. In supporting such an idea, Milton Friedman (1983) argued that the doctrine of social responsibility for businesses means acceptance of the socialist view that political mechanisms rather than market mechanisms are appropriate ways to allocate resources to alternative uses. However, altering people's cultural and ethical value systems is not the ultimate aim of globalization of enterprises. According to this mentality, some businesses may act unethically not because of a conscious desire to do wrong things or to commit unethical behavior regardless of the consequences of their decisions and actions, but simply because their objective is making profit. It is much easier to deal with money than to deal with ethical and moral valuable judgments.

The global social Darwinism theory views the free market economy as a jungle in which businesses are not ruled by fair play but by survival of the fittest. According to the naturalist theory of Social Darwinism, personal ethics exists in a separate compartment of society. Businesses, like plants and animal species, evolve by adapting to their environments through the natural selection of those individuals who are fittest to survive. For example, if a nation is oriented with payola, bribery, embezzlement, and fraud, it is obvious that those businesses are more active in such an unethical and immoral activities are the fittest to survive; "when you are in Rome do as Romans do."

AMORAL AMALGAMATION OF THE 20th CENTURY RICH AND POOR NATIONS

To highlight how poor countries have been abandoned in recent years, a few simple illustrations may suffice. First, debt service as a percentage of Gross National Product (GNP) for developing nations has risen from 1.5 percent in 1970 to 4.7 percent in 1990, while debt service as a percentage of exported goods and services has risen from 10.1 to 19.8 percent (see Table 10.2). Meanwhile, the average interest rates of such loans rose from 5.2 percent in 1970 to 6.8 percent in 1990 (although this is down from the average rate of 9.3 percent in 1980). More onerous for these borrowers is that variable rate financing as a percentage of total financing has risen from 2.3 percent in 1970 to

37.8 percent in 1990. The rising interest rate is increasingly a burden on shoulder of by debtor countries (Parhizgar and Jesswein, 1998).

Meanwhile, World Resources Institute figures show that average annual compensation for a citizen (or Gross Domestic Product per capita, which is as close to the same thing as we get in largely non-cash economies), in U.S. Dollars, is less than $100 in Mozambique and Tanzania, less than $200 in seven other African countries: Burundi, Chad, Malawi, Rwanda, Sierra Leone, Somalia, Uganda; plus Nepal and Vietnam, under $300 in another 15 countries worldwide (*World Resources*, 1996-1997: 166).

Table 10.2: Selected Debt Figures For All Developing Countries

	1970	1990
Debt service as percentage of GNP	1 5	4 7
Long-term debt as percentage of GNP	13 1	34 2
Interest payments as percentage of GNP	0 5	2 1
Debt service as percentage of exported goods/services	10.1	19 8
Average interest rates on loans	5 2	6 8
Variable rate loans as percentage of total debt	2 3	37 8

Source: World Bank (various issues).

The term *affordability* in the international economy refers not simply to the raw materials and components, and consequently to the abilities of production capabilities of nations, but also it refers to the solvency of the debtors paying their debts and compounded interest. In Third World Countries (TWCs) *solvency* refers to the acquisition of cash or monetary resources by exploring or trading off more valuable goods. Solvency would also mean that the country is able to appreciate burdens of individual citizens' educational, health, and welfare deficiencies, nation-states' weaknesses and national-international trade transactional deficits (Parhizgar, 1994: 109).

JUSTICE AND ECONOMIC DISTRIBUTION AROUND THE WORLD

The amoral free market economy has turned international business competition into a Darwinism jungle in which ethics is dictated by the survival of the fittest species' role. Darwin's evolutionary theory has popularized the notion of survival of the strongest species, evolved by adapting to their natural environments. Almost three hundred years ago, in1700, James Harington paraphrased Aristotle by stating: "power follows wealth." Business power has to be in alignment with econo-political power, and vice versa.

According to Social Darwinism Ideology, managers are viewed as guardians of power- holders to accumulate wealth. In 1994 *Business Week's* forty-fourth annual survey of the two highest-paid executives at 361 companies showed their average pay for the previous year approaching the $4 million mark, counting salary, bonuses, and other compensation *(Business Week,* 1994). *Business Week* (1993) conducted a survey on the growing gap between chief executive officers of American corporations between 1960-1992 (see Table 10.3). They found that American CEOs' salaries increased dramatically comparing to other professions.

Table 10.3: The Growing Gap Between CEO's Pay and What Other
          Workers Make

PROFESSION	1960	1970	1980	1992
Engineer	$9,828	$14,695	$28,486	$58,240
School Teacher	$4,995	$8,626	$15,970	$34,098
Factory Worker				
CEO	$4,665	$6,933	$15,008	$24,411
	$190,383	$548,787	$624,996	$ 3,842,247

Source: *Business Week, "Executive Pay: The Party Aren't Over Yet, "*
      (April 26, 1993).

Eckhouse (1990 and 1993), through another study of CEO's pay indicated that of all companies in the United States with annual sales levels of $100 million or more, CEO's pay (not including stock options) is 13.2 times higher than the pay of factory workers, a far higher ratio than other industrialized nations. Japan and the United Kingdom, for example, have a multiple of 9.4; France 8.5; Canada 8.4; Italy 8.2; Gernlany 6.7; Australia 5.9; and Sweden 4.4.

In 1996, Jack Welch, CEO of General Electric, received $21.4 million in annual salary and performance bonuses (and $18 million in stock options); Lawrence Coss of Green Tree Financial Corporation received $102.4 million in annual salary and bonus (plus stock options worth at least $38 million); Michael Disney added $196 million in stock to his previous holding, somewhere around a third or a billion. The list goes on: Intel's Andrew Grove took home $97.6 million.; Traveler's Group Sanford Weill made 94.2 million; and Citicorp's John Reed got $43.6 million (Cassidy, 1997).

According to Peter Drucker (1980: 192) management's job is to make human strength productive. Nevertheless, in a just society, the exercise of power should never be separated from the delineation of moral virtues and ethical values. Managerial neutrality should never lead, nor should it be equated with, value neutrality. The former is acceptable as a condition for a career - the latter is not (Dvorin and Simmons, 1972: 9).

This global Social Darwinism Ideology of business beliefs dictate that capitalization is the basic survival rule for managers to maximize profit. Since maximization of profit is considered as the means for capitalization, then the international business opportunities will be diverted from moral to amoral acts in order to pursue such an ideal. Maximization is the famous abstraction of theoretical economists because they believe in exploitation of resources including labor and nations.

Globalization of the free market economy in uneven sociocultural and econo-political conditions among nations has provided suitable opportunities for rich countries and miserable conditions for poor countries. According to research by the International Monetary Fund, the richest 25 percent of the world's population experienced a six-fold increase in real GDP per capita during the 20th century. By contrast, the lower quartile of world population enjoyed less than half that gain. These disparities are being exacerbated by the digital divide of; the contrast in economic opportunities between the computer literate and those lacking such skills (Roach, 2001: 14). Then the footprint of globalization leaves an obvious and important mark on the economic landscape. Those economically and socially retarded nations may pursue a radical motive to take inhumane actions against the rich nations. They may find themselves in a radical position in which survival may not be the most fundamental human emotion, and some people would choose to die rather than to live under such unjust conditions. These desperate people choose to experience bitter victory, because they believe that such a bittersweet victory is nonetheless a victory.

For example, Nike's child labor policy and low wages in production facilities in Indonesia with fifteen cents an hour is an example of profit maximization. However, in defense, the Nike chairman and CEO Philip Knight claims:

> Nike's foreign factories generally offer the highest pay and the best work conditions of any athletic shoe factories in that particular country. In China, a worker in a Nike factory makes higher wages than a professor at Beijing University, (Jackson, Miller, and Miller, 1997: 191).

Nike's wage policy brings up the following question: Should multinational corporations take moral and ethical considerations on human rights along with their mission when they do business abroad? The answer is not absolute.

In the international ethical philosophy of business maximization of profit makes no sense if it involves exploiting human rights. However, through ethical and moral responsibilities of businesses optimization is a fair deal to find the most favorable ratio efforts and risk on the one hand and opportunities on the other because no one in an ethical and moral sense knows how to maximize profits without contributing appreciative and fair returns to stakeholders. Therefore, through an amoral Social Darwinism Ideology the management role is neither ethicalization nor moralization of a business. The manager's role is to satisfy the shareholders capitalization motives. According to the evolutionary theory of Social Darwinism, the weakest nations must be abandoned in order for the most prosperous nations to survive.

Jackson, Miller, and Miller (1997: 35) believe:

> The concern is that excessive competition leads to continual ethical breakdowns in the business community. As these breakdowns have received more attention from the public, so has the idea that our competitive nature is somehow to blame.

However, in the Ethics of International Business, Donaldson (1989) argued that multinational corporations as well as individuals and nation-states must, at a minimum, respect international human rights. Brenkert (1992: 515) stated:

> For a purported right to be such a fundamental right it must satisfy three conditions: (1) the right must protect something of very great importance, (2) the right must be subject to substantial and recurrent threats, and (3) the obligations or burdens imposed by the right must satisfy a fairness-affordability test.

TAXATION AND SOCIAL DARWINISM ETHICS

Taxation is one of the instruments to be used by governments for redistributive justice through fair distribution of wealth among citizens in a nation. Within the philosophy of Social Darwinism, the government funnels money to the private sector through welfare-type programs for poor families and through business contracts for very rich families as public expenditures. With the passing of the Sixteenth Amendment to the U. S. Constitution in 1913, Congress granted the right to collect tax on the income of its citizens. Since then, the income tax laws have grown enormously complex.

The free-enterprise model of the American system is not static one. The intermingling of giant corporations, first class citizens, and government has been adjusted periodically. American citizens expect their government to consider fairness as a principle that concerns most citizens. It is very strange that American people cannot predict the exact nature of the fittest businesses in their society, because there are invisible hands that suddenly change the whole picture of the marketplace. Greider (1992: 80) writes:

> If Congress had done nothing since 1977 to alter the U.S. tax code, nine of ten American families would be paying less...Yet, paradoxically, the

government would be collecting more revenue each year; around $70 billion more.

The question is: Where did all that money go? Greider writes: "It went to corporations and to the one in ten families at the top of the income ladder, the fittest ones.

GLOBALIZATION OF BUSINESSES AS A PRACTICE OF SOCIAL DARWINISM

Globalization is a controversial term for free movements of capital and products around the world. In an analytical term, globalization can be viewed through two major dimensions: (1) causes and (2) effects. Champions of globalization look for influential expansion of rich people to create more freedom in international marketplace. Bosworth and Gordon (2001: 3) defined globalization broadly as follows: "Globalization is the expansion and intensification of linkages and flows; of people, good, capital, ideas, and cultures, across national borders." However, there is no consensus about this definition because globalization is a free movement of money-power around the world through borderless trades and integration of economic systems. Another issue is related to globalization of economy around the world. Ralph Nader said: "The essence of globalization is subordination of human rights, of labor rights, consumer rights, environmental rights, democracy rights, to imperatives of global trade and investment."

Greider (1997) pointed out that global economy made possible the accumulation and concentration of great wealth by wealthy people, but at the same time has serious flaws. Among them, first, is that global capitalism is repeating some of the shortcomings of capitalism experienced 100 years ago in the United States; for example, exploitation of workers, including children and women, and inequality of income distribution. Second, uncontrolled production capacity systems and overproduction of many products can cause drastic changes of the balance of natural resources. In addition, global corporations can show their loses through overproduction loses and escape from paying taxes at home and/or host countries. This provides an opportunity for the fittest to survive and weakest to demise. Third, the exuberant growth of global capitalism leads to degradation of the environment. Fourth, the extraordinary growth of money and its free flow of domestic economic movements and capital flights from poor nations to powerful countries inevitably will result in destabilizing financial markets and can cause more concentration of wealth in global oligopolies. Fifth, free market economy and political democracy should go together. Without democracy, free market economy will wither and fade away. Minority fittest interest groups will dominate majority and create economic and social crisis (Steiner and Steiner, 2003: 444).

financial markets and can cause more concentration of wealth in global oligopolies. Fifth, free market economy and political democracy should go together. Without democracy, free market economy will wither and fade away. Minority fittest interest groups will dominate majority and create economic and social crisis (Steiner and Steiner, 2003: 444).

It is a capitalistic assumption that rising nominal incomes (not real purchase power incomes) that are created by vigorous global capitalism will raise all boats. According to Summers (2000) such a perception demonstrably has not happened. Throughout the world the income gap between the fittest and the weakest has widen. He indicated:

> In Sub-Saharan Africa the global development effort has not succeeded when Lawrence Summers was the Secretary of the U.S. treasury Department... Per capita incomes in Africa in the late 1905 were lower than they were 30 years ago. Average incomes for a region of 600 million are now only 65 cents a day. And across large parts of the continent, children are more likely to die before their first birthday than to read.

CHAPTER SUMMARY

The evolution theory maintained that evolution occurred because some species were able to adapt to changing environmental conditions and thereby to survive while those less fit were destroyed. Darwin indicated that the natural selection of species is based upon adjustment to who are fittest to survive. Those that could escape or destroy their enemies and still obtain food thrived; the others died out. New species were the result of the survival of the strongest elements in older species.

International Business Social Darwinism doctrine presumes that in the global business environment there would be direct relationships between a majority and a minority, in terms of population and profit and that out of their interplay an international economic general rule would emerge. It is assumed that both majority and minority would be concerned with the entire spectrum of heavy competition. It is the rule that when population rises, the marginal profit goes down through high inflationary rate. A few small corporations, with marginal profit whose capital gain is indexed against inflation, can survive. It is assumed that small businesses stop considering profit and accept responsibility for earning the costs of majority population, the costs of staying in business, and the giant corporations escape from global citizenship responsibility and enjoy financial windfalls.

There is a debate about international business ethics. Some believe that international business transactions should be amoral. It is believed that business and personal ethics exist in separate compartments of universal multicultural value systems. Since each culture considers specific values, therefore international business activities could not be subject to the universal ethical and moral ideals. Managers may act according to selfish economic interest because the market mechanism distills such actions into benefits for shareholders including management.

Social Darwinism of international business promotes ruthless competitive pressures to make the business strong by all means and ends. It provides managers a release from the burden of guilt of unethical and immoral behavior. Since the business objective is to make profit, therefore managers do not care about personal guilt. In the highly industrial society like the United States of America, human species are under tremendous impact of the technology. This inanimate and blind force can cause the great gap between the dictates of reason and the world in which we live. Social Darwinism has offered a rationale for our contemporary society, explaining and justifying it to people by revealing the irrational elements underlying the development of societal life itself. Nevertheless, we are living in an era that the doctrine of the survival of the fittest has been employed to justify national and international policies regardless of ethics and morality. Also, Herbert Spencer in his *Synthetic Philosophy* attempted to set down a science of society along Comtian lines within the framework of evolution. Spencer showed that the doctrine of evolution provided the true explanation for the growth of industrialism and the concentration of wealth.

CHAPTER QUESTIONS

- What is the New World Order?
- What is the foundation of the evolutionary theory?
- What are foundational principles of the Social Business Darwinism?
- What is the syllogism application of moral virtues and ethical values in the field of business?
- How do you justify a comprehensive reasoning concerning survival of the fittest and the demise of the weakest and the sickest?
- Why do invisible hands of business alliances dominate international politics?
- How does humanity differ from practical Social Business Darwinism practices?
- How and why can moral and ethical values enhance the "existence needs?"
- What are the competitive conceptual perceptions concerning: the struggle to exist, survival of the fittest, natural selection, and the most favored races to exist?
- What are phases of neurongenesis evolutionary path of Social Business Darwinism ideology?
- What are analytical nature of business systems, the locus of control, and the practical models of business transactions?
- What are side effects of monopolies, monopsonies, oligopolies, oligarchies, and conglomeration in the field of international business?

- How do you criticize the practical processes of immoral, unethical, and illegal international business transactions?
- How do you analyze the impact of the Social Business Darwinism ideology in relationships between developed and developing countries?
- What is the relationship between business taxation and Social Business Darwinism ideology?

CASE STUDY

MICROSOFT CORPORATION AS THE BEST SELLER OF SOFTWARE AND ANTITRUST REGULATION IN THE US

Much has been written about the objectives of the antitrust laws. One of the best statements is that given in a Supreme Court opinion made in a Sherman Act case (U.S. v. Northern Pacific R.R. Co., 356 U.S. (1958):

> The Sherman Act was designed to be a comprehensive charter of economic liberty aimed at preserving free and unfettered competition as the rule of trade. It rests on the premise that the unrestrained interaction of competition forces will yield the best allocation of our economic resources, the lowest prices, the highest quality, and the greatest material progress, while at the same time proving an environment conductive to the preservation of our democratic political and social institutions But even were that premise open to question, the policy unequivocally laid down by the Act is competition.

Microsoft Corporation is the worldwide leader in the software industry. Its software products and Internet technologies serve all types of computing projects including personal, business, space, civilian, and military computing. The corporation offers updated software programs within a wide range of products and services designed to empower people through great software. Its main business activities are based on engineering, developing, manufacturing, and licensing software productions. With revenues of more than $14 billion annually, Microsoft is more than just the largest software company; it is a technological phenomenon. Microsoft's products consist of software, videogames, interactive television, and Internet access. The company has subsidiaries in many parts of the world such as Argentina, Brazil, Chile, Australia, Austria, Belgium, China, Colombia, Costa Rica, Croatia, Czech Republic, Denmark, Ecuador, Egypt, Mexico, and many others around the world. It has subsidiaries in more than 80 countries and employs nearly 44,000 people worldwide. It sells 74 percent in the United States and 26 percent in other countries.

THE SHORT HISTORY OF MICROSOFT

The founder of Microsoft, Bill Gates, was born in Seattle, Washington State. Bill Gates at age 14 and his best friend Paul Allen, were already in business writing and testing computer programs for fun and profit. In 1972, they established their first company named Traf-O-Data that sold a program that recorded and analyzed traffic data. As both engaged in writing versions for BASIC programming language, they dropped out of college and worked full time in developing programming languages for different companies like Altair and MITS. Microsoft was founded as a partnership on April 14, 1975, by Bill H. Gates III and Paul G. Allen, and incorporated on June 25, 1981. Microsoft stock was introduced to the public on March 13, 1986. Its net revenue $25.30 billion and net income $7.35 billion accounted at the end of the fiscal year ending June 2001.

THE MAJOR ROLE PLAYERS OF THE CASE

There are four major parties involved in this case: (1) Microsoft Corporation, 2) the U.S. Department of Justice, (3) The computing industry, and (4) the communication industry.

The Monopolistic Activities of Microsoft

Much of the antitrust violations deal with Internet competition. In 1995 Netscape had 70 percent of the market share because of Microsoft's Internet browser. Netscape's browser became a threat in Bill Gates eyes. Netscape was the competitor for the Windows 95 operating system. Microsoft was not about to lose the market share to its competitor; therefore it took on all means to distribute its own Internet browser called Internet Explorer. At one point Microsoft tried to make a deal with Netscape where they would divide that area of the market. Such an arrangement was not simple. On a bargaining table, Microsoft desired to be the only supplier of the browser with the Window 95 operating system. In order to accomplish its desire, 'Microsoft turned to a bundling strategy that focused on attaching weak products to more popular one. This was what Microsoft did with Internet Explorer in Windows. Microsoft distributed Internet Explorer freely with Windows 95. Such an operational strategy caused consumers to be oriented with Internet Explorer. In reality, it eliminated consumer shopping for alternatives.

The U.S. Department of Justice

The Antitrust Division of the Department of Justice became aware of Microsoft's dominance and sued the company for antitrust violations. In such a lawsuit several issues were addressed concerning Microsoft monopolistic performance. According to the United States' former General Attorney Janet Reno: "The Justice Department charged Microsoft with engaging in anti-competitive and exclusionary practices designed to maintain its monopoly in personal computer operating systems and to extend that monopoly to Internet browsing software." In order for Microsoft to enhance their monopoly, they engaged in anti-competitive arrangements with various vendors. The Justice Department based its case on the fact that Microsoft violated parts of two sections of the Sherman Antitrust Act.

The Joint Venturing Cooperation of the Computing Industry and Information Systems: Aside from this, the Justice Department identified other actions that were illegal and anti- competition such as bundling, exclusionary agreements with Internet service providers (ISPs), online services (OLSs), and Internet content providers (ICPs). Microsoft is also accused of putting restrictions on original equipment manufacturers (OEMs). In such a monopolistic networking several companies were involved such as America Online Inc. (AOL), Apple Computer, Intel, and Sun Microsystems.

The Communication Industry: Aside from the exclusionary agreements restricted computing companies' rights to provide services or resources to Microsoft's software competitors, Microsoft focused on some of the most popular communication Internet Service Providers and Online Services. Some of these companies include AT&T World Net, MCI's WorldCom, and Earthlink. These companies are link providers between the personal computer users and the Internet. Microsoft and these companies came to an agreement that no word was to be mentioned and no promotion was allowed with regards to all other browsers.

PROBLEMS AND ISSUES

In an industry in which substitution of products moves at lightning speed, innovation is critical to competitiveness. Microsoft is the world's best fitted retail of operating systems. It controls every delivery channel of information. As Microsoft took over the market in PC Windows' operating systems many legal problems arose.

ANALYSIS OF THE CASE

There are two key aspects to Microsoft's past and future success: first, its vision of technology and products and second, the values by which it provides for customers lives every day. The values are set of principles that have evolved since it's finding. These values are not new, but rather reinforcements of long-held corporation principles that tie customers, partners, and employees together.

Customers are a major part of Microsoft because it serves them to achieve their objectives. Microsoft listens to what customers demand and responds rapidly.

Microsoft's long-term strategic management approach to heavy investment in research and development - R&D -synergizes its constant efforts to anticipate customer needs, improve total quality management, and reduce costs to enable it to deliver the best products and technologies to the marketplace Another dimension of the Microsoft's success is due to successful partnerships with its associates and employees. At Microsoft, employees are the most important assets. It provides appropriate opportunities for employees' development and growth to their fullest potential. Microsoft's managers and employees are always act with the utmost integrity and they are guided by what is right for their customers. Microsoft's mission is based on a philosophy that indicates if they want to be the best at all they can, they need to respond to a fast-paced competitive environment. This philosophy facilitates Microsoft to be committed to encouraging cultural diversity in its workplace. Microsoft has realized that in order to be able to survive in a competitive market, it needs to contribute its resources to the communities in which it markets its products and services. The high value of Microsoft's mission places it on employees and customers to an extended well position beyond the corporation's mission. Microsoft has a strong belief that if its people are provided with appropriate power and resources they need, they can accomplish great things.

CONCLUSION OF THE CASE

By reviewing this case, there are two different categories of remedies: (1) ethical conduct remedies and (2) structural legal remedies. Ethical conduct remedies appear to do more harm than good to consumers. Structural legal remedies would not impose many barriers on Microsoft.

We should not forget that Microsoft is a leading corporation in the global computing industry. By having structural legal remedies it would replace the current monopoly with a global competitive market structure.

Microsoft Corp. took early steps to begin obeying court approved sanctions in its antitrust case, appointing three of its existing board members to a new committee responsible for making sure the software maker doesn't break the rules. Also, the judge ordered Microsoft to allow computer makers and customers to remove icons for some Microsoft features, share some to participate in exclusive deals that could hurt competitors.

CASE QUESTIONS FOR DISCUSSION

- What is the content of the Sherman Act?
- How do you define monopoly in the computing industry?
- Do you believe Microsoft has a monopoly?

- Should Microsoft be split into two companies? If yes explain advantages.
- Do you think Microsoft used its econo-political power to influence the outcome of the lawsuit?
- Do you believe Microsoft used its technological power in the marketplace to prevent potential competitors from challenging its dominant market position in operating systems?
- Do you believe the Department of Justice and the U.S. Court System were not severing enough customers in their final settlement agreements?

CASE SOURCES

S. Labaton,, "Microsoft Asks Supreme Court to Reverse Antitrust Finding," (*The New York Times,* August 8 2001).

MSNBC.com November 8, 2002, Justice vs. Microsoft, *Associate Press,* "Microsoft Obeys Antitrust Sanctions,"
<http ://www.msllbc.com/news/832386.as ?c1=1>

US v. *Northern Pacific R.R Co.,* 356 *U S.* 1(1958).

CHAPTER 11

JUSTICE, LAW, AND SOCIAL CONTRACTS BETWEEN BUSINESSES AND SOCIETY

We cannot expect to be treated justly unless we treat other people fairly.
(Whoever seeks justice must follow fairness).

We cannot judge on the outcomes of our behavior unless
we merit the equity between the equal equities.
(Wherever is the notion of equity, the equity must be equal to similar equities).

We cannot ignore our moral convictions unless
we give weight to ethical equity as a substance rather than a form.
(Without an equitable remedy for a wrongful action, equitable justice cannot be effective).

We cannot neglect those people who ignore their own rights unless
we are no longer morally and ethically committed to the notion of humanity.

(Whenever the notion of humanity is present, the notion of selfishness must be absent).

CHAPTER OBJECTIVES

When you have read this chapter you should be able to do the following:

- Develop conceptual skills in defining justice, law, and social contracts between businesses and society.
- Establish a foundation for analyzing philosophies of justice.
- Develop a framework of syllogistic reasoning for critical analysis of justice systems.
- Understand the importance of moral convictions in justice systems.
- Understand the importance of ethical, moral, and legal obligations in socialization.
- Make distinctions between different types of justice systems and their inherent means and ends.
- Analyze philosophical views on the issues of justice in the business world.
- Define and analyze components of law.
- Define and analyze philosophies of law.
- Know differences between the concepts of law.
- Know what are the relationships between constitutional law and other laws.
- Grasp the magnitude of today's global business responsibilities.
- Know why businesspeople should be honest during their trade transactions.
- Know what we mean by profit maximization and profit optimization concerning business ethics.
- Know the means and ends in signing a business contract between buyers and sellers or an employer and employees, or a business and community.

THOUGHT STARTER

Reasoning is an intellectual deliberated activity of the human mind for the expression of rational and peaceful solutions in the problem solving processes. Civilized people attempt to apply reasoning to settle their differences among themselves instead of using clubs or swords or bullets. These kinds of people rely on reasoning words to be used in order to establish and maintain justice. In the literature of justice, there is no room for using clubs or swords or bullets, because these fatal tools can cause vicious cycles of injustice.

Justice is an intellectual peaceful solution that people do not claim about it by fatal tools to get to final solutions. Justice is a rational convention as a factual reasoning process that everybody, regardless of his or her personal tastes or prejudice accepts. Justice is not by the expression of our selfish tastes or prejudicial feelings. Unjust people claim or assert that their way is the only way for safeguarding the dignity of humanity. Reasoning concerning how or why something is essential to use during cause-and-effect debates requires careful consideration of intellectual deliberation. In a justice system, we urge people to determine what causes and what effects follow from a particular action is just as often as we urge them to discover the nature of a decision and/or an action. Upon choosing reasoning, we may follow the cause-and-effect or the antecedent-consequence relationships. We must be careful to distinguish the reasoning based on one of the above alternatives. Cause-and-effect reasoning may work in two directions: (1) from cause to effect or (2) from effect to cause relationships. Both directions provide us with concrete reasoning to help us to understand, anticipate, and avoid the baneful effects of those causes predict will be harmful to us. We must also be careful to distinguish between the reasoning that is based on cause-and-effect relationships from reasoning that is based on antecedent-consequence relationships. Antecedent-consequence relationships are deceptively similar to cause and effect relationships with consideration of reasoning on the basis of contingent alternatives that when a certain condition or situation or disposition exists, something will follow. But something that follows (consequence) is not produced by, or is not caused by, what went before it (the antecedent). Potential effects do not invariably occur when the cause is present. Nevertheless, sometimes an existent cause will produce an unusual effect.

Moral reasoning in justified situations seeks only to win acceptable rational ideas or to persuade other people to adapt themselves with a certain course of ethical action. Nevertheless, sometimes people are caught in a savage web in which there is no room for intellectual deliberated reasoning. They find themselves in a deserted and polluted area in which corruption is the mainstream of survival. Savage people cannot use words to settle differences with one another. They turn to swords and bullets to destroy each other. In exchanging bullets, people target their objects with the intention to exterminate competitors with inhumane strategies. These kinds of people do not argue about facts. They argue about evidence. Usually, they argue about historical incidents that may no longer be possible for intellectuals to confirm or verify which precedent consequences or allegations have happened again.

Nevertheless, savage people pledge to some things that they never witnessed, about which they ever can get no firsthand information. We accept many ideas as facts simply on the basis of trusted authorities or on the conventions of a community regardless of their justifications.

Justice is more rational, valuable, and profitable than injustice, even in business. Philosophies of justice systems are viewed as crossroads through the surface of reasoning. You expect it to be faced with the exposition of criticism of several thoughts concerning justice philosophies that lead you through the terrain of morality and ethics. Philosophical highways of reasoning provide you with two directions (pros and cons), crossroads of thoughts (debates and arguments) and intersections put you in critical situations (conflicts on religious beliefs, cultural values, and political ideologies) in order to choose valuable alternatives. All these complexities offer you more possibilities of getting lost. This doesn't mean that you should not drive your thoughts on these highways of reasoning, but you should approach and proceed on them with wisdom and prudence in order to discover yourself direction you are heading.

PLAN OF THIS CHAPTER

This chapter provides you with a blueprint of our journey through an intellectual highway of wisdom to review the holistic reality of life in order to reach moral, ethical, and legal philosophies and practices of justice. The question of what constitutes the foundation of justice has been debated almost since the beginning of recorded history. In this chapter, we first look at the nature of virtues and values and then at meaning of justice, law, and organizational business ethics. We will examine the foundation of fundamental characteristics of the ethics of organizational culture. Then we describe the basic sources of law and some general classifications of law. We conclude with sections offering you practical guidance on business ethics with a contractual binding in relationship with a society.

WHAT IS JUSTICE?

Justice is expressed as a conventional conscientious societal idealistic system in terms of fairness in relation to what somebody deserves to have or get. Justice is defined as a dispassionate system of thought to treat people equally (e.g., through code law) and/or equitably (e.g., through common law) by intellectual reasoning. Justice is defined as a general foundation for legal treatments of equals equally as what is due to a person or thing as the requital of just desserts by punishment or reward. Justice is viewed as a legitimate claim for an individual or a group to be treated according to what is due or owed to them. The so-called formal principle of justice should guarantee that similar cases should be treated alike. The formal principle of justice necessarily should be considered to be different from moral and ethical doctrines.

Moralists believe that we are required to follow our conscience to treat similar cases alike except when there are some relevant differences. In a moral sense, if we believe in equality, justice requires that through our treatment of self and others, we should ponder our judgments on the basis of fundamental major principles and avoid minor differences. Conversely, in a legal sense, if we believe in equitability, justice requires that through our keen deliberation, not only we should focus on fundamental major principles in equality, but also, we must ponder valuable foundations of minor differences and then make a holistic final judgment. Justice is not the only virtue an individual or social institution can initiate and/or pursue.

It becomes very difficult when justice conflicts with other moral obligations and ethical convictions. For example, shoplifting is a major problem within the field of business. Through the philosophy of equality in justice, business owners are responsible to report cases of shoplifting to law enforcement in order to establish criminal records for these people. Some business owners through equality in justice report all cases to police regardless of the value of the stolen merchandises. They believe that shoplifting is stealing and it is wrong and illegal. The value of the stolen merchandise does not matter. Sometimes the value of the stolen goods is a few cents or a few dollars or more. For example, on November 14, 2002, the California Superior Court Judge Frank Ochoa ruled: "Roland Herrera, 57, a career criminal, was sentenced to 25 years to life in prison under California's three-strikes law for stealing $11 worth of wine, lip balm, and breath freshener" (*CNN*.com - $11 theft gets three-strikes career criminal 25 years to life - Nov. 15, 2002, *CNN*.com./Law Center).

Conversely, through the philosophy of equitability in justice, some business owners put a limit on the value of stolen merchandises that must be reported to law enforcement. That limit is usually around $10. In addition, they put some limits on the age brackets of shoplifters. They never report to law enforcement agencies those stolen merchandises that have value, for example, less than $10, or the age of shoplifters if they are less than ten years old.

There are some problems within a multicultural organization that does not identify which causes or motives of differences or categories of similarities and dissimilarities are relevant to moral and ethical decision-making processes or actions and which are not. Consequently, we will face some formal requirements that do not guarantee that justice is done. This principle of justice emphasizes the role of impartiality and consistency in decision-making processes and actions. From another point of view, justice is concerned with formulating what is due from whom to whom (Stewart, 1996:292). Also, it is defined as the quality of right, equitable, and justifiable grounds of reasoning for legal treatments of individuals in a society. In addition, through executive legal power, justice is defined as administration or maintenance of law by judicial or court proceedings.

Justice is viewed as the bedrock of a legal system. The monolithic foundation of such bedrock is based on different reasoning philosophies, arguments, and debates concerning causes, rights, duties, responsibilities, accountabilities, and equitable effects of a justice system. In addition, justice is viewed as a differentiated essence of rational equity.

Rationality is an intellectual ideal of human deliberation on right and just things. Rationality is free of sexual favoritism, passionate romance, and emotional sensitivity to the source of power. Rationality does not simply refer to the means-ends thinking known as instrumentality. It is an intellectual processing of cause-effect deliberation concerning validity and reliability of something or someone. Rationality is an appeal to an independent wisdom. It is caring about and maintaining the right things, a matter of ends and a matter of means. Rationality is always culture-bound; both in its determination and in its concerns.

Since justice is bound with the notion of rational public-good, not surprisingly, any system of justice ends up with a great deal of wealth distribution as a definite unit of societal worth. Nevertheless, wealth is not the only primary end of social goodness; it is also a mean in itself. Wealth is an instrument to provide social goods for the welfare of people.

In confrontation within a justice system, money-talk and money-power are two powerful instruments that people use to achieve their own interests. Why is money a position in a just society is used? It is used as an influential measurable standard for utility and comparable necessity of achieving intelligent selfishness. We need to analyze the philosophical utility of justice concerning material and non-material wealth.

PHILOSOPHICAL FOUNDATIONS OF JUSTICE

In today's life, the debates and arguments on intellectual reasoning for just and unjust ideas, intentions, judgments, and actions are more focused on legality rather than on moral and ethical concerns. Within the domain of justice, sometimes we forget our moral and ethical convictions to humanity. To claim something is unjust in the modem civilization is more specifically reflected on illegal actions rather than immoral and unethical ones. It has been observed that in some cases, through the legal mandates, many innocent people are treated unjustly because of inhumanity of people. In a moral and ethical sense not in a legal one, we are interested in knowing: What is unjust? Injustice involves violation of the rights of some identifiable people. In order to understand what is justice, it is important to identify sources of justice by appealing to the overlapping notions of moral, ethical, and legal rights, fairness, equality, and equitability.

A theory of justice defines what individuals must do for the common good of society and in return what society must do for the goodness of individuals. Reciprocal maintenance of rights and duties between parties are reasonably protected in an orderly, civil society. A basic principle of justice then, is to act for the common good of the community and its incumbents. In a broad moral and ethical sense, justice means acting fairly toward self and others. In a business life, the principle of justice defines fair relationships between producers and consumers or between buyers and sellers. Based on such a definition, each society defines its justice system on the basis of prioritized arrangements of beliefs among moral virtues, ethical values, cultural beliefs, and the prevailing political ideology (e.g., capitalism, socialism, communism).

Beauchamp (1982: 229) has found six philosophical foundations for establishing a justice system:

- To each person an equal share
- To each person according to individual needs
- To each person according to the person's rights
- To each person according to individual effort
- To each person according to his or her societal contributions
- To each person according to their merit

Each principle of the above philosophical foundation of justice identifies a relevant property on the basis of which burdens and benefits should be distributed. The above attributions are sample listings of major candidates for the position of valid principles of distributive justice. There is no obvious barrier to the acceptance of more than one of these principles, and some theories of justice accept all six as valid attributions. Most societies use several in the belief that different rules are appropriate to different situations.

By reviewing the first principle, Beauchamp (1982: 229) states that which domains of moral, ethical, and legal binding would constitute the basic foundation of justice depends upon religious faith, cultural beliefs, and political doctrine of a nation. Nevertheless, all justice systems in all nations share in one foundation. That foundation is human rights. In the previous chapter, we discussed entitlements of human beings through natural and societal right endeavors. Within this domain, justice is considered an ideal of liberty. Liberty is the prime value for maintenance of human dignity and integrity. Liberty immunizes people from the interference of others. Liberty is the freedom to live according to our own choices without coercion of others or by the force of others choices. For example, the right to life is reasonably protected in all civil societies and nobody has the right to take another human's life.

The second principle of justice identifies the rights to entitlements to be based on the voluntary cognitive perception of an individual's needs. The prevailing of justice should be based on the individual's needs to work and the priority for needy individuals to work. This means that people in socialization of their valuable things need to provide everybody with a fair and a just share of entitlements. They should not deprive needy people from a loaf of bread in order to give it to people who are full. This principle is varies profession to profession and culture to culture. In the field of business, recruitment of qualified people may be based on unemployment status of applicants or based on the notion of employment at will by employers. Therefore, justice in a business entity may consider two sides of a coin: employers' needs and employees' needs. The employers' needs are based on economic gains through employees' professional work habits: efficiency, effective, and productivity. But the employees' needs are based on their life-style necessities. For example, in the economic recession, in the Japanese business culture, employers do not layoff their excessive employees, while in the American culture; employers do it through cutbacks, turnaround, and rightsizing strategies.

The third principle of justice recognizes the rights of individuals. The terms of individuals, selves, or persons are conceived as whether they are isolated, atomic, and discrete entity, or are by their nature's parts of a social system. An individual's rights have been developed and established to provide general guidelines in determining what is permitted and what is prohibited. In all justice systems, individuals are viewed with their possessions of material and non-material rights. These rights are used to prove the distribution of burdens and benefits in a justified society. For example, in a capitalistic society, the rights of individuals depend on their social status, class position, economic fortune, intelligence, appearance, affiliation or linkage to a group, or the like.

The fourth principle of justice recognizes the truthful efforts of hard working individuals to be recognized in order to provide them with the appropriate rewards. This principle promotes innovativeness within a moral, ethical, and legal environment. Entitlements of super-rights or special-rights need to be based on a healthy competition. For example, justice in an organization means promotion of employees to higher positions and appropriation of pay raise cost of living adjustment (COLA) or merit pay should be based on the manifestation of their efforts, not on prejudice, connections, discrimination, and/or favoritism.

The fifth principle of justice is concerned with contributive degrees of efficiency, effectiveness, and productivity of individuals towards fulfillment of the mission of a corporation. This indicates that how individuals are contributing their skills, knowledge, wealth, and power for the increasing financial valuable wealth of an on-going organization or of the social welfare in a society alters how justice is distributed. Moral, ethical, and legal notions of equality or equitability, motivate individuals to manifest what a person has done or contributed his/her efforts to make justice more meaningful in an organization. Some people may think that this principle makes a managerial system unjust. For example, when an employee is very efficient and working very hard, he/she needs to be recognized and be provided with more supports in order to accelerate his/her potential for elevation of the organizational working people is spirit and welfare of self and others. Through equitability reasoning for justification of merit policy, this suggests that justice in these situations or conditions requires additional privileges and entitlements to be offered to those persons or groups not on the basis of equality (the equal minimum incentives for all) but on the bases of equitability (the appropriateness of incentives based on efforts of each individual).

The sixth principle states that the concerned with distribution of power and wealth should be based on merit systems. This would mean that everybody should have free access to sources of power and resources of wealth. In a just society, nobody should be deprived of these privileges. Everybody, on the basis of his/her entitlements and accomplishments, should be merited to higher privileges. This motivates individuals to be more productive and effective in order to serve better themselves and others.

Each of the above six principles of justice has its own advocates. Nevertheless, establishment and enforcement of principles of justice are two different domains. Within these two domains, there are some societies that claim that they have an impartial or neutral justice systems by the virtue that they have established all rights on paper, but never guarantee those entitlements in action. It is valid to claim that a justice system should protect the entitlements of possession of individuals' rights either by law or by voluntary actions through education and religious convictions.

In the book of *"A Theory of Justice,"* Rawls (1971: 12) speculated that:

> Rational persons are situated behind a hypothetical "veil of ignorance" and do not know their place in a society but know facts about their justice systems based on deliberations and choices of two rules of fairness. First, each person is to have an equal right to the most extensive basic liberty compatible with a similar liberty for others, and second, social and economic inequalities are to be arranged so that they are both (a) reasonably expected to be to everyone's advantage, and (b) attached to positions and offices open to all.

John Stuart Mill (1957: 62) stated:

> Whether justice consists in depriving a person of a possession, or in breaking faith with him, or in treating him worse than he deserves, or worse than other people who have no greater claims in each case the supposition implies two things: [1] a wrong done, and [2] some assignable person who is wronged...It seems to me that this feature to the moral obligation constitutes the specific difference between justice and generosity or benevolence. Justice implies something which is not only right to do, and wrong not to do, but which some individual person can claim from us as his moral right.

MORAL DEVELOPMENT AND JUSTICE

Psychologist Laurence Kohlberg (1973), Director of Harvard's Center for Moral Education, collected experimental data and traced individual's moral developments concerning justice. Kohlberg centered his research on analyzing the stages of moral development which individuals pass as they mature in their moral characters. He categorized moral development into three stages: (1) pre-conventional, (2) conventional, and (3) post-conventional. He assumed that in each of these three stages, there are two levels, giving a total of six possible stages of moral development (see Table 11.1). He believed in a universal guideline for human behavior concerning the intellectual foundations of justice. He believed that there should be some principles to serve as the guiding force in an individual's personal moral character. He believed in a moral behavioral development to such an extent that he has identified through his research experiences three major levels in the moral development. He believed most people operate sometimes on one level and sometimes on another level of moral stage and these types of behavioral patterns can serve as handy classificatory devices. Nevertheless, Kohlberg believed that ethical principles do not provide any quantifiable steps or stages of ethical development. In fact, he argued that people in different stages of moral development would have distinctive justifiable ethical judgments concerning self and others.

Table 11.1: Kohlberg's Moral Levels

MORAL LEVELS

Preconventional Level

1. The punishment-and-obedience orientation: The physical consequences of action determine its goodness or badness Avoidance of punishment and unquestioning deference to power are valued in their own right, not in terms of respect for an underlying moral order supported by punishment and authority.
2. The instrumental-relativist orientation: Right action consists of that which instrumentally satisfied one's own needs and occasionally the needs of others Human relations are viewed in terms like those of the marketplace. Elements of fairness, of reciprocity, and of equal sharing are present, but they always are interrelated in a physical, pragmatic way Reciprocity is a matter of "You scratch my back and I'll scratch yours," not out of loyalty, gratitude, or justice.

Conventional Level

1. The interpersonal concordance or "good boy-nice girl" orientation: Good behavior is that which pleases or helps others and is approved by them. There is much conformity to stereotypical images of what is majority or "natural" behavior Behavior is frequently judged by intention "He means well" becomes important for the first time One meets approval by being "nice."
2. The law-and-order orientation: There is orientation toward authority, fixed rules, and the maintenance of the social order Right behavior consists of doing one's duty, showing respect for authority, and maintaining the given social order for its own sake.

Postconventional Level

1. The social contract, legalistic orientation: This has utilitarian overtones The right action tends to be defined in terms of general individual rights and standards that have been critically examined and agreed to by the whole society. Emphasis upon the legal point of view but with the possibility of changing the law in terms of rational considerations This is the official morality of the American government and Constitution.
2. The universal-ethical principle orientation: Right is defined by the decision of conscience in accord with self-chosen ethical principles appealing to logical comprehensiveness, universality, and consistency. These principles are abstract and ethical (the Golden Rule, the categorical imperative * of Kant but not such concrete rules as the Ten Commandments).

* Kant's view that a moral principle is one that can be made a universal law.
Source: Lawrence Kohlberg , "The Claim to Moral Adequacy of a Highest Stage of Moral Judgment," *Journal of Philosophy,* (1973), 70, act. 25: 630-646.

Kohlberg in his research found that people move forward through the above stages of moral development of justice and never backward. Also, he found that individuals do not skip stages. They go through moral development of justice stage by stage and they can describe the preceding or lower stages but not the higher stages.

As previously indicated in this chapter, John Rawls's *A Theory of Justice* (1971:12) has received widespread public attention. He believed that social justice is neither merely a matter of personal morality nor of institutional ethics. In this regard he belongs to the tradition of Hobbes, Locke, Rousseau, and Kant, the tradition of social-contract theories. Rawls's principles of social justice are as follows.

First principle: Each person is to have an equal right to the most extensive total system of equal basic liberties compatible with a similar system of liberty for all.

Second Principle: Social and economic inequalities are to be arranged so that they are both (a) to the greatest benefit of the least advantaged and (b) attached to offices and positions open to all under conditions of fair equality of opportunity. The two principles, the equal liberty principle and the social and economic inequalities principle, are not correlative for Rawls. In addition, Rawls' moral theories are based on his theories of justice and what he called the *Veil of Ignorance*. Rawls believed that whether moral principles or practices are fair or just would be based on testing whether those principles or practices would be chosen by a society whose collective eyes were veiled to wealth, class, color, and the like. Also, Rowls (1971: 12) stated: "This ensures that no one is advantaged or disadvantaged in the choice of principles by the outcome of natural chance or the contingency of social circumstances."

JUSTICE AND MORAL REASONING

Philosophies of justice should not be finalized until all moral and ethical principles have demonstrated validity of neutral intellectual justness and fairness in practice. Justice is said to be within the domain of an intellectual reasoning in which everyone is dynamically engaged in reasoning while observing, sensing, deliberating, judging, and practicing life events. Reasoning for injustice is viewed as an assessment on reasoning either on the cause-and-effect or effect-and- cause argument. Arguing from cause to effect or from effect to cause is very tricky. Corbett (1991: 71) has provided some guidelines that might keep us from slipping into faulty cause-and-effect reasoning:

- A cause always comes before its effect.
- An effect could have a number of possible causes.

- The cause we assign to an effect must be capable of producing the effect.
- We must consider whether the hypothetical cause always produces the effect that it is capable of producing and whether it invariably produces the same effect.
- If something occurs repeatedly, the likeliest cause is the one that all the occurrences have in common.
- If an effect occurs in some situations but does not occur in other similar situation, the cause may be the single thing that is different in the similar situations.
- If a particular situation increases or decreases, you must find a plausible cause that acts in a similar or inverse fashion, that is, increases or decreases as the effect increases or decreases; or decreases as the effect increases or increases as the effect decreases

Philosophical studies about justness reasoning go back to ancient civilizations. For Plato (427-347 B.C.) and some of his followers, justice seems to have been the paramount of the sum of virtue in relation to self with surrounding things. Plato was Socrates' (469-399 B.C.) devoted recorder and faithful defender of justice. In 399 B.C., Socrates was condemned to death on the charge that he was "an evil-doer and curious person, searching into things under the earth and above the heaven, and making the worse appear the better cause, and teaching all this to others," (Albert, Denise, and Peterfreund, 1984: 9). By a moral sense do you find a justified ground for the conviction of Socrates? The answer is no, because he was living in a period of moral degeneration and continuous corrupted political system that only obeying the law was regarded justice; whether that law was rational or irrational. He was convicted for his devotion to searching and ascertaining the truth.

Aristotle (384-322 B.C.) was convinced that the development of moral character is the natural course of events over time and through intellectual habituation. He did not describe how this happens. Epicurus (342--270 B.C.) pointed out that although justice is the same for all when it is considered as a general principle, it manifests variations when it is applied in specific situations. After twenty-five centuries since the death of Socrates, Plato, Epicures and other ancient philosophers, we are observing that in some communities, the notion of injustice still is the most vicious instrument to suppress people and make them obedient to the wishes of non-democratic political regimes.

Confucius, who was born in 551 B.C., believed that the proper foundation for justice in a society is propriety based on respect for human dignity, which in turn is based on two principles: fairness and reversibility (De Mente, 1990: 18). While we are dynamically engaged in justice practices, we are supposedly having experience, and experience, by general consent, is the Great Teacher. Experiencing a justice system has two main ingredients: (1) action and (2) reflection. Observations from and judgments on actions become indispensable in cases where the consequences of a given moral and ethical situation cannot be gauged by mere legal decisions. But legal decisions must be supplemented with moral and ethical reflections to make a system of justice in the right direction.

Institutionalization of justice is the medium of both actions and reflections. Pursuing moral and ethical actions and reflections in conjunction with fitness of a justice system is the sheer love of rightness, justness, fairness, and worthiness. From reviewing the philosophical clashes of opinions on the nature of justice, we discover that the challenge of morality and ethics consists rather in the stimulation of their inherent questions than in the finality of their answers. Within the quest of wisdom, every human thought is the current issue of moral and ethical significance, and in all ages and places debates and arguments about morality and ethics are posed and answered differently. The initial problem of moral and ethical philosophy of justice is defining the nature of justice. If justice means to provide equal opportunities for everybody to have a good and safe life, then the objective of justice would be based upon searching for and discovering happiness and peace for all. If justice means to maintain a balance between virtue (good, better, best, and excellence) and vice (bad, worse, worst, and horrible), then it constitutes a moderate treatment of individuals on the basis of a balance between far right and far wrong. For example, there are two views concerning capital punishment:

- A murderer should be executed with lethal injection, or electric chair, or a gas chamber. It depends how justices make a choice among a multitude of inhumane actions (e.g., from electric chair to lethal injection) for executing a human being.
- Killing a human being by another human being or groups (even a murderer) is not moral and ethical. It is against humanity, because killing a murderer plus the murdered person is viewed as a double murder.

There are several questions arising from fairness and justness:

- What is true?
- What is fair?
- What is just?
- What is right?
- What is appropriate?

The general answer to these questions is: In a general term, human life is precious. We do expect our lives to be reasonable fair, because it is a natural gift or in a religious faith, it is God's gift. For such a reason, all human beings are entitled to such a liberty and no human being should take such a natural gift away from human beings. Such an idea is different culture to culture. For example, in the French justice system, there is no capital punishment. They believe that no other human being has the right to take the life of other human beings. Within this humane philosophy, human life or death is not subject to a justice system, because that system should not interfere with nature or God's will. Conversely, there are other justice systems like in Iran, Libya, Iraq, United States, China and other places in which a majority people believe that capital punishment is the right of a justice system. A murderer should be executed, because he/she has committed the worst crime.

JUSTICE PHILOSOPHIES IN BUSINESS

In the field of business, we expect to be treated fairly by producers, sellers, employers, and the justice system commensurately with our rights, duties, responsibilities, and productivity. We expect the rule of the law to be fair and just, treating each individual equally under its precepts. By an analytical discussion of 20th century justice systems, we may expose to two different views: (1) Equality, and (2) Equitability.

Equalitarian Philosophy of Justice

Equality means distribution of burdens and rewards in a society should be based on simply manifestation of equal weight among a numbering group. Equalitarian justice puts its view on the proposition that all human beings are equal in principles of their rights. Each individual is entitled to be treated equally and should have equal access to goods and services in a society. Having access to basic material needs such as food, shelter, and medicine should be the right of human beings and deviation from equality is considered unjust.

The notion of humanity is more oriented toward equal distribution of things rather than production. The distributive process varies from situation to situation and/or society to society. In equalitarian societies people believe in the doctrine that equal pay for equal work is the main criterion for a rewards system. The equalitarian justice philosophy requires equality in the assignment of all rights and duties without any exceptional cases. Each person is subject to the maximum amount of equal liberty compatible with a similar liberty for others.

Equitabilitarian Philosophy of Justice

In an equitable society, people believe in different pays for equal work on the basis of individual characteristics, qualifications, conditions, times, and places. They believe in a free market value system that is based on demand and supply. Values are subject to change and change agents. In equitable societies, the market places values on different occupations and the rewards, such as wages and salaries, are not necessarily subject to equal pay. There are some other factors that will be considered in addition to the general principles. In an equitable justice system, practitioners believe in the equitable pay for equal job doctrine, in which individuals are rewarded for the sweat of their brows according to what value the free market places on their services. Because the market places different values on different occupations, rewards, such as wages and incentives, are not necessarily equal (Hanson, 1991: 16). For example, to do the same job in a mild climate or in a very hot situation, or in a very sever cold condition is not subject to an equal pay for all. Fairness and justness say: there should be some incentives for very hot or very cold working environments for workers. Therefore, equitable social and economic incentives are to be arranged accordingly so that they are both (a) reasonably expected to be appropriated for an individual's specific entitlements (e.g., capabilities, efforts hardworking, work conditions, and innovativeness) and (b) attached to positions and offices open to specific qualified people as public authorities. As mentioned before, the equitability philosophy of justice according to Rawls' (1971: 60) philosophy of justice, formulates two basic principles as follows:

- First, each person is to have an equal right to the most extensive basic liberty compatible with similar liberty for all.

- Second, social and economic inequalities are to be arranged so that they are both: Reasonable expected to be everyone's advantage. Attached to positions and offices open to all.

Considering the above propositions, liberty is a function of rational reasoning concerning human dignity; consequently respect for liberty is viewed as respect for humanity. In addition, since liberty is a basic right for individuals to achieve their ends, people need to respect that liberty. Accordingly, Rawls' first principle serves human rights, and the second principle serves civil rights.

Now, within the domain of political ideologies, along the lines of the above discussion, we would like to examine both equalitarian and equitabilitarian philosophies of justice. Let us briefly consider two democratic and authoritarian political systems and their inherent relationships to the philosophy of justice. In the democratic justice system inequalities and the status of classes of people are based on the free will defense principle. What does the free will defense mean? For the purpose of answering to this question Plantinga (1974: 29) states:

If a person is free with respect to a given action, then he [she] is free to perform that action and free to refrain from performing it; no antecedent conditions and/or causal laws determine that he [she] will perform the action, or that he [she] won't.

Since the moral concern in a democratic society is based on liberty for all individuals, we cannot find an absolute moral action and ethical reflection on standardization of expected behavior. In addition, democracy, in its long history, has been analyzed through different econo-political and sociocultural perspectives. What can make a democratic system moral and ethical is based on three principles:

- The free will defense
- The property ownership rights including intellectual ones
- The free enterprises

The Free Will Defense: The free will defense is the idea of being free with respect to an action on the grounds of civil rights. Therefore, for such a reason, the exercise of other free will should never be separated from delineation of moral virtues and ethical values. Given these distinctive actions, we can claim a fundamental right of the free will as follows. The natural world has provided many opportunities for all creatures to be significantly free to be better in nature than evil. All creatures are equal to survive within nature. All creatures have been created by specific causes of universal justice. However, the natural causes or universal justice cannot force them to do only what is right or wrong. To behave morally and ethically depends on individual's free will on moral and ethical good.

The property Ownership Defense: The property ownership rights, including intellectual properties, are the second principle in a democratic society. This is a complementary principle along with the line of the free will defense. Ownership should not preclude the natural free will defense, of human beings. This means that the ownership of a production system does not mean one's entitled to the human ownership (e.g., slavery and sweatshop practices). Personal property excludes human beings, because all human beings are subject to equal rights to be free of ownership by another. Human beings are not properties to be owned. In a democratic society, all individuals are entitled to equal rights. Even such a right is denoted to husbands and wives, because a marriage is viewed as a loving contractual agreement between two parties to live together and share their joys and sorrows with each other. Nevertheless, ownership is denoted as the means and ends of production systems such as land, capital, raw materials, technology, information, and plants not human beings.

The Free Enterprises: The third characteristic of a democratic system is concerned with the establishment of free enterprises within the boundary of a free competitive market. A free enterprise is not controlled by the state or monopolized by a small capable elite group of individuals. Also, a free enterprise does not require to respond to the will of the government how to produce, distribute, and sale. However, this does not mean that a free enterprise is free of any societal rule including moral and ethical. On the other hand, the free competitive market is set by specific societal rules and regulations to safeguard the rights of producers and consumers. In a democratic society, the market share is bound to the free will of producers and consumers. When a justice system in a democratic society appears, it indicates that a small group of people are controlling the major portion of the market, then the government intervenes to safeguard the rights of all people. Within a just and fair marketplace, the government is responsible to resent *monopolies* (exclusive ownership rights of production systems or control of supply) and *monopsonies* (exclusive privileges of having control of demand by a special group of customers). For examples, there is a practice between two soft drink companies in the United States Coca Cola and Pepsi that restrict restaurants, hotels, vendors, and airlines who are customers of one of these companies, either by monopolistic desire of suppliers or by monopsonistic demand of businesses. They are bound not to have both soft drinks in their outlets. Such a business practice penetrates the principle rights of a democratic society. In addition, such an unethical business practice diminishes the notion of competition and free choices. Access to a market or to a product should be controlled neither by monopolies or monopsonies nor by any power including government or special interest groups. Free competition is driven in part by the quality of products or services in a free marketplace.

Now we would like to turn your attention to non-democratic societies or to authoritarian government systems. In the communistic justice systems (Marxism, Leninism, Stalinism, and Maoism) wages and salaries are based on services for society (actually for the powerful political party) in which burdens and rewards are distributed respectively to each individual according to their equal distribution of societal rights and privileges without consideration of their abilities and their basic needs (absolutism justice). If we make an effort to analyze these diverse views, we need to review the historical grounds for the establishment, maintenance, and reflections of philosophers in such an endeavor. The justice system in these countries is focusing equal production, distribution, sales, prices, and consumption systems. There are no motivational factors concerning profit making as equity or incentives for innovativeness. Both producers and consumers are convicted to the will of the state.

Marxism philosophy of justice is concerned with wage slavery. However, Marxists, in reality, believe in mass exploitation; mass slavery. Any socialistic and/or communistic political system cannot survive unless it imposes a limit on and controls the free will of citizens. In such a justice system, the system makes all citizens exploiters in order to minimize their efforts to the well being of a society. Also, exploitation by a government is a strong tool to make citizens obedient to the justice system that is affiliated with the elite powerful groups of government. Do you find any moral virtue and ethical value to be stemmed from this system concerning the dignity and integrity of individuals?

Different Types of Justice System

Throughout history, there have been numerous moral, ethical, legal, political, and economic doctrines concerning justice. These doctrines have emerged from different sociocultural and econo-political conditions. In viewing and analyzing different kinds of justice systems, there are three primary questions we should address:

- What are the main different philosophical principles that have been accepted throughout the centuries in a culture and what are their positions concerning justness and fairness in treating people whose rights are violated?
- What is adequate reasoning concerning rationalization and legitimization of a justice system in a society and how that justice system is serving its people?
- How would one apply a justice philosophy in the field of business and empower both producers and consumers in relationship to their rights and duties and how it creates an environment for a fair system to check the balance of power?

The issues, which we began with concerning justice, are analyzing the balance between selfishness versus altruism, cynical egoism versus gratified indulgence, the honest route versus the dishonest route, and the whims of lesser people versus the whims of supreme people. The appropriate answer to the above concerns emerges from rational principles in morality and ethics through honesty.

Successful business people have to be people of intellect in order to serve themselves and others. There are several kinds of justice that need to be defined and analyzed in this chapter.

Within the multitude domain of the above philosophical justice principles, managers may find moral, ethical, and legal guidelines in five basic spheres of organizational justice:

- Compensatory justice
- Retributive justice
- Procedural justice
- Commutative justice
- Distributive justice

Compensatory Justice: Compensatory justice consists in compensation someone or a group of people for harm suffers or injury received from another individual or groups of people; including business and non-business institutions. It is a just way for assessing and offering compensation for loses due to unjust treatment in the past. It is concerned with finding a just cause and a fair way for an individual or a group of people to be compensated for what they lost through intentional or unintentional harm or wrong doing by others. This type of compensation could be related to physical, psychological, and property harms that a person or a group has caused for others or vice versa.

- What moral and ethical ground for compensation of particular harm should be taken into account?
- What is ground for assuming a just compensation in both material and non-material terms?
- Who morally, ethically, and legally is liable for such compensatory rewards?
- Who is in authority or in charge to make that decision?
- How should damages and harms be assessed and with what rules and regulations?
- How can those compensatory rewards serve a justice system?

There are opponents to compensation for the historical unfair and unjust treatments of individuals or groups who have been abused by last generations. Opponents argue that the establishment of preferential and/or compensatory justice violates the integrity of all individuals' equitable rights, because historical compensatory justice offers extra privileges to some people that they can use to create injustice. Consequently, in such circumstances the justice system ignores the rights of other individuals in that society. Opponents believe that historical compensatory justice should come from those members of a group that committed some wrongdoing and be offered to those groups who suffered. Since both groups are dead, therefore there is nothing to do. Also, it is not just that compensation go equally to all members of a group that contains some injured and non-injured parties. Compensation should go only to those people who were injured. In sum, while historical compensatory justice can provide some preferential treatments for a special group of people, it can create injustice for other groups.

Equality for all can only be achievable through temporary preferences given to a group that historically suffered injuries or harms. In the field of business, when corporations are caught in organizational wrongdoing, there is a tendency for managers to find scapegoats in order to put guilt on those employees who have or haven't done it; right or wrong. In such a situation, managers usually deny wrongdoing and blame employees for some sort of character weaknesses. This occurs when they are caught and businesses will be sued by clients or fined by regulatory agencies. In return, employees request fair compensation, because they believe that it was the corporation's policy and/or procedures that they implemented, creating wrongdoing in the workplace. In such a situation, compensatory justice requires fair compensation to victims. For example, a business entity, which has damaged a nearby property by its employees, must restore it to its original state.

Retributive Justice: Retributive justice means that benefits and burdens should be equitably and fairly distributed among people. The retributive justice is a powerful force to override personal advantages. A corporation concerns it with specific punishment due to a law-breaker or wrongdoer, or illegal actions.

Within an organizational culture, retributive justice among employees is considered as a foundation for justness and fairness. They are ensuring that work burdens are proportionately distributed and compensated equitably by all parties involved. For example, while you are waiting in line to deposit your drafts in a bank, you may observe that all tellers are very busy and some other employees are sitting and doing nothing. It comes to your mind that wages for tellers are commensurate with the minimum and for other employees who have less work to do it is higher. You may conclude that it is a matter to your conscience that task performance is affected by the kind of retributive justice that should prevail equitable compensation for all. Also, retributive justice provides a rational ground on the bases of the principle of equity in which it can force a corporation to compensate all its employees equitably through sharing resources and information to perform their jobs better. Clearly, the retributive justice is an instrumentally valuable belief that can provide an ethical and moral harmony among all stakeholders'; employers, employees, customers, and others. Such a harmony creates trust and loyalty.

There are several issues concerning misbehavior, misappropriation of the corporation's funds, and misusage of the corporation's properties for the personal stakeholders' gains. Each requires that punishments should be evenhanded and be proportionately fair to transgressions of all organizational members. An employee should not be fired for the shortage of $10 (e.g., stealing or mistakes) if the corporate executives who have embezzled $100 millions are allowed to remain on the job. This is not justice.

Procedural Justice: Procedural justice is a kind of reasoning philosophy in which in an organization you may find justness through administrative moral and ethical convictions. Procedural justice preserves the integrity of a due process system. When managers have absolute power in decision- making processes, they should believe in a just due-process system. Managers should believe in the integrity of their institutions and fair processes themselves that respect and value the interest of that institution beyond their egoistic self-interest. Due process and participatory style management are indicatives of justness when allowing employees makes decisions give direct inputs. The decisions that emerge from procedural justice can be embraced and accepted as a legitimate outcome by all affected parties.

In the process of procedural justice, people find appropriate opportunities to express their viewpoints and feelings concerning the fairness and justness of a justice system. The fairness and justness of procedural justice reflects adequate structural and procedural mechanisms in policy making processes, in selecting decision-makers, in adequate proceedings for setting and communicating the ground rules for application of rules, in safeguarding against abusing or misusing of power, a chance for having appeals, and mechanisms for changes beyond the appeal process. In short, procedural justice, specifically in the field of business, provides mutual commitments between employers and employees, organization and society, and above all between producers. It requires that punishments should be evenhanded and proportionate to transgressions of all an effective team management outcome in order to designate fair-decision procedures, practices, and processes and above all arriving into just decisions and actions.

Since the distributive justice is more concerned that the size of merit raises or gains reflect true differences in contribution processes across people involved, it does not guarantee that in similar cases in future we will think the next one is fair. This is because distributive justice does not include assessments of the fairness of the methods or processes by which the decisions were made. Therefore, procedural justice emphasizes fairness on formulation and implementation of all policies and procedures across all organizational divisions. Folger and Greenberg (1985: 146) have identified six ethical and moral rules for procedural justice in an organization:

- *Consistency Rule*: Allocation procedures should be consistent across persons and over time.
- *Bias Suppression Rule*: Personal self-interest in allocation process should be prevented.
- *Accuracy Rule*: Decisions must be based on accurate information.
- *Correctability Rule*: Opportunities must exist to enable decisions to be modified.
- *Representative Rules*: All allocation processes must represent the concerns of all recipients.
- *Ethicality Rule*: Allocations must be based on prevailing moral and ethical standards.

Commutative Justice: Commutative justice refers to justice in decision-making and transactional or exchange processes of goods and services among specific parties. Commutative justice demands the equitable worth of exchanges to be traded. The goods or services should be valued in a competitive market for what they are worth according to the processing costs plus reasonable profits and consumers' effective demands and the worth of their purchase power. Commutative justice calls for just or fair prices, based on the utility of the necessitated causal demands of sellers (to cash their inventories) and buyers (to use their savings for meeting their needs). Within such a philosophical foundation of transactional or exchange of goods and services with cash or other forms of business deals, De George (1999: 102) states that the just or fair treatment of sellers and buyers is based on the following conditions:

- If all parties to the transaction have access to all the pertinent information about the transaction, then the deal is just.
- If all parties to the transaction enter it freely and without any coercion, the deal is just.
- If all parties to the transaction benefit from the transaction, the deal is just.

Distributive Justice: Distributive justice involves the equal distribution of rights, privileges, and duties among citizens by the state. Citizens might be given what they are due according to their rights, ability, work, performance, merit, needs, and so on by the state. Rawls developed a comprehensive theory of the distribution of justice, or what he has called distributive justice. His major hypothesis is based on questioning how within a society whose rules are designed through a veil of ignorance; one should then distribute the costs and benefits of all actions. Rawls suggested that several principles have to be followed in order to arrive at a set of rules. First, each and every individual within a society or affected by it must have equal right to the most extensive liberty that is compatible with a like liberty for all. Second, any inequalities, both social and economic, that are defined by a society's structural form or fostered by it must be considered arbitrary unless they are at the same time (1) arranged so that the least advantaged individuals obtain the greatest benefits and (2) the outgrowth of each individual's innate fair and equal chance to reach any social position.

One of the basic principles in distributive justice in a business entity is related to the value systems of stakeholders. The distributive justice is based on the perceived fairness of particular outcomes commensurate with each stakeholder's characteristics. It has to do with the distribution of rewards across people. This requires that the benefits and burdens of a corporation should equitably be distributed among stakeholders according to impartial criteria. Profit sharing and awarding pay raises based on friendship, favoritism, discrimination, and the like rather than performance criteria are unfair. Since distributive justice is viewed as a just foundation for law in a community, now we are turning your attention to law.

WHAT IS LAW?

The peaceful condition of societal life refers to the well-structured ordination in reasoning and practices concerning the inherent individual's natural and societal rights and duties. Ordination of reason signifies the establishment of cognitive judgments in searching for proper ends through rational means B justice. Social considerations raise ethical and legal issues in behavioral decision making processes and actions when the consequences conflict with differing objectives of an individual and a society in general. What is necessary to prevent such a fraction is prevailing of justice.

Law is not formally an act of "will," it is a pluralistic practicability of societal reasoning that determines behavioral means in relation to some predictable ends. Cross and Miller (2001: 2) state:

> One of the important functions of law in any society is to provide stability, predictability, and continuity so that people can have assurance of how to order their affairs... Law consists of enforceable rules governing relationships among individuals and between individuals and their society.

There have been and will continued to be different definitions of law through different cultures and political systems. Although the definition of law varies in their particular philosophical sources of rights and duties, they all are based on the genèral observation that, at a minimum:

- Law is something pertaining to intellectual reasoning.
- Law is the expression of what is reasonable to do under a sociocultural value doctrine and an econo-political system.
- Law mandates the social valuable standards of expected behaviors under which the community limits the power on what people can or cannot do.
- Law formalizes the socio-cultural and econo-political contracts under which the community limits the harm that can be done to others.
- Law establishes mandatory minimal standards in intellectual deliberation and conduct.
- Law is a mandate with respect to what to do or what not do.
- Law is an extrinsic means to achieve a productive moral ends.
- Law is an exterior principle of means that establishes discipline and order among human beings. It is a measure by which people induce their behavior to restraint their passion, desire, and greed.
- Law is something pertaining to reason. It is the expression of what is reasonable or unreasonable or just and unjust.
- Law is relevant here through moral convictions and ethical commitments to analyze the inherent characteristics of legal expectations by explaining rights, duties, viability, credibility, and accountability all citizens and institutions.

According to the above definitions, we are now focusing our attention on the rules of law. In a highly civilized and democratic nation, society expects individuals to provide a high standard of living and to protect the general quality of life by its members. In return, members of that society demand a high quality of lifestyle. They demand liberty in order to be able to express their ideas freely to anyone in the world and to quickly have access to the public information from around the globe. At the same time, they do not want their private information to be infringed upon because of the widespread availability of information. The moral fairness is an interior principle of goodness of law because it is qualitatively a modification of the most interior causes of action we have. The intellectual ethical values are the power of reasoning within the essence of the people's will. On the other hand law is an extrinsic principle of action. It is an exterior principle of peace making in the sense that it establishes an order of actions to be followed by all people in order to seek a common good-end. It is a measure by which we are induced to act or are restrained from acting.

The foundational bedrock of a legal system is based upon a political ideology and a distinct philosophy of intellectual reasoning. For such reasons, law possesses two different philosophical dimensions:

- The theological that is based upon moral theology; the law given by God through scriptures (e.g., Ten Commandments of Old Testament, Bible, Koran, etc.). This law is based on religious faith in the universal causes of justice.
- The teleological reasoning that is based on the ethical doctrine of equitable justness. In a moral, ethical, and legal environment, without an analytical grasp of the purpose of law, we cannot appreciate sufficiently the definition, needs and desirability of law.

Philosophies of Law

Each society according to its religious faiths, cultural values, political-legal ideologies, and economical doctrines establishes specific rights, duties, privileges, and entitlements for its members. While some communities believe in the integrity of the individualistic liberty, others believe in collectivistic shared materialistic goodness. By contrasting a private good and public well we mean that the good for an individual is the good for all. The moral good for a personal character whether, physical or metaphysical one like honesty cannot exclude possession of good for others. Nevertheless, many people can possess the public good simultaneously. The public good should come from individual good. Before we provide you with different types of law in general, it is necessary to have a precise notion of what is meant by the philosophy of law.

It is evident that any philosophy of justice carries the common goodness of means in order to reach to a good end by any law. Without a grasp of the purpose of law, we are not able to appreciate sufficiently the meaning, need, and finality of law. The public good is of necessity of spirituality or immaterial good. Honesty and altruism are based on humanitarian notion of being good that is denoted to spiritual goodness. It shares in such a way that it doesn't make any limitation on the sharing of goodness. All people can share humanity with each one possessing it wholly. There is a hierarchy in the state of public goodness. The most humanitarian organization is known as a family. Each member is trying to make it good on the basis of humanitarian public good intention and action for all its members. In a civil society, all people participate in a humanitarian culture that is based on trust, reciprocity, and confidence in the integrity of their society toward peace and order.

The philosophy of justice in a host country in which a firm is doing business usually has a greater impact on the firm's activities than does any other home countries' sources of law. Most national philosophical justice systems can be classified as belonging to one of the major legal systems B the civil law, common law, or Islamic law (see Figure 11.2).

Civil law or code law systems, as in France.

Common Law legal system, as in the United States (except in the State of Luisiana).

Islamic *Sharia* legal system, as in Iran.

Figure 11.2: Major Philosophical Foundations of Global National
                Justice Systems

Different Courts of Law

Among the above philosophical ideologies, there are others that they believe in spirituality. Despite what domain of justice philosophy you believe in, still there are some important questions concerning the nature of law. Part of the philosophical studies of law is often referred to as jurisprudence, which involves manifestation of the signs of different thoughts of jurisprudential approaches to law (see Table 11.2). Within the global judiciary environments, there are three systems of the court of law:

- The Court of Law and Remedies at Law
- The Court of Equity and Remedies in Equity
- The Court of the Islamic *Sharia* Law

These court systems make a distinction among laws of different lands. Not only should businesspeople know how they can seek justice, also, they should be aware how they will be able
to take the oath, and how the judge promptly proceeds with hearing of both parties and issues his verdict, in order to have access to justice in both home and host countries.

The Court of Law and Remedies at Law: These types of court system is concerned with the legal means to be recovered for commenting a right or redress a wrong action by awarding land, items of valuable things, or money through a jury or a judge. The three remedies of land, items of valuable things, or money are called remedies at law.

The Court of Equity and Remedies in Equity: This type of court system is concerned with the legal means when no adequate remedy at law is available. When individuals are not able to obtain adequate remedy in a court of law because of strict technicalities, they petition to the justice authorities for relief. The court's appointee for making a decree is called a chancellor, and the formal chancery court's remedies are called remedies in equity. Then benched judges rule about that case on the basis of so-called equitable maxims propositions or general statements of equitable rules.

Table 11. 2: Procedural Differences Among an Action at Law, an Action in Equity, an Action in *Sharia,* and an Action in the Organizational Administration Court

PROCEDURES	ACTION AT LAW	ACTION IN EQUITY	ACTION IN *SHARIA**	ACTION IN ORGANIZATIONAL ADMINISTRATION COURT
Initiation of claim	By filing a lawsuit	By filing a petition	By filing a claim	By filing a grievance
Judges, lawyers, and juries	Male and female	Male and female	Male only **	Male and Female, or a panel of experts
Parties	Plaintiffs and defendants	Petitioners and respondents	Claimants and accused	Complainers and accused or griever and grieved
Decision	By jury and by judge(s)	By Judge(s) only (not by jury)	By a religious jurisprudence	By the chief executive officer (CEO) or by a grievance committee
Result	Judgments	Decree	Writ (opinion) ***	Decision
Remedy	Monetary compensation	Injunction, specific performance, or rescission	*Ghesa (remedies)**** Monetary and non-monetary fines and/or imprisonment with corporal punishments	Reprimand and/or discharge

* Islamic Traditional Law
** The highest Islamic jurisprudence's order according to Koran by the Grand Ayatollah (Shia) or Grand Mofti, or Grand Ghazi (Sunni). Also, in exceptional cases appointment of a female judge or an attorney in the Women's Court, or Minor Children Courts is observed in the Islamic Republic of Iran.
*** Writ means the religious opinion or ruling of the Grand Ayatollah that needs to be executed.
**** Ghesas Law means legal remedies of the Islamic code-law.

The Islamic Sharia Court: The Islamic *Sharia* court initially is based on looking at the issues of guilt, sin, corruption, usurper, usury, adulatory, and others that are viewed against humanity and God.

The *Sharia* court needs to have two male witnesses, or one male witness and two female witnesses or four female witnesses to testify against an accused individual in the court for proving the proof and conviction of that person or an entity. In the Islamic law one male witness is equal to two female witnesses. Both claimant and accused are required to go under the Islamic oath. The procedure of the Islamic oath is based on swearing before the God with the right hand on the

Islamic religious script, *Koran*, to confirm or deny the allegations or to tell the truth. After taking the oath, the judge promptly proceeds with hearing of both sides and issues his verdict.

In the *Sharia* courts, only male judges are appointed to the bench and only male lawyers are permitted to practice law. However, it is observed in the Islamic Republic of Iran, in some occasions, female judges are appointed to the bench for the minor children courts and female lawyers are permitted to practice law for female parties in the women's courts. For example, Cross and Miller (2001: 170) indicate:

> An American businessperson was on trial in Saudi Arabia for assaulting and slandering a co-worker, an offense for which he might have been jailed or deported. He initially was required to present two witnesses to his version of events, but he had only one. Fortunately, he became aware that he could "demand the oath." In this procedure, he swore before God that he had neither kicked nor slandered the complainant. After taking the oath, he was promptly judged not guilty, as lying under oath is one of the most serious sins under Islamic law. Had he failed to demand the oath, he almost certainly would have been found guilty.

Legal philosophies are highly related to the practice of businesses in all societies. Civil or criminal disputes including disputes relating to domestic and international businesses depend upon their philosophical approaches to law. As we mentioned in the previous chapter, issues concerning virtues, values, rights, duties, and privileges are significant foundations to understand the reality of justness and fairness in each society. We review now some of significant schools of legal, or jurisprudential thoughts which have evolved in over time.

The Philosophies of Natural Law

Natural law denotes a universal system of humane fairness and justness in which moral and ethical principles are viewed as inherent characteristics in human nature and that people can discover it through the use of their natural intelligence by experience. Conscientious awareness serves as the basic principle to maintain the integrity of the universal law. The humanitarian notion indicates that all human beings are entitled to natural rights stems from the natural law tradition. The question of the universality of basic human rights including labor rights comes under analysis in the domains of international business operations. Should rights be similarly extended to workers in all countries? This question is rooted implicitly within the concept of universal rights or human rights. Should workers receive equal wages for equal jobs in all countries around the world? Or should workers receive equitable wages according to their countries' scale of economy? Answering the above questions is related to how a society has established its constitutional law.

Philosophies of Constitutional Law

The national constitutional philosophy of law refers to written or unwritten law of a given society. It applies only to those citizens who adhere to a political ideology that there can be no higher law than the nation's constitutional law. According to this philosophy, people believe that there is no such thing as natural rights. Rather, people's rights exist solely because of laws. If the laws are not enforced, injustice will result. However, constitutional laws of all nations can stem from the notions of democracy and liberty (e.g., the United States' Constitutional law) or from pure religious doctrines (e.g., Islamic law: the divine law or *Sharia*), or from pure political ideologies (e.g., the communistic law). Nevertheless, in all kinds of national laws, nations believe in the public good as the end of law. If a society is to survive, its members must be able to formulate what is legally right and legally wrong. People need to formulate peace and order for those who suffered as a result of others' wrongful acts.

Classification of Law

Since the body of law is so large, it is necessary to break it down by some means and ends of classification. A rainbow of mandatory ordination can represent the holistic peace and order in a society. Such a rainbow manifests a pluralistic value system with an aspiration of liberty, freedom, equality, rights, duties, and privileges for all. Nevertheless, the size, permanence, and influence of each segment of the national law vary nation to nation. There are numerous sources and types of law, including the following:

- *Constitutional Law*: The Constitutional law and the constitutions of the various states within a country represent general organizations, powers, and limits of their respective governments. Constitutional law is the supreme law for a nation. It spells out equal rights, duties, privileges, entitlements, and functions of all governmental constituencies in legal terms. All kinds of laws in a nation should be congruent with their Constitutional law. A law in violation of the Constitution, if challenged, will be declared unconstitutional and will not have the power to be enforced, no matter what its source is.

- *Statutory Law*: The laws enacted by legislative bodies at all levels of government (including laws passed by Congress, state legislatures, or local governing body) make up the body law generally referred to as statutory law. Congress, state legislators, and other representative bodies may enact laws or statutes.

- **Common Law:** The actions of courts and customs of the people constitute a body of law that is called common law. Common law rests primarily on decisions of courts: courts of laws and courts of equity. Common law is especially important in the area of procedure.

- *Administrative Law:* Different agencies of government (federal, state, and local) are often set up to function in specific tasks and apply particular statues, and the regulations and decisions issued by those agencies constitute administrative law. Rules issued by various administrative agencies affect business operations (e. g., safety, hiring and firing, union relationships, manufacturing and services, markets, mergers and others). The Food and Drug Administration (FDA), the Federal Trade Commission (FTC), the Securities and Exchange Commission (SEC), the Federal Communications Commission (FCC), the National Labor Relations Board (NLRB), the Environmental Protection Agency (EPA) and others are subject to the president's cabinet authorities who have the power to suggest to the President some related regulations and then President of the United States issues Executive Orders to implement them. Some of the other federal government executive offices are:
  - o The White House
  - o The Department of Justice
  - o The Antitrust Division
  - o The Bureau of Justice Statistics
  - o The Computer Crime and Intellectual Property Section
  - o The Civil Rights Division
  - o The Department of Labor
  - o The Employment and Training Administration (ETA)
  - o The Occupational Safety and Health Administration (OSHA)
  - o The Department of Commerce
  - o The Bureau of Census
  - o The International Trade Administration
  - o The Patent and Trademark Office
  - o The Department of the Treasury
  - o The Internal Revenue Services
  - o The Department of Health and Human Services
  - o The Food and Drug Administration (FDA)

- *Code Laws:* Code laws are ordered grouping of legal principles enacted into law by legislators, or other governing body or courts are required to interpret the code and apply the rules to individual cases. In theory, the code laws set forth all principles needed for the legal system. Components of the code law system are found in the courts of predominantly Muslim countries (*Sharia*). In the United States, the state of Louisiana, because of its predominant cultural ties to France, has a code law. The *Sharia* law is a type of code law on the ground of religious traditional legal system of the Islamic faith. The religious basis of these legal codes is based on the religious Islamic scripture, *Koran*. The pre-determined Judgment concerning penalties against criminals is known as "*Hadd*," and the monetary penalty is called "*Diyeyeh*." The religious Islamic basis of these traditional codes makes them far more difficult to alter on the basis of jurisprudence. The Islamic *Shari'*'s code law is not rules by a jury, because they believe that the jury members are not trained and qualified to understand the religious Islamic law. Therefore, the judgment or the decree needs to be issued by a highly qualified person who is so-called Grand Ayatollah (in *Shia*) or Grand *Mofti* (in *Sunni*), *Faqih*.

Wise international business managers should anticipate that their power often is restricted in Muslim dominated countries because the religious courts may challenge them. They need to know how to make legal decisions according to the rules of law. Governments in all countries from democratic to autocratic ones regulate business activities. At the same time, governments are viewed as the major customers and consumers of businesses. For such reasons the rest of this chapter will focus on the corporation's moral, ethical, and legal mandates.

THE CONCEPT OF A LEGAL CORPORATION

A corporation is a legal entity, which is entitled under a common name and owned by individuals or groups of investors. It can consist of one or more natural persons (as opposed to the artificial person of the corporation). A corporation is a legal entity with rights and duties.

The corporation substitutes itself for shareholders in conducting corporate business and incurring liability, yet its authority to act and the liability for its actions are separate and apart from the individuals who own it (Jeffcut, 1994: 225). It should be clear that there are two major terms within the domain of enterprises: businesses and corporations. The term of business no longer express the intended content of the word as applied to the larger enterprises. Traditionally, the person who owned and operated a small independent store used to be called businessperson.

Today, in giant corporations, the term of business basically has no more in common usage with the small trade-persons. Among characteristics of a businessperson is that they put their investments in risk, can fail, and go out of business through bankruptcy. But giant corporations can no more fail than can the public treasury. In the case of Enron and WordCom, Inc., there are some irregular, unprofessional, immoral, and unethical cover up operations which have caused them to go on bankrupt.

It has been a tradition in the capitalistic countries that giant corporations' risks have all marginal power, because they have the ability to change and control the direction of the national economy of all nations around the world. Some specialists in the field of business introduced the term super-corporations, which is better, as it indicates at least some sort of superiority or supremacy. What is superiority? Although legally these supreme corporations are artificial persons, in reality, they are community of persons working toward a similar objective to make profit by offering products and services to the large markets.

Entering into small businesses for oneself is now and always has been, a highly risky affair. Even those business people, who remain in business, operate on the thinnest of survival margins, constantly financed by lenders or bankers by short-term loans or credits and they are exposed frequently to economic recessions. Nevertheless, London and Waters (2002: 8) expressed their views concerning the failure of giant corporations in America as:

> A tornado is sweeping corporate America. Each day brings fresh evidence of upheaval. This week alone saw the bankruptcy of K-mart, one of the country's biggest retailers; the break-up of Tyco, one of its largest conglomerates; and further gusts from the direction of Enron, the biggest corporate failure of them all.

Individual investors that make up a corporate entity are not fixed. Most supreme corporations experience constant turnover of personnel on all levels and they go under re- engineering structural changes. Nevertheless, as a legal artificial person, corporations remain unchanged. Such a reality is evident to such an extent that English justice Edward Thurow (1731-1806) made a comment: "Did you expect a corporation to have a conscience, when it has no soul to be damned and no body to be kicked?" (Jackson, Miller, and Miller, 1997: 40).

Governments at all levels are viewed as one of the stakeholders of most corporations. Governments, also, set standards for many goods and services and regulate all aspects of a corporation's activities either through the court interventions and/or governmental regulatory agencies. In addition, business taxes finance a large part of all governments' expenditures. Then there is a close partnership between governments and businesses. Long (1949: 257) indicates that what is the most basic of government components is the urge to survive. An agency survival depends on alliances. In sum, government power flows from power, not from legal directives. It is doubtful that an agency's survival can ever become the ultimate moral virtue and ethical values of any democratic society.

WHY SHOULD BUSINESS PEOPLE BE HONEST?

Up to this point, we reviewed justice, law, and corporations' ethical, moral, and legal commitments. We have shown why moral and ethical convictions are altruistic virtues, and thereby why dishonesty is betrayal of human dignity and integrity. One concept important for discussion of having a successful business is that of customers' loyalty. Closely associated with customers' loyalty, is another term, business honesty.

We have discussed why the honest route in a long-run period of time can save the integrity of a corporation and prevent it from corruption, viciousness, and unfair business practices. Now we would like to return to the notion of the right causes and effects of a business.

That notion is business honesty. Within a general sense, it is almost impossible for a rational person to ignore immoral and unethical behavior through making conscious or subconscious distinctions between honest and dishonest decisions and actions. However, it is possible to make selective perceptions within the context of societal impressions of goodness and badness in order to decide to which direction your ethical business behavior is directed. A businessperson, clearly, has to make deliberated moral and ethical choice in multitude of decisions and actions. Business-deliberated choices, however, are not necessarily connected with desires or fantasies. Managers choose their choices in terms of deliberated good or evil rather than desires or fantasies.

Deliberation is a work of practical reason. We consider and valuate reasons for or against making or doing something. The connection of deliberation with choice becomes obvious. We cannot exercise a choice without deliberation. Thus we make choices on the basis of deliberation. That choice could be either oriented toward the honest route or the dishonest route of business transactions. To run a successful business is very difficult, because it requires a lot of right thoughts and efforts to be considered during paving the honest route.

The Honest Route of a Business Operation

Now we would like to consider the honest route for operating your business. Within this route the nature of decisions and actions are based upon the goodness for its stakeholders. Through the honest route of business transactions, every party involved in a deal enjoys an equitable share of profit. Producers obtain a fair share of monetary profit and consumers receive a fair share in the effectiveness of the utility of their consumed products. You will try to offer your products or services as a seller with fairly good end-results. These end-results can generate an equitable satisfaction for all parties B buyers and sellers. To conclude, we quote Ayn Rand (1957: 945): "Honesty is not a social duty, not a sacrifice for the sake of others, but the most profoundly selfish virtue man can practice: his refusal to sacrifice the reality of his own existence to the deluded consciousness of others."

The Dishonest Route of Business Operations

Now consider the dishonest route in your business transactions to cheat or deceive your customers. In this route, you may expose several possible end results. You may think that:

- Customers are stupid and do not have a cognitive sense of recognition to make distinction between good and bad, right and wrong, just and unjust, and finally workable products and defected products. If you think in this way, you are wrong.

- You may perceive that your customers are smart, but they do not have any other alternative choices available in your market. They have to buy your products. Such a perception in a short-term may be possible but in a long-term is impossible. Customers, eventually, will find other alternatives and you as a cheater or deceiver will pay a very heavy price by losing customers' loyalty. You may think that to cheat some customers is all right. But you know that cheating or deceiving customers is not right. You may think that a little poison will not kill you, but when your body is accustomed to poisonous substances, you generate more appetite to have more dosage consumption of poisonous substances. Eventually, poisonous substances that will conquer your body to such an extent so as to destroy your integrity and honesty will saturate your body. A dishonest business is like a poisonous body. Eventually, you will lose your customer's trust and loyalty. If a business is exposed to such a condition, it will lose its reputation and its customers. The only alternative for a successful business is to survive with customers' trust and loyalty. For example, Cutler (2002) reports:

> Three former Tyco International Ltd. Executives were charged Thursday (September 12, 2002) with looting the conglomerate of hundreds of millions of dollars in the latest move by prosecutors against alleged thievery in America's boardrooms. ...Former chief executive L. Dennis Kozlowski, 55, and former chief financial office Mark Swartz, 42, were charged with enterprise corruption and grand larceny. Former general counsel Mark Belnick, 55, was charged with falsifying business records.

- Business people who cheat customers may perceive that such a business practice is all right, because customers do not know about it. In this case, some of your employees may know something about it. Therefore, soon or latter corrupted business people will be exposed by whistleblowers. To some extent, law protects whistleblowers.

- A dishonest businessperson continuously and customarily will be accustomed to unethical and immoral business operations and will continue to cheat customers through their gullibility or blindness in order to make dishonest profit. The end-result is self-destruction by serving people low quality products and services. Low quality products do not make good profits.
- A dishonest businessperson through continuously cheating customers will shift their personalities from morality to immorality, from ethicality to unethical, and their business practices from legality to illegal. The end-result is shaping their businesses with deception and fraud. Deception and frauds are viewed as diseases and eventually will destroy businesses.
- As much as a dishonest businessperson practices more immoral, unethical, and illegal businesses and gains free-money, they generate more greedy appetite in their nature to such an extent that eventually they will be caught. Then, they pay all their earnings back both to the state or to the injured, harmed, and cheated customers as fines and punitive compensatory or retributive damages.

The end-result of the above and other possible consequences for a dishonest businessperson or a corporation's manager is to be at war with conscientiousness and to be blamed, condemned, convicted, fined, and imprisoned.

SOCIAL JUSTICE AND PROFIT-MAXIMIZATION OR PROFIT-OPTIMIZATION

Each nation may be said to have some characteristic fashions for formulating their justice systems to deal with their social system, economic system, and legal system. If each of these areas is conceived to involve at all levels of national activities in a nation, then the end-result may be described as a holistic area in which they overlap; social justice system. Figure 11.2 provides a diagrammatic identification of a social justice system in a society.

The social justice system is a differentiated form of the intersection of three systems: social, legal, and economic. Also, it shows that the other systems overlap two by two outside the social justice system. Thus, the social system and economic system overlap a great deal in areas other than justice, such as business ethics. Similarly, the legal system and economic system overlap broadly outside the justice system, such as elite interest group system. The social system and legal system overlap broadly out of the social justice system. They may provide a fair opportunity for a fair ground of practicing wealth distribution. Thus, we see that the social justice system is deeply embedded within the core concept of the framework of overlapping among different systems in a society. Nevertheless, society is perceived as a holistic entity in which includes all related systems interconnected and integrated. Within such a highly integrated and interrelated system, there are different interest groups who are solely pursuing specific paths of interest in order to achieve their own egoistic objectives; to gain power and to make profit.

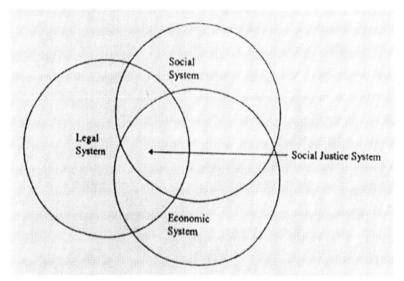

Figure 11.2: Identification of Integrated Justice Systems

Proponents of enlightenment of self-interest groups believe that it is the responsibility of a social justice system to formulate courses of actions in such a way to create a justified balance among all stakeholders. In reality, econopolitical campaigns promote a strong notion about the business profit-enhancement and regulatory agencies. Most of the interest group profit enhancements are aligned with maximization of self-interest objectives rather than the "social profit-enhancement" objectives.

As you may have observed above, there are two notions concerning profitability of a corporation in a social justice system: (1) enlightenment of self-interest profit and (2) enhancement of the social profit.   Most corporate managers believe in short-term profit making strategy on the basis of the notion of the enlightenment of self-interest groups. Executives who accept the notion of social profit-enhancement today must be willing to accept optimum profits rather than maximum profits. Therefore, according to the above assumptions, there are two different opinions among experts concerning business social responsibilities of a corporation: (1) profit maximization theory, and (2) profit optimization theory.

Profit Maximization Theory

Human beings are by nature acquisitive creatures that pursue profit with all the instinctual vigor of a cat chasing a mouse, or giant corporations dispose the integrity of small businesses. Humans are rational creatures who are pursuing profit in terms of a robust appetite for money profit. This money profit is for the sake of money and money-profit from money, not from manufacturing products and/or rendering services to consumers. This type of greedy profit motive makes people more motivated by their own economic self-interests and more likely to pursue the goal of profit maximization. Among profit maximization advocates, Milton Friedman (1971) took a strong position against social responsibilities of a corporation. Friedman stated that the doctrine of social responsibility for businesses means acceptance of the socialist view. He argued that the social doctrine of a business is based on political mechanisms rather than market mechanisms. He believed that business is business and it shouldn't be subject to a political ideology. He believed that the CEOs' responsibility is to tell the company's stockholders or shareholders that they will make every measure to ensure their maximum profits. In other words, as long as a corporation performs its economizing function well, it has fulfilled its social and ethical responsibilities and nothing more needs to be said. What is considered to be just and fair in a capitalistic global business environment is exactly the same as what is considered to be good business in a competitive market process.

A business firm is formed to provide goods and services that consumers are willing to buy at prices they can afford. The justified performance of a business is tied up with marketplace performance demand and supply. Therefore, according to the theory of profit maximization, a good business is a business with maximum profitability even at the expense of destroying the environment and national humanitarian objectives. In profit maximization, the producer is trying to lower the manufacturing cost and stretches the profitability to the maximum possibility. In such a theory those people who are viewed as losers or winners -- producers are winners and consumers are losers.

Profit Optimization Theory

In contrast to Friedman, Oliver Sheldon (1923: 285) in the discussion of strategy strongly advocated the development of a professional social creed for business organizations in the closing chapter of his book on management. He indicates:

> Industry exists to provide the commodities and services that are necessary for good life of the community; in whatever volume they are requested. ...It is for management to achieve the objective for which it exists by development of efficiency.

In addition, Sheldon believed that management is the one who stabilizes and balance the elements between demand and supply in an evolutionary process in a marketplace through profit optimization. Without a professional social creed, there can be no guarantee of efficiency.

Table 11.3: Comparative Ethical Factorial Decision-Making Processes
Between Profit Maximization and Profit Optimization

FACTORS	PROFIT MAXIMIZATION	PROFIT OPTIMIZATION
FIRM'S FINANCIAL CONCERN	Shareowners' profitability	Stakeholders' suitability
COSTS	Lowering costs by all means and ends	Lowering the operational costs with careful consideration
MARKET VALUE	Raising competitively the product and/or service pricing system	Lowering the product and/or service pricing system
QUALITY	Moderating the equitable product's quality	Enhancing the product's quality
PRODUCTION	Accelerating on mass production system with dumping strategy (Cash Cow Strategy)	Moderating production system according to the market demand and supply's fluctuation (Question Mark Strategy)
TIME-LINE VISION	Short-term profitability (Profitability Strategy)	Long-term profitability (Survival Strategy)
SATISFACTION	Shareowners' concern for corporation's efficiency	Stakeholders' concern for corporation's efficacy and productivity
CUSTOMER TRUST AND LOYALTY	Low	High
ACCOUNTABILITY AND LIABILITY	To the interest group's causes	To the social justice's effects

Sheldon's professional creed links the managerial functions to the wellbeing of the community in which a corporation is a part. Through this type of social justice philosophy, management needs to focus on stakeholders' interests by taking appropriate initiatives in raising the general ethical standards and conceptions of social justice that exists in the community. Sheldon believes that goods and services, produced by a firm, must be furnished at the holistic interests of the stakeholders' need disposition with an adequate standard of quality in order to promote the highest ends of the community's good utility. Such a view calls for management to take the social responsibilities of the wellbeing of community.

In addition, management's decisions in a free market economy should be based on long- run business objectives rather than short-run profitability. Therefore, according to the theory of profit optimization, management philosophy and strategy should be based on the most that could be made this year for optimum profits in the following years. In profit optimization, managers try to lower costs and prices. Who are winners in this theory? Both manufacturers and consumers are sharing some benefits from lowered costs and prices. Manufacturers will be able to expand their market size and product positions through lower pricing system, and consumers will enjoy paying less for their consumerable goods.

SOCIAL CONTRACT AND BUSINESS ETHICS

Before analyzing the social contract between a business entity and society, we should define some additional terms and reflections of a social contract. One concept important for discussing a business organization's obligations to society is related to the pursuit of profits for strengthening the national economy. Implicit in such an idea is the belief that national wealth and power are best served by the wellbeing of society. The emergence of a social justice system concerning ethical business responsibilities has been expressed in terms of a changing ethical contract between business and society that reflects changing expectations regarding the ethical social performance of a business (Anshen , 1974). On the one hand, according to economists, profits and loses are viewed as the basic functions of a free market economy. Profits to businesses mean to turn resources into their highest added-valued prices and use them for the benefit of shareholders or investors. Loses or negative profits are viewed as shifting the direction of added values of resources from one person to another, from a business to another, from an industry to another, and from one nation to another. Losers are motivated as much by the fear of not making profit as they are by the desire to make money. Also, profits are considered bait that induces entrepreneurs to take more risk; the greater the risk, the greater the profits or loses or rewards or punishments (Jackson, Miller and Miller, 1997: 37).

On the other hand, according to ethicists, profits are viewed as simply added values to the effective virtues of utility balanced production and consumption for the benefit of both buyers and sellers by providing them with a higher standard of living than previously imagined possible. Sellers, through a high volume of qualitative and quantitative sale volumes, can enjoy more profits and buyers, through an affordable qualitative acquisition of their necessities, can make their lives more meaningful. Within the contextual domain of such reciprocal ideas, the free enterprise systems and the free consumption choices through a fair doctrine of social justice place a legitimate premium on profit-making mechanisms between producers and consumers. That legitimate premium for profit-making enterprises is established and maintained through effective utility of a social justice system.

Harmonization of corporation's cultural slogans and national cultural sensitivity is critical to the wellbeing of a social justice system. Within such a contextual perception, competitive intelligence for balancing social justice system differs from country to country. Differences among moral virtues, cultural value systems, and legal doctrines can create problems at home and abroad. In today's international social justice systems, many of the units that we have structured and operated at home, may be appeared to be more value-destroying rather than value-enhancing in the global markets. Singer (1998: 124) states: "By the most cautious estimates, 400 million people lack the calories, protein, vitamins, and minerals needed to sustain their bodies and minds in a healthy state. Millions are constantly hungry... Children are the worst affected." It is a disturbing to consider what direction and with what consequences humanity is facing and moving to the future.

CHAPTER SUMMARY

Justice is expressed as a conventional conscientious societal idealistic system in terms of fairness and justness. Justice is defined as a dispassionate system of thoughts to treat people equally and/or equitably by intellectual reasoning. Justice is viewed as a legitimate claim for an individual or a group to be treated according to what is due or owed to them. Justice is not the only virtue an individual or social institution can initiate and/or pursue. From another point of view, justice is concerned with formulating what is due from whom to whom. Since justice is bound with the notion of rational public-good, not surprisingly, any justice system ends up with a great deal about distribution of wealth as a definite unit of societal worth.

In today's life, the debates and arguments on intellectual reasoning for just and unjust ideas, intentions, judgments, actions, and reflections are more focused on legality rather than on the whole moral and ethical concerns. In a moral and ethical sense, not in a legal one, we are interested to know: What is unjust? Injustice involves violation of the rights of some identifiable people. In order to understand what is justice, it is important to identify sources of justice by appealing to the overlapping notions of moral, ethical, and legal rights, fairness, equality, equitability, and just desserts.

A theory of justice defines what individuals must do for the common good of society and in return what society must do for the goodness of individuals. There are six philosophical foundations for establishing a justice system in a civil society. Those are: (1) to each person an equal share, (2) to each person according to individual needs, (3) to each person according to the person's rights, (4) To each person according to individual effort, (5) to each person according to their societal contributions, and (6) to each person according to their merit.

Philosophies of justice should not be finalized until all moral and ethical principles have demonstrated validity of neutral intellectual justness and fairness in practice. Justice is said to be within the domain of intellectual reasoning in which everyone is dynamically engaged in reasoning while observing, sensing, deliberating, judging, and practicing in life events. Reasoning in justice centers on the cause-effect of effect and cause arguments. There are some guidelines that might keep us from slipping into faulty cause-and-effect reasoning: A cause always comes before its effect; an effect could have a number of possible causes.

Causes we assign to an effect must be capable of producing the effect. We must consider whether the hypothetical causes always produce the effects that are capable of producing and whether they invariably produce the same effect, if something occurs repeatedly. The likeliest cause is the one that all the occurrences have in common. If an effect occurs in some situations but does not occur in other similar situation, the cause may be the single thing that is different in the similar situations, and if a particular situation increases or decreases causes, you must find a plausible reason that acts in a similar or in a reverse fashion.

Institutionalization of a justice system is the medium of both actions and reflections. Pursuing moral and ethical actions and reflections in conjunction with the fitness of a justice system is the sheer love of rightness, justness, fairness, and worthiness. If justice means to maintain a balance between virtue (good, better, best, and excellence) and vice (bad, worse, and worst), then it constitutes a moderate treatment of individuals on the basis of a balance between far right and far wrong. There are two different views on the philosophies of justice: equality and equitability. Equality means distribution of burdens and rewards in a society should be based on simply manifestation of equal weight. Equalitarian justice proposes that all human beings are equal in principles of their rights. In an equitable justice system practitioners believe in equitable pay for equal jobs doctrine, in which individuals are rewarded for the sweat of their brows according to what value the free market places on their services. Therefore, equitable social and economic incentives are to be arranged accordingly so that they are both: (1) reasonably expected to be appropriated for an individual's specific entitlements (e.g., capabilities, efforts, work conditions, and innovativeness), and (2) attached to positions and offices open to specific qualified people as public authorities.

A more democratic and ethical system is based on three principles: (1) the free will defense, (2) the property ownership rights including intellectual ones, and (3) the free enterprises. The free will defense is the idea of being free with respect to an action on the grounds of civil rights. The property ownership rights, including intellectual properties, are the second principle in a democratic society. This is a complementary principle along with of the free will defense. Ownership should not preclude the natural free will defense. The third is concerned about the establishment of free enterprises within the boundary of a free competitive market. A free enterprise is not controlled by the state or monopolized by a small capable elite group of individuals.

When a justice system in a democratic society appears, it indicates that it prevents monopolies. Within a just market system, the government is responsible to resist monopolies (exclusive ownership of production systems or control of supply) and monopsonies (exclusive control of demand by a special group of customers). Within the multitude domain of the above philosophical justice principles, managers may find moral, ethical, and legal guidelines in five basic spheres of organizational justice: (1) distributive justice, (2) procedural justice, (3) retributive justice, and (4) commutative justice, and (5) compensatory justice.

Law is not formally an act of will; it is a pluralistic practicability of societal reasoning that determines behavioral means in relation to some predictable ends. Each society, according to its religious faiths, cultural values, political-legal ideologies, and economical doctrines, establishes specific rights, duties, privileges, and entitlements for its members. While some communities believe in the integrity of the individualistic liberty, others believe in collectivistic shared materialistic goodness. There are three systems of the court of law: (1) the court of law and remedies at law, (2) the court of equity and remedies in equity, and (3) the court of the Islamic *Sharia* law.

QUESTIONS FOR DISCUSSION

- What does general justice mean?
- What is the definition of legal justice?
- Distinguish between objective and subjective right.
- Distinguish between natural law and constitutional law.
- Define particular justice philosophies.
- Define commutative justice.
- Define distributive justice.
- Define procedural justice.
- How do commutative justice and distributive justice differ?
- Explain why and how the mean and ends of distributive justice is one of proportional equality.
- What is the specific vice opposed to distributive justice?
- What are the interiors and exterior acts of justice?
- What are the basic philosophical foundations of code law, and *Sharia* law?
- What are different courts of law?
- Why should business people be honest in business transactions?
- Is general justice a perfect ethical and moral virtue?
- Is there any difference between general justice and legal justice?
- How can moral development justify foundational reasoning for general justice?
- What is Law?
- What are differences between profit maximization and profit optimization?

CASE STUDY

WHO WANTS TO BE MILLIONAIRE? MCDONALD'S PROMOTIONAL MONOPOLY GAME SCAM

On August 22, 2001, U. S. prosecutors alleged that McDonald's customers never really had much of a chance to win the biggest promotional prizes of the McDonald's Monopoly game. The FBI arrested eight people, ages between 44 to 58 years old, who were charged with fixing the outcome of McDonald's Monopoly.

MCDONALD'S CORPORATE PROFILE

McDonald's corporation incorporated in Delaware on March 1, 1965. The business was established around 1955. It started as one restaurant and then in May 1970, McDonald's Co. acquired five restaurants in Wisconsin. From there it started to open more and more restaurants. Cogently, McDonald's Worldwide Corporation is the world's leading fast food service retailer with more than 30,000 restaurants in 121 countries serving 46 million customers each day. It serves fast foods such as: World famous French Fries, Big Mac, Quarter Pounder, Chicken McNuggets, and Egg McMuffin.

The McDonald's Co. vision is: "To be the world's best quick service on its three-part growth strategy: Execution, Expansion, and Extension." The McDonald's corporation's social responsibility are: (1) To doing what is right, (2) To being a good neighbor and partner in communities, and (3) To conduct its business with the environment in mind.

What McDonald's Co. does is develop, operate, franchise, and provide service worldwide in order to prepare, assemble, package, and sell a limited menu of value-priced foods.

CASE ROLE PLAYERS

Specific members of a group relate this case to unethical, immoral, and illegal activities of McDonald's Co. concerning promotional deception and fraud. McDonald's Co. offered big prizes: $1 million in cash, diamonds or gold, cars, and vacations to Monopoly game winners. McDonald's Co. has offered the Monopoly promotion for ten years, according to McDonald's Web site. The U.S. prosecutors found that customers never really had much of a chance to win the biggest prizes. The FBI said the scheme began as early as 1995. Because this deceptive and fraudulent scam, eight people were arrested: Linda L. Baker, 49, of Westminister, South Carolina; John F. Davis, 44, of Granbury, Texas; Andrew M. Glomb, 58, of Fort Lauderdale, Florida; Michael L. Hoover, 56, of Westerly, Rhode Island; Ronald E. Hughey, 56, of Anderson, S. C.; Jerome P. Jacobson, 58, of Lawrenceville, Georgia; and Brenda S. Phenis, 50, of Fair Play, South Carolina. To know the personalities, social status, economical conditions, and religious faiths of these eight women and men, we need to conduct more research in order to be able to know in what ways how these people were unethical, immoral, and illegal. In addition, we need to analyze the managerial style of the McDonald's CEO, Jack M. Greenberg, who has been in charge of this corporation for more than twenty years.

CASE PROBLEMS

The scam was planned by eight individuals to provide winning game pieces to friends and associates who acted as recruiters. These recruiters then solicited individuals who falsely and fraudulently represented that they were the legitimate winners of the McDonald's Monopoly game. The eight people made off with some of the highest-value prizes in the McDonald's game.

ANALYSIS

Product promotion is an honest and straightforward communication that can be built and maintained to create favorable perceptions of customers about the goodness of a promoter. It is used to persuade customers to view a company more positively by providing them with effective products and/or services. While a company may pursue promotional objectives, the overall role of promotion is to stimulate product demand. McDonald's Co., for instance, promoted several programs, including the Monopoly game that helped selected groups and facilitated a boost of its sales and generated goodwill. In addition, sales promotion is an activity or material, or both, that acts as a direct inducement, offering added values or incentives for the products, to resellers, salespeople, or consumers. It encompasses all corporate professional activities and materials other than personal selling, advertising, and public relations.

The above statements indicate that an ethical product promotion is not primarily an attempt to mislead customers, but rather it is an informational attempt to persuade or influence consumers. On the other hand, marketing promotion is a social enterprise that is subject to moral expectations of society. This means that marketing practices cannot be evaluated solely on the basis of marketers effectiveness in promoting sales, but must also take into account the goals of the society in which they take place.

McDonald's Monopoly game provided customers with $13 million worth of grand prizes that supposedly customers had real opportunities to win. Unfortunately, there were some individuals who conspired a scheme to pocket those grand prizes. There is a problem within this case concerning McDonald's social responsibilities. It is related to truthful promotional activities of its marketing subcontractors.

On August 21, 2001 McDonald's CEO Jack M. Greenberg expressed his outrage at the scam and gratitude to the FBI for the investigation, and said: The fast-food giant will return all stolen money to the public via a new $10 million sweepstakes. It should be noted that most McDonald's restaurants do not participate activity in the Monopoly game any more.

CONCLUSION

In a democratic society, corporations have legal rights and duties and to that extent have a moral responsibility and ethical accountability. Since a corporation is known as an artificial person, its moral personality is exhausted by its legal personality. However, board of governance and top managers represents its ethical accountability. A corporation cannot act without some active participation by those managers who represent them. Therefore, corporations can act only through their representatives' managers and can do only those things that representatives can do. What corporate representatives can do is work in terms of rights and duties.

CASE QUESTIONS FOR DISCUSSION

- If you were one of the board members of McDonald's Co., how would you have initially question the McDonald's CEO's accountability to his social responsibilities?
- What would be your ground for questioning him? Why?
- Should the CEO conduct research to find deception and fraud in promotional activities of the McDonald's Monopoly game? Explain.
- Do you believe unethical, immoral, and illegal marketing subcontractors can diminish social responsibilities and accountability of McDonald's Corporation? Why?
- Do you believe McDonald's Corporation acted ethically and morally in this case? Explain.

CASE SOURCES

R. E. Ewin, "The Moral Status of the Corporation.," In Robert A. Larmer, *Ethics in the Workplace: Selected Readings in Business Ethics,* (Minneapolis/St. Paul: West Publishing Company, 1996), 363.

R. A. Larmer, *Ethics in the Workplace: Selected Readings in Business Ethics,* (Minneapolis/St. Paul: West Publishing Company, 1996), 330.

W. M. Pride and O. C. Ferrell, *Marketing Concepts and Strategies,* Twelfth Edition, (Boston: Houghton Mifflin Company, 2003), 501.

MSNBC August 22, 2001,
<http://www.msnbc.com/news/617154.asp?pne'msn,>, December 7, 2002.

CHAPTER 12

MANAGING MORAL AND ETHICAL
ISSUES IN THE WORKPLACE

The inescapement of time is a real function of growth and maturity,
which cannot be achieved without moral and ethical convictions.

So long as business people comply only with the laws of the land,
they cannot prove they are ethical and moral.

There are always a few rotten apples in every barrel;
this doesn't mean that the rest of the fruit isn't sound.

If econo-political figures take a drink during business socialization,
it doesn't mean that a drinking habit during prohibition is not considered sinful.

If we are dynamic in a competitive marketplace and look for profit however the
law permits,
it does not mean that we need to demote morality and ethics because we are
legal.

To play the business game in an industry means to comply with the rules of the
marketplace,
it does not mean that the game is only ideally molded in the economists,
abstractions.

CHAPTER OBJECTIVES

When you have read this chapter you should be able to understand the major issues concerning workplace and workforce as follows:

- What are different relationships between employers and employees and how do the outcomes of these relationships affect the organizational ethical responsibilities?
- What, if anything, binds employees to their organizations?
- What is the changing nature of the employer-employee social contract?
- How has this contract changed historically generation by generation?
- What is the state of civil liberties in the workplace?
- What is the philosophical foundation for practicing gender ethics in the workplace?
- How do employees expect their employers to treat them equally or equitably?
- What are the employer-employee efforts to respect their reciprocal rights and duties in the workplace?
- What are the pragmatic problems that arise with respect to personnel matters; namely, hiring, promotions, discipline, firing, appreciations, compensations, and wages?
- What are the ethical and moral obligations of a business entity to its stakeholders?
- What is the role of employee representatives in our economic system through collective bargaining power?
- What are three major philosophical foundations of wages and salaries: wage slavery, living survival wage, and sustainable just wage?
- How can an ethical and moral organizational culture develop?
- How can the quality of life be enhanced in an organization?
- What are the ethical and moral considerations of organizational life?
- What do we mean by economic wellbeing of organizational life?
- What do we mean by job ownership?
- What are the inherent problems with employment-at-will (EAW)?
- How do plant closing or moving out affect employees, life?
- How does insider trading affect employees, organizational life?
- What do we mean by job shop, expert knowledge, and trade secrets?
- What is gender ethics?
- What are sexual harassment and sexual favoritism in the workplace?
- Who is liable for sexual harassment in a firm?

THOUGHT STARTER

Within the context of moral and ethical judgments, impartiality typically has been recognized as fundamental awareness o f managers in the workplace to treat people equally. Impartiality requires weighing interests of each individual equally, permitting differentiation only on the basis of differences that can be shown to be ethically and morally relevant. Impartiality, thus, is linked conceptually to either equality of homogeneity or to heterogeneity equitability of assessing inherent superior or inferior characteristics of two related domains with rationality and objectivity.

Impartiality is interpreted as the absent of bias and/or prejudice in an individuals' judgment. Impartiality disregards favoritism in decision-making processes for particular identities within the domain of a rational judgment. It substitutes abstract variables for discovering the real characteristics of an individual as an agent. Williams (1973a, 1973b, & 1981) argues that the requirement of impartiality may determine our personal integrity because it may require us to abandon projects that are central to our identity, and he also suggests that acting from duty may sometimes be less valuable than acting from an immediate emotional response to a particular one. Also, impartiality avoids the feelings of emotionality in decision-making processes and judgments.

Impartiality is a pluralistic ethical judgment concerning both conventional and modern valuing systems. As we mentioned before, impartiality is a rational phenomenon that treats people either equally or equitably. In moral and ethical endeavors, emotional caring is not only hypocritical but also self-defeating.

Traditionally, the obligation of a management team to employees boils down to economic issues; mainly, "a fair wage or salary for an honest day's work or a work unit." Managers, professional obligations to workers have been formalized to pay them with a decent wage or salary. In return, workers were expected to work efficiently and to be loyal to their employers. This model of reciprocal relationships has been viewed through different types of management systems including gender management.

PLAN OF THIS CHAPTER

Ethical and moral considerations are the main points for a holistic organizational wellbeing. Within the contextual boundaries of such a holistic system of thought, there are two interdependent halves. One of the two halves or components of organizational structure is related to work ethics and the other half is related to the collective efforts of all stakeholders; namely known as economic productivity. By work ethics, we mean doing the right things; effectiveness, and by economic productivity, we mean doing the things right, efficiency. The medium between these two halves is the promotional valuable system of productivity by which we set interchangeable relations between the two. These two halves possess their own dynamic inherent spheres of activities that are known as *endeavor* and *development*. *Endeavor* refers to the contextual conditions of work deliberated ethical considerations in the workplace and *our assets know development as progressive trends in added economic values*. How these two phenomena can be promoted towards excellence depends on multiple linkages of interactive and counteractive communication systems between efficiency and effectiveness.

Within such a promotional cluster, there can of course be no action without reaction and/or any reaction without a precedent action. There is no organization to be known either as only employers or as only employees. Accordingly, organizations are composed of both employers and employees. When we act either as employers or employees, with the greatest enthusiastic spontaneity, we are to some extent led by economic incentives that motivate us to be more productive. Moreover, the very expanded synergy (which reveals the core concept of an organizational potency) is, ultimately, based upon employers, potential good faith and employees, good will to grow and progress. Each one of the good-faith decisions of employers and good will of employees, work can direct organizational synergy toward productivity. This is the mystical totality of goodness, rightness, and worthiness.

This chapter begins by addressing the changing characteristics of the workforce and the workplace with their emerging problems. To begin with in this chapter, we address the following issues in order to know:

- What are the different relationships between employers and employees and how do the outcomes of these relationships affect the organizational ethical responsibilities?
- What, if anything, binds employees to their organizations?
- What is the changing nature of the employer-employee social contract?
- How has this contract changed historically?
- What is the state of civil liberties in the workplace?
- What is the philosophical foundation for practicing gender ethics in the workplace?
- How do employees expect their employers to treat them equally or equitably?
- What are the employer-employee efforts to respect their reciprocal rights and duties in the workplace?
- What are the pragmatic problems that arise with respect to personnel matter; namely, hiring, promotions, discipline, firing, appreciations, compensations, and wages?
- What are the ethical and moral obligations of a business entity to its stakeholders?
- What is the role of employee representatives in our economic system through collective bargaining power?

CHARACTERISTICS OF THE TWENTIETH CENTURY GENERATIONS

By reviewing history, we can see both the workforce and workplaces in all countries around the world have changed dramatically. These changes have affected managerial moral and ethical decision-making processes. The workforce and the workplace are two different subjects that should carefully be analyzed in order to surface potential moral and ethical abuses by businesses. The ethical and moral workforce characteristics are aging, parents working conditions, child labor, women and minority discrimination, sexual harassment, and unequal pay including incentives and benefits. The moral and ethical workplace characteristics are competitive pay, benefits and opportunities to develop skills and enhance innovative conditions of the workplace, recognition of reciprocal employers-employees rights and duties, mutual respect and dignity among stakeholders, upgrading quality of lifestyle, and above all safety, security, health, and wellness in the workplace.

In order to review historical changes in the workplace, we need to first identify different types of generations from the beginning of the 20th century to the present time. Weiss (2003: 213) has identified five major generations with different characteristics within such a window time: (1) GIG, (2) GS, (3) GBB, (4) GX, and (5) GY.

GIG: General Issue Generation (Born 1901-1925)

This generation survived the Great Depression and the Environmental Epidemic problems. What does GI stands for? In a military term, GI is an old World War II term that means General Issue and/or Government Issue. It was used to describe regulation equipment, but it was applied to the common soldiers in WWII. So GI Joe sort of means "Average Joe," (http://www.joeheadquarters.com/faq.shtml). They were concerned about general issues in human life. Some of GIGs served in World War I and World War II. They were family oriented and fought for personal choices and freedom including working conditions. They tend to believe in upward-class-mobility, civic virtue, and better living conditions.

GS: Silent Generation (Born 1926-1944)

This generation was too young to fight in World War II. They were influenced by the patriotism and self sacrifice of the GIGs. Their dominant principles of beliefs were allegiance to resent aggression and racism. They fought for individual freedom and civil rights. They tried to create law, order, patriotism, and religious faith.

GBB: Generation of Baby Boomers (Born 1945-1964)

This generation is currently the most innovative and powerful demographic population. They developed the infrastructure of national economy and economic growth through working hard. They put too much emphasize on economic development by expanding educational opportunities for people. They fought for their political ideologies. They questioned political authorities and distribution of wealth among people. They refused to sacrifice their personal pleasure for the goodness of the interest groups. They blended their individualistic personal beliefs with religious traditions and avoided the dogma and teaching of superiority of a single race and a religion over others.

GX: Generation X (Born 1965-1981)

This generation is known as the baby busters. They were pressed between silent generation and baby boomers. They were born from a time of high national debt and bleak job markets. Also, they were labeled as the "Mac Job" generation, a phrase referring to holders of low-level, entry-level jobs with minimum wage. GXers have very high egoistic value and hope for a better future.   This generation received less familial financial support and socio-religious advice.

GY: Generation Y (Born 1982-2003)

The millennial generation has grown up with highly sophisticated technologies and communications, television, computers (instant communication Internet chat rooms), and micro robotics cybernetic products. The boomers grew up with radio and telephones, GYers grown up with multimedia and cyberspace communication. GXers believe GYers are selfish, creating a generation gap. GYers started grew up with economic prosperity. They are ambitious, motivated, extremely impatient and demanding. GYers were more exposed to criminal actions. They were unreliable to social illnesses and have had fewer chances to be devoted to moral and ethical convictions. They have learned brutality from the cult of football, hockey, and commercial adventurous sports. They have been oriented to the beat culture, the hip-hop culture, the Jazz culture, the Pop culture, the rap culture, and the popular cool culture. Because of such cultural orientations, youths have lost their identities to an extent that they are killing each other. GYers become rebellious and their ethical and moral learning has been converted from schools to the streets gangster culture, the MTV and the Internet violent game shows. If you look at the recent shooting incidents in the U.S. schools, you may find how generation Y has been exposed to unfitted situations (see Table 12.1).

Table 12.1: Recent Shooting at the US Schools

• February 19, 1997, Alaska: A 16-year-old shot and killed the principal and a student and injured two others
• October 1, 1997, Mississippi: A 16-year-old shot and killed two students and injured seven others after stabbing his mother to death
• December 1, 1997, Kentucky: A 14-year-old shot and killed three students and injured five others
• December 3, Indiana: A 14-year old boy shot and killed three girls and wounded five other students
• March 24, 1998, Arkansas: An 11-year old and a 13-year-old shot and killed four students and a teacher and wounded 10 others
• April 24, 1998, Pennsylvania: A 15-year-old shot and killed a teacher.
• May 19, 1998, Tennessee: An 18-year-old shot and killed a classmate
• May 21, 1998, Oregon: A 17-year-old shot and killed two students and injured more than 20 after killing parents
• April 20, 1999 Colorado: Two students at Columbine High School shot and killed 13 and wounded 23 before killing themselves.
• May 20, 1999, Georgia: A 15-year-old boy shot and wounded six students
• November 19, 1999, New Mexico: A 12-year-old shot and killed a 13-year-old girl.
• December 6, 1999: Oklahoma: A 13-year-old student fired at least 15 rounds wounding four classmates
• February 29, 2000, Michigan: A six-year-old boy shot and killed a classmate
• February 26, 2000, Florida: 13-year-old student shot and killed teacher.
• January 10, 2001, California: A 17-year-old fired shots before taking student hostage. Gunman later shot and killed by police
• March 5, 2001, California: A 15-year-old fired shot killed 2 students and injured 13 students and 2 teachers
• March 22, 2001, California: An 18-year-old fired shots and injured 6 students.
• March 30, 2001, Gary, Indiana: One dead in Indiana school shooting
• March 21, 2005, Lakeland, Minnesota: A 14 years old student fired shots and killed 9 students
Sources: Partially used from: C Parkes, "Cult of the Football Bully Lurks Behind School Shootings: Life is Made Miserable for the Misfits, the Overweight, the Underweight, the Newcomers, by the Swaggering Jocks," *Financial Time*,(Tuesday March 20, 2001), 7.

<Wysiwyg://2/http://dailynews netscape co .ry,20020426114750011722691& shortdate,0426>

<http://www.cnn com/2004/US/South/o2/02/school shooting ap/index html>

Laredo Morning Times (2003) "2 High School Boys Shot in Minnesota," (Thursday, September 25 2003), A. |

MORAL FOUNDATIONS OF EMPLOYERS-EMPLOYEES RIGHTS AND DUTIES

In a free market economy, employer and employee rights and duties are based on bargaining power assumptions and values. In the private sector of economy, employers try to control the labor force and consumption in the marketplace. They try to protect their intellectual properties and maximizing their productivity and profitability. Employees seek to increase their wages/salaries, incentives, and benefits in order to improve working conditions, to enhance their family lives, and to ensure their job security. Before discussing specific rights and duties between employers and employees, we need to discuss employer-employee relations within the contextual boundaries of two premises; workforce and workplace.

Mathis and Jackson (1997: 504) state three types of rights for employer-employee relationships as follows:

- Rights affecting the employment agreement, involving:
    o   Employment-at-will
    o   Implied employment contracts (employee handbooks)
    o   Due process
    o   Dismissal for just cause
- Employee privacy rights, involving:
    o   Employee review of records
    o   Substance abuse and drug testing
    o   Polygraph and honesty testing
- Other employee rights, involving:
    o   Workplace investigation
    o   Potential hazards and unsafe working conditions
    o   Free speech and whistle blowing
    o   Notification of plant closing
    o   Security and safety at work

EMPLOYER-EMPLOYEE RELATIONS IN THE WORKPLACE

The erosion of employees, rights by selfish desires of employers has become a common unethical and immoral theme in the business world as a result of a growing number of legal challenges to the common-law doctrine of employment-at-will (EAW). This has allowed employers to terminate an employee without considerations of due process or just cause. Employment-at-will is a uniquely American doctrine. It is traced back to the time of slavery.

Wood (1887) asserted such a right for employers in *"A Treatise of Law of Master and Servant,"* by having its source in the common-law principle. He believed that the employment relationship is not bound by a contract specifying the period of employment, the relationship is considered at-will and can be terminated without cause by either party. Such a doctrine has been in practice in the United States for three centuries. Hiley (1996: 85) reported: "Currently, approximately 70 percent of workers in America are considered at-will-employees." There are several questions that need to be answered as follows:

- Should each employer and employee know some inherent moral conviction and ethical principles about their workplace?
- How do the activities of employers and employees affect the lives of people in a community?
- Does it help a person to understand these matters?
- In what way?
- Who determines wages? How?
- On what authority?
- What is the source of the mind-set that is legitimate for some groups of people to be given for wages for their work that keeps them and their families at the lowest or highest levels in a community?
- What ethical and moral values and standards are operative?
- Who sets and enforces these standards?
- On what communal ground?
- How and why?

In discussing employees' rights including compensation, the question of wage levels often goes beyond organizational decision-making processes. Are we talking about wages that are legal, ethical, or moral? Such a discussion can be addressed by analyzing three major philosophies: (1) wage slavery, (2) living survival wage, and (3) sustainable just wage.

Wage Slavery: How is it possible for some employees within the context of economic competition to be forced to work for some employers and be paid on the basis of the philosophy of wage slavery? Examining this question helps us to look deeper into the underlying econo-political ideology of a nation. In a civilized world, no individual, no company, and no nation can ethically justify engaging in wage slavery. A person of dignity, a company of integrity, and a nation of honesty not only should have moral principles but they should live by them.

Wage slavery is a political ideology that allows for barely meeting immediate for needs of employees, including basic foods, used clothing, and minimal shelters. Human trafficking and forced labor in sweatshops and industrial homework settings are among those unethical and immoral activities of wage slavery. Some businesses in most countries around the world practice wage slavery. Practicing wage slavery raises critical issues such as forced labor, child labor, and harassment or abused workingwomen in some industries. The apparel industrial homework settings, sweatshops, child labor, and women discrimination are included in wage slavery. For example, as Halbert and Ingulli (2000: 245) reported:

> In 1997 coalition of women's groups (Ms Foundation for Women) wrote to Philip Knight, President of Nike, complaining of the >disconnect, between Nike's advertising appeals based on women' s empowerment and the way Nike pays and treats women workers worldwide, and calling for higher wages to women workers in Viet Nam, Indonesia, and China.

NO SWEAT
Help End Sweatshop Conditions for American Workers
Robert B. Reich, Secretary
U.S. Department of Labor

Help End Sweatshop Conditions for American Workers.

Sweatshops still exist for many garment workers in America—sweatshops where workers earn less than 70 cents an hour and live in slavery-like conditions.

As Secretary of Labor, I am committed to ending this shameful practice. Even though many retailers and manufacturers have agreed to help eradicate sweatshops, it's going to take more.

Consumers like you can make a difference. You can exercise your right as a consumer to avoid buying sweatshop-made clothing. Please carry this card with you as a guide to "No Sweat" shopping.

Thank you for your support.

Robert B. Reich
Robert B. Reich, Secretary
U.S. Department of Labor

Source: Robert Reich Poster, "Help End Sweatshop Conditions for
American Workers,"
< http: //www.dol.gov/dol/esa/public/nosweat/card.htm>

Living Survival Wages: The living survival wage system is balanced human resource costs with the ability to attract and keep employees busy with minimum compensation. Generally, the wage system has three components (1) pay, (2) incentives, and (3) benefits. The *pay* is defined as the basic compensation an employee receives in cash, usually as a wage or salary. The *incentives* are compensations that reward an employee for efforts beyond normal expected standard of performances. The *benefits* are indirect rewards given to an employee or group of employees as a part of organizational membership. Employees at work can be paid for the amount of time spent on the job or on the amount of work produced. Hourly pay is the most common means of payment based on time. Employees who are paid hourly are said to receive wages. *Wages* are payments directly calculated on the amount of time worked. In contrast, employees who are paid a *salary* receive payment that is consistent from period to period despite the number of hours worked on the basis of their work efficiency and effectiveness; productivity.

There are two types of wage or salary philosophies: (1) entitlement orientation, and (2) performance orientation. The entitlement orientation philosophy is based on labor law; commonly referred to as *cost-of-living*. This philosophy is tied specific economic indicators. Since the economic indicators are exposed to inflationary rates, every year employers adjust their employees, wages and salaries according to the *cost-of-living-adjustment; COLA.* Where the performance-oriented philosophy is followed, no one is guaranteed compensation according to the number of years of services; seniority. They are treated according to their productivity. Nevertheless, in the performance-orientation, employers should observe the labor law minimum wages or salaries. How have the federal government and some state authorities legally enacted legislation to establish the minimum wage on the basis of the philosophy of living wage? The answer is based on balancing the fair labor standards. The fair labor standard principles has three major objectives: (1) to establish a minimum wage floor, (2) to enforce limits on the number of weekly hours employees work through overtime provisions, and (3) to ban oppressive use of child labor and abusing women.

The philosophy of living wage is based on a marginal survival wage. This wage level does provide a minimum room for preventing starvation, illnesses, and early death among employees. It prevents malnutrition and forced labor. It promotes possibilities of a small amount of discretionary income. Such income allows employees for minimal planning beyond living from paycheck to paycheck. It provides a minimal opportunity for savings to meet their survival needs. The legal minimum wage means no more than what businesses may pay without violating the law of the country. Ethically and morally, legal wages are not predicted on human needs on an on-going basis. Often, they are predicted or based on the annual inflationary rate.

Sustainable Just Wages: Sustainable just wages or salaries meet a moderate level of needs including food, new clothing, housing, cars, boats, healthcare, education, and savings. It provides sufficient money to enable employees to enjoy a decent life. When we raise moral and ethical questions about wages and salaries, we are immediately forced to raise the question of fairness and justness. From a moral perspective of rightness, truthfulness, and goodness the wages and salaries proceed from the belief that all human beings by natural law have similar rights to fulfill their lives. Human beings are not to be seen as cybernetic robots, which need software programming in order to work. To be a human being means to be both a dignified individual and an individual in relationship with others, and therefore the wages or salaries that they should earn should reflects the truthfulness, worthiness, and goodness of those relationships. This means the ability to fulfill their natural convictions to be good parents within their families, to be productive workers within their organizations, and to be dynamic citizens in their communities. Wages should sufficiently provide them appropriate opportunities to meet all of the above objectives in their lifetime. In addition, morally all workers, like their employers, expect to have continuous incomes in order to have decent lives.

Just, fair, and worthy wages for workers should reflect the real contributions that employees make to their corporations. As corporations enjoy decent development, growth, and profitability through the hard working habits of their workers, commensurately employees expect to be paid fairly and justly through profit sharing. It is important in this endeavor to define decent wages or salaries not as bare minimum but as those maximum compensations in order to elevate employees, lifestyles and of their community members as a whole towards more progress and achievement.

HOW CAN WE PURSUE THE ETHICAL AND MORAL WORKPLACE LIFE?

Among the most important conditions of a healthy workplace life is the fact that decisions about the workplace by employers affect: (1) the quality of life, (2) the ethical and moral considerations of life, (3) the economic well-being of life, (4) the socio-cultural conditions of life, and (5) the politico-legal status of life.

The Quality of Life: The qualitative assessment of an individual's life depends upon the environmental conditions of the workplace. Such conditions determine the level of satisfaction by individuals and their attitudes they hold toward others.

The Ethical and Moral Considerations of Life: Many employees are ethically and morally committed to workplace ethics. An employee is first of all a human being and rational agent, self-determined concerning his/her contributions to the organization as a process, and an end in himself/herself and worthy of self-respect. As moral beings, they possess a sense of searching for excellence and are able to carry with them in all their endeavors and undertakings the moral obligations to do the right things and avoid doing what is wrong. Ethically, they are not bound in their lifestyles and have the freedom to do whatever they wish. They remain bound by ethical convictions in all their activities. Also, an employer as an individual or a group of people is bound by ethical convictions. Therefore, both sides are bound not only by law but also by workplace ethics.

The Economic Wellbeing of Life: The economic health of the employees, of their family members, and even of whole communities depends upon conditions of the working person. A simple approach to the economic wellbeing of employees states that employees have all those, and only those identified rights and duties that they negotiate with their employers as conditions of employment. The economic conditions of employees are not abstractions.

The Ssociocultural Conditions of Life: Business peoples' occupations and/or professions affect both employees and employers and their hierarchical social positions in modern life. Whether or not this is appropriate, it nevertheless affects all our lives. Decisions by employers; public or private agencies about jobs affect not only economic lives but our social lives as well.

The Political-Legal Status of Life: One of the main issues within the domain of at-will-employment is the collective bargaining contract. Employers and employees play a very significant role in our political life and affect decisions of government at all levels. They are often able to dispense large sums of money in political activities (although in most occasions such activities are illegal) and therefore may affect political decisions rather than legal ones. As a result, understanding the processes of self-government in a democratic society requires some knowledge of political practices.

CIVIL LIBERTIES IN THE WORKPLACE

Business organizations have all sorts of work-related power to manipulate working conditions. Generally speaking, they want to make profit. They believe profitability is the main path towards growth. Within such an endeavor of thought, growth seems so natural to us that it forces us to be nourished with productive actions in order to be successful. Employers must try to motivate employees to reveal themselves in terms of innovativeness and creativity. This means that employees need autonomy and liberty to work effectively in order to achieve their personal and organizational objectives. Prior to the 1930s there was little government interventions in business organizations. In the late nineteenth and early twentieth centuries strong majorities on the Supreme Court adhered to the *liberty of contract doctrine.* This constitutional law doctrine held that employers and employees should be free to negotiate all aspects of employment in the workplace, including wages, hours, duties, and conditions. The liberty of contract majority first emerged in *Allgeyer v. Louisiana* 106 U. S. 578 (1897), where justice Rufus W. Peckham grounded the process clause of the Fourteenth Amendment, which states that no state can deprive a person of life, liberty, or property without due process of law.

The great flaw in the liberty of contract was that it assumed equal bargaining power for all parties. In practice, such a law provided opportunities for employers to dominate employees and to exploit them. In reality, employees could be fired at-will by employers and forced to accept virtually any working conditions (Stainer and Stainer, 1994: 547).

Let us talk about the employees, potency and productivity through the notion of civil liberty. Employees desire to do well at their work assignments. They want to get along with their superiors, peers, and subordinates. They want to have their honest contributions and efforts be recognized and appreciated. The employees, job rights, working conditions, wages or salaries, and the possibilities of promotion are among the many things that occupy their day-to-day thoughts. Prior to their employment, employees desire employers recognize their rights by providing them with a prospective path of growth and development. What is important for employees is not only what they achieve, how well their employers treat them. Employees desire obedient to the good faith and legitimate desires of their employers. Frequently, employees find employers, treatment to be ethically deficient and complain that their employers violate their moral rights and civil liberties.

As opposed to specific saving employers, rights, concerning conditions of employment, employees' rights are general rights according to the society or system that is functioning. Natural and civil liberties hold that all human beings, no matter what politico-economic system has been constructed, are subject to a unified system of rights. For example, Shaw and Barry (1998: 249) have cited the case of Louise V. MacIntire, who worked for the Du Pont Company in Orange, Texas, for sixteen years. As a chemical engineer, he was paid well. He wrote a novel: *Scientists and Engineers: The Professionals Who Are Not.* In his novel, MacIntire wrote about various management abuses and argued for unionization of the plant that he was working for. Logan Chemical, as a subsidiary of Du Pont, decided to fire him because of such unexpected disloyalty in his writings. He was fired. Ewing (1983: 141) indicates that consequently, MacIntire sued Du Pont, claiming that his constitutional right of free speech had been violated. Consequently, a Texas district judge threw that charge out of court. Maybe such a judgment in the State of Texas was legal, but it avoided the ethical and moral principles governing the natural and civil liberties.

EMPLOYERS-EMPLOYEES STRENGTHS AND VULNERABILITIES

Often in developing and in some developed countries, a single employer personally hires and fires people, sets the conditions of work, and invites employees to take it or leave it. Today, many employees are organized collectively into unions, which bargain with management over the terms and conditions of their employment. There are inherent reasons why each employee should make an effort to know his/her rights in the workplace.

Table 12.2: Some General Attributions Concerning Employers and Employees' power

EMPLOYERS' STRENGHTS	EMPLOYEES' STRENGHTS
• Ownership of Jobs • Ownership of facilities • Control over business plans, decisions, and resources • Control over organizational structure • Legal protection through lobbying • Shared interests with political entities	• Ownership of expertise • Ownership of know-how skills • Control over workplaces • Control over technological devices • Legal protection through labor laws • Share interests with the labor market
EMPLOYERS' VULNERABILITIES	**EMPLOYEES' VULNERABILITIES**
• Survival requires economic stability • Survival depends upon resources accessibility, durability, suitability, productivity, and profitability • Profitability depends on customer satisfaction and customer loyalty • Financial survival depends upon wide-ranging laws and regulations	• Survival depends upon economic viability • Survival depends upon informational viability, availability, on time accessibility, capability, and efficacy • Employment continuity depends upon at-will-decisions of employers • Financial survival depends upon maintaining employment and professional membership

THE RIGHTS OF EMPLOYEES
WITHIN AND BEYOND A FIRM

By looking at Table 12.3 we can see the rights of employers and employees in a firm. Nevertheless, there are some countries that view employment as included in natural and civil rights and such rights are correlated with the obligation to work; an obligation that the government enforces against the able-bodied. De George (1996: 363) indicates:

> The right to employment is not a right that is recognized in the United States, where unemployment is both expected and accepted. The right can be derived from the right to work, another right that is not recognized in the United States, but one that is listed in Article 23 of the Universal Declaration of Human Rights and recognized in many countries. Whether there is truly a right to employment, which should be recognized in the United States, depends on whether it is a justifiable claim.

Table 12.3: The Rights of Employment-At-Will

RIGHTS	NATURAL RIGHTS	HUMAN RIGHTS	CIVIL RIGHTS	EMPLOYER S' RIGHTS	EMPLOYEE S' RIGHTS
COMMON RIGHTS	The rights to exist	The rights to live	The rights to be entitled to make profit	The rights to invest and make profit to continue the business	The rights to work and enjoy life
MORAL RIGHTS	The rights no to be harmed	The rights not to be ignored	The rights to be ecognized	The rights to make choices	The rights not to be forced to work
ETHICAL RIGHTS	The rights to know	The rights to legitimacy	The rights to privacy	The rights to have clean business environments	The rights to earn income
LEGAL RIGHTS	The rights to self-defense	The rights to advocacy	The rights to due process	The rights to manage their own capital	The rights to be paid justly
CULTURAL RIGHTS	The rights to free associations	The rights freely to communic-ate	The rights to job negotiation	The rights to protect their investments	The rights to the collective bargaining contracts

In a free-enterprise market, the right to employment is not a right that can be exercised against any particular employer. Employers, on the basis of their economic conditions, are free to hire or fire their employees with just cause, no cause, and even for morally wrong causes; economic causes. In the United States, because of the notion of free market economy and competition, no worker has a right to any particular job or position. The main argument for such a proposition is based upon the common law: unless there is an explicit contractual provision to the contrary, every employment is employment at-will, and either side is free to terminate it at any time without advance notice or reason. This is the main reason that in the United States, businesses are viewed amoral.

There are several issues concerning civil rights, just and unjust decisions, and fair and unfair actions by employers. In the following pages, we will examine inherent ethical and moral issues concerning the following workplace related issues: (1) job ownership, (2) at-will employment, (3) plant closings, (5) insider trading, (6) confidentiality and trade secrets, (7) conflict of interest, (8) privacy, (9) AIDS/HIV in the workplace, (10) sexual harassment, (11) job safety and security, and (12) job discrimination.

Job Ownership: Job ownership is a relatively new phenomenon and usually joined to some extent with government ownership. Job ownership spells out certain managerial saving rights by employers to own specific occupations either by a group of capital holders and investors or by a group of certified or licensed professionals (e.g., physicians, lawyers, taxi drivers, or special governmental owned groups like military and law enforcement officers, secret service and informant officers, inspectors, judges, etc.).

Job ownership is directly related to the ownership of production means (e.g., intellectual property rights, copyrights, patents, trade marks, trade secrets, and product's formula). In different societies job ownership denotes the legitimate exclusive rights for protecting the public interest (social ownership) or personal property rights and personal goods (private ownership). There is a widespread ethical and moral sentiment that indicates that every honest and hard-working employee should have an inherent right to continuing employment; unless employees perform their duties poorly. Within such an ethical and moral social contract, there are four major issues concerning job ownership:

- The extremely broad theory of breaching ethical and moral contracts of good faith to avoid fairness in employment provides opportunities for employers to act on the basis of self-interest.
- The specific managerial legal savings theory provides employers the opportunity to transfer targeted employees to remote or undesirable locations in order to coerce them into quitting their jobs. This intention illustrates how employers with bad-faith can ignore the job ownership by employees and abuse them.
- Firing an employee on the basis of trumped-up poor performance reports is another bad-faith employer's unethical and immoral decisions and actions. Employers through legal loopholes can harm employees in many ways. For example, when employees reach to certain levels of salary ceiling, some employers initiate new mandates for performance appraisal in order to build up just-causes for firing senior employees in order to replace them with new ones who will work for lower wages. Despite the laws, the employment-at-will doctrine is still in place.
- Firing an employee on the basis of defamation. Defamation refers to damaging professional credibility and reputation by spreading rumors concerning the misbehavior of an employee. Such a rumor makes it difficult for an employee to find other employment in the future. It is a

fact that some employers use specific immoral and unethical either verbal or written allegations against employees in order to get rid of them. Often these damaging allegations show incompetence behind charges of defamation. Since employers usually do not put these allegations in writing, however, defamation is often difficult to prove in the legal system.

The Doctrine of Employment-at-Will: We need to analyze the ethical doctrine of employment-at-will concerning how employers are free to hire whomever they choose and to fire them whenever they decide, for any just-cause, good-cause, or no-cause. The doctrine of employment-at-will regards employees as just a variable in the production system. According to this doctrine, workers may be hired and fired for many reasons, or for no reason at all at the pleasure of the employer. Likewise, employees can quit their jobs for any reason at all. There are several moral, ethical, and legal implications within the doctrine of at-will-employment.

In a free market economy the free flow of capital, resources, technology, and labor is considered as a matter of choice. All of the above resources are determined by the demand-supply trends in the marketplace with consideration of ethical, moral, and legal ramifications. The issue of employment is limited to certain societal mandates. We should indicate that employment rights should not be viewed as wage slavery. In any society, employment refers to certain reciprocal rights between employers and employees. Employment does not mean that employees give up human rights during and after their employment. Parties, employers and employees also have specific moral, ethical, and legal obligations. There are several issues that should be analyzed during and after employment. These questions are:

- What is the main attribution to employment concerning natural rights, human rights, employers, rights, and employees, rights?
- What are ethical, moral, and legal transactions among employers, employees, government, and society at large?
- Is the nature of employment based on a lawless foundation?
- Is the nature of employment bounded with written and/or non-written contracts and/or agreements between employers and employees?
- Is there any aspect of employment that cannot be subject to negotiation?
- Are there any ethical and moral obligations concerning employers-employees rights and duties?
- Are there any specific rights for employers to penetrate an individual's private life through employees, continuous background checking?
- Should employers have specific rights to check employees, performance background?
- What are employees, rights to check managerial misconduct, deception,

and fraud in the workplace?

- Who is protecting employees against employers, unfair, unjust, and wrongdoing decisions and action?
- Are governments more pro-employers rather than pro-employees?

To answer to the above questions, we need to look at the ethical, moral, and legal trends in a society concerning employment-at-will problems. Although in most democratic societies employees have a moral right to privacy, many employers possess the power to penetrate employees, privacy. The reason is twofold. First, the notion of privacy is declared to be natural and societal rights, but which agency can enforce such rights is a matter of the third party, namely governments, mass media, or interest groups. Second, the right to privacy, like other rights, is bound within arbitrary scaled rights from the pure zone of moral convictions to the impure zone of illegal actions, and it is not clear.

Each society possesses its own cultural and legal mandates to ordinate business employment. Some cultures are highly formalized through enacting legal statutes concerning the employers, right to dismiss and/or to layoff their employees. Typical of such legal statutes are protecting employees, employment rights through prohibitions against age, race, gender, religion, and national origin discrimination. In the United States the legal statutes of such prohibitions limited employers, ability to terminate employees on the bases of discrimination.

By looking at Table 12.4 you may notice that public policy shifted in attitudes from utilitarian employment-at-will to deontological concerns of fairness. This means that when an employer dismisses an employee, it must not be on grounds of gender, race, age, national origin, or other irrelevant factors. It must be based on performance and/or economic reasons.

Plant Closing or Moving Out: One of the major issues in the field of business is productivity. What is productivity? Productivity is a measure of efficiency doing the things right. Measuring the output of a particular product and dividing it by the number hours worked by the employees who produced product would obtain a measure of employee productivity. While this may seem a simple concept, it in fact reflects a very complex calculation. Such an assessment cannot be assigned to any particular employee because labor productivity measures the rate of synergized output of the group as a whole. Also, the amount measured depends upon quality of raw materials and technology.

Plant closing and/or moving the plant location are serious issues in the economic condition of a community. Through such adverse situations, employees lose their jobs. Specifically, plant closing and moving the plant out of a community occur when the economic condition of a country faces heavy recession. In these situations, employers search for alternatives to save money. Besides economic recession, there are other reasons that employers decide to close their plants, including confrontation with unions. In unionized businesses, there are some measures of protection for workers who lose their jobs due to plant closing and plant movement.

Table 12.4: The Federal Legislated Statutes of Employer-Employee Relations

DATE	FEDERAL LAW
1934	National Industrial Recovery Act (NIRA)
1934	The Antikickback Law (Copeland Act)
1935	The National Labor Relations Act (NLRA)
1936	The Prevailing Wage Law (Davis-Bacon Act)
1936	The Overtime Law (Walsh-Healy Act)
1963	The Equal Pay Act
1964	Title VII of the Civil Rights Act
1965	The Service Contract Act (McNamara- O'Hara Act)
1968	Age Discrimination in Employment Act
1970	Occupational Safety and Health Act (OSHA)
1972	Equal Employment Opportunity Act
1973	The Nonretaliation Provisions of Fair
1973	Labor Standards Act
1974	Rehabilitation Act
1974	Federal Privacy Act
1977	Employment Retirement Income Security Act
1978	Federal Mine Safety & Health Act
1981	The Labor-Management Cooperation Act
1986	The Fair Labor Standards Act
1988	Employee Polygraph Protection Act
1990	Americans With Disabilities Act

The lack of ethical principles and legislative mandates provide unfair opportunities for employers to abandon their communities and to relocate their plants to other communities in order to get rid of unions. Harrison (1984:387) indicates that in some countries, including Germany, there is a legislative prenotification before closing or moving a plant. In Germany, the pre-notification time is a requirement introduced as part of the 1976 Co-Determination Act.

Many employers simply prefer to close the least efficient plants and move their production systems elsewhere for the following reasons:

- The plant is facing serious regulatory measures.
- The development of program remedy either is very expensive or defective
- The failure of employees and union to improve productivity.
- The lack of disciplinary culture for tightening work ethics.
- The frequent confrontation and/or resistance by unions to improve productivity.
- Changing the technological infrastructure of a plant to an advanced technology (e.g., automation to robotics or robotics to cybernetic robotics).
- The frequent exposure of employers to strikes, stoppages, boycotts, picketing, and class file lawsuits.
- Excessive demands for higher wage rates, new expertise, new physical setups, new equipments, and new labor agreements.
- The heavy cost for outsourcing.

In plant closing and plant moving both employers and employees may be considered as losers. Nevertheless, since employers possess more financial capabilities, they may be able to regain their loses in the new places. There are three scenarios in solving plant productivity: (1) collective bargaining productivity enhancement, (2) authoritative management productivity enhancement, and (3) joint venturing partnership productivity enhancement (see Figure 12. 2).

Enhancement Plan: Consensus on productivity enhancement plan through joint venturing partnership between the management team and employees is the result of having agreed decisions based on an equation between corporate profitability and the wage management system. Such a concession can come from a formatted forum table concerning work rules or work rights and duties in a workplace. A concession forum is a promotional one where all organizational members perceive their roles to pursue institutional effectiveness; doing the right things. This provides an ethical ground for establishing fewer workplace hierarchical rules and more indulgence of self-motivated deliberation for improving productivity in the workplace.

Some people consider the joint venturing partnership productivity enhancement plan a necessary response to the strategic long-term profitability conditions of a corporation. Productivity concession also guarantees continuity of employment security.

Authoritative Management Productivity Enhancement Plan: Some authoritative managerial styles demand concessions from employees where the problems are not well defined and/or not clearly needed. In other words, some companies cried wolf. This makes the task of developing a comprehensive plan for productivity enhancement more difficult.

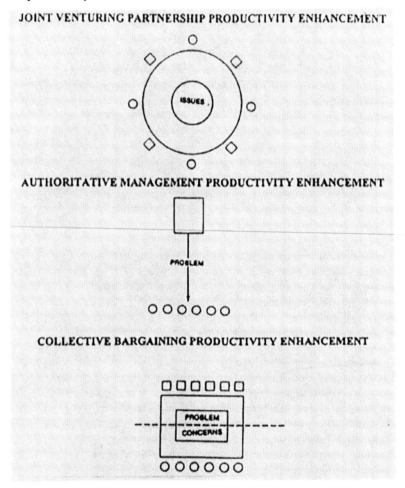

Figure 12.2: Three Pronged Problem Solving Processes in Plant
Productivity Enhancement

Source: Partially adapted from John Belcher, Jr., "The Role of Unions in
Productivity Management," *Personnel,* (1988, 65: 1, 57).

Employees are concerned about two major issues concerning their employment: (1) job security; guarantees for specific jobs, and (2) employment security; guarantees for overall employment. It is a matter of choice for employees to be concerned about either having flexible work rules governing workplace in job assignments, hours of work, seniority, wages, incentive pay and teamwork or permanent employee guarantees. Such a discrepancy can cause interruption in the workplace.

Collective Bargaining Productivity Enhancement Plan: According to the collective bargaining agreements, the productivity enhancement agenda brings two major issues to the negotiation table: (1) managerial problems and (2) employees concerns. We need to analyze these two domains concurrently. Through a deontological approach we may discover what causal factors lie beneath the collective bargaining contracts concerning productivity enhancement outcomes. In collective bargaining negotiations, we find two hard-core groups confronting each other: (1) management teams and (2) union leaders. Management concern is focused on meritocracy (utilitarianism) while union concern is focused on seniority (deontologicalism). Each industry, company, and plant has a unique persuasive objective to have profitability through long-run synergistic productivity enhancement plans. Each union is concerned about employment security. Layoffs occur where plants are being closed or moved, companies are bankrupted, and/or companies are restructured. Each situation provides specific conditions to be considered by management teams to safeguard stakeholders' interests. This requires a serious negotiation and consensus agreements on a company's survival trends. Therefore, collective bargaining productivity enhancement plans could be either a cosmetic agreement or a drastic surgical restructuring task towards reassignment of an agreement. The end result depends upon conditional circumstances.

INSIDER TRADING

We are living in a highly sophisticated information era. Information about one's own company that is obtained through one's employment and/or by a regulatory agency (governmental or professional), and that has not been publicly disclosed to those outside the company, is known as insider information. Insider informants sometimes profit from insider information. Insider informants may learn, for example, about approval or disapproval of a drug by the Food and Drug Administration (FDA) to be or not be licensed for a pharmaceutical company. This information can help or hurt the company's stock values (e.g., the Imclone Company's disapproval of a cancer drug by FDA and the Martha Steward case). Using insider information before it is publicly announced can make a huge difference in the buying or selling of the stock of a company. Insider trading scandals go back to many years, including during 1980s when so-called financial geniuses such as Ivan Boseky, Michael Milken, Martin Siegel, and Dennis Levine made billions of dollars and were caught.

Although there is no precise definition of insider trading, it can be broadly defined as buying and selling securities while in possession of nonpublic information about a corporation or about the market for a corporation's securities (Buchholz and Rosenthal, 1998: 391). Larmer (1996: 224) defines:

> Insider trading as buying or selling of stocks on the basis of privileged information available only to a select few. It is widely regarded as unethical and is illegal in the United States, as well as a large number of European and Asian countries.

Also, Moore (1996: 225) defines the term of insider trading as: "The buying or selling of securities on the basis of material, non-public information... Insider trading makes for exiting headlines, and stories of the unscrupulousness and unbridled greed of traders abound."

Within contextual fair and just conditions of buying or selling securities in the stock market there are two major views concerning insider trading:

- The view widely held that acquiring insider information as a basic foundation for buying or selling stocks of a corporation by specific interest groups is wrong, unethical, and some countries illegal. They believe that using insider information for one's own profit is wrong primarily because the information is put in the hands of an interest group in order to acquire free money.
- The other view of insider trading as ethically acceptable and should not be illegal. They argue that invisible hands can stimulate the economy and concurrently, insider trading can in many instances be viewed as good for the economy, the corporation whose shares are traded and the insiders who trade the shares. In addition, they believe that it does not necessarily involve defrauding investors. They argue that today information is viewed as a commodity to be bought and possesses value in the marketplace. There is nothing wrong with a trader buying information and using it in his/her decision-making processes for buying or selling a company's stocks. They believe that the nature of stock market is based on buying or selling information concerning the performance of corporations. Therefore, if buying and selling information is a legitimate deal and a trader pays for a vital piece of information, it is ethical and legal to use it in his/her decision making process and stock transaction. These groups of traders believe that the nature of the stock market is based on information. They don't believe that the stock market is like a casino in which one gamble monies without insider information.

Ethical and Legal Arguments Concerning Insider Trading

The argument concerning ethics of insider trading remains a hotly contested topic in a variety of fiduciary judgments because it is difficult to detect it in many cases. Some scholars believe that the nature of free competition in the stock market should be based upon fairness and justness and others believe that it should be based upon property rights in acquisition of information. In reality, the nature of the stock market is based on the infusion of buyers, and sellers, wealth potential, socio-cultural valuable competitive corporations, efficiencies, econo-political influential bargaining power of a corporation's affiliates, and acquisition of information at the right time in order to make the right decisions and to execute them in the right places.

There are two opposing arguments concerning insider trading: (1) moral fairness in equal opportunities for acquisition of public information for all buyers and sellers and (2) amoral competitive infusion of wealth, power, and information only for stockholders of a corporation.

Moral Fairness in Equal Opportunities For Acquisition of Public Information: Moral fairness focuses on the disparity of information between the two parties namely buyers and sellers of securities to the transaction. Moralists believe that trading in securities should take place on an open level playing field and disparities in acquisition of information tilt the field toward one player and away from the other. Regardless of the ownership of information, parties as buyers and sellers should be provided with all information related to publicly privately owned securities. Both ordinary investors and exceptional investors should have access to the public records of all publicly owned private corporations. Specifically, ordinary investors should be provided with daily information concerning the values of their shares and any insider trading information. It is not fair or just to keep ordinary investors in dark. For example, in case of a merging decision, if such a decision should not be publicly announced, ordinary investors may sell their shares too early and be deprived of the advantages that the stocks of merging companies would generate rise. Some people including Werhane (1989: 841) argue that insider trading thwarts the very basis of market competition because the same information is not available to everyone, so competition, which depends on the availability of equal advantage of all parties, is precluded. Insider trading allows the insider to indulge in greed. Thus, insider trading is economically inefficient for the very reason it is immoral.

Another serious ethical issue is the harming thesis that holds that insider trading erodes investors, confidence in the security exchange market and causes investors to pull out their investments from the stock market. If investors do not have assurance that the security exchange processes functions impartially, consequently they will not have any inclination to invest their monies in the security exchange market. The market will be harmed accordingly and will not be able to perform its role of allocating capital resources in our economy (Moore, 1996: 225).

Amoral Competitive Infusion of Wealth, Power, and Information: There are amoral investors who believe that insider information can be seen as a form of property, much like trade secrets and inventions. Insider trading information concerning a corporation is viewed as a competitive key for success. Therefore, those investors who own information are entitled to sell them to any other investors as they wish. These informants are known as infopreneurs. Since the nature of the stock market is based upon quick decision-making processes, there are many consultant firms acting as infopreneurs that provide insider-trading information for investors for a fee. The major issue in such a case raises the question: "Are infopreneurs, business activities immoral, unethical, and illegal?" The answer is no. We need to realize that the international security exchange market is a global phenomenon. Is there any international rule to control all related decisions and actions around the globe? The answer is no. Then, how will we be able to regulate the international security exchange market?

According to the amoral theses of insider trading information ownership, business is business. There is no room for fairness in the stock market because everybody is looking for very quick profit. Useem (1999: 121) indicates: "It's a devil of a dilemma, but the upshot for corporate America is fairly simple: Companies that learn to cannibalize themselves today will rule tomorrow's business jungle. Those that don't will find themselves in someone else's pot." Therefore, the international exchange security role is based on Social Darwinism: the survival of the fittest, and the demise of the weakest or the sickest.

If investors desire to invest their capital in the international stock market, they need to be aware of stockholder sharks that are waiting for them. If investors are equipped with the best information, they will avoid collision with those sharks and they can safely swim along with them. If they don't, sharks will beat them. In order to survive, they need to be strong through the acquisition of insider trading information, because in reality, acquisition of insider trading information is the key for survival. Therefore, according to this type of reasoning there is no room for fairness in the international stock market. It is a very risky business in which all investors are trying to acquire free-money. Is there any ethical and moral rule in the process of free money making? The answer is no.

JOB SHOP RIGHTS, EXPERTISE KNOWLEDGE, AND TRADE SECRETS

Job shop rights, employees, rights for making free choices of their employers, and trade secrets are very complex and challenging issues in the field of business. Expert knowledge including know-how knowledge, know-what knowledge, know-where knowledge, know-for knowledge, and know-whom knowledge are subjects of controversial ethical and moral issues in today's competitive market. Who owns technical production procedures and operational skills in an organization employer as investors or employees as experts? Who owns scientific knowledge patent holders and copyrighters or researchers? Who owns a corporation's trade secrets; employers or employees? How an expert may keep a company's trade secret and not to disclose it to others? Can an expert carry it to his/her new employer and disclose his/her expert knowledge to them? Are experts virtually viewed as a company's permanent employees or they are employers, slaves beyond their employment termination? These issues are highly complicated through moral, ethical, and legal deliberations. For example, Shaw and Barry (1998: 353) indicate:

> Donald Wohlgemuth, who worked in the spacesuit department of B. F. Goodrich... became general manager of spacesuit division and learned Goodrich's highly classified spacesuit technology for the Apollo flights. Shortly thereafter, Wohlgemuth, desiring a higher salary, joined Goodrich's competitor International Latex Corporation in Dover, Delaware, as manager of engineering for the industrial area that included making spacesuits in competition with Goodrich. Goodrich protested by seeking an order restraining Wohlgemuth from working for Latex or for any other company in the space field.

Questioning the ethical and moral convictions of Goodrich and Wohlgemuth has raised the mutual issue of employer-employee loyalty. When asked by Goodrich management whether he thought his action was moral, Wohlgemuth replied: "Loyalty and ethics have their price and International Latex has paid the price."

Expertise knowledge is defined as acquisition, integration, and transformation of specific knowledge for problem solving in a pragmatic condition. Knowledge expert, expert systems, diagnostic, and prognostic systems are viewed as highly integrated domains of knowledge. There is an old debate concerning expert systems in the field of business, about whether ethics in business is more *pervasive* or *persuasive*.

The first view is that expert systems are *amoral* and that experts should act based solely on economic-self-interest through legal considerations. For example, in the Japanese culture, there are four concentric cultural pervasive circles: (1) family, (2) fellows close associates, (3) a combination of open competition and long-term give-and-take, and (4) the world (Muskin, 2000: 285). Experts need to function according to their preferred hierarchical cultural value systems and their self-interests. Experts tend to view the inner circles as operational bases supported by reciprocal cooperative behavior between employer and employees while the outer expert circles are seen as battlegrounds of intensive competition. Nevertheless, the aim of experts is based on economic self-interest for their inner circle. Such a notion of expert system is taken from naturalist, Loyal Watson (1995: 48) who provides evidence that a parallel to the four convincing circles exists in nature: (1) be nasty to outsiders, (2) be nice to insiders, and (3) cheat whenever possible for survival. Fukuyama (1995) indicates:

> The feature would appear to be that you trust your family absolutely,

your friends and acquaintances to the degree that mutual dependence has been established and face invested in them. With everybody else you make no assumptions about their good will. You have the right to expect their politeness and their following of social proprieties, but beyond that you must anticipate that, just as you are, they are looking primarily at their own, i.e., their family's best interest.

The second view is that expert knowledge should be persuasive. This is a view of socio-ethical incorporating unity among all three ethical dimensions along with the notion of work ethics: employers, integrity, employees, dignity, and professionals, responsibilities. This means that expertise autonomy should not be only expressed by the general expected legal or lawful mandates, but also they should be expressed by the incorporation of general societal ethical standards, professional codes of conducts, and personal professional commitments.

In a broad sense, the terms job-shop-rights, trade secrets, and an expertise's autonomy are viewed as moral, ethical, and legal intellectual property rights like patents, copyrights, and trademarks. Job-shop rights are defined as the exclusive rights of total manufacturing information, experience, operational procedures, and technical skills that have been developed by a corporation through heavy research and development (R&D) investment to manufacturing a unique set of products in a highly competitive manner. The job-shop-rights are based either the data that is maintained in a database inventory system or kept in a scientific procedural manual. The database must be integrated through purposeful objectives. By integration, it is understood that a unification of several distinct data sources or files has occurred, and that any redundancies that resulted from the unification have been removed, either completely or in part (Date, 1990).

The concept of trade secret is broad and imprecise. The trade secret as Bock (1983:136) defines: "Is any formula, patent, device, or compilation of information which is used in one's business and which gives him an opportunity to obtain an advantage over competitors who do not know or use it." Patents and copyrights are generally defended on the ground that without them technological innovation would be hampered.

In today's high-tech firms, one of the major moral and ethical issues is an employee, having to sensitive organizational information and disclosure to competitors at the time of separation from one in order to become an employee of a rival company. O'Connor (1993: 1A) indicates: "The average job tenure of an executive in the software industry is a scant twenty-two months." Two major factors conspire to make this a morally and ethically complicated problem: (1) the individual's right to seek employment with higher salary and benefits as experts and (2) the difficulty of separating trade secrets from expert knowledge, experience, and skills known as the employees, own intellect and talents of expertise. Respect for an individual's autonomy, respect for rights, duties, and responsibilities, and respect for privacy lie behind the ethical and moral obligations to control self-indulged desires to disclose organizational secrets.

Clearly, one of the ethical problems facing an organization is preventing trade secrets to the public and proprietary data from being misused by its own employees. Boatright (1993: 155) states that there are at least three arguments for legally protecting trade secrets:

- Trade secrets are intellectual property of the company.
- The theft of trade secrets is unfair competition.
- Employees who disclose trade secrets violate the confidentiality owed to their employers.

GENDER ETHICS IN THE WORKPLACE

Every business organization functions in a society differently. Nevertheless, societal business ethics defines which behaviors are moral and which are unethical within that society. Through history, it has been the recognition of gender as sometimes contradictory but always pervasive in constructing social norms that regulates biological characteristics of genders. Biological gender characteristics like other natural issues are so deep as to be invisible in all societies. Such a phenomenon has created gender classification in different forms such as masculine and feminine or male and female.

Men and women can speak the same language universally. Can men communicate with women as men communicate among themselves or *vice versa*? One must answer these and other similar questions case by case. However, we assume that similarly they should be able to perceive and understand each other equally. If the latter proposition is true, then in an organization do women exert the same managerial power within the workplace as men do? Some researchers indicate that the gender typing of referent-power is less straightforward, because referent-power is based on perceived identification. Johnson (1976) views it as being open to either gender, but more aligned with female than male gender-role stereotypes due to the personal nature of power. One reason for this disparity is gender differences in power. While power is a critical factor in upward mobility, females tend to have less power in organizations than males. In recognition of this problem, researchers and practitioners have focused on the need to provide females with equivalent power resources as males.

By nature, women are communicative, intuitive, nurturing, sensitive, supportive, and persuasive (Schwartz, 1989:65). Researchers found that most women have a higher sense of the importance of long-term relationships (Covey, 1993). Women's sense of importance to long-term relationships and their natural instinct bring to mind the more personal issues. It is a traditional fact in the Western civilization, when an Occidental culturally oriented women considers an advancement in her career, she elevates personal career over family concerns; such trends is not are acceptable in Oriental cultures (Coser, 1975) on the other hand, by nature men are aggressive, very competitive, risk-takers, self-reliant, and predictable to women. This is primarily why they work so well in positions of power and influence and why they like to take advantage of their position. As Covey (1993) indicates, men tend to have a management mindset, and management focuses primarily on control and efficiency and on turning people into things. Nevertheless, Simon and Cornwall (1989: 42) indicate:

> The obstacles in cross-gender communication are often greater than those between foreign cultures... Despite a quarter century of feminist progress and the many changes in gender roles in society, at a most basic and unconscious level, men and women consistently continue to be: talked to and talked about differently; touched and approached differently; dressed and dealt with out of role assumptions and expectations that are significantly different.

As Parhizgar (1994: 525) indicates:

> In all cultures, human organizations were mostly managed by male-oriented philosophies of management, and had patriarchal organizational approaches. History indicates that men with command, control, communication, and cooperative leadership styles through many centuries ran organizations. In keeping with history men and women still do not enjoy equal shares in the workplace.

Linda Wirth (2001: VIII) reports:

> Only 2 percent of those senior posts in companies [in the private sector] are held by women in France and less than 3 percent in Germany. The portion is 3.6 percent in the UK, and as low as 1.3 percent in Australia In the U.S., a gap of 16 percent exists between the earnings of the average male and female manager. The divide is 15 percent in the UK, 12 percent in Australia and a massive 35 percent in Finland.

It is interesting that Taylor (2001: VIII) reports:

> The gender gap is less apparent in developing countries. The ILO report has found that as many as 40 percent of employees in administrative and managerial positions in Colombia are women, the same portion as in Bermuda. In Honduras the portion is an impressive 47 percent and in the Philippines 37 percent.

Do you think men prevent women from having equal opportunities? If your answer is yes, then men are less moral and ethical in the workplace. Therefore, we need to analyze gender ethics in more depth.

Socio-cultural norms and trends of gender phenomenon have influenced not only on the basis of the types of dressing, occupation, and sexuality, but also bodily compartments, patterns of communication and speech, emotional and sensational appeal, and moral and ethical developments. Biologically, can we claim that both genders possess the same physiological characteristics? The answer is no. However, from another view, can we claim that the distinction between males and females and other societal norms is variable rather than a constant? The answer is yes. Biologically, men and women are different, but through legality, they are equally before the law in some societies like European and American countries, and they are unequal in the Moslem countries.

Are gender ethics and morality sex-blind? Should men be assimilated into women's ethics and morality or *vice versa*? This creates some types of double standard policy in the workplace. For instance, mandating special leaves for disability on account of pregnancy or childbirth provides rational special incentives for women. Gender ethics defines the behaviors of both genders, male and female, that are considered ethical within and beyond a business entity. There are several topics that need to be analyzed and discussed within the boundary of gender ethics. These topics are gender management, gender bias, gender prejudice, and gender ethics including masculine ethics and feminine ethics. We need to make it clear that gender ethics is completely another dimension of human life in organizations. Also, we need to mention that "sexual harassment" is another legal and cultural dimension of organizational life. Within the domain of all of the above kinds of discussions, there are two general types of philosophical foundations for gender ethics: (1) equalitarianism gender ethics and (2) equitabilitarianism gender ethics.

Equalitarianism Gender Ethics: There are two different types of analysis to view gender ethics in the workplace. First, we assume that both genders; male and female should be equally treated as a unified system known as equalitarianism. Second, we assume that both genders possess distinctive characteristics within and beyond domain of their gender characteristics, which should be, analyzed separately known as equitabilitarianism.

Equalitarianism gender ethics is identified as assuming equal rights and duties in an organization for both genders, masculine and feminine goodness. According to this view employees are considered as abstract variables that represent societal reminiscent of equalitarian discussions of the encumbered. According to the general views both genders masculine and feminine are viewed within a holistic context of natural rights as interdependent entities whose assessments are based on uniformity of treatments in an organization. This view indicates that there is no difference between male and female leadership. Both genders possess equal characteristics that match with general societal ethical and moral values. Such a system is based on essential similar characteristics that form human beings distinct from other creatures; essentialism.

Ahistoric essentialists believe that gender ethics is related to a partial historical tradition in ethics that covers a portion (not the whole) of traditional moral characteristics to be extended from the past to the present. The roots of the traditional ahistorical essentialism gender ethics are mainly related to the well being of adult work, workplace, and finally lifestyles of both genders. In fact ahistorical essentialism gender ethics analyzes the gender power struggle to stabilize the disparity of the power-distance between genders.

Essentialism gender ethics emphasizes uniformity in moral and ethical characteristics between masculine and feminine behaviors. They deny the existence of sexual harassment in the workplace. They do not view any behavior (verbal or physical) by a gender male can cause harm to another gender female in a dominant subjugated power form of harassment.

Essentialism ethics provides a macro characteristic, which is shared by both genders, and naturally they should be treated equally. This assumption is based upon the universalism perception of unity between both genders. Both genders have common values and naturally expect to be treated equally. Though it is true that a lot of unethical and immoral treatments occur between genders unequally, they believe that it is false to say that a gender has always-absolute power to dominate the other and/or to manipulate the other because both genders are equal. For example, liability of a gender's comment concerning the type of a dress to the opposite gender has been found unethical and immoral only when the comment has been so outrageous in character, and so in extreme degree, as to go beyond all possible bounds of decency, and to be regarded as atrocious and utterly intolerable in a moralized and ethicalized form.

There is an essential fact that women are more in tune with physical beautification and attractiveness. Beautification is a generally expected female characteristics bestowed on females by society. The masculine gender expects to see beautification as a moral and ethical value system to praise females, beauty and elegance. Nobody can deny this fact. In addition, honest aesthetic comments for a female's physical and psychological beauty in some cultures such as in France pertain to the sense of beautification characterized by love of beauty. It is not fair for the masculine gender either to be denied and/or having injunction from such a form of aesthetic expression. Also, it is cruel for beautiful females or handsome males to be denied praiseworthiness.

From a different viewpoint, if it is ethical for a gender to enjoy some possible incentives, essentialists believe that there should be a unified clause of me too for both genders. If women are cultivated to love beauty, it is not fair for males to be deprived. For example, if there is a maternity leave for mothers why not such an entitlement for a father. Therefore, organizations should not provide some privileges for one gender and deprive the other gender from such privileges. Within equalitarian gender ethics, there is no particularity for each gender. Such an ethical view is known as ahistorical ethics. Ahistorical ethics tells a portion of the historical truth not the whole.

Equitabilitarian Gender Ethics: Equitabilitarian gender ethics is assuming that rights and duties for masculine and feminine individuals in an organization should be equitable with their particular characteristics. Since genders are different, therefore their rights and duties would be different too. Nevertheless, such differences should be considered relatively when we are considering gender ethics. According to this view, employees are considered as particular variables that represent their rights and duties on the basis of their gender characteristics.

This means that we need to recognize particularism in conceptualizing their moral and ethical justice.

According to moral and ethical principles both genders are viewed as two different independent entities within the context of natural and civil rights and duties. Accordingly, a major question arises: Do women manage organizations differently than men? The answer is yes and no. According to Higgins (1994: 648) the following paragraphs summarizes the views of female entrepreneurs:

> Women manage differently than men, and they should. Women are generally more concerned about people than men. This helps them deal with the majority of problems in businesses, which are people problems... Women tend to be more cooperative than competitive. They are also horizontally rather than vertically oriented. That is, they are less on power than on a peer, group, or shared authority perspective, in contrast to men, who depend more on the power of the organizational hierarchy to support their decisions.

Equitabilitarianism gender ethics views masculine and feminine ethics as the same in principle but in practical reality they are slightly different from each other. Sometimes women and men are independent entities whose assessments are based on particular treatments in an organization that creates double standard policies and procedures. This view indicates that there are differences between male and female leadership. Both genders possess particular characteristics that match with their historical societal ethical and moral values. Such a system is based on essential characteristics that form the nature of genders. Therefore, we cannot treat men and women equally, but we need to treat them equitably.

What is Elite Equitabilitarian Ethics? As we have indicated above, each individual, group and gender possess unique characteristics and outcomes. Accordingly, they are entitled to different outcome assessments. Some people through their genetic and social characteristics are more intellectually oriented and some less. Those who are more intellectually are oriented are very few. We have called them elites. The elite equitabilitarianism ethics is consistent with free competitive philosophy because the most efficient combination of resources should be with those best abilities and talented people in order to get to the best end result; the best job done, the best chances to start a business, the best investment opportunities, and the best possible fair competition among business entities. Regardless of gender characteristics, society is better off with considering an equitable system of treatment to be based on knowledge and skills rather than equal gender characteristics. The meritocracy is the ultimate objective of the elite equitabilitarianism ethics to respect talents and skills of men and women in a fair competitive process, because men and women will end up in positions where their abilities can best be utilized and fit into the business environment.

The principles of equal opportunities for men and women help business organizations ensure that the best qualified competitors function in the marketplace, no matter what their genders and have a chance to promote businesses based on their proven ability to efficiently and effectively use society's resources. In other words, to compete progressively mandates that businesses enrich societal economic wellbeing in order to get commensurately rewards. This wise concept never held that men and women would be of equal and/or unequal ability or that such a free and open competition for existing opportunities would bring about equal results in terms of economic conditions. It depends on their abilities.

Merit and meritocracy are the heart of the elite equitabilitarian ethical concept. They dictate that society should reward those who deserve it on the basis of their abilities regardless of gender discrimination. Carl Marx challenged the ahistoricalism of this model and deconstructed the model to reveal fractures rather than unitary identities. The elite equalitarian ethics mandates society reward those capable businesses whatever they deserve. The rewards are supposed to go to those men and women who perform the best and thus are able to compete most efficiently and effectively.

Prejudice, bias, and discrimination are three ugly words that easily contaminate business processes with subtle greed and stinginess. These terms inherently contain egoistic selfishness in human nature. Therefore, in equalitarian business ethics there is no particularism between general gender characteristics. Both genders are equal in their rights, duties, responsibilities, and accountabilities but they will be different according to their outcomes.

SEXUAL HARASSMENT AND SEXUAL FAVORITISM IN THE WORKPLACE

There are several issues concerning gender ethics in an organization. These issues are office romance, sexual favoritism, sexual abuses, and sexual harassment. What are the inherent causes and effects of gender ethics in the workplace? How can organizations create ethical, moral, and productive work environments? How can organizations prevent office romance incidents, sexual favoritism, sexual abuses, and sexual harassment in the workplace? To answer the above questions, we need to analyze them with an in depth rational argument.

The Office Romance: Sexual favoritism, request for sexual favors, office romances, sexual jokes, and consensual sexual advances between supervisors and subordinates and/or among peers are not uncommon. Office romance between male and female employees including managers and subordinates has created a minefield that sometimes abuses organizational integrity. Some organizations forbid dating within a firm, or sexual favoritism prohibitions the hiring of spouses or requiring one spouse to transfer or quit when co-workers have intimate relationships and/or marry. Others take less dramatic action, requiring employees to report certain in-house relationships so they can be monitored. Other organizations prohibit appointment of one spouse as a supervisor over the other. Some organizations create specific procedural policies for a couple to be as co-supervisors in a firm. In each of the above cases, there are inherent unethical and immoral issues that employers cannot afford to practice. Ethically and morally there is noting wrong for two coworkers to marry but legally there are some complexities when two coworkers work in a department; specifically if one of the spouses is the immediate supervisor of the other.

Sexual Harassment: Every year many employees experience sexual harassment in their workplace. Sexual harassment exists in various forms of different genders and between individuals from the same gender. However, the major workplace problems are harassment of women by selfish men and deception of men by some immoral women. Sexual harassment creates hostile, intimidating, and derogatory remarks such as "You are a woman, what do you know?" or offensive work environment. On November 16, 2000, Suffolk Superior Court Judge Maria I. Lopez admitted that as she took the witness stand in her own disciplinary hearing that she behaved inappropriately during her handling of the child sexual assault case in September 2000. Judge Lopez acknowledged that she harassed Assistant District Attorney Loera Joseph by saying: "She belonged in the suburbs and the kind of woman who stays home, does her nails and goes to the beauty parlor (*CNN*: 2002).

Verbal words, body language, body exposures, and vulgar hints of a sexual nature or with sexual overtones affect employees, work quality and performance. More direct forms of sexual harassment are staring with touching, full and partial exposure of sexual organs, joking, and gratuitous discussion of sex.

In 1993 the Supreme Court set up a test for hostile environments. Tresa Harris, a manager in a Nashville company that rented forklifts, filed an EEOC complaint due to the misbehavior of the company president, Charles Hardy. Over years Hardy asked Harris to serve coffee in meetings. He asked Harris and other female employees to fish coins out of his front pants pockets and sometimes threw objects on the floor, asking the women to pick them up while he commented on their breasts and clothing. He proposed negotiating Harris's pay rises at a Holiday Inn and suggested that she try giving sexual favors to get forklift rentals. When Harris complained and threatened to quit, Hardy apologized and she stayed, but his boorishness resumed (Stainer and Stainer, 2003: 645).

The Title VII, the Equal Employment Opportunity Commission (EEOC) guidelines (1980) define sexual harassment as follows:

> Unwelcome sexual advances, requests for sexual favors, and other verbal or physical conduct of a sexual nature constitute sexual harassment when (1) submission to such conduct is made either explicitly or implicitly a term or condition of an individual's employment, (2) submission to or rejection of such conduct by an individual is used as the basis for employment decisions affecting such an individual, or (3) such conduct

has the purpose or effect of unreasonably interfering with an individual's work performance or creating an intimidating, hostile, or offensive working environment.

The courts in the United States have recognized sexual harassment as offensive conducts ranging from blatant grabbing and touching to more subtle hints and suggestions about sex. Also, within ethical and moral contextual conducts there have recognized seven types of sexual harassment. The most serious forms include touching and blatant grabbing of sexual organs and demand for sexual favors or physical assaults. Heyes (1991: B1) found different forms of sexual harassment:

1. Unwelcome sexual advances.
2. Sexual coercion.
3. Sexual favoritism.
4. Indirect sexual harassment through creating hostile work environments.
5. Physical contacts including touching and blatant grabbing.
6. Visual harassment including graffiti was written on men's bathroom walls about a female employee and when pornographic pictures or movies were displayed in the workplace.
7. Psychologically, sexual harassment can threat health and safety conditions of employees in the workplace.
8. When pornographic pictures and/or videotapes were displayed and/or shown in the workplace.

These unethical and immoral behaviors reinforce male or female power in work settings. By treating young females as sex objects, male employees place them in the stereotyped role of submissive females, thereby subordinating and marginalizing them. Cockburn (1991: 142) interpreted such a stereotyping perception as: "You're only a woman, that's the way I see you. And at that level you are vulnerable to me and any man."

The Supreme Court of the United States ruled in 1986 that sexual harassment is illegal under Title VII of the 1964 Civil Rights Act and that when a hostile environment is created through sexual harassment in the workplace, thereby interfering with an employee's performance, the law is violated, regardless of whether economic harm is done or whether demands for sexual favors in exchange for raises, promotions, bonuses, and other employment-related opportunities are granted (Machlowitz and Machlowitz, 1986).

There is no mathematically precise testing and/or proving what constitutes a hostile work environment and/or sexual harassment. Nevertheless, through moral convictions and ethical principles sexual harassment should be examined with respect to its truthful claims, frequency, and severity whether it is physically threatening or humiliating, and/or whether it is unreasonably interferes with work. In addition, according to several European experts, sexual harassment is a workplace menace. The Dutch Ministry of Social Affairs has compared it to the risk of stumbling over equipment, or of excessive noise-dangers that responsible employers try to minimize (Bernstein: 2000: 157).

WHO IS LIABLE IN SEXUAL HARASSMENT IN A FIRM?

To keep the workplace environment morally and ethically clean is one of the tasks of the management team. But to keep the personal behavior of individuals moral and ethical is related to the societal cultural value systems and managers on behalf of employers are liable for subordinates, good conduct. If the managers know of any unethical and immoral actions have happened in the workplace, they need to take immediate and appropriate action to correct the situation. Sometimes employers need to provide managers and subordinates with ethical and moral training programs. Employers need to develop policies to prevent sexual harassment and hostile environments. Employers may be liable for harassment of non-employees under the same conditions as stated for coworkers.

There are three distinctive international sexual harassment liabilities:

- *An individual Employee's Moral Liability Style*: Since each individual employee is responsible for his/her own conduct, therefore, he/she will be liable for any type of misbehavior in an organization. The company will not be liable for sexual harassment because it is not related to the task of that organization. There is an argument that sexual harassment is not viewed as an organizational work behavior. It is an individual's personal behavior. Therefore, there is no legal binding ground for sexual behavioral standardization in an organization.

- *A company's ethical liability style*: Since a corporation is viewed legally as an artificial person, therefore any misbehavior within the contextual activities of such an entity can cause a corporation to be liable. With regard to the workplace ethical and moral environment, the courts have treated sexual harassment as a form of discrimination and distinguished two types. The first, *quid pro quo* (This for that or giving of one thing for another) occurs when sexual favors are made the condition of employment opportunities. The second occurs when a sexually hostile environment affects an employee's ability to function effectively. Therefore, sexual harassment cannot be resolved independently of the moral issues surrounding it.

- *An interconnected individual employee and a company's cultural style*: Since sexual harassment is viewed as a cultural trend in the workplace, it cannot be viewed as a sole liability of a supervisor. It is viewed as violating cultural dignity of labor. The civil rights of workers respect freedom of the community. In American culture, sexual harassment refers to a firm's beliefs about ethicality and default. Dignity refers to human rights. Labor dignity connects harassed workers with documented unjust treatment of workers in the workplace. Through such an interpretation, sexual harassment violates civil rights of employees and prevents them from enjoying freedom, rights, and entitlements. Europeans, generally speaking, are more likely to believe that outsiders, particularly courts of law, are ill-qualified to sort out the merits of all but the simplest sexually charges situations (Bernstein, 2000: 158). Pollack (2000: 160) indicates: "Hence sexual harassment has not pervaded the social conscientiousness of Japan... Experts say the root cause of sexual harassment in Japan is that women have a secondary status in society over all."

CHAPTER SUMMARY

The ethical and moral workforce characteristics are aging, parents working conditions, child labor, women and minority discrimination, sexual harassment, and unequal pay including incentives and benefits. The moral and ethical workplace characteristics are competitive pay, benefits and opportunities to develop skills and enhance innovative conditions of the workplace, recognition of reciprocal employers-employees rights and duties, mutual respect and dignity among stakeholders, upgrading quality of lifestyle, and above all safety, security, health, and wellness in the workplace.

In a free market economy, employer and employee rights and duties are based on bargaining power assumptions and values. In the private sector of economy, employers try to control the labor force and consumption in the marketplace. Employees seek to increase their wages/salaries, incentives, and benefits in order to improve working conditions, to enhance their family lives, and to ensure their job security.

The erosion of employees, rights by selfish desires of employers has become a common unethical and immoral theme in the business world as a result of a growing number of legal challenges to the common-law doctrine of employment-at-will (EAW). This has allowed employers to terminate an employee without considerations of due process or just cause. Employment-at-will is a uniquely American doctrine. It is traced back to the time of slavery.

In discussing employees, rights including compensation, the question of wage levels often goes beyond organizational decision-making processes. Are we talking about wages that are legal, ethical, or moral? Such a discussion can be addressed by analyzing three major philosophies: (1) Wage Slavery, (2) Living Survival Wage, and (3) Sustainable Just Wage.

Wage slavery is a political ideology that allows for barely meeting immediate for needs of employees, including basic foods, used clothing, and minimal shelters. Human trafficking and forced labor in sweatshops and industrial homework settings are among those unethical and immoral activities of wage slavery. The living survival wage system is balanced human resource costs with the ability to attract and keep employees busy with minimum compensation. Generally, the wage system has three components (1) pay, (2) Incentives, and (3) Benefits. The pay is defined as the basic compensation an employee receives in cash, usually as a wage or salary. Wages should sufficiently provide them appropriate opportunities to meet all of the above objectives in their lifetime. In addition, morally all workers, like their employers, expect to have continuous incomes in order to have decent lives.

Just, fair, and worthy wages for workers should reflect the real contributions that employees make to their corporations. As corporations enjoy decent development, growth, and profitability through the hard working habits of their workers, commensurately employees expect to be paid fairly and justly through profit sharing. It is important in this endeavor to define decent wages or salaries not as bare minimum but as those maximum compensations in order to elevate employees, lifestyles and of their community members as a whole towards more progress and achievement.

Among the most important conditions of a healthy workplace life is the fact that decisions about the workplace by employers affect: (1) the quality of life, (2) the ethical and moral considerations of life, (3) the economic well-being of life, (4) The socio-cultural conditions of life, and (5) The politico-legal status of life.

Job ownership is a relatively new phenomenon and usually joined to some extent with government ownership. Job ownership spells out certain managerial saving rights by employers to own specific occupations either by a group of capital holders and investors or by a group of certified or licensed professionals (e.g., physicians, lawyers, taxi drivers, or special governmental owned groups like military and law enforcement officers, secret service and informant officers, inspectors, judges, etc.).

One of the major issues in the field of business is productivity. What is productivity? Productivity is a measure of efficiency; doing the things right. Measuring the output of a particular product and dividing it by the number hours worked by the employees who produced threat product would obtain a measure of employee productivity.

Insider trading as buying or selling of stocks on the basis of privileged information available only to a select few. It is widely regarded as unethical and is illegal in the United States, as well as a large number of European and Asian countries. Moral fairness focuses on the disparity of information between the two parties; buyers and sellers of securities; to the transaction. Moralists believe that trading in securities should take place on an open level playing field and disparities in acquisition of information tilt the field toward one player and away from the other. Another serious ethical issue is the harming theses that hold that insider trading erodes investors, confidence in the security exchange market and causes investors to pull out their investments from the stock market. If investors do not have assurance that the security exchange processes functions impartially, consequently they will not have any inclination to invest their monies in the security exchange market. The market will be harmed accordingly and will not be able to perform its role of allocating capital resources in our economy. There are amoral investors who believe that insider information can be seen as a form of property, much like trade secrets and inventions. Insider trading information concerning a corporation is viewed as a competitive key for success. Therefore, those investors who own information are entitled to sell them to any other investors as they wish.

Job shop rights, employees, rights for making free choices of their employers, and trade secrets are very complex and challenging issues in the field of business. Expert knowledge including know-how knowledge, know-what knowledge, know-where knowledge, know-for knowledge, and know-whom knowledge are subjects of controversial ethical and moral issues in today's competitive market. Who owns technical production procedures and operational skills in an organization; employers as investors or employees as experts? Who owns scientific knowledge; patent holders and copyrighters or researchers? Who owns a corporation's trade secrets; employers or employees? How an expert may keep a company's trade secret and not to disclose it to others? Can an expert carry it to his/her new employer and disclose his/her expert knowledge to them? Are experts virtually viewed as a company's permanent employees or they are employers, slaves beyond their employment termination? These issues are highly complicated through moral, ethical, and legal deliberations.

Men and women can speak the same language universally. Can men communicate with women as men communicate among themselves or *vice versa*? One must answer these and other similar questions case by case. However, we assume that similarly they should be able to perceive and understand each other equally. If the latter proposition is true, then in an organization do women exert the same managerial power within the workplace as men do? Some researchers indicate that the gender typing of referent-power is less straightforward, because referent-power is based on perceived identification. By nature, women are communicative, intuitive, nurturing, sensitive, supportive, and persuasive. Researchers found that most women have a higher sense of the importance of long-term relationships. Women's sense of importance to long-term relationships and their natural instinct bring to mind the more personal issues. It is a traditional fact in the Western civilization, when an Occidental culturally oriented women considers an advancement in her career, she elevates personal career over family concerns; such trends is not are acceptable in Oriental cultures. There are two different types of analysis to view gender ethics in the workplace. First, we assume that both genders of male and female should be equally treated as a unified system. This is known as equalitarianism. Second, we assume that both genders possess distinctive characteristics within and beyond domain of their gender characteristics that should be analyzed separately This is known as equitabilitarianism.

Equalitarianism gender ethics is identified as assuming equal rights and duties in an organization for both genders; masculine and feminine goodness. According to this view employees are considered as abstract variables that represent societal reminiscent of equalitarian discussions of the encumbered. Equitabilitarian gender ethics is assuming that rights and duties for masculine and feminine individuals in an organization should be equitable with their particular characteristics. Equitabilitarianism gender ethics views masculine and feminine ethics as the same in principle but in practical reality they are slightly different from each other. Sometimes women and men are independent entities whose assessments are based on particularism treatments in an organization that creates double standard policies and procedures.

Sexual favoritism, request for sexual favors, office romances, sexual jokes, and consensual sexual advances between supervisors and subordinates and/or among peers are not uncommon. Office romance between male and female employees including managers and subordinates has created a minefield that sometimes abuses organizational integrity.

Verbal words, body language, body exposures, and vulgar hints of a sexual nature or with sexual overtones affect employees, work quality and performance. More direct forms of sexual harassment are staring with touching, full and partial exposure of sexual organs, joking, and gratuitous discussion of sex.

CHAPTER QUESTIONS

- Identify five major moral and ethical trends in five generations of the Twentieth century.
- Identify moral tensions and ethical conflicts associated with five types of the 20th century generations.
- What are inherent moral and ethical side effects of employment-at-will?
- How does employment-at-will serve the economic objectives of employers?
- What does the term moral entitlement mean as it relates to community wellbeing?
- Do you agree that employees should have legal entitlements to some rights in the workplace? If yes explain why.
- How do you assess the present equal or equitable wages and salaries of managers and employees in the workplace?
- Do you believe sexual harassment refers only to women? If yes, explain why.
- What are some arguments for and against sexual favoritism for male and female employees?
- In sexual favoritism which gender benefits?
- Describe criteria used to determine whether verbal or physical actions constitute sexual harassment.
- Have you been sexually harassed by your supervisors and/or coworkers in your workplace? Explain how.

- Have you been sexually harassed by the opposite gender? Explain how and why.
- What should be the ethical and moral rights and duties in the workplace?
- Should corporate managers prevent sexual harassment in the workplace? Explain how and why.
- What are different philosophical foundations of gender discrimination of equalitarianism and equitabilitarianism.

CASE STUDY

WHEN A CEO IS DISLOYAL TO THE STAKEHOLDERS: THE FRAUD AND CORRUPTION IN ADELPHIA CABLE CORPORATION

Adelphia Business Solutions Inc. is one of the nation's leading cable companies with more than 5.5 million residential customers nationwide. In addition to cable entertainment, Adelphia offers digital cable, high-speed Internet access, long distance telephone service, home security and paging. Adelphia Media Services, the cable advertising division, continues to grow in magnitude along with the Adelphia organization. Adelphia, which is a public company, is now the sixth-largest cable company in the United States.

The founder and chief executive of the company, John J. Rigas, along with two of his sons and two other Adelphia executives were recently indicted by a federal grand jury, charging them with conspiracy, securities fraud, wire fraud and bank fraud. The five of them were accused of stealing hundreds of millions of dollars from Adelphia, which is considered the most serious of the Bank fraud and can carry a penalty of as much as 30 years in prison.

The bankruptcy occurred primarily due to the centralization of authority. As the Rigas were founders of the company, they could utilize their authority in manipulating the company's policies and money according to their convenience. Hence, they could misappropriate public funds from Adelphia and use it for buying stocks and their personal use.

The Rigases set up a system of buying stock in Adelphia whenever the company issued new shares so that their holdings would not be diluted. To assure themselves the capital to buy the stock for a total of about $423 million, the indictment says, they set up a credit line that allowed the family to borrow the same, with the loans guaranteed by Adelphia, while increasing the company's debt load. False documents were drawn up to make it look as if the family members paid money for their stock, according to the indictment.

The Rigas family was accused of using $252 million in company money to buy stock through margin loans, interest payments on loans for which they had put up Adelphia stock as collateral. The fraud caused losses to stockholders amounting to more than $60 billion, the complaint said. The Rigases are also accused of taking an additional $52 million from the company for their personal use, including development of a golf course. Each of the defendants is charged with one count of conspiracy, 16 counts of securities fraud, five counts of wire fraud and two counts of bank fraud.

Defending himself, John Rigas said that he and his sons were not guilty and that borrowing agreements were "legal and entirely proper and were approved and ratified by Adelphia's outside directors and audited by its independent accountants. John Rigas's lawyer Peter Fleming Jr. scolded prosecutors for forcefully arresting a 78-year old man at 6 A.M. when he volunteered to surrender. Jermey H. Temkin, lawyer of Timothy, son of John Rigas, hints public arrest may have been politically motivated as part of Washington's effort to demonstrate its prosecution of corporate fraud amid crumbling confidence among investors in stock market.

CASE QUESTIONS FOR DISCUSSION

•   What immoral and unethical factors do you think have caused the problems in the above case? Present your arguments.
•   What changes do you suggest should be made in the management policies of a corporation in order to avoid the kind of problems faced in the above case?
•   In what way could the bankruptcy of the Rigas family have affected the company's shares?
•   Explain.The Rigas family could misappropriate funds from the company and use them for personal gain due to the centralized authority in their hands. How far do you support the above statement?
•   What should be the role of the Security Exchange Commission – SEC – concerning this type of corporate fraud and corruption? Explain.

CASE SOURCES

Andrew Ross Sorkin (2002). "Founder of Adelphia and 2 Sons Arrested"
Late Edition – Final, Section C, Page 1, Column 3. (July 25); Business Desk.

Geraldine Fabricant (2002). "Fraud Indictments at Adelphia" (May 15).

CHAPTER 13

ETHICS OF CAPITAL FLIGHT MOVEMENTS AND MONEY LAUNDERING AROUND THE WORLD

If you are expecting you and all other people to be normal,
what you find is abnormality because normality is an ideal.

If your mind is contaminated with greed, your life proceeds with stinginess,
and you will be as greedy at the end as you were without greed at the beginning.

If you have not the eyes to see where are you walking through in your life,
you will learn nothing about coping with fear and deceit.

If you keep your mind and your judgmental perception clean,
you can learn a great deal of clean thoughts from intellectual people.

If you want to get away from inhumane dilemmas,
you need to polish your mind and open your eyes with interest in humaneness.

CHAPTER OBJECTIVES

When you have read this chapter you should be able to do the following:

- Develop conceptual skills to understand the concept and magnitude of the capital flight movements around the globe.
- Analyze ethical and moral attributions concerning the concepts of capital ownership and capital control.
- Develop a framework of critical analysis to discuss issues concerning the capital flight movement rights.
- Define different types and spheres of money-power from the standpoint of moral, ethical, and legal value systems.
- Understand global econo-political implications and visible and invisible money-power role players in the international free market economy.
- Understand the complexity of the global financier alliances strategies and how they maintain their financial power in the global markets.
- Analyze the holistic characteristics of money-power free markets and the black money-power market.
- Define global perceptions concerning clean money-power, dirty money-power, free-money-power, money-power cleansing, and money laundering.
- Define and analyze the twelve techniques for money-power cleansing in the global financial markets.
- Understand different types of money-cleansing: Smurfing, Legitimate Businesses, Foreign Currency Exchange, Daisy, Chaining, Brokerage House, Double Invoicing, Reverse Flip, Loan Back, Underground Banking, Sex Industry, Illegal Sale of Wildlife, and *Havala*.

THOUGHT STARTER

Switzerland, New York City, and London are known as three major financial hobs in the world for the daily international capital flight movements. Some of the financial transactions are legitimate and legal and some are illegitimate and illegal. Nevertheless, bribery, corruption, tax evasion, and embezzlement are evident at all levels of the international financial community. There are different types of unethical, immoral, and illegal capital flight movements around the world ranging from petty corruption to huge criminal operations. In addition to the sale of illegal drugs and arms, there are other corrupt activities such as the illegal sale of wildlife, prostitution, frauds, briberies, payolas, kickbacks, embezzlements, inside trading and securities fraud, tax evasion, siphoning off international financial aid funds, the illegal and irregular sale of mineral substances (such as Uranium), the sale of information, kidnapping for ransoms, slavery, sweat shops, human trafficking, and others.

What a horrible world of unethical, immoral, and illegal we live in.
Johnson (2001: 122) states:

> The Durban Declaration called for the return of wealth plundered by
> corrupted leaders. The Financial Task Force (FATF), the Financial
> Stability Forum (FSF), and the OECD all identified countries with
> unregulated or poorly regulated financial systems, which encourage
> money laundering and the US Senate, identified problems with
> corresponding banking.

Wright (2002: 239) reports:

> In July (2001), a London solicitor was sentenced to seven years'
> imprisonment for laundering 30 million British pounds, being the proceeds
> of drugs and other unaccustomed substances that one of his clients had
> smuggled into the country. In 1998, the operator of a bureau de change in
> Notting Hill Gate in west London was sentenced to 14 years in prison four
> laundering an even larger sum.

Corruption of some governmental authorities in conjunction with private
financial sectors for what used to be called receiving, or fencing the proceeds of
crime is a kind of dirty money-power movement which is notable in the survival
of some authoritarian political leaders. It is not ethical to rule that all solicitors,
auditors, accountants, bankers, inspectors, governmental authorities, and
professionals in the financial services are dishonest. In addition to the above
unethical and illegal authorities, casinos and the more down-market betting
shops are other uncontrolled methods for the international capital flights from
one country to another. Casinos use camouflaged businesses through securities
and commodities brokers to move capital around the world. The most dynamic
camouflaged business persons and/or institutions are bankers, accountants,
auditors, real estate agents, legal advisors, diamond traffickers, precious metal
dealers, airlines, ship-lines, railroads, trucking companies, casino operators,
foreign exchange agencies, arms dealers, drug dealers, terrorist organizations,
organized crime authorities, import and export traders, forwarding agencies,
immigrants, hotel and resort chains, cabaret and nightclub operators, and others.
In sum, the purpose of all these unethical and illegal individuals and entities is to
make free-money with profit. What type of profit? Huge profits. It doesn't
matter whether it is through fraud or trafficking in drugs, arms, or immigrants.
These individuals and institutions are looking for huge profits, which cannot be
conveniently, be kept in cash.

PLAN OF THIS CHAPTER

The ethics of financial institutions including the banking system has come
under increased scrutiny as a result of the September 11, 2001 terrorists attacks

on the World Trade Towers in New York and on the Pentagon in Washington DC. The United States and the United Nations have tried to freeze assets of those terrorist individuals and groups who supported international terrorist acts. Also, the unethical capital flight movements among nations and businesses are many. In this chapter we shall deal with ethical and moral issues in capital flight movements along with analysis of clean-money, dirty-money, cleansing-money, free-money, and money laundering.

Circulation of dirty-money through the black money-power market is a complex process. A number of unethical and illegal activities other than the sale of illegal drugs, arms, and human trafficking feed the dirty money-power cycle. They include, but are not limited to, illegal wildlife sales, sex industry, child pornographic movies and internet sites, fraud and embezzlement, inside trading and securities fraud, bribery and corruption, tax evasion, siphoning off of aid funds to developing nations, and the sale of oil outside of OPEC or UN sanctions. These and other types of dirty-money power go hand in hand with the activities of business criminal rings around the world.

INTRODUCTION

Power has evolved through different types of material and non-material ownerships of different valuable things, including money-power. The old beliefs associated with the individualism ideology of utilizing physical and mental power to pursue self-interest through personal enjoyments are still valid today. However, the older view of unrestrained individualism money-power has been modified by the concepts of either pluralism or collectivism through socio-cultural value systems, econo-political doctrines, and religious combination of material and spiritual faiths in organizations -- namely nations, states, locals, corporations, companies, firms, organizations, institutions, groups, shrines, and places of worship (e.g., Temples, Churches, Mosques, Ministries, *Atashgah, Madares, Mahfel,* and *Khonegah)*. These concepts have been modified and protected by global governmental power-holding competition. Specifically, capital flight movements around the globe have emerged through identification of moral and immoral, ethical and unethical, and legal and illegal aspects of economic activities. Over ground and underground capital flight movements; either explicitly criminal or merely informal (which may mean evading taxes on otherwise lawful activities) interact at many levels with legal ones.

In developing countries, the masses of street vendors in large cities sell goods that might be smuggled, brand counterfeits, stolen from legitimate businesses, or confiscated by governmental authorities that may pay no sales or income taxes, but provide payments to governmental officials (as bribery) and/or drug dealers that control the streets or cities where they operate. Then the drug dealers, bootleggers, and corrupted governmental authorities use the protection money as operational capital to finance wholesale purchases of legitimate commodities and/or drugs by individuals or arms by governmental partisan groups to channel the funds, perhaps paying in cash, in *havala,* or in precious stones, gold bars, and gold coins. The result of these and many other similar sorts of money transactions is an economic complexity that cannot easily be explained by the differences between clean-money and dirty-money. Within such a complex process, the role of banks and financial institutions is very crucial. The banking industry and financial institutions typically make profit by serving their customers through their investments or loaning money they receive as deposits at higher rates of return than the interest they pay on deposits. In addition, within the international banking systems these institutions receive forwarding fees as a commission. Also, as much as possible of the client funds remain in the bank accounts, so bankers will be able to circulate them by lending to other people and receive interest. Bankers lend money to viable and credible customers as mortgage loans, business loans, car loans, student loans, credit card loans and others. As bankers and financial institutions as much as receive more deposits, they profit more. Bankers and financial institutions are looking for those customers that deposit large sum of money either as their certified deposits (CDs) and/or transferred funds. Therefore, banks and financial institutions are viewed as a safe heaven for investors to deposit their legal and legitimate assets and/or for business rings and criminals to use as offshore reserved institutions.

THE GLOBAL OFFSHORE FINANCIAL CENTERS

Global power-holding competition is viewed as a techno-political rivalry among wealthy individuals and nations. There is no doubt that the capital flight movements have drifted to offshore finance centers and/or to accounts of individuals and groups who have lucrative economic gains. Within the international financial market place, there are specific countries that are known as Offshore Finance Centers (e.g., Swiss banks, Caribbean Islands banks, Cayman Islands banks, etc.). Historically these banks have provided tax shelters for global capital holders by offering them with very low or zero tax rates along very low interest rates too, and very safe and secret accounts. Generally, in the global politico-financial markets, there are two major invisible power groups: (1) the invisible new world order and (2) the invisible black-market world order. Sometimes these two power groups are highly coordinated through some countries' camouflaged front businesses organizations that are affiliated with the secret national security and information agencies.

The international and national banking industry has gone through different phases of regulations according to their chartering characteristics. There are different types of banks and financial institutions. The International Monetary Fund, The World Bank, central banks, investment banks, commercial banks, industrial and mines banks, savings banks and others are different banks. There are also a variety of other financial institutions, such as savings and loan associations, insurance companies, pension funds, and brokerage houses, which are involved in financing and investing. A large number of ethical issues arise when considering the capital flight movements of these financial institutions. Specifically, among the more crucial problems, savings and loan associations, or thrifts, have been established to provide mortgages for individual homeowners. The original mission of these associations was to provide mortgages for local real estate owners both residential and commercial loans. These institutions receive deposits from local patrons who would get a basic rate of interest, and in return they lend those funds to local people with higher interest rates for buying and/or for building homes. The Federal Government in the United States, through the Federal Savings and Loan Insurance Corporation (FSLIC), guaranteed the safety of all patrons' deposits made in such institutions up to $100,000.00 per depositor. In 1989, fraud and corruption contaminated some of the 3,000 U.S. Savings and Loan Associations. Of these associations, 515 thrifts were insolvent. Since all certified deposits up to $100,000.00 were covered through insurance by the federal government, no depositor lost money. American taxpayers, for an estimated total of up to $200 billion, covered the losses. Among these thrifts, the famous highly corrupted CEO Charles Keading was fined and sentenced to jail for the crime of fraud and embezzlements.

As De George (1990: 309) indicates, in 1972, Agha Hasan Abedi, a Pakistani banker, convinced Sheik Zayed of Abu Dhabi (one of the rulers of the United Arab Kingdom) to use some of his vast oil-generated income to fund a Karachi-based bank that would compete with Western banks and serve to help less developed countries. The bank was chartered in Luxembourg and grew to control more than $20 billion in 400 branches and subsidiaries located in over 70 countries. BCCI effectively escaped any effective government control for almost twenty years. BCCI was a safe haven for corrupt authoritarian governments, money launderers, drug lords, international illegal arms dealers, wealth siphoned by corrupted rulers of developing countries, and secret governmental agencies, the PLO, Manuel Noriega of Panama, Saddam Hussein of Iraq, and others. Finally, in 1991, authorities in the United States and Britain closed all its branches and depositors could receive their monies through federally insured policies. Other individuals and countries lost their deposits an estimated $10 billion in losses. These are among numerous banking irregularities and fraud cases. The ethical question is raised: How can some governments use such a group of rogue banks to deposit their monies? Unfortunately, amoral statements label the answer to this question.

THE UNITED NATIONS TEN LAWS FOR CAPITAL FLIGHT MOVEMENTS

Blum *et al.*, (1998) identified certain international rules for capital flight movements around the world that are mandated by the United Nations. The United Nations-commissioned team has developed the following ten laws for its members:

- Law One: the more successful a money-laundering apparatus is in imitating the patterns and behavior of legitimate transactions, the less the likelihood of it being exposed.
- Law Two: the more deeply embedded illegal activities are within the legal economy, the less their institutional and functional separation, the more difficult to detect money laundering.
- Law Three: the lower the ratio of illegal to legal financial flows through any given business institution, the more difficult it will be to detect money laundering.
- Law Four: the higher the ratio of service to physical goods protection in any economy, the more easily money-laundering can be conducted in that economy.
- Law Five: the more the business structure of production and distribution of non-financial goods and services is dominated by small and independent firms or self-employed individuals, the more difficult the job of separating legal from illegal transactions.
- Law Six: the greater the facility for using cheques, credit cards and other non-cash instruments for effecting illegal financial transactions, the more difficult is the detection of money-laundering.
- Law Seven: the greater the degree of financial deregulation of legitimate transactions, the more difficult will be the job of tracing and neutralizing criminal money flows
- Law Eight: the lower the ratio of illegally to legally earned income entering any given economy from outside, the harder the job of separating criminal from legal money.
- Law Nine: the greater the progress towards the financial services supermarket, the greater the degree to which all manner of financial services can be met within one integrated multidivisional institution, the less the functional and institutional separation of financial activities, the more difficult the job of detecting money-laundering.
- Law Ten: the worse the current contribution between global operation and national regulation of financial markets becomes, the more difficult the detection of money laundering.

Hampton and Levi (1999: 648) constructed an international index of *susceptibility* to money laundering using the above criteria. They added another law that indicates the degree of *corruptibility* that is necessary only if regulation national or international is attempted.

ANALYSIS OF CAPITAL OWNERSHIP AND CAPITAL CONTROL

Within the contextual analysis of capital ownership, there are two major views concerning possession of wealth: (1) physical or material ownership and (2) non-physical or conventional valuable phenomena. Property ownership is identified only with physical objects like houses, cars, computers, and video recorders. Non-physical ownership is identified by a simple relationship between the owner and the things owned. Within this category, one can have property rights over things that are not simple physical objects, as we own money, stocks of a company, copyrights, patents and others. Non-physical ownerships involve a generally complex bundle of rights and duties governing how, under what circumstances, and in what ways both the owners and users can possess, use, dispose of, and have access to the things in question.

Within property ownership, we need to clarify who *owns* and who is in *control* of those properties. In the field of business, company managers, whether themselves owners or non-owners are always in charge of operations, by tacit or explicit leave of the big owners. The ethical issue of control is seldom raised in resources allocation in a corporation. But when it is, as most recently with large corporations such as Enron, WorldCom, Adelphia, Kmart and others, the stockholders walked away with nothing and CEOs walked away with everything. After bankruptcy of the above corporations, it is assumed that all large U.S. Corporations are owned by everybody and nobody, and are run or only controlled by executives.

The concept of ownership is directly related to the trends of territorial protectionism. In the publicly owned corporations, capital control rests with a small number of owners (as distinct from non-owning executives and many small stockholders). In no cases, except when a company is under court-sanctioned trustees, can it be shown that ownership is divorced from control. This means that governments in all nations represent their citizens and residents in exchanging material and non-material thing with other alien individuals and groups. Both material and non-material ownerships are viewed as the results of governmental regulations concerning the values of properties including material and intellectual properties monetary values.

As the direct result of government regulations, societies have been faced with comparative societal value systems, the rights of property ownerships, and the rights of property value movements. Although intellectuals in democratic nations enjoy considerable autonomy in the use and movements of their intellectual properties such as copyrights, patent rights, trade mark rights, brand name rights, shop rights, and theoretical and practical innovative rights, both material properties such as money, precious mineral stones and metals, and real estates (e. g., commercial buildings and plants, residential premises, and industrial and agricultural lands and fields) are more defined, regulated, and managed through monetary value systems.

THE CAPITAL FLIGHT MOVEMENT RIGHTS

When people move from one geographical location to another, they may move their movable properties including intellectual rights, physically moveable material things and/or their valuable things in terms of capital (e.g., stocks, shares, trust, cash money, savings, credits, etc.). In collectivistic societies both human physical and monetary material movements are highly limited and regulated, while in pluralistic countries such as the United States only monetary material movements are highly regulated through "The Bill of Rights." Through The Bill of Rights, there seemed to be no limit to the numbers of groups and individuals seeking rights in all financial transactions. Capital flight movements to or from a country create econo-political complexities.

Businesses, as the major institutions of society, have an ever-expanding array of capital flight movements with specific entitlements. The capital right movements are interrelated with moral, ethical, and legal power-commitments within different sectors of society. Critics' capital flight movements in the global markets say businesses are too powerful by having money-power. Businesses pollute the environment, exploit people for their own gains, take advantage of workers and consumers, and very easily move their capitals from one location to another. People complain that businesses use and abuse nations for the sake of material gains. Some of the points of friction between businesses and the public include globalization, corporate bankrolling of politicians, sweatshops, urban sprawl, wages, money laundering, and tax evasion. The major criticism of businesses is to be that in addition to the use or abuse of money-power is related to engaging questionable or unethical money-power movements.

WHAT IS MONEY-POWER?

What is money-power? The nature of money is related to neutral valuable purchase power. Money, by its nature through long historical events, is valuable because people invented it in order to represent appreciation of their hard work at the time of exchange. Money has been used as a medium for exchanging and measuring values. It is considered as a property with reference to its pecuniary value. Money could be perceived in the forms of metal coins (e.g., gold, silver, bronze, etc), bank certificates, bank drafts, bank checks, travelers' checks, or banknotes generally accepted in payment of debts and current transactions.

Whether money is perceived as good or evil depends on the behavioral perceptions of money owners and money controllers. Money-power refers to the ability or capacity of individuals, groups, organizations, and nations to produce an effect (good or evil) or to bring influence to bear on a situation or provide people with some privileges for the benefit of money-power holders. Money-power, in and of it, may be good or evil, positive or negative, legitimate or illegitimate, ethical or unethical, and legal or illegal. It depends who owns it or who controls it. Money certainty carries enormous power. In sum, when money-power intermingles with political-power, then their synergistic result creates an enormous power to manipulate the market place and to be conceived as threats to the liberty of citizens. Within the global political diplomacy, money-power plays enormous roles in peace and war. If a nation has not been successful in its commercial productive trade, then politicians turn that nation towards corruption.

In political systems, there are two major systems of money-power: (1) campaign contributions and (2) kickbacks. Campaign contributions come from the affluent and well positioned businesses the wealthy individuals, corporate executives and lawyers, government contractors including hoodlum and hoodwink businesses, stock brokers, influence-seekers, and friends of the candidates. Kickbacks are illegitimate soft-monies that flow secretly among political and wealthy people in order to manipulate the public interest for the purpose of personal gains. Kickbacks are viewed as capital flight movements among power holders and affluent individuals and/or organizations in the forms of *informal* money allocations. It is viewed as a considerable deviation from the *formal* ethical, moral, and legal script in a nation and among nations. Money-power possesses the ability to bend freely ethical, moral, and legal rules in a corrupted society. As Lundberg (1972: 893) indicates:

> More diligent members will of necessity exercise power not exercised by dilatory members of any functioning organization, a universal rule applying to corruption, fraternal societies, and labor unions as well as to government.

We will not settle this issue here, but the allegation that money-power very easily can abuse people remains the central part of business ethics.

Sphere of Money-Power

In addition to the kinds of money-power, there are also many different spheres or arenas in which money-power may manifest good or evil consequences. Sometimes the nature of money-power is causal (deontological); that is, it is not wielded intentionally but nevertheless exerts its influence even though no attempt is made to exercise it (Epstein, 1973: 11). Sometimes the nature of money-power is consequential (teleological) such as when a landlord or a corporation purchases huge parcels of land within a city or around a city. That money-power will generate enormous power within the various city institutions and their effective functions. If those parcels of land have been purchased for establishing factories, land fields, industrial plants, commercial buildings, or residential properties, each will carry different effects over the neighboring land values. There are three major spheres of money-power: (1)

international money-power market, (2) national based money-power market, and (3) black money-power market.

The International Money-Power Market

The international money-power market refers to economic, political, sociocultural, technological, ecological, and individual status of money-power holding nations. For example, representatives of the major allied powers established the international money-power institutions such as International Monetary Fund (IMF in 1944). They met at Britton Woods, New Hampshire, in 1944 to plan for future stabilization of currencies values and international exchange rates and/or floating or fluctuating exchange rates. To achieve its goal, the Britton Woods Conference established the International Monetary Fund (IMF). On the basis of economic synergy of the United States of America, IMF agreed the U.S. dollar to be the only currency directly convertible into gold for official monetary purposes. An ounce of gold was agreed to be worth U. S. $35.00 and other currencies were assigned so called par values in relationship to the U.S. dollar. For example, the British pound's par value was U.S. $2.40, the French franc's was U. S. $0.18, and the German mark's was U.S. $0.2732. Such an agreement is found to be the basic criteria for valuing all nations' wealth.

The National Based Money-Power Market

Despite Karl Marx's claim that social justice is the ethical means and ends of classless societies, it is impossible to find any society classless. Therefore, all societies are hierarchical and a small number of influential people and/or institutions dominate all lay people. Within the context of national based money-power market, the concepts of *economic class, ruling class, elite class*, and *lay people class* put individuals on guard. The Industrial Revolution has dramatically changed money-power, shifting it from one industry to another. If we look at inventions and innovative technological trends throughout recorded civilization, we may find different periods of money-power shifting with rapid decreasing time-spans. The Industrial Revolution started 1785 with the inventions of waterpower, mass production of textiles, and iron beams. The first wave of invention was from 1785 to 1845. It took 60 years to move to the second wave. The second wave of inventions occurred between with 1845 and 1900. Within 55 years, steam engines, railroads, and standardized steel manufacturing had been invented. Foundations of modern automated technology changed the features of all industries. The third wave of inventions occurred between 1900 and 1950. Within 50 years of new inventions and two worldwide wars, the First World War and the Second World War, industries such as electricity, chemical, and internal- combustion engine changed the total life style of all nations. Between the years of 1950 and 1990 for 40 years, new technologies emerged and attracted the international money-power to petrochemical, electronic, and aviation industries. From 1990 to the present time new industries such as digital networking and fiber-optic communication, software and hardware, the space industry, E-commerce and the Internet, pharmaceutical, and biotechnology emerged. In the 19th and 20th centuries new inventions and innovations have been pivotal in accelerating economic and population growth. The shortening successive waves of inventions and innovativeness reveal a speeding up of technological change and money-power shifting (The Economist, 1999: 8).

From a micro-economic point of view, everyone recognizes that money-power is extremely complex. Individuals and groups view economic classes of people from different perspectives. One of these new trends is shifting accumulation of wealth from older millionaires to younger billionaires (e.g., Bill Gates, Pear Omidvar, and others). Such a shifting is viewed as the result of technological advancement and entrepreneurial innovations. The condition of these new young billionaires depends upon their interrelationships with the nature of money-power, and the volume of money-power, the processes of money-power including shifting from one industry to another (e.g., the 1970s' Seven Sisters Oil Companies; the 1980s' Oligopolistic Auto Industry; the 1990s' Computer Industry; the 2000s' biotech; biosciences; and pharmaceutical industry). The billionaires may differ radically in their motivations, moral commitments, and roles to play in societal problem making or problem solving. In addition, people may differ in their societal hierarchical levels in relationship with money-power, and they may have more influence than others. Therefore, it is important to know the fundamental conceptual frameworks that people use in viewing money-power in the levels of national marketplace.

The *economic-class* money-power visualizes the industrial organizations and institutions as substantially emerged from socio-economic forces in its environment and focuses on the primacy of money-market economy (e.g., the stock market, the bond market, the gold market, the international monetary market, etc.). The economic class people do not work for bureaucracies. Instead, they manifest their money-power through the activities of a wide variety of organizations and institutions. These organizations and institutions are financed and directed by the wealthy people. For example, as Ferraro (1995: 271) indicates: "The upper class people in the United States comprises approximately 4 percent of the population."

The *ruling-class* money-power by its virtue dominates the econo-political infrastructure and processes of governmental bureaucracies as the national regulatory agencies. These ruling class people are highly cohesive and active in dominating the great mass of ordinary people. This does not deny that the basic form of private economy has evolved from personal ownership and partnership between economic class and ruling class and shifted the money-power from families to social clubs, and think-tank institutions. Ferraro (1995: 271) indicates the upper middle-class comprises about 12 percent of the American population.

The *elite-class* money-power functions on the basis of the economic-class people's wishes or desires to be transmitted to the bulk of lay-class people. The elite-class money-power is highly dominated by both economic-class and ruling-class or in another word; plutocrats and bureaucrats dominate their money-power. It is a fact that the elite-class is viewed as a sort of monolithic intellectual power that tells people what they must do. This thesis is found in John Kenneth Galbraith's (1958) works.

The *lay-class* money-power can be included lower middle class, working-class, and lower class people's purchase power through their hard working earnings. Ferraro (1995: 271) indicates the U.S. lower middle class constitutes approximately one-third (33 percent) of the population, the working-class people comprises 45 percent of the population, and the lower-class comprises around 6 percent of the population. All of the above classes of people comprise the total money-power according to the national exchanging values that the daily rates of the American dollar's values.

The Black Money-Power Market

The underground money-power is called the *black economy* in England, the *shadow economy* in Germany, the *submerged economy* in Italy, the *black work* in France, the *underreporting economy* in the United States and the *second economy* in most other developing countries. The black money-power market is responsible for all kinds of distortions of economic data.

To clarify the nature of money-power one must recognize that it resides in and may be manifested by several kinds of means and ends. In order to examine different types of money-power through ethical principles and legal doctrines we first define different kinds of money-power such as: (1) clean money-power, (2) dirty money-power, (3) free money-power, (4) money-power cleansing, and (5) money-power laundering.

Clean Money-Power: Clean-money refers to the honest processes of capital earnings and movements within and beyond of the national borders of a country by which an individual, an institution, a group of capital holders, or governments discloses the sources of its existence, legal application of incomes, and appearance of its nature in the form of regular reporting system to the public and/or to the governmental specific agencies such as the Internal Revenue Services (IRS) or other law enforcement agencies.

Dirty Money-Power: Dirty-money may infect anyone's mind who thinks about and/or who approaches it. So people try to avoid risk-creating behavior by not approaching, thinking about or touching dirty-money. Unfortunately, there is no effective tool to regulate how dirty-money should be controlled in both micro and macro capital flight movements. International capital flight movements depend on the size, volume, and values of comparative commodities and currencies. Jurith (2002: 212) indicates:

> Large amounts of cash are difficult to transport compared to drugs. $1 million worth of heroin weighs just 22 lbs, whereas $1 million in equal amounts of $5, $10, and $20 notes weighs 271 lbs. That is more than ten times the weight of the drugs sold. Attorney General John Ashcroft recently estimated that the amount of dirty-money generated by illegal drug sales in the USA would weigh 13 million lbs.

Free Money-Power: Bribery, payola, grease money, kickbacks, under-the-table money, and illegal secret campaign contributions for political means and ends are known as free money and their symptoms are evidence of corruption at all levels of society. In a number of countries petty corruption is almost a routine way of life and considered as an unfortunate necessity for daily survival. Within the contextual boundaries of moral, ethical, and legal assessments of the above situations, the amount of money paid and/or received could be from very large amounts to one dollar.

Money-Power Cleansing: Sweatshops in big cities hire illegal aliens brought in by international human smuggling rings that may also deal in banned or restricted commodities. They are unethical, immoral, and illegal activities and financed by international loan sharks who may be recycling drug money, bribery, and making cartel agreements with transportation firms run by organized business rings. The end result of such unethical, immoral, and illegal acts is to clean their dirty-money by selling the products of these sweatshops thus cleaning their money. Also, some money launderers are very active in the tourism industry. They establish a number of camouflaged businesses as ethical and legal entities in resort areas or islands through which they intend to clean their dirty-money. These businesses provide very cheap airfares, sea-fares, or land-fares with lucrative entertainment facilities in order to absorb as many as possible tourists. These businesses will even be competitive as the profit margin is irrelevant. The main purpose is to launder the funds generated from unethical and illegal activities such as drug, sex, gambling, and bootlegging activities. In order to further launder the money, they create more businesses alongside financial institutions such banks and lending agencies. They eventually will be able to regain business power through money laundering. Although it may seem that the resort chains of businesses are benefiting from legitimate activities, the opposite is true (Munro, 2001: 135). Cacheris and O'Malley (2001:115) indicate:

> Theoretically, by perpetually and severely criminalizing all transactions where parties know they are using or receiving illegally derived proceeds, secondary parties will be reluctant to further the ablution and primary party will find it impossible to wash his hands of a criminal matter. In other words, dirty money may infect anyone who touches it.

Senguder (2002:196) has identified nine types of money cleansing: (1) smurfing, (2) legitimate Business, (3) foreign currency exchange, (4) Daisy chaining, (5) brokerage houses, (6) double-invoicing, (7) reverse flip, (8) loan back, (9) underground banking, and we are adding three more as (10) sex industry, (11) *Havala* (popular in the Asian and Middle Eastern countries), (12) illegal sale of wildlife, and (13) oil Smuggling.

Smurfing: Money traffickers employ so called *smurfs*, people of innocuous appearance to make large numbers of small transactions (less than $10,000.00) at various financial institutions. The smurf purchases either money orders or bank drafts and then deposits them in his/her various bank accounts. Smurfs are also hired to convert small denominations to larger bills or vice versa. This process is also called either money refining or money-cleansing.

Legitimate Businesses: Money traffickers often take over or invest in businesses that customarily handle a high volume of cash transactions. Retail stores, restaurants, and food stores are popular. Such a strategy creates very high cash flow for different purposes including acquisition of business loans for the purpose of business development and transferring money back to their original countries. Then the payments of the loans will be paid with dirty-money.

Foreign Currency Exchange: By buying foreign monies, traffickers can avoid conventional banks because currency exchanges keep no records that would identify the customer. In such a case the audit trail is broken. Then traffickers buy money orders, or bank drafts, and very easily they can either carry or forward it through the overnight delivery systems.

Daisy - Chaining: Similar to corporate layering, by which ultimate ownership is disguised through a series of interlocking companies that legitimate firms use to reduce taxes, money launderers employ this method as a way to legitimize income. By chaining, it becomes progressively more difficult to trace illegitimate business income either forward to the ultimate recipient or backward to the crime. The basic requirement is an offshore tax haven with bank secrecy laws.

Brokerage Houses: The money launderers place orders for securities through a brokerage house, then they stipulate payments to the brokers and forward them by couriers. Because brokerage houses generally accept large cash deposits if they believe that they are executing orders from a foreign bank, or an important customer of that bank, the drug traffickers have their dirty-money delivered through their shielded businesses. The result of such a process is money cleansing by selling securities for cash at later dates.

Double Invoicing: Another favorite tax-avoidance method by illegitimate dirty-money owners involves a trafficking organization's gaining control of corporate entities in two different jurisdictions. Then one firm orders goods from the offshore corporation at inflated prices. The difference between the inflated price and the real value is deposited in another offshore account, sometimes even in a third jurisdiction. In a capitalistic decentralized economy, the domestic corporations show a low level of profit as the last agent for such a sophisticated purchasing ordering system. Then they show low or no profit in order to avoid taxes.

Reverse Flip: The capital owner finds a co-operative property seller who agrees to a reported purchase price either below the actual market-value or separate fixed property value from movable equipments and accessories (e.g., refrigerators, dishwashers, draperies, washers and dryers, ladders, garbage compactors, air-conditioning units, mirrors, fixtures, moveable closets and kitchen tables, etc.) as depreciative goods and then accepts the difference either under the table or as non-recording valuable deals. This way a capital holder or a buyer can purchase a $1 million piece of property for $800,000.00 as the price of property and $200,000.00 as for accessories. Then, the title company can only record the $800,000,00 can as the original price of property to be recorded and taxed. Then later on the buyer can sell the property for $2,000,000.00 and cleanse his/her dirty- money.

Loan Back: International dirty-money rings try to cleanse their money through camouflaged and/or legitimate front businesses. Having established a corporation in a tax haven country, traffickers then purchase those businesses with nominal deposit. The balance is in the form of a loan from their secretly held offshore corporations. Then the traffickers borrow money from one of their own subsidiaries. Once the money launderers set up businesses at home, then they make scheduled payments on the loan as if it had been legitimate they not only repatriate illegal money, but they also pay themselves interest.

Underground Banking: This system operates through worldwide financial networking of gold shops, money changers, and trading and forwarding companies, often owned and controlled by the same conglomerate oligarchies and/or oligopolies. A money launderer merely has to deposit his/her funds in an oligarchic-owned business and/or oligopoly in one country and withdraw them from a relative business in another country. This is a very dynamic and synergistic money cleansing in most Asian and Middle Eastern countries. In these countries, corruption and bribery among government authorities and big businesses are very popular even in the secret banking systems.

Sex Industry: One of the other methods directly related to money cleansing is to the sex industry. Johnson (2001: 124) reports:

Estimates of prostitution in London alone range from 250-500 million British pounds per year. As this is mostly a cash business, the amount of money creamed off by organized criminal gangs means that a significant amount needs laundering. Another side of the sex industry is the trafficking in women, tricked and coerced into industry with offers of jobs in foreign countries.

Hughes (2000:625) reports that estimates of the global trade in women are between US $7-12 billion annually. The trade is highly profitable with relatively low risks compared to the trade in drugs and firearms. The UN estimates that a quarter of the four million people trafficked each year are for the sex industries. By looking at these issues and figures, we will find out how international trade has been converted into unethical and immoral human activities for accumulation of wealth by some nations. Nations are expanding and promoting unethical and immoral industries without regard to human dignity, integrity, and rights.

Illegal sale of wildlife

Selling wildlife products and animals are related to money laundering in the international market place. Schiffer (1997) reports:

Havala Each year, approximately US $5 billion of illegal wildlife shipments are traded around the world. There is said to be more profit generated from these sales than is generated from illegal arms sales. Bird smuggling rings are extensive and profitable.

Havala is an Arabic word that refers to a money trafficker who transfers sum of money through oral promises among traders without leaving a trace of document. In the field of international business, there are two types of agreements between traders and/or buyers and sellers: (1) the contractual agreement (2) *Havala*.

The contractual agreement: This system is a *written formal legal agreement* between parties to make a deal. Moon and Woolliams (2000: 113) have provided five types of contracts:

- A contract is a contract. It means precisely what its terms say. If the world price had risen we would not be crying, nor should they. What partnership are they talking about? We had a deal. We bargained We won. That is the end of story.
- A contract symbolizes the underlying relationship It is an honest statement of original intent. However, such rigid terms are too brittle to withstand turbulent environments. Only tacit forms of mutuality have the flexibility to survive.

- A contract is a function of both the underlying relationship and the legal system covered by it. We should split the difference.
- A contract symbolizes the underlying relationship. It is an honest statement of original intent. Where circumstances transform the mutual spirit of that contract, then terms must be negotiated to preserve the relationship.
- A contract is a contract. It means precisely what the terms say. If the world price had risen we would not be crying, nor should they. We would, however, consider a second contract whose terms would help offset their losses.

Havala: Havala is an oral moral and ethical (not legal) agreement between parties to make a deal in transferring money from one location to another. *Havala* is very popular business transaction in the Middle Eastern and some Asian countries. *Havala* is a traditional cultural system for allocation of wealth among businesses. In addition, in Moslem countries *havala* plays an important role in their systems of economy. In Moslem countries, trust and trustees among traders play an important role. Religiously, Moslems believe that they should not take any property of others by force. It is prohibited. In addition, while they are in trust to take money from others they need to return it to the original owner without taking a penny out of it. If a Moslem acts against his/her faith, it is considered a big sin. Therefore, according to their religious obligations, the process is expected to be completed during the process of transferring money from a person to another through a third party, that. Not only are both parties committed to fulfill their obligations; they are accountable to their religious faiths to fulfill their agreements, even when governments have confiscated the money. Therefore, a *havala* is viewed not only as a social contract, but also it is a religious contract with God presiding over the process of such an agreement. There are several attributions attached to *havala* as follows:

- *Havala* is viewed as a moral, ethical, and religious obligation to be executed by all parties.
- *Havala* is based on trust among parties.
- *Havala* is viewed as a very convenient system among business people avoiding the interference of governmental agencies from private business transactions.
- *Havala* is the main vehicle to facilitate agreements between buyers and sellers.
- *Havala* is the quickest method of exchanging currencies in the international money market with merely a phone call between a sender and receiver.

Oil Sale: Oil smuggling and sale outside of OPEC and the United Nations sanctions is considered a traditional unethical activity significant in its profitability to be profitable to smugglers. Iraq has taken advantage of high oil prices and smuggling has increased considerably. Iraq's refineries are producing approximately 1000,000 barrels of oil a day in excess of domestic consumption. The U. S. Navy in the Persian Gulf estimates that around 400,000 tons of Iraqi oil, worth U. S. $50-60 million, was smuggled out in January 2000 alone (Pirontin, 2000). The exporting oil industry is a very lucrative business that generates very large profits so there is always a temptation for governmental officials in the Eastern and Western oil exporting and importing countries to cheat their own nations. For example, a former senior official of Elf-Aquitaine, France's former state-owned oil company, admitted in July 2000 that Elf had paid bribes for the past 25 years to top African politicians and officials by allegedly diverting oil revenues directly to bank accounts in Liechtenstein (*Global Witness*, 2000). Most of these bribes have been deposited in Swiss banks. Hall (2001:10) reports that Switzerland is a country which has been regarded as one of European's most secretive financial centers, has an estimated 60 percent share of the European banking market for wealthy individuals who like to do their banking offshore and out of sight of their national domestic tax authorities. Unlike most Western countries that have just one financial center, Switzerland has four: Geneva, Zurich, Basle, and Lugano, plus a number of specialist tax havens, such as Zug and Schwyz. Recently after the September 11, 2001 terrorist attacks in the United States, Switzerland put in place "know your customer rules and anti-money laundering legislation."

Money-Power Laundering

Money laundering is a specific transnational method of allocating *dirty-money* in order that it looks clean, as it has come from legitimate business sources. As *business rings* have grown so has the amount of money laundering activities. Money laundering is a very complex phenomenon with multiple facets. By nature, it is the result of unethical, immoral, and in some countries, illegal business transactions. Money laundering refers to the capital flight movements by which one conceals the existence, sources of income, channels of transferred money, the name and addresses of owners and brokers, and then disguises that income to make it appear legitimate. It could be through food stamps, health care, and prescription fraud to kidnapping, espionage, drug trafficking, and organized racketeering in most cases, it is very difficult to determine exactly how much money from business rings is being laundered. Some experts have estimated that annual worldwide money laundering amounts range from $450 billion to as much as $1,500 trillion (Johnson, 2001: 122).

Cacheris and O'Malley (2002: 266) define money laundering as: "The process by which one conceals the existence, illegal sources, or illegal application of income, and then disguise that income to make it appear legitimate." Money launderers are typically domestic or international business ring leaders or governmental authorities or agencies who have very influential contacts with authorities such as corrupt law enforcement, political figures, customs agencies, bankers, commercial traders, organized crime teamsters, international exchange agencies, and some ambassador offices. Wright (2002: 240) states: "The process can cover all those ways in which the profits of crime are controlled and converted, stored, transported or transferred, managed, obscured, anonymous, invested and enjoyed." Usually, money-laundering processes go along with its market characteristics black market.

In the U.S. the main source of an illegal activity of money laundering has come to include dirty-money transactions such as ransom for kidnapping, food stamps, medical and health care frauds, criminal pharmaceutical transactions, drug trafficking, racketeering, embezzlement, insider trading, tax evasion, sex workers' commissions, bribery, payola, kickbacks, grease money, capital flight without paying taxes, human trafficking, sex slavery trade commissions, illegitimate commissionaire money for international arms brokers, illegal arms trades, and even espionage. As can be seen by these wide ranging forms of money laundering, sometimes not only business rings are involved in these activities, but also some governmental authorities and agencies directly or indirectly are viewed as the main sources of money laundering. Because of such a general definition of money laundering, each country has developed its own definition of money laundering. These definitions may or may not respond to the ethical and moral nature of the money laundering processes. The kinds of business rings that are most active in money laundering are trading international agencies, the international construction agencies (e. g., airports, hospitals, dams, plants, roads, and railroads, etc.), arms sales, drug traffickers, and international bankers.

Money launderers, before they can spend their dirty-money from unethical and illegal activities, must first convert it into clean-money. Cleansing the money is defined as monies funneled through specifically designed banking and financial routes of legal transactions. There are a variety of methods through which dirty money can be laundered. Applying pressure on banks and international financial institutions only targets a fraction of the dirty-money that is laundered, since bankers are not the only institutions involved.

The Internet and non-financial institutions including philanthropic, humanitarian, and educational non-profit agencies have widened the scope of money laundering. By non-financial institutions, we mean law firms and attorneys, medical and health care institutions and doctors, contractors, and even some embassies can be included in money laundering activities. Anti-globalization groups state that money laundering is a new legitimate form of international money flight without repercussions.

In the past, there were three major routes of money laundering: (1) communication services (e.g., international postal services, telephone services, telex, and telegraph agencies), (2) banking drafts (e.g. traveler checks, transferable banking drafts, cashing exchanged drafts, etc.), and (3) Transportation of cash monies to other countries and or through conversion of money into precious stones, diamonds, gold, rare commodities, artworks, and antiques.

While it may seem that money laundering has little affect upon a single person, it may deteriorate morality in a society. Money laundering promotes unethical, immoral, and illegal activities, since there is a direct linkage between drug trafficking, sexual pleasurable images sales such as movies, bars and other activities.

Governments every year should appropriate a huge portion of their expenditures to fight these activities and divert their resources from education, health and medical care, and social activities into anti-drug addiction, jails, and law enforcement. The judiciary system must work together to capture and prosecute money launderers. In some countries, on the one hand governments promote activities of money laundering by having access to free money as one of the main sources of income by catching illegal funds, and on the other hand allow the flow of capital to enter to their countries as an economic stimulant. As Richard Small (1999), assistant director in the division of Banking Supervision and Regulation of the Federal Reserve, observed:

> *We have long felt that banking organizations and their employees are the first and strongest line of defense against money laundering and other financial crimes As a result, the Federal Reserve emphasizes the importance of financial institutions putting in place controls to protect themselves and their customer from illicit activities*

As a result of international banking agreements, the Wolfsberg Principles constitutes a set of standards that has the potential to become a set of banking industry standards. It took two years of negotiation among eleven international banks to create the Wolfsberg Principles. These banks are: the United Bank of Switzerland, ABN Amro Bank NV, Banco Santander Central Hispano, SA, Barclays Bank, The Chase Manhattan Private Bank, Citibank NA, Credit Suisse Group, Deutsche Bank AG, Hongkong Shanghai Bank Corporation, JP Morgan, Societe Generale and UBS AG.

The Wolfsberg Principles are:

Principle 1. 1: Wolfsberg Principle 1.1 states that:

The primary purpose of the Wolfsberg Principles is to ensure that the services offered by banks and their worldwide operations are not abused for criminal purposes. The primary means by which this is to be accomplished is by... accepting only those clients whose source of wealth and funds can be reasonably established as legitimate.

Under Wolfsberg Principles 1.1, banks will try to deal with only those clients whose money has been established as derive from a legitimate source.

***Principle* 1. 2:** Wolfsberg Principle 1.2 deals with identification and states that: "The bank will take reasonable measures to establish the identity of its client and beneficial owns and will only accept clients once this process has been completed." Under Wolfsberg Principle 1.2, banks should take reasonable measures to obtain sufficient information about the true identity of the person on whose behalf an account is opened or a transaction conducted if there are any doubts as to whether these clients or customers are acting on their own behalf.

***Principle* 1. 2. 1:** Woflfsberg Principles 1. 2. 1 focuses on the documentation in establishing a client's true identity. It recommends that:

Banks should be required ... to identify, on the basis of an official or other reliable identifying document, and record the identity of their clients, either occasionally or usual, when establishing business relations or conducting transactions.

Under Wolfsberg Principle 1. 2. 1, banks should take reasonable measures for natural persons to show specific identification such as a passport, driver license, social security card, or other evidence appropriate for the circumstances.

***Principle* 1. 2. 2:** Wolfsberg Principle 1. 2. 2 focus on the need to establish the beneficial ownership of each account. It recommends that:

Banks should take reasonable measures to obtain information about the true identity of the persons in whose behalf an account is opened or a transaction conducted if there are any doubts as to whether these clients or customers are acting on their own behalf.

Under Wolfsberg Principle 1. 2. 2, banks with consideration of artificial persons (corporations, companies, firms, organizations etc) should understand the structure of the company very well to determine the provider of funds, principal owner(s) of the shares and those board members and executive officers who have control over the funds. In addition, Wolfsberg's Principle 1. 2. 2, in respect to trusts where the natural or artificial person is a trustee, the banker will understand the structure of the trust sufficiently to determine the provider of funds, those who have control over the funds, and any person or entities who have the power to remove the trustees.

***Principle* 1. 2. 3:** Wolfsberg Principle 1.2.3, focuses on making clear all reasonable identities of money managers and similar intermediaries to be known. It states: "The private banker will perform due diligence on the intermediary and establish that the intermediary has a due diligence process for its clients, or a regulatory obligation to conduct such due diligence, that is satisfactory to the bank."

Principle **1. 2. 4:** Wolfsberg Principle 1. 2. 4, focuses on powers of attorney and authorized signers. It mandates bankers to observe the following guideline: "Where the holder of a power of attorney or another authorized signer is appointed by a client, it is generally sufficient to do due diligence on the client."

Principle **1. 2. 5:** Wolfsberg Principle 1. 2. 5, concerns walk-in clients ad electronic banking relationships. It recommends: "A bank will determine whether walk-in clients or relationships initiated through electronic channels require a higher degree of due diligence prior to account opening."

Principle **1. 3:** Wolfsberg Principle 1. 3 sets out what is required with respect to the due diligence process. It states:

> It is essential to collect and record information concerning the following categories: purpose and reason for opening the account, anticipated account activity, source of wealth (description of the economic activity which has generated the net worth), estimated net worth, source of funds (description of the origin and the means of transfer for monies that are accepted for the account opening), and reference to other sources to corroborate reputation information where available.

Principle **1. 4:** Wolfsberg Principle 1.4 states: "There will be a requirement that all new clients and new accounts be approved by at least one person other than the private banker."

Principle **2:** Wolfsberg Principle 2 concerns customer acceptance and sets out situations that require additional due diligence and attention. Under Wolfsberg principle 2: "Numbered or alternate name accounts will only be accepted if the bank has established the identity of the client and the beneficial owner." Under Wolfsberg Principle 2, banks in consideration of the Privacy Act should keep the name of customers anonymous. Therefore, banks should convert the name of customers into coded numbers. Debate as to whether numbered accounts should be kept or not carries serious implications.

Principle **3:** Wolfsberg Principle 3 concerns updating client files "The private banker is responsible for updating a client's file on a defined basis and/or when there are major changes."

Principle **4:** Wolfsberg Principle 4 focuses on the practices related to identification of unusual or suspicious activities. Wolfsberg Principle 4 states: "The bank will have a written policy on the identification of and follow-up on unusual or suspicious activities. This policy will include a definition of what is considered to be suspicious or unusual and give examples thereof."

Principle **5:** Wolfsberg Principle 5 focuses on monitoring and states: "A sufficient monitoring program must be in place."

Principle **6:** Wolfsberg Principle 6 concerns control responsibilities. It states: "A written control policy will be put in place by each bank establishing standard control procedures to be undertaken by the various control layers, meaning private banker, independent operating unit, compliance, internal audit etc."

Principle **7:** Wolfsberg Principle 7 concerns reporting. It states: "There will be regular management reporting established on money laundering issues."

Principle **8:** Wolfsberg Principle 8 concerns education, training, and information for employees. It states: "The bank will establish a training program on the identification and prevention of money laundering for employees who have client contact and for compliance personnel."

Principle **9:** Wolfsbeg Principle 9 states: "A bank will establish record retention requirements for all anti-money laundering related documents. ...The documents are to be kept for a minimum of five years."

Principle **10:** Wolfsbeg Principle 10 states: "The bank will establish a exception and deviation procedure that requires risk assessment and approval by an independent unit."

Principle **11:** Wolfsberg states: "The bank will establish a adequately staffed and independent department responsible for the prevention of money laundering (e.g., compliance, independent control unit, legal)."

DEONTOLOGICAL AND UTILITARIAN ETHICAL LEGITIMACY CONCERNING EARNEST MONEY

Through an ethical, moral, and legal analysis, we need to identify what type of money is clean or dirty. In order to verify the type of money, we need to analyze it through ethical, moral, and legal legitimacy. What is legitimacy? Legitimacy is a common syllogistic reasoning to establish a valuable-based rule or a claim that an individual and/or an institution need to establish their logical power.

There are two types of legitimate arguments concerning legitimacy of the earnest money:

- Legitimacy concerning the actual inherent value of an object; money.
- Legitimacy concerning the operative utility of object different types of coins and/or notes.

Deontologically, ethical legitimacy is viewed as dealing with the language used in perceiving the inherent actual value of an object itself, not the denominated market value. Teleologically, ethical legitimacy refers to the operative suitability and profitability of an object. Therefore, such types of legitimacy can be perceived either on the level of perceptual causal (deontological) values or on the level of operative effective (utilitarian) experiences.

Our discussion here is related to earnest money. The ethical legitimacy of earnest money stems from the belief that a certain person and/or an institution has the right to possess, control, and enjoy a certain volume of valuable wealth in a society. Such legitimacy mandates others to be obligated to accept it. In an ethical analysis of earnest money only two kinds of perceptions are meaningful and therefore genuine: (1) *empirical* or *synthetic* and (2) *analytic*.

An empirical legitimacy is one that can be confirmed to a high degree of probability by observation and experiment. An analytic legitimacy is one that can be established as true or false by an examination of the definitions of its logical terms. Beyond of the above domains of legitimacy there are utterances that are neither empirical nor analytic. They are termed literal nonsense, that is, even though they may seem to be valuable to some people, they do not really assert or deny confirmable fact, nor are they true or false by their definitions. Expressions like, everything has a value in the natural order, are typical of this class of legitimate expression.

In the field of business, the logic of legitimacy for earning, possessing, controlling, and enjoying money depends on the preferred ethical, moral, and legal socio-cultural and econo-political value systems in a nation. There are no fixed perceptions concerning the inherent values of each nation's currency in relation to others. Global perception concerning the inherent values of a nation's currency is based on the market values to be denominated as hard currencies or soft. Hard currencies are fully convertible to other currencies. They also are relatively stable in value or tend to be strong in comparison with other currencies. The hard currencies are desirable assets to hold. Currencies that are not convertible are often called soft currencies, or weak currencies.

Our discussion here is no concerned with the inherent values of a nation's currency. It is concerned with the ethical legitimacy of type of business and/or the behavior and activities of a businessperson. Which type of earning is legitimate or illegitimate? The answer is how people in a society through their socio-cultural values, econo-political doctrines, and religious faiths judge those earnings. Within and beyond a nation's value systems, there are different ethical legitimacies concerning clean money and dirty money.

Establishing and operating a business line may be ethical, moral, and legal in a country, while it may be unethical, immoral, and illegal in other countries. It depends on how people perceive their values and contributions to their lifestyles. For example, alcohol consumption, brewing, buying and selling, and profit making in the Moslem and Bahaii faiths, because of their religious value systems, are forbidden and prohibited, while in the Christian and Jewish faiths they are legitimate. Nevertheless, in some Moslem, Christian, or Jewish dominated countries, conducting such a business could be legal. If we examine the legitimacy of such a business in relationship with ethicality and legality we will find two contradictions. One, an ethical point of view indicates that it is unethical as a businessperson to sell alcohol to drivers who may become drunk and kill other people, and a legal viewpoint selling alcohol increases the income of the government through taxation. Sometimes, legitimacy of ethical and legal propositions in different cultures carry different value systems. This is a deontological perception concerning the analytic judgments about money; clean-money and dirty money.

CHAPTER SUMMARY

Within the contextual analysis of capital ownership, there are two major views concerning possession of wealth: (1) physical or material ownership, and (2) non-physical or conventional valuable phenomena. Property ownership is identified only with physical objects like houses, cars, computers, and video recorders. Non-physical ownership is identified by relationships between the owner and the things owned. Within this category, one can have property rights over things that are not simple physical objects, as we own money, stocks of a company, copyrights, patents and others. Non-physical ownerships involve a generally complex bundle of rights and duties governing how, under what circumstances, and in what ways both the owners and users can possess, use, dispose of, and have access to the things in question.

Within property ownership, we need to clarify who *owns* and who is in *control* of those properties. In the field of business, company managers, whether themselves owners or non-owners are always in charge of operations, by tacit or explicit leave of the big owners. The ethical issue of control is seldom raised in resource allocation in a corporation. The concept of ownership is directly related to the trends of territorial protectionism. In publicly owned corporations, capital control rests with a small number of owners. In no cases, except when a company is under court-sanctioned trustees, can it be shown that ownership is divorced from control. This means that governments in all nations represent their citizens and residents in exchanging material and non-material things with other alien individuals and groups. Both material and non-material ownerships are viewed as the results of governmental regulations concerning the values of properties including material and intellectual properties monetary values. Businesses, as society's major economic institutions, have an ever-expanding array of capital flight movements with specific entitlements. The capital flight movements are interrelated with moral, ethical, and legal power-commitments within different sectors of society.

What is money-power? The nature of money is related to neutral valuable purchase power. Money, by its nature through long historical events, is valuable because people invented it in order to represent appreciation of their hard work at the time of exchange. Money has been used as a medium for exchanging and measuring values. It is considered a property with reference to its pecuniary value. Money could be perceived in the forms of metal coins (e.g., gold, silver, bronze, etc), bank certificates, bank drafts, bank checks, traveler's checks, or banknotes generally accepted in payment of debts and current transactions. If money is to be perceived good or evil depends on the behavioral perceptions of money owners and money controllers. Money-power refers to the ability or capacity of individuals, groups, organizations, and nations to produce an effect (good or evil) or to bring influence to bear on a situation or give people some privileges for the benefit of money-power holders. Money-power, in and of it, may be good or evil, positive or negative, legitimate or illegitimate, ethical or unethical, and legal or illegal. It depends on who owns it or who controls it. Money certainty carries enormous power. In sum, when money-power intermingles with political-power, then their synergistic result creates an enormous power to manipulate the market place and to be conceived as threats to the liberty of citizens. There are three major spheres of money-power: (1) international money-power market, (2) national based money-power market, and (3) black money-power market.

In order to examine different types of money-power through ethical principles and legal doctrines we first define different kinds of money-power such as: (1) clean money-power, (2) dirty money-power, (3) free money-power, (4) money-power cleansing, and (5) money-power laundering. Clean-money refers to the honest processes of capital earnings and movements within and beyond of the national borders of a country by which an individual, an institution, a group of capital holders, or governments discloses the sources of its existence, legal application of incomes, and appearance of its nature in the form of regular reporting systems to the public and/or to the governmental specific agencies such as the Internal Revenue Services (IRS) or other law enforcement agencies. Dirty-money may infect anyone's mind who thinks about and/or who approaches it. So people try to avoid risk-creating behavior by not approaching, thinking about or touching dirty-money.

Bribery, payola, grease money, kickbacks, under-the-table money, and illegal secret campaign contributions for political means and ends are known as free-money and their symptoms are evidence of corruption at all levels of society. In a number of countries petty corruption is almost a routine way of life and considered as an unfortunate necessity for daily survival. Within the contextual boundaries of moral, ethical, and legal assessments of the above situations, the amount of money paid and/or received could be from very large amounts to one dollar.

Sweatshops in big cities hire illegal aliens brought in by international human smuggling rings that may also deal in banned or restricted commodities. They are unethical, immoral, and illegal activities and financed by international loan sharks who may be recycling drug money, bribery, and making cartel agreements with transportation firms run by organized business rings. The end result of such unethical, immoral, and illegal activities is to clean their dirty-money by selling the products of these sweatshops. Also, some money launderers are very active in tourism industry. They establish a number of camouflaged businesses as ethical and legal entities in resort areas or islands through which they intend to clean their dirty-money. These businesses provide very cheap airfares, sea-fares, or land-fares with lucrative entertainment facilities in order to absorb as many as possible tourists. These businesses will even be competitive as the profit margin is irrelevant. The main purpose is to launder the funds generated from unethical and illegal activities such as drugs, sex, gambling, and bootlegging activities. In order to further launder the money, they create more businesses alongside financial institutions such banks and lending agencies. The dirty money may infect anyone who touches it. There are twelve types of money cleansing: (1) smurfing, (2) legitimate business, (3) foreign currency exchange, (4) daisy - chaining, (5) brokerage houses, 6) double-invoicing, 7) reverse flip, (8) loan back, (9) underground banking, and we are adding three more: (10) sex industry, (11) *Havala* (popular in the Asian and Middle Eastern countries), (12) illegal sale of wildlife and (13) oil and other mineral substances smuggling.

Money laundering refers to the capital flight movements by which one conceals the existence, sources of income, channels of transferred money, the name and addresses of owners and brokers, and then disguises that income to make it appear legitimate. It could be through business practices such as food stamps, health care and prescription fraud to kidnapping, espionage, drug trafficking, and organized racketeering. Money launderers, before they can spend their dirty- money from unethical and illegal activities, must first convert it into clean-money. Cleansing the money is defined as fueling money through specifically designed banking and financial routes of legal transactions. There are a variety of methods that dirty money can be laundered. Applying pressure on banks and international financial institutions only targets a fraction of the dirty-money that is laundered, since bankers are not the only institutions involved.

The Internet and non-financial institutions including philanthropic, humanitarian, and educational non-profit agencies have widened the scope of money laundering. By non-financial institutions, we mean law firms and attorneys, medical and health care institutions and doctors, contractors, and even some embassies. Anti-globalization groups state that money laundering is a new legitimate form of international money flight without repercussion.

In the past, there were three major routes of money laundering: (1) communication services (e.g., international postal services, telephone services, telex, and telegraph agencies), (2) banking drafts (e.g. traveler checks, transferable banking drafts, cashing exchanged drafts, etc.), and (3) Transportation of cash monies to other countries and or through conversion of money into precious stones, diamonds, gold, rare commodities, artworks, and antiques.

QUESTIONS FOR DISCUSSION

- What is the general definition of capital flight movements?
- How do you define and analyze ethical and moral attributions concerning the concepts of capital ownership and capital control?
- What is the legitimacy of capital flight movement rights?
- How do you define different types and spheres of money-power from the standpoint of moral, ethical, and legal value systems?
- How do you assess the econo-political implications and visible and invisible money-power role players in the international free market economy?
- What is your opinion concerning the global financier alliances strategies?
- How to global financial alliances maintain their econo-political power in the global markets?
- How do you compare the holistic money-power effectiveness in the free market and the black market?
- How do you define clean money-power, dirty money-power, free-money-power, money-power cleansing, and money laundering?
- How do you analyze the twelve techniques for money-power cleansing in the global financial markets?
- How do you understand the differences among money-cleansing techniques?
- What is scuffing?
- What is daisy chaining money cleansing?
- What do we mean by *havala*?
- What is the ethical and moral attribution concerning *havala* in a free market economy?

CASE STUDY

ILLEGAL CAPITAL FLIGHT FROM RUSSIA TO AMERICA: THE BANK OF NEW YORK

The Bank of New York was established in 1784. It is one of the oldest banks in the world, since in the in the form we know it today was just beginning to emerge in the second half of the 18th century. BNY transfers more money around the world than almost any other bank, with some $600 billion passing through its coffers everyday. Alexander Hamilton, a New York attorney, who went on to become the secretary of the treasury in George Washington's first cabinet, wrote the BNY's constitution. In 1792 the New York Stock Exchange was formed and the first corporate stock to be traded was The Bank of New York.

During the 1880s, the BNY made investments in early railroad and utility, as well as in the construction of the New York City subway system. By 1918, the U. S. became the largest creditor nation as well as the world's new international money center. In July 1922, the BNY and the New York Life Insurance and Trust company merged. The Bank of New York Company Inc., with its assets of $77 billion, is the 17th largest financial holding company in the United States. It provides a complete range of banking and other financial services to corporations and individuals worldwide through its five basic businesses, corporate banking, securities servicing and global payment services, BNY asset management and private client services, financial market services and retail banking.

In recent years, the prestigious image of Bank of New York has been gradually diminishing due to the Russian underground's apparent $10 billion dollar money-laundering scheme at the Bank and company officials' alleged involvement in it. Money laundering is the term used to describe the transfer of illegally obtained funds through a series of accounts in order to hide the origin of the money.

PROBLEMS AND ISSUES OF THE CASE

Nancy Birdsall was senior associate at the Carnegie Endowment for International Peace and Devesh Kapur was an assistant professor at Harvard University. Through their research the above researchers, in September 13, 1999, have found one of the huge capital flights from Russia destined to

America. They state:

> The perennial problems of money laundering and corruption in emerging
> markets have been highlighted again by Russia. The Bank of New York is
> alleged to have helped shift more than $10 billion in ill-gotten gains out of
> Russia into private bank accounts in the west, at the same time as the
> number of Russians below the official poverty line has risen from 33
> million to 55 million in the past year (1999). How should the international
> community respond?

The problem of money laundering at the Bank of New York by the transfer
of funds from overseas banks occurred basically due to corruption of higher-
level management of the company and due to the bank's and the government's
inefficiency in maintaining a unique identity of individual accounts and assets
and due to ineffective implementation of taxation. Capital flight movements
around the world are a serious security issue. Not only can illegal capital flights
the harm the economy of a nation, but also it provides some opportunities for
organized crime to manipulate the sovereignty of nations.

THE MAJOR ROLE PLAYERS OF THE CASE

The major role player of the case was Semyon Yukovich Mogilevich, a
shadowy Russian businessman with alleged links to organized crime and the
world of drugs and arms trafficking; Sobinbank, a Russian bank founded in
Moscow and one of the most politically connected financial institutions in that
country. The counterpart role player in America was Thomas Renyi, chairman of
the board and Chief Executive Officer (CEO) of the Bank of New York. The
third major party is the American media that played the most important role in
disclosing invisible issues in American society. Because of the alleged
involvement of the bank and the Russian government's underground ties,
Mogilevich could conduct a major money-laundering operation, by illegal
transferring of around $10 billion dollars through the Bank of New York with
impunity.

ANALYSIS OF THE CASE

Over the years, the Bank of New York has gained popularity and customer
confidence and has been developing in every aspect of banking. Since its
inception, BNY has expanded its boundaries by acquisitions and mergers and
today it has grown into one of the major financial institutions in the world. But,
the recent allegations that the company's higher officials were involved in a $10
billion money-laundering operation by a Russian businessman has hindered its
expansion and reputation.

The accounts under scrutiny at the Bank of New York have been linked to Semyon Yukovich Mogilevich, who is believed to be a major figure in Russian organized crime. As much as $10 billion have been channeled through the bank in what was believed to be a major money-laundering operation by Russian organized crime.

A shareholder lawsuit alleged that the chairman of The Bank of New York, Thomas Renyi personally profited from the complex Russian scheme that moved money to offshore accounts. The suit alleged that the chairman was paid an unspecified amount through interests assigned to him in offshore companies that received funds allegedly stolen from Russian banks.

After around two years of investigation federal-law enforcement officials said that much of the money involved was from tax evasion by Russian businesses. The inquiry also showed that the system for moving funds through The Bank of New York was used to transfer money to individuals connected with organized crime in Russia. In Russia, Sobin Bank was put together by a collection of larger powerful banks that had strong political ties with Russian governmental authorities. If Russian authorities decided to pursue a case against The Bank of New York and/or Sobin Bank, that could mean taking on some of the most influential political authorities in Russia.

Such a situation raises many questions in both countries; Russia and America. Within the political corruption on the Russian side, Mogilevich had advantages because the corrupted Russian figures are part of the government. The BNY, however, denied the allegations as baseless and has not been accused of any wrongdoing. It said it is fully cooperating with government investigators.

CASE QUESTIONS FOR DISCUSSION

- What problems do you think could have caused money-laundering through The Bank of New York? Explain them.
- Suggest some solutions to the problems identified in the case.
- What effects do you think the Western investors have on the Russian market after the money-laundering scheme at The Bank of New York?
- Do you think that the Federal-law enforcement officials gave a biased judgment by not accusing The Bank of New York of any wrongdoings? Why or why not?
- What are inherent ethical and moral problems with the banking system concerning money laundering?
- How, econo-politically, do you perceive the shifting of Russian's government plan economy to the free market economy?
- How do you assess corruption in today's free market economy?
- How Russian people have accessed to democracy through shifting their communistic ideology to capitalistic world?

- How business ethics is observed in the Russian's international business institutions?
- What is the role of International Monetary Fund (IMF) to prevent capital flights from Russia to other nations?
- How American government is fighting against money laundering?
- Why Bank of America has been used as an agent to launder Russian's laundered money?
- How money laundering can hurt American economy and/or help other nations?
- How American judiciary system should put CEO's of Bank of America in trial?
- Do you find moral and ethical convictions in the international banking systems?

CASE SOURCES

N. Birdsall and D. Kapur, "Clearing Muddy Waters: The International Financial Community Must Be More Transparent If Money Laundering of Ill-Gotten Gains from Emerging Markets Is to Be Stopped," *Financial Times,* (Monday September 13,1999), 14.

S. Lemieszewski, "Sobinbank-Berezovsky-Russian Mafia and Bank of New York Money-Laundering," *New York Times*, (September 15, 2000).

V. Olevich, "Bank of New York Chairman Is Accused of Profiting on Russian Schemes in Suit," *Wall Street Journal,* (September 12, 2000).

CHAPTER 14

PROFESSIONALISM, PARAPROFESSIONALISM, OCCUPATIONALISM, AND VOCATIONALISM INTEGRITY, LOYALTY, AND ACCOUNTABILITY

There is no perfect man or woman to be ever found on this planet
because each person possesses unique strong and weak characteristics.

There is no perfect altruistic man or women to be found
because they have learned how to be aggressive in order to survive.

There is no perfect society to be reached
because men and women are selfish and self-centered.

There is no fixed value system to be found for having a spiritual life
because life values are dynamically changing.

There is no way to calculate the holistic life value of an individual
because there are different objectives for calculating the value of human life.

With all material and spiritual value perceptions for assessing an individual's life
values,
we can identify them in terms of effective and efficient economic value systems.

CHAPTER OBJECTIVES

When you read this chapter you should be able to do the following:

- Develop conceptual knowledge concerning what is a profession.
- Distinguish differences between a profession and a paraprofession.
- Distinguish differences between a profession and an occupation.
- Distinguish differences between professional codes of ethics, and occupational codes of conduct.
- Define what are special rights, duties, entitlements, privileges, and autonomy of a professional person.
- Understand why society has allowed professionals more autonomy and self-management than paraprofessionals and occupations.
- Be able to ague in favor or against of allowing a profession to govern itself.
- Develop a sense of logic for understanding under what conditions self-governance by a profession is justifiable.
- Know why a professional code of ethics is justifiable for a professional's autonomy to perform their duties.
- Be familiar with the characteristic and procedures the codes of ethics should have in a profession.
- Argue that an occupational and/or a paraprofessional person should not have the same rights and duties in democratic society as professionals.
- Be able to make distinctions among different themes and objectives of professional academies, associations, and organizations.
- Know the limits of moral, ethical, and legal ordinations among professions.
- Be familiar with members of a profession with the issue of collective bargaining power.
- Know what is the difference between restricted professionalism and extended professionalism.
- Understand the logic behind the differences among registered, licensed, and licensor paraprofessionals.
- Know what are different types of management philosophy concerning moral, ethical, legal, and amoral behavior and conduct.
- Be familiar with prohibitions and injunctions against advertising by professional members concerning justification of the professional codes of ethics.
- Analyze different moral and ethical commitments through professionalization of a group of experts.
- Be familiar with professional expertise and their moral and ethical commitments in relationship with different governmental agencies.
- Know the relationship between professional employees and employers.

- Know what are ethical, moral, and legal boundaries between experts and their organizations.
- Know how to perceive business organizations as professional entities.
- Know how amoral behavior differs from moral behavior.

THOUGHT STARTER

The notion of morality is what you think to find in an ideal state of excellence. Morality is a general idealistic picture of spiritual characteristics of men and women devoted to causing and achieving the state of goodness. Goodness is a complex and mixture of personal, social, and professional commitments to conduct courses of actions towards happiness. We need to be concerned with what are characteristics of ethical professionalism concerning the following questions:

- How can professionalism and moralism characteristics affect behavior of experts?
- How can a professional person hope for and strive for achieving a state of moral happiness?
- Why is it important to do what is right as long as the job gets done?
- Where should a professional's main ethical integrity lie in relation to self-morality, to clients or customers, to coworkers, to employers, and to the society or to humanity at large?
- What can a professional do when integrity, loyalty, and accountability appear to be in irreconcilable conflict?
- Has society the right and power to provide individuals with opportunities to be moral or immoral?
- Is morality a matter for private judgments and ethics a matter for public auditing?
- Does freedom of choice and action offered to professionals provide the freedom of choice to be moral or immoral?
- How does societies value moral and immoral, ethical and unethical, and legal and illegal decisions and actions?

Society cannot live without assessments of moral, ethical, and legal values. A rational society, which is also a good society, may have other standards such as financial, economical, and technological value systems. It has no valuable standards at all if it is not a good society and will not survive.

Within our socio-cultural and econo-political contextual boundaries, every year employers, insurance agents, legal experts, scientists, and governmental agencies routinely calculate our economic life values ranging from few dollars to many billions of dollars; depending on which set of criteria or standards are used, which incidents are considered, who is valuing, and how values are valued. Nevertheless, valuing is a rational mandated principle for survival.

Materialistically, one of the most ways of calculating the value of a human life is to break it down into its chemical elements. Some econometric experts have determined that the value of a human life on the basis of material criteria is about $8.37 in 1984, which has increased $1.09 in every six years because of the inflationary rates (French, 1984: 163).

Spiritually and psychologically, human life is not subject to monetary values. It is beyond economic gains. Spiritual values of human life are invaluable. If you do not develop your intellectual mind to perceive things and wisely value them, you will learn nothing. If you are tightly bound by prejudice, you can assess your surroundings and go through it and be as ignorant at the end as you were at the beginning. If you want to get benefit from material things, you must be spiritually open-minded person. If you want to be a professional person, you need to first intellectually think, professionally talk, and then occupationally walk through your life.

Material and spiritual value conflicts exist among people when they are obsessed with passion and greed. We efficiently need to work to avoid such a miserable life. We should not complain about our weaknesses or abnormality. We should accelerate our strengths and opportunities in order to succeed at our legitimate objectives.

There is no underlying value system into which other values can be interpreted. Life is dynamic. Each individual's life is subject to the natural law to begin with and there is a certain date to end it. Nevertheless, selfishness and kindliness, idealism and realism, smartness and laziness, attractiveness and disinterestedness, and altruism and egoism all exist in a single person, a human being. We tend to think about a miser as being nothing more than miserly, the fop as being foppish, and the glutton as being gluttonous.

PLAN OF THIS CHAPTER

There are several moral, ethical, and legal issues concerning decision-making processes and operations in an organization. Accordingly, there are several obligations concerning individual moral commitments, professional grouping ethical convictions, and organizational legal mandates. In addition, there are several attributes such as trust, loyalty, and rationalism among people in a working place. As we defined in chapter one, morality is related to conscious awareness of an individual to pursue right things. Ethicality is defined as excellent cultural behavioral values that fit into customs and traditions. Ethicality is referred to as a societal benchmark or instrumental assessment of society as a whole for the guidance of good social behavior for individuals and groups.

We hear constantly of professional ethics: medical ethics, business ethics, legal ethics, bioethics, teachers' ethics, administrative ethics, and many more. Are these professional ethics making up their own specific ethics? Are they each distinctive? The answer is "no." Our view of professional ethics is roughly analogous to our practical convictions about certain ethical rules. Our plan in this chapter is to provide you with a professional ethical framework and the conceptual tools to sufficiently to allow you professionally to behave morally and ethically in your operations. We shall devote primary attention to the following questions:

- Is professionalism bound with ethics?
- Is occupationalism bound with professionalism?
- Are there any other terms than professionalism and occupationalism such as paraprofessionalism and vocationalism in the workplace?

We may begin by recognizing a broad moral and ethical distinction among ideas of professionalism, occupationalism, and paraprofessionalism.
We have seen that corporations have ethical convictions and legal mandates not to harm, abuse, misuse, neglect, or defraud the public. These ethical convictions and legal mandates fall primarily on those who manage corporations. Yet other organizational members are not ethically and legally allowed to take part in any illegal activity. In this chapter, we are going to examine what responsibilities managers have, what duties employees have, and how both managers and employees can be accountable to the public.

INTRODUCTION

People have different ideas and perceptions concerning the kind of world in which they want to live. Some strive to build their own personal power through manipulation, domination, and greed and while others feel fear, sadness, empathy, anger, depravation, and injustice. Some are very materialistically oriented, while others are spiritual. Some are very prudent, conservative, and value only their own personal lives and benefits and others sacrifice their lives for the happiness of others. Nevertheless, such visions must be realistic and pragmatic. Those people who are highly materialistically oriented, their visions are based upon cost-benefit analysis. Those people who are spiritualistically oriented, their visions are based on humanistic concerns. Accordingly, we recognize two major groups of people: (1) altruistic and (2) egoistic. Altruistic people are very generous in their mind-set and egoistic people are very stingy and greedy. You need to evaluate your own personality according to these characteristics. Those groups of people who are altruistic are called professionals.

WHAT IS PROFESSIONALISM?

We may begin our discussion by recognizing a broad distinction between ideas of professionalism, paraprofessionalism, and occupationalism. Since such a debate is arguable, certain types of activities reflect a certain vacillation among professional, paraprofessional, and occupational concepts. First, in this section we will describe all relevant ethical and moral characteristics of professionalism, and then in the following sections we will define and analyze the other three terms as paraprofessionalism, occupationalism, and vocationalism.

The notion of professionalism does seem to be more impersonally regulated concepts and often has been structured in terms of serving beyond self. Everyday we hear the terms of profession, professional, and professionalism. At one level, we describe a member of profession as related to a group of experts who are committed to certain rules and regulations through observing a pluralistic professional code of ethics. These professional codes of ethics mandate a member of a profession to observe them in addition to the legal mandated rules. Edgar Schein (1966: 3-11) sketched out the basic elements in conceiving the concept of professional as follows:

> A professional is someone who knows better what is good for his client than the client himself does.... If we accept this definition of professionalism ... we may speculate that it is the vulnerability of the client that has necessitated the development of moral and ethical codes surrounding the relationship. The client must be protected from exploitation in a situation in which he is unable to protect himself because he lacks the relevant knowledge to do so...If [a manufacturer] is... a professional, who is his client? Who needs protection against the possible misuse of these skills? Any economists argue persuasively... that the consumer has not been in a position to know what he was buying and hence was, in fact, in a relatively vulnerable position.... clearly, then, one whole area of values deals with the relationship between the [manufacturer] and consumer.

In an economical term, professionalism is more oriented towards elitism. This means more should be given to those who have developed their intelligence rather than more is given to those who have not.

Although all ethical concepts of professionalism, paraprofessionalism, and occupationalism refer to human social activities, there are significant differences, as well as interesting emphases among them. Colleges and universities train individuals for the practice of professions that require systematically studied knowledge for their practice and which are necessary for the well being of society as a whole. Such professions include medicine, law, higher education, engineering, architecture, and the administration of private and public institutions. Also, it should be noted that colleges and universities are not the same as a vocational school or a polytechnic institution.

It is common for the incumbents of a profession to regard themselves as people whose services are given to others in a way that leave room for their personal selfishness. The idea of professionalism does seem to be more impersonally regulated and has often been viewed as client-centered, precise separation of selfishness from altruistic perceptions. In a philosophical term, professionals have been supposed to enter their professions for love rather than money. In practice, professionals have been paid more than occupations.

Professionals are conceived as practitioners of a specific scientific branch of knowledge and practitioners of a pragmatic profession who set voluntarily values and standards for the integrity of their own professions. They possess all possible pluralistic competencies to practice their jobs and morally, ethically, and legally are accountable for their success or failure. This perception enshrines a range of virtues more than a set of scientific skills. This means that professionals practice their skills with very high levels of virtuous standards.

Professionalism is known as a concept and practice that resents in bureaucratizational objectives of a group of people who are loyal to their specializations. This notion conduces the level of performances more to avoid the self-serving interests than to meet the needs of clients. Professionalism avoids dehumanization of a group of people whose intentions and practices serve clients rather making self-profit. Within the practice of professionalism philosophy, clients easily perceive the integrity of practitioners who are judged to be on their side. Professionalism avoids hypocrisy and professionals are authentic in dealing morally and ethically with their clients.

Specific Common Criteria for Professionals

Carr (2000: 23) and De George (1995: 468) indicate that the idea of a profession should serve specific commonly altruistic criteria of professionalism as follows:

- Professionals should provide important public services beyond their self-interests.
- Professionals should be involved theoretically as well as practically in-grounded expertise.
- Professionals should have a distinct ethical dimension that calls for expression in the code practical ethics.
- Professionals should require structural organizational regulations and practices for the purposes of recruitment and discipline in their fields.
- Professionals require a higher degree of autonomy in their decision-making processes and actions than do others B independent judgments B for effective practices.
- Professional should impose upon themselves pluralistic codes of ethics and live up with them.
- The specific demands for careful considerations in a profession should protect the welfare of society. Such careful considerations should protect the public interest, the rights of clients, and the duties of professionals within the domain of their expertise.
- The monolithic document of the professional codes of ethics for each profession should be assumed as the bedrock foundation for judgments

in the process of legal actions.

- Professionals not only should fulfill their expertise roles to share their knowledge and experiences with colleagues and peers, but also they should exercise their individual moral obligations without fear.
- Professionals relentlessly should strive for restructuring their professional mechanical performances according to the legitimate environmental forces if they pluralistically need to reform their professional codes of ethics.
- Professionals are sometimes faced with moral and ethical problems and issues, because of conflict of interests and conflicts between one's professional ethical obligations and the demand of civilian bureaucratic authorities. They should wisely resent and express their truthful professional opinions as experts.
- Professionals within the domain of their judgments first are viewed as moral agents, ethically responsible second, and legal accountable third. To decide to be a member of a profession is to choose greater, not lesser, personal moral commitments, professional ethical convictions, and legal expertise in decision-making processes and actions.
- Professionals have been offered by a general societal trustful rule to govern themselves by their autonomous collective professional codes of ethics. They need to implement these codes without prejudice and/or favoritism.
- Professionalism depends in a large part on the quality of personal deliberations and reflection upon novel problems. In critical situations with good faith and good will they need to make extraordinary decisions and actions to solve problems.
- Any profession is governed by professional codes of ethics, which reflect clearly their expertise's obligations and responsibilities by recurrence to the rights of clients. They need to be faithful to their clients.

Different Types of Professionalism

There are two types of professionalism: (1) the restricted professionalism and (2) The extended professionalism. Although the distinction between the two is usually observed in the interests of arguing in favor of the latter over the former, both notions of professionalism appear to be within the holistic context of professionalism.

The Restricted Professionalism: The restricted professionalism is defined as the notions of procedural specialization competence, mechanical operational skills, and contractual bounded commitments to the profession. These notions are more along the lines of exchanging expertise than the notion of acquisition of knowledge. The responsibilities of restricted professionalism are exclusively defined in terms of procedural competition among professionals, and more directed toward accountability or conformity to the to the relationships among peers.

The Extended Professionalism: An extended professionalism perception aspires precisely with relentless acquisition of knowledge through practicing a profession. It is related to maintaining continuous independent judgment rather than merely to be obedient to the bureaucratic authorities. For example, in the business of medical and health insurance, according to this perception, anyone who has professional medical training should in the position to issue appropriate permission on behalf of an insurance company for covering expenses of an insured person. It is vital to practice medicine within the boundary of financial commitments by a physician. To direct the decisions of doctors concerning diagnosis, treatments, and prognosis is a matter of professional policy and practice rather than an administrative or financial one. In addition, within the domain of health and medical care system, the notion of extended professionalism is related to the level of superiority in knowledge acquisition and seniority in professional pragmatic services.

Notoriously, however, recent general erosion of professional autonomy in the field of medicine in relationship with health insurance industry has shifted from professionalism to occupationalism. Professionalism has been marked by more centrally prescribed by de-professionalization or de-skilling of restricted professionalism governmental and/or insurance superiority over physician autonomy. One effect of such a restricted professionalism can be seen in the popularity of HMOs in which the medical and health industry is focusing upon more managerial, particularly economic-administrative aspects of the quality care system.

DIFFERENCES BETWEEN CODES OF ETHICS AND CODES OF CONDUCT

The argument for making a distinction between a profession and an occupation in a moral, ethical, and legal term is based on two claims: (1) codes of ethics and (2) codes of conduct. We discussed above in a general term in some organizations (e.g., a hospital, a law firm, a laboratory, a plant, etc.) there may be three groups of employees working together: (1) professionals, (2) paraprofessionals, and (3) occupationals. Within the field of business ethics their own turf regulates each group. Professionals are highly educated and skillful people and serve their clients beyond selves. Paraprofessionals are trained to help professionals perform their duties. Occupassionals are trained to safeguard their personal interest by serving others. In terms of moral, ethical, and legal boundaries each group possess specific disciplinary codes of behavior. In a general term, all three groups must comply with law and in addition, professionals must observe codes of ethics.

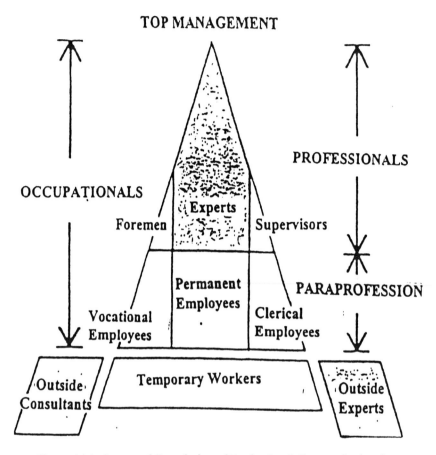

Figure 14.1: Structural Foundation of Professional, Paraprofessional,
Occupational, and Vocational Staff in a Corporation

What Are Professional Codes of Ethics?

What is a code of professional ethics? The Hippocratic oath, generally
recognized as the earliest expression of such a code in relation to medical
practice, seems to be a simple principle to the effect that the physician's first
concern should be for the wellbeing of his/her patients above any personal
interest or profit. Within the domain of professional ethics, professionals always
must treat people as *ends* not as *means*. Kant's distinction of the morally
grounded categorical imperative from the hypothetical imperatives of
instrumental agency seems tailor-made to distinguish the endeavors of
professionals from those of occupations as trade-people or sale-persons.

Professionals are required to possess in addition to specific theoretical expertise and technical skills, a range of distinctive personal moral virtues, cultural values, and legal knowledge to elevate the interest and needs of their clients above their selves-interest.

Within the contextual boundary of a code of professional ethics there are three main attributions: (1) the basic human needs, (2) the civil needs, and (3) the quiddity needs. The basic human needs extend through essential needs for survival. The civic needs, such as medical and health care needs, judiciary and justice service needs, and educational opportunity needs, are the prime societal needs in a society for achieving peace and harmony. As Parhizgar (2002: 126) stated: "The *quiddity* needs are matters common to all concepts of the existence of a person. In Latin and Arabic languages, quiddity means what is it? This concept in English-speaking cultures is closely related to holistic essence of humanity.

It is said, morally and ethically, the basic human needs are viewed as natural needs: (1) the right to exist (2) the right to live. The civil needs are viewed as liberty and freedom in intellectual expressions within the establishment of structural justice systems concerning how to live? The quiddity needs are related to holistic essence of humanity concerning what is good to live? The basic needs are known as *natural rights*. The civil needs are apt to be known as *welfare rights*. The quiddity needs are known as *human rights*. Also, the quiddity needs are known as holistic needs. They demand freedom from diseases, injustice, and ignorance. Therefore, a professional code of ethics spells out what constitutes appropriate education, adequate experiential skills, genuine justice, and sufficient careful consideration in a profession?

The professional codes of ethics require not only acquisition of appropriate theoretical knowledge (e.g., scientific, evidential, observational, deductive, tacit, technological, legal, and ethical) they also require competencies and experiences in practicing knowledge. The professional codes of ethics sufficiently must include enough matters of normative, evaluative, and behavioral criteria rather than sole scientific or theoretical reflections of problem solving. The professional codes of ethics must focus on the pursuit of what is true and good rather than upon the discovery of what seems to be good or true. For example, in biotechnology, biosciences, and pharmaceutical industries, the experiment in human cloning seems to be a rational method to change the defected genes of human species. Such an attribution apparently is evidential because biosciences, biotechnologists, pharmacologists, and chemists pursue their professional research upon the normative or evaluative experiments as the good and truthful evidential reasoning for changing the natural path of the evolution to a desirable artificial one. Since all present research activities emphasize upon the domain of trial and error, researchers are not sure about strategic prodigical consequences of cloning in human species. Therefore, they need to first know what is a good and truthful ethical and moral consequence of their experiments, and then continue it with careful consideration. Such a recommendation provides a clear guideline for establishing a code of ethics in these professions.

Professional codes of ethics should have the following characteristics:

- A profession should be regulated by pluralistic self-rule of professional members. This means that all members are entitled to freely express their moral, ethical, and specialized concerns through collective debates, hearings, and testimonies. Inclusion of ideal codes of ethics is not necessarily inappropriate.
- Authoritative societal representatives provide appropriate room for professional ethical autonomy concerning performance of their services. Government will not interfere in regular practices of professionals, unless to find a serious harm to be rendered to the social fabric. Professionals for customers must make expected professional moral norms, ethical behavior, and technical procedures publicly available before providing them with any type of services.
- Professional codes of ethics should provide both providers and clients appropriate rights and duties.
- Professional codes of ethics should not be self-serving for individual objectives of professionals. Codes should be initiated to consider the interests of the profession and the total interests of society as whole.
- Professional codes of ethics prohibit professionals to compete with peers and colleagues through spreading false rumors.
- Professional codes of ethics should prevent false advertisement and promotion of a professional person. It must prevent negative comments by peers against colleagues in a profession.
- Professional advertisement should be designed as honest pieces of information not for promotion of their businesses but also for awareness of the public concerning their availability of their public services.
- Professional codes of ethics should provide sufficient room for professional institutions to regulate immoral, unethical, and illegal practices by professionals.
- Professional codes of ethics should provide society with appropriate procedural channels to enforce punishment for unprofessional actions and those who have broken the codes of ethics. In return, society must appropriately provide special channels for controlling illegal activities of professional members.

A survey of corporate officers by the Ethics Resource Center in 1990, a nonprofit organization based in Washington, DC, revealed the following benefits that companies get from enforcing codes of ethics:

- Legal protection for the company (78 percent)
- Increased company pride and loyalty (74 percent)
- Increased consumer/public goodwill (66 percent)
- Improved loss prevention (64 percent)

- Reduced bribery and kickbacks (58 percent)
- Improved product quality (14 percent)
- Increased productivity (12 percent)

Professional Causal and Consequential Responsibilities

Some responsibilities are moral and ethical, some are legal, some are moral, ethical, and legal, and some are amoral. We need to identify in what sense we are responsible. Sometimes, we are causally responsible or consequentially responsible in our moral judgments and actions. Causal responsibilities are ingredients in moral, ethical, and legal deliberations. This means that an individual is responsible for specific courses of decisions and actions. Consequential responsibilities are ingredients of sole conscientious judgments and behaviors. This notion indicates that the individual's judgment and/or actions are based on knowingly and willingly deliberations.

There are degrees of knowledge and degrees of deliberation in moral and ethical judgments. Such a variety of responsibility is based on conditional and situational factors. The conditions that diminish moral and ethical responsibilities are known excusable conditions. A pathologist may not be responsible for informing an attending physician in a hospital and/or an outpatient right a way after detecting a cancerous cell either because of not having the address and telephone of the attending physician, a patient, or both because of the sloppiness of medical records. This condition provides the room for lessening professional negligence. This condition is viewed as a managerial responsibility rather than a professional responsibility. Those conditions that preclude or diminish the excusing responsibilities of judgments and actions fall into one of the three following categories:

- Those conditions that preclude the possibility of actions; this means that to be morally and ethically obligatory, an action must be possible.
- That condition that precludes or diminishes the required knowledge a bioscientist and/or a biotechnologist is morally and ethically responsible to be highly skilled and specialized in the domain of his/her expertise. The excusable responsibilities could be lessened when one of the conditions is absent. With respect to knowledge, there are two excusing conditions:

  o *Excusable ignorance* is related to insufficiency of knowledge.
  o *Invincible ignorance* is related to unpredictable consequences of our judgments or actions. Professionals are responsible for the immediate and obvious consequences of their judgments and actions. Nevertheless, both excusable and invincible ignorance are failure of the lack of sufficient knowledge.

- Those conditions that preclude or diminish the required freedom; a bioscientist or pilot may be excused from the lack of freedom in innovative judgments. They need to follow standard procedures in their performances. This means excusable conditions may be viewed as the result of four conditional factors:

o   The absences of alternatives
o   The lack of control in courses of actions
o   The external coercive forces
o   The internal coercion (De George, 1995: 115)

WHAT IS PARAPROFESSIONALISM?

The words of paraprofession and ancillary refer to the engagement of specific training and pragmatic skillful activities in which individuals regularly devote their daily activities to assist professionals in order to acquire living income. Most paraprofessional groups aspire to the rule ethics (e.g., physician aids, nurses, paralegal, lab technicians, etc.). Greenwood (1962: 206) states:

There are a number of component parts to the definition of a paraprofessional person:

• Paraprofessionals need to acquire formal theoretical education, practical skills, technical training, and qualifying examination in order to be certified and serve in their areas of careers (e.g., Registered Nurses - RNs).
• Paraprofessionals are required to be certified for having specific qualifications reflecting community sanctions or approvals (e.g., Certified Teachers, Certified Occupational Therapists, Licensed Appraisers, Certified Custom Brokers, etc.),
• Paraprofessionals are required to acquire licenses through skillful tests in order to be allowed to practice independently their jobs in specific communities (e.g., Midwives, Licensed Psychologists, etc.).
• Paraprofessionals need to have specified qualifications in order to be a member of local, regional, or national associations (e.g., American Nursing Association, American Dietician Association, American Physical Therapist Association, etc.)
• Paraprofessionals are required to observe certain codes of conduct.
• Paraprofessionals are required to follow certain legal mandates.

Different Types of Paraprofessionals

As modern society becomes more complex, it requires greater specialized knowledge and practical skills. We may recognize differences among paramedical, paralegal, and paraeducational people with variety of ideas and mandated patterns of responsibilities and accountabilities. Within the contextual boundary of a broad distinction between paraprofessionals and occupations, we may find certain vacillation between these concepts. Genealogically, there are significant and illuminating tensions as well as interesting differences of emphasis between paraprofessional and occupational people. It is common for the incumbents of so-called paraprofessionals to give their career lives to the services of others in a way that leaves relatively little room for their personal gains (e.g., firefighters, police officers, soldiers, emergency crews of medical helicopter pilots, co-pilots, and nurses). Wilson and Neuhauser, (1976: 52) indicate that there are three major groups of paraprofessionals: (1) registered, (2) certified, and (3) licensed paraprofessionals.

Registered Paraprofessionals: Registration is a legal process by which qualified individuals are included in a listed roster maintained by governmental or non-governmental agencies. Registration in some cases allows individuals to carry designated recognizable titles after their names. This group of people needs to have sufficient experience and knowledge in sensitive lines of professional activities. Nevertheless, this group of people is not required to have maximum theoretical educational expertise in their own fields. They are more practical. For example, a cytotechnologists registered by the Board of Registry of the American Society of Clinical Pathologists may use the designation title of CT (ASCP).

Certified Paraprofessionals: Certification is a process by which a non-governmental agency and/or a scientific association grant recognition to an individual who has certain predetermined qualifications specified by that agency or association. A *diploma* is one certified by an agency recognized an individual competent to grant such a certificate.

Licensed Paraprofessionals: Licensed paraprofessional degree is the process by which a qualified governmental agency grants permission to people meeting predetermined qualifications to engage in a given occupation and/or use a particular title.

DIFFERENCES BETWEEN PROFESSIONALISM AND PARAPROFESSIONALISM

As modern society becomes more complex, it requires greater specialized knowledge experts. Most highly specialized groups in the medical and health field aspire to be considered professionals. We may recognize a variety of different ideas and innovations among medical and health occupations. Within the contextual boundary of a broad distinction between *vocation* and *profession,* we may find a certain vacillation between these conceptions. Genealogically, there are significant and illuminating tensions as well as interesting differences of emphasis between vocational and professional conceptions. It is common for the incumbents of so-called vocational researchers in the field of biosciences, rightly or wrongly, to give their lives to the services of others in a way that leaves relatively little room for their personal gain. Identically, this idea of significant bioscientific vocational researchers' continuity between personal and occupational concerns and interests has probably been one reason why traditional vocations have been less financially rewarded than other professions such as physicians and lawyers. Maybe one of the moral reasoning for such a discrepancy is the fear that raising the salaries of bioscientists and bioresearchers would attract the wrong kind of people, those of mercenaries into the vocations. There can be little doubt that teaching and researching in the field of biosciences has often been regarded as a vocation, that it has also been regarded as the kind of occupation which people enter for love rather than money, and that it has also frequently been woefully underpaid.

In any organization there are two types of employees: (1) professional experts and (2) auxiliary staff. Professional experts perform their duties beyond their personal interest, while paraprofessionals perform their duties on the basis of receiving economic incentives. As we analyzed professional codes of ethics, we will analyze occupational codes of conduct in the following pages.

WHAT IS OCCUPATIONISM?

We may begin our discussions by recognizing a broad distinction among professionalism, paraprofessionalism, and occupationism. These ideas carry different definitions, power, authority, responsibility, and accountability in society. Although all of the above terminologies refer to specific breadth of activities, there are significant and illuminating differences among them. Occupationism is viewed as a societal bureaucratic ordering system concerning values, contributions, effectiveness, and efficiency of all types of jobs in a society. It mainly focuses on distribution of wealth and resources among citizens according to the econo-political doctrine of a nation. One consequence concerning a person to be engaged in a type of vocation with specific legal mandates is called an occupation. Therefore, an occupation is a kind of vocation in which people perform specific jobs for receiving economic incentives as incomes; wages, salaries, commission, and fees. It is common for the incumbents of so-called vocations to regard themselves as occupationals.

Whereas professionalism seems to be viewed as loyalty to the notion of expertise codes of ethics, occupationalism is more viewed to have loyalty to the civil codes of conduct. The expertise codes of ethics mean that physicians' professional commitment is to provide diagnosis, treatment, and prognosis to all types of people within the boundary of humanity without any discriminating policy such as race, religion, color, ethnicity, political ideology, nationality, and wealth. The civil codes of conduct mean that jobholders must act within the legal boundaries of their power and authority. For example, peacekeeper officers' (e.g., a police, constable, or state trooper) responsibilities mandate them to perform their duties according to their geographical areas of jurisdiction and /or services.

Occupationalism is enshrined with legal standards and requires a specific set of skillful training programs. Occupationals are not professionals, because they do not require the same equivalent qualifications of professional expertise. The main objective for an occupation is to pursue self-interest. From this perspective, if university professors, lawyers, or physicians convert their jobs from professionalism to occupationalism by self-interest their clients will suffer from such self-interest. Then they will not be trusted to serve people.

Another dimension of occupationalism is related to the priority of the notion of economic self-means and ends. From this perspective, occupationalism priority is to first fulfill self-interest and second serve others. As we indicated before, the notion of professionalism is personal attachment to a kind of expertise job that requires avoidance of personal welfare and/or self-interest. It is a fact that all occupations in society are no more than that they get paid for what they do; fee for services. Within this sense of understanding in an occupation, specifically in the field of business or trade, we may find that some people can fairly compare their responsibilities with the quality of their performances. For example, the job of a plumber, electrician, or auto mechanic is a differentiation of economic equity between service providers and customers. This means that a well-executed job in the field of occupation requires to be compensated adequately. Therefore, occupationalism is the requirement of an economic relationship between buyers and sellers or customers and service providers.

One consequence of regarding human social activities as an occupation rather than as a profession turns the idea of significant continuity between selfish and altruistic values and concerns in terms of moral commitments and ethical convictions. The notion of occupationalism is focuses on the nature of the division of labor the economic value of work. Although much recent emphasis has been put upon the economic status of paid work; fee for services and has therefore sought to stress the broader econo-political values of work the urgent need for total quality care systems has been neglected. Thus, it is common for the incumbents of so-called an occupation to regard themselves as people whose services are totally dominated by financial rewards. Occupationals are known as having a cultural custodian view of performing their jobs for receiving a specific financial reward. One reason for including such a financial view among different types of occupationalism is that a certain anti-professionalism stance has been found within the organizational bureaucratic mandates. Thompson (1961: 170) states:

> The bureaucratic culture makes certain demands upon clients as well as upon organizational employees. There are people in our society who have not been able to adjust themselves to these demands. To them, bureaucracy is a curse. They see no good in it whatsoever, but view the demands for modern organization simply as a reaction to bureaupathology. Its source will be found within the critics of themselves, not within the organization. It is, in fact, a kind of social disease that we propose to call it bureausis.

Occupational Codes of Conduct

The argument in favor of the following issues concerning codes of conduct is based on two claims. The first is that the know-how knowledge and skills that members of an occupation have mastered have usefulness for the economical welfare of a society. The second is that members of an occupation are expected to observe legal standards for themselves that society is expecting of them. Codes of conduct in an occupation do not exhaust the issues of ethics. Ethical codes of conduct are general behavioral and procedural rules for both professions and occupations. They specify particular legal prohibitions and ideals, each of which can be evaluated from moral and ethical point of view. For instance, bioethical issues in biosciences and biotechnology often gain media attention as results of advances in cloning. These issues raise moral, ethical, and legal legitimacy not only for those in research centers but also for those in society concerning their religious faith. The ethics of organ transplant, the use of fetal tissues, the various genetic engineering, and the stem cell cloning press issues in socio-cultural and econo-political endeavors. Therefore, bioscientists and biotechnologists are not under oath like physicians to observe codes of ethics what are they expected to observe is the codes of conduct.

Occupational codes of conduct spell out a corporation's expected behavioral standards for effectively communicating those standards to all employees including managers. A study by the Ethics Resource Centers in 1990 revealed the following topics in the codes of conduct:

- Conflict of interest
- Receiving gifts, gratuities, entertainment
- Protecting company proprietary information
- Giving gifts, gratuities, entertainment
- Discrimination
- Sexual harassment
- Kickbacks
- General conduct
- Employee theft
- Proper use of company assets

Schwartz (2001: 247) indicated that there are eight themes in which employees perceive codes of conduct as follows:

- As *a rulebook,* the code acts to clarify what behavior is expected of employees
- As a *signpost,* the code can lead employees to consult other individuals or corporate policies to determine the appropriateness of behavior
- As a *minor,* the code provides employees with a chance to

confirm whether their behavior is acceptable to the company
- As a *magnifying glass,* the code suggests a note of caution to be more careful or engage in greater reflection before acting
- As a *shield,* the code acts in a manner that allows employees to better challenge and resist unethical requests
- As a *smoke detector,* the code leads employees to try to convince others and warn them of their inappropriate behavior
- As a *fire alarm,* the code leads employees to conduct the appropriate authority and report violations
- As a *club,* the potential enforcement of the code causes employees to comply with the code's provision

The point is that whereas the professional codes of ethics are self-sustainable, the occupational expected conducts are authoritative tailor-made rules. In professional codes of ethics, professionals are known as guardians of their professions, while in occupational custodian view; job occupants are viewed as guardians of their institutions. In addition, within the philosophy of professionalism, professionals strive for precisely how to be *neutral* and observe a clear line between professional obligations and institutional loyalty.

Whereas professionalism seems to be viewed as loyalty to the notion of expertise policy, occupationalism is more viewed to the notion of being loyal to the civil policy. Expertise policy is a set of shared values flowing from the side of individual's self-disciplinary perceptions of professional membership and civil policy is viewed as top-down desired conceptions of elite group of power-holders in a society.

DIFFERENT VIEWS BETWEEN PROFESSIONS AND OCCUPATIONS

The distinction between an occupation and a profession is a notion that clearly makes what are general and specific characteristics of these two phenomena. That distinction clearly makes a difference between private or personal, and public or professional. In a profession, there are specific pluralistic rules and regulations plus knowledge and skills in terms of professional self-imposed disciplines namely, the codes of ethics, while in occupations specific qualifications and expected behavior which are prescribed and imposed by authorities are defined as the organizational codes of conduct. The point is that whereas the professional codes of ethics are viewed as self-sustained sanctions against self-interest, the occupational expected codes of conduct are authoritatively tailored-rules made by societal authorities.

In professional codes of ethics, professional are known as guardians of their conscientious commitments for respecting their peers and their work integrity, while in occupational custodial view, the codes of conduct are viewed as guardians of their own self-interest and their institutions. In addition, within the philosophy of professionalism, professionals strive for cooperative enhancement of their tasks, while in occupations; occupationals compete with each other in order to win the market edge. Professionals share their findings from experimental research towards more accomplishments, while occupationals keep their achievements secret in order to maintain their competitive superiority. In addition, within the philosophy of professionalism, professionals strive for precisely how to be neutral and observe a clear line between professional obligations and institutional loyalty.

Professionalism is viewed as commitment to the cause of altruism and promulgation of the scientific partisan doctrine. Professionals believe and act according to the sincerity of their expertise and pragmatic values. Professionals strive to achieve pragmatic scientific outcomes to be measured by good-intention, good will, good operations, and good consequences.

Whereas professionalism seems to be viewed us having loyalty to the notion of expertise policy, occupationals strive to have loyalty to the civil policy. For example, we may question the role of a physician in the wartime in battlefield. According to the professional expertise policy, a physician's professional responsibility is to cure injured people, both friends and foes. If that physician changes his/her ideology to occupationalism, then he/she has to cure only friend solders and ignores foes because friends paid him not by foes. Then, the latter connotation is against the spirit of medical ethics.

Expertise rules are professional sets of shared humanistic values that follow goodness of humanity. Professionals put aside their self-interest and/or prejudice in order to serve humanity. The civil rules are viewed as top-down ideological political desires concerning the elite interest groups of power-holders in a society. For example, the role of a business in international trade is to follow their home political ideology, capitalistic, socialistic, communistic, and nationalistic. Each political ideology applies specific strategy to fulfill such an ideology.

WHAT IS VOCATIONALISM?

The word vocation connotes the relation of self and a pragmatic technical problem solving. To have a vocation is to have more meaning than an occupation. Also, vocation is more than a job, a role, or even a career that one arbitrarily chooses on the basis of personal preference or inclination because one is forced to answer the perennial question posed to the self.

Vocationalism depends on relationships between an individual and a technical task to be done; plumbing, carpentering, and trading. Vocationalism conveys a pragmatic commitment to solve problems of others rather than self-fulfillment. Vocation is a profoundly ethical question of the good: What is good for myself and for my customers and/or clients? Any response to this question affects primarily both the self and others and their relationships. Since the notion of occupationalism is more focused on self-fulfillment; my job, my position, and my pay the ethical question of vocationalism can be neither posed nor answered by the self-alone. Parks (1993: 217) states: "Vocation conveys a sense of being called to a relationship and to an interdependence that is larger than self." Therefore, vocationalism is a vehicle for social mobility of pragmatic problem solving. Within such endeavor of thinking, society needs a group of people to be involved in vocations and trades.

Vocationalism is the notion of developers the necessary skills and docility to be successful employees within a capitalistic framework system. It channels working-class people into working-class jobs. Indeed, it seems to be a fairly common sociological view that such distinctions reflect differences of social or class status. Within such a magnitude of ethical deliberation there are two types of arguments concerning vocationalism: (1) ethical functionalism and (2) ethical instrumentalism.

Ethical Functionalism of Vocationalism: Ethical functionalists tend to come to the defense of vocationalism by describing several vital social necessities. Social ethics mandates some people in society to serve pragmatic problem solving by training middle-level workers, and to preserve the notion of expertise excellent. Vocationalism provides such a facility to democratize vocational options and keep lower prices for rendering services to community. Vocationalism will serve society with all different types of needs. This means that when a kitchen is flooded because of a burst water pipe, it is likely to be more urgent that there is a plumber than there is a doctor or lawyer in the vicinity. Therefore, it is not necessary to ask a mechanical engineer to come and fix it and charge the homeowner with excessive rates. Because of social necessities, there should be another group of workers with lower cost to fulfill this social task. Ethical functionalism is a matter for normative or evaluative rather than scientific or theoretical reflection, focused on the pursuit of what is *good* rather than upon discovery of what is *true*. The evaluative or normative ethics is considered by the evidential patterns of social necessities; goodness.

Ethical Instrumentalism of Vocationalism: Ethical instrumentalists tend to come to the defense of vocationalism by describing several vital *civil necessities*. There are three major reasons for having vocationalism as an instrument in balancing civil needs. First, vocationalism provides those workers who have developed the necessary pragmatic skills and docility to be successful as small business owners. These opportunities allow society to enjoy lower costs for having immediate services by small businesses and avoid bureaucratic red tape processes and/or systematic expensive sophisticated technological systems. Second, vocationalism is used as an instrument to serve professionalism in order to avoid class confusion in a capitalistic society. Third, vocationalism maintains class equitability reward systems by channeling *working-class people into working-class jobs*. This facilitates changing the trends of the labor market from unemployment to employment. Also, this converts scienticized aspects of problem solving to technicalized; territorial societal ideology. It is important to provide grounds for distinguishing professionalism and paraprofessionalism from vocationalism such as trades, manufacturing industries, and mercantile enterprises. It is important to emphasize here that this sense is focused upon the idea that enterprises such as medicine, law, and education are implicated in questions and considerations of a particular ethical and moral character which are not to the forefront of, for instance, plumbing, joinery, auto repair, wholesale or retail and hairdressing. Any communities possess numerous vocations. We are not able to analyze ethical and moral issues of each in this text. Therefore, for the clarity of such an issue, we only will examine one of the vocations, namely automotive repair shops.

ETHICAL AND MORAL IMPLICATIONS OF AUTO REPAIR SHOPS

Operating a personal transportation vehicle is viewed as a social necessity in an industrialized nation. To operate, maintain, and service personal vehicles need frequent trips to auto repair shops every year. There are varieties of auto repair centers. Each type has advantages and disadvantages. There are generally five types of businesses within the domain of automotive repair services:

- Department Stores
- Car Dealerships
- Automotive Retail Chains
- Service Stations
- Small Specialty Mechanical Shops

Since the auto repair industry is included within the domain of vocationalism, they are not subject to codes of ethics and/or codes of conduct. Also, they are not highly regulated by governmental agencies. Every year customers pay 20 billion dollars for automotive repairs either for unnecessary repairs or by being grossly overcharged for services and parts that they never received (http://www.bfrconvertibleventures.com/free_eports/car_repairs.htm). This is partially due to fraud and partially due to the incompetence of the mechanics. Let us go through moral and ethical behavior of these businesses and discover how customers may be ripped off. Although in any industry there are honest enterprises with integrity and high moral standards, there are few with dishonest behavior. Therefore, within this type of business, the chance to being ripped off is very high. Automotive Service Excellence BASE certifies some mechanics and others are not. Those mechanics who are certified by ASE in eight categories are subject to: Breaks, Engine Repair, Front and End, Tune-up and Emission-Control systems, Electrical Systems, Air Conditioning and Heating, Manual Transmission and Rear Excel, and Automatic Transmissions.

Since customers are not allowed to visit the shop floor because of safety insurance policy, they do not know who is working on their cars with what types of valid certificates. A good mechanic frequently attends training courses sponsored by different manufacturing auto corporations or vocational colleges and schools.

There are inherent problems in the automotive repair and service industry. Since most people are not familiar with the functional parts of their cars, the probability of being ripped off is very high. The best customer for an auto repair center is the most susceptible group of customers who do not understand functional operation of their cars. Within the auto repair and service industry, it is a mandate to maintain a library of technical service bulletins. These are bulletins distributed by the car manufacturers and consist of technical updates, special repair instructions, and service hints on different models and years of cars. Without these bulletins the repair center can charge you skyrocketing fees and still not correctly fix your car.

It is possible to be cheated by automotive repair shops with different unethical and immoral techniques. Some mechanical shops build up their customer profile with long-range strategic plans. Their strategies formulated to provide first time customers with high discounts and serve them with the best possible ways. When customers frequently visit their shops for repairing their cars, then they accelerate the fees for services and replacing new parts. This system is not unusual for many other businesses such as clinics and hospitals. There are usually three basic methods the repair shops to set up their customer profiles:

- Manufacturing car factories assembled low quality parts in a new car in order to reduce the competitive pricing system in the marketplace. Then owners of new cars immediately will face with defected parts that are not covered in the warranty. Then the dealership service centers charge their customers with very high fees in order to compensate their low competitive price system. This strategy is very popular for foreign cars.
- Some non-dealership repair centers charge their customers very little for their work the first few times. This practice portrays them as honest, reliable, and cheap repair shops. Then once customers become loyal to them, suddenly in one of the repair time, they accelerate charges skyrocketing. Nevertheless, in the automotive repair industry, the words of trust, reliability, and promise fulfillment are almost never associated with a cheap repair shop.
- Some repair centers including dealership services charge heavily for the repairs done, but treating their customers with courtesy and good hospitality providing customers with coffee and donuts and/or with soft drinks and very luxurious comfortable waiting rooms, in the hope that customers will return. As customers come back more, they reduce their charges more. Customers believe that they are loyal to them.

Fraud and deception in the automotive repair shops are not unusual. There are different unethical and immoral and in most occasions, legal ways that customers can be charged for new parts which are not necessary to be changed. Sometimes customers are charged for new parts while mechanics installed rebuilt parts that are cheaper than new parts.

The next problem is related to the billing rip-offs. Within the automotive repair industry there are two systems of calculating wages for mechanics as following:

- *The Flat Rate System (FRS)*: The FRS is the most abused one. Each car manufacturer has a specific manual listing for parts and average time to remove and replace parts known as "re & re fees." Customers are charged for "re & re fees" on the basis of number of hours found in the manuals multiplied by hourly mechanical rates. Usually, there is two types manuals: (1) factory manual rates and (2) shop manual rates. Factory manuals rates are those that repair shops charge manufacturing companies for warranty repairs. Shop manual rates are issues by headquarter repair shop corporations to charge their customers. The shop manual rate is higher than the factory manual rate. Under the flat rate system if the job takes the mechanic minimum time he/she receives for the maximum rate minus the shop's commissions. This is why mechanics and shop owners love the flat rate system.

- *The Clock Hour System (CHS)*: The CHS is where customers are charged for the real actual time for "re & re." This system is related to diagnosing. This is known as milking customers. The CHS is led to camp out or hood up sham (mechanics pretend to be testing with using magic boxes or black boxes), but in reality they are not doing anything; other than adding additional hour fees to customers' repair bills.

Up to this point you have been shown possible frauds and deceptions in the automotive repair centers. We will define and describe problems and issues concerning five types of repair ventures as follows:

- *Department Store Mechanical Shops*: Many department stores have found a market niche in maintaining and operating auto repair shops because they have learned how this type of business is very profitable. These department stores like Wall Mart, K-Mart, Sears, and others, specialize in a few major repair items that are profitable. Because of their volume buying and aggressive promotional strategy, these competitive chain stores provide good deals for their customers. Also, these department stores push their customers to buy their own brand name parts in order to make more profit. Department Stores usually have set repair and service prices for each job calculated by clock hour system of wages.

- *Car Dealership Services*: Car dealerships tell their customers that their new cars must have all the repairs performed at their authorized dealerships or their warranty would be void. By ethical and legal terms such a declaration is wrong. The truth is that all simple repairs and maintenance items including oil change, brakes, etc. can be repaired elsewhere without voiding the warranty. Within a dealership service system, there are two types of mechanics: (1) service advisor and (2) mechanics. The service advisor represents the employer or the owner of the dealership and seeks to maximize profitability. The mechanic looks at the technical problems; the real problems. Ethically, if the service advisor writes some problems which are not the real problems and the mechanic doesn't find such a problem, then the dealership will charge customers with diagnoses charges. This kind of strategy to maximizes income of a dealership auto center. Customers should not pay for what the service advisor has written. The dealerships sometimes may be setting a policy for some customers to delay some types of repairs in order for the warranty to expire, causing customers to pay the cost for the repair. Timing is crucial in such a strategy. In the field of ethics, there is a clause that we call extending chain of warranty. This means that if the problem of some warranty parts start before expiration date, then customers need not to pay for those parts that are expired. In such occasions, the dealerships cheat their customers.

- *Automotive Retail Chains*: There are the places that claim they can perform specialized jobs while you are waiting. These retail chains are Midas Muffler, Goodyear, Penzoil Pit Shop, etc. The rates usually charged at these quick shops are very competitive due to aggressive competition. Their charges are based on package deals on brake work, muffler work, tires, and oil changes. Any services beyond the package deal will be excessively high. The advantage to these chains is that they offer very competitive prices because of high volume of sales. Nevertheless, these chains are accustomed to two irregular and unethical practices: (1) sometimes they replace rebuilt and reconditioned parts instead of new ones, and/or (2) use cleaned old parts and reuse them as new parts. The automotive chains are usually independently owned and operated franchises, not regulated or monitored regularly like the big department store chains and dealerships. A franchise automotive chain usually has quota systems that force them to meet certain volume of sales per month. If they are not able to meet such a quota, they will charge their customers excessively or provide unnecessary repairs without merit. One of the problems of the automobile retail chains is that employers or owners who do not send their mechanics to be updated with mechanical skills, because they do not want to give up a payday work. The worst scenario indicates that most mechanics are not qualified skill-workers.

- *Service Stations*: Mom and Pop service stations are the oldest automotive repair shops. These stations are really independent shops. These shops are to be used for emergency work. Nevertheless, the most important issue for these service stations is customer satisfaction. There are two types of service stations: (1) very ethical and (2) very unethical. These service stations treat their customers on the basis of knowing their addresses and the future customer loyalty profiles. In most cases, if they find that, the customer is from out of town and has to fix his/her car right a way, then they charge with maximum. They start with very low price, and gradually they increase it by demonstrating that there more problems with the car. Customers need to fix their cars as soon as possible and get out of the town. This provides a golden opportunity for the mechanics to charge excessively. On the other hand, if mechanics find out the customer is from town, they extend the work-time. If customers demand very quickly repair then the charge customers with an additional percentage for repairing theirs cars out of turn. At both cases, all possible unethical and immoral actions could be happened in these shops.

- *Small Specialty Mechanical Shops*: They maintain their business with integrity and customer loyalty. They ask customers to shop around for cheaper spare parts and allow their customers to watch their work. Customers not only receive very high quality of services, they will learn about the functional areas of their cars. Sometimes, customers receive special discounts by auto part dealers when they provide them with the service station's codes (e.g., 10-20 percent discounts). These shops look for reliability and good reputation of their mechanicals.

IS A BUSINESSPERSON OCCUPATIONAL OR VOCATIONAL?

Occupational and vocational people are inextricably involved with business transactions. Since both occupational and vocational people are directly providing services for customers, they are assumed to receive some fair economic rewards. Nevertheless, both occupational and vocational people provide services either for professionals or for their customers. From the viewpoint of ethics and morality these people may cause special problems in society. For example, unethical and immoral actions in the field of automotive repair businesses are an international phenomenon. Some auto repair centers are famous for ripping customers off. They often have a polite greeting conduct along with a smile motto, being friendly as possible while grossly overcharge their customers.

Professionalism, paraprofessionalism, occupationalism, and vocationalism raise problems from the viewpoints of ethics and morality. Their rapid integrated scientific advancement, technological breakthroughs, legal implications, and ethical commitments make socio-cultural and politico-economical problems more pressing. The major differences between professionalism and occupationalism are the degree of autonomy and justifications for moral, ethical, and legal rules. Professionalism is not compatible with loyalty and obedience to employers. They should be loyal to their professions. For example, the professional role of physicians is to provide patients with diagnoses, treatments, and prognoses according to their professional codes of ethics, not "codes of health care insurance systems." Or we perceive accountants as auditors who are in professional trust to audit business accounts, they are not supposed to commit immoral, unethical, and illegal activities to cook books for their clients (e.g., Arthur Andersen's case for Enron). They should not deceive the public by overvaluing their assets, equity, and return on investments in orders to booster their client's stock market. However, it should be indicated that there are many professionals who are self-employed; therefore, they are expected to professionally conduct their businesses without fraud and deception.

The notion of professions and occupations are denoted in the activities of people who are serving their clients beyond their self-interests. Some are known as to be expected to serve society with careful considerations, and others serve themselves within the legal breath of society for achieving both interests of their clients and themselves (e.g., lawyers). This makes the differences between pure professionalism and occupationalism. If we state services beyond self in a profession, we are not excluding profitability in their works. For example, when lawyers charge their clients with hourly fees (e.g., $ 400 per hour) regardless of the outcomes of trial, they perceive that their cases are not very strong in order to sign a flat rate for contingency contract with their clients. Nevertheless, in both options lawyers need to defend interests of their clients with maximum care. In some unethical and immoral legal cases, lawyers have settled their clients' cases out of the court with a perception of per unit case cost. If clients do not express their consent, they withdraw from the case and put a lien (e.g., 45% plus court costs and administrative fees) on the case for receiving full percentage of the case. Clients have to hire another lawyer with another contingency percentage (e.g., 45% plus court costs and administrative fees). In the end, clients will receive only five or zero percent of the final settlement. This is fraud within the legal professional system; it is not professional. It is occupational. Therefore, the professional profitability is based on just and fair rates for clients' added values to their costs.

According to the above discussions, you may find differences between fairness and justness in profitability for professionalism and occupationalism. In professional codes of ethics, professionals perceive themselves with altruistic desires to serve their clients' interests first and themselves second. In occupational codes of conduct, occupationals perceive their egoistic search for self-interests first and clients' interests second. Usually, professionals do not charge their first time clients for consultation, but occupationals charge their clients for consultation and providing them with the fee for services. For example, a thoracic open heart surgeon never charge his/her patient for consultation, but an orthodontist charges first time patients with double charges of usual fees with an assumption that if patients agree with the fee for service, they deduct it from the general contract. With such a strategy, orthodontists lock their patients with consultation fees. This provides unfair and unjust consequences for patients not be able to shop around for their medical costs. The problem in orthodontic services is that employees are provided with a flat lifetime fee from health care insurance companies; usually with $1000 benefits. The cost is estimated for $5000-$8000 per patient with retainers. There are many unethical loopholes in the profession of orthodontic.

DIFFERENT TYPES OF AMORAL, MORAL, ETHICAL, AND LEGAL MANAGERS

Organizations' ethical commitments are central to their internal stabilized alignment and external valuable market effectiveness. There are different types of managers who maintain moral, ethical, and legal social responsibilities for three types of corporate objectives: stability, survival, and profitability. The sole responsibility of a social entity like a business is not simply to make profit. While this is one of the legitimized and rationalized objectives, there are other concurrent objectives that protect a company's existence. The perception of integration or fragmentation of a company's mission spells out different beliefs for managers to examine the extent to which direction the management system is committed.

Ethical and legal issues for individual employees and managers are very different. Hence, employees may not be legally accountable in any activity that they know will cause harm. Do they still have ethical and legal obligations to prevent harm? Since individual managers are role models for the workers in their organizations, they provide advice to employees who find themselves in an ethical quandary. Also, since managers are responsible for employee supervision, they are increasingly being held accountable for wrongdoing. According to the theme of this chapter, we will review four different managerial perceptions concerning amoral, legal, ethical, and moral commitments of managers in an organization (see Table 14.1).

Amoral Managers: The amoral managers are known as manipulative managers. These managers follow a Machiavellian strategy to justify their ends through their means. These managers do not believe in morality and ethicality. They believe morality and ethics are oxymora; types of perceptions in which produce effects by seeming self-contradictions. A manager has legitimate power to be enforced to reach ends. These types of manipulative motives can be justified to profit-maximization. This type of managerial style denies fairness and justness because it is an egoistically and essentially economically motivated system to make profit. It lacks trust, sincerity, and loyalty to their clients. Although the motives underlying this style may be amoral, the end result could be unethical and immoral for those affected customers and consumers. For example, in a free market economy, having the stock option policy for employees at large including managers is an amoral objective. The bottom line of such an option for managers is ending up with freedom to cash their stocks at any desirable time of their employments in a corporation and prohibiting employees not to have the full access to their pension funds during their employments is an oxymoron; unethical and immoral (e.g., the Enron's stock options for executives to cash their stocks before bankruptcy and restrictions for its employees not to be able to cash their retire funds before bankruptcy).

The justification of such a Machiavellian amoral reasoning is to tell a portion of the truth to have option to buy the Enron's stocks; but not employees being able to sell them before the fire gets to their courtyards. This means that getting into the option stock plan is a privilege, but getting out of it is a hassle; a cruel kindness.

***Bureaucratic Managers*:** Bureaucratic managers are known as rule-based legal leaders. Based on the Sociologist Max Weber, theory of bureaucracy is very rational. Bureaucratic managers act on the traditional principles embodied in an ideal organizational bureaucracy; fixed rules that explain legitimized purposes (Gerth, 1946). The rational driving force behind this type of management system is based upon *efficient processes, doing things right*. This type of managerial system is more oriented toward political economy. The moral and ethical problem with this system is the quantitative legitimization of the organizational rule; the sin of omission. That is, a manager legally may follow all legitimate rules exactly but hurts someone; a bittersweet victory is nonetheless a victory. In the field of business, if a commitment to certain fundamental values is accepted as a by-product of evolutionary maturity, then perhaps the bureaucratic managerial style needs to mature intellectually. Rules cannot solve all business problems. To be blind folded legally without ethical and a moral commitment is a prescriptive remedy for problem solving without qualitative objectives. Bureaucratic efficient processes without ultimate rationalized objectives force organizations to be oriented with uselessness. Bureaucratic processes must be concerned with the notions of ethicality. It is within this context that the crisis of imbalance emerges from legal principles.

***Professional Managers*:** The most basic ethical duty that a business firm owes to its stakeholders is the duty to provide them with truthful means and ends. This means that professional managers ethically and morally are under specific commitments to disclose truthful information. Professional managers should aim to achieve effectiveness (doing the right things), efficiency (doing the things right) and productivity (doing the right things rightly).

In the Platonic term, experts have specific purposes or proper functions. Their values depend upon their effectiveness in fulfilling these functions. Professional managers in Platonic terms are those experts who are *wise, temperate, courageous,* and *just* (Albert, Denise, and Peterfreund, 1980: 10).

Professional managers act on the basis of *groupthink.* Groupthink ethics is based on deliberated intellectual pluralistic knowledge and expertise. It is consensus-dominated intentions, decision-making processes, and unbiased professional operations concerning formulation and implementation of codes of ethics. Professional group thinkers possess expertise and tools for accomplishing their functions effectively through their functional areas.

***Transforming Managers*:** Transforming managers are grounded in personal moral commitments. Modern transforming managers' mode of moral thoughts has been labeled Nietzschean. Frederiche Nietzsche (1844-1900) was a philosopher who attacked what he called *herd morality or ethicality.* He did not intend his doctrine for the transformation *of values for the common herd,* but for the few *free spirits* of the day who are intellectually fit to receive it. He argued that an individual must move beyond good and evil in order to create his/her moral value systems (Nietzsche, 1924). As society changes towards more developments and progresses in all aspects of life, simultaneously goodness must move towards excellence. Therefore, the transforming morality should be based on the level of intellectual ability in order to be fitted to the new conditions.

Table 14-1: Different Types of Moral, Ethical, Legal, and Amoral
Managers

AMORAL (Paraprofessionals)	LEGAL (Occupationals)	ETHICAL (Professionals)	MORAL (Theologicals)
Manipulative managers	Bureaucratic managers	Professional managers	Transforming managers
Machiavellian end-perceivers	Weberian rule-perceivers	Platonic social contract and altruistic operations	Kantian personal conscience intentions and actions
Disclosers of a portion of truth	Disclosing only the legal truth	Disclosing the real truth	Disclosing spiritual truth

Transforming managers should search for what is the right thing to do rightly in particular moral situations. Within this type of moral framework, managers are urged to use their personal conscientiousness to formulate supreme moral commitments for distinguishing moral from immoral and ethical from unethical.

The transformational managers should be involved in the process of intellectual development and growth of a company by manifestation of self-actualization according to the ultimate objective of work ethics. This provides managers success in their careers. Managers need to be empowered with moral commitments to promote and praise subordinates' aspirations to achieve the ultimate state of innovativeness. They should relentlessly promote creativity in order to strengthening organizational dignity and integrity. Accordingly, transforming managers should search for true reasoning with their aggressive "will to power" in order to dominate their organizational performances. They should believe that the strongest and highest "the will to manage," could initiate "the will to overcome problems by finding appropriate solutions."

ACADEMIA, ASSOCIATIONS, ORGANIZATIONS, AND UNIONS

The primary determination for establishing an academy, an association, an organization, and a union is related how society expects its members to fairly and justly relate and behave to each other and towards their customers or clients. According to social ordinations professionals, paraprofessionals, occupationals and vocationals form either pluralistic or collectivistic gatherings that are known as academia, associations, organizations, and unions. In a democratic society these institutions strive to create an enhanced social system in the areas of their expertise, practices, concerns, and benefits in order to establish a societal balance system to protect their rights and duties.

The primary objective of members of academic institutions is to promote scientific knowledge by a group of academicians. Academia's mission is to promote the doctrine of scientific free expression of ideas without interference from institutions, social and governmental authorities. Academia is viewed as scientific forums for discussions, analysis, and dissemination of scientific knowledge concerning societal issues and problems (e.g., Academy of Management). Also, the primary mission of academia is to establish a collective scientific understanding system for scientists, researchers, and practitioners to enhance and promote theoretical and practical knowledge discovery by conducting annual conferences for sharing their discoveries, innovations, and inventions of new methods and procedures with their peers and colleagues.

Professional associations also tend to establish self-ruled professional policing system concerning behavior and practices of their members. In addition, professional associations tend to establish and enforce their professional codes of ethics in addition to their legal occupational obligations (e.g., American

Medical Association, American Association of University Professors, and American Bar Association).

Societies are those ethical, moral, legal, and social entities that strive to maintain the highest disciplinary standards of personal conduct of their members in society. Societies emphasize codes of conduct. Affiliated members of a society strive enhance their humanitarian and philanthropic awareness by raising voices against injustice, unfairness, and wrong doings of authorities or organizations. Societies try to improve public understanding of organizational roles, public and private, and their power, authorities, responsibilities, and accountabilities (e.g. Society for Civil Rights, Society for Advancement of Management, Cancer Society, etc.).

Organizations in the field of business are known as those entities which are committed to specific causes and effects such as commercial, trade, exchange materials, goods, and services either as buyers or sellers. The best example of such organizations is known as trusts, monopolies, cartels, and consumer organizations. Domestically and internationally, these organizations play very important functional roles in the marketplace.

The illicit activity of organized criminals for receiving continuous profit is one of the ladders of social mobility for some political and financial authorities in all nations. Indeed it is not too much to say that the whole question of organized crime in the international market cannot be understood unless one appreciates: (1) the distinctive role of organized gambling as a function of mass-consumption economy, (2) the specific role various demographic movements around the world have in creating marginal businesses and crime, and (3) the relationship of criminals with some societal authorities to the changing character of national and international machines (Bell, 1960). Nevertheless, we should indicate that not all uncharted domestic or international organizations are criminals. Some have specific business causes for organizing their collective power and others organize their power to protect their rights (e.g., International Labor Organizations, ILO).

International organizations include some oil cartels such as OPEC B Organization of Petroleum Exporting Countries (Algeria, Gabon, Indonesia, Iran, Iraq, Kuwait, Libya, Nigeria, Qatar, Saudi Arabia, United Arab Emirates, Venezuela). The members of OPEC control prices of energy by establishing oil production quotas in the international marketplace. These organizations may not be directly harmful to their own countries and others. They possess uncontrollable financial power to influence moral and ethical issues for good or evil. Ralph Nader (2000: 3) indicates:

> Over the past twenty years, big business has increasingly dominated our political economy. This control by corporate government over our political government is creating a widening >democracy gap.' ... The unconstrained behavior of big business is subordinating our democracy to the control of a corporate plutocracy that knows few self-imposed limits to the spread of its power to all sectors of our society.

There are two other types of organizations: (1) unions and (2) employee organizations. Both types of organizations gather employees of public and private organizations. A union is a formal and legal association of workers that promotes the employment rights and duties of its members by collective decisions and actions. Unions' primary concerns are related to wages, benefits, incentives, work rules, sanitation, safety, and security of employees. The status of unions varies among countries depending on the culture and the laws that define employer-employee and/or union-management relationships. Employees in different nations are represented by many different kinds of unions such as craft unions, industrial unions, and federations. A craft union is a type of collective bargaining system members do one type of work, often using specialized technical or vocational skills and training (e.g., International Association of Bridge, Structural and Ornamental Iron Workers). An industrialized union includes many workers working in the same industry or company, regardless of jobs held (e.g., United Food and Commercial Workers, The United Auto Workers). The federations are groups of autonomous national and international unions. This type of union is the most complex organization in which individual unions work together and present a more unified front to the public, legislators, and members (e.g., American Federation of State, County, and Municipal Employees and American Federation of Labor and Congress of Industrial Organizations- AFL-CIO), (Mathis and Jackson, 1997:528).

Employee organizations in contrast were said to have a greater concern for the occupational aspects of employment, including the quality of public services and of the people performing it. Employees of state and local governments serve in a variety of capacities. Among public employees are police, firefighters, sanitation workers, nurses, health aids, clerks, prison guards, utility workers, and others. This is substantial range of occupations demonstrates the wide range of matters with which public employees are concerned.

CHAPTER SUMMARY

There are several moral, ethical, and legal issues concerning decision-making processes and operations in an organization. Accordingly, there are several obligations concerning individual moral commitments, professional grouping ethical convictions, and organizational legal mandates. Our plan in this chapter was to provide you with a professional ethical framework and the conceptual tools to sufficiently to allow you professionally to behave morally and ethically in your operations. We have devoted our primary attention to analyze why professionalism bound with ethics? Are there any other terms than professionalism and occupationalism such as paraprofessionalism and vocationalism in the workplace?

The notion of professionalism does seem to be more impersonally regulated concepts and often has been structured in terms of serving beyond self. Everyday we hear the terms of profession, professional, and professionalism. At one level, we describe a member of profession as related to a group of experts who are committed to certain rules and regulations through observing a pluralistic professional code of ethics. These professional codes of ethics mandate a member of a profession to observe them in addition to the legal mandated rules. In an economical term, professionalism is more oriented towards elitism. This means more should be given to those who have developed their intelligence rather than more is given to those who have not. Although all ethical concepts of professionalism, paraprofessionalism, and occupationalism refer to human social activities, there are significant differences, as well as interesting emphases among them. Professionals are conceived as practitioners of a specific scientific branch of knowledge and practitioners of a pragmatic profession who set voluntarily values and standards for the integrity of their own professions. They possess all possible pluralistic competencies to practice their jobs and morally, ethically, and legally are accountable for their success or failure. This perception enshrines a range of virtues more than a set of scientific skills. This means that professionals practice their skills with very high levels of virtuous standards. Finally, professionalism is known as a concept and practice that resents in bureaucratic objectives of a group of people who are loyal to their specializations.

There are two types of professionalism: (1) The restricted professionalism, and (2) The extended professionalism. The restricted professionalism is defined as the notions of procedural specialization competence, mechanical operational skills, and contractual bounded commitments to the profession. An extended professionalism perception aspires precisely with relentless acquisition of knowledge through practicing a profession. It is related to maintaining continuous independent judgment rather than merely to be obedient to the bureaucratic authorities.

The argument for making a distinction between a profession and an occupation in a moral, ethical, and legal term is based on two claims: (1) Codes of ethics and (2) Codes of conduct. What is a code of professional ethics? Professionals are required to possess in addition to specific theoretical expertise and technical skills, a range of distinctive personal moral virtues, cultural values, and legal knowledge to elevate the interest and needs of their clients above their selves-interest. The professional codes of ethics require not only acquisition of appropriate theoretical knowledge (e.g., scientific, evidential, observational, deductive, tacit, technological, legal, and ethical), they also require competencies and experiences in practicing moral knowledge. The professional codes of ethics sufficiently must include enough matters of normative, evaluative, and behavioral criteria rather than sole scientific or theoretical reflections of problem solving. The professional codes of ethics must focus on the pursuit of what is true and good rather than upon the discovery of what seems to be good or true.

The words of paraprofessional and ancillary refer to the engagement of specific training and pragmatic skillful activities in which individuals regularly devote their daily activities to assist professionals in order to acquire living income. Most paraprofessional groups aspire to the rule ethics (e.g., physician aids, nurses, paralegal, lab technicians, etc.).

There are three major groups of paraprofessionals: (1) registered, (2) certified, and (3) licensed. Registration is a legal process by which qualified individuals are included in a listed roster maintained by governmental or non-governmental agencies. Registration in some cases allows individuals to carry designated recognizable titles after their names. Certification is a process by which a non-governmental agency and/or a scientific association grant recognition to an individual who has certain predetermined qualifications specified by that agency or association. Licensed paraprofessional degree is the process by which a qualified governmental agency grants permission to people meeting predetermined qualifications to engage in a given occupation and/or use a particular title.

Occupationalism is enshrined with legal standards and requires a specific set of skillful training programs. Occupationals are not professionals, because they do not require the same equivalent qualifications of professional expertise. The main objective for an occupation is to pursue self-interest. From this perspective, if university professors, lawyers, or physicians convert their jobs from professionalism to occupationalism by self-interest their clients will suffer from such self-interest. Then they will not be trusted to serve people.

Codes of conduct in an occupation do not exhaust the issues of ethics. Ethical codes of conduct are general behavioral and procedural rules for both professions and occupations. They specify particular legal prohibitions and ideals, each of which can be evaluated from moral and ethical point of view. Occupational codes of conduct spell out a corporation's expected behavioral standards for effectively communicating those standards to all employees including managers.

The word vocation connotes the relation of self and a pragmatic technical problem solving. To have a vocation is to have more meaning than an occupation. Also, vocation is more than a job, a role, or even a career that one arbitrarily chooses on the basis of personal preference or inclination because members in society. Societies emphasize codes of conduct. Affiliated members of a society strive to enhance their humanitarian and philanthropic awareness by raising voices against injustice, unfairness, and wrong doings of authorities or organizations. Organizations in the field of business are known as those entities which are committed to specific causes and effects such as commercial, trade, exchange materials, goods, and services either as buyers or sellers. The best example of such organizations is known as trusts, monopolies, cartels, and consumer organizations. Domestically and internationally, these organizations play very important functional roles in the marketplace.

The illicit activity of organized criminals for receiving continuous profit is one of the ladders of social mobility for some political and financial authorities in all nations. Indeed it is not too much to say that the whole question of organized crime in the international market cannot be understood unless one appreciates: (1) the distinctive role of organized gambling as a function of mass-consumption economy, (2) the specific role various demographic movements around the world have in creating marginal businesses and crime, and (3) the relationship of criminals with some societal authorities to the changing character of national and international machines. Nevertheless, we should indicate that not all uncharted domestic or international organizations are criminals. Some have specific business causes for organizing their collective power and others organize their power to protect their rights (e.g., International Labor Organizations, ILO).

International organizations include some oil cartels such as OPEC; Organization of Petroleum Exporting Countries (Algeria, Gabon, Indonesia, Iran, Iraq, Kuwait, Libya, Nigeria, Qatar, Saudi Arabia, United Arab Emirates, Venezuela). The members of OPEC control prices of energy by establishing oil production quotas in the international marketplace. These organizations may not be directly harmful to their own countries and others. They possess uncontrollable financial power to influence moral and ethical issues for good or evil. Over the past twenty years, big business has increasingly dominated our political economy. This control by corporate government over our political government is creating a widening democracy gap. There are two other types of organizations: (1) unions and (2) employee organizations. Both types of organizations gather employees of public and private organizations. A union is a formal and legal association of workers that promotes the employment rights and duties of its members by collective decisions and actions. Unions' primary concerns are related to wages, benefits, incentives, work rules, sanitation, safety, and security of employees. The status of unions varies among countries depending on the culture and the laws that define employer-employee and/or union-management relationships. Employees in different nations are represented by many different kinds of unions such as craft unions, industrial unions, and federations. A craft union is a type of collective bargaining system members do one type of work, often using specialized technical or vocational skills and training (e.g., International Association of Bridge, Structural and Ornamental Iron Workers). An industrialized union includes many workers working in the same industry or company, regardless of jobs held (e.g., United Food and Commercial Workers, The United Auto Workers). The federations are groups of autonomous national and international unions. This type of union is the most complex organization in which individual unions work together and present a more unified front to the public, legislators, and members (e.g., American Federation of State, County, and Municipal Employees and American Federation of Labor and Congress of Industrial Organizations- AFL-CIO).

Employee organizations in contrast were said to have a greater concern for the occupational aspects of employment, including the quality of public services and of the people performing it. Employees of state and local governments serve in a variety of capacities. Among public employees are police, firefighters, sanitation workers, nurses, health aids, clerks, prison guards, utility workers, and others. This is substantial range of occupations demonstrates the wide range of matters with which public employees are concerned.

QUESTIONS FOR DISCUSSION

- What is a profession?
- What are distinguishing differences between a profession and a paraprofession?
- Distinguish differences between a profession and a occupation.
- Distinguish differences between professional codes of ethics and occupational codes of conduct?
- Define special rights, duties, entitlements, privileges, and autonomy of a professional person.
- Why does society allow professionals more autonomy and self-rulership than paraprofessionals and occupationals?
- Argue in favor or against allowing a profession to govern itself.
- Under what conditions is self-governance by a profession justifiable?
- Why is a professional code of ethics justifiable for a professional's autonomy to perform their duties?
- What characteristics and procedures should codes of ethics have in a profession?
- Argue that an occupational and/or a paraprofessional person should not have the same rights and duties in a democratic society as other professionals.
- Make distinctions among different themes and objectives of professional academies, associations, organizations, and unions.
- What are the limits of moral, ethical, and legal ordinations among professions?
- What is the difference between restricted professionalism and extended professionalism?
- What are differences among registered, licensed, and certified paraprofessionals?
- What are different types of management philosophy concerning moral, ethical, legal, and amoral behavior and conduct?
- Analyze different moral and ethical commitments through professionalization of a group of experts.
- What are relationships between professional employees and employers?
- What are ethical, moral, and legal boundaries between experts and their organizations?
- How do you perceive business organizations as vocational entities?

CASE STUDY

THE ETHICAL, PROFESSIONAL ENGINEERING CONVICTIONS AND THE MANAGERIAL BUREAUCRATIC RESPONSIBILITIES OF THE MORTON HIOKOL CORPORATION ON THE NIGHT BEFORE THE 1986 CHALLENGER EXPLOSION

The following information is related to the events of the night before January 28, 1986 when the Challenger headed into space. To refresh your memory, in the cold freezing morning of January 28, 1986, *The Kennedy Space Center* in Florida was busy preparing the launch of the 25th space shuttle into space. *Mission 51-L, the Tenth flight of Orbiter Challenger.* Before January 28, 1986, the launch of Challenger had been delayed five times due to bad weather. Unfortunately, almost no testing had been done below 40 degrees F and no lift-off had occurred after a night as cold as that day. The engineers had to extrapolate. But, with the lives of seven astronauts at stake, including a civilian for the first time B a teacher -- the decision seemed clear enough that safety was not the first priority for Morton Thiokol Corporation. January 28, 1986 was the coldest day that NASA had ever launched a shuttle. The time of the flight was at 11:38 AM Easter Standard Time which the Challenger with seven crews left Pad 39B at Kennedy. Seventy-three seconds into flight, the Orbiter Challenger exploded, killing all seven of its crew.

THE CATASTROPHIC EVENT

While *The Kennedy Space Center* engineers were counting down for a launch the next morning B the night before January 28, 1986, Robert Lund, Vice President for engineering at Morton Thiokol, presided at a meeting of engineers that unanimously recommended against the launch for the sixth time. Lund had concurred and informed his boss, Jerald Mason. Mason informed *The Space Center*. Lund had expected the flight to be postponed. Nevertheless, the State of the Union message was only a day away. Everyone in *The Space Center* supposed the President was anxious to announce the first teacher among astronauts to be in space. If *The Space Center* not launches that day, they would have to wait at least a month. It was not clear why *The Space Center* wanted to launch. They didn't say, but the reasons were obvious. Previous five times delay had put them well behind schedule already.

The Space Center wanted to launch, but they would not launch without Thiokol's engineering approval. They urged Mason to reconsider. Lund recalled Thiokol's engineers and all engineers repeated their objections. Mason was present in that meeting. Mason had drowned the flight managers to one side of the meeting room and said something that made Lund think again. Mason had urged Lund to take off [your] engineering hat and put on [your] management hat. Finally, Lund did and changed his mind despite of professional engineering objections and signed the document to lift-off for the shuttle the next morning.

THE TECHNICAL CONDITION OF THE LIFTOFF

On January 28, 1986, the temperature at ground level at the launching pad was around 36 degrees F, which was 15 degrees F cooler than any other previous launch by NASA. It was the policy of NASA to preauthorize the safety of the crew to be first. NASA had a very good experience in safety record., because NASA would not allow a launch unless the technical people approved.

The Solid Rocket Boosters (SRB) was ignited. At 68 seconds after ignition, videotape showed black smoke coming from the aft (bottom) field joint of the right SRB. The black smoke suggested that grease, joint insulation, and rubber O-rings were being burned. The black smoke was an indication that the aft joint was not sealing correctly.

In flight, flashed were seen on Challenger. Three bright flashes shot across the Challenger's wings, 45 seconds after lift-off. Each of the three flashes lasted only 1/13 of a second. At 58.8 seconds into flight on enhanced film a flame was seen coming from the right SRB at 305 degrees. As the flame increased in size, the flame grew with an intense heat of 5600 degrees F, making it hot and weak. The main explosion occurred in both Hydrogen and Oxygen tanks. All technical defects happened during a short period of time within 73.62 seconds after lift-off.

PROFESSIONAL ETHICAL ANALYSIS

This case illustrates different views between professional engineers who believed that the lift-off was not safe, and the management team who believed that the schedule of the lift-off had to be implemented by all means and ends. While no one broke the law, but there was an ethical and moral wrongdoing. Immediately, after that sad historical day, Mason took early retirement and Lund was moved to a new office. When managers ignore professional opinions of experts and make their own minds without technical considerations, the end result is a catastrophe.

CASEE QUESTIONS FOR DISCUSSION

- How do you perceive the role of a manager as a professional or as an occupational? Explain why.

- Do you find any professional codes of ethics in today's business world?
- What is the difference between the engineering hat and management hat?
- What were the NASA's responsibilities concerning the safety procedural code of lift-off of the Tenth *flight of Challenger?*
- Why Mr. Lund and Mason changed their minds in spite of all engineering objections for the lift-off of the Challenger?
- Who should be blamed in the Challenger's explosion? Explain why.
- Do you find any wrongdoing in the above case? If yes explain them.
- What was the ethical, moral, and legal role of government concerning this catastrophe?
- Who paid the price of managerial wrongdoing in this case?
- Do you find any difference between managerial professional code of ethics, and managerial code of conduct?

CASE SOURCES

M. Davis, "Explaining Wrongdoing," In Robert A. Larmer (Ed.), *Ethics in the Workplace: Selected Readings in Business Ethics,* (Minneapolis/St. Paul: West Publishing Company, 1996), 17-28.

The Presidential Commission on the Space Shuttle Challenger Disaster, (Washington DC: June 6, 1986, Esp. V. I), 82-103.

Report of the Presidential Commission on the Space Shuttle Challenger Accident: In Compliance With Executive Order 12546 of February 3, 1986. <Http://www.jlhs.nhusd.k12.ca.us/Classes/Social_Scienc/Challenger.html/ Challenger.html>.

CHAPTER 15

PROFESSIONAL INTEGRITY, WHISTLE BLOWING, AND ORGANIZATIONAL LOYALTY

No honest professional system is corrupted,
unless people who operate it corrupt it.

No honest system can be established,
unless all individuals who design and operate it are honest.

No honest system can claim what cause is morally right,
unless it wants to do the right things correctly.

No honest system can operate in the business world,
unless it creates a sense of honesty, loyalty, and fidelity.

No honest whistle blower can be effective in society,
unless the fear of retaliatory personal professional consequences are eliminated.

CHAPTER OBJECTIVES

When you have read this chapter, you will be able to do the following:

- Learn what we mean by employees' loyalty and fidelity to employers.
- Learn what we mean by employers' obligations to employees private information.
- Learn how reciprocal employer-employee relationships should be established on the basis of trust.
- Define the terms of whistle blowing; internal whistle blowing; external whistle blowing; personal whistle blowing, impersonal whistle blowing; and governmental whistle blowing.
- Understand the rational philosophy behind whistle blowing.
- Learn how and when whistle blowing is permissible even though it may violate one's obligation of loyalty to colleagues, peers, profession/corporation, and humanity at large.
- Whether serious threat and harm to the public interest actually, ethically, and morally obligates one with knowledge of this threat or harm to make this knowledge public.
- Know how whistle blowing fosters or destroys public trust.
- Know how whistle blowing betrays unethical and/or illegal business decisions and operations.
- Know how whistle blowing protects employees and shareholders from selfish decisions and/or operations of CEOs.
- Learn how someone argues that whistle blowing is always morally permitted or prohibited.
- Learn how much fidelity, if any, a worker owes an organization.
- Argue under what conditions is whistle blowing ethically permitted.
- Know under what circumstances law protects a whistle blower.
- Learn how a business firm can prevent whistle blowing.

THOUGHT STARTER

Any meaningful altruistic judgment in the field of business must be based upon the equitable concept of the public interest and the stakeholders' rights that are indigenous to society's goodness. To accept any other option is to deny that businesses originate some policies as well as modify their original organizational vision and mission in the face of glutinous interest. The default doctrinal separation between the declared mission and pragmatic practices of businesses is converting legal businesses into anarchical behavior. Formulating legal business laws without professional codes of ethics in a meaningful enforcement of law jeopardizes the stakeholders' rights and violates the public trust. One of the issues of today's stock market is the negligence of the Security Exchange

Commission to control and oversee over book keeping of the publicly owned private corporations. We have seen how many executives of publicly owned private corporations illegally transferred billions of dollars of corporate assets into their own pockets. Such illegal actions are mainly based upon book cooking of accounting firms such as Arthur Andersen Company (e.g., Enron, Adelphia, WordCom, AOL, and many others).

Unethical business power and influence in shaping the image of public trust through lobbying can abuse the public interest and consumer rights. Business decisions and operations either lead toward preconceived moral and ethical ends or they do not. If they do; they are complying with stakeholders' legal rights, if they don't, they violate the public trust. This is the current situation of business ethics in the international market. The power and influence of businesses, specifically the giant ones, in econo-political systems has grown prodigiously, while the intellect trust and honesty has become flabby. With the compounded gluttonous appetite of some businesses, the public conscience can no longer tolerate dishonest decisions and operations of executives in the field of business. How can the public prevent such unethical and immoral actions? The answer is either through whistle blowers or governmental regulatory agencies.

Democratic governments, however, have little meaning except within the context of certain ethical and moral transcendent value systems. The job of a citizen as a whistle blower and the duty of governmental regulatory agencies are fused; one makes little sense without the other.

The difference between a whistle blower's objective and the governmental regulatory obligation to the public raises serious questions about the safety and security of consumers. Such a disparity creates a twofold issue:

- The narrow citizenship responsibility of the whistle blower
- The expanded governmental regulatory obligations in the recognition a sense of community wellbeing

The twofold issue has one common threat, the necessity for the whistle blower to embark upon a voyage of discovery, seeking to inform the public of "what is" rather than "what ought to be" this is the center of ethical and moral concern. Such a legitimate concern promises to be a long process for the public interest. The quest for a better understanding of the fused responsibilities of a whistle blower and obligations of a governmental regulatory agency is the first step to the development of a moral and ethical system in a nation.

Employees' dignity is enhanced by that which contributes to their individual sense of worth when working for a business. This implies that the working environment should not be demeaning to the human spirit, both within and beyond the business environment. Employers and employees must regard human dignity as the ultimate goal of their investments conducting an honest and safe business. The conflictive interest between private or publicly owned businesses (non-governmental business entities) and society at large can no longer tolerate slight-of-hand semantic deceptions which distort the meanings of trust and confidence, because the public interest is not susceptible to quickie justifications. Nevertheless, business interest needs to be fused with humanizing ethics.

Today's businesses are not like previous conventional businesses. They are now businesses in the domain of public interest. The dividing line between most privately owned businesses such as family businesses, and publicly private owned businesses is being eroded because of a reciprocal fusion among the family businesses and publicly owned businesses. As that line gradually fades, businesses should exercise their ethical and legal power in a civilized manner.

PLAN OF THIS CHAPTER

There are several moral, ethical, and legal issues concerning decision-making processes and operations in an organization. Accordingly, there are several obligations concerning individual moral commitments, professional grouping ethical convictions, and organizational legal mandates. In addition, there are several attributes such as trust, loyalty, fidelity ethical, moral, and legal mandates of whistle blowing.

In a democratic society, we believe that businesses have moral, ethical, and legal obligations not to harm consumers, employees, and above all the environment. This obligation falls on the board of governance and their selected individuals as executive officers who manage their businesses. In addition, other professional employees such as engineers, managers, accountants, and legal experts according to their professional codes of ethics are not ethically allowed to take part in any immoral and unethical activities.

Legally individual employees within the holistic operational procedures of a corporation are not liable for organizational wrongdoing. Do employees further have a moral obligation and ethical conviction to prevent harmful actions? If they detect corruption and deception in a corporation what are their duties and responsibilities? If they do so, should they proceed to announce them to the public? If they are able to do so, how should they assess the equity between their moral and ethical obligations and their consequential harmful cost to themselves? As the fear of personal cost increases, the moral duties and ethical obligations decrease.

While, employees may not be legally accountable in any activity that they know will cause harm to other employees, consumers, and the environment, they need to ask themselves the following questions:

- Do employees have ethical and legal obligations to prevent harm?
- Isn't it a selfish desire to destroy others' lives at the expense of saving ones life?
- Are we morally and ethically obliged to ignore others' safety and security in the workplace for the benefit of self?

- What are the moral, ethical, and legal obligations of employees and former employees of a corporation when they know that their employers are harming the public?

Answering to the above questions is very complicated and leads us to consider *informants* or *whistle-blowers*.

From another point of view what is the role of managers in the above situations? Since individual managers are representing role models for their workers in their organizations, they provide advice to employees who find themselves in an ethical quandary. Also, since managers are responsible for employees' supervision, they are increasingly being held accountable by organizational wrongdoing.

It is a basic legitimate responsibility of a corporation not to harm any individual or entity. We have seen that corporations have ethical convictions and legal mandates not to abuse, misuse, neglect, or cheat the public. These ethical convictions and legal mandates fall primarily on those who manage the corporation. Yet while other organizational members are not ethically and legally allowed to take part in any illegal activity, there are several discussions concerning employee loyalty and fidelity in contrast with sincere ethical commitments to the social fabric.

In this chapter, we are going to examine what responsibilities managers have what duties employees have and how both managers and employees can be accountable to the public. In this chapter we first will define the definitions of trust, responsibilities, loyalty, and fidelity of whistle-brewers and informants as these terms relate to their professions and the public. Second we will discuss whether and when it is permissible to violate one's obligation of loyalty to colleagues, peers, profession/corporation, and humanity at large. Third, we will examine whether serious threat and harm to the public interest actually legally and/or morally oblige with knowledge of this threat or harm make this knowledge public. Fourth, we will examine whether whistle blowing fosters or destroys the public trust. Fifth, we will assess how whistle blowing can betray unethical and/or illegal decisions and operations for the benefit of humanity. Sixth, we want to know how whistle blowing protects employees and shareholders from selfish decisions and/or operations of CEOs or the governing board of directors of a corporation.

In particular, this chapter looks at the following topics:

- What we mean by blowing the whistle?
- How do we define whistle blowing?
- How an employee's loyalty to the firm can cause him/her to ignore citizenship duties?
- How blowing the whistle creates conflicts of interest problems.
- What are the moral, ethical, and legal choices faced when a corporation's present or former employees are whistle-blowers?

- What are moral and ethical obligations of employers to employees and customers as informants?
- What are the rights and privileges in a democratic society concerning the freedom of speech?
- How far does this right extend into the business world?
- What are the obligations and limits of free speech?
- What are the mutual obligations of employees and employees to the public?
- Under what circumstances should an employee or a manager blow the whistle?
- How big is your whistle?
- When, for how long, and how loud should an employee or a manager blow the whistle?
- Through what channels of mass media should an employee or a manager blow the whistle?
- When and how should the whistle blower be protected?

DUTIES AND OBLIGATIONS OF EXPERTS

Personal moral responsibilities and professional ethical duties are closely related. In general, we have an obligation or duty to fulfill our responsibilities, and we are responsible for fulfilling our obligations and duties. Duties are viewed as notions of "completeness." Duty is a constraint on the scope of permissible actions, but not all constraints are duties. Duties, to begin with, apply directly only to actions. A duty might correspond to a specific right held by a specific person. To make the issue clear, we must say that what is meant is a duty that we would have to discharge by doing what results in our rights. Moral duties, however, are always somebody else's; indeed, everybody else's business. Society may compel us to what is our moral duty. Ethical professional duties are what we owe in consequence of our social condition. Such duties are essentially to others, even though the considerations that give rise to them are, no doubt, anchored in our interests as humans, because there are general relations to each other as persons interacting in a society.

For example, in the field of bioethics, if the category of professional duty applies at all scientific testing systems, it stems from ethical principles. Moral duties are distinct from legal duties, and the necessary conditions of each are distinct. A necessary condition of the validity of legal duties is the validity of the procedure by which the law imposing them is enacted. Moral duties do not presuppose the validity of any legal procedure. An agent might find that a legal duty contradicts a moral duty, unless conformity with moral duty is among the criteria of legitimacy of legal enactments.

Integrative scientific advancement and technological development have established a diffusing responsibility among experts. In order for a relationship to exist between what professionals think is right and what they do, they must feel responsibility and accountability for the consequences of their actions. Therefore, the feeling of personal responsibility is a prerequisite for moral action. The communities of academicians, researchers, and practitioners often become disconnected from the consequences of their actions and do not feel personally responsibility for their own actions. Then, an expert's responsibilities and accountabilities become *diffusive*. Trevino and Nelson (1995: 161) argue that there are at least four reasons why individuals may not feel personally responsible for their ethical team efforts:

- Individuals are often encouraged to turn responsibility over to those at higher levels. This translates into believing the ethical problems or decisions are someone else's responsibility.
- Important diffusive scientific and technological efforts are often made in groups. Therefore, responsibility for the ethical decisions becomes diffused among all research team members.
- Ethical responsibility in physiological and psychological research is often so divided that individuals see themselves as only a small cog in a large machine. Therefore, they see only what is directly ahead of them and no one sees the whole picture of wrongdoing.
- Ethical responsibilities can be diffused because of the physiological and/or psychological distance between the researchers and potential victims. Therefore, when potential victims are distant or out of sight, it is more difficult to see oneself as responsible for any negative outcomes.

EMPLOYEES' LOYALTY TO THE FIRM AND CONFLICTS OF INTEREST

It will be helpful to begin with an ethical attribution concerning honesty, trust, loyalty, and fidelity of employees to their organizations. When employees accept a firm's employment offers,   ethically they are agreeing to perform certain tasks, usually during certain shifts, in exchange for financial remuneration. Whether such employments are based upon legal contracts or oral promises, both parties, employers and employees, establish specific relationships with reciprocal obligations to be met. Within the contextual boundary of such reciprocal contracts, there are certain governing ethical, moral, and legal bindings in which employers and employees are entitled to. Employees are obligated to establish loyalty to their employers and in return, employers are obligated to maintain the integrity of the workplace by not abusing, misusing, or violating organizational policy and societal general rules and regulations concerning employees' rights.

Table. 15.1: Bradley's View: My Station and Its Duty

What is it then that I am to realize? We have said it is in 'my station and its duties.' To know what a man is (as we have seen) you must not take him in isolation. He is one of a people, he was born in a family, and he lives in a certain society, in a certain state. What he has to do depends on what his place is, what his function is, and that all comes from his station. ... We must content ourselves by pointing out that there are such facts as the family, then in a middle position a man's own profession and society, and, over all, the larger community of the state. Leaving out of sight the question of a society wider than the state, we must say that a man's life with its moral duties is in the main filled up by his station in that system of wholes which the state is, and that this, partly by its laws and institutions, and still more by its spirit, gives him the life which he does live and ought to live... In short, man is a social being; he is real only because he is social, and can realize himself only because it is as social that he realizes himself. The mere individual is a delusion of theory; and the attempt to realize it in practice is the starvation and mutilation of human nature, with total sterility or the production of monstrosities... The point here is that you can not have the moral world unless it is willed; that to be willed it must be willed by persons; and that these persons not only have the moral world as the content of their wills, but also must in some way be aware of themselves as willing this content... We must never let this out of our sight, that, where the moral world exists, you have and you must have these two sides; neither will stand apart from the other; moral institutions are carcasses without personal morality, and personal morality apart from moral institutions is an unreality, a soul without body.

Source: Bradley, F. H. (1876, 1927). *Ethical Studies*. First published in
    1876, Second Edition, 1972. Oxford: Clarendon   Press,
    Excerpts from Chapter 5.

In a document prepared for the American Philosophical Association's Committee for Education in Business Ethics, Baier (1965: 146) defined fidelity as an agent's willingness to promote the interests of someone ahead of the interest of others due to the agent's obligation to someone. To put it in more meaningful terms, an employee incurs an obligation to the employer by accepting employment. In addition, both employers and employees are expected to manifest their trust to the public by good faith through conducting honest and legitimate business activities. Within such a contract, all parties are expected to carry out their obligations. Nevertheless, employers' promises and employees' loyalty bind both parties together to establish very clear expectations from each other. Sometimes such expectations exceed the boundaries of their relationships and cause conflict of interest. Morally and ethically, neither parties should promise the other blind loyalty or total submission to the wishes of the other, because they may lose their personal autonomy.

Specifically, in the field of business, as we mentioned in chapter thirteen, there are different types of employees – professionals, paraprofessionals, and occupationals; who possess certain moral, ethical, and legal obligations to the public through their "professional codes of ethics," or "occupational codes of conduct." Some writers believe that professionals can't be loyal to their employers and ignore their obligations to their professions, because professionals understand that business organizations are the kind of institutions that sometimes can't properly perform their social roles and be loyal to the public. Why not? Because business entities operate in all societies for making profit – self interest. Nevertheless, employers or employees' loyalty to each other and to society depend upon conditions or circumstances, which emerge during their relationships.

Since loyalty is based upon self-sacrifice, both employers and employees on the basis of their economic conditions are not able to keep the promise of permanent loyalty. When a corporation is facing economic hardship, managers have to trim their excessive workforce and lay off people. Such a condition can't fulfill a corporation's obligation of loyalty to employees. Also, when employees find better job opportunities in the market place with higher salaries and benefits, immediately they quit their old jobs. Neither employers nor employees will sacrifice their lives and personal interests for the sake of each other. Therefore, morally and ethically loyalty by its own term, is conditional.

It is clear that a business organization could not function without employees' and customers' loyalty. Arguably, some obligations of loyalty come from employee jobs and customers' quality of products. For example, the obligation to warn the organization of danger, the obligation to act in a way that protects its legitimate interests, and the obligation to cooperate activity in the furtherance of legitimate corporate objectives create a general sense of loyalty among employees (Fiedler, 1992: 87).

Conflict of interest is the result of a clash between employers' objectives and employee's desires. In order not be pushed into a confrontation between employers and employees, we need not only comply with societal rules, also, we need to enhance both "professional codes of ethics," and "occupational codes of conduct." Weiss (2003: 328) suggests seven recommendations for integrating "ethical professional codes of ethics" along with "occupational codes of conducts" with social legal mandates as follows:

- Confidentiality should not be so restrictive that it prohibits employees from consulting with internal personnel regarding ethical questions.
- A fair and objective hearing process should follow any report of an ethical problem or conflict.
- Assurance should be given to all employees that their rights with respect to discrimination and to adequate notice and compensation in the event of a layoff will be protected.
- In order to facilitate open communication and clarity expectations, employee rights and terms of employment should be clearly stated in codes of conduct and ethics codes.
- Executive support of the code of conduct should be demonstrated in the form of clear sanctions against those who violate it.

- Conflicts of interest revolving around ownership interest in related concerns need to be addressed, as these conflicts can cloud judgments.
- Consider any external ethical codes of conduct that influence employees in the corporation, and design the corporate code so it does not conflict with these.

MORAL, ETHICAL, AND LEGAL CHOICES FACING WITH A CORPORATION'S PRESENT OR FORMER EMPLOYEES

Theoretically, the reciprocal obligations between business organizations and their employees could be perceived as having a fair and equitable balance between performance and pay for an honest piece of work (unit work), and/or an honest day's work (time work). Such a philosophical perception is based upon employees' conscience to work truly for a corporation and to be paid by their employers a decent wage, salary, and/or commission. In addition, employers expect employees to be loyal and obedient to them. This theoretical model on the surface is obviously very rational and too simple, but in reality there are other major moral and ethical issues that arise between employers and employees. These issues are as follows:

- Should professional employees be committed to their "professional codes of ethics," and/or to their "occupational codes of conduct," and ignore organizational loyalty?
- How should employers believe in employees' civil liberties concerning their rights and duties?
- How should employers successfully respect and maintain employees' moral dignity and institutional integrity?
- How should institutional policies and practices concerning matters of hiring, promotion, discipline, separation, compensation, salaries or wages, and benefits morally, ethically, and legally be practiced?
- How should employees be organized in the forms of unions, associations, and other types of gathering for the purpose of collective bargaining processes?
- What should be the relationships between employers and employees concerning safety and security of their workplace and business environments?
- Can or should employees expect their employers to treat them as human beings?
- Can or should employees expect to treat their consumers and customers in a manner that does not violate their civil liberties?
- How can a business entity be in harmony with the natural environment?

Ewing (1983: 141) believes that business organizations very frequently invade employees' civil liberties and expresses his opinion in the following manner:

> In most ...organizations, during working hours, civil liberties are a will-o'-the-wisp. The Constitutional rights that employees have grown accustomed to in family, school, and church life generally must be left outdoors, like cars in the parking lot. As in totalitarian countries, from time to time a benevolent chief executive or department head may encourage speech, conscience, and privacy, but these scarcely can be called rights, for management can take them away at will... It is fair to say that an enormous corporate archipelago has grown which, in terms of civil liberties, is as different from the rest of America as day is from night. In this archipelago... the system comes first, the individual second or [the profit first and consumers second].

Such a disparity causes employees or former employees to go to the public and disclose the corporation illegal, unethical, and immoral practices. These types of current or former employees are called either informants or whistle blowers.

WHAT ARE THE MORAL AND ETHICAL OBLIGATIONS OF EMPLOYERS TO OTHER EMPLOYEES AND CUSTOMERS AS INFORMANTS?

It is no secret that most institutions frequently seek, store, communicate, and sell personal information about their employees and customers without their consent. Nowadays, it is very popular to bug employees' offices, lounges, cafeterias, and vehicles hoping to discover who is responsible for disclosing corporate secrets and pilfering and conspiring against management team. Another firm may use an informal grapevine managerial communication system through supervisory meetings to exchange obtained information from employees or to hear organizational rumors and gossips, and/or opening employees' personal mails and E-mails with the hope of discovering potential troublemakers and troubleshooters. Still another corporation may keep detailed files on the personal private lives of its employees either to insure compatibility with organizational vision, mission, and reputation or to spy on their short and long term illnesses in order to avoid paying higher health insurance premiums. These are some examples of collecting information about employees and customers without their knowledge and/or consent.

Someone else defines informed consent as having deliberation and free choice to have access and permission to disclose personal information.

Employees and customers must understand what they are agreeing to allow to be done with their personal information. Deliberation requires not only the in-depth cause and effects of facts but also a full understanding of consequential results. Free choice is providing the voluntary consent to the informants to permit them to disclose personal information. Sometimes information is completed and sometimes it is not. If it is not are complete, then informants have to pursue one step further to discover them. We will explain ethical and moral implications of assimilative integrated discovery systems in the following pages.

WHAT IS ASSIMILATIVE INTEGRATED DISCOVERY SYSTEM (AIDS)?

There are two types of AIDS in the modern world:

- Social Diseases known as Integrated Discovery Systems, (AIDS)
- Ecological diseases Known as Acquired Immune Deficiency Syndrome (AIDS)

The first AIDS is a kind of disease, which causes people to lose their liberty and freedom, and the second is a communicative biological one. Both types of AIDSs have similarities in the form of social contacts; one is the result of sexual contact and the other is the result of informants' contact.

Parhizgar and Lunce (1996:393) have made efforts to present ethical and moral implications of assimilative integrated discovery systems in the workplace by employers. They analyzed the development of knowledge-based information techniques and employees' information profiles in modern organizations. These systems have access through processing to both deep and broad domains of information in corporations and industries as well as modern societies. Through these systems organizations can predict future trends in promotions, training, and retention of their employees. These techniques are new and produce new information, which organizations can use without the help and consent of the knowledge sources because of the existence of highly sophisticated computerized networks and database management systems.

The ontological moral, ethical, and legal approaches to dissimilation and disclosure of employees' information profiles are interdisciplinary issues. Ethical genealogy insists that knowledge-power and information-power are implicated in each other. It shows how knowledge-power not only is a product of information-power but also it can be itself a non-neutral form of abusive power. Therefore, knowledge-based information systems containing the employees' and customers' personal information should be organizationally regulated.

Knowledge-based information systems often are successful precisely when they deny their power to intervene. The question: "What would happen if everyone has access to other's private information systems?" is one with which we are all familiar. We have some familiarity with the sort of ethical, moral, and legal context in which it would be appropriate to ask such a question. Thus, we understand that it is either elliptical for or a prelude to say: "If everyone has access to other's information systems, the consequences would be disastrous," and this is often considered a good reason for concluding that one ought not to have access to others' information systems.

Ethical, moral, and legal genealogy not only investigates obscured continuities of traditional cultural beliefs and political ideologies of employees through a highly sophisticated networking access, such as the knowledge-based and information-system connections, it also can be regarded as the social history of continuous and current knowledge as lacking their traditionally asserted intellectual unity. In such a domain, there are two major issues to be addressed. First, knowledge-based information systems containing employee data are highly disciplined within the field of computer science; however, they may not be highly disciplined within the fields of organizational behavior in which scientific and technological order is imposed on dispersed information systems. Discipline in its ethical and moral terms is the infrastructure of truthful embodiment of information that should be extended to the behavior and conduct of both informants and information users. Second, attention to the use of knowledge-based information systems containing employee data is not merely about organizational societal commitments, it is above all the concern about the integrity of human identity. Therefore, knowledge-based information systems containing the employees' data in businesses should be regulated.

Disciplinary organizational institutionalization of knowledge-based information systems containing data is scheming the protection and appreciation of individual freedom and privacy. It also respects the organizational societal commitments to the legal privacy of social citizens' rights, and the individual professionalization is the moral and ethical responsibilities of knowledge-based information system informants and users. The often-neglected point in modern society is the abusive disseminative power of information contents through unethical and immoral objectives. Through some legal perceptions, "truthful" knowledge is not objective or socially independent, but it is a system of ordered procedures for the production, regulation, distribution, circulation, and operation of information contents. However, the truthful knowledge, through ethical and moral commitments, is based on cultural and individual value systems, which are dynamically changing human perceptual thoughts and judgments.

According to the law of physics, any reaction is based upon some emerged actions. Up to this point we have tried to orient you with one side of organizational immoral and unethical issues, the disclosure of employees' information without their consent. For the following pages we will turn to the other side that refers to the task of whistle blowers. As the early Twentieth century Noble Prize Winner, Rudyard Kipling (1998) said: *"The strength of the pack is the Wolf, and the strength of the Wolf is the pack."*

WHAT IS WHISTLE BLOWING?

Some writers like Martin and Schinzinger (1989: 213) believe that whistle blowing is any act of reporting corporate wrongdoing, regardless of the position of the one doing the reporting. This definition, therefore, could include acts of public reporting by journalists, public interest groups, even a single individual who becomes aware of activity that is either harmful, illegal, or both. Whistle blowing is a new mode of ethical and moral obligation generated by conscientious awareness of an individual or a group of informants concerning serious wrongdoings against intrinsic and extrinsic rights of stakeholders by a corporation. Whistle blowers spotlight a corporation's negligence, intended harm, and/or abusive behavior of managerial decision-making processes and operations that threaten the public interest. Bok (1980: 2) states:

> The stakes in whistle blowing are high. Take the nurse who alleges that physicians enrich in her hospital through unnecessary surgery; the engineer who discloses safety defects in the braking systems of a fleet of new rapid-transit vehicle; the Defense Department official who alerts Congress to military graft and overspending: all know that they pose a threat to those whom they denounce and that their own careers may be at risk.

Nolan (1996: 222) questions the moral and ethical positions of a whistle blower who is working in a corporation:

> If you report the violation to your immediate supervisor, has that fulfilled your ethical obligation? What if the supervisor ignores the report? Should you attempt to over supervisor's head, to your boss's boss, know that the company frowns upon this sort of behavior? Should you take your suspicions to a professional organization, such as a local engineering association? To a news reporter? To a regulatory agency? To a political leader? ... When it is ethically acceptable to violate the principle of loyalty to your employer?

Organizational whistle blowing has been defined as a truthful public disclosure by an employee or a group of employees and/or a former employee or a group of former employees about what "certainly" they believe to be wrongdoing by other employees including managers in or by the organization (Hoffman and Moore, 1990). Whistle blowing occurs when an informant informs the public of inappropriate and devious activities going on inside the organization. In other words, whistle blowing is an effort to make others aware of wrongdoing practices one considers illegal, immoral, and unethical (Buchholz and Rosenthal, 1998: 398).

More limited definitions of the whistle blowing term include the requirement that it is a kind of disclosure activity in which an individual or a group of people makes public a disagreement with an authority or an institution that there has been something very wrong with their decisions and/or operations. Whistle blowing has the narrower objective of shedding light on intentional and deliberated negligence, abuses, harms, or disclosing the wrongdoings to a normal decision-making processes and/or operations.

From the standpoint of psychosocial obligation, whistle blowing is a heroic activity in which an individual feels a courageous humanitarian obligation to disclose serious decisions and/or covert operations that may be harmful to the public. The whistle blower acts on the basis of conscientious obligation to be act in the public interest or institutional interest. Bowie 1982: 142) indicates that it is important to note that the consensus of contemporary moral philosophers is that whistle blowing should be defined as the action of a person within an organization, for it is only in this context that the full moral complexity of the act becomes apparent. Boartright (1993: 133) defines:

> Whistle-blowing is the voluntary release of nonpublic information, as a moral protest, by a member or former member of an organization outside the normal channels of communication to an appropriate audience about illegal and/or immoral conduct in the organization or conduct in the organization that is opposed in some significant way to the public interest.

ANALYSIS OF THE NATURE
OF WHISTLE BLOWING

Under what ethical and legal conditions is whistle blowing morally justified?

- When a corporation is in the process of legal litigation, the whistle blowers are committed to disclose the truth. They should not protect a criminal action by covering up wrong doing decisions and/or covert operations by misrepresenting the truth.
- It should be done based upon an individual's appropriate moral conscientious altruistic motive. The informants deliberately need to inform and/or communicate with organizational authorities to stop organizational wrongdoings.
- The informants should believe that the inappropriate organizational misconduct is based upon evidence that would harm either stakeholders and/or consumers.
- The whistle blowers should honestly analyze organizational negligence, carelessness, harms, and inappropriate conduct that carry totally the nature of wrongdoings.
- The whistle blowers should clearly disclose the immediacy of the violation of consumer rights and the specificity of the violation of the stakeholders' rights.

- The whistle blower should predict some chances of success by disclosing organizational negligence, fraud, harms, abuses, and greed.

THE POSSIBLE RETALIATION AGAINST THE WHISTLE BLOWERS

History is full of incidents when real whistle blowers have sacrificed their lives for the cause of altruism. In some business environments, most whistle blowers are fired. If they are not fired, they have been shunted aside at promotion time and treated as pariahs. Those who consider making a firm's wrongdoings public must therefore be aware that they may be fired, ostracized, and condemned by others. Whistle blowers are honest people and those business people who are morally and ethically (not necessarily legally) guilty of endangering the lives of others, even of indirectly killing their customers, frequently get promoted either by their companies or by their industry towards higher jobs with higher salaries (De George, 1995: 227). For example in the early of 1970, Lee Iacocca, the Vice-President of the Ford Motor Company, initiated an idea to manufacture a new compact car to compete with Japanese' automobile industry. He ordered the Ford's engineers to design and manufacture a type of car to be weighted less than 2,000 pounds, to be priced at less than $2,000.00, to be designed and manufactured within two years not four years, and the new model to be known as the Ford Pinto. Because of accelerated designing and production systems, the Ford Pinto was not tested for rear-end accidents until it was produced. The Ford engineers knew about the Pinto's fatal defect. After manufacturing and selling thousands of the Pinto model, Ford did a study and determined that if a baffle (estimated at costing between $6.65 and $11) were placed between the bumper and the gas tank, the Pinto would save passengers' lives and the gas tank would not be punctured by a bolt from the bumper causing it to burst into flame. As the new Ford Motor Company president, Iacocca made an unethical and immoral decision not to recall all Ford Pinto cars designed from 1971 to1978, because he found that based on calculation of cost-benefit analysis, it was financially beneficial to the Ford Company to proceed to the legal systems and settle life loses of those drivers and passengers with less money rather than to spend millions of dollars for the recall. Ford's unethical and immoral actions have been widely criticized. A Ford Motor Company's executive and engineer, Harley Copp, as a whistle blower, was critical of the Pinto from the start. He was forced to leave the company and voiced his criticism, which was later on taken up by Ralph Nader. As a result of making profit for the Ford Company, in 1980, Lee Iacocca became as a famous "amoral executive" in the American automobile industry. He was promoted as the Chief Executive Officer of the Chrysler Company. Then he saved the bankrupted Chrysler Company through his amoral skills (De George, 1981; Strobel, 1980; and Dowie, 1977).

Business people possess very influential political links in industrialized societies. Their influences are very effective in the judiciary systems by when they hire very capable lawyers to find legal loopholes to turn around all allegations. Only rarely have whistle blowers been praised and supported by industrialized societies. This is not surprising, because industrialized societies have not established a safe mechanistic justice procedure to support truthful and honest whistle blowers. By this token, businesses have found many loop holes in law to do what they are not morally and ethically supposed to do.

As the preceding discussion mentioned, employees and/or former employees sometimes learn or experience about the illegal or immoral actions of a business organization or executives' misconduct. When such an informant tries to correct the situation within institutional channels and is thwarted, central ethical and legal questions emerge: Should the employees avoid organizational loyalty and go public with the information? Should society; specifically the Department of Justice protects them? Should society provide sufficient protections for the informants and/or whistle blowers against retaliatory actions either by a company or an industry?

In a democratic society, it is responsibility of all citizens to disclose wrong doings in their societies in order to not let a group of corrupted people to fool or harm the public. Nevertheless, in reality deciding to go public and blowing the whistle creates harsh consequences and/or life threats for the whistle blowers. Among the most famous cases of whistle blowers is the case of Karen Silkwood. Sass (2001: 222) reports: "Karen Silkwood was killed on November 12, 1974, at 28 years of age while driving to meet a reporter from the New York Times with documentation about plutonium fuel rod tampering at the Kerr-McGee uranium and plutonium plants in Cimarron, Oklahoma." In another case, Kermit Vandivier, who blew the whistle on the B. F. Goodrich Aircraft Brakes scandal in 1975, also lost his job. James Pope claimed that the Federal Aviation Administration (FAA) found in 1975 an effective device, known as an airborne collision avoidance system, which would prevent mid-air crashes; but it chose instead to pursue an inferior device it had a hand in developing. Mr. Pope was retired early by the FAA.

The most famous whistle blower of all may be A. Ernest Fitzgerald, the U.S. Air Force cost analyst who found huge cost overruns on Lockheed cargo planes that were being developed for the Air Force. After his revelations, he was discharged from the Air Force. He fought for 13 years to be reinstated, which he was, at full rank, in 1982 (Fitzgerald, 1989).

Another famous whistle blower is Charles Atchinson who blew the whistle on the Comanche Park nuclear plant in Glen Rose, Texas, a power plant that was unsafe. It cost him his job. Shaw (1996: 290) reports:

> Morris H. Baslow, a 47-year-old biologist and father of three, won't forget the day he dropped an envelope in the mail to Thomas B. Yost, an administrative law judge with the Environmental Protection Agency (EPA). For later that day, Baslow was fired from his job with Lawler,

Mtusky & Skelly, an engineering consulting firm that had been hired by Consolidated Edison of New York to help it blunt EPA demands. The EPA was insisting that the power company's generating plants on the Hudson River had to have cooling towers to protect fish from excessively warm water that it was discharging into the river.

Shaw and Barry (1998: 360) report that shortly after being fired, Baslow sent seventy-one company documents supporting his allegation to the EPA, the Federal Energy Regulatory Commission, and the Justice Department. In the month following these disclosures, Baslow's employers accused him of stealing the documents and sued him for defamation. Baslow countersued. A year later, Lawler, Matusky & Skelly dropped all legal action against Baslow and gave him a cash settlement, reportedly of around $100,000.00 and in return Baslow was forced to write a letter to EPA and other governmental agencies to withdraw his charges of wrongdoing.

All of the above and other similar cases illustrate the unethical problems and personal risks facing employees who blow the whistle on what they perceive as organizational misconduct and wrong doing. It should be noted that there is a huge gap between ethical convictions and legal litigations.

THE 1992 U.S. FALSE CLAIMS ACT

Barton (1995: 154) reports:

When President George Bush signed into law the U.S. False Claims Act in 1992, he did so after Congress and agency policy makers recognized that many government contractors and employees had historically abused the public trust by accepting or paying bribes or other illegal activities. ... The 1992 act rectifies this deficiency by promising to pay any U.S. citizen up to 25 percent of the value of any loss, cost overrun, or fraud that is proven.

The 1992 U.S. False Claim Act has provided honest and truthful whistle blowers an opportunity to be protected. Such an act has encouraged whistle blowers to disclose wrong doings in governmental agencies and/or in subcontractors who are serving the government.

GENERAL MORAL CHARACTERISTICS OF WHISTLE BLOWERS

Based on several studies of researchers to identify mutual characteristics of whistle blowers Glazer and Glazer (1989: 6) indicate:

Whistle blowers, we discovered, are conservative people devoted to their works; whether as professionals, managers, or workers, by confirming to the requirements of bureaucratic life. Most had been successful until they were asked to violate their own standards of appropriate behavior. Invariably, they believed that they were defending the true mission of their organization by resisting illegal practices and could not comprehend how their superiors could risk the good name of their company by producing defective products, the reputation of their hospital by abusing and neglecting patients or the integrity of their agency by allowing their safety reports to be tampered with or distorted.

The real whistle blowers are really attempting to stop unethical, immoral, and illegal activities of businesses. Generally, whistle blowers have similar characteristics. These characteristics could be summarized as follows:

- Whistle blowers possess very strong feelings concerning their self-confidence and self-determination. They have high self-esteem.
- Whistle blowers are very courageous people who believe in honesty and strive for cleansing organizational problems.
- Whistle blowers are highly educated and put their intellectual abilities and wisdom to work in order to serve society.
- Whistle blowers are fearless people. They are not afraid of retaliation by being discharged or to be killed.
- Whistle blowers possess strong religious faith to goodness and worthiness.
- Whistle blowers are very sensitive people who perceive that they should not be deceived or cheated by greedy business people.
- Whistle blowers try to obtain praiseworthiness by their peers and colleagues in disclosing the truthful allegations of wrong doings for business operations.
- Whistle blowers try to provide honest advise to their peers, colleagues, and friends how to say no to powerful selfish authorities and prevent their wrongdoings.
- Whistle blowers talk and walk according to their conscientious judgments not based upon their self-interest.
- Whistle blowers look for psychological self-satisfaction.

TYPES OF WHISTLE BLOWING

Let us begin with the obvious reasons for blowing a whistle. No matter how large or small, every organization includes two different types of employees:

Obedient and Loyal Employees: These groups of employees seek to justify their behavior according to the desires of superiors and they are loyal to and/or dominated by the organizational authorities. Employees' conversation is limited to what must be perceived and said to carry the task of organization. Ordinary life, ordinary attitudes, and rigidity in organizational hierarchical structure permeate employees to work together and protect the interest of an organization. Much of what makes these types of organizational success or failure goes on within the broad and deep intentions, decisions, and actions of management team. Which manager likes or dislikes employees for whatever reason is a general characteristic of these types of organizations.

Organizational high performance is not simply a matter of technical knowledge or professional skills. Managers are looking for loyalty and confidentiality in their businesses. Managers like "Yes Sir or Yes Ma'am" people. Ethical and moral issues are not related to these types of organizations.

Professional and Outspoken Employees: As discussed earlier, our concept of business ethics is influenced by our conscientious awareness and institutional integrity. In all organizations, there are different groups of employees who perceive their works based on the legitimate public interest, including the employer's profitability. These types of employees expect their organizations conduct an honest business without fraud, deception, and wrongdoings. If they find something wrong, they prefer to refer either to the internal organizational authorities or external channels of societal hierarchy to stop the organization from doing something that they believe morally wrong or to force it to something they believe is ethically required. Usually, these types of employees are highly educated and act professionally. In return, managers accuse these types of employees of being disloyal to their managerial style, and try to fire them if they can – whether they are right or wrong. The most important finding among researchers in such situations reveals that egocentric managers like revenge. Those who mistreat whistle blowers do so because they expect to benefit from having fewer whistle blowers. The egoistic self-interest of managers or their organizations explains the mistreatment.

The nature of whistle blowing, good or bad, depends upon employees including managers' perceptions about the goodness of society over a long period of time. Moralists and ethicists perceive whistle blowing is the job of honest citizens. Since organizational members are citizens of a community, they first need to be loyal to their society's causes and effects and second to be loyal to business organizations. Larmer (1992: 127) indicates:

> Loyalty does not imply that we have a duty to refrain from reporting immoral actions of those to whom we are loyal. An employer who is acting immorally is not acting in her own best interests and an employee is not acting disloyally in blowing the whistle. Indeed, the argument can be made that the employee who blows the whistle may be demonstrating greater loyalty than the employee who is simply ignoring the immoral conduct, inasmuch as she is attempting to prevent her employer from engaging in self-destructive behavior.

It is a fact that if businesses today are more willing to play the role of informants by disclosing information related to their employees to outsiders, employees in return are also more willing to disclose the employer's wrongdoing to the public. Generally there are two types of whistle blowing: (1) Internal, and (2) External.

Internal Whistle Blowing: Internal whistle blowing occurs when a company employee goes to the top organizational authority without following the corporate chain of command to disclose the immoral conduct of their superiors, peers, and coworkers or unethical operations including petty or grand theft in a department. Also, internal whistle blowing may take place when a group of employees reveal their concerns to persons outside of their organizations within their business system. The incidental internal harm tends to be shadowed by managerial authorities, perhaps because so much of it seems deserved. Internal whistle blowing is always proof of organizational trouble. Employees do not go outside the institutional channels because they believe that the institution has an adequate moral and ethical responsibility to prevent or to stop wrongdoings. Internal whistle blowing also is proof of management failure. Management also is very sensitive to receiving bad news from whistle blowers – specifically those types of employees who are not on their sides. Managers immediately react to the bad news that is in the spot light. They have to be reactive to such bad news, because they need to act as "damage control." They need to prevent it, because they are worried about the effect of publicity on their own career.

The internal whistle blowing for the disclosure or allegation of inappropriate conduct of an individual and/or operation of a department requires further investigation to impose sanction against immoral and unethical behavior or operations. Traditionally, in a university system, there are two groups of faculty members: (1) tenured and (2) non-tenured including full time tenure track and part time lecturers. If faculty members are tenured, according to the concept of academic freedom and institutional integrity, both institution and tenured faculty members are guardians of academic freedom. They have agreed to professionally speak out concerning immoral, unethical, and illegal conducts of their peers, administrators, and students. It is their obligations to resist any wrong doing, cheating, or misconduct by employees and students. In these cases, the charges against faculty members, staff, and students are about an offense not against the organization or system. If faculty members are not tenured, they are not professionally obligated to report wrong doings to the public media and other authorities including boards of regents or trustees. A similar analysis applies in a business firm.

Clearly, from a moral and ethical view of the conditions under which type of internal whistle blowing is permitted, prohibited, or mandatory is a matter of self-conscientious awareness. Internal moral and ethical whistle blowing is not an act of institutional loyalty. It usually conveys loyalty to professional codes of conducts or codes of ethics. If whistle blowing is done from professional codes of ethics or moral motives, the intent and action of such an action is to stop unprofessional conduct or dishonesty in order to protect individual's rights, professional duties, and reputation of their institution.

External Whistle Blowing: Discussion concerning external whistle blowing tends to emphasize the undesirable news concerning corporate corruption and fraud. If whistle blowing carries the message that an organization has trouble using bad news to be publicized in the community, they need to improve the organizational ability to use bad news. This means that there is no doubt that bad news is bad and harming to the reputation of a corporation in the market place. We will analyze consequential ends of bad news to be spread by external whistle blowers.

One approach we might call the "proactive tactic." This approach builds invitations to report bad news into the ordinary expected accidents of doing business. This can be quite simple; with good faith the company's representative announces the products' default and he/she recalls defected products for the purpose of eliminating the faulty parts. This confirms the ethical corporate convictions towards goodness and loyalty of management to the moral integrity. Revealing corporate bad news is more likely to seem part of the business.

Sometimes employees identify a serious threat of a product to the consumers or to the general public. They perceive that executives are careless and ignore bad news. Then the whistle blowers must have, or have accessible, documented evidence that would convince the public of the corporation's wrongdoings. In such situations, to exhaust the internal procedures and possibilities is the key requirement here. Employees need to act on the basis of their citizenship duties to inform the media of such a continued wrongdoing. There should be a very well scientific documentation either to submit them to media and/or governmental authorities.

Some psychologists believe that employees do not have an obligation to the public to put themselves at serious risk by blowing the whistle. Some ethicists believe that loyalty to the crooks corrupts society and individual citizens are responsible to the well being of their society. In these conditions several difficulties emerge. Should it be the responsibility of the media or the appropriate regulatory agencies to carry out investigations based on whistle blowers' claims? Is it the responsibility of the Department of Justice to register all whistle blowers claims and proceed with them through legal channels for discovering the wrong doings of businesses? It is reasonable in such a formal proceeding, that laws protect whistle blowers. If the wrong doings are criminal ones, then an investigation by a law enforcing is appropriate. If the wrong doings are civil ones, then it's the responsibility of the Justice Department through the Office of Attorney General to investigate allegations.

Nevertheless, co-workers rarely honor whistle blowers because coworkers believe that whistle blowers have broken the code of promise and loyalty to their organization. In return, whistle blowers believe that co-workers who did not join them to blow the whistle are guilty of immorality and unethicality, and complicity in the wrongdoings of the organization and that such negligence jeopardizes the goodness of society.

CHAPTER SUMMARY

An ethical dilemma can occur when a loyal employee observes that the employer is committing or assisting an illegal, or immoral, or unethical act and must decide what to do. There are several moral, ethical, and legal issues concerning decision-making processes and operations in an organization. Accordingly, there are several obligations concerning individual moral commitments, professional grouping ethical convictions, and organizational legal mandates. In addition, there are several attributes such as trust, loyalty, fidelity, and blowing whistle as parts of ethical, moral, and legal mandates.

Legally, individual employees within the holistic operational procedures of a corporation are not liable for organizational wrongdoings. Do employees have a further moral obligation and ethical conviction to prevent harmful actions to other employees and/or customers by a corporation? If employees detect corruption and deception in a corporation what are their duties and responsibilities? If they do so, should they proceed to announce them to the public? If they are able to do so, how should they assess the equity between their moral and ethical obligations and their consequential harmful cost to themselves? As the fear of personal cost increases, the moral duties and ethical obligations decrease. In particular, this chapter looks at the specific topics such as what we mean by blowing whistle? How do we define whistle blowing? How often employees' loyalty to the firm justify ignoring citizenship duties? How blowing the whistle creates problems of conflicts of interest? What are the moral, ethical, and legal choices facing a corporation when present or former employees act as whistle blowers? What are moral and ethical obligations of employers to employees and customers as informants? What are the rights and privileges in a democratic society concerning the freedom of speech? How far does this right extend into the business world? What are the obligations and limits of free speech? What are the mutual obligations of employees and employees to the public? Under what circumstances should an employee or a manager blow the whistle? How big is your whistle? When, for how long, and how loud should an employee or a manager blow the whistle? Through what channels of mass media should an employee or a manager should the whistle? When and how should the whistle blower be protected?

Personal moral responsibilities and professional ethical duties are closely related. In general, do experts have rights, and obligations or duties to fulfill their professional responsibilities? Rights are legitimate claims which one person and/or an institution has or can make on another, whether those claims are based upon innate moral feelings, or cultural ethical convictions. Rights can be thought of as legal privileges or entitlements that invoke corresponding duties on the part of others. Duties are viewed as notions of "completeness." Duties are constraints on the scope of permissible actions, but not all constraints are duties. Duties, to begin with, apply directly only to actions. A duty may correspond to a specific right held by a specific person. Responsibilities are closely associated with duties. An individual who has a specific right and duty to do something he/she has a commitment to carry that duty. The self-commitment is called responsibility. Fidelity is a moral commitment to keep one's word and doing what has agreed to do either as result of making promises or by entering into contracts with others. Loyalty is closely related with fidelity. It is the willingness to promote the interests of someone to whom one has a moral obligation, such as an employer.

It is no secret that most institutions frequently seek, store, communicate, and sell personal information about their employees and customers without their consent. Someone else defines informed consent as having deliberation and free choice to access and permission to disclose personal information. Integrative scientific advancement and technological development have established a diffusing responsibility among experts. Employees and customers must understand what they are agreeing to be done with their personal information. Deliberation requires not only the in-depth cause and effects of facts but also a full understanding of consequential results.

Assimilative integrated discovery systems (AIDS) have access through processing to both deep and broad domains of information in both corporations and industries as well as modern societies. Through these systems organizations can predict future trends in promotions, training, and retention of their employees. Knowledge-based information systems often are successful precisely when they deny their power to intervene.

Whistle blowing is a new mode of ethical and moral obligation generated by conscientious awareness of an individual or a group of informants concerning serious wrongdoings against intrinsic and extrinsic rights of stakeholders by a corporation. Whistle blowers spotlight a corporation's negligence, intended harm, and/or abusive behavior of managerial decision-making processes and operations that threaten the public interest. Whistle blowing has the narrower objective of shedding light on intentional and deliberated negligence, abuses, harms, or disclosing the wrongdoings into a normal decision-making processes and/or operations. In a democratic society, it is responsibility of all citizens to disclose wrong doings in their societies in order not to let a group of corrupted people fool and harm the public. Nevertheless, in reality deciding to go public and blowing the whistle create harsh consequences and/or life threats for the whistle blowers.

It is a fact that if businesses today are more willing to play the role of informants by disclosing information related to their employees to outsiders, employees in return are also more willing to disclose the employer's wrongdoing to the public. Generally there are two types of whistle blowing: (1) Internal and (2) External. Internal whistle blowing occurs when a company employee goes to the top organizational authority without following the corporate chain of command to disclose the immoral conduct of their superiors, peers, and coworkers or unethical operations including petty or grand theft in a department. Also, internal whistle blowing may take place when a group of employees reveal their concerns to persons outside of their organizations within but their business system. Sometimes employees identify continuity of a serious threat of a product to consumers or to the general public. They perceive that executives are careless and ignore bad news. Then the whistle blowers must have, or have accessible, documented evidence that would convince the public of the corporation's wrongdoings. In such situations, to exhaust the internal procedures and possibilities is the key requirement here. Employees need to act on the basis of their citizenship duties to inform the media of such continued wrongdoing. There should be a very clear scientific documentation to submit either to media and/or governmental authorities.

QUESTIONS FOR DISCUSSION

- What do we mean by employees' loyalty and fidelity to employers?
- What do we mean by employers' obligations to employees' private information?
- How should reciprocal employer-employee relationships be established on the basis of trust?
- Define the terms of whistle blowing; internal whistle blowing; external whistle blowing; personal whistle blowing, impersonal whistle blowing; and governmental whistle blowing.
- What is the rational reasoning behind whistle blowing?
- How and when should whistle blowing permissible not to violate one's obligation of loyalty to colleagues, peers, profession/corporation, and humanity at large?
- What are the psychosocial side effects of assimilative integrated discovery system – AIDS?
- How does whistle blowing foster or destroy public trust? Why?
- How does whistle blowing betray unethical and/or illegal business decisions and operations?
- How does whistle blowing protect employees and shareholders from selfish decisions and/or operations of CEOs?
- Can someone argue that whistle blowing is always morally permitted or prohibited?
- How much fidelity, if any, does a worker owe an organization?
- Under what conditions is whistle blowing ethically permitted?
- Under what circumstances does law protect a whistle blower?
- How can a business firm prevent whistle blowing?

CASE STUDY

THE WHISTLE-BLOWERS: SMITHKLINE BEECHAM PLC

Whistle-blowing can be considered as morally, ethically, and legally neutral act of an employee and/or an informant making public some wrong doings of a firm's internal operation, practice, or policies that affect the public interest. Bribing government authorities and cheating the public funds are illegal in the United States and in many other countries. This case is about a "Labscam" investigation by the Department of Justice in a multinational corporation in the United States of America.

Smithkline Beecham PLC (SBPLC) was incorporated on January 24, 1989, under the name Goldslot PLC. On April 11, 1989, SBPLC entered into an agreement for the merger of Beecham Group PLC and Smithkline Beckman Corp. excluding Allergan Inc., Beckman Instruments Inc. and their respective subsidiaries. This transaction was implemented on July 26, 1989, through an exchange of securities. In 1992 the company acquired the Corsodyl business from ICI Pharmaceutical. During 1992, Smithkline Beecham PLC disposed of the Manetti Roberts Toiletries business in Italy and the Personal Care Products business in North America. SBPLC listed Pharmaceutical in Germany and the Collistar cosmetics business in Italy. Also, during 1992, SBPLC acquired the Clinical Trials Division of Winchester Research Laboratories and many others.

The SBPLC continuously produces innovative medicine and consumer health care products. The company specializes in the development and manufacture of pharmaceutical, vaccines, over-the-counter medicines and consumer health care services. In addition, SBPLC is better known for its clinical laboratory testing and disease management. Some of the testing services they offer include blood, urine and tissue testing for use in screening and diagnosis, and central laboratory testing for clinical trials for pharmaceutical and biotechnology companies in Europe and North America. It offers emergency 24-hours toxicology tests, and substance abuse testing certified by the United States Department of Health and Human Services.Smithkline Beecham PLC has its main headquarters in New Horizons Court, Brentford, Middlesex, United Kingdom. This company has several subsidiaries all over the world. Some of the places where they are located in France, Germany, Argentina, China, India, Italy, Mexico, Japan, Austria, Panama and many other countries. This company runs its operation with a total of 52,400 employees. It also has 119,136 stockholders.

Sometime in 1997, through a nationwide "labscam" investigation done by the Justice Department of the United States and the help of three whistle-blowers (Robert J. Merena, Charles W. Robinson, Jr, and Glen Grossenbacher), Smithkline Beecham Clinical Laboratories Inc., a strategic business unit (SBU) of Smithkline Beecham PLC, was found to be involved in Medicare fraud. The company was accused of paying *kickbacks* to doctors, billing the U.S. Government for laboratory tests not performed and other violations. Although the company has denied the allegations by saying the violations were unintentional and a misunderstanding of regulations and guidelines, through a Court hearing process, it agreed to pay the U.S. Government $325 million in 1997.

One issue of the settlement was the problem of payments for the three whistle-blowers. The Justice Department had resisted paying the three men the 15% to 25% share of the SBPLC's settlement specified for the whistle-blowers by the federal False Claim Act. The Justice Department argued that most of the $325 million settlement was obtained through its nationwide "Labscam" investigations that had nothing to do with the three men. Nonetheless, the U.S. District Judge Donald W. VanArtsalen ruled that the three whistle-blowers made a major contribution to the government's case and that they helped bring in nearly all of the settlement.

In relation to this case, Smithkline Beecham PLC acted unethical, immoral, illegal and inhumane to the U.S. society and specifically to American old patients (Senior Citizens). They betrayed the medical profession by paying kickbacks to medical doctors. They misled the government by billing for the Medicare patients the fees for tests never performed, and provided false laboratory results for Senior Citizens to be kept in their medical record files. Finally, Judge Van Artsdalen said the three whistle-blowers accounted for all but about $15 million of that total. The U.S. government agreed to pay the three whistle-blowers a minimum of $9.7 million but only if they dropped claims to a larger portion. However, the Justice Department did not perpetuate SBPLC's fraud by providing doctors and patients with false laboratory results and side effects of the consequential results of misdiagnosis and mistreatment of patients. The government's concern was only the financial side of the case. The case was closed (*The Wall Street Journal*, 1998 and *Moody* 1998).

CASE QUESTIONS FOR DISCUSSION

- How do you assess the ethical, moral, and legal behavior of the Smithkline Beckman Co.?
- What was the motive of SBC?
- Was SBC greedy to do anything to further their own financial interest?
- How do you analyze the SBC's professional and social responsibilities?
- Did SBC ignore humaneness and the rights of its customers?

CASE SOURCES

The Wall Street Journa, "U.S. Judge Says Whistle-Blowers to Get $42.3 Million," (April 10, 1998), 1.

Moody's International Manual, D. A. Zoholi Jr., Publisher, (New York: Moody's Investors Service, Inc., 1998), 10777-10779.

REFERENCES

Chapter 1

Abraham, P. (1999). "Japanese Debt Collector Told Client to Sell a Kidney." *Financial Times*. Monday, November 1.

Albert, E. M., Denise, T. C., and Peterfraund, S. P. (1984). *Great Traditions in Ethics*. Belmont, California: Wadsworth Publishing Company, 1-7.

Aristotle (384-322 B.C.). In L. Strauss and J. Cropsey, (Eds.) (1987). *History of Political Philosophy*. Chicago, IL: University of Chicago Press, 138-139.

Barton, L. (1995). *Ethics: The Enemy in the Workplace* Cincinnati, Ohio: South-Western College Publishing, 83.

Baumhart, R. C. (1961). "How Ethical Are Businessmen?" *Harvard Business Review*. Vol. 39, No. 4, 6-8.

Berenheim, R. E. (1987). *Corporate Ethics*. New York: The Conference Board, Inc.

Brooks, L. J. (1989). "Corporate Codes of Ethics." *Journal of Business Ethics* Vol. 8, 117.

Business Week January 10, 1977.

Carroll, A. B. (1975). "Linking Business Ethics to Behavior in Organizations." *S A M. Advanced Management Journal*. Vol. 4, No. 3, 4-11.

Catan, T. (2000). "Suspects Admit Laundering at Least $7bn Through BoNY." *Financial Times*, Thursday, February 17, 18.

Cherrington, J. O. and Cherrington, D. J. (1989). "Ethics: A Major Business Problem." *Exchange*, (Fall), 30.

Clarkham, J. P. (1994). *Keeping Good Company*. Oxford, England: Clarendon Press, 174.

Colgrove, D., "Singer Company Files Chapter 11." <wysiwyg://7/http://sewing.about.com/hobbies/sewing/library/weekly/aa091499a.htm.Sheila>.

Dahlinger, J. D. (1978). *The Secret Life of Henry Ford*. New York: Bobbs-Merill Company, Inc., 124.

De George, R. T. (1995). *Business Ethics,* Fifth Edition. Upper Saddle River, New Jersey: Prentice Hall, 5, 38, 39.

de Jonquieres, G., (2000). "Multinationals Making Lower Profits Abroad." *Financial Times*, Thursday, (April 27), 8.

Deresky, H. (1997). *International Management: Managing Across Borders and Cultures*. Second Edition. New York: Addison-Wesley , 493.

Dobson, J. (1990). "The Role of Ethics in Global Corporate Culture," *Journal of Business Ethics* Vol. 9, 481-484.

Dowie, M. (1977). "How Ford Put Two Million Fire Traps on Wheels?" *Business and Society Review*, Vol. 23, 51-55.

Drucker, P. (1980), *Managing in Turbulent Times*. New York: Harper & Row, 191.

English, H. and English, A. C. (1958). *A Comprehensive Dictionary of Psychological and Psychoanalytical Terms.* New York: David McKay, 64.

Farmer, R. N. and Hogue, W. D. (1973). *Corporate Social Responsibility.* Chicago: Science Research Associates, Inc., vii.

Ferraro, I. (1995). *The Cultural Dimension of International Business.* Second Edition. Englewood Cliffs, NJ: Prentice Hall, 321.

Financial Times (2000). "Jury Convicts Former KBW Chief of Insider Trading." (Friday, April 28), 1.

Fraedrich, J. and Ferrell, O. C. (1991). *Business Ethics.* Boston: Houghton Mifflin, 5.

Freud, S. (1926). "Inhibitions, Symptoms, and Anxiety." *Standard Edition.* Vol. 18, 19, 20.

Friedman, T. (2000). *The Lexus and the Olive Tree.* New York: Anchor Books, 20-24.

Gates, D. (2000). "Fundamentalism 101: Why That Old-Time Religion Is Thoroughly Modern." *Business Week.* March 20.

Getz, Kathleen A. (1990). "International Codes of Conduct: An Analysis of Ethical Reasoning." *Journal of Business Ethics.* Vol. 9, 567-577.

Gibbons, S. (Ed.) (1992). *Media Report to Women.* Vol. 20, (Fall), 88.

Gioia, D. (1995). In Trevino, L. K. and Katherine, A. N. *Managing Business Ethics: Straight Talk About How To Do It Right.* New York: John Wiley & Sons, Inc., 80-85.

Gudykunst, M. B. (1994). *Bridging Differences: Effective Intergroup Communication.* Thousand Oaks, California: Sage, 4.

Halbert, T. and Ingulli, E. (2000). *Law & Ethics in the Business Environment.* Cincinnati, Ohio: West Legal Studies in Business, South Western College Publishing, 1.

Hartley, R. F. (1993). *Business Ethics: Violation of the Public Trust.* New York: John Wiley & Sons, 112-125.

Harvey, C. and Allard, M. J. (1995). *Understanding Diversity: Readings, Cases, and Exercises.* New York: Harper Collins College Publishing, 3.

Honigmann, D. (2000). "Disunited Children of Slavery." *Financial Times.* Weekend May 13-14, V.

Hume, D. (1955). *Writing in Economics.* In Eugene Rotwein (Ed.). Madison: University of Wisconsin Press. (Quote in Text Is Taken from Essay: "An Enquiry Concerning the Principles of Morals." (Originally Published in 1751).

Jackson, J. H., Miller, R. L. and Miller, S. H. (1997). *Business and Society Today: Managing Social Issues.* Cincinnati, Ohio: West Publishing Company, 173, 500.

Ketz, K. A. (1990). "International Codes of Conduct: An Analysis of Ethical Reasoning." *Journal of Business Ethics.* Vol. 9, 567-577.

Kirrane, D. E. (1990). "Managing Values: A Systematic Approach to Business Ethics." *Training and Development Journal.* (November), 53-60.

Kreithner, R. (1998). *Management.* Seventh Edition. Boston: Houghton and Mifflin, 131.

Laczniak, G. R. and Naor, J. (1985). "Global Ethics: Wrestling With the Corporate Conscience." *Business.* (July-August-September), 3-10.

Manakkalathil, J. (1995). "Corporate Social Responsibility in Globalizing Market." *SAM Advanced Management Journal.* (Winter), 29.

McIntyre, A. (1983). "Utilitarianism and Cost-Benefit Analysis: An Essay on the Relevance of Moral Philosophy to Bureaucratic Theory." In Donald Scherer and Thomas Attig (Eds.). *Ethics and the Environment.* Englewood Cliffs, NJ: Prentice-Hall, 145-146.

Mohrman, S. A. and Mitroff, I. I. (1987). "Business Not Just as Usual." *Training and Development Journal.* Vol. 4, No. 6, 37.

Moody's International Manual (1998). Zoholi Jr., D. A. Publisher. New York: Moody's Investors Service, Inc., 10777-10779.

Nelson, C. C. (1977). Preface. In Walton, C. (Ed.). *The Ethics of Corporate Conduct: The Discipline Dealing With What is Good and Bad or Right and Wrong or With Moral Duty and Obligation.* Englewood Cliffs, New Jersey: Prentice-Hall, Inc., vii.

Nussbaum, M. (1993). "Non-Relative Virtues: An Aristotelian Approach." In Nassbuam, M. and Sen, A. (Eds.). *The Quality of Life.* Oxford, Clarendon Press, 243.

Payne, D., Raiborn, C., and Askvik, J. (1997). "A Global Code of Business Ethics." *Journal of Business Ethics.* Vol. 16, 1727-1728.

Parhizgar, K. D. and Landeck, M. (1997). "Characteristics and Perceptions of Female Workers Regarding Their Work Environment in Mexican Maquiladoras." In Lemaster, J. (1977). *Southwest Review of International Business Research: Proceedings of the 1997 Academy of International Business Conference,* 427.

Parhizgar, K. D. (1999). "Comparative Analysis of Multicultural Paradigm Management System and Cultural Diversity Models in Multinational Corporations." *Journal of Global Business.* (Spring), Vo. 10, No. 18, 43.

Parhizgar, K. D. (1999). "Globalization of Multicultural Management." *Journal of Transnational Management Development.* Vol. 4: No. 3/4, 16.

Parhizgar, K. D. (2000). "Globalization of Multicultural Management." In Becker, K. *Culture and International Business.* New York: Haworth Press, Inc., 1-23.

Peikoff, L. (1999). *"Why Businessmen Need Philosophy?"* In Ralston, R. E. (Ed.). *Why Businesses Need Philosophy.* United States of America: The Ayn Rand Institute, 7-23.

Poste, G. (2001). "Rude Awakening to the Forces of Good and Evil." *Financial Times.* Tuesday November 27, IV.

Raclin, L. L. (1995). "Environmental Audits: Risks and Rewards." *Kirkpatrick and Lockhart Business Law Update.* (Summer), 4-6.

Randall, J. and Treacy, B. (2000). "Digital Buccaneers Caught in a Legal Web." *Financial Times.* (Tuesday, May 30), 6.

Rothman, B. K. (1999). "The Potential Cost of the Best Genes Money Can Buy." *The Chronicle of Higher Education.* (June 11), A52.

Shankar, S. and Pilling, D. (2000). "India Seeks a Cure for Tough Patent Laws." *Financial Times.* (Wednesday, May 24), 12.

Shaw, W. H. (1996). *Business Ethics.* Second Edition. New York: Wadsworth Publishing Company, 12.

Steiner, G. A. and Steiner, F. S. (1994). *Business, Government, and Society: A Managerial Perspective.* McGraw-Hill Book Company, 181.

Tait, N. (2000). "Cargill to Pay $100m in Genetic Seed Case Settlement." *Financial Times.* (Wednesday, May 17), 17.

The Wall Street Journal (1998). "U.S. Judge Says Whistle-Blowers to Get $42.3 Million." (April 10), 1.

Tong, H. M. and Welling, P. (1981). "What American Business Managers Should Know and Do About International Bribery." *Baylor Business Review.* (November-December), 8.

Trevino, L. K. and Nelson, K. A. (1995). *Managing Business Ethics: Straight Talk About How To Do It Right?* New York: John Wiley & Sons, Inc., 7.

Walton, C. (1977). *The Ethics of Corporate Conduct.* Englewood Cliffs, New Jersey: Prentice-Hall, Inc., 8-9, 25-27.

Watson Jr., T. J. (1963). *A Business and Its Beliefs.* New York: McGraw Hill Book Company, Inc. 3-5.

Williams, F. (2000). "Swiss Broaden Bribes Claims." *Financial Times.* (Friday, February 18), 2.

Chapter 2

Adair v. United States, 208 U.S. 161, 174-75, 1908.

Ahmed, M. M. (1999). "Cultural and Contextual Aspects in Business Ethics: Three Controversies and One Dilemma." *Journal of Transnational Management Development.* Vol.4, No.1, 111-129.

Albert, E. M., Denise, T. C., and Peterfreund, S. P. (1984). *Great Traditions in Ethics.* Belmont, California: Wadsworth Publishing Company, 1-7,128.

Barton, L. (1995). *Ethics: The Enemy in the Workplace.* Cincinnati, Ohio: South-western College Publishing, 109.

Benn, S. (1967). "Power." In Paul Edwards (Ed.). *The Encyclopedia of Philosophy.* New York: The Free Press, Vol. 6, 424-427.

Bierman, L. and Fisher, C. D. (1984). "Anti-Nepotism Rules Applied to Spouses: Business and Legal Viewpoints." *Labor Law Journal.* 634-642.

Council on Ethical and Judicial Affairs (1998-1999). *Code of Medical Ethics: Current Opinions. American Medical Association.* Chicago, Illinois: Annotations prepared by the Southern Illinois University Schools of Medicine and Law, 61.

De George, R. (1995). *Business Ethics.* Englewood Cliffs, New Jersey: Prentice Hall., Vol. 5, No. 19, 87, 256.

De Mente, B. L. (1989). *Chinese Etiquette & Ethics in Business: A Pene-*

trating Analysis of the Morals and Values that Shape the Chinese Business Personality. Chicago, Illinois: NTC Publishing Group, 27-28.

Drucker, P. (1980). *Managing in Turbulent Times.* New York: Harper & Row, Publishers, 191.

Drucker, P. (1981). "What Is Business Ethics?" *The Public Interest.* 18-36.

Emerson, R. M. (1962). "Power-Dependent Relations." *American Sociological Review.* (February), Vol. 27, 31-41.

Enron Oil & Gas Company. <http://www.eog.enron.com/main.htm>.

Flecher, G. J. O., and Ward, C. (1988). Attribution Theory and Processes: A Cross-Cultural Perspective." In Bond, M. H. (Ed.). *The Cross-Cultural Challenge to Social Psychology.* Newbury Park, CA: Sage, 230-244.

Fortune v. National Cash Register Co., 373, Mass. Vol. 96, No. 36 NE Second 1251, 1977.

Frankena, W. K. (1963). *Ethics.* Englewood Cliffs, NJ: Prentice-Hall, Inc., 6.

French, W. A. and Granrose, J. (1995). *Practical Business Ethics.* Englewood Cliffs, New Jersey: Prentice Hall, 9.

French, J. R. P. and Raven, B. (1959). *Studies in Social Power.* Ann Arbor: Institute for Social Research.

Halbert, T. and Ingulli, E. (2000). *Law and Ethics in the Business Environment.* Canada: West Legal Studies, 19, 40.

Hemingway, E. (1932). *Death in the Afternoon.* New York: Charles Scibner's Sons, 4.

Hobbes, T. (1839). *Leviathan and Philosophical Rudiments.* From *The English Works of Thomas Hobbes.* Vol. II, III, Sir William Molesworth (Ed.). London: John Bohn.

Holmes, Jr., O. W. (1938). *The Common Law.* Boston, Mass: Little, Brown, first published, 1881.

Hook, S. (1946). Education for Modern Man. New York: Dial Press.

Human Rights Watch. AU.S. Corporation Complicated in Abuses in India." January (1999). <http://www.hrw.org/hrw/press/1999/enr0124.hym>.

Kant, I. (1969). *Foundation of the Metaphysics of Morals.* Reprinted. Translated by Lewis White Beck. Indianapolis: Bobbs-Merrill Educational Publishing, (Originally Published in 1785).

Kant, I. 1984. *Duty and Reason.* In Albert, E.M. and Denise, T. C. (Eds.), *Great Traditions in Ethics.* Belmont, California: Wadsworth Publishing Company, 199-218.

Lilla, M. T. (1981). "Ethos, Ethics, and Public Service." *The Public Interest.* 3-11.

Mills, D. Q. (1989). *Labor-Management Relations.* Fourth Edition, New York: McGraw-Hill Publishing Company, 100.

Nash, R. J (1996). *Real World Ethics: Frameworks for Educators and Human Services Professionals.* New York: Teachers College, Columbia University, 11.

Newton, L.H. and Schmidt, D. P. (1996). *Wake up Calls: Classic Cases in*

Business Ethics. United States of America: Wadsworth Publishing Company, 3.

NYSE, Market Guide. "The Benchmark of Quality Financial Information." February 4, 1999. <http://yahoo.marketguide.com/mgi/ratio/3052N.htm>.

Oesterle, J. A. (1957). *Ethics: The Introduction to Moral Science*. Englewood, New Jersey: Prentice Hall, Inc. 5, 20, 201.

Parhizgar, K. D. and Jesswein, K. R. (1998). "Ethical and Economical Affordability of Developing Nation's Repayment of International Debt." In Baker, J. C. (1998). *Selected International Investment Portfolios*. Great Britain: Pergamon Publishing Co., 141.

Parhizgar, K. D. (2002). *Multicultural Behavior and Global Business Environments*. New York: Haworth Press, 297.

Park, J. and Barron, R. W. (1977). "Can Morality Be Taught?" In Stiles, L. J. and Johnson, B. D. (Eds.). (1977). *Morality Examined: Guidelines for Teachers*. Princeton, NJ: Princeton Book Company, Publishers, 3-23.

Paul, R. W. and Elder, L. (2002). *Critical Thinking*. Upper Saddle River, NJ: Prentice Hall, 48.

Price Waterhouse vs. Ann B. Hopkins, 618 F. Supp. at 1117,57 LW at 4471 (1989).

Randall, J. and Treacy, B. (2000). "Digital Buccaneers Caught in a Legal Web." *Financial Times*. (Tuesday May 30), 4 Mastering Risk, 6.

Shaw, W. H. (1996). *Business Ethics*. Second Edition, Belmont, California: Wadsworth Publishing Company, 4, 12.

Steiner, G. A. and Steiner, J. F. (1988). *Business, Government, and Society*. New York: Random House Division, 592.

The Asian Wall Street Journal, (1999). "Human-Rights Group Denounces Enron." (February 4), 11.

The Equal Employment Opportunity Commission. "Guideline on Sexual Harassment." 29 CFR 1604.11(a).

The Oxford English Dictionary (1963). Oxford, Britain: At the Clarendon Press, 287, 312-314, 554, 656.

Thorne, J. D. (1995). "How to Head Off Termination Suits." *Nation's Business*. (May Edition), 28.

Trevino, L. K. and Nelson, K. (1995). *Managing Business Ethics: Straight Talk About How To Do It Right*. New York: John Wiley & Son, Inc., 52.

Walton, C. C. "Overview." In C.C. Walton (Ed.) (1977). *The Ethics of Corporate Conduct*. Englewood Cliffs, New Jersey: Prentice-Hall, Inc., 6.

Whately, R. (1859). *Play's Moral Philosophy: With Annotations*. London: John W. Parker & Son, 68-90.

Yinger, J. M. (1970). *The Scientific Study of Religion*. London: The Macmillan Company, 45.

Zottoli, D. A., Jr. (1999). *Moody's Investors Service, Inc.*3210.

Chapter 3

Adler, N. (1986). *International Dimensions of Organizational Behavior.* Boston, MA: Kent Publishing Company, 12, 13.

Aquinas, T. (1945). *Basic Writings of St. Thomas Aquinas.* Vol. II, A. C. Pegis (Ed.). New York: Random House, Article V, 356-357.

Bentham, J. (1823). *An Introduction to the Principles of Morals and Legislation.* 2nd Edition, Ch. XII, Part 2.

De George, R. T. (1995). *Business Ethics Fourth Edition.* Englewood Cliffs, New Jersey: Prentice Hall, 63.

Dupuios, A. M. (1985). *Philosophy of Education in Historical Perspective.* Landham, MD: Rand McNally and Company, 10.

Freud, S. (1949). *An Outline of Psycho-Analysis.* New York: Norton.

Geertz, C. (1970). "The Impact of the Concept of Culture on the Concept of Man." In Hammel, E. A. and Simmonson, W. S. (Ed.). Man Makes Sense. Boston: Little Brown, 47.

Herbart, J. (1806). *General Principles of Pedagogy Deduced from the Aims of Education.* (Tr. By A. F. Lange with annotations by C. De Garmo) London: Macmillan, 1913.

Hobbes, T. (1839) *Leviathan and Philosophical Rudiments.* London: Sir William Molesworth, (Ed.), Part I, Chapter 13, Paragraph 13; Chapter 14, Paragraph 3, and Chapter 15, Paragraph 10.

Kant, I. (1898). *Fundamental Principles of Metaphysics of Morals.* Tr. T. K. Abbott, From *Kant's Critique of Practical Reason and Other Works on the Theory of Ethics.* London: Longmans, Green, 10 & 539.

Kluckhohn, F. R. and Strodtbeck, F. L. (1961). *Variation Value Orientations.* Evanston, IL: Row, Peterson, and Company, 11.

Locke, J. (1924). *An Essay Concerning Human Understanding.* (Abr. and Ed. by): A. S. Pringle-Pattison. Oxford: Clarendon Press.

Locke, J. (1693). *Some Thoughts Concerning Education.*

Marshal, K. P. (1999). "Has Technology Introduced New Ethical Problems?" *Journal of Business Ethics.* Vol.19, 81-90.

Marshal, L. (1997). "Facilitating Knowledge Management and Knowledge Sharing." *Online,* Vol. 21, No. 5, 92-98.

Montague, W. P. (1930). *Beliefs Unbound. A Promethean Religion for the Modern World.* New Haven, Conn.: Yale University Press, 44.

Moran, R. T. and Harris, P. R. (1982). *Managing Cultural Synergy.* Vol. 2. Houston: Gulf Publishing Company, 19.

Parhizgar, K. D. (2002). *Multicultural Behavior and Global Business Environments.* New York: Haworth Press, 124, 221-254.

Parhizgar, K .D., and Lunce, S. E. (1994). "Genealogical Approaches to Ethical Implications of Informational Assimilative Integrated Discovery Systems (AIDS) in Business." In Beardwell, I. (Ed.), *Contemporary Developments in Human Resource Management.* Montpellier, France: An International Publication of the Scientific Committee of the Montpellier Graduate Business School, Editions ESKA, 55-60.

Plato, (1892). *The Dialogues of Plato*. Vols. I, II. and III. Translated by B. Jowett. 3rd Edition. New York: Oxford University Press, 26.

Reid, T. (1764). *Inquiry into the Human Mind on the Principles of Common Sense.*

Smith, E. D. and Pham, C. (1998). "Doing Business in Vietnam: A Cultural Guide." In Maidment, F. (Ed.). *International Business 98/99*. Seventh Edition. Guilford, Connecticut: Dushkin/McGraw-Hill, 174.

Spencer, H. (1888). *Education, Intellectual, Moral, and Physical.* New York: D. Appleton.

Watson, Jr., T. J. (1963). *A Business and Its Beliefs: The Ideas That Helped Build IBM.* New York: McGraw-Hill Book Company, Inc., 36.

Chapter 4

Aristotle (1925). *Nichomachean Ethics*. Translated by W. D. Ross. *Works of Aristotle*. Vol. IX, W. D. Ross, (Ed.). Oxford: Clarendon Press.

Bentham, J. (1838). Edited by J. Bowring. *The Works of Jeremy Bentham.* London: Simpkin, Marshall, Vol. 1, 16, note.

Buchholz, R. A. and Rosenthal, S. B. (1998). *Business Ethics: The Pragmatic Path Beyond Principles to Process*. Upper Saddle River, NJ: Prentice-Hall, 5.

Butler, J. (1949). Five Sermons. New York: Liberal Arts Press, 45.

Carroll, A. B. and Buchholtz, A. K. (2003). *Business and Society: Ethics and Stakeholder Management*. United States: Thomson, South-western, 167.

Corbett, E. P. J. (1991). *The Elements of Reasoning*. New York: Macmillan Publishing Company, 24.

De George, R. T. (1995). *Business Ethics*. Englewood Cliffs, NJ: Prentice-Hall, 256.

Epicurus, (1866). *The Work of Epictetus*. Translated by T. W. Higginson, Boston, Mass.: Little, Brown.

Hosmer, L. R. T. (1987). *The Ethics of Management*. Homewood, IL: Irwin, 12, 98.

Johnson and Johnson Web Site:
<http://www.jnj.com/who_is_jnj/cr_usa.html>.

McCollum, K. (1998). "Founder of Utilitarianism Is Present in Spirit at 250th Birthday Teleconference." *The Chronicle of Higher Education.* February 27, A28.

Mill, J. S. (1897). *Utilitarianism*. London: Longmans, Green.

Moore, G. E. (1948). *Principa Ethica*. New York: Cambridge University Press, vii.

Moore, G. E. (1922). *Philosophical Studies*. London: Kegan Paul, Trench, Trubner, 273.

Multinational Monitor. (1996, June, Vol. 17, No. 6):

< http:multinationalmonitor.org/hyper/mm0696.01.html>.

Plato. *Apology, Crito, Republic I-II.* Great Books Foundation (Regency), 343.

Plato. *The Republic. Everyman's Library (Dutton).*

Ross, W. D. (1930). *The Right and the Good.* New York: Oxford University Press, 41-42.

Sartre, J. P. (1947). *Existentialism.* New York: Philosophical Library, 27.

Shaw, W. H. (1996). *Business Ethics.* Second Edition. New York: Wadsworth Publishing Company, 11.

Zadeh, L. A. (1965). "Fuzzy Sets." *Information Control.* Vol. 8, 338-353.

Chapter 5

Adiga, A. (2000). "Dads Hope to Have Nice DNA: US Fathers Flock to Patiently Test Labs." The Book of Life." *Financial Times.* (Monday, June 26), 16.

Baumhart, R. C. (1961). "How Ethical Are Businessmen?" *Harvard Business Review.* Vol. 39, No. 4, 6.

Branner, S. N. and Molander, E. A. (1977). "Is the Ethics of Business Changing?" *Harvard Business Review.* Vol. 55, 57.

Brown, H. R. (1953). *Social Responsibilities of the Businessman.* New York: Harper & Brothers, 6.

Buchholz, R.A. and Rosenthal, S. B. (1998). *Business Ethics.* Upper Saddle River, NJ: Prentice Hall, 111, 401, and 396.

Buchman, E. S. (1980). *The Use of Humor in Psychotherapy.* Boston, Mass.: Boston University: Dissertation Abstract International, Vol. 41, No. 5-B, 1715.

Butler, J. (1849). "Advertisement" Prefixed to *The Analogy of Religion, Natural and Revealed, to the Constitution and Course of Nature.* New York: Robert Carter.

Butler, J. K. and Cantrell, R. S. (1984). "A Behavioral Decision Theory Approach to Modeling Dyadic Trust in Supervisors and Subordinates." *Psychological Reports.* August 1994. 19-28.

Carroll, A. B. (1975). "Linking Business Ethics to Behavior of Organizations." *S. A. M. Advanced Management Journal.* Vol. 3, 4.

Carroll, A.B. (1989). *Business and Society: Ethics & Stakeholder Management.* Cincinnati, Ohio: South-Western Publishing Co., 30.

Chaudhry, P. E. and Walsh, M. G. (1995). "Intellectual Property Rights." *Columbia Journal of World Business.* Vol. 30, No. 2, 80.

Comte, A. In Edwards, P. (Ed.), (1967). "Comte, August." *Encyclopedia of Philosophy.* New York: The Macmillan Company and the Free Press, 173.

Conner, K. R. (1995). "Obtaining Strategic Advantage From Being Imitated: When Can Encouraging 'Clones' Pay?" *Management Science.* Vol. 41, 209.

Coser, L. R. (1960). "Laughter Among Colleagues." *Psychiatry.* Vol. 23, No. 1, 81-95.

Daley, W. (2000). "Bribe Affect $165bn Worth of Global Contracts." *Financial Times*. (Friday, June 30), 4.

Davis, K. (1960). "Can Business Afford to Ignore Social Responsibilities?" *California Management Review*. (Spring), 70.

Day, G. S. (1997). "Maintaining the Competitive Edge: Creating and Sustaining Advantages in Dynamic Competitive Environments." In Day, G. S., and Reibstein, D. J. *Wharton on Dynamic Competitive Strategy*. New York: John Wiley & Sons, 48.

De George, R. T. (1995). *Business Ethics*. Fourth Edition. Englewood Cliffs, NJ: Prentice Hall, 63.

Dooley, L. (1941). "The Relation of Humor to Masochism." *Psychoanalytic Review*. Vol. 28, 37.

Edwards, P. (Ed.), (1967). "Comte, August." *Encyclopedia of Philosophy*. New York: The Macmillan Company and the Free Press, 173.

Eichenwald, K. (1993). "Commissions Are Many, Profits Few." *New York Times*. May 24, C1.

Epstein, M. A. (1989). *Modern Intellectual Property*. New York: Law & Business, Inc./Harcourt Brace Jovanovich, 3, n.3.

Financial Times. (2000). "Freedom to Grow." (Friday June 30), 12.

Financial Times. (2000). "The Book of Life." (Monday June, 26), 16.

Financial Times. (2000). "World News." (Friday, April 28), 1.

Financial Times. (2001). "Former Sotheby's Chairman Convicted of Price Fixing." (Thursday, December 6), 1.

Freud, S. (1960). *Jokes and their Relation to the Unconscious*. New York: W. W. Norton. (Originally, 1905).

Freud, S. (1928). "Humour." *International Journal of Psychoanalysis*. Vol. 9, 2.

Grotjahn, M. (1956). *Beyond Laugher*. New York: McGraw-Hill.

Guerrera, F. and Jennen, B. (2001). "European Groups Face Record Fines for Roles in Price-Fixing." *Financial Times*. (Wednesday, November 21), 1.

Hayek, F. (1948). *Individualism and Economic Order*. Chicago: University of Chicago Press, 114.

Heidigger, M. (1962). *Being and Time*. (Trans.) Macquarrie, J., and Robinson, E., New York: Harper & Row Publishers, Inc.

Hitt, M. A., Ireland, R. D., and Hoskinsson, R. E. (1999). *Concepts and Cases: Strategic Management, Competitiveness and Globalization*. Cincinnati, Ohio: South-Western College Publishing, 167 & 186-191.

Hueber, G. (1990). "Pharmacists and Clergy Again Rate Highest for Honesty and Ethical Standards." *Gallup Poll Monthly*. (February), 23.

Jackson, S. and Collingwood, H. (1987). "Harris Poll: Is an Antibusiness Backlash Building?" *Business Week*. (July 20).

Jackson, J. H., Miller, R. L., and Shawn, G. M. (1997). *Business and Society Today: Managing Social Issues*. Cincinnati, Ohio: West Publishing Company, 195.

Kant, I. (1898). *Fundamental Principles of the Metaphysic of Morals.* (Trans.) Abbott, T. K. *From Kant's Critique of Practical Reason and Other Works on the Theory of Ethics.* London: Longmans, Green.

Kempton, W., Boster, J. S., and Hartley, J. A. (1995). *Environmental Values in American Culture.* Cambridge, Massachusetts: The MIT Press, 1& 27.

Knight, F. (1921). *Risk, Uncertainty and Profit.* Houghton Mifflin Company.

Laredo Morning Times (2000) ACC Trustees Tabs Trial a Witch Hunt." (Friday, May 19), 10A.

Locke, J. (1924). *An Essay Concerning Human Understanding.* (Abr. and Ed. By Pringle-Pattison, A. S.) Oxford: Clarendon Press.

Markham, J. W. (1951). "The Nature and Significance of Price Leadership." *The American Economic Review.* Vol. 41, 891.

Nietzsche, F. (1917). *The Will to Freedom.* New York: Charles Scribner's.

Nietzsche, F. (1917). Common, T. (Trns.), New York: Modern Library, Prologue, No. 3, as Found in Titus and Keeton, *Ethics for Today,* 178.

Newton, L. H. and Ford, M. M. (1990). *Taking Sides.* Guilford, CT: Dushkin.

Norton, M. B., Katzman, D. M., Escott, P. D., Chudacoff, H. P., Peterson, H. P., and Tuttle, Jr., W. M. (1990). *A People and a Nation: A History of the United States.* Boston: Houghton Mifflin Company, 215.

Oesterle, J. A. (1957). *Ethics: The Introduction to Moral Science.* Englewood Cliffs, NJ: Prentice Hall, 17 & 156.

Olasky, M. N. (1985). "Ministers or Panderers: Issues Raised by the Public Relations Society Code of Standards." *Journal of Mass Media Ethics.* Vol. 1, No. 1.

Peikoff, L. (1999). "Why Businessmen Need Philosophy?" In Ralston, R. (Ed.), Why Businessmen Need Philosophy: United States: The Ayn Rand Institute, 9.

Punnett, B. J. and Ricks, D. A. (1992). *International Business.* Boston: PWS-Kent Publishing Company, 237.

Ridpath, J. B. (1980). "The Philosophical Origins of Antitrust." *The Objectivist Forum.* (June), 14.

Rosenbloom, B. (1999). *Marketing Channels: A Management View.* New York: The Dryden Press, 336.

Ross, W. D. (1930). *The Rights and the Good.* London: Oxford University Press, 42.

Royce, J. (1916). *The Philosophy of Loyalty.* The MacMillan Co., 16-17 & 25.

Salameh, W. A. (1983). "Past Outlooks, Present Status, and Future Frontiers." In McGhee, P. and Goldstein, J. (Eds.). *Handbook of Humour.* New York: Springer, Verlag.

Schindler, P. L. and Thomas, C. C. (1993). "The Structure of Interpersonal Trust in the Workplace." *Psychological Reports.* October 1993, 563-573.

Schwartz, A. (1991). "Mining a Mountain." *Far Eastern Economic Review.* (July 4), 47.

Sethi, S. P. (1982). *Up Against the Corporate Wall, Modern Corporations and Social Issues of the Eighties.*(4th Ed.). Englewood Cliffs, NJ: Prentice Hall, 288.

Shaw, W. H. (1996). *Business Ethics.* Belmont, CA: Wadsworth Publishing Company: 61.

Shaw, W. H. and Barry, V. (1998). *Moral Issues in Business.* Belmont, CA: Wadsworth Publishing Company, 36, 283.

Sonnenberg, F. K. (1993). Trust Me...Trust Me Not." *Industry Week.* August 16, 22.

Spanner, R. A. (1986). *Who Owns Innovation?* Homewood, IL: Dow Jones-Irwin, 10.

Stewart, D. (1996). *Business Ethics.* New York: The McGraw-Hill Companies, Inc., 281-282.

Steiner, G. A. and Steiner, J. F. (1994). *Business, Government and Society: A managerial Perspective.* Seventh Edition,. New York: McGraw-Hill, Inc., 180.

Stuart, R. (1977). In Walton, C. (Ed.). *The Ethics of Corporate Conduct.* Englewood Cliffs, New Jersey: Prentice Hall, Inc., 181-182.

The Economist (1992). "Fake Drugs." (May, 2), 85.

Velasquez, M. G. (1998). *Business Ethics: Concepts and Cases.* (Second Edition). Englewood Cliffs, NJ: Prentice Hall, 201 & 364.

<wysiwyg://http://www.cnn.com/2002/WORLD/europe/07/19/shipman.vic tims/index.html>.

Waldmeir, P. (2001). Copyright Extended to Digital Data." *Financial Times.* Tuesday June 26: 4.

Walton, C. (1997). (Ed.). *The Ethics of Corporate Conduct.* Englewood Cliffs, New Jersey: Prentice Hall, Inc., 181-182.

Williams, J. R. (1992). "How Sustainable Is Your Competitive Advantage?" *California Management Review.* Vol. 34, (Spring), 29.

Chapter 6

Albert, S. and Whetten, D. (1985). "Organizational Identity." In L. L. Cummings and B. M. Staw (Eds.). *Research in Organizational Behavior.* Greenwich, Conn.: JAI Press, 263-295.

Awadudi, A. A. (1989). *Towards Understanding Islam.* Jamaica, New York: The Message Publications, 121.

Ball, D. A., and McCulloch, Jr., W. H. (1988). *International Business: Introduction and Essentials.* Third Edition. Homewood, IL: Irwin, 269.

Beals, R. L. and Hijer, H. (1959). *An Introduction to Anthropology.* New York: Macmillan, 9.

Behdad, S. (1989). "Property Rights in Contemporary Islamic Economic Thought: A Critical Perspective." *Review of Social Economy*. Vol. 47, No. 2, 185-211.

Berelson, B. and Steiner, G. A. (1964). *Human Behavior*. New York: Harcourt, Brace, And World, 16-17.

Blackler, F. (1995) "Knowledge, Knowledge Work and Organizations: An Overview and Interpretation." *Organization Studies*. Vol. 16, No.6, 1021-1046.

Buchholz, R. A. and Rosenthal, S. B. (1998). *Business Ethics*. Upper Saddle River, NJ: Prentice Hall, 60.

Carroll, A. B. (1979). "A Three Dimensional Conceptual Model of Corporate Performance." *Academy of Management Review*. (October Issue), 499.

Collins, H. (1993). "The Structure of Knowledge." *Social Research*. Vol. 60, 95-116.

De George, R. T. (1990). *Business Ethics*. Fourth Edition. Englewood Cliffs, New Jersey: Prentice Hall, Inc., 119.

Dewey, J. (1929). *The Quest for Certainty*. New York: Mint Balch.

Drucker, P. (1993). *Post-Capitalist Society*. Oxford: Butterworth Heineman, 5.

Financial Times (2001). "The Danger of Knowing Too Much." Weekend May 12/May 13, 11.

Flack, J. (1997). "Contingent Knowledge and Technology Development." Technology Development. *Technology Analysis for Strategic Management*. Vol. 9, No. 4, 383-397.

Freud, Z. (1856-1939). "Re-Examining Freud." *Psychology Today*. September 1989, 48-52.

Garvin, D. A. (1998). "Building a Learning Organization." *Harvard Business Review on Knowledge Management*. Boston, Mass.: President and Fellows of Harvard College, 47.

Gold, J. (2000). "Ex-Penny Stock Mogul Arrested on Fraud Charges." *San Antonio Express News*. Wednesday, August 2, 2E.

Hall, W. (2000). "Banks Agree Money Laundering Rules." *Financial Times*. Tuesday, October 31, 10.

Harvey, C. and Allard, M. J. (1995). *Understanding Diversity: Readings, Cases, and Exercises*. New York: Harper Collins College Publishers, 11.

Lundvall, B. A. (1996). "The Social Dimension of the Learning Economy." *Department of Business Studies*. Aalborg University, Denmark.

Luthans, F. (1985) *Organizational Behavior*. New York: McGraw-Hill, 30-39.

Meyes, B. T. and Allen, R. W. (1977). "Toward a Definition of Organizational Politics." *Academy of Management Review*. Vol. 2, No. 4, 672-678.

Miller, J., David, A., and Quintas, P. (1997). "Trans-Organizational Innovation: A Framework for Research." *Technology Analysis of Strategic Management*. Vol. 9, No. 4, 399-418.

Morgan, C., and King, R. (1966). *Introduction to Psychology*. 3rd Edition, New York: McGraw-Hill, 22.

Palmer, J. D. (1989). "Three Paradigms for Diversity Challenge Leaders." *OD Practitioner*. Vol. 21, 15-18.

Parhizgar, K. D. (2002). *Multicultural Behavior and Global Business Environments*. New York: Haworth Press, 84, 125.

Parhizgar, K. D., Pena-Sanchez, R., and Parhizgar, F. F. (2002). "Development of Corporate Technology Along With Know-What, Know-Why, Know-How, Know-Whose, Know-Where, and Know-For Knowledge." *Proceedings of the Eleventh World Business Congress*, July 10-14, 2002, Antalya, Turkey.

Parhizgar, K. D. and Lunce, S. E. (1996). "Implications of Employees' Informational Integrated Discovery Systems." In Beardwell, I. (Ed.). *Contemporary Developments in Human Resource Management*. Montpelier: France: An International Publication of the Scientific Committee of the Montpelier Graduate Business School, Editions ESKA, 393-403.

Parhizgar, K. D. (1996). "Cross-Cultural Implications of the Popular Cultural Damping in the International Movie Market." In Lemaster, J., and Islam, M.M., *Southwest Review of International Business Research, Proceedings of the 1996 Academy of International Business, Southwest Regional Meeting*, 309.

Parhizgar, K. D. (1994). "Affordability and Solvency Implications of Privatization of Government-Owned Industries in the Third World Countries." *Journal of Business and Society*. Vol. 7, No. 1, 110.

Steidlmeier, P. (1993). "The Moral Legitimacy of Intellectual Property Claims: American Business and Developing Country Perspectives." *Journal of Business Ethics*. February, Vol. 12, No. 2, 157.

Terpstra, V. and David, K. (1991). *The Cultural Environment of International Business*. Third Edition. Cincinnati. Ohio: College Division South-Western Publishing Co., 136.

The Oxford English Dictionary (1989). Second Edition. Prepared by Simpson, J. A. and Weiner, E. S. C. Oxford: Clardon Press.

Weber, C. O. (1960). *Basic Philosophies of Education*. New York: Rinehart and Winston, 13-14.

Wundt, W. (1879). In Luthans, F. (1985) *Organizational Behavior*. New York: McGraw-Hill, 36.

Zack, M. H. (1999). "Managing Codified Knowledge." *Sloan Management Review*. Vol. 40, No. 4, Summer, 45-58.

Zadeh, L. A. (1965). "Fuzzy Sets." *Information Control*. Vol. 8, 338-353.

Chapter 7

abcNEWS.com (Monday July 21, 2002). "Investors Fear Another Tough Week." <wysiwyg://11/http://ancnews.go.com/wire/Business/ap20020721_826.html.>.

Abrams, F. (1951). Management's Responsibilities in a Complex World." *Harvard Business Review*. Vol. 24, No. 3, 29-34.

Adler, N. (1986). *International Dimensions of Organizational Behavior*. Boston, Massachusetts: The Kent International Publishing Company, 18.

Albert, E. M., Denise, T. C., and Peterfreund, S. P. (1984). *Great Traditions in Ethics*. Belmont, CA: Wadsworth, Publishing Company, 40.

Aristotle, *Nicomachean Ethics*, 1097a, 35.

Atkins, R. (2001). "Kunnast Refuses to Rule Out Danger to Milk." *Financial Times*. Tuesday January 16, 2001, 2.

Atkins, R. (2000). "Germany Bans Sale of Untested Beef." *Financial Times*. Friday December 1, 2000, 3.

Bahadori, R. S. and Bohne, B. A. (1993). "Adverse Effects of Noise on Hearing." *American Family Physician*. April 1, 12-19.

BBC News (2002). "Rise and Fall of an Energy Giant." <http://news.bbc.co.uk/hi/english/business/newsid_1681000/1681758.stm >.

Buchholz, R. A. and Rosenthal, S. B. (1998). *Business Ethics: The Pragmatic Path Beyond Principles to Process*. Upper Saddle River, NJ: Prentice Hall, 56.

Calderia, K. and Kasting, J. F. (1993). "Insensitivity of Global Warming Potentials to Carbon Dioxide Emission Scenarios." *Nature*. Vol. 366, November 18, 251-253.

Cohen, E. (2002). "Family of Only U. S. Mad Cow Case Blame U. K." *CNN News* Friday, October 18 <http://www.cnn.com/2002/HEALTH/conditions/10/17/madcom.us/index.html >

Cookson, C. (2000). "BSE Could Have Happened Anywhere." *Financial Times*. November 4 & 5, Weekend FT, 11.

Crawford, L. (2001). "Spanish Fear Mad Cow Among the Bulls." *Financial Times*. Tuesday, January 23, 1.

Danley, J. R. (1990). "Corporation Moral Agency: The Case for Anthropological Bigotry." In Business Ethics: W. M. Hoffman and J. M. Moore (1990). *Reading and Cases in Corporate Morality*. New York: McGraw-Hill, 165-170.

De Mente, B. (1990). *Chinese Etiquette and Ethics in Business: A Penetrating Analysis of the Morals and Values that Shape the Chinese Business Personality* Lincolnwood, IL: NTC Business Books, 21.

Fabrikant, G. (1995). "Battling for Hearts and Minds at Time Warner." New York Times, February 26, 9.

Financial Times (2000). "The Cost of BSE." Wednesday December 6, 2000, 14.

Frankena, W. K. (1973). *Ethics*. Second Edition. Englewood Cliffs, NJ: Prentice-Hall, Inc., 64.

Frederick, W. C. (1992). "Social Issues in Management: Coming of Age or Prematurely Gray?" Paper presented to the Doctoral Consortium of the Social Issues in Management Division of the *Academy of Management*. Las Vegas, Nevada, August: 5.

Freeman, R. F. (1984). *Strategic Management: A Stakeholder Approach.* Boston: Pitman.

Garrett, T. M. (1966). *Business Ethics*. New York: Appleton-Century-Crofts, 8.

Geertz, C. (1964). "Ideology as a Cultural System." In David E. Apter (Ed.). *Ideology and Discontent.* New York: The Free Press, 47-76.

George, N. (2000). "Ethical Practices May Have Prevented Outbreak in Sweden." *Financial Times.* Thursday November 30, 2000, 2.

Jackson, J. H., Miller, R. L., and Miller, S. G. (1997). *Business and Society Today: Managing Social Issues.* Cincinati, OH: West Publishing Company, 61.

Jonquieres, G. de and Bilefsky, D. (2001). "Herd Instinct: Europe's >Mad Cow' Crisis can be Blamed on the Politicization of Food Regulation and National Governments that Put Sovereignty Before Safety." *Financial Times.* Wednesday January 17, 14.

Kempton, W., Boster, J. S., and Hartley, J. A. (1995). *Environmental Values in American Culture.* Cambridge, Massachusetts: The MIT Press, 30.

Kluckhohn, F.R. and Strodtbeck, F. L. (1961). *Variation in Value Orientations.* New York: Row and Peterson, 11.

Koran: Surat: Al Hajj, Ayat 18.

Labate, J. (2001). "Madden to Pay $7.8m Penalty for Stock Fraud." *Financial Times.* Thursday May 24: Week 21, 15.

Leopold (1970). *A Sand Country.* New York: Ballantine, 239-240.

Locke, J. (1980). *Second Treatise of Government.* Indianapolis, MN: Hackett Publishing, 23-24.

Lui, H., Farr-Jones, S., Ulyanov, N.B., Llinas, M., Marqusee, S. Groth, D., Cohen, F.E., Prusiner, S.B., and James, T.L. (1999). "Solution Structure of Syrian Hamster Prion Protein rPrP(90-231)." *Biochemistry.* Vol. 38, 5362-5377.

Mawdudi, A. A. (1986). *Towards Understanding Islam.*U.S. A.: The Message Publications, 61.

McCollum, K. (1998). "Founder of Utilitarian Is Present in Spirit at 250th-Birthday Teleconference." *The Chronicle of Higher Education.* February 27, A28.

McIntyre, A. (1984). *After Virtue.* Second Edition. Notre Dame, IN: University of Notre Dame Press, 6.

Morrison, S. (2000). "Mad Cow Panic Blights Farmer of Water Buffalo." *Financial Times.* Weekend December 9-10, 2000, 3.

Neale, R. and Mindel, R. (1992). "Rigging Up Multicultural Teamworking." *Personnel Management.* January, 27-30.

Oesterle, J. A. (1957). *Ethics: The Introduction to Moral Science.* Englewood Cliffs, NJ: Prentice-Hall, Inc., 172.

Office of Technology Assessment (OTA), (1991). *Changing By Degrees: Steps to Reduce Greenhouse Gases.* OTA-O-482, February. Washington, D.C.: U.S. Government Printing Office.

O'Reilly, B. (1994). "The New Deal: What Companies and Employees Owe One Another." *Fortune.* June 13, 44.

Paikoff, L. (1999). "The Evil of Respecting Nature." In Ralston, R. (Ed.). *Why Businessmen Need Philosophy?* United States of America: The Ayn Rand Institute Publication, 67.

Parhizgar, R. R., Parhizgar, S. S., and Parhizgar, K. D. (2001). "Assessment of the Meat and Bone Meal (MBM) on Livestock and Financial Effects of Mad Cow Disease on International Trade." The paper presented at the *Eleventh Conference of the International Trade and Finance Association.* May 26-29, Washington DC.

Parhizgar, K. D. (2002). *Multicultural Behavior and Global Business Environments.* New York: Haworth Press, 40 and 73.

Parsons, T. (1960). *Structure and Process in Modern Societies.* Glencoe, IL: The Free Press, 59.

Patrick Primeaux, S. M. (2002). "Maximizing Ethics and Profits." In L. P. Hartman (Ed.). *Perspectives in Business Ethics.* New York: McGraw-Hill, Irwin. 242-247.

Peters, F. E. (1967). *Greek Philosophical Terms.* New York: New York University Press, 25.

Peters, R. L. and Lovejoy, T. E. (1990). "Terrestrial Fauna." In B. L. Turner et al. *The Earth as Transformed by Human Action: Global and Regional Changes in the Biosphere over the Past 300 Years."* 353-369.

Peters, T. J. and Waterman Jr., R. H. (1982). *In Search of Excellence: Lessons from America's Best-Run Companies.* New York: Harper & Row.

Prusiner, S. B (1997). "Molecular Biological, Genetic, and Protein Structural Studies of Prion Disease." *Noble Foundation.* Stockholm, Sweden. Reprinted in (1998) *Proceedings: National Academy of Science,* U.S.A. Vol. 95, 13363-13383.

Rand, A. (1999). "The Money-Making Personality." In R. E. Ralston (1999). *Why Businessmen Need Philosophy.* U.S.A.: Ayn Rand Institute Press, 27-38.

Reuters (2001). "U.S. Quarantines Texas Cattle Over Mad Cow Rules." <*Netscape*: wysiwyg://6/http:// dailynews.netscape.com...able'n&cat'50100&id' 200101251849000210734>.

Ridpath, J. B. (1999). "The Philosophical Theory of Antitrust." In R. E. Ralston (1999). *Why Businessmen Need Philosophy.* U.S.A.: Ayn Rand Institute Press, 169.

Rokeach, M. (1973). *The Nature of Human Values.* New York: The Free Press.

Salsman, R. M. (1999). "Antitrust Returns With a Vengeance." In R. E. Ralston (1999). *Why Businessmen Need Philosophy.* U.S.A.: Ayn Rand Institute Press, 191.

Shabecoff , P. (1987). "Dozens of Nations Reach Agreement to protect Ozone." *New York Times.* September 17, A1.

Smith, M. (2000a). "Brussels May Ban Meat-Based Feed." *Financial Times.* Thursday November 30, 6.

Smith, M. (2000b). "Fischler Warns on Cost of Mad Cow Measures." *Financial Times.* Wednesday December 6, 2 and 6.

Sproul, L. S. (1981). "Beliefs in Organizations." In Nystrom. P. C. and Starbuck, W. H. (Eds.). *Handbook of Organizational Design*. New York: Oxford University Press, 204-205.

Steiner, G. A. and Steiner, F. S. (1994). *Business, Government, and Society: A Managerial Perspective*. Seventh Edition. New York: McGraw-Hill, Inc., 5 & 29.

Steiner, G. A. and Steiner, J. F. (1980). *Business Government, and Society: A Managerial Perspective*. New York: Random House, 273.

Stainer, G. A. and Stainer, J. F. (1994). *Business, Government, and Society: A Managerial Perspective*. Seventh Edition. New York: McGraw-Hill, Inc., 29.

Sullivan, R. (2001). "Mad Cow Findings Surprise Officials." *Financial Times*. Wednesday January 10, 26.

Sullivan, E. T. (1991). *The Political Economy of the Sherman Act: The First One Hundred Years*. New York: Oxford University Press, 13 & 22.

Supattapone, S. Bosque, P., Muramoto, T., White, H., Aagaard, C., Peretz, D., Nguyen, H., O.B., Heinrich, C., Torchia, M. Safar, J., Cohen, F.E., DeArmond, S.J., Prusiner, S.B., and Scott, M. (1999). "Prion Prottein of 106 Residues creates an Artificial Transmission Barrier for Prion Replication in Transgenic Mice." *Cell*. Vol. 96, 869-878.

Viles, J.H., Cohen, F.E., Prusiner, S.B., Goodin, D.B., Wright, P.E., and Dyson, H.J. (1999). "Copper Binding to the Prion Protein: Structural Implications of Four Identical Cooperative Binding Sites." *Proceeding· National Academy of Science*, USA. Vol. 96, 2042-2047.

Wilson, E. O. (1989). "Threats to Biodiversity." *Scientific American*. Vol. 261, No. 3, 108-116.

Woolf, H. B. (1981), (Ed.). *Webster's New Collegiate Dictionary*. Sprinfield, MA: G. & C. Merriam Company.

World Resources Institute (1992). *World Resources* 1992-93: A Guide to the Global Environment. New York: Oxford University Press, 128.

Wrong, M. (2000). AEU to Prop up French Beef Market." *Financial Times*. Thursday November 16, 6.

Chapter 8

Albert, E. M., Denise, T. C., and Peterfreund, S. P. (1984). *Great Traditions in Ethics*. Belmont, CA: Wadsworth Publishing Company, 10.

Botwin, M. D. and Buss, D. M. (1989). " Structure of Act-Report Data: Is the Five-Factor Model of Personality Recaptured." *Journal of Personality and Social Psychology*. Vol. 56, 988-1001.

Buchholz, R. A. and Rosenthal, S. B. (1998). *Business Ethics: The Pragmatic Path Beyond Principles to Process*. New York: McGraw-Hill Book Company, 30 and 297.

Cairncross, F. (1991). *Costing the Earth*. Boston: Harvard Business School Press, 56.

De George, R. T. (1995). *Business Ethics*. Fourth Edition. Englewood Cliffs, NJ: Prentice Hall, 113.

Dewey, J. (1929). *The Quest for Certainty*. New York: Mint, Baloch, 260-261.

Donaldson, T. (1989). *The Ethics of International Business*. New York: Oxford University Press, 81.

Dutka, A. (1999). *Competitive Intelligence For Competitive Edge*. Chicago, IL: NTC Basic Books, 18.

Fried, M. H. (1967). *The Evolution of Political Society: An Essay in Political Anthropology*. New York: Random House.

Hawes, F. and Kealey, D. J. (1981). "An Empirical Study of Canadian Technical Assistance." *International Journal of Intercultural Relations*. Vol. 5, 239-258.

Hegel, G. W. In Loewenberg, J. (Ed.), (1929). *Hegel Selections*. New York: Harper, 468.

Kant, I. (1898). *Fundamental Principles of the Metaphysic of Morals*. Translated by T. K. Abbott, from *Kant's Critique of Practical Reason and Other Works on the Theory of Ethics*. London: Longmans, Green: First Section, 10, 12-14.

Loewenberg, J. (Ed.), (1929). *Hegel Selections*. New York: Harper, 468.

Locke, J. (1924). *An Essay Concerning Human Understanding*. A. S. Pringle-Pattison (Abr. and Ed.). Oxford: Claredon Press.

Meiklejohn, A. (1942). *Education Between Two Worlds*. New York: Harper, 57 & 83.

Moore, G. E. (1922). *Philosophical Studies*. London: Kegan Paul, Trench, Trubner, 273.

Piaget, J. (1977). *The Development of Thought: Equilibrium of Cognitive Structures*. New York: Viking Press.

Pope, J. (2002). "CFOs Pressure to Lie." <wysiwyg://13http://www.cbsnews.com/stories/2002/07/25/national/main51629 9.shtml>.

Segal, T. and Del Valle, C. (1993). "They Didn't Even Give at the Office." *Business Week*. January 25, 68-69.

Shaw, W. H. (1996). *Business Ethics*. Second Edition. Belmont, CA: Wadsworth Publishing Company, 18.

Steiner, G. A. and Steiner, J. F. (1994). *Business, Government, and Society: A Managerial Perspective*. New York: Seventh Edition. McGraw-Hill, Inc., 47.

Stewart, D. (1996). *Business Ethics*. New York: The McGraw-Hill Companies, Inc., 297.

Terpstra, V. and David, K. (1991). *The Cultural Environment of International Business*. Cincinnati, OH: South-Western Publishing Co., 55.

Velasquez, M. G. (1992). *Business Ethics: Concepts and Cases*. 3rd Edition. Englewood Cliffs, NJ: Prentice Hall. 59.

Weber, C. O. (1960). *Basic Philosophies of Education*. New York: Rinehart and Winston, 29.

Weber, M. (1946). *The Theory of Social and Economic Organization.* Translated by T. Parsons. New York: Oxford University Press.

Welch, J. (1993). "Jack Welch's Lessons for Success." *Fortune* January 25, 86-93.

Chapter 9

Abrams, F. W. (1951). "Management's Responsibilities in a Complex World." *Harvard Business Review.* May Edition, 29-35.

Adler, N. (1986). *International Dimension of Organizational Behavior* Boston, MA: Kent Publishing Company, 18.

Ayers, E. L., Gould, L. L., Oshinsky, D. M., and Soderlund, J. R. (2001). *American Passages: A History of the United States.* New York: Harcourt College Publishers, 50 and 299.

Barrett, M. (1991). *The Politics of Truth: From Marx to Foucault.* Stanford, CA: Stanford University Press, Viii,194.

Barry, D. D. and Barner-Barry, C. (1987). *Contemporary Soviet Politics.* Third Edition. Englewood Cliffs, NJ: Prentice-Hall, Inc., 25.

Brzezinski, Z. (1970). *Between Two Ages B America's Role in the Technocratic Era.* New York: Penguin Books, 72, 83, 300-304.

Burn, T. and Stalker, G. M. (1961). *The Management of Innovation.* London: Tavistock Institute of Human Relations Press.

Cohen, G. A. (1988). *History, Labour, and Freedom.* Oxford: Oxford University Press, 84.

Collier's Encyclopedia (1985). Ed., S. V. "Knights Templars."

Council on Foreign Relations Annual Report (1936). New York.

Council on Foreign Relations Annual Report (1987). New York: 103-104.

Council on Foreign Relations Annual Report (1990). New York: 6, 141, 142, 185-186.

Dalton, C. B. (1985). *Constitutional Money and the Banking Procedure.* Oreana, IL: Illinois Committee to Restore the Constitution, 4.

Duncan, M. (1974). *Duncans' Masonic Ritual and Monitor.* Rev. Ed. Chicago: Charles T. Powner Co., 42-47.

Editorial Perspectives (1994). "Socialism: Dead Again, Born Again." *Science & Society.* Vol. 58, No. 2, Summer, 131.

Epperson, R. (1985). *The Unseen Hand.* Tucson: Publius Press: 186 and 196.

Griffith, V. (2001). "Samoa to Get Percentage of Aids Drug Profits." *Financial Times.* Thursday December 13, 3.

Harding, J. (2001). "Globalization's Children Strike Back." *Financial Times.* Tuesday, September 11, 4.

<http://libreray.thinkquest.org/17823/data/irancontra.html)>.

Hofstede, G. (1980). *Culture's Consequences: International Differences in Work Related Values* Beverly Hills, CA: Sage Publications.

Holbrook, M. B. (1994). "The Nature of Customer Value." In R. T. Rust and R. L. Oliver (Eds.). *Service Quality: New Directions in Theory and Practice.* Thousand Oaks, CA: Sage Publications, 21-71.

Jeffcut, P. (1994). "The Interpretation of Organization: A Contemporary Analysis and Critique." *Journal of Management Studies.* March, 225.

Kah, G. (1991). *En Route To Global Occupation: A High Ranking Government Liaison Exposes the Secret Agenda for World Unification.* Lafayette, Louisiana: Huntington House Publishers, 13 and 45.

Kaminarides, J. S. and Nissan, E. (1993). "The International Debt and its Effects on the Economic Growth of Selected Developing Countries." *Journal of Business and Society.* Vol. 6: No. 2, 123-138.

Kodoma, F. (1992). "Technology Fusion and the New R&D." *Ministry of International Trade and Industry.* Vol. 70, (July/August), 70-78.

Lane, R. E. (1965). *Political Life.* New York: The Free Press: 106.

Lane, R. E. (1962). *Political Ideology: Why the American Common Man Beliefs What He Does.* New York: Free Press, 3, 15.

Lundberg, F. (1968). *Who really owns America? How Do They Keep Their Wealth and Power? The Rich and the Super-Rich.* New Jersey: Little Stuart Inc., 305.

Marger, M. N. (1985). *Race and Ethnic Relations: American and Global Perspectives.* Belmont, California: Wadsworth Publishing Company, 16.

Marx, K. (1991). *Capital.* Vol. III. Harmonsworth, England: Penguin 359.

Marx, K. (1848). *The Communist Manifesto.*

Marx, K. (1867). *Das Kapital.*

Marx, K. (1938). *Critique of the Gotha Program.* New York: International Publisher.

Meadows, D. L., Meadows, D. M., Randers, J. and Behrens, W. W. (1974). *The Limit to Growth -- A Report for the Club of Rome's Project on the Predicament of Mankind.* Second Edition. Washington DC: Potomac Associates; New York: Universe Books: 9.

Mesarovic, M. and Pestel, E. (1974). *Mankind at the Turning Point -- The Second Report to the Club of Rome.* New York: E. P. Dutton & Co., Inc./Readers's Digest Press, 203.

Miller, R. W. (1984). *Analyzing Marx.* New Jersey: Princeton University Press, 237.

Miller, M. H. (1997). *Merton H. Miller on Derivatives.* New York: John Wiley.

Moszkowska, N. (1935). *Zur Kritik Moderner Krisentheorien.* 97.

Mullins, E. (1985). *The World Order.* Staunton, VA: Ezra Pound Institute of Civilization: 33-34 and 196.

Mullins, W.A. (1972). "On the Concept of Ideologies in Political Science." *American Political Science Review.* Vol. 66, 498-511.

Parhizgar, K. D., Willman, E., and Parhizgar, F. F. (2002). "Analysis of Different Types of Businesses." *Journal of Global Competitiveness.* Vol. 10, No. 1, 353-362.

Parhizgar, K. D. and Parhizgar, F. F. (2002). "Analysis of Ecological Business Ethics Commitments." In Mostapha Abdelsamad (Ed.). *Proceedings Society for Advancement of Management BSAM.* 826-833.

Parhizgar, K. D. "Ethical Analysis of the Kinetic and Quiddity Existence Need Theory (KQENT) in Multicultural Organizations." *Journal of Transnational Management Development.* Vol. 5, No. 3, 47-59.

Parhizgar, K. D. (1994). "Affordability and Solvency Implications of Privatization of Government-Owned Industries in the Third World Countries (TWCs)." *Journal of Business and Society.* Vol. 1, No. 1, 109-119.

Parhizgar, K. D. and Jesswein, K. R. (1998). "Ethical and Economical Affordability of Developing Nations' Repayment of International Debt." In Baker, J. C. (Ed.). *Selected International Investment Portfolios.* Great Britain: Pergamon, Biddles Ltd., 141-150.

Parhizgar, K. D. (2002). *Multicultural Behavior and Global Business Environments.* New York: Haworth Press, 71.

Peikoff, L. (1999)."The Evil of Respecting Nature." In Ayn Rand (Ed.) (1999). *Why Businessmen Need Philosophy?* U.S.S.: The Ayn Rand Institute, 66.

Pike, A. (1966). *Morals and Dogma of the Ancient and accepted Scottish Rite of Freemasonry.* Washington DC: House of the Temple, 816.

Pilling, D. (2001). A WHO Backs South African Law on Drug Patents." *Financial Times.* March 17/18, 4.

Rich, P. and de los Reyes, G. (1998). "Freemasonry and Popular Culture: creating Mystiques." *Popular Culture Review.* Vol. 9, No. 1, 59.

Rich, P. and de los Reyes, G. (1996). "California Freemasonry: Early Masonic Lodges of California." *Popular Culture Review.* February, Vol. 7, No. 1, 20.

"Rivalry in the Persian Gulf" (1981). *The Middle East Congressional Quarterly Inc.,* Fifth Edition, Washington, DC, 71-98.

Roberts, A. E. (1979). *Emerging Struggle for State Sovereignty.* Fort Collins: Betsy Ross Press: 185.

Roberts, A. E. (1984). *The Most Secret Science.* Forth Collins: Betsy Ross Press, 56.

Roberts, A. E. (1985). *State Sovereignty.* Fort Collins: Betsy Ross Press: 203.

Roberts, A. E. (1986). "Bulletin-Should the United States Participate and Encourage Development of the United Nations Organization?" Committee to Restore the Constitution (July), 4-5

Shaw, W. H. and Barry, V. (1998). *Moral Issues in Business.* Seventh Edition. Belmont, CA: Wadsworth Publishing Company, 144.

Smith, A. (1869). *An Inquiry into the Nature and Causes of the Wealth of Nations.* Vols. 1 and 2.

Sproul, L. S. (1981). "Beliefs in Organizations" in P. C. Nystrom and W. H. Starbuck (Eds). *Handbook of Organizational Design.* New York: Oxford University Press, 204.

Chapter 10

Ayala, F. J. (1994). "On the Scientific Method, Its Practice and Pitfalls." *His., Phil., Life Science.* Vol. 1. No. 16, 205-240.

Beatie, A. (2000). "U.S. Blocked Planned Trade Privileges for Poor Countries." *Financial Times.* (Friday April 7), 5.

Bosworth, B. and Gordon, P. H. (2001). "Managing a Globalizing World." *Brookings Review.* Fall Edition, 3.

Brenkert, G. G. (1992). "Can We Afford International Human Rights?" *Journal of Business Ethics.* Vo.l.11, No. 7, 515-521.

Bush, G. (1991). "State of the Union -Bush Seeks to Inspire Support for His Persian Gulf Mission." *Congressional Quarterly.* (February 2), 308-310.

Business Week (1993). "Executive Pay: The Party Ain't Over Yet." April 26.

Business Week (1994). "The Eye-Popping Executive Pay." April25.
Cassidy, J. (1997). "Gimme." *New Yorker.* April, 21.

Coss, L. (1997). In Cassidy, *I. "Gimme." New Yorker.* April21.
Cowan, w. M. (1978). "Aspects of Neural *Development."Int. Rev. Physiol.* Vol. 17, No. 902 &150.
Darwin, C. (1859). *On the Origin of Species.* London: John Murray.

Darwin, C. R. (1958). *The Autobiography of Charles Darwin* 1809-1882 *With Original Omissions Restored.* London: Collins, 120.

De George, R. T. (1999). *Business Ethics.* Upper Saddle River, New Jersey: Prentice Hall, 5

De George, R. T. (1995). *Business Ethics.* Englewood Cliffs, NJ: Prentice Hall, 5.

Donaldson, T. (1989). *The Ethics of International Business.* New York: Oxford University Press.

Donaldson, T. (1996). "Values in Tension: Ethics Away From Home." *Harvard Business Review.* Vol. 74, No.5, 48-62.

Drucker, P. F. (1980). *Managing in Turbu/ent Times.* New York: Harper & Row, Publishers, 11 and 192.

Dvorin, E. P. and Simmons, R. H. (1972). *From Amoral to Humane Bureaucracy.* New York: Harper & Row, Publishers, Inc., 9.

Friedman, M. (1983). "The Social Responsibility of Business Is to Increase Profits." In Beauchamp, T. L. and Bowie, N. E. (Eds.). *Ethical Theory in Business.* Second Edition., 81-83.

Greider, W. (1992). *Who Will Tell the People: The Betrayal of American Democracy.* New York: Simon & Schuster, 80.

Greider, W. (1997). *One World, Ready or Not: The Manic Logic of Global Capitalism.* New York: Simon & Schuster.

Hegel, G. W. (1770-1831). In Loewenberg, J. (Ed.), (1929) *Hegel Selections.* New York: Scriber's

Hofstadter, R. (1945). *Darwinism in American Thought,* 1860-1915. Philadelphia: University of Pennsylvania Press.

International Investment Portfolios. Great Britain: Pergamon, Biddles Ltd., 141-150.

Iyre, G. R. (1999). "Approaches to Ethics in International Business *Education."Journal of Teaching in International Business.* Vol. 11, No.1, 9.

Jackson, J. H., Miller R. L. and Miller, S. G. (1997). *Business and Society Today: Managing Social Issues.* Cincinnati, Ohio: West Publishing Company, 35,23, and 191.

Labaton, S. (2001). "Microsoft Asks Supreme Court to Reverse Antitrust Finding." *The New York Times.* August 8.

Loewenberg, J. (Ed.), (1929). *Hegel Selections.* New York: Scriber's.

Maitland, A. (2000). "Human Rights Weigh Heavier with Investors." *Financial Times.* Thursday, April 6, London, 3.

Marx, K. (1867). *Das Kapital.*

MSNBC.com, November 8,2002, Justice vs. Microsoft, *Associate Press.* "Microsoft Obeys Antitrust Sanctions."
<httD://www.ms11bc.com/news/832386.asQ?cQ 1 '1>.

Nader, R. (2000). Transcript of "Globalization and Human Rights." A PBS Program, <www .pbs.org./ globalization/prologue.html>.

Parhizgar, K. D. (1994). "Affordability and Solvency Implications of Privatization of Government-Owned Industries in the Third World Countries (TWCs)." *Journal of Business and Society.* Vol. 1, No.1, 109-119.

Parhizgar, R. R. and Parhizgar, S. S. (2000). "Analysis of Three Types of Personhood: Genotype, Phenotype, and Phylontype in Biotech Enterprise." In Maniarn, B. and Mitha, S. A. (Eds.), Proceedings of the 51 Annual Conference of the Decision Sciences Institute Southwest Region. San Antonio, Texas, 185.

Parhizgar, K. D. and Jesswein, K. R. (1998). "Ethical and Economical Affordability of Developing Nations' Repayment of International Debt." In Baker, J. C. (Ed.). *Selected International Investment Portfolios.* Great Britain: Pergamon Publishing Company, 141-152.

Powell, J. M. (1967). *The Civilization of the West: A Brief Interpretation.* New York: The Macmillan Company, 415.

Parhizgar, K. D. (2002). *Multicultural Behavior and Global Business Environments.* New York: Haworth Press, 125

Rhinesmith, S. H. (1991). "An Agenda for Globalization." *Training and Development Journal.* (February), Vol. 45, No.2, 24-27.

Smith, C. G.. (1994). "The New Corporate Philosophy." *Harvard Business Review.* May-June, 107.

Smith, C. G. and Cooper, A. C. (1988). "Establish Companies Diversity into Young Industries: "Comparison of Firms With Different Levels of Perforn1ance." *Strategic Management Journal.* Vol. 9, March-April, 111-121.

Social Darwinism (1940). "The Sins of Legislators." In *The Man Versus the State.* London: Watts & Co. Originally Published in 1884.

Spencer, H. (1888). *Education, Intellectual, Moral, and Physical.* New York: D. Appleton.

Steiner, G. A. and Steiner, F. S. (1994). *Business, Government, and Society: A Managerial Perspective* McGraw-Hill Book Company, 444.

Steinmann, H. and Scherer, A. G. (1997). "Intercultural Management Between Universalism and Relativism-Fundamental Problems in International Business Ethics and the Contribution of Recent German Philosophical Approaches." In Urban, S. (Ed.), *Europe in Global Competition: Problems-Markets-Strategies.* Wiesbaden, Germany: Gabler, 77 -143.

Summers, L. H. (2000). "Rising to the Challenge of Global Economic Integration." In a Speech to the School of Advanced International Studies. Washington, DC, September 20.

Svyantek, D. J. Hendrick, H. L. (1988). "The Nature of Change: An Extension of New Development in Evolutionary Theory to the Study of Organizational Systems." *The Association of Human Resources Management and Organizational Behavior Proceedings.* Volume 1, 243.

US. v. Northern Pacific R.R. Co., 356 U.S. 1(1958).

Walton, C. (1977). *The Ethics of Corporate Conduct.* Englewood Cliff, New Jersey: Prentice Hall, Inc., 9.

Walton, C. (Ed.), (1990). *Enriching Business Ethics.* Penguin Press, ix.

Watson, T. J. (1963). *A Business and its Beliefs: The Ideas that Helped Build IBM.* New York: McGraw-Hill Book Company, Inc. 5.

Weber, C. (1960). *Basic Philosophies of Education.* New York: Holt, Rinehart and Winston, 252.

Welch, J. In Cassidy, J. (1997). *"Gimme." New Yorker.* April 21.

World Bank (various issues) *World Bank Development Report.* World Bank, Washington D.C.

World Resources (1996-1997). World Resources Institute. 166.

Chapter 11

Abrams, F. (1951). "Management's Responsibilities in a Complex World." *Harvard Business Review.* Vol. 24, No 3, 29-34.

Albert, E. M., Denise, T. C., and Peterfreund, S. P. (1984). *Great Traditions in Ethics.* Fifth Edition. Belmont, CA: Wadsworth Publishing Company, 9.

Anshen, M. (1974). *Managing the Socially Responsible Corporation.* New York: Macmillan.

Beauchamp, T. L. (1982). *Philosophical Ethics: An Introduction to Moral Philosophy.* New York: McGraw-Hill, 229.

CNN.com - $11 theft gets three-strikes career criminal 25 years to life - Nov. 15, 2002, *CNN.com./Law Center.*

Corbett, E. P. J. (1991). *The Elements of Reasoning.* New York: Macmillan Publishing, Company, 71-73.

Cross, F. B. and Miller, R. L. R. (2001). *West's Legal Environment of Business: Text, Cases, Ethical, Regulatory, International, and E-Commerce Issues* Fourth Edition. United States: West, Thomson Learning: 2, 170.

Cutler, S. M. (2002). "New Charges for Ex-Tyco Honchos." <Http://www.cbsnews.com/stories/2002/08/07national/main517820.shtml. >.

De George, R. T. (1999). *Business Ethics.* Upper Saddle River, NJ: Prentice Hall: 102.

De Mente, B. L. (1990). *Chinese Etiquette and Ethics in Business: A Penetrating Analysis of the Morals and Values that Shape the Chinese Business Personality.* Lincolnwood, IL: NTC Business Books, 18.

Fabrikant, G. (1995). "Battling for Hearts and Minds at Time Warner." *New York Times.* February 26, 9.

Folger, R. and Greenberg, J. (1985). "Procedural Justice: An Interpretive Analysis of Personnel Systems." *Research in Personnel and Human Resources Management.* Vol. 3, 141-183.

Frankena, W. K. (1973). *Ethics.* Second Edition. Englewood Cliffs, NJ: Prentice-Hall, Inc., 64.

Frederick, W. C. (1992). "Social Issues in Management: Coming of Age or Prematurely Gray?" Paper presented to the Doctoral Consortium of the Social Issues in Management Division of the Academy of Management. Las Vegas, Nevada, August 5.

Freeman, R. F. (1984). *Strategic Management: A Stakeholder Approach.* Boston: Pitman.

Friedman, M. (1971). "Does Business Have a Social Responsibility?" *Bank Administration.* (April Edition).

Hanson, D. P. (1991). "Managing for Ethics: Some Implications of Research on the Prisoner's Dilemma Game." *SAM Advanced Management Journal.* Winter, 16.

Jackson, J. H., Miller, R. L., and Miller, S. G. (1997). *Business and Society Today; Managing Social Issues.* United States: West Publishing Company, 37, 40,61.

Jeffcut, P. (1994). "The Interpretation of Organization: A Contemporary Analysis and Critique." *Journal of Management Studies.* March, 225.

Kohlberg, L. (1969). "Stages and Sequence: The Cognitive-Developmental Approach to Socialization." In David A. Goslin (Ed.). *Handbook of Socialization Theory and Research.* Chicago, IL: Rand McNally.

Kohlberg, L. (1973). "The Claim to Moral Adequacy of a Highest Stage of Moral Judgment." *Journal of Philosophy.* Vol. 70, Act. 25, 630-646.

London, S. and Waters, R. (2002). "All Shook Up." *Financial Times.* Weekend January 26 and 27, 8.

Long, N. E. (1949). "Power and Administration." *Public Administration Review.* Vol. 9, Autumn, 257-264.

Mill, J. S. (1957). *Utilitarianism. Indianapolis.* IN: Bobbs-Merrill, 62.

Plantinga, A. (1974). *God, Freedom, and Evil.* New York: Harper and Row, Publisher, 29.

Rand, A. (1957). *Atlas Shrugged.* New York: Penguin Books (Signet), 945.

Rawls, J. (1971). *A Theory of Justice.* Cambridge, Mass.: Harvard University Press: 12 and 60-71.

Sheldon, 0. (1923). *The Philosophy of Management.* London: Sir Isaac Pitman & Sons, LTD., 280-291.

Singer, P. (1998). "Rich and Poor." In W. H. Shaw and V. Barry (Eds.), (1998). *Moral Issues in Business.* 7th Edition. Belmont, CA: Wadsworth Publishing Company, 124-130.

Stewart, D. (1996). *Business Ethics.* New York: McGraw-Hill Companies, Inc., 292.

Chapter 12

Belcher, Jr., J. (1988). "The Role of Unions in Productivity Management." *Personnel.* Vol. 65, No. 1, 57.

Bernstein, A. (2000). "Law Culture, and Harassment." In Terry Halbert, P. 157. & Elaine Ingulli (2000). *Law & Ethics in the Business Environment.* U. S. A.: West Legal Studies in Business, Thomson Learning, 157.

Boatright, J. R. (19993). *Ethics and the Conduct of Business.* Englewood Cliffs, NJ: Prentice Hall, 155-168.

Bock, S. (1983). *Secrets.* New York: Vintage, 136.

Buchholz, R. A. and Rosenthal, S. B. (1998). *Business Ethics: The Pragmatic Path Beyond Principles to Process.* Upper Saddle River, NJ: Prentice-Hall, Inc., 391.

Coser, R. L. (1975). "Stay Home Little Sheba: On Placement, Displacement, and Social Change." *Social Problems.* Vol. 22, 470 - 480.

Cockburn, C. (1991). *In the Way of Women: Men's Resistance to Sex Equality in Organizations.* Ithaca, NY: ILR Press, 142.

Covey, S. R. (1993). "Transforming a Swamp." *Training and Development.* Vol. 47, No. 5, 42-46.

De George, R. T. (1996). *Business Ethics.* Fourth Edition. Englewood Cliffs, NJ: Prentice Hall, 363.

Date, C. J. (1990). *An Introduction to Database Systems.* Volume 1, Fifth Edition. Readings, MA: Addison Wesley Publishing, Company.

Ewing, D. W. (1983). A Civil Liberties in the Corporation." In Tom L. Beauchamp and Norman E. Bowie (Ed.). *Ethical Theory and Business.* 2nd Edition. Englewood Cliffs, NJ: Prentice Hall, 141.

Fukuyama, F. (1995). *Trust.* New York: The Free Press, 75.

Halbert, T. and Ingulli,E. (2000). *Law & Ethics in the Business Environment.* U. S. A.: West Legal Studies in Business, Thomson Learning, 245.

Harrison, B. (1984). "The International Movement for Prenotification of Plant Closures." *Industrial Relations.* Vol. 23, No. 3, Fall Edition, 387-409.

Heyes, A. (1991). "How the Courts Define Harassment." *Wall Street Journal.* B1.

Higgins, J. M. (1994). *The Management Challenge: An Introduction to Management.* Second Edition. New York: Macmillan Publishing Company, 648.

Hiley, D. R. (1996). "Employee Rights and the Doctrine of At-Will-Employment.' In Robert A. R (Ed.), (1996). *Ethics of the Workplace· Selected Readings in Business Ethics.* Minneapolis/St. Paul: West Publishing Company, 85.

<http://www.cnn.com/2002/LAW/11/19/judge.underfire.ap/index.html.>.

<http://www.joeheadquarters.com/faq.shtml).>.

Johnson, P. (1976). "Women and Power: Toward a Theory of Effectiveness." *Journal of Social Issues.* Vol. 32, No. 3, 99-110.

Larmer, R. A. (1996), (Ed.). *Ethics in the Workplace. Selected Readings in Business Ethics.* Minneapolis/St. Paul: West Publishing Company, 224.

Machlowitz, M. and Machlowitz, D. (1986). "Hug by the Boss Could Lead to a Slap From the Judge." *Wall Street Journal.* September 20, 20.

Mathis, R. L. and Jackson, J. H. (1997). *Human Resources Management.* Eight Editions. Minneapolis/St. Paul, MN: West Publishing Company, 504.

Moore, J. (1996). "What is Really Unethical About Insider Trading?" In Robert A. Lamar (1996), (Ed.). *Ethics in the Workplace: Selected Readings in Business Ethics.* Minneapolis/St. Paul: West Publishing Company, 225.

Muskin, J. B. 2000). "Interorganizational Ethics: Standards of Behavior." *Journal of Business Ethics.* Vol. 24, 283-297.

O'Connor, R. J. (1993). "Trade Secrets Case Casts Chill." San Jose Mercury News. March 7, 1A.

Parkes, C. (2001). "Cult of the Football Bully Lurks Behind School Shootings: Life is Made Miserable for the Misfits, the Overweight, the Underweight, the Newcomers, by the Swaggering Jocks." *Financial Times.* Tuesday March 20, 2001, 7.

Parhizgar, K. D. (1994). "Conceptual and Perceptual Paths of Cultural Power-Gender Philosophies Towards Entrepreneurial Management." *Proceedings: 5ᵗʰ ENDEC World Conference on Entrepreneurship* July 7-9, Marina Mandarin Singapore, 524-534.

Pollack, A. (2000). "In Japan, It's See No Evil; Have No Harassment." In Terry Halbert, 157. & Elaine Ingulli (2000). *Law & Ethics in the Business Environment.* U.S.A.: West Legal Studies in Business, Thomson Learning, 160.

Reich, Robert. B. Poster, "Help End Sweatshop Conditions for American Workers." <hhtp://www.dol.gov/dol/esa/public/nosweat/card.htm.>.

Schwartz, F. N. (1989). "Management Women and the New Facts of Life." *Harvard Business Review.* Vol. 67, No. 1, 65-67.

Show, W. H. and Barry, V. (1998). *Moral Issues in Business.* 7ᵗʰ Edition. Belmont, CA: Wadsworth Publishing Company, 249, 353.

Simons, G, and Cornwall, S. (1989). "Managing Gender Differences." *Supervisory Management.* August, 42.

Stainer, G. A. and Stainer, J. F. (2003). *Business, Government, and Society: A Managerial Perspective.* Tenth Edition. New York: McGraw-Hill, Inc., 645.

Stainer, G. A. and Stainer, J. F. (1994). *Business, Government, and Society: A Managerial Perspective.* New York: Seventh Edition. McGraw-Hill, Inc., 547.

Taylor, R. (2001). "Failing to Shatter the Glass Ceiling." *Financial Times.* Friday, July 13, VIII.

Useem, J. (1999). "Internet Defense Strategy: Cannibalize Yourself." *Fortune.* September 6, 121-134.

Werhane, P. H. (1989). "The Ethics of Insider Trading." *Journal of Business Ethics.* No. 8, 841-845.

Watson, L. (1995). *Dark Nature: A Natural History of Evil.* New York: HarperCollins, 48-76.

Weiss, J. W. (2003). *Business Ethics: A Stakeholder and Issues Management Approach.* 3ʳᵈ Edition. United States: Thompson, South-western, 213.

Williams, B. (1973a). "A Critique of Utilitarianism." *Utilitarianism: For and Against.* Cambridge: Cambridge University Press.

Williams, B. (1973b). "Morality and Emotions." *Problems of Self.* Cambridge: Cambridge University Press.

Williams, B. (1981). "Persons, Character and Morality." Moral Luck," and "Utilitarianism and Moral Self Indulgence." *Moral Luck.* Cambridge, Cambridge University Press.

Wood, H. G. (1887). *A Treatise of Law of Master and Servant.* Now York: John D. Parsons.

Wirth, L. (2001). In Taylor, R. (Ed.). "Failing to Shatter the Glass Ceiling." *Financial Times.* Friday, July 13, VIII.

<Wysiwyg://2/http://dailynews.netscape.co..ry=2002042611475001172269 1&shortdate=0426>.

Chapter 13

Blum, M., Levi, M., Naylor, R. and Williams, P. (1998). *Financial Heavens, Banking Secracy and Money Laundering*. Vienna: United Nations.

Cacheris, P. and O'Malley, E. S. (2001). "Frankencrime: America's Harsh Money Laundering Penalties." *Journal of Money Laundering Control*. Vol. 5, No. 2, 266.

CNN. Com, (2005). <http://www.cnn.com/2005/WWIRLD/meast/10/27/ oil.food.report.ap/index.htm>.

De George, R. T. (1990). *Business Ethics*. Fourth Edition. Englewood Cliffs, New Jersey: Prentice Hall, 309.

Dwyer, P., Solomon, S., Smith, G., and Parry, J. (1998). "The Citi that Slept?" *Business Week*. November 2.

Epstein, E. M. (1973). "Dimensions of Corporate Power: Part I." *California Management Review*. Winter Edition, 11.

Ferraro, G. (1995). *Cultural Anthropology: An Applied Perspective*. Second Edition. New York: West Publishing Company, 271.

Galbraith, J. K. (1958). *The Affluent Society*. Boston: Houghton Mifflin.

Global Witness. (2000). "Bribes Paid by State-Owned Oil Company." July 12.

Hall, W. (2001). "Bankers' Veil of Secrecy Begins to Lift." *Financial Times*. Friday November 16, 10.

Hampton, M. P. and Levi, M. (1999). "Fast Spinning into Oblivion? Recent Development in Money-Laundering Policies and Offshore Finance." *Third World Quarterly*. June. Vol. 20, No. 3, 648-656.

Hughes, D. M. (2000). "The 'Natasha' Trade: The Transnational Shadow Market of Trafficking in Women." *Journal of International Affairs*. Vol. 53, No. 2, 625-651.

Johnson, J. (2001). "In the Pursuit of Dirty Money: Identifying Weaknesses in the Global Financial System." *Journal of Money Laundering Control*. Vo. 5, No. 2, 122-132.

Jurith, E. H. (2002). International Cooperation in the Fight Against Money Laundering." *Journal of Financial Crime*. Vol. 9, No. 3, 212-216.

Lundberg, F. (1972). *The Rich and the Super Rich: A study in the Power of Money Today*. New York: Bantam Book/ Lyle Stuart, Inc., 893.

Moon, C. J. and Woolliams, P. (2000). "Managing Cross Cultural Business Ethics." *Journal of Business Ethics*. Vol. 27, 113.

Munro, N. (2001). "Internet-Based Financial Services: A New Laundering." *Journal of Financial Crime*. Vol. 9, No. 2, 134-152.

Pironti, A. (2000). "OPEC Decision Might End Iraq's Profit from Smuggled Oil." *Deusche Press-Agentur*, March 22.

Schiffer, L. J. (1997). "Statement Concerning Enforcement of Environmental Laws, Before the Committee on Environment and Public Works, US Senate."*Assistant Attorney General, Environmental and Natural Resources Division, US Department of Justice.* June 10.

Senguder, T. (2002). "An Examination of Money Laundering Prevention in the United States of America." *The Journal of Academy of Business.* Cambridge, Mass.: 196.

Small R. (1999). "Reporting Requirements Under the Bank Secrecy Act, Testimony Before the Subcommittee on General Oversight and Investigations, and the Subcommittee on Financial Institutions and Customer Credit, Committee on Banking and Financial Services, US House of Representatives, 20th April 1999, <www.federalreserve.org.>

The Economist (1999). "A Survey of Innovation in Industry." February 20, 8.

Wright, R. (2002). "The Hiding Wealth: The Implications for the Prevention and Control of Crime and the Protection of Economic Stability." *Journal of Financial Crime.* Vol. 8, No. 3, 239-243.

Chapter 14

Albert, E. M., Denise, T. C., and Peterfreund, S. P. (1980). *Great Traditions in Ethics.* Belmont, CA: Wadsworth Publishing Company, 10.

Carr, D. (2000). *Professionalism and Ethics in Teaching* London/New York: Routledge, Taylor and Francis Group, 23.

Davis, M. (1996). "Explaining Wrongdoing." In Robert A. Larmer (Ed.), (1996). *Ethics in the Workplace: Selected Readings in Business Ethics.*

De George, R. (1995). *Business Ethics.* Englewood Cliffs, NJ: Prentice Hall, 115, and 454-464.

Ethics Resource Center (1990). "Creating a Workable Company Code of Ethics." Washington, DC: Ethics Resource Center Publication, VIII, 1.

Ethics Resource Center (1990). "Ethics Policies and Programs in American Business." Washington, DC: Ethics Resource Center Publication, 23-24.

French, P. A. (1984). "Corporate Model Agency." In W. Michael Hoffman and Jennifer Mills Moore (Eds.). *Business Ethics: Readings and Cases in Corporate Morality.* New York: McGraw-Hill, 163-171.

Gerth, H. (1946). *From Max Weber: Essay in Sociology.* (Trans.) C. Wright Mills. Cambridge: Oxford University Press.

Gert, B., Culver, C. M. and Clouser, K. D. (1977). *Bioethics. A Return To Fundamentals.* New York/Oxford; Oxford University Press, 98.

Greenwood, E. (1962). "Attributes of a Profession. In Nosow, S. and Form, W. H. (Eds.). *Man, Work, and Society.* New York: Basic Books, 206.

<http://www.bfrconvertibleventures.com/free_reports/car_repairs.htm.>.

Nader, R. (2000). *The Ralph Nader Reader.*New York: Seven Stories Press, 3-4.

Nietzsche, F. (1924). *The Common Work of Friedrich Nietzsche.*Vol. XII, VIII, XVI; Levy, O. (Ed.). New York: Macmillan.

Parhizgar, K. D. (2002). *Multicultural Behavior and Global Business Environments.* New York: Haworth Press, 126.

Parks, S. D. (1993). "Young Adults, Mentoring Communities, and the Conditions of Moral Choice." In Andrew Garrod (Ed.). *Approaches to Moral Development: New Research and Emerging Themes.* New York: Teachers College Press, Columbia University, 217.

Schein, E. H. (1966). "The Problem of Moral Education for Business Manager." *Industrial Management Review.* Vol. 8, 311.

Schwartz, M. (2001). "The Nature of Relationship Between Corporate Codes of Ethics and Behavior." *Journal of Business Ethics.* Vol. 32, 247-256.

Thompson, V. G. (1961). *Modern Organization.* New York: Knopf, 170.

Wilson, F. A. and Neuhauser, D. (1976) *Health Services in the United States.* Cambridge, Mass.: Balinger Publishing Company, 52.

Chapter 15

Baier, K. (1965). *The Moral point of View: A Rational Basis of Ethics.* New York: Random House, 146.

Barton, L. (1995). Ethics: *The Enemy in the Workplace.* Cincinnati, Ohio: South-Western College Publishing, 154.

Boartright, J. R. (1993). *Ethics and the Conduct of Business.* Englewood Cliffs, NJ: Prentice-Hall, P. 133.

Bok, S. (1980). "Whistle Blowing and Professional Responsibility." *New York University Education Quarterly.* Vol. 11, Summer Edition, 2-7.

Bowie, N. (1982). *Business Ethics.* Englewood Cliffs, NJ: Prentice-Hall, 142.

Bradley, F. H. (1876, 1927). *Ethical Studies.* First published in 1876, Second Edition, 1972. Oxford: Clarendon Press. Excerpts from Chapter 5, " My Station and Its Duties."

Buchholz, R. A. and Rosenthal, S. B. (1998). *Business Ethics: The Pragmatic Path Beyond Principles to Process.* Upper Saddle River, NJ: Prentice Hall, 398.

De George, R. T. (1981). "Ethical Responsibilities of Engineers in Large Organizations: The Pinto Case." *Business and Professional Ethics Journal.* Vol. 1, No. 1, 1-14.

De George, R. (1995). *Business Ethics.* Englewood Cliffs, New Jersey: Prentice Hall, 115, 227, & 454-464.

Dowie, M. (1977). "Pinto Madness." *Mother Jones.* September/October Edition, 24-28.

Ewing, D. W. (1983). "Civil Liberties in the Corporations." In Tom L. Beauchamp and Norman E. Bowie (Eds.). *Ethical Theory and Business.* Second Edition. Englewood Cliffs, NJ: Prentice-Hall, 141.

Fiedler, J. H. (1992). "Organizational Loyalty." *Business and Professional Ethics Journal.* , Vol. 11, Spring Edition, 87.

Fitzgerald, A. E. (1989). *Pentagonists: An Insider's View of Waste, Mismanagement, and Fraud in Defense Spending:* Boston: Houghton Mifflin.

Glazer, M. and Glazer, P. (1989). *The Whistle Blowers.* New York: Basic Books, 6.

Hoffman, H. and Moore, J. (1990). "Whistle Blowing: Its Moral Justification." In James, G. *Business Ethics: Readings and Cases in Corporate Morality.* Second Edition. New York: Mc-Graw Hill.

Kipling, R. (1998). *The Law of the Jungle.* Oxford: Oxford University Press.

Larmer, R. A. (1992). "Whistle-Blowing and Employee Loyalty." *Journal of Business Ethics.* Vol. 11, 127.

Martin, M. W. and Schinzinger, R. (1989). *Ethics in Engineering.* Second Edition. New York: McGraw-Hill, 213.

Nolan, H. E. (1996:). "Company Loyalty and Whistle-Blowing." In David Stewart (1996). *Business Ethics.* New York: The McGraw-Hill Companies, Inc., 219-235.

Parhizgar, K. D. and Lunce, S.E. (1996). "Implications of Employees' Informational Integrated Discovery Systems." *Contemporary Developments in Human Resource Management.* Montpellier, France: *Sup de CO,* An International Publication of the Scientific Committee of the Montpellier Graduate Business School, Editions ESKA, 393-403.

Sass, R. (2001). "The Killing of Karen Silkwood: The Story Behind the Kerr-McGee Plutonium Case." *Winter Relations Industrials,* Vol. 56, 222.

Shaw, W. (1996). *Business Ethics.* Second Edition. New York: Wadsworth Publishing Company, 290.

Shaw, W. H. and Barry, V. (1998). *Moral Issues in Business.* Seventh Edition, New York: Wadsworth Publishing Company, 360.

Strobel, L. P. (1980). *Reckless Homicide? Ford's Pinto Trial.* South Bend, Ind.: And Books.

Trevino, L. K. and Nelson, K. A. (1995). *Managing Business Ethics· Straight Talk About How to Do it Right.* New York: John Wiley & Sons, Inc., 161.

Weiss, J. W. (2003). *Business Ethics: A Stakeholder and Issues Management Approach.* 3rd Edition. Canada: South-Western Publishing Company, 328.

SUBJECT INDEX

ABOUT THE AUTHORS

Kamal Dean Parhizgar, PhD, is Professor of Management and International Business Strategy at the Texas A&M International University, Texas. Previously in the United States, he has taught at California State University campuses, in Hayward, Dominguez Hills, and Los Angeles; The University of the District of Columbia; George Mason University; Georgetown University; YMCA College in Chicago; as well as at Iranian colleges and universities. Before the Iranian Islamic Revolution in 1979, he served as the Director of the Iranian Scientific Research Center for the Ministry of Sciences and Higher Education.

Professor Parhizgar obtained his undergraduate and graduate degrees from the University of Shiraz and The University of Teheran, and his PhD in 1972 from Northwestern University, Evanston, Illinois. His postdoctoral fellowship was at Northwestern University in 1983, and he spent his Hospital Administrative Residency and Intenrship Assignments in St. Paul Ramsey Hospital, University of Minnesota; National Iranian Oil Company (NIOC) Hospitals; and Firoozgar Medical Center.

Professor Parhizgar's extensive multicultural interests are illustrated by his research and teaching activities in the field of strategic cultural management. He has published numerous text books including 2002 Edition of *Multicultural Behavior and Global Business Environments,* articles in refereed journals, and conference proceedings research papers, and has presented research papers at the regional, national, and international conferences in the United States and overseas. He has been Co-Program Chair, Division Chair, Track Chair, Session Chair, Discussant, and Reviewer for the ABI, IAoM, IMDA, SAM, ITFA, and GCA. He has served as the Editor of the *Newsletter for the International Management Development Association.* He has served in the editorial review boards of the *Journal of Transnational Management Development, Avances in Competitiveness Research,* and *Journal of Teaching in International Business.*

Robert R. Parhizgar, MS, is a medical student in the School of Medicine, Texas Tech University Health Sciences Center, Lubbock, Texas. Also, he is a graduate student in the field of business administration in the College of Business Administration, Texas Tech University. He obtained his Master's Degree in Health Services Research and Management, School of Medicine, Texas Tech University, Lubbock, Texas in 2002. He spent his Management Research Internship Assignment in Caroline Nursing Home, Lubbock, Texas. He has published an article in the refereed *Journal of Cardiology*, presented and published papers at professional conferences of the *American Society for competitiveness, the World Business Congress, the International Management Development,* and *The International Trade and Finance Association.*

LaVergne, TN USA
26 September 2010
198524LV00004B/27/P